PENGUIN BOOKS

THE NEW PENGUIN BOOK OF ROMANTIC POETRY

Jonathan Wordsworth is descended from William Wordsworth's younger brother, Christopher. He is Chairman of the Wordsworth Trust, Grasmere, retired Professor of English Literature at Oxford, and Fellow Emeritus of Exeter and St Catherine's colleges. He has edited much of Wordsworth's poetry, including the recent Penguin *The Prelude: The Four Texts*, and over 180 titles in the Woodstock Facsimile Series Revolution and Romanticism. He is the author of *The Music of Humanity*, *The Borders of Vision*, *Ancestral Voices*, *Visionary Gleam* and *The Bright Work Grows.*

Jessica Wordsworth graduated from Mount Holyoke College, Massachusetts and took her Master's degree at Oxford. She is Administrator of the Wordsworth Winter School and Summer Conference at Grasmere, and is preparing the Penguin *Selected Coleridge.*

THE NEW PENGUIN BOOK OF

Romantic Poetry

Edited by Jonathan and Jessica Wordsworth

PENGUIN BOOKS

PENGUIN BOOKS

Published by the Penguin Group
Penguin Books Ltd, 80 Strand, London WC2R 0RL, England
Penguin Putnam Inc., 375 Hudson Street, New York, New York 10014, USA
Penguin Books Australia Ltd, 250 Camberwell Road, Camberwell, Victoria 3124, Australia
Penguin Books Canada Ltd, 10 Alcorn Avenue, Toronto, Ontario, Canada M4V 3B2
Penguin Books India (P) Ltd, 11, Community Centre, Panchsheel Park, New Delhi – 110 017, India
Penguin Books (NZ) Ltd, Cnr Rosedale and Airborne Roads, Albany, Auckland, New Zealand
Penguin Books (South Africa) (Pty) Ltd, 24 Sturdee Avenue, Rosebank 2195, South Africa

Penguin Books Ltd, Registered Offices: 80 Strand, London, WC2R 0RL, England

www.penguin.com

This collection first published in hardback 2001
Published in paperback 2003
3

Set in 11/12.5 pt Monotype Bulmer
Printed in England by Clays Ltd, St Ives plc

For the twins, Helen Emily and Giles Philip

a child more than all other gifts
Brings hope with it and forward looking thoughts

CONTENTS

THE POETRY

PREFACE

Romanticism is the mood in which 'we recognize / A grandeur in the beatings of the heart', in which 'We feel that we are greater than we know' (Wordsworth). It is a valuing of emotion, of imagination, a belief in human potential taken beyond its ordinary limits. It belongs to no period. Philip Sidney invoked it when he saw in his Elizabethan contemporaries 'a want of inward touch'. Wallace Stevens evokes it in the 1940s as

> the yes of the realist spoken because he must
> Say yes, spoken because under every no
> [Lies] a craving for yes that [has] never been broken.

There is every reason to think of Plato in certain moods as a Romantic. In Hazlitt's words, it is a way of thinking 'as old as the heart of man'.

Yet there are times when Romantic thinking, feeling, understanding are more likely. Something happens in the years following the French Revolution that is unique. Not that all writers suddenly became Romantic. The vast majority didn't – either because their values remained those of an earlier period (Jane Austen, Crabbe, Peacock), or because they could not make the act of faith that is implied. Romanticism is an aspiring, a hopefulness – an exalting, and exulting, of the imagination. For reasons that we associate with political hope roused, and defeated, in the Revolution, the spirit of the age seems for two generations after 1789 to have been especially favourable to this outgoing of imagination. But the Revolution was symptom as well as cause. Blake in 1784 (first *Innocence* poetry), Burns in his Kilmarnock *Poems* (1786), show that something was already in the air. Collins, MacPherson ('Ossian'), Chatterton, Barbauld, Cowper tempt us to think of quite a gradual late eighteenth-century moving into Romantic ways of thinking and writing. At the end of the period, similarly, we see in Hemans, Landon, Hood, Clare and Norton (all writing in the 1820s and early 1830s) a Victorianism before its time. In his eighty years (1770–1850) Wordsworth offers the completed cycle. Born in the early days of the reign of George III, he writes his first published poem, *An Evening Walk*, aged seventeen, in a mode that is clearly pre-Romantic. Yet he lives to be Victoria's Poet Laureate.

If the Romantic period didn't begin or end conveniently, there are dates and happenings that present themselves as landmarks: Burns' *Poems* 1786, Blake's *Songs of Innocence* (1789), Wollstonecraft's *Vindication of the Rights of Woman* (1792), Wordsworth and Coleridge's *Lyrical Ballads* (1798) cluster about the Revolution, offering a suitably flexible sense of an opening, an outset. The deaths in succession of the second-generation Romantic poets – Keats in 1821, Shelley in 1822, Byron in 1824 – cannot fail to suggest a coming-to-an-end. The Reform Bill of 1832, though hardly a fulfilment of Romantic political ideals, is (to quote Byron) a point 'where the Fates change horses'. Publication of Tennyson's *Poems Chiefly Lyrical* in 1830, and Victoria's Coronation, aged seventeen, in 1837, are clearly the start of something new.

With all this in mind, we have allowed ourselves flexibility in making selections for *The New Penguin Book of Romantic Poetry*. Cowper has been accepted as a forerunner of Romanticism, not because he was the best-selling English poet through much of the period, or because he is now wrongly unregarded, but that to leave him out would be to deny readers a means of testing what is and is not new. More extreme is the case of Anna Laetitia Barbauld, whose Unitarian poetry, published in 1773, a generation before Coleridge, just seemed to contain too much of the story of Romanticism to be omitted:

> At this still hour the self-collected soul
> Turns inward, and beholds a stranger there
> Of high descent and more than mortal rank,
> And embryo God, a spark of fire divine . . .
> (*Summer Evening's Meditation*)

At the other end of the period we have included few poets who were born after 1800, and none whose first publication was later than the 1820s.

Rather than presenting Romantic poetry writer by writer, offering a separate mini-selections of each, we have arranged the volume by theme, and to some extent by genre. The result has been to emphasize both likeness and difference. It is strange, but not unuseful, to think that Robinson's *Sappho and Phaon*, Wordsworth's *Ruined Cottage*, Blake's *Crystal Cabinet*, Tighe's Spenserian *Psyche*, Shelley's *Alastor*, Byron's *Bride of Abydos* and the Haidee episode of *Don Juan* are all Narratives of Love (Section II, below). How, one is led to ask, does romanticism with a small 'r' relate to Romanticism with a big one? But there is the further bonus that comes from this principle of arrangement.

Chronology, obscured in arrangement by author, comes to be quietly central. Working through, section by section (in whatever order he or she may choose), the reader gains imperceptibly a sense of the period as it unfolds; and gains a sense of the power and versatility of poets who impress themselves again and again under the different headings. Byron one might think of as the poet of the Oriental Tales and *Don Juan*, but he is everywhere. Women writers, who perhaps have not to the same extent stamped themselves on a particular genre, emerge as strong in their variety: Smith and

Tighe are more restricted, but Robinson, Hemans, Landon and Norton have the technique, and the power of mind, to make themselves felt on many different issues.

Section I, Romantic Hallmarks, is offered to the browsing, or the sharply analytical, reader, as a way into Romanticism, and into this book. Poems in the section have been chosen as in some important way definitive of their writers and the period – no one but Coleridge could have written *Kubla Khan*, and at no other period could it have been written. The same is surely true of Lamb and *Old Familiar Faces*, Wordsworth and the Lucy Poems, Blake's *And Did Those Feet*, Scott and *Lochinvar*, Byron and 'Revelry by Night', not to mention Keats and *To Autumn*, Shelley and *The Skylark*, Hood and *I Remember, I Remember*. These are poems that touch us emotionally, draw us in imaginatively, depending often on the power of the numinous and unexplained:

> Season of mists and mellow fruitfulness,
> Close bosom-friend of the maturing sun,
> Conspiring with him how to load and bless
> With fruit the vines that round the thatch-eves run . . .
>
> (*To Autumn*)

In its strangeness, broadly definitive of Romanticism, this imaginative power is to be felt everywhere in the twelve sections presented below, dominating (as one might expect) IV, Ennobling Interchange: Man and Nature, V, Romantic Odes, and XII, On Poets and Poetry, and strongly present in III, Romantic Solitude, Suffering and Endurance, VI, Romantic Lyric and Song, VII, The Romantic Sonnet, and XI, Poets in Relationship. Thanks to Byron and (more surprisingly) to Wordsworth, it is recurrent in II, Narratives of Love, and IX, Romantic Comedy and Satire. Even in X, Protest and Politics, it is to be found (rather as a working of the spirit of the age, than in its own right), for instance, in Shelley's *Mask of Anarchy*. Section VIII, The Gothic and Surreal, is a special case – the Gothic, for all its crudities, shading in its use of the supernatural into the Romantic sublime (of which it is a sort of mimicry).

Texts in *The New Penguin Book of Romantic Poetry* are those read by the Romantics themselves, or where this is impossible (as in the case of *The Prelude*, first published after Wordsworth's death in 1850) they are presented from manuscript, as originally written. Where there is a choice of printed versions, the earlier have in general been preferred, as closer to the poet's original creative impulse, and most influential on his contemporaries. *The Ancient Mariner* will therefore be found with its 'antique' spelling, as published in *Lyrical Ballads* 1798, rather than tidied up and replete with marginal glosses, as it appears in *Sybilline Leaves* 1817. More controversially, *Frost at Midnight* is presented in the text of 1798, not because the early version is better than that of 1828 (it probably isn't), but because in its original form it is the climax of Coleridge's Conversation Poems, and a vital influence on the Wordsworth of *Tintern Abbey*. Nowhere else can we read Coleridge's marvellous intuition:

> the living spirit in our frame
> That loves not to behold a lifeless thing
> Transfuses into all its own delights,
> Its own volition . . .

With such niceties in mind, attention has been paid in this volume to dates at which the poetry is originally composed. Where the gap between writing and publication is large, or for some other reason significant, both dates are provided. Thus the Spring Odes of Keats are composed April–May 1819, when he was at the height of his powers, and published in 1820, when he knew himself to be dying, and was forbidden by his doctors to write poetry.

Texts have been annotated and lightly repunctuated. Some inevitably have been abridged, or presented in the form of excerpts, but in every case the original numbering has been preserved. Spelling has been standardized, except in dialect poetry (Burns, in particular), and in cases elsewhere when rhyme would be affected. Contractions (apostrophe 'd', typically) have been spelt out, and final 'ed's marked where they should be sounded for the metre. Initial capitals, misread by the modern reader as a form of emphasis, have been removed except where they mark conscious abstraction ('Nature' is thus distinct from 'nature'). In general the editors' wish has been not so much to modernize and standardize, as to make the poetry accessible. Annotation is at times quite heavy, but there has been no fudging, no silence at points where the editors themselves are in difficulties. Every case where a modern reader might have problems of interpretation has been noted – even the Serbonian-bog complexities of Shelley's *Epipsychidion* are seriously attempted. But above all, the passing of 200 years since *Lyrical Ballads* has had the effect of limiting awarenesses. Early readers of Romantic poetry knew Latin, knew the Bible in detail, and *Paradise Lost* almost as a second Bible. Notes cannot take the place of the countless pleasurable recognitions that we have lost, but they can help.

INTRODUCTION: THE ROMANTIC PERIOD

1. Origins

The ideals, values and belief of the Romantic period – never those of the majority, even among the educated upper classes – are commonly thought to have been formed in opposition to neo-classicism and the Age of Reason. No doubt there is truth in this, but Romantic assumptions evolve gradually, and over a length of time, before finding expression in the verse (sometimes in the prose) of the great imaginative writers whose work for us defines the period. Reaction sets the process in motion – reaction in politics against oppression, reaction in literature against artifice, reaction in belief against the stereotypes of Christian thinking – but at a secondary stage a new optimism, a new momentum, is created that is forward-looking, positive in itself.

(i) *Revolution and Romantic Vision*

Few persons but those who have lived in it, can conceive or comprehend what . . . the French Revolution was, nor what a visionary world seemed to open up upon those who were just entering it. Old things seemed passing away, and nothing was dreamt of but the regeneration of the human race. (Southey: letter of 1824)

The Revolution of 1789 didn't just happen. It was predictable, unstoppable. Five years before the fall of the Bastille, Cowper had addressed the great fortress-prison, symbol of the Ancien Régime and its silent iniquities:

> Ye dungeons and ye cages of despair,
> That monarchs have supplied from age to age
> With music such as suits their sovereign ears,
> The sighs and groans of miserable men!
> There's not an English heart that would not leap
> To hear that ye were fallen at last . . .
>
> (*Task* V, 385–90)

There were shrewder political commentators than Cowper, but a knowledge of English seventeenth-century history (much studied in France) made clear that the Bastille was bound to go. Lack of money had forced Charles I to summon the Long Parliament in 1640, leading to demands for reform, to war, to the imprisonment, trial and execution of the King, and to the setting up of a republic. In May 1789, lack of money would force Louis XVI to summon the Estates General, a thing which no French monarch had done since 1611. From then on the King would be in the hands of his people. Those who attacked the Bastille were speeding up an inevitable process. Inspired not only by the Civil War, but by the bloodless English Revolution of 1688 (at which Parliament had sacked one king and appointed another), members of the French Assembly tried hard to impose on Louis a constitutional monarchy. But he had no intention of keeping the oaths he swore of allegiance, and in the end he too was beheaded.

Repeating a pattern set elsewhere, and in the previous century, hardly amounts to the opening up of a 'visionary world', but there were other factors at work to associate revolution and regeneration. Radicals across the known world saw the French as re-enacting the American rebellion of 1776, and assumed that liberty would come to their countries too. Richard Price (whose speech to the Revolution Society in November 1789 provoked Burke to his immoderate *Reflections on the French Revolution*) had proclaimed in 1784 that 'Next to the introduction of Christianity among mankind, the American Revolution may prove the most important step in the progressive course of human improvement'. Price, be it said, was an authority on taxes as well as a dissenting minister; in 1778 he had been invited by Congress to become an American citizen and give assistance 'in regulating their finances'; in 1781 he had received an honorary doctorate at Yale, alongside Washington. He was no fool. Nor was William Godwin, who wrote in 1793 *Political Justice*, Book IV:

> only six years elapsed between the completion of American liberty and the commencement of the French revolution. Will a term longer than this be necessary before France, the most refined and considerable nation in the world, will lead other nations to imitate and improve upon her plan?

Price and Godwin (though Price is a theologian and Godwin an atheist) think in terms of progress. It is this millenarian aspect of Revolution that makes it so attractive. It is 'the progressive course of human improvement' visibly taking place. News of the fall of the Bastille was initially welcomed as Cowper said it would be ('There's not an English heart that would not leap'): even Pitt assumed it would be for the good. The backlash was rapid, though, leaving only the most resolute supporters unperturbed when Louis was executed and Robespierre created the Reign of Terror. After Robespierre's death (July 1794) it again became possible to hope that things would come right in political terms. But increasingly the Revolution was becoming an ideal – or a cautionary tale, if one took the Establishment view. France *as a fact* was at war with England, France *as an ideal* was unaffected. Based on the American Declaration of Independence, the French Declaration of the Rights of Man was beyond political fact, a statement of how things should be, and one day must become. The optimism (or naivity) to be seen in this keeping faith with the Revolution is a major characteristic of the earlier Romantic poets. They have both to come to terms with disappointment, and to quell disillusion by finding an apolitical basis for confidence in humanity and hope for the future. To some it seemed at first that Godwin's faith in reason might provide the answer, but instinctively they were drawn rather to feeling and imagination.

From this point of view – the point of view of the relation of the Revolution to Romanticism – it is Wordsworth who proves the indispensable chronicler. Writing not as an historian, but as one who feels afresh every stage and turn in the Revolution's progress, he gives in the *Prelude* episodes printed in Section X below (Protest and Politics) an extraordinary insight into the hopes and disappointments and rethinkings forced upon radicals of the day – and is in the process nowhere doctrinaire. Faith in the Revolution comes to him not through books, or even from persuasion by the republican nobleman, Michel Beaupuy, with whom he walks beside the Loire in the summer of 1792, but through sympathy with suffering humanity:

And when we chanced
One day to meet a hunger-bitten girl
Who crept along fitting her languid self
Unto a heifer's motion – by a cord
Tied to her arm, and picking thus from the lane
Its sustenance, while the girl with her two hands
Was busy knitting in a heartless mood
Of solitude – and at the sight my friend
In agitation said, ''Tis against *that*
Which we are fighting!' I with him believed
Devoutly that a spirit was abroad
Which could not be withstood . . .
– whence better days
To all mankind.

Rejoicing, affectation, terror, alienation, glee, confusion and imaginative transcendence take each other's place in a sequence of vivid, always credible episodes, as Wordsworth, writing ten to fourteen years after the events described, offers an example both of the continuing power of the Revolution over the minds of his contemporaries, and of the power of political hope transmuted into art.

(ii) *A New Style and a New Spirit*

That morning, as soon as breakfast was over, we strolled out into the park, and seating ourselves on the trunk of an old ash-tree, Coleridge read aloud with a sonorous and musical voice the ballad of Betty Foy [*The Idiot Boy*]. I was not critically or sceptically inclined. I saw touches of truth and nature, and took the rest for granted. But in *The Thorn*, *The Mad Mother* and *The Complaint of a Poor Indian Woman* [sic], I felt that deeper power and pathos which have since been acknowledged . . . as the characteristics of this author, and the sense of a new style in poetry, and a new spirit, came over me. It had to me something of the effect that arises from the turning up of the fresh soil, or the first welcome breath of spring.

(Hazlitt: *My First Acquaintance with Poets*, 1823)

Hazlitt is talking of the visit he paid in May 1798, aged twenty, to Coleridge and Wordsworth at Alfoxden in Somerset. The lyrical ballads were just being written. Given the sharpness of his critical perceptions, and the genius of Coleridge and Wordsworth, there is no reason to doubt that he sensed at the time 'a new style in poetry, and a new spirit'. But the characteristics of this style – its extreme simplicity of language and openness of emotion – had antecedents that went back forty years to the period of MacPherson's spurious Celtic epics, *Fingal* and *Temora*, and Blair's *Dissertation on Ossian*, authenticating the ancient Scottish bard who never existed, yet at the same time beautifully establishing a criterion for early Romantic poetry:

The two great characteristics of Ossian's poetry are tenderness and sublimity . . . He moves perpetually in the high region of the grand and the pathetic. One note is struck at the beginning, and supported to the end; nor is any ornament introduced but what is perfectly concordant with the general tone or melody.

More than twenty years before the death of Dr Johnson (1784), a primitivist view of poetry as naturalness is being advanced. Offering the public what it wanted to believe in, Chatterton created in 1768–70 a second major primitivist fake in his pseudo-medieval *Rowley Poems* – then took arsenic at the age of eighteen. The faking was still more blatant than MacPherson's cobbling together his own work with Highland fragments (old, but nothing like as old as 'Ossian' was claimed to be) as the basis of his 'epics'. But, again there were those determined to believe the poetry authentic; controversy in each case going on into the next century. Percy's *Reliques* (1765), meanwhile, and other ballad-collections, were offering genuine (and more or less genuine) survivals of oral poetry.

In 1784 Blair emerged with his *Lectures on Rhetoric and Belles Lettres*, presenting both the primitivist claims for spontaneity – stirred by patriotism etc 'the ancient bard arose and sang . . . native effusions of his heart' – and a more subtle view of the origins of poetic language that will be assimilated in 1800 into the Preface to *Lyrical Ballads*:

In the infancy of societies, men live scattered and dispersed, in the midst of solitary rural scenes, where the beauties of Nature are their chief entertainment . . . Their passions have nothing to restrain them, their imagination has nothing to check it. They display themselves to one another without disguise, and converse and act in the uncovered simplicity of Nature. As their feelings are strong, so their language, of itself, assumes a poetical turn.

Compare Wordsworth:

Low and rustic life was generally chosen because in that situation the essential passions of the heart find a better soil in which they can attain their majority, are less under restraint, and speak a plainer and more emphatic language; because in that situation our elementary feelings exist in a state of greater simplicity, and consequently may be more accurately contemplated and more forcibly communicated . . . and lastly, because in that situation the passions of men are incorporated with the beautiful and permanent forms of Nature.

The difference between the primitivist critic and the Romantic poet is that Blair (who never ceased to believe in Ossian) continues to think in terms of a distant past, Wordsworth looks through similar eyes at the 'solitary rural scenes' of contemporary England.

Two years after Blair's *Lectures*, Burns was to publish his Kilmarnock *Poems*. Once more the impetus was Scottish, but this time it was the real thing – an authentic primitivist voice, yet new:

Gie me ae spark o' Nature's fire,
That's a' the learning I desire . . .
My Muse, though hamely in attire,
May touch the heart.
(*Epistle to J. Lapraik, An Old Scotch Bard*)

To complete the pattern, in January 1798 Coleridge (two months before the first poetry is written for *Lyrical Ballads*) takes Blair's *Lectures* out of the Bristol Public Library. In March, Wordsworth selects Burns' quoted lines ('Gie me ae spark') as the epigraph for *The Ruined Cottage*, first of his own great poems of the human heart. That Blair should lie behind the writing both of the 1798 *Lyrical Ballads*, and of the 1800 Preface, adds a final touch. Hazlitt's 'new style' was new all right, but only in the sense that three great poets – Burns, Coleridge, Wordsworth – had made it new. Not that it was a new thing to attempt.

(iii) *'And All Things In Himself': Romantic Platonism*

So shalt thou see and hear
The lovely shapes and sounds intelligible
Of that eternal language, which thy God
Utters, who from eternity doth teach
Himself in all, and all things in himself.
(Coleridge: *Frost at Midnight*, 1798)

This is Coleridge, as the great Unitarian poet of spring 1798, celebrating a God who is the divine principle of the universe. Such thinking, according to his contemporary, Thomas Taylor, the Platonist, is 'coeval with the universe itself'. Other beliefs may break its continuity, but Platonism 'will make its reappearance at different periods of time, as long as the sun himself shall continue to illuminate the world' (*Eleusinian Mysteries* 1790). In the Romantic period Coleridge shares it with his fellow Unitarians, Lamb and Hazlitt; in different forms, with Blake, Wordsworth and Shelley; even at times with Keats and Byron. Those who were attracted to it could turn to philosophers and poets of the mid seventeenth century, Vaughan and Marvell among them, but it goes back at least to Plotinus, in the third century AD. To confuse matters, it could take either its traditional idealist form or a materialist one. In the 1770s it is promoted by Joseph Priestley, scientist, polymath, founder of modern Unitarianism, and (as discoverer of oxygen) effectively founder of modern chemistry too. Attracted by the possibility that science will reveal the nature of God's immanent presence – could it be as electricity? – Coleridge is a follower of Priestley. But he is also a traditional Platonist philosopher, disciple of the Cambridge Platonist, Cudworth, on whom he bases his 1795 *Lectures on Revealed Religion*.

Not everybody could bring together opposing systems so happily – Taylor in his 1792 translation of Plotinus' *Essay on the Beautiful* sneers at the 'truly modern' genius, for whom 'the crucible and the air-pump [symbols of Priestley's experiments on oxygen] are alone the standards of truth'. But Coleridge had an interesting precedent in Anna Laetitia Aikin, protégée of Priestley at Warrington Dissenting Academy, whose *Poems* were published in 1773, and significantly reprinted in 1792. Showing her reading of Heraclitus, Aikin (aged twenty-one, and soon to marry Rochemont Barbauld) speculates that

mind, as ancient sages taught,
A never-dying flame,
Still shifts through matter's varying forms,
In every form the same . . .
(*The Mouse's Petition*)

– that 'There is a tongue in every star that talks with man, / And woos him to be wise' (*A Summer Evening's Meditation*).

Priestleyan Unitarianism taught that Jesus was a man, son of Joseph the carpenter of Nazareth; Trinitarian views (standard in other Christian denominations) were 'idolatry', a splitting of the one God into three that amounted to worshipping idols. In some ways it was a rather down-to-earth religion. 'Consult common sense', wrote Frend, Priestley's disciple and Coleridge's future role-model at Cambridge,

> Could God lie in the womb of a woman? Could God expire on the Cross? Could God be buried in the grave? Shocking suppositions! . . . Search the Scriptures, point out one single passage in which Jesus Christ declared himself to be God. Point out one in which the Apostles declared him to be God.
>
> (*To the Citizens of Cambridge*, 1788)

Coleridge could be pretty down-to-earth himself. 'Quere', he writes in March 1796,

> How is it that Dr Priestley is not an atheist? He asserts in three different places that God not only *does*, but *is*, everything? But if God *be* everything, everything is God – which is all the atheists assert – an eating, drinking, lustful God, with no *unity* of consciousness.

More often, though, he sought ways of understanding the 'unity of consciousness' in which above all he needed to believe. If Jesus was not God – a 'person' of the Trinity – what was he? 'Thou more bright than all the angel blaze, / Despiséd Galilean', Coleridge writes in *Religious Musings* (1794–6), not his most readable poem, but the repository of his Unitarian understandings:

> For chiefly in the oppresséd good man's face
> The Great Invisible (by symbols seen)
> Shines with peculiar and concentred light,
> When, all of self regardless, the scourged saint
> Mourns for the oppressor.

Christ, as the 'oppresséd good man', the 'scourged saint', who has no care for himself (praying for his tormentors, 'Father, forgive them, for they know not what they do'), is pervaded by the 'light' of God's invisible presence. We might see God also in a tree, or in a fallible human being, but we see him especially in the face of the crucified Christ, because in his death Jesus has achieved perfection. It comes as a surprise that Priestleyan Unitarianism should accept the Resurrection, but it does. Christ as perfect man rises from the dead – becomes fully spiritual. In doing so he offers us not merely an example but a guarantee. Finally there is no distinction between matter and spirit. Christ, as man, has shown us the way – which he could not do as God.

Refusal to believe in the divinity of Christ raises the question, how is God present on earth? One answer is that Nature is 'animated' by his breath, consisting of

> organic harps, diversely framed,
> That tremble into thought as o'er them sweeps
> Plastic [creative] and vast one intellectual breeze,
> At once the soul of each and God of all.
> (*The Eolian Harp*, 1795)

Another is that the Great Invisible is 'by symbols seen', that it is our task to read the Book of Nature, interpret the 'eternal language that [our] God utters'. It is this last implication that gives to Coleridge his lifelong preoccupation with imagination – the power that in its 'primary' form (at once perceptive and creative) enables us to perceive the godhead, and perceive ourselves to be at one with it. ' 'Tis the sublime of man', as Coleridge put it in *Religious Musings*,

> Our noontide majesty, to know ourselves
> Parts and proportions of one wondrous whole . . .

adding for good measure, 'But 'tis God / Diffused through all that doth make all one whole.'

To Blake (a true Platonist in this respect) it seemed that 'If the doors of perception were cleansed, everything would appear to man as it is, infinite' (*Marriage of Heaven and Hell*, 1790) – or, to put it another way, that man would regain the lost fourfold vision of eternity. For Wordsworth, things were less certain: imagination was associated with an 'obscure sense of possible sublimity', 'something evermore about to be'. But he did believe that we may be 'laid asleep / In body and become a living soul', that 'with an eye made quiet' we may 'see into the life of things'. Shelley's Humean scepticism denied him the possibility of outright belief: 'God is an hypothesis, and as such in need of proof.' Plato took him on a quest for his epipsyche (soul-mate), rather than Coleridgean definitions of the one. But he was drawn nonetheless to Coleridgean/Wordsworthian pantheism: the 'unknown power' of *Hymn to Intellectual Beauty*, 'the secret strength of things' that 'inhabits' Mont Blanc, are not very far from the 'motion and . . . spirit' that 'rolls through all things in *Tintern Abbey*. It was under the influence of Shelley, and through him, of Wordsworth, that the unsettled

Byron of 1816 briefly accepted this Romantic Platonism. But there was nothing half-hearted about the acceptance: 'I live not in myself, but I become / Portion of that around me' –

> Then stirs the feeling infinite, so felt
> In solitude, where we are least alone –
> A truth which through our being then doth melt,
> And purifies from self; it is a tone,
> The soul and source of music, which makes known
> Eternal harmony . . .

'Wherein lies happiness', Keats asks himself in *Endymion*, and answers:

> In that which becks
> Our ready minds to fellowship divine,
> A fellowship with essence, till we shine
> Full alchemized, and free from space.

Plotinus would have agreed.

2. The Romantic Poets In Context

(i) *The First Generation*

When Burns' Kilmarnock *Poems* came out in 1786, George III had been on the throne for twenty-six years; the American colonists had declared their independence (4 July 1776), and won it after five years of a bloody and unnecessary war; Kant's *Critique of Pure Reason*, Rousseau's *Confessions* and Schiller's *Robbers*, had all emerged in 1781; Pitt had become Prime Minister aged twenty-four in 1783 (and would remain in power almost continuously till 1801); on the English literary scene Charlotte Smith's *Elegiac Sonnets* had appeared and Dr Johnson had died, in 1784; in 1786 Mozart's *Marriage of Figaro* had received its first performance. There was no clear sense of the end of one era, or the beginning of another, but in 1787 the American Constitution would be drafted and signed, and in 1789 would come the storming of the Bastille. In 1786, Burns was an unsuccessful farmer and rather too successful lover. His finances were desperate; publishing his songs was a last attempt to earn some money before emigrating to the West

Indies. Wordsworth was an orphan, well educated at a Cumbrian grammar school (and by the Cumbrian mountains), and about to go south to Cambridge, where he would complete his first major poem, *An Evening Walk*, Romantic in neither form nor vision. The big issue in 1788 was slavery: a bill restricting, but not abolishing, the carriage of slaves in British ships brought out poems by Cowper (*Sweet Meat Has Sour Sauce*), Hannah More and Ann Yearsley. To 1789, but yet uninfluenced by the Revolution, belong the new voice of Blake's *Songs of Innocence* (earliest poems 1784), and the unabashed nostalgia of Bowles' *Fourteen Sonnets*.

Initial British response to the Revolution was that the French had got there in the end. It was partly complacency, partly that by chance the previous year had been the hundredth anniversary of the English 'Glorious Revolution' of 1688, when the Catholic James II had been forced into exile, and replaced by Parliament with William of Orange, Dutch Protestant husband of Charles II's daughter Mary. Traditionalists saw the terms imposed in 1688 as establishing painlessly the glories of British constitutional monarchy, radicals (many of them dissenters, barred from the universities, and from holding civil office) saw them as offering precedent for the people's sacking and replacing of a king. It was to the anniversary meeting of the Society for Commemorating the Revolution in Great Britain that Richard Price in November 1789 preached the sermon that provoked Edmund Burke to his attack on the French, setting off a debate which ensured that readers and writers of the early Romantic period were forced to take sides. Fastest in their responses to Burke were Mary Wollstonecraft and Catherine Macaulay, most important in the long run was Thomas Paine. 'I am contending', he wrote magnificently in *The Rights of Man*, Part I (March 1791), 'for the rights of the living, and Mr Burke is contending for the authority of the dead.'

As author of the pamphlet *Common Sense* which had precipitated the Declaration of Independence, Paine took it for granted that the American and French Revolutions should, and would, be followed by an up-to-date English one. Part II of *The Rights of Man* offered a blueprint for an egalitarian state. Workingmen's clubs were set up to buy and read the pamphlets, and an estimated 200,000 were sold (each doubtless reaching many readers). Though impressive in its indignation, Wollstonecraft's *Vindication of the Rights of Men* was hurried to the press, and based on no comparable experience. But she too followed her first pamphlet with a sequel – the now-famous *Vindication of the Rights of Woman* (1792). Feminism became an issue. For good reason those who followed Wollstonecraft's lead tended to examine the problems at greater length in novels, or prose polemics, rather than verse. But there is the great exception of Blake's *Visions of the Daughters of Albion*, equating the lives of British women (Albion's daughters) with those of American slaves, protesting with passionate eloquence against male dominance, and celebrating female independence of mind and will:

> I cry love, love, love! Happy, happy love!
> Can that be love that drinks another as a sponge drinks water?

Of the big Romantic poets only Blake was of an age to greet the Revolution at its outset, and his attempt is perhaps the one outright failure in his writing, detail deadening his imagination. Coleridge, aged sixteen, made a shot at it, demanding in *On the Fall of the Bastille*, 'Shall France alone a despot spurn?' and concluding hopefully, 'Let favoured Britain ever be / First of the first, and freest of the free!' Two years older than Coleridge, Wordsworth emerges, not as the immediate commentator (a role filled by Helen Maria Williams' prose *Letters from France*), but as an on-the-spot observer who stored his material for later composition. The evidence of his own eyes as he walked beside the Loire in 1792, led him to give his heart to the people. Under the guidance of the aristocrat-republican, Michel Beaupuy, he came to believe that 'poverty . . . would in a little time / Be found no more' – that we should see

> All institutes for ever blotted out
> That legalized exclusion, empty pomp
> Abolished, sensual state, and cruel power
> (Whether by edict of the one or few),
> And finally, as sum and crown of all,
> Should see the people having a strong hand
> In making their own laws – whence better days
> To all mankind!
>
> (1805) *Prelude*, XI)

Back in England, in 1793 Wordsworth writes his republican pamphlet (justifying firmly the execution on Louis XVI), and a clumsy, vehement anti-war poem, *Salisbury Plain* – neither of them published. For different reasons similarly unknown at the time, was Blake's great imaginative response to repression, *Songs of Experience*, drafted in 1791–2, and sold to a handful of readers from 1794 in illuminated individual copies:

> How the chimney-sweeper's cry
> Every blackening church appals,
> And the hapless soldier's sigh
> Runs in blood down palace-walls.

It is Coleridge who at this time is beginning to take the public eye, embarking as he leaves Cambridge in December 1794 on his series of political sonnets, celebrating heroes of world revolution – Godwin, Lafayette, Kosciusko. Without even a degree to show for his time at the university, he settled (aged twenty-two) into his role of the mid Nineties – an amalgam of poet, political agitator and Unitarian philosopher, lecturing in Bristol to considerable audiences, and writing on the side his early Conversation Poems and Unitarian *Religious Musings*: 'There is one mind, one omnipresent mind / Omnific, his most holy name is love.' The poetry was clumsy, Miltonic, passionate, and unsteadily improved. With hindsight we can see it leading, via *The Eolian Harp* and *This Lime-Tree Bower, My Prison*, to *Frost at Midnight*, and giving expression to the underlying beliefs of *The Ancient Mariner*.

The great Romantic poetry was slow to emerge. Blake was producing his own entirely private version, that would take him from *The Book of Urizen* (foundation of his personal myth) to the vastly impressive, not very accessible, epics, *Vala*, *Milton*, *Jerusalem*. Burns, after twelve years of poetry (1784–96), was dead, leaving a penniless family and a mass of poetry scattered through different song-books, including his masterpiece, *Tam O' Shanter*:

> Kings may be blest, but Tam was glorious,
> O'er a' the ills o' life victorious!

Southey was coming through, with his pro-French epic, *Joan of Arc* (1796) and the humanitarian protest-poetry of his 1797 and 1799 collections. Probably the most accomplished poet, though, of this pre-*Lyrical Ballads* moment was Mary Robinson. Like Charlotte Smith (whose *Elegiac Sonnets* continued to expand though she had turned novelist to support her immense family), Robinson was a woman writer overcoming difficulties that did not afflict her rising male contemporaries. Like Smith, she valued the sonnet-form for its concentration; unlike her, she employed it for narrative, distancing emotion through a dramatizing of Sappho, earliest and (by reputation) greatest of women poets.

For no evident reason it was in 1797 that Wordsworth and Coleridge suddenly started writing at their best. Coleridge had published, and published again, his early poems, without ever showing his true greatness. Wordsworth had written and rewritten *Salisbury Plain*, and composed his Shakespearean tragedy, *The Borderers*. Then, as if feeling he'd learnt his trade, Wordsworth wrote in May–early June 1797 a fluent first version of *The Ruined Cottage*. It would be convenient to ascribe the change to the two poets' effect on each other, which was immense in the year that followed. But a completed text of *The Ruined Cottage* was read to Coleridge on 5 June, when he appeared at Racedown (the west Dorset farmhouse where Wordsworth and his sister, Dorothy had been living since September 1795) and persuaded them to come and live close to him at his cottage at Nether

Stowey in the Quantock Hills of Somerset. Wordsworth's influence on Coleridge is at all times more difficult to judge, but one certainly wouldn't guess that it was important to *Kubla Khan*, first of Coleridge's great poems, and written in November. Be that as it may, Coleridge in the six month's period, November 1797–April 1798, wrote his four most famous poems, *Kubla Khan*, *The Ancient Mariner*, *Frost at Midnight* and *Christabel*, Part I, as well as *France: An Ode* and *The Nightingale*. Wordsworth in a similar period, beginning January 1798, wrote *The Discharged Soldier*, the bulk of the *Lyrical Ballads*, and finally, in mid July, *Tintern Abbey*. For good measure, Dorothy, who contributed much to this year of inspiring companionship, composed alongside the poetry the first of her *Journals*. By chance 1798 saw the writing of Jane Austen's *Northanger Abbey* alongside Wordsworth's *Tintern*.

Containing as it does *The Ancient Mariner* and *Tintern Abbey*, the two seminal poems of the Romantic period, *Lyrical Ballads* 1798 has to be considered a high point. Coleridge would write little poetry in the years that followed: *Genevieve* and a second less inspired part of *Christabel* in 1800; *Letter to Sara Hutchinson* (and its rewriting, *Dejection: An Ode*) in 1802; *To William Wordsworth* in 1807, and not a lot more. In 1801 Coleridge, by now irrecoverably addicted to opium and German philosophy, grumbled that he was no more than 'a species of metaphysician'. As journalist, critic and philosopher, he was for the rest of his life a prose-writer, and merely an occasional poet. Not so Wordsworth. He too famously lived to be past his best, but before his great decade ended with *Poems in Two Volumes* (1807) he had written the Lucy Poems, the Matthew Poems, and two-part *Prelude* of 1798–9; *The Brothers*, *Michael* (and Preface to *Lyrical Ballads*) in 1800; the inspired sonnets of 1802; *The Leech Gatherer*, *The Immortality Ode*, *Daffodils*, and other Grasmere lyrics of 1802–4; *The Solitary Reaper* and *Elegiac Stanzas* of 1805–6; the thirteen-book *Prelude* of 1805 – and much, much more. Had he not thought it too egotistical to publish the autobiographical *Prelude* when it was completed and revised in 1806, the course of literary history would have been quite different; even so, his influence on the second-generation Romantics and on the Victorians was pervasive.

(ii) *A Gap*

The gap that is felt to exist between the first- and second-generation Romantics is widened by the fact that so little major poetry was published between 1800 and 1810. By rights it should have been the period when the women writers came into their own. But Robinson died at Christmas 1800, aged forty-one, the last phase of her remarkable life seeing her as a purveyor of poetry (alongside Coleridge) to the *Morning Post*, and author of *Lyrical*

Tales (more in the manner of Southey than Wordsworth). Smith died in 1807, worn out with Dickensian legal battles (concluded after thirty-seven years, when she was long dead) over money intended for the children (six of the original twelve being alive at her death). Yet in her last years she wrote the quite new poetry of *Beachy Head*, going back to the landscape of her childhood as she had often done in the Elegiac Sonnets, but with a wider sweep and greater assurance. Helen Maria Williams, who with Smith had seemed in the 1780s more than a match for her male contemporaries, had emigrated and turned to prose; Joanna Baillie, after her impressive (anonymous) *Poems* 1790, had turned playwright; Anna Laetitia Barbauld had turned editor, on a large scale, but would make a comeback as poet with *Eighteen Hundred and Eleven*. Only Mary Tighe came forward at this period, publishing in 1805 her wonderfully controlled Spenserian allegory, *Psyche* – but publishing it in Ireland and in numbers so small that it was virtually unknown until the three posthumous London editions of 1811.

Among the men, Southey (like Wordsworth) went unconcernedly on, publishing a sequence of epics, or romances, including *Thalaba* (1801, a Mohammedan spiritual quest, admired by Newman) and *Madoc* (a legend of Welsh benevolent conquistadors, 1805) both original in their documented bookish way. As difficult to revive as Southey, would now be Campbell (*Gertrude of Wyoming*, 1809) and Moore (*Lalla Rookh*, 1817) both of whom were rated more highly in their day than any save Byron of those we now think of as the major Romantics. Still more important to our understanding of the age, and selling in record numbers, is Scott. Wordsworth was not best pleased, managing to be grumpy even to Scott himself (the most affable of men), but there could be no doubt that historical romance was to the public's liking. *The Lay of the Last Minstrel* (1805), *Marmion* (1808) and *The Lady of the Lake* (1810) sold between them more than 70,000 copies. It is a reminder that our version of the Romantic period is a reflection of our taste, not that of the time. We refuse a place among the great to Scott, who sold in tens of thousands, and award one to Blake, whose best-seller, the combined *Songs of Innocence and Experience*, sold thirty-seven copies. Byron in *English Bards and Scotch Reviewers* (1809) and Hunt in *Feast of the Poets* (1814) both in the same way refused a place to Wordsworth, though they came to know they had been wrong. Shelley and Keats among the second generation were almost wholly unregarded by their contemporaries, yet hindsight places them with the best-selling Byron.

(iii) *The Second Generation*

Romantic poets of the first generation (Smith, Burns, Robinson, Blake, Southey, Coleridge and Wordsworth) are all writing at the height of their powers by the end of the 1790s. Those of the second generation (Byron, Shelley, Hunt, Hemans, Keats, Landon and Hood) come into their own twenty years later, in the 'teens of the new century. Bridged by a war that lasts twenty-two years, 1793–1815, the two periods have much in common in terms of restrictive governments, poverty and social unrest. But for all the failure of the Revolution, and of hope in political causes (constitutional reform, anti-slavery legislation), the 1790s have an optimism that has gone in the later period – an optimism curiously linked to the Revolution that failed. Romanticism emerges from hope transmuted – perhaps in the first generation it *is* hope transmuted. Blake, Coleridge and Wordsworth are at times openly millenarian; they view man as godlike in his potential. Their theme is imagination, the human power that can enable man to perceive, and to share in, the godhead. Merely to name imagination is for us to bring to mind *Biographia Literaria* and Coleridge's definitions: 'the prime agent of all human perception', 'a repetition in the finite mind of the infinite I AM'. But *Biographia* was an irrelevance when it came out (as *The Prelude* would be when finally published in 1850) – old-fashioned, out-of-date, a lingering on of concerns of the earlier generation. No second edition of *Biographia* was called for.

For all their genius, the first generation are a part of what is going on – quite a humble part. They seek earnestly to influence things through their writing, but have no power – that is in the hands of the aristocracy (Byron and Shelley's class, not theirs). With the exception of Blake (who as a low-bred Londoner is still further from the ruling elite), they are provincials, for the most part working and publishing outside London. Smith, Robinson, Southey, Coleridge and Wordsworth belonged to the gentry: their daughters could have told Lady Catherine, as did Elizabeth Bennett, that they were the same class as Mr Darcy. But Darcy had land. And land, despite industrialization and the rise of the entrepreneur, was power – could enter where it would, marry where it chose. The first-generation Romantics, by these standards, were dowdy, lacking in style. Byron and Shelley were noblemen, Byron with a seat in the House of Lords, Shelley the son of a Whig baronet, with a thousand a year and relatives in the Lords who were useful to him when his political goings-on drew the attention of the Home Office.

Radicalism in the two generations brings the differences into focus. Wordsworth in 1792 was drawn into the Revolution by seeing a 'hunger-bitten' girl on the banks of the Loire; Coleridge was a known Bristol agitator opposing the Two Bills of autumn 1795; Southey was singled out for parody in the *Anti-Jacobin*, 1797, because he was seen as dangerously articulate in his humanitarian poetry. Byron's maiden speech in the Lords was a protest at the government's wish to hang Nottinghamshire machine-breakers. It was sincere, but though his interest in the weavers' cause came from their being his neighbours at Newstead Abbey, he knew little of them. Perhaps if *Childe Harold* had not been such a success, there would have been more of the caring Byron, but as it was he dropped politics for Lady Caroline Lamb and the Regency social scene. Shelley's compassion was no less distant. Aged nineteen, but already blending pragmatism with his ideals, he crossed to Ireland ready to take part in a rebellion. Discovering the actualities of working-class poverty and ignorance, he returned disgusted to England, resolved to dedicate his revolutionary poem, *Queen Mab*, not to the lower classes but to the sons and daughters of the nobility (who, like himself, might care). Even *The Mask of Anarchy*, great political poem as it is, and written to express the poet's shock at the Peterloo Massacre (1819) could hardly be further from the people it was designed to help.

Where, one might ask, are Keats and others in all this? Norton (*A Voice from the Factories*) and the Landon of *The Factory* had strong political feelings and Hood too; Hemans didn't. Hunt went to prison for libelling the Prince Regent. He had his family and possessions around him, though, and as a political martyr enjoyed his visitors' admiration; his one moment of recorded discomfort came on the first night when he was put in a room where he could hear the working-class prisoners shaking their chains. With Hunt and Hazlitt as friends, Keats ought to be politically minded, and critics now claim that he was. Lack of a single major political poem doesn't strengthen the case. It was Wordsworth (rebuked for his 'egotistical sublime'), not Keats, who showed his 'negative capability' by getting inside the minds of beggars and forsaken Indian women. Keats, if the truth be told, was in a different way as aloof as Byron and Shelley. *Tintern Abbey* speaks of moods in which 'the affections gently lead *us* on', in which '*we* see into the life of things'; *Ode to a Nightingale* in its solepsistic beauty shares with no one, values only the moods of the writer.

If the first-generation Romantics got rather slowly under way, the second did so with a flourish. It is true that Byron had published his precocious *Hours of Idleness* at the age of nineteen in 1807, and the polemic *English Bards and Scots Reviewers* in 1809, but these gave no warning of the impact he would make in March 1812 with *Childe Harold* I and II. He awoke, as he said, and found himself famous: 500 copies were sold on the first day. 1812 was the year in which Dickens and Browning were born, the United States declared war on Britain, Napoleon disastrously invaded Russia, and the Tory Prime Minister, Spencer Percival, was shot in the lobby of the House of Commons. George III was still technically on the throne, but because his madness was now unremitting, the Prince of Wales had been Regent for a year. Shelley had contrived to be sent down from Oxford for publishing a pamphlet on the *Necessity of Atheism*, and was, at nineteen, at work on *Queen Mab* ('privished' 1813), denouncing monarchy, war and organized religion. Keats was seventeen, and had for two years been apprenticed to an apothecary-surgeon. Felicia Hemans (born Felicia Browne) put out her second volume, *Poems of the Domestic Affections*, in 1812 and married the ne'er-do-well Captain Alfred, who resented her writing and left her in 1818 when she was carrying their fifth son.

The years 1813–15 saw the final stages of the French War. Napoleon had fatally weakened himself with the invasion of Russia, and appalling losses of the wintertime retreat from Moscow. In 1813 he was defeated near Leipzig at the Battle of the Nations; Paris was captured in April 1814, the worthless Bourbons were reinstated, and the Emperor was exiled to Elba, off the coast of Italy. The story of the Hundred Days – Napoleon's escape in March 1815, his triumphant return to Paris, and raising of a new Grand Army – deserved a more romantic ending than defeat at Waterloo and final sad exile on faraway St Helena. On the literary scene (and the aristocratic social scene) these were Byron's years. Switching from the travelogue of *Childe Harold* to the eastern romance, he created from his travels an exotic genre all his own. In 1813 *The Bride of Abydos* was written in a week, and *The Corsair* in ten days. *The Giaour* followed and, in 1814, *Lara*. Educated in romance by Scott, readers were delighted by this more stylish variant – and the Byronic hero was born. The old guard, meanwhile, were quietly advancing themselves. Southey (once a leading Jacobin, now a Tory reviewer with the *Quarterly*) became Poet Laureate; Wordsworth came out with *The Excursion* (1814) in a handsome quarto, and took a sinecure job in the gift of the Lowther family (who, be it said, had employed his father and grandfather before him); Coleridge earned a little money when his play (written as *Osorio*, 1797, rechristened *Remorse*, 1813) ran for thirteen nights at Drury Lane, and went through three editions. Scott, after refusing the Laureateship in 1814, turned to the novel, publishing *Waverley* anonymously in 1815, and proving just as successful as he had been as a poet. From his prison, Hunt offered in *Feast of the Poets* an assessment of how his contemporaries were doing, with Southey at the top table, but still not Wordsworth (a nineteen-page footnote shows Hunt's anxiety at leaving him out). Coleridge, as poet, was little known, his poems being scattered here and there in early editions and newspapers, and some as yet unpublished.

In October 1815 Keats became a student at Guy's Hospital, and in the following year he wrote the first of his great poems: 'Much have I travelled in the realms of gold' (*On First Looking into Chapman's Homer*). Shelley's *Alastor* appeared in 1816, again establishing an unmistakable new voice. Beginning with Byron's separation (after one-year's troubled marriage), and his exile to the Continent, this was to be one of the great years of Romantic achievement. Coleridge's *Kubla Khan* and *Christabel* were published, after almost twenty years in manuscript. Byron, as a Bonapartist, made his public goodbye in the tones of Napoleon –

> Farewell to the land where the gloom of my glory
> Arose and o'ershadowed the earth with its fame!
> She abandons me now, but the page of her story,
> The brightest or blackest, is filled with my name

– and his private ones in the impassioned lyric voices of *Fare Thee Well* (to his wife) and *Stanzas to Augusta* (to his half-sister and closest companion, mother of his child, Medora). Joining up with Shelley on Lake Geneva, he wrote also *The Prisoner of Chillon* and the powerful third Canto of *Childe Harold*. Shelley contributed *Hymn to Intellectual Beauty* and *Mont Blanc*, and the eighteen-year-old Mary Godwin (soon to be Mary Shelley) embarked on *Frankenstein*.

1817 saw the death of Jane Austen, whose novels were published between 1811 and 1818 (though *Sense and Sensibility*, *Pride and Prejudice* and *Northanger Abbey* go back to 1796–8). Coleridge finally brought together his poems (except for *Kubla Khan* and *Christabel*, published the previous year) in *Sybilline Leaves*, and Keats published the first of his three volumes, containing *Chapman's Homer* (perhaps the greatest Romantic sonnet of them all) and *Sleep and Poetry*. Talking-point of the year was Moore's eastern romance, *Lalla Rookh*. Shelley was at work on *Laon and Cythna* (later, *The Revolt of Islam*), and at the end of the year wrote *Ozymandias*. Frere meanwhile published his delightful *Whistlecraft*, which would provide Byron with the metre of *Don Juan* – begun in 1818, the year in which Shelley (by now in Italy) translates Plato's *Symposium*, writes *Julian and Maddalo* and begins *Prometheus Unbound*. In England, Keats' brother Tom dies of TB (handing it on in the process); in Prussia, Karl Marx is born. Queen Victoria and Walt Whitman are born in 1819, most productive of years for the later Romantics. Keats writes *The Eve of St Agnes*, *La Belle Dame Sans Merci*, the Odes, *Lamia*, *To Autumn* and *The Fall of Hyperion*. Byron publishes Cantos I and II of *Don Juan*, including the episode of Juan and Julia, and the Shipwreck. Shelley completes *Prometheus Unbound*, writes *The Mask of Anarchy*, *Ode to the West Wind* and *Peter Bell the Third*. The last, an acute and brilliant satire of Wordsworth, who had published the eccentric *Peter Bell* (after holding it twenty years in manuscript), and been parodied – in advance! – by Keats' friend Reynolds in *Peter Bell, A Lyrical Ballad*.

1820 saw, at long last, the death of George III. As Poet Laureate, Southey celebrated in sychophantic hexameters his reception into Heaven, unwisely choosing to attack Byron and the 'Satanic School' as he did so. Using Southey's title, *A Vision of Judgment* (but replacing the tentative 'A' with 'The'), Byron in Venice set aside *Don Juan* to write a beautifully scathing double-lampoon, on Southey as vainglorious turncoat and George as incompetent monarch. 'The New World shook him off', Satan comments to the Archangel Michael at the gates of Heaven,

> the Old yet groans
> Beneath what he and his prepared, if not
> Completed. He leaves heirs on many thrones
> To all his vices . . .

Wordsworth's *Duddon Sonnets* (memorable for the *Afterthought*, almost the last of his great poems) appeared in 1820, alongside Shelley's *Prometheus Unbound and Other Poems*, and Keats' *Lamia, Isabella and The Eve of St Agnes.* On 18 September Keats departed for Italy – to die. Shelley in Pisa was writing great poetry, including *Epipsychidion*, *To a Skylark* and *The Cloud*, despite the deaths of his two children, and the sad alienation of Mary. Byron was living in Venice and Ravenna with Countess Guiccioli, plotting revolution with her family, the Gambas, and completing the great Haidee episode of *Don Juan* (Cantos III–V, published 1821). Deserted by her husband in 1818, Hemans had embarked on her programme of yearly publications to feed the five children; nine years younger, L. E. L. (Letitia Elizabeth Landon) was beginning to intrigue readers of the *Literary Gazette* with the charm and skill of her initialled contributions. Clare's *Poems Descriptive of Rural Life* had emerged in 1820, carefully packaged by Keats' publisher, Taylor and Hessey – and gained much more success than Keats. Already seeing the skull beneath the skin, Beddoes (later to write *Death's Jest-Book*) had in 1821 published *The Bride's Tragedy*, a version of the Gothic closer to Webster than to Radcliffe: 'Who put this iron aspic in my hand?' Hood had now become assistant editor of the *London Magazine*, in which De Quincey (*Confessions of an English Opium Eater*), Lamb (*Essays of Elia*) and Hazlitt (*Spirit of the Age*), all tried out the prose masterpieces for which they are famous.

Keats' death came (after more than a year of being forbidden by his doctors to excite himself by writing poetry or seeing Fanny Brawne) on 23 February 1821 in Rome, in a small room above the bustle and life of the Spanish Steps. With his experience of nursing Tom, and his medical training, he had known from the first what would be the outcome. Shelley heard the news in Pisa, and with Milton's *Lycidas* in mind wrote the great elegy for his fellow-poet, *Adonais*, revealing as he did so an extraordinary death wish, and rising in his conclusion to an apocalyptic grandeur:

> The breath whose might I have invoked in song
> Descends on me – my spirit's bark is driven
> Far from the shore, far from the trembling throng
> Whose sails were never to the tempest given.

> The massy earth and spheréd skies are riven!
> I am borne darkly, fearfully, afar,
> Whilst, burning through the inmost veil of Heaven,
> The soul of Adonais like a star,
> Beacons from the abode where the Eternals are.

That Shelley, on 8 July 1822, should drive the new boat he had had built into the eye of a Mediterranean storm, refusing to take in sail, has a frightening appropriateness; that he should have in his pocket, when his body was washed ashore, a copy of Keats' 1820 Poems, completes the picture. Byron, who sat in his carriage as Hunt burned Shelley on the beach to comply with quarantine regulations, was thinking rather of death in battle than at sea. The Greek War of Independence had begun the previous year; though he enjoyed the company and the plotting of the Gambas, Byron had never been fully convinced by the Carbonari – now here was a cause that touched him. In the period before he set sail for Greece at Christmas 1823 he was writing exceedingly fast: Cantos VI–VIII of *Don Juan* are finished by July, IX–XI belong to August, XII–XIV are complete by December. Meanwhile in England the literary scene was changing. Poetry, which had sold well up to the period when Scott turned novelist and Byron went into exile, was no longer profitable. There were no more than five poets worth publishing, Murray told Southey in 1818. The new money-makers were the albums and annuals: *The Gem*, *The Casket*, *The Amulet*, *Fisher's Drawing-Room Scrap-Book* – the last edited by Landon in the early 1830s. Illustrations were as important as the poetry, in fact they literally came first. Steel-engraving offered the possibility of multiple copies at a very high finish, as the plates didn't wear. Poets were supplied with pictures to 'illustrate' in words. Landon became immensely skilled at this new art, writing almost the whole of the *Scrap-book* herself, taking up different topics, voices, viewpoints, some evidently connected with the engravings, others more ingenious in their quest for variety. Significantly *The Improvisatrice*, 1823, which provided her first major success, offers a medley of stories and metres artfully woven together. It was the style of the day.

Byron's death at Missolonghi on 19 April 1824 was not the 'soldier's grave' that he had pictured for himself, fighting in a just cause at the head of the 'Byron Brigade', troops whom he had armed and trained. It came instead from marsh fever, and the attentions of a doctor who weakened his patient's resistance by frequent bleeding to lower his temperature. And it came after months of disillusion, not with the cause, but with the Greek leaders, who bickered among themselves instead of fighting the Turks. Keats,

> Now more than ever seems it rich to die,
> To cease upon the midnight with no pain . . .

– Shelley,

> Death is the veil which those who live call life:
> They sleep, and it is lifted.

– Byron,

> Seek out – less often sought than found –
>   A soldier's grave (for thee the best);
> Then look around, and choose thy ground,
>   And take thy rest.

had all in different moods found death attractive. Now it had come, and within a space of three years. It was almost an irrelevance that Blake, Wordsworth and Coleridge lived on. Their deaths would have changed nothing; those of their successors (Keats aged twenty-six, Shelley thirty, Byron thirty-six) changed forever our perception of Romantic poetry and the Romantic period. It came to be about young writers – and writers whose ideals were young. In retrospect, this worked for the first generation too. They hadn't died – hadn't even found death attractive – but Coleridge's great poetry was written when he was twenty-five, Wordsworth's between the ages of twenty-seven and thirty-six; Blake is more sustained, but the inspiration that carries into his later work both as poet and painter belongs to the 1790s, when he was in his thirties.

(iv) *The Sense of an Ending*

A cluster of moments, events and publications defines the last stage of the Romantic period: Hazlitt, at work on *The Spirit of the Age*, for instance, and writing about *Don Juan*. Byron, he tells us, 'is that anomale in letters, a noble poet' – aristocrats should be idle, and leave the field to others, poets should be needy and come from more restless classes. News reaches him, as he writes, of Byron's death. He has the opportunity to modify some quite harsh criticism – and doesn't. Death is the leveller, cancels all, yet Hazlitt owes it to truth, to the period, to Byron himself, to say what he has said. *The Spirit of the Age* is no mere collection of portraits; Hazlitt writes because he feels the period he has lived through to *be* an age, a portion of history, with its own integrity.

Blake dies in 1827, amid a circle of disciples, the Ancients, among whom is a young Romantic painter and occasional poet, Samuel Palmer. Clare's *Shepherd's Calendar* is published, having been kept back for three years by Taylor, who revises it (not always for the worse) and holds it because he knows the time has passed for Nature-poetry of dedicated observation:

The tottergrass upon the hill,
And spiders' threads, are standing still . . .

Hood and Hunt go on writing, sometimes very well, in the later Twenties and Thirties, but it is the women poets – Hemans, Landon and Norton – who make the end of the Romantic period memorable. Hemans especially stands out. *Records of Woman* (1828) is written by a woman about women, and quite largely (one supposes) for women. But it is not feminist in the sense of championing one sex against the other, or claiming for it equality or similarity. Rather it sets out to give women their due in an imperfect world. In the 1790s Robinson had identified with Sappho more as a woman betrayed by her lover than as a poet. In her greatest poem, *Properzia Rossi*, Hemans offers us a Roman sculptress consciously shaping the brow of her 'Forsaken Ariadne' to take on her own history, yet quarreling with her art as she does so, as cause of the suffering that she imparts. It is through these layers of implication that we approach Hemans herself, also deserted, but an artist of extraordinary subtlety and strength:

It comes – the power
Within me born flows back – my fruitless dower
That could not win me love! . . .
Line by line,
I fix my thought, heart, soul, to burn, to shine,
Through the pale marble's veins. It grows – and now
I give my own life's history to thy brow,
Forsaken Ariadne!

Hemans gives to Properzia, who gives to Ariadne, who is and is not marble, the predicament of the woman creative artist. She dies aged forty-one in 1835, two years before Victoria comes to the throne, and is celebrated in his *Extempore Effusion* by Wordsworth (who knows that it is the ending of an era) alongside Scott, Crabbe, Coleridge and Lamb, all recently dead:

but why
O'er ripe fruit, seasonably gathered,
Should frail survivors heave a sigh?

Mourn rather for that holy spirit,
Sweet as the spring, as ocean deep –
For her who, ere her summer faded,
Has sunk into a breathless sleep.

Though Wordsworth himself would live on until 1850, the future lay with Tennyson, whose *Poems Chiefly Lyrical* had appeared in 1830, and with Browning, *Pauline*, 1833.

THE POETRY

I. Romantic Hallmarks

A reader who browses through Romantic Hallmarks will hear, not so much the themes – those develop through later sections – as the voices and the tones of Romantic poetry: 'Ah, hills beloved . . .', 'In Xanadu did Kubla Khan . . .', 'Oft had I heard of Lucy Gray . . .', 'And did those feet in ancient time . . .', 'On with the dance, let joy be unconfined . . .', 'Season of mists and mellow fruitfulness . . .', 'I remember, I remember . . .', 'Abou Ben Adhem, may his tribe increase . . .'. This is what Romanticism is like, this is what makes it so touching and special. It has an immediacy rarely found in other periods. Many will know the magic of these poems; those who do not will find themselves captured by something that is at once high art, and a part of themselves – something that stirs the imagination, yet seems to come from within. It is a valuing of all that is most precious in existence: of love, of feeling, of imagination in its highest form, which is an awareness of the sacred. It celebrates the ordinary because that is what we have, it celebrates the exotic because that which is different, strange, brings out in us our own creativity. It is a poetry for those who love life, who feel with Blake that everything that lives is holy. It needs no introduction.

1. CHARLOTTE SMITH

To the South Downs (*Elegiac Sonnets* 1784)

Ah, hills beloved! where once, a happy child,
   Your beechen shades, 'your turf, your flowers among',
I wove your bluebells into garlands wild,
   And woke your echoes with my artless song –
Ah, hills beloved! your turf, your flowers, remain,
   But can they peace to this sad breast restore –
For one poor moment soothe the sense of pain,
   And teach a breaking heart to throb no more?
And you, Aruna, in the vale below,
   As to the sea your limpid waves you bear,
Can you one kind Lethean cup bestow
   To drink a long oblivion to my care?
Ah no! when all, e'en hope's last ray, is gone,
There's no oblivion – but in death alone.

2. ROBERT BURNS

To a Mountain Daisy, on Turning One Down with the Plough, April 1786

(Kilmarnock 1786)

Wee, modest, crimson-tippéd flower,
Thou's met me in an evil hour;
For I maun crush amang the stoure
   Thy slender stem:
To spare thee now is past my power,
   Thou bonnie gem.

Alas! It's no thy neebor sweet,
The bonnie lark, companion meet,
Bending thee 'mang the dewy weet,
   Wi' spreckled breast,
When upward-springing, blythe, to greet
   The purpling east.

Cauld blew the bitter-biting north
Upon thy early, humble birth;
Yet cheerfully thou glinted forth
   Amid the storm,
Scarce reared above the parent-earth
   Thy tender form.

The flaunting flowers our gardens yield,
High sheltering woods and wa's maun shield;
But thou, beneath the random bield
   O' clod or stane,
Adorns the histie stibble-field,
   Unseen, alane.

There, in thy scanty mantle clad,
Thy snawie bosom sun-ward spread,
Thou lifts thy unassuming head

3 *stoure* dust. **9** *'mang the dewy weet* among the dewy wet.
20 *wa's* walls. **21** *bield* protection, cover. **23** *histie* dry, stony.

In humble guise;
But now the share uptears thy bed,
And low thou lies!

Such is the fate of artless maid,
Sweet floweret of the rural shade,
By love's simplicity betrayed,
And guileless trust;
Till she, like thee, all soiled, is laid
Low i' the dust.

Such is the fate of simple bard,
On Life's rough ocean luckless starred!
Unskilful he to note the card
Of prudent lore,
Till billows rage, and gales blow hard,
And whelm him o'er!

Such fate to suffering Worth is given,
Who long with wants and woes has striven,
By human pride or cunning driven
To misery's brink;
Till, wrenched of every stay but Heaven,
He, ruined, sink!

Even thou who mournst the Daisy's fate,
That fate is thine – no distant date –
Stern Ruin's plough-share drives elate,
Full on thy bloom,
Till crushed beneath the furrow's weight
Shall be thy doom!

38 *luckless starred* fated to be unlucky. **39** *note the card* chart the course.
47 *of every stay* from every support.

3. MARY ROBINSON

A London Summer Morning (1794; publ. 1804)

Who has not waked to list the busy sounds
Of summer morning in the sultry smoke
Of noisy London? On the pavement hot
The sooty chimney-boy, with dingy face
And tattered covering, shrilly hawks his trade,
Rousing the sleepy housemaid. At the door
The milk-pail rattles, and the tinkling bell
Proclaims the dustman's office, while the street
Is lost in clouds impervious. Now begins
The din of hackney coaches, wagons, carts;
While tin-men's shops, and noisy trunk-makers,
Knife-grinders, coopers, squealing cork-cutters,
Fruit-barrows, and the hunger-giving cries
Of vegetable vendors, fill the air.
Now every shop displays its varied trade,
And the fresh-sprinkled pavement cools the feet
Of early walkers. At the private door
The ruddy housemaid twirls the busy mop,
Annoying the smart 'prentice, or neat girl
Tripping with bandbox lightly. Now the sun
Darts burning splendour on the glittering pane,
Save where the canvas awning throws a shade
On the gay merchandise. Now spruce and trim
In shops where beauty smiles with industry,
Sits the smart damsel, while the passenger
Peeps through the window, watching every charm.
Now pastry dainties catch the eyes minute
Of hummy insects, while the slimy snare
Waits to enthral them. Now the lamp-lighter
Mounts the slight ladder, nimbly venturous,
To trim the half-filled lamp, while at his feet
The pot-boy yells discordant. All along
The sultry pavement, the old-clothes man cries
In tone monotonous, and sidelong views
The area for his traffic. Now the bag
Is slily opened, and the half-worn suit
(Sometimes the pilfered treasure of the base
Domestic spoiler) for one half its worth

Sinks in the green abyss. The porter now
Bears his huge load along the burning way,
And the poor poet wakes from busy dreams
To paint the summer morning.

4. SAMUEL TAYLOR COLERIDGE

Kubla Khan (Nov. 1797; publ. 1816)

In the summer of the year 1797, the author, then in ill health, had retired to a lonely farmhouse between Porlock and Linton, on the Exmoor confines of Somerset and Devonshire. In consequence of a slight indisposition, an anodyne had been prescribed, from the effects of which he fell asleep in his chair at the moment when he was reading the following sentence, or words of the same substance, in *Purchase's Pilgrimage*: 'Here the Khan Kubla commanded a palace to be built, and a stately garden thereunto. And thus ten miles of fertile ground were enclosed with a wall.' The author continued for about three hours in a profound sleep, at least of the external senses, during which time he has the most vivid confidence that he could not have composed less than from two to three hundred lines – if that indeed can be called composition in which all the images rose up before him as *things*, with a parallel production of the correspondent expressions, without any sensation or consciousness of effort. On awakening he appeared to himself to have a distinct recollection of the whole, and taking his pen, ink, and paper, instantly and eagerly wrote down the lines that are here preserved. At this moment he was unfortunately called out by a person on business from Porlock, and detained by him above an hour, and on his return to his room, found, to his no small surprise and mortification, that . . . with the exception of some eight or ten scattered lines and images, all the rest had passed away . . .

In Xanadu did Kubla Khan
A stately pleasure-dome decree,
Where Alph the sacred river ran
Through caverns measureless to man
   Down to a sunless sea.
So twice five miles of fertile ground
With walls and towers were girdled round –

And there were gardens bright with sinuous rills,
Where blossomed many an incense-bearing tree;
And here were forests ancient as the hills,
Enfolding sunny spots of greenery.

But oh, that deep romantic chasm, which slanted
Down the green hill athwart a cedarn cover!
A savage place, as holy and enchanted
As e'er beneath a waning moon was haunted
By woman wailing for her demon lover!
And from this chasm, with ceaseless turmoil seething
As if this earth in fast thick pants were breathing,
A mighty fountain momently was forced,
Amid whose swift half-intermitted burst
Huge fragments vaulted, like rebounding hail
Or chaffy grain beneath the thresher's flail;
And mid these dancing rocks, at once and ever,
It flung up momently the sacred river.
Five miles meandering with a mazy motion
Through wood and dale the sacred river ran,
Then reached the caverns measureless to man
And sank in tumult to a lifeless ocean –
And mid this tumult Kubla heard from far
Ancestral voices prophesying war!

    The shadow of the dome of pleasure
    Floated midway on the waves,
    Where was heard the mingled measure
    From the fountain and the caves.
It was a miracle of rare device –
A sunny pleasure-dome with caves of ice!

    A damsel with a dulcimer
    In a vision once I saw:
    It was an Abyssinian maid,
    And on her dulcimer she played
    Singing of Mount Abora.
    Could I revive within me
    Her symphony and song,
    To such a deep delight 'twould win me,
That with music loud and long

I would build that dome in air –
That sunny dome, those caves of ice!
And all who heard should see them there,
And all should cry 'Beware! Beware!'
His flashing eyes, his floating hair!
Weave a circle round him thrice,
And close your eyes with holy dread,
For he on honey-dew hath fed
And drunk the milk of Paradise.

5. CHARLES LAMB

Old Familiar Faces (1798)

Where are they gone, the old familiar faces?

I had a mother, but she died, and left me,
Died prematurely in a day of horrors –
All, all are gone, the old familiar faces.

I have had playmates, I have had companions,
In my days of childhood, in my joyful schooldays –
All, all are gone, the old familiar faces.

I have been laughing, I have been carousing,
Drinking late, sitting late, with my bosom cronies;
All, all are gone, the old familiar faces.

I loved a love once, fairest among women;
Closed are her doors on me, I must not see her –
All, all are gone, the old familiar faces.

I have a friend, a kinder friend has no man;
Like an ingrate, I left my friend abruptly,
Left him, to muse on the old familiar faces.

Ghost-like, I paced round the haunts of my childhood.
Earth seemed a desert I was bound to traverse,
Seeking to find the old familiar faces.

Friend of my bosom, thou more than a brother,
Why wert not thou born in my father's dwelling?
So might we talk of the old familiar faces –

How some they have died, and some they have left me,
And some are taken from me – all are departed –
All, all are gone, the old familiar faces.

6. WILLIAM WORDSWORTH

Lucy Poems

(winter 1798–9; publ. *Lyrical Ballads* 1800)

(i) *Lucy Gray* (c. Nov.)

Oft had I heard of Lucy Gray,
And when I crossed the wild
I chanced to see at break of day
The solitary child.

No mate, no comrade, Lucy knew:
She dwelt on a wild moor,
The sweetest thing that ever grew
Beside a human door!

Yet you may spy the fawn at play,
The hare upon the green,
But the sweet face of Lucy Gray
Will never more be seen.

'Tonight will be a stormy night,
You to the town must go,
And take a lantern, child, to light
Your mother through the snow.'

'That, father, will I gladly do,
'Tis scarcely afternoon!
The minster-clock has just struck two,
And yonder is the moon.'

At this the father raised his hook
And snapped a faggot-band;
He plied his work, and Lucy took
The lantern in her hand.

Not blither is the mountain-roe:
With many a wanton stroke
Her feet disperse the powdery snow
That rises up like smoke.

The storm came on before its time;
She wandered up and down,
And many a hill did Lucy climb
But never reached the town.

The wretched parents all that night
Went shouting far and wide,
But there was neither sound nor sight
To serve them for a guide.

At daybreak on a hill they stood
That overlooked the moor,
And thence they saw the bridge of wood
A furlong from their door.

And now they homeward turned, and cried,
'In Heaven we all shall meet' –
When in the snow the mother spied
The print of Lucy's feet.

Then downward from the steep hill's edge
They tracked the footmarks small,
And through the broken hawthorn-hedge,
And by the long stone wall.

And then an open field they crossed –
The marks were still the same –
They tracked them on, nor ever lost,
And to the bridge they came.

They followed from the snowy bank
The footmarks one by one,
Into the middle of the plank,
And further there were none.

Yet some maintain that to this day
She is a living child,
That you may see sweet Lucy Gray
Upon the lonesome wild.

O'er rough and smooth she trips along
And never looks behind,
And sings a solitary song
That whistles in the wind.

(ii) *Strange Fits of Passion I Have Known*

(c. Dec.)

Strange fits of passion I have known,
And I will dare to tell
But in the lover's ear alone
What once to me befell.

When she I loved was strong and gay
And like a rose in June,
I to her cottage bent my way
Beneath the evening moon.

Upon the moon I fixed my eye
All over the wide lea;
My horse trudged on, and we drew nigh
Those paths so dear to me.

And now we reached the orchard-plot,
And as we climbed the hill
Towards the roof of Lucy's cot
The moon descended still.

In one of those sweet dreams I slept,
Kind Nature's gentlest boon,
And all the while my eyes I kept
On the descending moon.

My horse moved on – hoof after hoof
He raised and never stopped –
When down behind the cottage-roof
At once the planet dropped.

What fond and wayward thoughts will slide
Into a lover's head:
'Oh mercy', to myself I cried,
'If Lucy should be dead!'

(iii) *She Dwelt Among the Untrodden Ways* (c. Dec.)

She dwelt among the untrodden ways
Beside the springs of Dove,
A maid whom there were none to praise
And very few to love –

A violet by a mossy stone
Half-hidden from the eye,
Fair as a star when only one
Is shining in the sky.

She *lived* unknown, and few could know
When Lucy ceased to be;
But she is in her grave, and oh,
The difference to me!

(iv) *A Slumber Did My Spirit Seal* (c. Dec.)

A slumber did my spirit seal –
I had no human fears –
She seemed a thing that could not feel
The touch of earthly years.

No motion has she now, no force,
She neither hears nor sees,
Rolled round in Earth's diurnal course
With rocks and stones and trees.

(v) *Three Years She Grew* (Feb.)

Three years she grew in sun and shower,
Then Nature said: 'A lovelier flower
On earth was never sown –
This child I to myself will take,
She shall be mine, and I will make
A lady of my own.

Myself will to my darling be
Both law and impulse, and with me
The girl – in rock and plain,
In earth and heaven, in glade and bower –
Shall feel an overseeing power
To kindle or restrain.

She shall be sportive as the fawn
That wild with glee across the lawn
Or up the mountain springs;
And hers shall be the breathing balm,
And hers the silence and the calm,
Of mute insensate things.

The floating clouds their state shall lend
To her, for her the willow bend;
Nor shall she fail to see
Even in the motions of the storm
Grace that shall mould the maiden's form
By silent sympathy.

The stars of midnight shall be dear
To her, and she shall lean her ear
In many a secret place
Where rivulets dance their wayward round,
And beauty born of murmuring sound
Shall pass into her face.

And vital feelings of delight
Shall rear her form to stately height,
Her virgin bosom swell –
Such thoughts to Lucy I will give
While she and I together live
Here in this happy dell.'

Thus Nature spake: the work was done.
How soon my Lucy's race was run!
She died – and left to me
This heath, this calm and quiet scene,
The memory of what has been
And never more will be.

7. THOMAS CAMPBELL

Hohenlinden (1801; publ. 1809)

On Linden, when the sun was low,
All bloodless lay the untrodden snow,
And dark as winter was the flow
Of Iser, rolling rapidly.

But Linden saw another sight
When the drum beat at dead of night,
Commanding fires of death to light
The darkness of her scenery.

By torch and trumpet fast arrayed,
Each horseman drew his battle-blade,
And furious every charger neighed
To join the dreadful revelry!

Then shook the hills with thunder riven,
Then rushed the steed to battle driven,
And louder than the bolts of heaven
Far flashed the red artillery!

But redder yet that light shall glow
On Linden's hills of stainéd snow,
And bloodier yet the torrent flow
Of Iser, rolling rapidly.

'Tis morn, but scarce yon level sun
Can pierce the war clouds, rolling dun,
Where furious Frank and fiery Hun
Shout in their sulphurous canopy.

The combat deepens. On, ye brave,
Who rush to glory, or the grave!
Wave, Munich, all thy banners wave!
And charge with all thy chivalry!

Few, few shall part where many meet!
The snow shall be their winding-sheet,
And every turf beneath their feet
Shall be a soldier's sepulchre.

8. ROBERT SOUTHEY

The Inchcape Rock (1803)

No stir in the air, no stir in the sea,
The ship was still as she could be,
Her sails from heaven received no motion,
Her keel was steady in the ocean.

Without either sign or sound of their shock
The waves flowed over the Inchcape Rock:
So little they rose, so little they fell,
They did not move the Inchcape Bell.

The Abbot of Aberbrothok
Had placed that bell on the Inchcape Rock –
On a buoy in the storm it floated and swung,
And over the waves its warning rung.

When the Rock was hid by the surge's swell
The mariners heard the warning bell;
And then they knew the perilous Rock,
And blest the Abbot of Aberbrothok.

The sun in heaven was shining gay,
All things were joyful on that day:
The sea-birds screamed as they wheeled around,
And there was joyance in their sound.

The buoy of the Inchcape Rock was seen,
A darker speck on the ocean green;
Sir Ralph the Rover walked his deck,
And he fixed his eye on the darker speck.

He felt the cheering power of spring,
It made him whistle, it made him sing;
His heart was mirthful to excess,
But the Rover's mirth was wickedness!

His eye was on the Inchcape float –
Quoth he, 'My men, put out the boat,
And row me to the Inchcape Rock,
And I'll plague the Abbot of Aberbrothok!'

The boat is lowered, the boatmen row,
And to the Inchcape Rock they go;
Sir Ralph bent over from the boat,
And he cut the Bell from the Inchcape float!

Down sunk the Bell with a gurgling sound,
The bubbles rose and burst around;
Quoth Sir Ralph, 'The next who comes to the Rock
Won't bless the Abbot of Aberbrothok!'

Sir Ralph the Rover sailed away,
He scoured the seas for many a day;
And now, grown rich with plundered store,
He steers his course for Scotland's shore.

So thick a haze o'erspreads the sky
They cannot see the sun on high;
The wind hath blown a gale all day,
At evening it hath died away.

On the deck the Rover takes his stand,
So dark it is they see no land;
Quoth Sir Ralph, 'It will be lighter soon,
For there is the dawn of the rising moon.'

'Canst hear', said one, 'the breakers roar?
For methinks we should be near the shore.'
'Now where we are I cannot tell,
But I wish I could hear the Inchcape Bell.'

They hear no sound, the swell is strong,
Though the wind hath fallen, they drift along,
Till the vessel strikes with a shivering shock –
'Oh Christ! it is the Inchcape Rock!'

Sir Ralph the Rover tore his hair –
He cursed himself in his despair –
The waves rush in on every side,
The ship is sinking beneath the tide.

But even in his dying fear
One dreadful sound could the Rover hear,
A sound as if with the Inchcape Bell
The Devil below was ringing his knell!

9. WILLIAM BLAKE

And Did Those Feet

(1802–4; engraved *Milton* c. 1808)

And did those feet in ancient time
Walk upon England's mountains green?
And was the holy Lamb of God
On England's pleasant pastures seen?

And did the Countenance Divine
Shine forth upon our clouded hills?
And was Jerusalem builded here
Among these dark satanic mills?

Bring me my bow of burning gold!
Bring me my arrows of desire!
Bring me my spear – oh clouds unfold!
Bring me my chariot of fire!

I will not cease from mental fight,
Nor shall my sword sleep in my hand,
Till we have built Jerusalem,
In England's green and pleasant land.

10. WALTER SCOTT

Lochinvar (*Marmion* 1808)

Oh young Lochinvar is come out of the west,
Through all the wide Border his steed was the best,
And save his good broadsword, he weapons had none –
He rode all unarmed, and he rode all alone.
So faithful in love, and so dauntless in war,
There never was knight like the young Lochinvar!

He stayed not for brake, and he stopped not for stone,
He swam the Esk river where ford there was none;
But ere he alighted at Netherby gate,
The bride had consented – the gallant came late!
For a laggard in love, and a dastard in war,
Was to wed the fair Ellen of brave Lochinvar.

So boldly he entered the Netherby Hall,
Among bride's-men, and kinsmen, and brothers, and all;
Then spoke the bride's father, his hand on his sword
(For the poor craven bridegroom said never a word),
'Oh come ye in peace here, or come ye in war,
Or to dance at our bridal, young Lord Lochinvar?'

'I long wooed your daughter – my suit you denied –
Love swells like the Solway, but ebbs like its tide,
And now am I come, with this lost love of mine
To lead but one measure, drink one cup of wine.
There are maidens in Scotland more lovely by far,
That would gladly be bride to the young Lochinvar.'

The bride kissed the goblet, the knight took it up –
He quaffed off the wine, and he threw down the cup.
She looked down to blush, and she looked up to sigh,
With a smile on her lips, and a tear in her eye.
He took her soft hand, ere her mother could bar –
'Now tread we a measure!' said young Lochinvar.

So stately his form, and so lovely her face,
That never a hall such a galliard did grace –
While her mother did fret, and her father did fume,

And the bridegroom stood dangling his bonnet and plume;
And the bride-maidens whispered, ' 'Twere better by far
To have matched our fair cousin with young Lochinvar.'

One touch to her hand, and one word in her ear,
When they reached the hall-door, and the charger stood near;
So light to the croup the fair lady he swung,
So light to the saddle before her he sprung!
'She is won! We are gone, over bank, bush, and scar –
They'll have fleet steeds that follow!' quoth young Lochinvar.

There was mounting 'mong Graemes of the Netherby clan;
Forsters, Fenwicks, and Musgraves, they rode and they ran;
There was racing and chasing on Cannobie Lee,
But the lost bride of Netherby ne'er did they see –
So daring in love, and so dauntless in war,
Have ye e'er heard of gallant like young Lochinvar?

11. THOMAS MOORE

Oh! Blame Not the Bard (1810)

Oh! blame not the bard, if he fly to the bowers
   Where Pleasure lies carelessly smiling at Fame;
He was born for much more, and in happier hours
   His soul might have burned with a holier flame.
The string that now languishes loose o'er the lyre
   Might have bent a proud bow to the warrior's dart,
And the lip which now breathes but the song of desire
   Might have poured the full tide of a patriot's heart.

But alas for his country! Her pride is gone by,
   And that spirit is broken which never would bend;
O'er the ruin her children in secret must sigh,
   For 'tis treason to love her, and death to defend!
Unprized are her sons, till they've learned to betray;
   Undistinguished they live, if they shame not their sires;
And the torch that would light them through dignity's way
   Must be caught from the pile where their country expires.

Then blame not the bard, if in passion's soft dream
He should try to forget what he never can heal:
Oh, give but a hope – let a vista but gleam
Through the gloom of his country – and mark how he'll feel!
That instant his heart at her shrine would lay down
Every passion it nursed, every bliss it adored;
While the myrtle, now idly entwined with his crown,
Like the wreath of Harmodius, should cover his sword.

But though glory be gone, and though hope fade away,
Thy name, loved Erin, shall live in his songs:
Not e'en in the hour when his heart is most gay
Will he lose the remembrance of thee and thy wrongs!
The stranger shall hear thy lament on his plains;
The sigh of thy harp shall be sent o'er the deep –
Till thy masters themselves, as they rivet thy chains,
Shall pause at the song of thy captive and weep.

12. LORD BYRON

'Revelry by Night'

(*Childe Harold* III, stanzas 16–18, 21–8) April 1816; publ. Dec.

16

Self-exiled Harold wanders forth again,
With nought of hope left – but with less of gloom.
The very knowledge that he lived in vain,
That all was over on this side the tomb,
Had made despair a smilingness assume,
Which, though 'twere wild (as on the plundered wreck
When mariners would madly meet their doom
With draughts intemperate on the sinking deck),
Did yet inspire a cheer, which he forbore to check.

17

Stop! for thy tread is on an Empire's dust!
An earthquake's spoil is sepulchred below!
Is the spot marked with no colossal bust?
Nor column trophied for triumphal show?

None. But the moral's truth tells simpler so –
As the ground was before, thus let it be!
How that red rain hath made the harvest grow!
And is this all the world has gained by thee,
Thou first and last of fields – king-making victory?

18

And Harold stands upon this place of skulls,
The grave of France, the deadly Waterloo!
How in an hour the power which gave annuls
Its gifts, transferring fame as fleeting too!
In 'pride of place' here last the Eagle flew,
Then tore with bloody talon the rent plain,
Pierced by the shaft of banded nations through;
Ambition's life and labours all were vain –
He wears the shattered links of the World's broken chain . . .

21

There was a sound of revelry by night,
And Belgium's capital had gathered then
Her beauty and her chivalry – and bright
The lamps shone o'er fair women and brave men.
A thousand hearts beat happily, and when
Music arose with its voluptuous swell,
Soft eyes looked love to eyes which spake again,
And all went merry as a marriage-bell –
But hush, hark, a deep sound strikes like a rising knell!

22

Did ye not hear it? No – 'twas but the wind,
Or the car rattling o'er the stony street –
On with the dance! Let joy be unconfined!
No sleep till morn, when youth and pleasure meet
To chase the glowing hours with flying feet –
But hark! that heavy sound breaks in once more
As if the clouds its echo would repeat,
And nearer, clearer, deadlier, than before.
Arm! Arm! It is, it is, the cannon's opening roar!

23

Within a windowed niche of that high hall
Sat Brunswick's fated Chieftain; he did hear
That sound the first amidst the festival,
And caught its tone with death's prophetic ear –

And when they smiled because he deemed it near,
His heart more truly knew that peal too well
Which stretched his father on a bloody bier,
And roused the vengeance blood alone could quell:
He rushed into the field, and, foremost fighting, fell!

24

Ah! then and there was hurrying to and fro,
And gathering tears, and tremblings of distress,
And cheeks all pale which but an hour ago
Blushed at the praise of their own loveliness –
And there were sudden partings, such as press
The life from out young hearts, and choking sighs
Which ne'er might be repeated. Who could guess
If ever more should meet those mutual eyes,
Since upon night so sweet such awful morn could rise!

25

And there was mounting in hot haste! The steed,
The mustering squadron, and the clattering car,
Went pouring forward, with impetuous speed
And swiftly forming in the ranks of war –
And the deep thunder, peal on peal, afar;
And near, the beat of the alarming drum
Roused up the soldier ere the morning star;
While thronged the citizens, with terror dumb,
Or whispering, with white lips: 'The foe! They come! they come!'

26

And wild and high the *Cameron's Gathering* rose –
The war-note of Lochiel, which Albyn's hills
Have heard, and heard too have her Saxon foes.
How in the noon of night that pibroch thrills,
Savage and shrill! But with the breath which fills
Their mountain-pipe, so fill the mountaineers
With the fierce native daring which instils
The stirring memory of a thousand years –
And Evan's, Donald's, fame rings in each clansman's ears!

27

And Ardennes waves above them her green leaves,
Dewy with Nature's tear-drops, as they pass,
Grieving, if aught inanimate e'er grieves,
Over the unreturning brave – alas,

Ere evening to be trodden like the grass
Which now beneath them, but above shall grow
In its next verdure, when this fiery mass
Of living valour, rolling on the foe
And burning with high hope, shall moulder cold and low.

28

Last noon beheld them full of lusty life,
Last eve in Beauty's circle proudly gay,
The midnight brought the signal-sound of strife,
The morn the marshalling in arms – the day,
Battle's magnificently-stern array!
The thunder-clouds close o'er it, which, when rent,
The earth is covered thick with other clay
Which her own clay shall cover, heaped and pent,
Rider and horse – friend, foe – in one red burial blent!

13. JOHN KEATS

To Autumn (Sept. 1819; publ. 1820)

Season of mists and mellow fruitfulness,
Close bosom-friend of the maturing sun,
Conspiring with him how to load and bless
With fruit the vines that round the thatch-eaves run –
To bend with apples the mossed cottage-trees,
And fill all fruit with ripeness to the core;
To swell the gourd, and plump the hazel-shells
With a sweet kernel; to set budding more,
And still more, later flowers for the bees,
Until they think warm days will never cease,
For Summer has o'erbrimmed their clammy cells.

Who hath not seen thee oft amid thy store?
Sometimes whoever seeks abroad may find
Thee sitting careless on a granary floor,
Thy hair soft-lifted by the winnowing wind;
Or on a half-reaped furrow, sound asleep,
Drowsed with the fume of poppies, while thy hook
Spares the next swath and all its twinéd flowers;
And sometimes like a gleaner thou dost keep

Steady thy laden head across a brook,
Or by a cider-press, with patient look,
Thou watchest the last oozings hours by hours.

Where are the songs of Spring? Aye, where are they?
Think not of them, thou hast thy music too –
While barred clouds bloom the soft-dying day,
And touch the stubble-plains with rosy hue.
Then in a wailful choir the small gnats mourn
Among the river sallows, borne aloft
Or sinking as the light wind lives or dies;
And full-grown lambs loud-bleat from hilly bourn;
Hedge-crickets sing; and now, with treble soft,
The redbreast whistles from a garden-croft,
And gathering swallows twitter in the skies.

14. PERCY BYSSHE SHELLEY

To a Skylark (1820)

Hail to thee, blithe spirit,
Bird thou never wert
That from heaven, or near it,
Pourest thy full heart
In profuse strains of unpremeditated art!

Higher still and higher
From the earth thou springest
Like a cloud of fire;
The blue deep thou wingest,
And singing still dost soar, and soaring ever singest.

In the golden lightning
Of the sunken sun
O'er which clouds are brightning,
Thou dost float and run;
Like an unbodied joy whose race is just begun.

The pale purple even
Melts around thy flight;
Like a star of heaven
In the broad daylight
Thou art unseen, but yet I hear thy shrill delight.

Keen as are the arrows
Of that silver sphere,
Whose intense lamp narrows
In the white dawn clear,
Until we hardly see – we feel that it is there.

All the earth and air
With thy voice is loud,
As, when night is bare,
From one lonely cloud
The moon rains out her beams, and heaven is overflowed.

What thou art we know not –
What is most like thee?
From rainbow clouds there flow not
Drops so bright to see
As from thy presence showers a rain of melody.

Like a poet hidden
In the light of thought,
Singing hymns unbidden
Till the world is wrought
To sympathy with hopes and fears it heeded not;

Like a high-born maiden
In a palace tower,
Soothing her love-laden
Soul in secret hour
With music sweet as love, which overflows her bower;

Like a glow-worm golden
In a dell of dew,
Scattering unbeholden
In aërial hue
Among the flowers and grass, which screen it from the view;

Like a rose embowered
In its own green leaves,
By warm winds deflowered,
Till the scent it gives
Makes faint with too much sweet those heavy-wingéd thieves –

Sound of vernal showers
On the twinkling grass,
Rain-awakened flowers –
All that ever was
Joyous, and clear, and fresh, thy music doth surpass!

Teach us, sprite, or bird,
What sweet thoughts are thine;
I have never heard
Praise of love or wine
That panted forth a flood of rapture so divine.

Chorus hymeneal,
Or triumphal chant,
Matched with thine would be all
But an empty vaunt,
A thing wherein we feel there is some hidden want.

What objects are the fountains
Of thy happy strain?
What fields, or waves, or mountains?
What shapes of sky or plain?
What love of thine own kind? What ignorance of pain?

With thy clear keen joyance
Languor cannot be;
Shadow of annoyance
Never came near thee!
Thou lovest – but ne'er knew love's sad satiety.

Waking or asleep,
Thou of death must deem
Things more true and deep
Than we mortals dream,
Or how could thy notes flow in such a crystal stream?

We look before and after,
And pine for what is not:
Our sincerest laughter
With some pain is fraught –
Our sweetest songs are those that tell of saddest thought.

Yet if we could scorn
Hate, and pride, and fear;
If we were things born
Not to shed a tear,
I know not how thy joy we ever should come near.

Better than all measures
Of delightful sound
Better than all treasures
That in books are found,
Thy skill to poet were, thou scorner of the ground!

Teach me half the gladness
That thy brain must know,
Such harmonious madness
From my lips would flow,
The world should listen then, as I am listening now.

15. JAMES HOGG

When the Kye Comes Hame (1823)

Come all ye jolly shepherds that whistle thro' the glen,
I'll tell ye of a secret that courtiers dinna ken.
What is the greatest bliss that the tongue of man can name?
'Tis to woo a bonny lassie when the kye comes hame.
When the kye comes hame, when the kye comes hame,
'Tween the gloaming an' the mirk, when the kye comes hame.

4 *when the kye comes hame* (refrain) when the cows come home at milking time:

In the title and chorus of this pastoral song, I choose rather to violate a rule in grammar, than a Scottish phrase so common, that when it is altered into the proper way, every shepherd and shepherd's sweetheart account it nonsense. I was once singing it at a wedding with great glee the latter way ('when the kye came hame') when a tailor, scratching his head, said, 'It was a terrible affectit way that!' I stood corrected, and have never sung it so again. (Hogg note, 1834)

'Tis not beneath the burgonet, nor yet beneath the crown,
'Tis not on couch of velvet, nor yet in bed of down –
'Tis beneath the spreading birch, in the dell without a name,
Wi' a bonny, bonny lassie, when the kye comes hame,
When the kye comes hame, when the kye comes hame,
'Tween the gloaming an' the mirk, when the kye comes hame.

There the blackbird bigs his nest for the mate he lo'es to see,
And up upon the topmost bough, oh, a happy bird is he!
There he pours his melting ditty, and love 'tis a' the theme,
And he'll woo his bonny lassie when the kye cames hame.
When the kye comes hame, when the kye comes hame,
'Tween the gloaming an' the mirk, when the kye comes hame.

When the bluart bears a pearl, and the daisy turns a pea,
And the bonny lucken gowan has fouldit up his ee,
Then the lavrock frae the blue lift drops down, and thinks nae shame
To woo his bonnie lassie when the kye comes hame.
When the kye comes hame, when the kye comes hame,
'Tween the gloaming an' the mirk, when the kye comes hame.

Then the eye shines sae bright, the hale soul to beguile,
There's love in every whisper, and joy in every smile:
O wha wad choose a crown, wi' its perils and its fame,
And miss a bonny lassie when the kye comes hame?
When the kye comes hame, when the kye comes hame,
'Tween the gloaming an' the mirk, when the kye comes hame.

See yonder pawky shepherd, that lingers on the hill,
His ewes are in the fauld, and his lambs are lying still;
Yet he downa gang to bed, for his heart is in a flame,

7 *burgonet* helmet.
12 *'Tween the gloaming an' the mirk* between dusk and dark. **13** *bigs* builds.
19 *When the bluart bears a pearl* when the cornflower has its dew drop (in autumn). *turns a pea* turns to a round seed-head.
20 *lucken gowan* buttercup. **21** *lavrock* lark. *lift* heaven, sky.
25 *hale* whole. **31** *pawky* sly, up to no good.
33 *downa* does not.

To meet his bonny lassie when the kye comes hame.
When the kye comes hame, when the kye comes hame,
'Tween the gloaming an' the mirk, when the kye comes hame.

Away wi' fame and fortune, what comfort can they gie?
And a' the arts that prey on man's life and liberty:
Gie me the highest joy that the heart o' man can frame,
My bonny, bonny lassie, when the kye comes hame.
When the kye comes hame, when the kye comes hame,
'Tween the gloaming an' the mirk, when the kye comes hame.

16. JOHN CLARE

The Shepherd's Calendar

(*July*, 90–131) c. 1824; publ. 1827

Loud is the Summer's busy song,
The smallest breeze can find a tongue,
While insects of each tiny size
Grow teasing with their melodies,
Till noon burns with its blistering breath
Around, and day dies still as death.
The busy noise of man and brute
Is on a sudden lost and mute;
Even the brook that leaps along
Seems weary of its bubbling song,
And, so soft its waters creep,
Tired silence sinks in sounder sleep.
The cricket on its banks is dumb,
The very flies forget to hum;
And, save the wagon rocking round,
The landscape sleeps without a sound.
The breeze is stopped, the lazy bough
Hath not a leaf that dances now;
The tottergrass upon the hill,
And spiders' threads, are standing still;
The feathers dropped from moorhen's wing,
Which to the water's surface cling,
Are steadfast, and as heavy seem
As stones beneath them in the stream;

Hawkweed and groundsel's fanning downs
Unruffled keep their seedy crowns;
And in the oven-heated air,
Not one light thing is floating there,
Save that to the earnest eye
The restless heat seems twittering by!
Noon swoons beneath the heat it made,
And flowers e'en wither in the shade,
Until the sun slopes in the west,
Like weary traveller, glad to rest,
On pillowed clouds of many hues;
Then Nature's voice its joy renews,
And chequered field and grassy plain
Hum, with their summer songs again,
A requiem to the day's decline,
Whose setting sunbeams coolly shine,
As welcome to day's feeble powers
As falling dews to thirsty flowers.

17. THOMAS HOOD

I Remember, I Remember (1826)

I remember, I remember,
The house where I was born,
The little window where the sun
Came peeping in at morn;
He never came a wink too soon,
Nor brought too long a day;
But now, I often wish the night
Had borne my breath away!

I remember, I remember,
The roses, red and white,
The violets, and the lily-cups,
Those flowers made of light!
The lilacs where the robin built,
And where my brother set
The laburnum on his birth-day –
The tree is living yet!

I remember, I remember
Where I was used to swing,
And thought the air must rush as fresh
To swallows on the wing;
My spirit flew in feathers then,
That is so heavy now,
And summer-pools could hardly cool
The fever on my brow!

I remember, I remember
The fir-trees dark and high;
I used to think their slender tops
Were close against the sky:
It was a childish ignorance,
But now 'tis little joy
To know I'm farther off from heaven
Than when I was a boy.

18. FELICIA HEMANS

Casabianca (1824; publ. 1826)

Young Casabianca, a boy about thirteen years old, son to the Admiral of the Orient, remained at his post (in the Battle of the Nile), after the ship had taken fire and all the guns had been abandoned, and perished in the explosion of the vessel, when the flames had reached the powder.

The boy stood on the burning deck
   Whence all but he had fled;
The flame that lit the battle's wreck,
   Shone round him o'er the dead.

Yet beautiful and bright he stood,
   As born to rule the storm –
A creature of heroic blood,
   A proud, though childlike form!

The flames rolled on! He would not go
   Without his father's word –
That father, faint in death below,
   His voice no longer heard.

He called aloud: 'Say, Father, say
  If yet my task is done?'
He knew not that the chieftain lay
  Unconscious of his son.

'Speak, Father!' once again he cried,
  'If I may yet be gone!' –
And but the booming shots replied,
  And fast the flames rolled on.

Upon his brow he felt their breath,
  And in his waving hair,
And looked from that lone post of death,
  In still, yet brave despair –

And shouted but once more aloud,
  'My Father! must I stay?'
While o'er him fast, through sail and shroud,
  The wreathing fires made way.

They wrapt the ship in splendour wild,
  They caught the flag on high,
And streamed above the gallant child
  Like banners in the sky.

There came a burst of thunder-sound –
  The boy – oh! where was he?
Ask of the winds that far around
  With fragments strewed the sea:

With mast, and helm, and pennon fair,
  That well had borne their part –
But the noblest thing which perished there
  Was that young faithful heart!

19. LETITIA ELIZABETH LANDON

Lines of Life (1829)

Well, read my cheek, and watch my eye –
Too strictly schooled are they
One secret of my soul to show,
One hidden thought betray.

I never knew the time my heart
Looked freely from my brow:
It once was checked by timidness,
'Tis taught by caution now.

I live among the cold, the false,
And I must seem like them –
And such I am, for I am false
As those I most condemn.

I teach my lip its sweetest smile,
My tongue its softest tone;
I borrow others' likeness, till
Almost I lose my own.

I pass through flattery's gilded sieve
Whatever I would say;
In social life, all, like the blind,
Must learn to feel their way.

I check my thoughts like curbéd steeds
That struggle with the rein;
I bid my feelings sleep, like wrecks
In the unfathomed main.

I hear them speak of love, the deep,
The true, and mock the name –
Mock at all high and early truth –
And I too do the same.

I hear them tell some touching tale,
I swallow down the tear;
I hear them name some generous deed,
And I have learnt to sneer.

I hear the spiritual, the kind,
The pure, but named in mirth;
Till all of good, aye, even hope,
Seems exiled from our earth.

And one fear, withering ridicule,
Is all that I can dread;
A sword hung by a single hair
For ever o'er the head.

We bow to a most servile faith,
In a most servile fear,
While none among us dares to say
What none will choose to hear.

And if we dream of loftier thoughts,
In weakness they are gone,
And indolence and vanity
Rivet our fetters on.

Surely I was not born for this!
I feel a loftier mood
Of generous impulse, high resolve,
Steal o'er my solitude!

I gaze upon the thousand stars
That fill the midnight sky;
And wish, so passionately wish,
A light like theirs on high.

I have such eagerness of hope
To benefit my kind,
And feel as if immortal power
Were given to my mind.

I think on that eternal fame,
The sun of earthly gloom,
Which makes the gloriousness of death
The future of the tomb –

That earthly future, the faint sign
Of a more heavenly one:
A step, a word, a voice, a look –
Alas! my dream is done.

And Earth, and Earth's debasing stain,
Again is on my soul;
And I am but a nameless part
Of a most worthless whole.

Why write I this? because my heart
Towards the future springs,
That future where it loves to soar
On more than eagle wings.

The present, it is but a speck
In that eternal time,
In which my lost hopes find a home,
My spirit knows its clime.

Oh! not myself – for what am I? –
The worthless and the weak,
Whose every thought of self should raise
A blush to burn my cheek?

But song has touched my lips with fire,
And made my heart a shrine;
For what, although alloyed, debased,
Is in itself divine.

I am myself but a vile link
Amid life's weary chain;
But I have spoken hallowed words –
Oh do not say in vain!

My first, my last, my only wish,
Say will my charméd chords
Wake to the morning-light of fame,
And breathe again my words?

Will the young maiden, when her tears
Alone in moonlight shine –
Tears for the absent and the loved –
Murmur some song of mine?

Will the pale youth by his dim lamp,
Himself a dying flame,
From many an antique scroll beside,
Choose that which bears my name?

Let music make less terrible
The silence of the dead;
I care not, so my spirit last
Long after life has fled.

20. CAROLINE NORTON

My Arab Steed (1830)

My beautiful, my beautiful, that standest meekly by
With thy proudly arched and glossy neck, and dark and fiery eye,
Fret not to roam the desert now, with all thy wingéd speed –
I may not mount on thee again – thou'rt sold, my arab steed!
Fret not with that impatient hoof – snuff not the breezy wind!
The further that thou fliest now, so far am I behind!
The stranger hath thy bridle-rein – thy master hath his gold –
Fleet-limbed and beautiful, farewell! Thou'rt sold, my steed, thou'rt sold!
Farewell! Those free untiréd limbs full many a mile must roam
To reach the chill and wintry sky which clouds the stranger's home;
Some other hand, less fond, must now thy corn and bed prepare;
The silky mane I braided once, must be another's care!
The morning sun shall dawn again, but never more with thee
Shall I gallop through the desert-paths, where we were wont to be:
Evening shall darken on the earth, and o'er the sandy plain
Some other steed, with slower step, shall bear me home again.
Yes, thou must go! The wild free breeze, the brilliant sun and sky,
The master's home – from all of these, my exiled one must fly!
Thy proud dark eye will grow less proud, thy step become less fleet,
And vainly shalt thou arch thy neck thy master's hand to meet.
Only in sleep shall I behold that dark eye glancing bright,
Only in sleep shall hear again that step so firm and light;
And when I raise my dreaming arm to check or cheer thy speed,
Then must I, starting, wake, to feel – thou'rt sold, my arab steed!
Ah, rudely then (unseen by me) some cruel hand may chide,
Till foam-wreaths lie, like crested waves, along thy panting side;
And the rich blood that is in thee swells, in thy indignant pain,
Till careless eyes which rest on thee may count each started vein.
Will they ill-use thee? If I thought – but no, it cannot be! –
Thou art so swift, yet easy curbed; so gentle, yet so free.

And yet if haply when thou'rt gone my lonely heart should yearn,
Can the hand which casts thee from it now, command thee to
return?
Return! Alas, my arab steed, what shall thy master do
When thou, who wert his all of joy, hast vanished from his view –
When the dim distance cheats mine eye, and through the gathering
tears
Thy bright form, for a moment, like the false mirage appears?
Slow and unmounted will I roam with weary foot, alone,
Where with fleet step, and joyous bound, thou oft hast borne me on;
And, sitting down by that green well, I'll pause and sadly think,
'It was here he bowed his glossy neck, when last I saw him drink!'
When last I saw thee drink! Away – the fevered dream is o'er! –
I could not live a day, and know that we should meet no more!
They tempted me, my beautiful, for hunger's power is strong –
They tempted me, my beautiful, but I have loved too long!
Who said that I had given thee up? Who said that thou wert sold?
'Tis false – 'tis false, my arab steed! I fling them back their gold!
Thus, thus, I leap upon thy back, and scour the distant plains –
Away! Who overtakes us now, shall claim thee for his pains!

21. JAMES LEIGH HUNT

Abou Ben Adhem (1834)

Abou Ben Adhem – may his tribe increase –
Awoke one night from a deep dream of peace,
And saw, within the moonlight in his room,
Making it rich, and like a lily in bloom,
An angel writing in a book of gold.
Exceeding peace had made Ben Adhem bold,
And to the presence in the room he said:
'What writest thou?' The vision raised its head
And with a look made all of sweet accord,
Answered, 'The names of those who love the Lord.'
'And is mine one?' said Abou. 'Nay, not so',
Replied the angel. Abou spoke more low,
But cheerly still, and said, 'I pray thee, then,
Write me as one who loves his fellow men.'
The angel wrote, and vanished. The next night
It came again, with a great wakening light,
And showed the names whom love of God had blest,
And lo! Ben Adhem's name led all the rest.

II. Narratives of Love

Love is the great bringer-together: all writers write love-stories, all readers read them. A sameness might be expected in the telling – but not among the Romantics. If they all respond to love, they respond with the individuality that is the hallmark of the period. Blake's strange powerful myth of the crystal cabinet –

> The maiden caught me in the wild
> Where I was dancing merrily;
> She put me into her cabinet
> And locked me up with a golden key.

– is as much an insight into the nature of love as Byron's recapturing of lost innocence with Juan and Haidee, or Wordsworth's tale in *The Ruined Cottage* (at once elemental and up to the moment), of the 'silent suffering' of a war widow: 'Yet still she loved this wretched spot, / Nor would for worlds have parted hence'. For Robinson, writing of Sappho, first and most famous of women poets, who had died 2,000 years before, and Hemans, writing of Arabella Stuart (dead a mere 200 years), historical figures mask and enact an anguished personal love: 'It was no dream, I saw the stag leap free.' Byron in *The Bride of Abydos*, Moore in *Lalla Rookh*, Landon in *The Indian Bride* find in the oriental a high romance that is just one aspect of Romanticism. Keats in *The Eve of St Agnes* blends the Gothic, so popular at the time, with Shakespeare's *Romeo and Juliet*, to create a fantasy of wish-fulfilment. For Shelley in *Alastor* erotic love is the acting out of a death wish. To bring these poets, and these poems, together under the banner of love is to feel above all their powerful diversity.

1. MARY ROBINSON

from *Sappho and Phaon* (1796)

To The Reader

The story of the Lesbian muse, though not new to the classical reader, presented to my imagination such a lively example of the human mind, enlightened by the most exquisite talents, yet yielding to the destructive control of ungovernable passions, that I felt an irresistible impulse to attempt the delineation of their progress, mingling, with the glowing picture of her soul, such moral reflections as may serve to excite that pity which, while it proves the susceptibility of the heart, arms it against the danger of indulging too luxuriant a fancy.

The unfortunate lovers, Heloïse and Abelard, and the supposed platonic Petrarch and Laura, have found panegyrists in many distinguished authors. Ovid and Pope have celebrated the passion of Sappho for Phaon, but their portraits, however beautifully finished, are replete with shades tending rather to depreciate than to adorn the Grecian poetess . . . Among the many Grecian writers, Sappho was the unrivalled poetess of her time: the envy she excited, the public honours she received, and the fatal passion which terminated her existence, will, I trust, create that sympathy in the mind of the susceptible reader which may render the following poetical trifles not wholly uninteresting. (St James's Place, 1796)

Love taught my tears in sadder notes to flow,
And tuned my heart to elegies of woe.

(Pope, *Sappho to Phaon*, 7–8)

1. *Sonnet Introductory*

Favoured by Heaven are those, ordained to taste
The bliss supreme that kindles fancy's fire;
Whose magic fingers sweep the muse's lyre
In varying cadence, eloquently chaste!
Well may the mind, with tuneful numbers graced,
To fame's immortal attributes aspire,
Above the treacherous spells of low desire
That wound the sense, by vulgar joys debased.
For thou, blest Poesy, with godlike powers
To calm the miseries of man, wert given;
When passion rends, and hopeless love devours,
By memory goaded and by frenzy driven,
'Tis thine to guide him midst Elysian bowers
And show his fainting soul – a glimpse of Heaven.

2. *The Temple of Chastity*

High on a rock, coëval with the skies,
A temple stands, reared by immortal powers
To chastity divine! Ambrosial flowers,
Twining round icicles, in columns rise,
Mingling with pendent gems of orient dyes!
Piercing the air, a golden crescent towers,
Veiled by transparent clouds; while smiling Hours
Shake from their varying wings – celestial joys!
The steps of spotless marble, scattered o'er
With deathless roses, armed with many a thorn,
Lead to the altar. On the frozen floor,
Studded with tear-drops petrified by scorn,
Pale vestals kneel the goddess to adore,
While Love, his arrows broke, retires forlorn.

3. *The Bower of Pleasure*

Turn to yon vale beneath, whose tangled shade
Excludes the blazing torch of noonday light:
Where sportive fawns and dimpled loves invite,
The bower of pleasure opens to the glade.
Lulled by soft flutes, on leaves of violets laid,
There witching beauty greets the ravished sight,
More gentle than the arbitress of night
In all her silvery panoply arrayed!

The birds breathe bliss, light zephyrs kiss the ground
Stealing the hyacinth's divine perfume;
While from pellucid fountains glittering round,
Small tinkling rills bid rival flowerets bloom!
Here, laughing cupids bathe the bosom's wound;
There, tyrant passion finds a glorious tomb!

4. *Sappho Discovers her Passion*

Why, when I gaze on Phaon's beauteous eyes,
Why does each thought in wild disorder stray?
Why does each fainting faculty decay,
And my chilled breast in throbbing tumults rise?
Mute on the ground my lyre neglected lies,
The Muse forgot, and lost the melting lay;
My down-cast looks, my faltering lips, betray
That stung by hopeless passion Sappho dies!
Now on a bank of cypress let me rest –
Come, tuneful maids, ye pupils of my care,
Come, with your dulcet numbers sooth my breast,
And, as the soft vibrations float on air,
Let pity waft my spirit to the blest,
To mock the barbarous triumphs of despair!

5. *Condemns its Power*

Oh how can love exulting reason quell?
How fades each nobler passion from his gaze –
E'en fame, that cherishes the poet's lays,
That fame ill-fated Sappho loved so well?
Lost is the wretch, who in his fatal spell
Wastes the short summer of delicious days,
And from the tranquil path of wisdom strays
In passion's thorny wild forlorn to dwell.
Oh ye who in that sacred temple smile
Where holy innocence resides enshrined,
Who fear not sorrow, and who know not guile
(Each thought composed, and every wish resigned),
Tempt not the path where pleasure's flowery wile
In sweet, but poisonous, fetters holds the mind.

6. *Describes the Characteristics of Love*

Is it to love, to fix the tender gaze,
   To hide the timid blush, and steal away –
   To shun the busy world, and waste the day
In some rude mountain's solitary maze?
Is it to chant one name in ceaseless lays,
   To hear no words that other tongues can say,
   To watch the pale moon's melancholy ray,
To chide in fondness, and in folly praise?
   Is it to pour the involuntary sigh,
To dream of bliss, and wake new pangs to prove –
   To talk, in fancy, with the speaking eye,
Then start with jealousy, and wildly rove?
   Is it to loath the light, and wish to die?
For these I feel – and feel that they are love.

7. *Invokes Reason*

Come, Reason, come! Each nerve rebellious bind,
   Lull the fierce tempest of my feverish soul –
   Come, with the magic of thy meek control,
And check the wayward wanderings of my mind:
Estranged from thee, no solace can I find.
   O'er my rapt brain, where pensive visions stole,
   Now Passion reigns and stormy tumults roll:
So the smooth sea obeys the furious wind!
   In vain, Philosophy unfolds her store –
O'erwhelmed is every source of pure delight;
   Dim is the golden page of Wisdom's lore;
All nature fades before my sickening sight:
   For what bright scene can fancy's eye explore
Midst dreary labyrinths of mental night?

8. *Her Passion Increases*

Why, through each aching vein, with lazy pace
   Thus steals the languid fountain of my heart,
   While from its source each wild convulsive start
Tears the scorched roses from my burning face?
In vain, oh Lesbian vales, your charms I trace –
   Vain is the poet's theme, the sculptor's art!
   No more the lyre its magic can impart,
Though waked to sound with more than mortal grace.

Go, tuneful maids, go bid my Phaon prove
That passion mocks the empty boast of fame –
Tell him no joys are sweet, but joys of love,
Melting the soul, and thrilling all the frame!
Oh may the ecstatic thought his bosom move,
And sighs of rapture fan the blush of shame!

9. *Laments the Volatility of Phaon*

Ye, who in alleys green and leafy bowers
Sport, the rude children of fantastic birth;
Where frolic nymphs, and shaggy tribes of mirth,
In clamorous revels waste the midnight hours –
Who, linked in flaunting bands of mountain-flowers,
Weave your wild mazes o'er the dewy earth,
Ere the fierce lord of lustre rushes forth
And o'er the world his beamy radiance pours!
Oft has your clanking cymbal's maddening strain,
Loud-ringing through the torch-illumined grove,
Lured my loved Phaon from the youthful train,
Through rugged dells, o'er craggy rocks to rove –
Then how can she his vagrant heart detain,
Whose lyre throbs only to the touch of love?

10. *Describes Phaon*

Dangerous to hear is that melodious tongue,
And fatal to the sense those murderous eyes,
Where in a sapphire sheath love's arrow lies,
Himself concealed the crystal haunts among!
Oft o'er that form, enamoured, have I hung,
On that smooth cheek to mark the deepening dyes,
While from that lip the fragrant breath would rise,
That lip, like Cupid's bow, with rubies strung!
Still let me gaze upon that polished brow,
O'er which the golden hair luxuriant plays;
So, on the modest lily's leaves of snow
The proud sun revels in resplendent rays!
Warm as his beams this sensate heart shall glow,
Till life's last hour with Phaon's self decays!

11. *Rejects the Influence of Reason*

Oh Reason, vaunted sovereign of the mind –
Thou pompous vision with a sounding name!
Canst thou the soul's rebellious passions tame?
Canst thou in spells the vagrant fancy bind?
Ah no, capricious as the wavering wind
Are sighs of love that dim thy boasted flame,
While Folly's torch consumes the wreath of fame,
And Pleasure's hands the sheaves of truth unbind.
Pressed by the storms of fate, hope shrinks and dies;
Frenzy darts forth in mightiest ills arrayed;
Around thy throne destructive tumults rise,
And Hell-fraught jealousies thy rights invade!
Then, what art thou, oh idol of the wise? –
A visionary theme! A gorgeous shade!

12. *Previous to her Interview with Phaon*

Now, o'er the tesselated pavement strew
Fresh saffron, steeped in essence of the rose,
While down yon agate column gently flows
A glittering streamlet of ambrosial dew!
My Phaon smiles! The rich carnation's hue,
On his flushed cheek in conscious lustre glows,
While o'er his breast enamoured Venus throws
Her starry mantle of celestial blue!
Breathe soft, ye dulcet flutes, among the trees
Where clustering boughs with golden citrons twine;
While slow vibrations, dying on the breeze,
Shall soothe his soul with harmony divine.
Then let my form his yielding fancy seize,
And all his fondest wishes blend with mine!

13. *She Endeavours to Fascinate Him*

Bring, bring, to deck my brow, ye sylvan girls,
A roseate wreath – nor for my waving hair
The costly band of studded gems prepare,
Of sparkling chrysolite, or orient pearls!
Love o'er my head his canopy unfurls,
His purple pinions fan the whispering air;
Mocking the golden sandal, rich and rare,
Beneath my feet the fragrant woodbine curls.

  Bring the thin robe, to fold about my breast,
White as the downy swan; while round my waist
  Let leaves of glossy myrtle bind the vest,
Not idly gay, but elegantly chaste!
  Love scorns the nymph in wanton trappings dressed;
And charms the most concealed, are doubly graced.

14. *To the Eolian Harp*

Come, soft Eolian harp, while zephyr plays
  Along the meek vibration of thy strings,
  As Twilight's hand her modest mantle brings,
Blending with sober grey the western blaze!
Oh prompt my Phaon's dreams with tenderest lays,
  Ere night o'ershade thee with its humid wings,
  While the lorn philomel his sorrow sings
In leafy cradle, red with parting rays!
  Slow let thy dulcet tones on ether glide –
So steals the murmur of the amorous dove;
  The mazy legions swarm on every side,
To lulling sounds the sunny people move!
  Let not the wise their little world deride,
The smallest sting can wound the breast of love.

15. *Phaon Awakes*

Now round my favoured grot let roses rise,
  To strew the bank where Phaon wakes from rest!
  Oh happy buds, to kiss his burning breast,
And die beneath the lustre of his eyes!
Now let the timbrels echo to the skies,
  Now damsels sprinkle cassia on his vest,
  With odorous wreaths of constant myrtle dressed,
And flowers, deep tinted with the rainbow's dyes!
  From cups of porphyry let nectar flow,
Rich as the perfume of Phoenicia's vine!
  Now let his dimpling cheek with rapture glow,
While round his heart love's mystic fetters twine;
  And let the Grecian lyre its aid bestow,
In songs of triumph to proclaim him mine! . . .

35. *Reproaches Phaon*

What means the mist opaque that veils these eyes?
Why does yon threatening tempest shroud the day?
Why does thy altar, Venus, fade away,
And on my breast the dews of horror rise?
Phaon is false! Be dim, ye orient skies,
And let black Erebus succeed your ray!
Let clashing thunders roll, and lightnings play –
Phaon is false! and hopeless Sappho dies!
'Farewell, my Lesbian love', you might have said
(Such sweet remembrance had some pity proved),
Or coldly thus, 'Farewell, oh Lesbian maid' –
No task severe for one so fondly loved!
The gentle thought had soothed my wandering shade,
From life's dark valley, and its thorns, removed!

36. *Her Confirmed Despair*

Lead me, Sicilian maids, to haunted bowers,
While yon pale moon displays her faintest beams
O'er fading woodlands, and enchanted streams
Whose banks infect the breeze with poisonous flowers.
Ah, lead me where the barren mountain towers,
Where no sounds echo, but the night-owl's screams;
Where some lone spirit of the desert gleams,
And lurid horrors wing the fateful hours!
Now goaded frenzy grasps my shrinking brain,
Her touch absorbs the crystal fount of woe!
My blood rolls burning through each bursting vein:
Away, lost lyre – unless thou canst bestow
A charm to lull that agonising pain
Which those who never loved can never know!

37. *Foresees Her Death*

When, in the gloomy mansion of the dead,
This withering heart, this faded form shall sleep;
When these fond eyes at length shall cease to weep,
And earth's cold lap receive this feverish head –
Envy shall turn away, a tear to shed,
And Time's obliterating pinions sweep
The spot where poets shall their vigils keep
To mourn and wander near my freezing bed!

Then my pale ghost upon the Elysian shore
Shall smile, released from every mortal care,
While (doomed love's victim to repine no more)
My breast shall bathe in endless rapture there –
Ah no, my restless shade would still deplore,
Nor taste that bliss, which Phaon did not share!

38. *To a Sigh*

Oh sigh, thou stealest (the herald of the breast)
The lover's fears, the lover's pangs, to tell;
Thou bidst with timid grace the bosom swell,
Cheating the day of joy, the night of rest!
Oh lucid tears, with eloquence confessed,
Why on my fading cheek unheeded dwell,
Meek as the dew-drops on the flowret's bell
By ruthless tempests to the green-sod pressed.
Fond sigh, be hushed! Congeal, oh slighted tear –
Thy feeble powers the busy Fates control!
Or if thy crystal streams again appear,
Let them, like Lethe's, to oblivion roll –
For love the tyrant plays when hope is near,
And she who flies the lover, chains the soul!

39. *To the Muses*

Prepare your wreaths, Aonian maids divine,
To strew the tranquil bed where I shall sleep;
In tears, the myrtle and the laurel steep,
And let Erato's hand the trophies twine.
No Parian marble there, with laboured line
Shall bid the wandering lover stay to weep;
There holy silence shall her vigils keep
Save when the nightingale such woes as mine
Shall sadly sing; as twilight's curtains spread,
There shall the branching lotus widely wave,
Sprinkling soft showers upon the lily's head,
Sweet drooping emblem for a lover's grave!
And there shall Phaon pearls of pity shed
To gem the vanquished heart he scorned to save!

40. *Visions Appear to Her in a Dream*

On the low margin of a murmuring stream,
As rapt in meditation's arms I lay,
Each aching sense in slumbers stole away,
While potent fancy formed a soothing dream.
O'er the Leucadian deep, a dazzling beam
Shed the bland light of empyrean day –
But soon transparent shadows veiled each ray,
While mystic visions sprang athwart the gleam!
Now to the heaving gulf they seemed to bend,
And now across the sphery regions glide;
Now in mid-air their dulcet voices blend:
'Awake! awake!' the restless phalanx cried,
'See ocean yawns the lover's woes to end;
Plunge the green wave, and bid thy griefs subside!'

41. *Resolves to Take the Leap of Leucata*

Yes, I will go, where circling whirlwinds rise,
Where threatening clouds in sable grandeur lour;
Where the blast yells, the liquid columns pour,
And maddening billows combat with the skies!
There, while the Demon of the Tempest flies
On growing pinions through the troublous hour,
The wild waves gasp impatient to devour,
And on the rock the wakened vulture cries!
Oh! dreadful solace to the stormy mind –
To me, more pleasing than the valley's rest,
The woodland songsters, or the sportive kind
That nip the turf, or prune the painted crest;
For in despair alone, the wretched find
That unction sweet, which lulls the bleeding breast!

42. *Her Last Appeal to Phaon*

Oh! canst thou bear to see this faded frame
Deformed and mangled by the rocky deep?
Wilt thou remember, and forbear to weep,
My fatal fondness and my peerless fame?
Soon o'er this heart, now warm with passion's flame,
The howling winds and foamy waves shall sweep –
These eyes be ever closed in death's cold sleep,
And all of Sappho perish, but her name!

Yet, if the Fates suspend their barbarous ire,
If days less mournful, Heaven designs for me,
If rocks grow kind, and winds and waves conspire
To bear me softly on the swelling sea –
To Phoebus only will I tune my lyre,
'What suits with Sappho, Phoebus, suits with thee!'

43. *Her Reflections on the Leucadian Rock Before She Perishes*

While from the dizzy precipice I gaze,
The world receding from my pensive eyes,
High o'er my head the tyrant eagle flies,
Clothed in the sinking sun's transcendent blaze!
The meek-eyed moon, midst clouds of amber plays,
As o'er the purpling plains of light she hies,
Till the last stream of living lustre dies,
And the cool concave owns her tempered rays!
So shall this glowing, palpitating soul,
Welcome returning reason's placid beam,
While o'er my breast the waves Lethean roll,
To calm rebellious fancy's feverish dream.
Then shall my lyre disdain love's dread control,
And loftier passions prompt the loftier theme!

44. *Sonnet Conclusive*

Here droops the Muse! while from her glowing mind,
Celestial Sympathy, with humid eye,
Bids the light sylph (capricious Fancy) fly,
Time's restless wings with transient flowers to bind!
For now, with folded arms and head inclined,
Reflection pours the deep and frequent sigh
O'er the dark scroll of human destiny,
Where gaudy buds and wounding thorns are twined.
Oh, sky-born Virtue! sacred is thy name –
And though mysterious Fate, with frown severe,
Oft decorates thy brows with wreaths of fame
Bespangled o'er with Sorrow's chilling tear,
Yet shalt thou more than mortal raptures claim,
The brightest planet of the eternal sphere!

2. WILLIAM WORDSWORTH

The Ruined Cottage

(1797–8; *Excursion* 1814/from MS 1908)

First Part

'Twas summer and the sun was mounted high;
Along the south the uplands feebly glared
Through a pale steam, and all the northern downs,
In clearer air ascending, showed far off
Their surfaces with shadows dappled o'er
Of deep embattled clouds. Far as the sight
Could reach those many shadows lay in spots
Determined and unmoved, with steady beams
Of clear and pleasant sunshine interposed –
Pleasant to him who on the soft cool moss
Extends his careless limbs beside the root
Of some huge oak whose agéd branches make
A twilight of their own, a dewy shade
Where the wren warbles while the dreaming man,
Half-conscious of that soothing melody,
With sidelong eye looks out upon the scene,
By those impending branches made more soft,
More soft and distant.
Other lot was mine.
Across a bare wide common I had toiled
With languid feet which by the slippery ground
Were baffled still; and when I stretched myself
On the brown earth my limbs from very heat
Could find no rest, nor my weak arm disperse
The insect host which gathered round my face
And joined their murmurs to the tedious noise
Of seeds of bursting gorse that crackled round.
I rose and turned towards a group of trees
Which midway in that level stood alone;
And thither come at length, beneath a shade
Of clustering elms that sprang from the same root
I found a ruined house, four naked walls
That stared upon each other. I looked round,
And near the door I saw an agéd man
Alone and stretched upon the cottage bench;
An iron-pointed staff lay at his side.

With instantaneous joy I recognized
That pride of Nature and of lowly life,
The venerable Armytage, a friend
As dear to me as is the setting sun.
Two days before
We had been fellow-travellers. I knew
That he was in this neighbourhood, and now
Delighted found him here in the cool shade.
He lay, his pack of rustic merchandise
Pillowing his head. I guess he had no thought
Of his way-wandering life. His eyes were shut,
The shadows of the breezy elms above
Dappled his face. With thirsty heat oppressed
At length I hailed him, glad to see his hat
Bedewed with water-drops, as if the brim
Had newly scooped a running stream. He rose
And pointing to a sun-flower, bade me climb
The broken wall where that same gaudy flower
Looked out upon the road.
It was a plot
Of garden-ground now wild, its matted weeds
Marked with the steps of those whom as they passed,
The gooseberry-trees that shot in long lank slips,
Or currants hanging from their leafless stems
In scanty strings, had tempted to o'erleap
The broken wall. Within that cheerless spot,
Where two tall hedgerows of thick alder boughs
Joined in a damp cold nook, I found a well
Half covered up with willow-flowers and grass.
I slaked my thirst and to the shady bench
Returned, and while I stood unbonneted
To catch the motion of the cooler air
The old man said, 'I see around me here
Things which you cannot see. We die, my friend,
Nor we alone, but that which each man loved
And prized in his peculiar nook of earth
Dies with him, or is changed, and very soon
Even of the good is no memorial left.
The poets, in their elegies and songs
Lamenting the departed, call the groves,
They call upon the hills and streams to mourn,
And senseless rocks – nor idly, for they speak
In these their invocations with a voice
Obedient to the strong creative power
Of human passion. Sympathies there are

More tranquil, yet perhaps of kindred birth,
That steal upon the meditative mind
And grow with thought. Beside yon spring I stood,
And eyed its waters till we seemed to feel
One sadness, they and I. For them a bond
Of brotherhood is broken: time has been
When every day the touch of human hand
Disturbed their stillness, and they ministered
To human comfort. When I stooped to drink
A spider's web hung to the water's edge,
And on the wet and slimy foot-stone lay
The useless fragment of a wooden bowl.
It moved my very heart.
The day has been
When I could never pass this road but she
Who lived within these walls, when I appeared,
A daughter's welcome gave me, and I loved her
As my own child. Oh sir, the good die first,
And they whose hearts are dry as summer dust
Burn to the socket. Many a passenger
Has blest poor Margaret for her gentle looks
When she upheld the cool refreshment drawn
From that forsaken spring, and no one came
But he was welcome, no one went away
But that it seemed she loved him. She is dead,
The worm is on her cheek, and this poor hut,
Stripped of its outward garb of household-flowers,
Of rose and sweetbriar, offers to the wind
A cold bare wall whose earthy top is tricked
With weeds and the rank speargrass. She is dead,
And nettles rot and adders sun themselves
Where we have sat together while she nursed
Her infant at her breast. The unshod colt,
The wandering heifer and the potter's ass,
Find shelter now within the chimney-wall
Where I have seen her evening hearthstone blaze
And through the window spread upon the road
Its cheerful light. You will forgive me, sir,
But often on this cottage do I muse
As on a picture, till my wiser mind
Sinks, yielding to the foolishness of grief.
She had a husband, an industrious man,
Sober and steady. I have heard her say
That he was up and busy at his loom

In summer ere the mower's scythe had swept
The dewy grass, and in the early spring
Ere the last star had vanished. They who passed
At evening, from behind the garden-fence
Might hear his busy spade, which he would ply
After his daily work till the daylight
Was gone, and every leaf and flower were lost
In the dark hedges. So they passed their days
In peace and comfort, and two pretty babes
Were their best hope next to the God in Heaven.
        You may remember, now some ten years gone,
Two blighting seasons when the fields were left
With half a harvest. It pleased Heaven to add
A worse affliction in the plague of war;
A happy land was stricken to the heart –
'Twas a sad time of sorrow and distress.
A wanderer among the cottages,
I with my pack of winter raiment saw
The hardships of that season. Many rich
Sunk down as in a dream among the poor,
And of the poor did many cease to be,
And their place knew them not. Meanwhile, abridged
Of daily comforts, gladly reconciled
To numerous self-denials, Margaret
Went struggling on through those calamitous years
With cheerful hope. But ere the second autumn,
A fever seized her husband. In disease
He lingered long, and when his strength returned
He found the little he had stored to meet
The hour of accident, or crippling age,
Was all consumed. As I have said, 'twas now
A time of trouble: shoals of artisans
Were from their daily labour turned away
To hang for bread on parish charity,
They and their wives and children – happier far
Could they have lived as do the little birds
That peck along the hedges, or the kite
That makes her dwelling in the mountain rocks.
        Ill fared it now with Robert, he who dwelt
In this poor cottage. At his door he stood
And whistled many a snatch of merry tunes
That had no mirth in them, or with his knife
Carved uncouth figures on the heads of sticks;
Then idly sought about through every nook

Of house or garden any casual task
Of use or ornament, and with a strange
Amusing but uneasy novelty
He blended where he might the various tasks
Of summer, autumn, winter, and of spring.
But this endured not, his good humour soon
Became a weight in which no pleasure was,
And poverty brought on a petted mood
And a sore temper. Day by day he drooped,
And he would leave his home, and to the town
Without an errand would he turn his steps,
Or wander here and there among the fields.
One while he would speak lightly of his babes
And with a cruel tongue, at other times
He played with them wild freaks of merriment,
And 'twas a piteous thing to see the looks
Of the poor innocent children. 'Every smile',
Said Margaret to me here beneath these trees,
'Made my heart bleed.'
At this the old man paused,
And looking up to those enormous elms
He said, ' 'Tis now the hour of deepest noon.
At this still season of repose and peace,
This hour when all things which are not at rest
Are cheerful, while this multitude of flies
Fills all the air with happy melody,
Why should a tear be in an old man's eye?
Why should we thus with an untoward mind,
And in the weakness of humanity,
From natural wisdom turn our hearts away,
To natural comfort shut our eyes and ears,
And, feeding on disquiet, thus disturb
The calm of Nature with our restless thoughts?'

Second Part

He spake with somewhat of a solemn tone,
But when he ended there was in his face
Such easy cheerfulness, a look so mild,
That for a little time it stole away
All recollection, and that simple tale
Passed from my mind like a forgotten sound.
A while on trivial things we held discourse,
To me soon tasteless. In my own despite

I thought of that poor woman as of one
Whom I had known and loved. He had rehearsed
Her homely tale with such familiar power,
With such an active countenance, an eye
So busy, that the things of which he spake
Seemed present, and, attention now relaxed,
There was a heartfelt chillness in my veins.
I rose, and turning from that breezy shade
Went out into the open air, and stood
To drink the comfort of the warmer sun.
Long time I had not stayed ere, looking round
Upon that tranquil ruin, I returned
And begged of the old man that for my sake
He would resume his story.
                                        He replied,
'It were a wantonness, and would demand
Severe reproof, if we were men whose hearts
Could hold vain dalliance with the misery
Even of the dead, contented thence to draw
A momentary pleasure, never marked
By reason, barren of all future good.
But we have known that there is often found
In mournful thoughts, and always might be found,
A power to virtue friendly; were't not so
I am a dreamer among men, indeed
An idle dreamer. 'Tis a common tale
By moving accidents uncharactered,
A tale of silent suffering, hardly clothed
In bodily form, and to the grosser sense
But ill adapted – scarcely palpable
To him who does not think. But at your bidding
I will proceed.
                        While thus it fared with them
To whom this cottage till that hapless year
Had been a blesséd home, it was my chance
To travel in a country far remote;
And glad I was when, halting by yon gate
That leads from the green lane, again I saw
These lofty elm-trees. Long I did not rest –
With many pleasant thoughts I cheered my way
O'er the flat common. At the door arrived,
I knocked, and when I entered, with the hope
Of usual greeting, Margaret looked at me
A little while, then turned her head away

Speechless, and sitting down upon a chair
Wept bitterly. I wist not what to do,
Or how to speak to her. Poor wretch, at last
She rose from off her seat, and then, oh sir,
I cannot tell how she pronounced my name.
With fervent love, and with a face of grief
Unutterably helpless, and a look
That seemed to cling upon me, she enquired
If I had seen her husband. As she spake
A strange surprise and fear came to my heart,
Nor had I power to answer ere she told
That he had disappeared – just two months gone,
He left his house. Two wretched days had passed,
And on the third by the first break of light,
Within her casement full in view she saw
A purse of gold. "I trembled at the sight",
Said Margaret, "for I knew it was his hand
That placed it there. And on that very day
By one, a stranger, from my husband sent,
The tidings came that he had joined a troop
Of soldiers going to a distant land.
He left me thus. Poor man, he had not heart
To take a farewell of me, and he feared
That I should follow with my babes, and sink
Beneath the misery of a soldier's life."
This tale did Margaret tell with many tears,
And when she ended I had little power
To give her comfort, and was glad to take
Such words of hope from her own mouth as served
To cheer us both. But long we had not talked
Ere we built up a pile of better thoughts,
And with a brighter eye she looked around
As if she had been shedding tears of joy.
We parted. It was then the early spring;
I left her busy with her garden-tools,
And well remember, o'er that fence she looked,
And, while I paced along the foot-way path,
Called out and sent a blessing after me,
With tender cheerfulness, and with a voice
That seemed the very sound of happy thoughts.
I roved o'er many a hill and many a dale
With this my weary load, in heat and cold,
Through many a wood and many an open ground,
In sunshine or in shade, in wet or fair,

Now blithe, now drooping, as it might befall;
My best companions now the driving winds
And now the "trotting brooks" and whispering trees,
And now the music of my own sad steps,
With many a short-lived thought that passed between
And disappeared.
                                    I came this way again
Towards the wane of summer, when the wheat
Was yellow, and the soft and bladed grass
Sprang up afresh and o'er the hayfield spread
Its tender green. When I had reached the door
I found that she was absent. In the shade,
Where we now sit, I waited her return.
Her cottage in its outward look appeared
As cheerful as before, in any show
Of neatness little changed – but that I thought
The honeysuckle crowded round the door
And from the wall hung down in heavier tufts,
And knots of worthless stonecrop started out
Along the window's edge, and grew like weeds
Against the lower panes. I turned aside
And strolled into her garden. It was changed.
The unprofitable bindweed spread his bells
From side to side, and with unwieldy wreathes
Had dragged the rose from its sustaining wall
And bent it down to earth. The border tufts,
Daisy, and thrift, and lowly camomile,
And thyme, had straggled out into the paths
Which they were used to deck.
                                                        Ere this an hour
Was wasted. Back I turned my restless steps,
And as I walked before the door it chanced
A stranger passed, and guessing whom I sought,
He said that she was used to ramble far.
The sun was sinking in the west, and now
I sat with sad impatience. From within
Her solitary infant cried aloud.
The spot though fair seemed very desolate –
The longer I remained more desolate –
And looking round I saw the corner-stones,
Till then unmarked, on either side the door
With dull red stains discoloured, and stuck o'er
With tufts and hairs of wool, as if the sheep
That feed upon the commons thither came

Familiarly, and found a couching-place
Even at her threshold.
The house-clock struck eight:
I turned and saw her distant a few steps.
Her face was pale and thin, her figure too
Was changed. As she unlocked the door she said,
"It grieves me you have waited here so long,
But in good truth I've wandered much of late,
And sometimes – to my shame I speak – have need
Of my best prayers to bring me back again."
While on the board she spread our evening meal
She told me she had lost her elder child,
That he for months had been a serving-boy,
Apprenticed by the parish. "I perceive
You look at me, and you have cause. Today
I have been travelling far, and many days
About the fields I wander, knowing this
Only, that what I seek I cannot find.
And so I waste my time: for I am changed,
And to myself", said she, "have done much wrong,
And to this helpless infant. I have slept
Weeping, and weeping I have waked. My tears
Have flowed as if my body were not such
As others are, and I could never die.
But I am now in mind and in my heart
More easy, and I hope", said she, "that Heaven
Will give me patience to endure the things
Which I behold at home."
It would have grieved
Your very soul to see her. Sir, I feel
The story linger in my heart. I fear
'Tis long and tedious, but my spirit clings
To that poor woman. So familiarly
Do I perceive her manner and her look
And presence, and so deeply do I feel
Her goodness, that not seldom in my walks
A momentary trance comes over me
And to myself I seem to muse on one
By sorrow laid asleep or borne away,
A human being destined to awake
To human life, or something very near
To human life, when he shall come again
For whom she suffered. Sir, it would have grieved
Your very soul to see her: evermore

Her eyelids drooped, her eyes were downward cast,
And when she at her table gave me food
She did not look at me. Her voice was low,
Her body was subdued. In every act
Pertaining to her house-affairs appeared
The careless stillness which a thinking mind
Gives to an idle matter. Still she sighed,
But yet no motion of the breast was seen,
No heaving of the heart. While by the fire
We sat together, sighs came on my ear –
I knew not how, and hardly whence, they came.
I took my staff, and when I kissed her babe
The tears stood in her eyes. I left her then
With the best hope and comfort I could give:
She thanked me for my will, but for my hope
It seemed she did not thank me.

I returned
And took my rounds along this road again
Ere on its sunny bank the primrose flower
Had chronicled the earliest day of spring.
I found her sad and drooping. She had learned
No tidings of her husband. If he lived,
She knew not that he lived: if he were dead,
She knew not he was dead. She seemed the same
In person or appearance, but her house
Bespoke a sleepy hand of negligence.
The floor was neither dry nor neat, the hearth
Was comfortless,
The windows too were dim, and her few books,
Which one upon the other heretofore
Had been piled up against the corner-panes
In seemly order, now with straggling leaves
Lay scattered here and there, open or shut,
As they had chanced to fall. Her infant babe
Had from its mother caught the trick of grief,
And sighed among its playthings. Once again
I turned towards the garden-gate, and saw
More plainly still that poverty and grief
Were now come nearer to her. The earth was hard,
With weeds defaced and knots of withered grass;
No ridges there appeared of clear black mould,
No winter greenness. Of her herbs and flowers
It seemed the better part were gnawed away
Or trampled on the earth. A chain of straw,

Which had been twisted round the tender stem
Of a young apple-tree, lay at its root;
The bark was nibbled round by truant sheep.
Margaret stood near, her infant in her arms,
And, seeing that my eye was on the tree,
She said, "I fear it will be dead and gone
Ere Robert come again."
                                        Towards the house
Together we returned, and she enquired
If I had any hope. But for her babe,
And for her little friendless boy, she said,
She had no wish to live – that she must die
Of sorrow. Yet I saw the idle loom
Still in its place. His Sunday garments hung
Upon the self-same nail, his very staff
Stood undisturbed behind the door. And when
I passed this way beaten by autumn winds,
She told me that her little babe was dead
And she was left alone. That very time,
I yet remember, through the miry lane
She walked with me a mile, when the bare trees
Trickled with foggy damps, and in such sort
That any heart had ached to hear her, begged
That wheresoe'er I went I still would ask
For him whom she had lost. We parted then,
Our final parting; for from that time forth
Did many seasons pass ere I returned
Into this tract again.
                                Five tedious years
She lingered in unquiet widowhood,
A wife and widow. Needs must it have been
A sore heart-wasting. I have heard, my friend,
That in that broken arbour she would sit
The idle length of half a sabbath-day –
There, where you see the toadstool's lazy head –
And when a dog passed by she still would quit
The shade and look abroad. On this old bench
For hours she sat, and evermore her eye
Was busy in the distance, shaping things
Which made her heart beat quick. Seest thou that path?
The green-sward now has broken its grey line –
There to and fro she paced through many a day
Of the warm summer, from a belt of flax
That girt her waist, spinning the long-drawn thread

With backward steps. Yet ever as there passed
A man whose garments showed the soldier's red,
Or crippled mendicant in sailor's garb,
The little child who sat to turn the wheel
Ceased from his toil, and she, with faltering voice,
Expecting still to learn her husband's fate,
Made many a fond enquiry; and when they
Whose presence gave no comfort, were gone by,
Her heart was still more sad. And by yon gate,
Which bars the traveller's road, she often stood
And, when a stranger horseman came, the latch
Would lift, and in his face look wistfully,
Most happy if from aught discovered there
Of tender feeling she might dare repeat
The same sad question.
Meanwhile her poor hut
Sunk to decay; for he was gone, whose hand
At the first nippings of October frost
Closed up each chink, and with fresh bands of straw
Chequered the green-grown thatch. And so she lived
Through the long winter, reckless and alone,
Till this reft house, by frost, and thaw, and rain,
Was sapped; and when she slept, the nightly damps
Did chill her breast, and in the stormy day
Her tattered clothes were ruffled by the wind
Even at the side of her own fire. Yet still
She loved this wretched spot, nor would for worlds
Have parted hence; and still that length of road,
And this rude bench, one torturing hope endeared,
Fast rooted at her heart. And here, my friend,
In sickness she remained; and here she died,
Last human tenant of these ruined walls.'
The old man ceased; he saw that I was moved.
From that low bench rising instinctively
I turned aside in weakness, nor had power
To thank him for the tale which he had told.
I stood, and leaning o'er the garden gate
Reviewed that woman's sufferings; and it seemed
To comfort me while with a brother's love
I blest her in the impotence of grief.
At length towards the cottage I returned
Fondly, and traced with milder interest
That secret spirit of humanity
Which, mid the calm oblivious tendencies

Of Nature, mid her plants, her weeds and flowers,
And silent overgrowings, still survived.
The old man seeing this resumed, and said,
'My friend, enough to sorrow have you given,
The purposes of wisdom ask no more:
Be wise and cheerful, and no longer read
The forms of things with an unworthy eye.
She sleeps in the calm earth, and peace is here.
I well remember that those very plumes
Those weeds, and the high spear-grass on that wall,
By mist and silent raindrops silvered o'er,
As once I passed did to my mind convey
So still an image of tranquillity,
So calm and still, and looked so beautiful
Amid the uneasy thoughts which filled my mind,
That what we feel of sorrow and despair
From ruin and from change, and all the grief
The passing shows of being leave behind,
Appeared an idle dream that could not live
Where meditation was. I turned away,
And walked along my road in happiness.'
   He ceased. By this the sun declining shot
A slant and mellow radiance, which began
To fall upon us where beneath the trees
We sat on that low bench. And now we felt,
Admonished thus, the sweet hour coming on:
A linnet warbled from those lofty elms,
A thrush sang loud, and other melodies
At distance heard peopled the milder air.
The old man rose and hoisted up his load;
Together casting then a farewell look
Upon those silent walls, we left the shade,
And ere the stars were visible attained
A rustic inn, our evening resting-place.

3. SAMUEL TAYLOR COLERIDGE

Love (Nov. 1799; publ. 1817)

All thoughts, all passions, all delights,
Whatever stirs this mortal frame,
All are but ministers of Love,
   And feed his sacred flame.

Oft in my waking dreams do I
Live o'er again that happy hour,
When midway on the mount I lay
   Beside the ruined tower.

The moonshine, stealing o'er the scene,
Had blended with the lights of eve,
And she was there, my hope, my joy,
   My own dear Genevieve!

She leant against the armèd man,
The statue of the armèd knight –
She stood and listened to my lay,
   Amid the lingering light.

Few sorrows hath she of her own,
My hope! my joy! my Genevieve!
She loves me best whene'er I sing
   The songs that make her grieve.

I played a soft and doleful air,
I sang an old and moving story –
An old rude song, that suited well
   That ruin wild and hoary.

She listened with a flitting blush,
With downcast eyes and modest grace,
For well she knew I could not choose
   But gaze upon her face.

I told her of the Knight that wore
Upon his shield a burning brand,
And that for ten long years he wooed
   The Lady of the Land.

I told her how he pined – and ah!
The deep, the low, the pleading tone
With which I sang another's love,
   Interpreted my own.

She listened with a flitting blush,
With downcast eyes, and modest grace,
And she forgave me that I gazed
   Too fondly on her face!

But when I told the cruel scorn
That crazed that bold and lovely Knight,
And that he crossed the mountain-woods,
   Nor rested day nor night;

That sometimes from the savage den,
And sometimes from the darksome shade,
And sometimes starting up at once
   In green and sunny glade,

There came and looked him in the face
An angel beautiful and bright;
And that he knew it was a fiend,
   This miserable Knight!

And that unknowing what he did,
He leaped amid a murderous band,
And saved from outrage worse than death
   The Lady of the Land!

And how she wept, and clasped his knees;
And how she tended him in vain,
And ever strove to expiate
   The scorn that crazed his brain –

And that she nursed him in a cave,
And how his madness went away
When on the yellow forest-leaves
   A dying man he lay.

His dying words – but when I reached
That tenderest strain of all the ditty,
My faltering voice and pausing harp
   Disturbed her soul with pity!

All impulses of soul and sense
Had thrilled my guileless Genevieve –
The music and the doleful tale,
   The rich and balmy eve –

And hopes, and fears that kindle hope,
An undistinguishable throng,
And gentle wishes long subdued,
   Subdued and cherished long!

She wept with pity and delight,
She blushed with love and virgin-shame,
And like the murmur of a dream
   I heard her breathe my name.

Her bosom heaved, she stepped aside –
As conscious of my look she stepped –
Then suddenly, with timorous eye,
   She fled to me and wept.

She half enclosed me with her arms,
She pressed me with a meek embrace,
And, bending back her head, looked up
   And gazed upon my face.

'Twas partly love, and partly fear,
And partly 'twas a bashful art,
That I might rather feel, than see,
   The swelling of her heart.

I calmed her fears, and she was calm,
And told her love with virgin pride –
And so I won my Genevieve,
   My bright and beauteous bride.

4. WILLIAM BLAKE

(i) *The Crystal Cabinet* (c. 1803; from MS 1905)

The maiden caught me in the wild
Where I was dancing merrily;
She put me into her cabinet
And locked me up with a golden key.

This cabinet is formed of gold
And pearl and crystal shining bright,
And within it opens into a world
And a little lovely moony night!

Another England there I saw,
Another London with its Tower,
Another Thames and other hills,
And another pleasant Surrey bower,

Another maiden like herself,
Translucent, lovely, shining clear,
Threefold each in the other closed –
Oh what a pleasant trembling fear!

Oh what a smile, a threefold-smile,
Filled me, that like a flame I burned!
I bent to kiss the lovely maid,
And found a threefold-kiss returned;

I strove to seize the inmost form
With ardour fierce and hands of flame,
But burst the crystal cabinet
And like a weeping babe became!

A weeping babe upon the wild
And weeping woman pale reclined –
And in the outward air again
I filled with woes the passing wind!

(ii) *The Mental Traveller* (c. 1803; from MS 1905)

I travelled through a land of men,
A land of men, and women too –
And heard and saw such dreadful things
As cold-earth wanderers never knew.

For there the babe is born in joy
That was begotten in dire woe,
Just as we reap in joy the fruit
Which we in bitter tears did sow;

And if the babe is born a boy,
He's given to a woman old
Who nails him down upon a rock,
Catches his shrieks in cups of gold –

She binds iron thorns around his head,
She pierces both his hands and feet,
She cuts his heart out at his side
To make it feel both cold and heat.

Her fingers number every nerve
Just as a miser counts his gold,
She lives upon his shrieks and cries
And she grows young as he grows old;

Till he becomes a bleeding youth
And she becomes a virgin bright,
Then he rends up his manacles
And binds her down for his delight –

He plants himself in all her nerves
Just as a husbandman his mould,
And she becomes his dwelling place
And garden fruitful seventy-fold!

An agéd shadow soon he fades
Wandering round an earthly cot,
Full filled all with gems and gold
Which he by industry had got –

And these are the gems of the human soul:
The rubies and pearls of a lovesick eye,
The countless gold of the aching heart,
The martyr's groan and the lover's sigh.

They are his meat, they are his drink;
He feeds the beggar and the poor
And the wayfaring traveller –
For ever open is his door.

His grief is their eternal joy:
They make the roofs and walls to ring,
Till from the fire on the hearth
A little female babe does spring!

And she is all of solid fire
And gems and gold, that none his hand
Dares stretch to touch her baby form,
Or wrap her in his swaddling-band.

But she comes to the man she loves,
If young or old or rich or poor,
They soon drive out the agéd host,
A beggar at another's door –

He wanders weeping far away
Until some other take him in,
Oft blind and age-bent, sore distressed,
Until he can a maiden win;

And to allay his freezing age
The poor man takes her in his arms –
The cottage fades before his sight,
The garden and its lovely charms!

The guests are scattered through the land,
For the eye, altering, alters all!
The senses roll themselves in fear
And the flat earth becomes a ball;

The stars, sun, moon all shrink away,
A desert vast without a bound,
And nothing left to eat or drink
And a dark desert all around.

The honey of her infant lips,
The bread and wine of her sweet smile,
The wild game of her roving eye,
Does him to infancy beguile –

For as he eats and drinks he grows
Younger and younger every day,
And on the desert wild they both
Wander in terror and dismay.

Like the wild stag she flees away
(Her fear plants many a thicket wild)
While he pursues her night and day
By various arts of love beguiled –

By various arts of love and hate;
Till the wide desert planted o'er
With labyrinths of wayward love
Where roams the lion, wolf, and boar;

Till he becomes a wayward babe
And she a weeping woman old!
Then many a lover wanders here
The sun and stars are nearer rolled,

The trees bring forth sweet ecstasy
To all who in the desert roam,
Till many a city there is built
And many a pleasant shepherd's home.

But when they find the frowning babe
Terror strikes through the region wide,
They cry, 'The babe, the babe is born!'
And flee away on every side –

For who dare touch the frowning form
His arm is withered to its root;
Lions, boars, wolves, all howling flee,
And every tree does shed its fruit.

And none can touch that frowning form,
Except it be a woman old –
She nails him down upon the rock,
And all is done as I have told.

5. MARY TIGHE

'A Glimpse of Love'

(*Psyche* I, stanzas 16–32) 1802–3; publ. 1805

16

Mid the blue waves, by circling seas embraced,
A chosen spot of fairest land was seen,
For there with favouring hand had Nature placed
All that could lovely make the varied scene:
Eternal Spring there spread her mantle green;
There high surrounding hills deep-wooded rose
O'er placid lakes; while marble rocks between
The fragrant shrubs their pointed heads disclose,
And balmy breathes each gale which o'er the island blows.

17

Pleasure had called the fertile lawns her own,
And thickly strewed them with her choicest flowers;
Amid the quiet glade her golden throne
Bright shone with lustre through o'erarching bowers:

There her fair train, the ever-downy Hours
Sport on light wing with the young Joys entwined;
While Hope, delighted, from her full lap showers
Blossoms, whose fragrance can the ravished mind
Inebriate with dreams of rapture unconfined.

18

And in the grassy centre of the isle,
Where the thick verdure spreads a damper shade,
Amid their native rocks concealed awhile,
Then o'er the plains in devious streams displayed,
Two gushing fountains rise; and thence conveyed,
Their waters through the woods and valleys play,
Visit each green recess and secret glade,
With still unmingled, still meandering way,
Nor widely wandering far, can each from other stray.

19

But of strange contrast are their virtues found,
And oft the lady of that isle has tried
In rocky dens and caverns under ground,
The black deformèd stream in vain to hide –
Bursting all bounds her labours it defied!
Yet many a flowery sod its course conceals
Through plains where deep its silent waters glide,
Till secret ruin, all corroding, steals,
And every treacherous arch the hideous gulf reveals.

20

Forbidding every kindly prosperous growth,
Where'er it ran, a channel bleak it wore;
The gaping banks receded, as though loth
To touch the poison which disgraced their shore:
There deadly anguish pours unmixed his store
Of all the ills which sting the human breast,
The hopeless tears which past delights deplore,
Heart-gnawing jealousy which knows no rest,
And self-upbraiding shame, by stern remorse opprest.

21

Oh, how unlike the pure transparent stream
Which near it bubbles o'er its golden sands!
The impeding stones with pleasant music seem
Its progress to detain from other lands;

And all its banks, enwreathed with flowery bands,
Ambrosial fragrance shed in grateful dew.
There young Desire enchanted ever stands,
Breathing delight and fragrance ever new,
And bathed in constant joys of fond affection true.

22
But not to mortals is it e'er allowed
To drink unmingled of that current bright.
Scarce can they taste the pleasurable flood,
Defiled by angry Fortune's envious spite,
Who from the cup of amorous delight
Dashes the sparkling draught of brilliant joy,
Till, with dull sorrow's stream despoiléd quite,
No more it cheers the soul nor charms the eye,
But mid the poisoned bowl distrust and anguish lie.

23
Here Cupid tempers his unerring darts,
And in the fount of bliss delights to play;
Here mingles balmy sighs and pleasing smarts,
And here the honied draught will oft allay
With that black poison's all-polluting sway,
For wretched man. Hither, as Venus willed,
For Psyche's punishment he bent his way;
From either stream his amber vase he filled –
For her were meant the drops which grief alone distilled.

24
His quiver, sparkling bright with gems and gold,
From his fair pluméd shoulder graceful hung,
And from its top in brilliant chords enrolled,
Each little vase resplendently was slung.
Still as he flew, around him sportive clung
His frolic train of wingéd zephyrs light,
Wafting the fragrance which his tresses flung;
While odours dropped from every ringlet bright,
And from his blue eyes beamed ineffable delight.

25
Wrapt in a cloud unseen by mortal eye,
He sought the chamber of the royal maid;
There, lulled by careless soft security,
Of the impending mischief nought afraid,

Upon her purple couch was Psyche laid,
Her radiant eyes a downy slumber sealed;
In light transparent veil alone arrayed,
Her bosom's opening charms were half revealed,
And scarce the lucid folds her polished limbs concealed.

26

A placid smile plays o'er each roseate lip!
Sweet severed lips, while thus your pearls disclose
That slumbering thus unconscious she may sip
The cruel presage of her future woes.
Lightly, as fall the dews upon the rose,
Upon the coral gates of that sweet cell
The fatal drops he pours; nor yet he knows
(Nor, though a god, can he presaging tell)
How he himself shall mourn the ills of that sad spell!

27

Nor yet content, he from his quiver drew,
Sharpened with skill divine, a shining dart.
No need had he for bow, since thus too true
His hand might wound her all-exposéd heart,
Yet her fair side he touched with gentlest art,
And half relenting on her beauties gazed!
Just then, awaking with a sudden start,
Her opening eye in humid lustre blazed –
Unseen he still remained, enchanted and amazed.

28

The dart which in his hand now trembling stood,
As o'er the couch he bent with ravished eye,
Drew with its daring point celestial blood
From his smooth neck's unblemished ivory.
Heedless of this, but with a pitying sigh
(The evil done now anxious to repair),
He shed in haste the balmy drops of joy
O'er all the silky ringlets of her hair;
Then stretched his plumes divine, and breathed celestial air.

29

Unhappy Psyche! Soon the latent wound
The fading roses of her cheek confess,
Her eyes' bright beams, in swimming sorrows drowned,
Sparkle no more with life and happiness

Her parents' fond exulting heart to bless.
She shuns adoring crowds, and seeks to hide
The pining sorrows which her soul oppress,
Till to her mother's tears no more denied,
The secret grief she owns, for which she lingering sighed.

30

A dream of mingled terror and delight
Still heavy hangs upon her troubled soul,
An angry form still swims before her sight,
And still the vengeful thunders seem to roll –
Still crushed to earth she feels the stern control
Of Venus unrelenting, unappeased.
The dream returns, she feels the fancied dole:
Once more the furies on her heart have seized,
But still she views the youth who all her sufferings eased.

31

Of wondrous beauty did the vision seem,
And in the freshest prime of youthful years –
Such at the close of her distressful dream
A graceful champion to her eyes appears!
Her loved deliverer from her foes and fears
She seems in grateful transport still to press;
Still his soft voice sounds in her ravished ears.
Dissolved in fondest tears of tenderness
His form she oft invokes her waking eyes to bless.

32

Nor was it quite a dream, for as she woke,
Ere heavenly mists concealed him from her eye,
One sudden transitory view she took
Of Love's most radiant bright divinity.
From the fair image never can she fly,
As still consumed with vain desire she pines;
While her fond parents heave the anxious sigh,
And to avert her fate seek holy shrines
The threatened ills to learn by auguries and signs.

6. THOMAS CAMPBELL

Gertrude of Wyoming II (1809)

1

A valley, from the river-shore withdrawn,
Was Albert's home, two quiet woods between
Whose lofty verdure overlooked his lawn;
And waters to their resting-place serene
Came freshening, and reflecting all the scene –
A mirror in the depth of flowery shelves!
So sweet a spot of earth you might (I ween)
Have guessed some congregation of the elves
To sport by summer moons had shaped it for themselves.

2

Yet wanted not the eye far scope to muse,
Nor vistas opened by the wandering stream;
Both where at evening Allegany views,
Through ridges burning in her western beam,
Lake after lake interminably gleam –
And past those settlers' haunts the eye might roam,
Where earth's unliving silence all would seem,
Save where on rocks the beaver built his dome
Or buffalo remote lowed far from human home.

3

But silent not that adverse eastern path
Which saw Aurora's hills the horizon crown:
There was the river heard, in bed of wrath
(A precipice of foam from mountains brown),
Like tumults heard from some far distant town –
But, softening in approach, he left his gloom
And murmured pleasantly, and laid him down
To kiss those easy curving banks of bloom
That lent the windward air an exquisite perfume.

4

It seemed as if those scenes sweet influence had
On Gertrude's soul, and kindness like their own
Inspired those eyes affectionate and glad,
That seemed to love whate'er they looked upon.

Whether with Hebe's mirth her features shone,
Or if a shade more pleasing them o'ercast
(As if for heavenly musing meant alone),
Yet so becomingly the expression past
That each succeeding look was lovelier than the last.

5

Nor, guess I, was that Pennsylvanian home,
With all its picturesque and balmy grace,
And fields that were a luxury to roam,
Lost on the soul that looked from such a face!
Enthusiast of the woods, when years apace
Had bound thy lovely waist with woman's zone,
The sunrise-path at morn I see thee trace
To hills with high magnolia overgrown,
And joy to breathe the groves, romantic and alone.

6

The sunrise drew her thoughts to Europe forth
That thus apostrophized its viewless scene:
'Land of my father's love, my mother's birth!
The home of kindred I have never seen!
We know not other – oceans are between –
Yet say! far friendly hearts from whence we came,
Of us does oft remembrance intervene?
My mother sure, my sire, a thought may claim,
But Gertrude is to you an unregarded name.

7

And yet, loved England! when thy name I trace
In many a pilgrim's tale and poet's song,
How can I choose but wish for one embrace
Of them, the dear unknown, to whom belong
My mother's looks – perhaps her likeness strong?
Oh parent! with what reverential awe,
From features of thine own related throng,
An image of thy face my soul could draw –
And see thee once again whom I too shortly saw!

8

Yet deem not Gertrude sighed for foreign joy –
To soothe a father's couch her only care,
And keep his reverend head from all annoy.
For this, methinks, her homeward steps repair

Soon as the morning-wreath had bound her hair,
While yet the wild deer trod in spangling dew,
While boatman carolled to the fresh-blown air,
And woods a horizontal shadow threw,
And early fox appeared in momentary view.

9

At times there was a deep untrodden grot,
Where of the reading-hours sweet Gertrude wore;
Tradition had not named its lonely spot,
But here, methinks, India's sons explore
Their father's dust, or lift, perchance, of yore,
Their voice to the Great Spirit – rocks sublime
To human art a sportive semblance wore,
And yellow lichens coloured all the clime
Like moonlight battlements, and towers decayed by time.

10

But high, in amphitheatre above,
His arms the everlasting aloes threw –
Breathed but an air of Heaven, and all the grove
As if with instinct living spirit grew,
Rolling its verdant gulfs of every hue.
And now suspended was the pleasing din,
Now from a murmur faint it swelled anew –
Like the first note of organ heard within
Cathedral aisles, ere yet its symphony begin.

11

It was in this lone valley she would charm
The lingering noon, where flowers a couch had strewn,
Her cheek reclining, and her snowy arm
On hillock by the palm-tree half o'ergrown –
And aye that volume on her lap is thrown
Which every heart of human mould endears:
With Shakespeare's self she speaks and smiles alone,
And no intruding visitation fears
To shame the unconscious laugh, or stop her sweetest tears.

12

For, save her presence, scarce an ear had heard
The stock-dove plaining through its gloom profound,
Or winglet of the fairy humming-bird
Like atoms of the rainbow fluttering round,

Till chance had ushered to its inmost ground
The stranger-guest of many a distant clime.
He was (to weet) for eastern mountains bound,
But late the equator suns his cheek had tanned,
And California's gales his roving bosom fanned.

13

A steed, whose rein hung loosely o'er his arm,
He led dismounted; ere his leisure pace
Amid the brown leaves could her ear alarm
Close he had come, and worshipped for a space
Those downcast features – she her lovely face
Uplift on one whose lineaments and frame
Wore youth and manhood's intermingled grace:
Iberian seemed his boot, his robe the same,
And well the Spanish plume his lofty looks became.

14

For Albert's home he sought – her finger fair
Has pointed where the father's mansion stood.
Returning from the copse, he soon was there;
And soon has Gertrude hied from dark green wood,
Nor joyless, by the converse, understood,
Between the man of age and pilgrim young –
That gay congeniality of mood
And early liking from acquaintance sprung.
Full fluently conversed their guest in England's tongue,

15

And well could he his pilgrimage of taste
Unfold, and much they loved his fervid strain
While he each fair variety retraced
Of climes, and manners, o'er the eastern main:
Now happy Switzer's hills, romantic Spain,
Gay lilied fields of France, or, more refined,
The soft Ausonia's monumental reign –
Nor less each rural image he designed
Than all the city's pomp, and home of human kind.

16

Anon some wilder portraiture he draws:
Of Nature's savage glories he would speak –
The loneliness of Earth that overawes
Where, resting by some tomb of old cacique,

The lama-driver on Peruvia's peak
Nor voice, nor living motion, marks around,
But storks that to the boundless forest shriek,
Or wild-cane arch high flung o'er gulf profound,
That fluctuates when the storms of El Dorado sound!

17

Pleased with his guest, the good man still would ply
Each earnest question, and his converse court;
But Gertrude, as she eyed him, knew not why
A strange and troubling wonder stopped her short.
'In England thou hast been, and by report
An orphan's name', quoth Albert, 'mayst have known.
Sad tale! When latest fell our frontier-fort
One innocent, one soldier's child, alone
Was spared, and brought to me, who loved him as my own.

18

Young Henry Waldegrave – three delightful years
These very walls his infant sports did see –
But most I loved him when his parting tears
Alternately bedewed my child and me.
His sorest parting, Gertrude, was from thee –
Nor half his grief his little heart could hold!
By kindred he was sent for o'er the sea,
They tore him from us when but twelve years old,
And scarcely for his loss have I been yet consoled.'

19

His face the wanderer hid, but could not hide
A tear, a smile, upon his cheek that dwell.
'And speak, mysterious stranger!' Gertrude cried,
'It is – it is –I knew – I knew him well!
'Tis Waldegrave's self, of Waldegrave come to tell!'
A burst of joy the father's lips declare,
But Gertrude speechless on his bosom fell:
At once his open arms embraced the pair –
Was never group more blest in this wide world of care!

20

'And will ye pardon then', replied the youth,
'Your Waldegrave's feignéd name, and false attire?
I durst not in the neighbourhood, in truth,
The very fortunes of your house inquire,

Lest one that knew me might some tidings dire
Impart, and I my weakness all betray;
For had I lost my Gertrude, and my sire,
I meant but o'er your tombs to weep a day –
Unknown I meant to weep, unknown to pass away.

21

But here ye live, ye bloom! In each dear face
The changing hand of time I may not blame:
For there it hath but shed more reverend grace,
And here, of beauty perfected the frame –
And well I know your hearts are still the same!
They could not change – ye look the very way
As when an orphan first to you I came!
And have ye heard of my poor guide, I pray –
Nay, wherefore weep we, friends, on such a joyous day?'

22

'And art thou here – or is it but a dream?
And wilt thou, Waldegrave, wilt thou leave us more?'
'No, never! Thou that yet dost lovelier seem
Than aught on earth – than even thyself of yore –
I will not part thee from thy father's shore,
But we shall cherish him with mutual arms,
And hand-in-hand again the path explore
Which every ray of young remembrance warms,
While thou shalt be my own with all thy truth and charms!'

23

At morn, as if beneath a galaxy
Of over-arching groves in blossoms white
(Where all was odorous scent and harmony,
And gladness to the heart, nerve, ear and sight),
There if, oh gentle love, I read aright
The utterance that sealed thy sacred bond,
'Twas – listening to these accents of delight –
She hid upon his breast those eyes beyond
Expression's power to paint, all languishingly fond.

24

'Flower of my life, so lovely and so lone!
Whom I would rather in this desert meet,
Scorning (and scorned by) Fortune's power, than own
Her pomp and splendours lavished at my feet!

Turn not from me thy breath, more exquisite
Than odours cast on Heaven's own shrine – to please –
Give me thy love, than luxury more sweet,
And more than all the wealth that loads the breeze
When Coromandel's ships return form Indian seas!'

25

Then would the home admit them – happier far
Than grandeur's most magnificent saloon –
While here and there a solitary star
Flushed in the darkening firmament of June,
And silence brought the soul-felt hour, full soon,
Ineffable, which I may not portray –
For never did the Hymenean moon
A paradise of hearts more sacred sway
In all that slept beneath her soft voluptuous ray!

7. LORD BYRON

The Bride of Abydos (stanzas 22–7) 1814

22

Zuleika mute and motionless
Stood, like that statue of distress
When (her last hope forever gone)
The mother hardened into stone –
All in the maid that eye could see
Was but a younger Niobe!
But ere her lip, or even her eye,
Essayed to speak or look reply,
Beneath the garden's wicket-porch
Far flashed on high a blazing torch –
Another – and another – and another!
'Oh fly – no more, yet now my more than brother!'
Far, wide, through every thicket spread,
The fearful lights are gleaming red –
Nor these alone, for each right hand
Is ready with a sheathless brand.
They part, pursue, return and wheel,
With searching flambeau, shining steel;

And last of all, his sabre waving,
Stern Giaffir in his fury raving!
And now almost they touch the cave –
Oh, must that grot be Selim's grave?

23

Dauntless he stood – ' 'Tis come – soon past –
One kiss, Zuleika – 'tis my last!
But yet my band, not far from shore,
May hear this signal, see the flash –
Yet now too few, the attempt were rash –
No matter – yet one effort more!'
Forth to the cavern-mouth he stepped –
His pistol's echo rang on high –
Zuleika started not, nor wept,
Despair benumbed her breast and eye.
'They hear me not! Or if they ply
Their oars, 'tis but to see me die!
That sound hath drawn my foes more nigh –
Then forth my father's scimitar –
Thou ne'er hast seen less equal war!
Farewell, Zuleika! Sweet, retire –
Yet stay within – here linger, safe –
At thee his rage will only chafe.
Stir not, lest even to thee perchance
Some erring blade or ball should glance.
Fearst thou for him? May I expire
If in this strife I seek thy sire!
No – though by him that poison poured!
No – though he called me coward!
But tamely shall I meet their steel?
No – as each crest, save *his*, may feel!

24

One bound he made, and gained the sand:
Already at his feet hath sunk
The foremost of the prying band,
A gasping head, a quivering trunk!
Another falls – but round him close
A swarming circle of his foes.
From right to left his path he cleft,

And almost met the meeting wave!
His boat appears – not five oars' length –
His comrades strain with desperate strength!
Oh, are they yet in time to save?
His feet the foremost breakers lave,
His band are plunging in the bay –
Their sabres glitter through the spray –
Wet, wild, unwearied, to the strand
They struggle – now they touch the land!
They come – 'tis but to add to slaughter –
His heart's best blood is on the water.

25

Escaped from shot, unharmed by steel,
Or scarcely grazed its force to feel,
Had Selim won – betrayed, beset –
To where the strand and billows met.
There, as his last step left the land,
And the last death-blow dealt his hand,
Ah, wherefore did he turn to look
For her his eye but sought in vain?
That pause, that fatal gaze he took,
Hath doomed his death, or fixed his chain.
Sad proof, in peril and in pain
How late will lover's hope remain!
His back was to the dashing spray –
Behind, but close, his comrades lay –
When, at the instant, hissed the ball:
'So may the foes of Giaffir fall!'
Whose voice is heard? Whose carbine rang?
Whose bullet through the night-air sang
Too nearly, deadly, aimed to err?
'Tis thine, Abdallah's murderer!
The father slowly rued thy hate,
The son hath found a quicker fate:
Fast from his breast the blood is bubbling,
The whiteness of the sea-foam troubling –
If aught his lips essayed to groan,
The rushing billows choked the tone!

26

Morn slowly rolls the clouds away,
   Few trophies of the fight are there.
The shouts that shook the midnight-bay
Are silent; but some signs of fray
   That strand of strife may bear,
And fragments of each shivered brand;
Steps stamped; and, dashed into the sand,
The print of many a struggling hand
   May there be marked – nor far remote
   A broken torch, an oarless boat.
And, tangled on the weeds that heap
The beach where shelving to the deep,
   There lies a white capote!
'Tis rent in twain – one dark-red stain
The wave yet ripples o'er in vain –
   But where is he who wore?
Ye, who would o'er his relics weep,
Go, seek them where the surges sweep
Their burden round Sigaeum's steep
   And cast on Lemnos' shore.
The sea-birds shriek above the prey,
O'er which their hungry beaks delay,
As shaken on his restless pillow
His head heaves with the heaving billow.
That hand, whose motion is not life,
Yet freely seems to menace strife,
Flung by the tossing tide on high,
   Then levelled with the wave –
What recks it, though that corse shall lie
   Within a living grave?
The bird that tears that prostrate form
Hath only robbed the meaner worm!
The only heart, the only eye,
Had bled or wept to see him die,
Had seen those scattered limbs composed,
   And mourned above his turban-stone –
That heart hath burst, that eye was closed,
   Yea – closed before his own!

27

By Helle's stream there is a voice of wail!
And woman's eye is wet, man's cheek is pale.
Zuleika – last of Giaffir's race –
Thy destined lord is come too late:
He sees not, ne'er shall see, thy face!
Can he not hear
The loud wull-wulley warn his distant ear?
Thy handmaids weeping at the gate,
The Koran-chanters of the hymn of fate,
The silent slaves with folded arms that wait,
Sighs in the hall, and shrieks upon the gale,
Tell him thy tale.
Thou didst not view thy Selim fall:
That fearful moment when he left the cave
Thy heart grew chill!
He was thy hope, thy joy, thy love, thine all,
And that last thought on him thou couldst not save
Sufficed to kill –
Burst forth in one wild cry, and all was still!
Peace to thy broken heart and virgin grave!
Ah happy, but of life to lose the worst –
That grief, though deep, though fatal, was thy first!
Thrice happy, ne'er to feel or fear the force
Of absence, shame, pride, hate, revenge, remorse,
And oh, that pang where more than madness lies –
The worm that will not sleep, and never dies –
Thought of the gloomy day and ghastly night,
That dreads the darkness, and yet loathes the light,
That winds around, and tears, the quivering heart!
Ah, wherefore not consume it, and depart?
Woe to thee, rash and unrelenting chief!
Vainly thou heapst the dust upon thy head,
Vainly the sackcloth o'er thy limbs dost spread –
By that same hand Abdallah, Selim, bled!
Now let it tear thy beard in idle grief:
Thy pride of heart, thy bride for Osman's bed,
She whom thy Sultan had but seen to wed,
Thy daughter's dead!
Hope of thine age, thy twilight's lonely beam,
The star hath set that shone on Helle's stream –
What quenched its ray? The blood that thou hast shed.
Hark to the hurried question of despair:
'Where is my child?' An echo answers, 'Where!'

8. PERCY BYSSHE SHELLEY

Alastor (lines 140–222) 1816

The poem entitled *Alastor* may be considered as allegorical of one of the most interesting situations of the human mind. It represents a youth of uncorrupted feelings and adventurous genius led forth, by an imagination inflamed and purified through familiarity with all that is excellent and majestic, to the contemplation of the universe. He drinks deep of the fountains of knowledge, and is still insatiate. The magnificence and beauty of the external world sinks profoundly into the frame of his conceptions, and affords to their modifications a variety not to be exhausted. So long as it is possible for his desires to point towards objects thus infinite and unmeasured, he is joyous, and tranquil, and self-possessed. But the period arrives when these objects cease to suffice. His mind is at length suddenly awakened, and thirsts for intercourse with an intelligence similar to itself. He images to himself the being whom he loves. Conversant with speculations of the sublimest and most perfect natures, the vision in which he embodies his own imaginations unites all of wonderful, or wise, or beautiful, which the poet, the philosopher, or the lover, could depicture. The intellectual faculties, the imagination, the functions of love, have their respective requisitions [demands] on the sympathy of corresponding powers in other human-beings. The Poet is represented as uniting these requisitions, and attaching them to a single image. He seeks in vain for a prototype of his conception. Blasted by his disappointments, he sinks to an early grave. (Shelley, Preface)

The Poet wandering on, through Araby
And Persia, and the wild Carmanian waste,
And o'er the aerial mountains which pour down
Indus and Oxus from their icy caves,
In joy and exultation held his way,
Till in the vale of Cashmire, far within
Its loneliest dell, where odorous plants entwine
Beneath the hollow rocks a natural bower,
Beside a sparkling rivulet he stretched
His languid limbs.
A vision on his sleep
There came – a dream of hopes that never yet
Had flushed his cheek. He dreamed a veiléd maid
Sat near him, talking in low tones.
Her voice was like the voice of his own soul

Heard in the calm of thought: its music long,
Like woven sounds of streams and breezes, held
His inmost sense suspended in its web
Of many-coloured woof and shifting hues.
Knowledge and truth and virtue were her theme,
And lofty hopes of divine liberty
(The thoughts most dear to him), and poesy –
Herself a poet. Soon the solemn mood
Of her pure mind kindled through all her frame
A permeating fire: wild numbers then
She raised, with voice stifled in tremulous sobs
Subdued by its own pathos. Her fair hands
Were bare alone, sweeping from strange harp
Strange symphony, and in their branching veins
The eloquent blood told an ineffable tale.
The beating of her heart was heard to fill
The pauses of her music, and her breath
Tumultuously accorded with those fits
Of intermitted song.
                                        Sudden she rose,
As if her heart impatiently endured
Its bursting burden. At the sound he turned,
And saw by the warm light of their own life
Her glowing limbs beneath the sinuous veil
Of woven wind, her outspread arms now bare,
Her dark locks floating in the breath of night,
Her beamy bending eyes, her parted lips
Outstretched and pale, and quivering eagerly.
His strong heart sank and sickened with excess
Of love. He reared his shuddering limbs and quelled
His gasping breath, and spread his arms to meet
Her panting bosom. She drew back a while,
Then, yielding to the irresistible joy,
With frantic gesture and short breathless cry
Folded his frame in her dissolving arms.
Now blackness veiled his dizzy eyes, and night
Involved and swallowed up the vision; sleep,
Like a dark flood suspended in its course,
Rolled back its impulse on his vacant brain.
   Roused by the shock, he started from his trance –
The cold white light of morning, the blue moon
Low in the west, the clear and garish hills,
The distinct valley and the vacant woods,
Spread round him where he stood. Whither have fled

The hues of heaven that canopied his bower
Of yesternight, the sounds that soothed his sleep,
The mystery and the majesty of Earth,
The joy and exultation? His wan eyes
Gaze on the empty scene as vacantly
As Ocean's moon looks on the moon in heaven.
The spirit of sweet human love has sent
A vision to the sleep of him who spurned
Her choicest gifts.
He eagerly pursues
Beyond the realms of dream that fleeting shade –
He overleaps the bounds! Alas, alas,
Were limbs, and breath, and being, intertwined
Thus treacherously? Lost, lost, for ever lost,
In the wide pathless desert of deep sleep,
That beautiful shape! Does the dark gate of Death
Conduct to thy mysterious paradise,
Oh Sleep? Does the bright arch of rainbow clouds,
And pendent mountains seen in the calm lake,
Lead only to a black and watery depth,
While Death's blue vault, with loathliest vapours hung
(Where every shade which the foul grave exhales
Hides its dead eye from the detested day),
Conduct, oh Sleep, to thy delightful realms?
This doubt, with sudden tide, flowed on his heart;
The insatiate hope which it awakened stung
His brain even like despair.

9. JAMES LEIGH HUNT

Paulo and Francesca

(*Rimini* III, lines 482–564) 1816

All the green garden, flower-bed, shade, and plot,
Francesca loved but most of all this spot:
Whenever she walked forth, wherever went
About the grounds, to this at last she bent.
Here she had brought a lute and a few books;
Here would she lie for hours, with grateful looks,
Thanking at heart the sunshine and the leaves,
The summer rain-drops counting from the eaves,

And all that promising, calm smile we see
In Nature's face, when we look patiently.
Then would she think of Heaven; and you might hear
Sometimes, when everything was hushed and clear,
Her gentle voice from out those shades emerging,
Singing the evening anthem to the Virgin.
The gardeners and the rest, who served the place
And blest – whenever they beheld – her face,
Knelt when they heard it, bowing and uncovered,
And felt as if in air some sainted beauty hovered.
One day – 'twas on a summer afternoon,
When airs and gurgling brooks are best in tune,
And grasshoppers are loud, and day-work done,
And shades have heavy outlines in the sun –
The princess came to her accustomed bower
To get her, if she could, a soothing hour,
Trying, as she was used, to leave her cares
Without, and slumberously enjoy the airs
And the low-talking leaves, and that cool light
The vines let in, and all that hushing sight
Of closing wood seen through the opening door,
And distant plash of waters tumbling o'er,
And smell of citron blooms – and fifty luxuries more!
She tried, as usual, for the trial's sake –
For even that diminished her heartache,
And never yet (how ill soe'er at ease)
Came she for nothing midst the flowers and trees.
Yet somehow or another, on that day,
She seemed to feel too lightly borne away –
Too much relieved – too much inclined to draw
A careless joy from everything she saw;
And looking round her with a new-born eye,
As if some tree of knowledge had been nigh,
To taste of Nature, primitive and free,
And bask at ease in her heart's liberty.
Painfully clear those rising thoughts appeared,
With something dark at bottom that she feared;
And snatching from the fields her thoughtful look,
She reached o'er-head, and took her down a book,
And fell to reading with as fixed an air,
As though she had been wrapt since morning there.
'Twas *Launcelot of the Lake*, a bright romance,
That like a trumpet made young pulses dance,

Yet had a softer note that shook still more.
She had begun it but the day before,
And read with a full heart, half sweet, half sad,
How old King Ban was spoiled of all he had
But one fair castle – how one summer's day
With his fair queen and child he went away
To ask the great King Arthur for assistance;
How, reaching by himself a hill at distance,
He turned to give his castle a last look,
And saw its far white face – and how a smoke,
As he was looking, burst in volumes forth,
And good King Ban saw all that he was worth,
And his fair castle, burning to the ground,
So that his wearied pulse felt over-wound,
And he lay down, and said a prayer apart
For those he loved, and broke his poor old heart.
　Then read she of the Queen with her young child,
How she came up, and nearly had gone wild,
And how, in journeying on in her despair,
She reached a lake and met a lady there
Who pitied her, and took the baby sweet
Into her arms, when lo, with closing feet
She sprang up all at once, like bird from brake,
And vanished with him underneath the lake!
The mother's feelings we as well may pass –
The fairy of the place that lady was,
And Launcelot (so the boy was called) became
Her inmate, till in search of knightly fame
He went to Arthur's court, and played his part
So rarely, and displayed so frank a heart,
That what with all his charms of look and limb,
The Queen Genevra fell in love with him.
And here, with growing interest in her reading,
The princess, doubly fixed, was now proceeding.
　Ready she sat with one hand to turn o'er
The leaf, to which her thoughts ran on before,
The other propping her white brow, and throwing
Its ringlets out, under the sky-light glowing.
So sat she fixed; and so observed was she
Of one, who at the door stood tenderly –
Paulo – who, from a window seeing her
Go straight across the lawn, and guessing where,

Had thought she was in tears, and found, that day,
His usual efforts vain to keep away.
  'May I come in?' said he. It made her start,
That smiling voice – she coloured, pressed her heart
A moment (as for breath), and then with free
And usual tone said 'Oh yes, certainly!'
There's apt to be, at conscious times like these,
An affectation of a bright-eyed ease,
An air of something quite serene and sure,
As if to seem so, was to be, secure:
With this the lovers met, with this they spoke,
With this they sat down to the self-same book,
And Paulo, by degrees, gently embraced
With one permitted arm her lovely waist;
And both their cheeks, like peaches on a tree,
Leaned with a touch together, thrillingly;
And o'er the book they hung, and nothing said,
And every lingering page grew longer as they read.
  As thus they sat, and felt with leaps of heart
Their colour change, they came upon the part
Where fond Genevra, with her flame long nurst,
Smiled upon Launcelot when he kissed her first!
That touch, at last, through every fibre slid,
And Paulo turned, scarce knowing what he did,
Only he felt he could no more dissemble,
And kissed her, mouth to mouth, all in a tremble.
Sad were those hearts, and sweet was that long kiss:
Sacred be love from sight, whate'er it is!
The world was all forgot, the struggle o'er –
Desperate the joy! That day they read no more.

10. THOMAS MOORE

The Fire-Worshippers

(from *Lalla Rookh* III, lines 201–453) 1817

She loves – but knows not whom she loves,
  Nor what his race, nor whence he came –
Like one who meets, in Indian groves,
  Some beauteous bird, without a name,

Brought by the last ambrosial breeze
From isles in the undiscovered seas
To show his plumage for a day
To wondering eyes, and wing away!
Will *he* thus fly – her nameless lover?
   Allah forbid! 'Twas by a moon
As fair as this, while singing over
   Some ditty to her soft kanoon,
Alone, at this same witching-hour,
   She first beheld his radiant eyes
Gleam through the lattice of the bower
   Where nightly now they mix their sighs,
And thought some spirit of the air
(For what could waft a mortal there?)
Was pausing on his moonlight way
To listen to her lonely lay!

This fancy ne'er hath left her mind,
   And though, when terror's swoon had passed,
She saw a youth of mortal kind
   Before her in obeisance cast,
Yet often since, when he has spoken
Strange, awful words, and gleams have broken
From his dark eyes too bright to bear,
   Oh, she hath feared her soul was given
To some unhallowed child of air,
   Some erring spirit, cast from Heaven,
Like those angelic youths of old,
Who burned for maids of mortal mould,
Bewildered left the glorious skies,
And lost their Heaven for woman's eyes!
Fond girl – nor fiend nor angel he,
Who woos thy young simplicity,
But one of Earth's impassioned sons
   As warm in love, as fierce in ire,
As the best here whose current runs
   Full of the Day-God's living fire!

But quenched tonight that ardour seems,
   And pale his cheek, and sunk his brow.
Never before, but in her dreams,
   Had she beheld him pale as now –

And those were dreams of troubled sleep
From which 'twas joy to wake and weep,
Visions that will not be forgot
   But sadden every waking scene
Like warning ghosts, that leave the spot
   All withered where they once have been.

'How sweetly', said the trembling maid,
Of her own gentle voice afraid
(So long had they in silence stood,
Looking upon that moonlight flood) –
'How sweetly does the moonbeam smile
Tonight upon yon leafy isle!
I've wished that little isle had wings,
And we, within its fairy-bowers,
   Were wafted off to seas unknown
Where not a pulse should beat but ours
   And we might live, love, die, alone,
Far from the cruel and the cold,
   Where the bright eyes of angels only
Should come around us to behold
   A paradise so pure and lonely!
Would this be world enough for thee?'

Playful she turned, that he might see
   The passing smile her cheek put on;
But when she marked how mournfully
   His eyes met hers, that smile was gone,
And, bursting into heart-felt tears,
'Yes, yes', she cried, 'my hourly fears,
My dreams, have boded all too right –
We part, for ever part, tonight!
I knew, I knew, it *could* not last –
'Twas bright, 'twas heavenly, but 'tis past!

Oh ever thus, from childhood's hour,
   I've seen my fondest hopes decay –
I never loved a tree or flower,
   But 'twas the first to fade away!
I never nursed a dear gazelle,
   To glad me with its soft black eye,
But when it came to know me well,
   And love me, it was sure to die!

Now too, the joy most like divine
   Of all I ever dreamed or knew,
To see thee, hear thee, call thee mine –
   Oh misery! must I lose *that* too?
Yet go! On peril's brink we meet:
   Those frightful rocks, that treacherous sea –
No, never come again – though sweet,
   Though heaven, it may be death to thee!
Farewell, and blessings on thy way
   Where'er thou goest, belovéd stranger!
Better to sit and watch that ray,
   And think thee safe, though far away,
Than have thee near me and in danger!'

'Danger – oh tempt me not to boast!'
The youth exclaimed, 'Thou little knowest
What he can brave, who, born and nursed
In Danger's paths, has dared the worst –
Upon whose ear the signal-word
   Of strife and death is hourly breaking,
Who sleeps with head upon the sword
   His fevered hand must grasp in waking!
Danger!'
            'Say on! Thou fearest not then,
And we may meet – oft meet again?'

'Oh look not so! Beneath the skies
I now fear nothing but those eyes.
If aught on earth could charm or force
My spirit from its destined course –
If aught could make this soul forget
The bond to which its seal is set,
'Twould be those eyes – they, only they,
Could melt that sacred seal away!
But no – 'tis fixed – my awful doom
Is fixed! On this side of the tomb
We meet no more – why, why, did Heaven
Mingle two souls that Earth has riven,
Has rent asunder, wide as ours?
Oh arab maid – as soon the powers
Of light and darkness may combine
As I be linked with thee, or thine!

Thy father –'
'Holy Allah save
His gray head from that lightning glance!
Thou knowest him not – he loves the brave,
Nor lives their under heaven's expanse
One who would prize, would worship thee
And thy bold spirit, more than he!
Oft when in childhood I have played
With the bright falchion by his side,
I've heard him swear his lisping maid
In time should be a warrior's bride.
And still, whene'er at haram-hours,
I take him cool sherbets and flowers,
He tells me (when in playful mood)
A hero shall my bridegroom be –
Since maids are best in battle wooed,
And won mid shouts of victory!
Nay, turn not from me – thou alone
Art formed to make both hearts thy own!
Go, join his sacred ranks – thou knowest
The unholy strife these Persians wage –
Good Heaven, that frown! Even now thou glowest
With more than mortal warrior's rage!
Haste to the camp by morning's light,
And when that sword is raised in fight
Oh still remember love and I
Beneath its shadow trembling lie!
One victory o'er those slaves of fire –
Those impious Ghebers, whom my sire
Abhors –'
'Hold, hold – thy words are death!'
The stranger cried, as wild he flung
His mantle back, and showed beneath
The Gheber belt that round him clung:
'Here, maiden, look – weep – blush, to see
All that thy sire abhors in me!
Yes! *I* am of that impious race –
Those 'slaves of fire' who, morn and even,
Hail their Creator's dwelling-place
Among the living lights of Heaven!
Yes! *I* am of that outcast few,
To Iran and to vengeance true,

Who curse the hour your arabs came
To desolate our shrines of flame –
And swear, before God's burning eye,
To break our country's chains, or die!
Thy bigot sire – nay, tremble not –
   He who gave birth to those dear eyes
With me is sacred as the spot
   From which our fires of worship rise!

But know, 'twas he I sought that night
   When from my watch-boat on the sea
I caught this turret's glimmering light,
   And up the rude rocks desperately
Rushed to my prey! Thou knowest the rest –
I climbed the gory vulture's nest,
And found a trembling dove within!
Thine, thine, the victory – thine the sin –
If Love has made one thought his own
Which Vengeance claims first – last – alone!
Oh, had we never, never met,
Or could this heart even now forget
How linked, how blest, we might have been,
Had Fate not frowned so dark between!

Hadst thou been born a Persian maid,
   In neighbouring valleys had we dwelt,
Through the same fields in childhood played,
   At the same kindling altar knelt,
While all those nameless ties
In which the charm of Country lies
Had round our hearts been hourly spun,
Till Iran's cause and thine were one –
While in thy lute's awakening sigh
I heard the voice of days gone by
And saw in every smile of thine
Returning hours of glory shine –
While the wronged spirit of our land
   Lived, looked and spoke, her wrongs through thee!
God! who could then this sword withstand?
   Its very flash were victory!

But now, estranged, divorced for ever
Far as the grasp of Fate can sever,
Our only ties what love has wove
   (Faith, friends, and country, sundered wide),
And then, then only, true to love,
   When false to all that's dear beside;
Thy father Iran's deadliest foe,
Thyself perhaps even now– but no!
Hate never looked so lovely yet!
   No – sacred to thy soul will be
The land of him who could forget
   All but that bleeding land for thee!
When other eyes shall see, unmoved,
   Her widows mourn, her warriors fall,
Thou'lt think how well one Gheber loved,
   And for *his* sake thou'lt weep for all.
But look!'
            With sudden start he turned
   And pointed to the distant wave
Where lights, like charnel meteors, burned
   Bluely, as o'er some seaman's grave,
And fiery darts at intervals
   Flew up all sparkling from the main,
As if each star that nightly falls
   Were shooting back to heaven again.

   My signal-lights! I must away –
   Both, both, are ruined if I stay.
   Farewell, sweet life – thou clingst in vain –
   Now, Vengeance, I am thine again !'
Fiercely he broke away, nor stopped,
Nor looked, but from the lattice dropped
Down mid the pointed crags beneath,
As if he fled from life to death –
While pale and mute young Hinda stood,
Nor moved, till in the silent flood
A momentary plunge below
Startled her from her trance of woe.
Shrieking, she to the lattice flew:
   'I come, I come – if in that tide
Thou sleepst tonight, I'll sleep there too,
   In death's cold wedlock by thy side.

Oh, I would ask no happier bed
   Than the chill wave my love lies under –
Sweeter to rest together dead,
   Far sweeter, than to live asunder!'

But no, their hour is not yet come:
   Again she sees his pinnace fly,
Wafting him fleetly to his home
   (Where'er that ill-starred home may lie),
And calm and smooth it seemed to win
   Its moonlight way before the wind,
As if it bore all peace within
   Nor left one breaking heart behind!

11. JOHN KEATS

The Eve of St Agnes (Jan.–Feb. 1819; publ. 1820)

1

St. Agnes' Eve – ah, bitter chill it was!
The owl, for all his feathers, was a-cold;
The hare limped trembling through the frozen grass,
And silent was the flock in woolly fold;
Numb were the Beadsman's fingers, while he told
His rosary, and while his frosted breath,
Like pious incense from a censer old,
Seemed taking flight for Heaven, without a death,
Past the sweet Virgin's picture, while his prayer he saith.

2

His prayer he saith, this patient holy man;
Then takes his lamp, and riseth from his knees,
And back returneth, meagre, barefoot, wan,
Along the chapel-aisle by slow degrees.
The sculptured dead, on each side, seem to freeze,
Imprisoned in black, purgatorial rails:
Knights, ladies, praying in dumb oratories,
He passeth by, and his weak spirit fails
To think how they may ache in icy hoods and mails.

3

Northward he turneth through a little door,
And scarce three steps, ere music's golden tongue
Flattered to tears this agéd man and poor;
But no – already had his deathbell rung;
The joys of all his life were said and sung –
His was harsh penance on St Agnes' Eve!
Another way he went, and soon among
Rough ashes sat he for his soul's reprieve,
And all night kept awake, for sinners' sake to grieve.

4

That ancient Beadsman heard the prelude soft –
And so it chanced, for many a door was wide
From hurry to and fro. Soon, up aloft,
The silver snarling trumpets gan to chide;
The level chambers, ready with their pride,
Were glowing to receive a thousand guests;
The carvéd angels, ever eager-eyed,
Stared, where upon their heads the cornice rests,
With hair blown back, and wings put cross-wise on their breasts.

5

At length burst in the argent revelry,
With plume, tiara, and all rich array,
Numerous as shadows haunting fairily
The brain, new stuffed in youth with triumphs gay
Of old romance. These let us wish away,
And turn, sole-thoughted, to one lady there,
Whose heart had brooded all that wintry day
On love, and winged St Agnes' saintly care –
As she had heard old dames full many times declare.

6

They told her how upon St Agnes' Eve
Young virgins might have visions of delight,
And soft adorings from their loves receive
Upon the honeyed middle of the night,
If ceremonies due they did aright –
As, supperless to bed they must retire,
And couch supine their beauties, lily white;
Nor look behind, nor sideways, but require
Of Heaven with upward eyes for all that they desire.

7

Full of this whim was thoughtful Madeline:
The music, yearning like a god in pain,
She scarcely heard; her maiden eyes divine,
Fixed on the floor, saw many a sweeping train
Pass by – she heeded not at all. In vain
Came many a tiptoe amorous cavalier,
And back retired – not cooled by high disdain,
But she saw not. Her heart was otherwhere:
She sighed for Agnes' dreams, the sweetest of the year.

8

She danced along with vague regardless eyes,
Anxious her lips, her breathing quick and short.
The hallowed hour was near at hand – she sighs
Amid the timbrels, and the thronged resort
Of whisperers in anger, or in sport,
Mid looks of love, defiance, hate, and scorn,
Hoodwinked with faery fancy – all amort,
Save to St Agnes and her lambs unshorn,
And all the bliss to be before tomorrow morn.

9

So, purposing each moment to retire,
She lingered still. Meantime, across the moors
Had come young Porphyro, with heart on fire
For Madeline. Beside the portal-doors,
Buttressed from moonlight, stands he and implores
All saints to give him sight of Madeline
But for one moment in the tedious hours,
That he might gaze and worship all unseen –
Perchance speak, kneel, touch, kiss! In sooth such things have been.

10

He ventures in! Let no buzzed whisper tell –
All eyes be muffled, or a hundred swords
Will storm his heart, love's feverous citadel.
For him, those chambers held barbarian hordes,
Hyena foemen and hot-blooded lords,
Whose very dogs would execrations howl
Against his lineage. Not one breast affords
Him any mercy in that mansion foul,
Save one old beldame, weak in body and in soul.

11

Ah, happy chance – the agéd creature came,
Shuffling along with ivory-headed wand,
To where he stood, hid from the torch's flame
Behind a broad hall-pillar, far beyond
The sound of merriment and chorus bland.
He startled her; but soon she knew his face
And grasped his fingers in her palsied hand,
Saying, 'Mercy, Porphyro! Hie thee from this place –
They are all here to-night, the whole bloodthirsty race!

12

Get hence! Get hence! There's dwarfish Hildebrand;
He had a fever late, and in the fit
He curséd thee and thine, both house and land –
Then there's that old Lord Maurice, not a whit
More tame for his grey hairs! Alas me, flit!
Flit like a ghost away!' 'Ah, Gossip dear,
We're safe enough – here in this armchair sit,
And tell me how – ' 'Good saints not here, not here!
Follow me, child, or else these stones will be thy bier.'

13

He followed through a lowly archéd way,
Brushing the cobwebs with his lofty plume,
And as she muttered, 'Well-a – well-a-day!'
He found him in a little moonlight room,
Pale, latticed, chill, and silent as a tomb.
'Now tell me where is Madeline', said he,
'Oh tell me, Angela, by the holy loom
Which none but secret sisterhood may see,
When they St Agnes' wool are weaving piously.'

14

'St Agnes? Ah, it is St Agnes' Eve –
Yet men will murder upon holy days:
Thou must hold water in a witch's sieve,
And be liege-lord of all the elves and fays,
To venture so! It fills me with amaze
To see thee, Porphyro! St Agnes' Eve!
God's help! My lady fair the conjuror plays
This very night – good angels her deceive!
But let me laugh awhile, I've mickle time to grieve.'

15

Feebly she laugheth in the languid moon,
While Porphyro upon her face doth look,
Like puzzled urchin on an agéd crone
Who keepeth closed a wondrous riddle-book,
As spectacled she sits in chimney nook.
But soon his eyes grew brilliant, when she told
His lady's purpose; and he scarce could brook
Tears at the thought of those enchantments cold,
And Madeline asleep in lap of legends old.

16

Sudden a thought came like a full-blown rose,
Flushing his brow, and in his painéd heart
Made purple riot. Then doth he propose
A stratagem that makes the beldame start:
'A cruel man and impious thou art!
Sweet lady, let her pray, and sleep, and dream
Alone with her good angels, far apart
From wicked men like thee. Go, go! – I deem
Thou canst not surely be the same that thou didst seem.'

17

'I will not harm her, by all saints I swear',
Quoth Porphyro. 'Oh may I ne'er find grace
When my weak voice shall whisper its last prayer,
If one of her soft ringlets I displace,
Or look with ruffian passion in her face!
Good Angela, believe me by these tears;
Or I will, even in a moment's space,
Awake, with horrid shout, my foemen's ears,
And beard them, though they be more fanged than wolves and
bears.'

18

'Ah, why wilt thou affright a feeble soul –
A poor, weak, palsy-stricken, churchyard thing,
Whose passing-bell may ere the midnight toll,
Whose prayers for thee each morn and evening
Were never missed?' Thus plaining, doth she bring
A gentler speech from burning Porphyro,
So woeful, and of such deep sorrowing,
That Angela gives promise she will do
Whatever he shall wish, betide her weal or woe –

19

Which was, to lead him in close secrecy
Even to Madeline's chamber, and there hide
Him in a closet of such privacy
That he might see her beauty unespied,
And win perhaps that night a peerless bride,
While legioned fairies paced the coverlet
And pale enchantment held her sleepy-eyed.
Never on such a night have lovers met,
Since Merlin paid his demon all the monstrous debt!

20

'It shall be as thou wishest', said the dame,
All cates and dainties shall be storéd there
Quickly on this feast-night – by the tambour-frame
Her own lute thou wilt see – no time to spare
For I am slow and feeble, and scarce dare
On such a catering trust my dizzy head!
Wait here, my child, with patience; kneel in prayer
The while. Ah! thou must needs the lady wed,
Or may I never leave my grave among the dead!'

21

So saying, she hobbled off with busy fear.
The lover's endless minutes slowly passed;
The dame returned, and whispered in his ear
To follow her – with agéd eyes aghast
From fright of dim espial. Safe at last,
Through many a dusky gallery, they gain
The maiden's chamber, silken, hushed, and chaste;
Where Porphyro took covert, pleased amain –
His poor guide hurried back with agues in her brain.

22

Her faltering hand upon the balustrade,
Old Angela was feeling for the stair,
When Madeline, St Agnes' charméd maid,
Rose, like a missioned spirit, unaware.
With silver taper's light, and pious care,
She turned, and down the agéd gossip led
To a safe level matting. Now prepare,
Young Porphyro, for gazing on that bed –
She comes, she comes again, like ring-dove frayed and fled.

23

Out went the taper as she hurried in –
Its little smoke in pallid moonshine died –
She closed the door, she panted, all akin
To spirits of the air, and visions wide.
No uttered syllable (or, woe betide!)
But to her heart, her heart was voluble,
Paining with eloquence her balmy side,
As though a tongueless nightingale should swell
Her throat in vain, and die, heart-stifled, in her dell.

24

A casement high and triple-arched there was,
All garlanded with carven imageries
Of fruits, and flowers, and bunches of knot-grass,
And diamonded with panes of quaint device,
Innumerable of stains and splendid dyes
As are the tiger-moth's deep-damasked wings;
And in the midst, 'mong thousand heraldries,
And twilight saints, and dim emblazonings,
A shielded scutcheon blushed with blood of queens and kings.

25

Full on this casement shone the wintry moon,
And threw warm gules on Madeline's fair breast
As down she knelt for Heaven's grace and boon;
Rose-bloom fell on her hands, together prest,
And on her silver cross soft amethyst,
And on her hair a glory, like a saint:
She seemed a splendid angel, newly drest,
Save wings, for Heaven – Porphyro grew faint:
She knelt, so pure a thing, so free from mortal taint.

26

Anon his heart revives. Her vespers done,
Of all its wreathéd pearls her hair she frees,
Unclasps her warméd jewels one by one,
Loosens her fragrant bodice – by degrees
Her rich attire creeps rustling to her knees.
Half-hidden, like a mermaid in sea-weed,
Pensive awhile she dreams awake, and sees,
In fancy, fair St Agnes in her bed,
But dares not look behind, or all the charm is fled.

27

Soon, trembling in her soft and chilly nest,
In sort of wakeful swoon, perplexed she lay,
Until the poppied warmth of sleep oppressed
Her soothéd limbs, and soul fatigued away –
Flown, like a thought, until the morrow-day;
Blissfully havened both from joy and pain;
Clasped like a missal where swart Paynims pray;
Blinded alike from sunshine and from rain,
As though a rose should shut, and be a bud again!

28

Stolen to this paradise, and so entranced,
Porphyro gazed upon her empty dress
And listened to her breathing, if it chanced
To wake into a slumberous tenderness –
Which when he heard, that minute did he bless,
And breathed himself; then from the closet crept,
Noiseless as fear in a wide wilderness,
And over the hushed carpet, silent, stepped
And 'tween the curtains peeped, where, lo – how fast she slept!

29

Then by the bedside, where the faded moon
Made a dim silver twilight, soft he set
A table, and, half anguished, threw thereon
A cloth of woven crimson, gold, and jet –
Oh for some drowsy Morphean amulet!
The boisterous, midnight, festive clarion,
The kettle-drum and far-heard clarionet,
Affray his ears, though but in dying tone:
The hall door shuts again, and all the noise is gone.

30

And still she slept an azure-liddéd sleep,
In blanchéd linen, smooth and lavendered,
While he from forth the closet brought a heap
Of candied apple, quince, and plum, and gourd;
With jellies soother than the creamy curd,
And lucent syrops, tinct with cinnamon;
Manna and dates, in argosy transferred
From Fez; and spicéd dainties, every one,
From silken Samarcand to cedared Lebanon.

31
These delicates he heaped with glowing hand
On golden dishes and in baskets bright
Of wreathéd silver – sumptuous they stand
In the retiréd quiet of the night,
Filling the chilly room with perfume light:
'And now, my love, my seraph fair, awake!
Thou art my Heaven, and I thine eremite!
Open thine eyes, for meek St Agnes' sake,
Or I shall drowse beside thee, so my soul doth ache.'

32
Thus whispering, his warm, unnervéd arm
Sank in her pillow. Shaded was her dream
By the dusk curtains – 'twas a midnight charm
Impossible to melt as icéd stream!
The lustrous salvers in the moonlight gleam;
Broad golden fringe upon the carpet lies:
It seemed he never, never could redeem
From such a stedfast spell his lady's eyes,
So mused awhile, entoiled in wooféd fantasies.

33
Awakening up, he took her hollow lute
Tumultuous, and, in chords that tenderest be,
He played an ancient ditty, long since mute,
In Provence called *La Belle Dame Sans Mercy*,
Close to her ear touching the melody.
Wherewith disturbed, she uttered a soft moan –
He ceased – she panted quick – and suddenly
Her blue affrayéd eyes wide open shone:
Upon his knees he sank, pale as smooth-sculptured stone.

34
Her eyes were open, but she still beheld,
Now wide awake, the vision of her sleep.
There was a painful change, that nigh expelled
The blisses of her dream so pure and deep –
At which fair Madeline began to weep,
And moan forth witless words with many a sigh,
While still her gaze on Porphyro would keep;
Who knelt, with joinéd hands and piteous eye,
Fearing to move or speak, she looked so dreamingly.

35
'Ah, Porphyro!' said she, 'but even now
Thy voice was at sweet tremble in mine ear,
Made tuneable with every sweetest vow,
And those sad eyes were spiritual and clear.
How changed thou art! How pallid, chill, and drear!
Give me that voice again, my Porphyro,
Those looks immortal, those complainings dear –
Oh leave me not in this eternal woe,
For if thou diest, my love, I know not where to go.'

36
Beyond a mortal man impassioned far
At these voluptuous accents, he arose,
Ethereal, flushed, and, like a throbbing star
Seen mid the sapphire heaven's deep repose,
Into her dream he melted, as the rose
Blendeth its odour with the violet –
Solution sweet! Meantime the frost-wind blows
Like love's alarum pattering the sharp sleet
Against the window-panes. St Agnes' moon hath set.

37
'Tis dark – quick pattereth the flaw-blown sleet:
'This is no dream, my bride, my Madeline!'
'Tis dark – the icéd gusts still rave and beat:
'No dream, alas! alas! and woe is mine!
Porphyro will leave me here to fade and pine –
Cruel! What traitor could thee hither bring?
I curse not, for my heart is lost in thine,
Though thou forsakest a deceivéd thing,
A dove forlorn and lost with sick unpruned wing.'

38
'My Madeline! Sweet dreamer! Lovely bride!
Say, may I be for aye thy vassal blest –
Thy beauty's shield, heart-shaped and vermeil dyed?
Ah, silver shrine, here will I take my rest
After so many hours of toil and quest,
A famished pilgrim saved by miracle!
Though I have found, I will not rob thy nest,
Saving of thy sweet self – if thou thinkst well
To trust, fair Madeline, to no rude infidel.

39

Hark! 'Tis an elfin-storm from faery land,
Of haggard seeming, but a boon indeed!
Arise, arise! The morning is at hand –
The bloated wassaillers will never heed –
Let us away, my love, with happy speed!
There are no ears to hear, or eyes to see,
Drowned all in Rhenish and the sleepy mead.
Awake! Arise, my love, and fearless be,
For o'er the southern moors I have a home for thee!'

40

She hurried at his words, beset with fears,
For there were sleeping dragons all around,
At glaring watch, perhaps with ready spears;
Down the wide stairs a darkling way they found.
In all the house was heard no human sound:
A chain-drooped lamp was flickering by each door;
The arras, rich with horseman, hawk, and hound,
Fluttered in the besieging wind's uproar;
And the long carpets rose along the gusty floor.

41

They glide, like phantoms, into the wide hall –
Like phantoms, to the iron porch, they glide –
Where lay the porter, in uneasy sprawl,
With a huge empty flagon by his side!
The wakeful bloodhound rose, and shook his hide,
But his sagacious eye an inmate owns;
By one, and one, the bolts full easy slide,
The chains lie silent on the footworn stones;
The key turns, and the door upon its hinges groans,

42

And they are gone – aye, ages long ago
These lovers fled away into the storm!
That night the Baron dreamt of many a woe,
And all his warrior-guests, with shade and form
Of witch, and demon, and large coffin-worm,
Were long be-nightmared. Angela the old
Died palsy-twitched, with meagre face deform;
The Beadsman, after thousand avés told,
For aye unsought for, slept among his ashes cold.

12. LORD BYRON

Juan and Haidee (from *Don Juan* II–IV) 1819–21

Canto II

111

How long in his damp trance young Juan lay
He knew not, for the earth was gone for him,
And Time had nothing more of night nor day
For his congealing blood, and senses dim;
And how this heavy faintness passed away
He knew not, till each painful pulse and limb,
And tingling vein, seemed throbbing back to life,
For Death, though vanquished, still retired with strife.

112

His eyes he opened, shut, again unclosed,
For all was doubt and dizziness; he thought
He still was in the boat, and had but dozed,
And felt again with his despair o'erwrought,
And wished it death in which he had reposed,
And then once more his feelings back were brought,
And slowly by his swimming eyes was seen
A lovely female face of seventeen.

113

'Twas bending close o'er his, and the small mouth
Seemed almost prying into his for breath;
And chafing him, the soft warm hand of youth
Recalled his answering spirits back from death;
And, bathing his chill temples, tried to soothe
Each pulse to animation, till beneath
Its gentle touch and trembling care, a sigh
To these kind efforts made a low reply.

114

Then was the cordial poured, and mantle flung
Around his scarce-clad limbs; and the fair arm
Raised higher the faint head which o'er it hung,
And her transparent cheek (all pure and warm)

Pillowed his death-like forehead. Then she wrung
   His dewy curls, long drenched by every storm,
And watched with eagerness each throb that drew
A sigh from his heaved bosom – and hers, too.

115

And lifting him with care into the cave,
   The gentle girl, and her attendant (one
Young, yet her elder, and of brow less grave,
   And more robust of figure), then begun
To kindle fire, and as the new flames gave
   Light to the rocks that roofed them, which the sun
Had never seen, the maid, or whatsoe'er
She was, appeared distinct, and tall, and fair.

116

Her brow was overhung with coins of gold
   That sparkled o'er the auburn of her hair –
Her clustering hair, whose longer locks were rolled
   In braids behind – and though her stature were
Even of the highest for a female mould,
   They nearly reached her heel; and in her air
There was a something which bespoke command,
As one who was a lady in the land . . .

124

I'll tell you who they were, this female pair,
   Lest they should seem princesses in disguise;
Besides, I hate all mystery, and that air
   Of clap-trap, which your recent poets prize!
And so, in short, the girls they really were
   They shall appear before your curious eyes –
Mistress and maid – the first was only daughter
Of an old man, who lived upon the water.

125

A fisherman he had been in his youth,
   And still a sort of fisherman was he;
But other speculations were, in sooth,
   Added to his connection with the sea,
Perhaps not so respectable, in truth:
   A little smuggling, and some piracy,
Left him, at last, the sole of many masters
Of an ill-gotten million of piastres.

126

A fisher, therefore, was he – though of men,
  Like Peter the Apostle, – and he fished
For wandering merchant-vessels, now and then,
  And sometimes caught as many as he wished.
The cargoes he confiscated, and gain
  He sought in the slave-market too, and dished
Full many a morsel for that Turkish trade,
By which, no doubt, a good deal may be made.

127

He was a Greek, and on his isle had built
  (One of the wild and smaller Cyclades)
A very handsome house from out his guilt,
  And there he lived exceedingly at ease;
Heaven knows what cash he got, or blood he spilt –
  A sad old fellow was he, if you please –
But this I know, it was a spacious building,
Full of barbaric carving, paint, and gilding.

128

He had an only daughter, called Haidee,
  The greatest heiress of the Eastern Isles;
Besides, so very beautiful was she,
  Her dowry was as nothing to her smiles!
Still in her teens, and like a lovely tree,
  She grew to womanhood, and between whiles
Rejected several suitors, just to learn
How to accept a better in his turn.

129

And walking out upon the beach, below
  The cliff, towards sunset, on that day she found,
Insensible – not dead, but nearly so –
  Don Juan, almost famished, and half drowned;
But being naked, she was shocked, you know,
  Yet deemed herself in common pity bound,
As far as in her lay to 'take him in' –
'A stranger' dying, with so white a skin!

130

But taking him into her father's house
  Was not exactly the best way to save,
But like conveying to the cat the mouse,
  Or people in a trance into their grave;

Because the good old man had so much *nous*
   Unlike the honest arab thieves so brave,
He would have hospitably cured the stranger,
And sold him instantly when out of danger.

131

And therefore, with her maid, she thought it best –
   A virgin always on her maid relies –
To place him in the cave for present rest.
   And when, at last, he opened his black eyes
Their charity increased about their guest,
   And their compassion grew to such a size
It opened half the turnpike-gates to Heaven
(St Paul says 'tis the toll which must be given).

132

They made a fire, but such a fire as they
   Upon the moment could contrive with such
Materials as were cast up round the bay –
   Some broken planks, and oars, that to the touch
Were nearly tinder, since so long they lay
   A mast was almost crumbled to a crutch –
But, by God's grace, here wrecks were in such plenty,
That there was fuel to have furnished twenty.

133

He had a bed of furs, and a pelisse,
   For Haidee stripped her sables off to make
His couch; and, that he might be more at ease,
   And warm, in case by chance he should awake,
They also gave a petticoat apiece,
   She and her maid, and promised by daybreak
To pay him a fresh visit, with a dish
For breakfast, of eggs, coffee, bread, and fish.

134

And thus they left him to his lone repose:
   Juan slept like a top – or like the dead,
Who sleep at last, perhaps (God only knows) –
   Just for the present, and in his lulled head
Not even a vision of his former woes
   Throbbed in accurséd dreams, which sometimes spread
Unwelcome visions of our former years,
Till the eye, cheated, opens thick with tears.

135

Young Juan slept all dreamless – but the maid
Who smoothed his pillow, as she left the den
Looked back upon him, and a moment stayed,
And turned, believing that he called again.
He slumbered; yet she thought, at least she said
(The heart will slip even as the tongue and pen),
He had pronounced her name–but she forgot
That at this moment Juan knew it not.

136

And pensive to her father's house she went,
Enjoining silence strict to Zoë, who
Better than her knew what in fact she meant,
She being wiser by a year or two –
A year or two's an age when rightly spent,
And Zoë spent hers, as most women do,
In gaining all that useful sort of knowledge
Which is acquired in Nature's good old college.

137

The morn broke, and found Juan slumbering still
Fast in his cave, and nothing clashed upon
His rest; the rushing of the neighbouring rill,
And the young beams of the excluded sun,
Troubled him not, and he might sleep his fill;
And need he had of slumber yet, for none
Had suffered more – his hardships were comparative
To those related in my grand-dad's *Narrative.*

138

Not so Haidee; she sadly tossed and tumbled,
And started from her sleep, and, turning o'er,
Dreamed of a thousand wrecks, o'er which she stumbled,
And handsome corpses strewed upon the shore;
And woke her maid so early that she grumbled,
And called her father's old slaves up, who swore
In several oaths – Armenian, Turk, and Greek –
They knew not what to think of such a freak.

139

But up she got, and up she made them get,
With some pretence about the sun, that makes
Sweet skies just when he rises, or is set –
And 'tis, no doubt, a sight to see, when breaks

Bright Phoebus, while the mountains still are wet
   With mist and every bird with him awakes,
And night is flung off like a mourning-suit
Worn for a husband, or some other brute.

140

I say, the sun is a most glorious sight,
   I've seen him rise full oft, indeed of late
I have sat up on purpose all the night,
   Which hastens, as physicians say, one's fate –
And so all ye, who would be in the right
   In health and purse, begin your day to date
From daybreak, and when coffined at fourscore,
Engrave upon the plate, you rose at four.

141

And Haidee met the morning face to face!
   Her own was freshest, though a feverish flush
Had dyed it with the headlong blood, whose race
   From heart to cheek is curbed into a blush,
Like to a torrent which a mountain's base,
   That overpowers some alpine river's rush,
Checks to a lake, whose waves in circles spread –
Or the Red Sea (but the sea is not red).

142

And down the cliff the island virgin came,
   And near the cave her quick light footsteps drew,
While the sun smiled on her with his first flame,
   And young Aurora kissed her lips with dew,
Taking her for a sister – just the same
   Mistake you would have made on seeing the two,
Although the mortal, quite as fresh and fair,
Had all the advantage too of not being air.

143

And when into the cavern Haidee stepped
   All timidly, yet rapidly, she saw
That like an infant Juan sweetly slept;
   And then she stopped, and stood as if in awe
(For sleep is awful) and on tiptoe crept
   And wrapped him closer, lest the air, too raw,
Should reach his blood – then o'er him still as death
Bent, with hushed lips, that drank his scarce-drawn breath.

144
And thus like to an angel o'er the dying
   Who die in righteousness, she leaned; and there
All tranquilly the shipwrecked boy was lying,
   As o'er him lay the calm and stirless air;
But Zoë the meantime some eggs was frying,
   Since, after all, no doubt the youthful pair
Must breakfast, and betimes–lest they should ask it,
She drew out her provision from the basket.

145
She knew that the best feelings must have victual,
   And that a shipwrecked youth would hungry be;
Besides, being less in love, she yawned a little,
   And felt her veins chilled by the neighbouring sea;
And so, she cooked their breakfast to a tittle;
   I can't say that she gave them any tea,
But there were eggs, fruit, coffee, bread, fish, honey,
With Scio wine – and all for love, not money!

146
And Zoë, when the eggs were ready, and
   The coffee made, would fain have wakened Juan;
But Haidee stopped her with her quick small hand,
   And without word, a sign her finger drew on
Her lip, which Zoë needs must understand,
   And, the first breakfast spoilt, prepared a new one,
Because her mistress would not let her break
That sleep which seemed as it would ne'er awake.

147
For still he lay, and on his thin worn cheek
   A purple hectic played like dying day
On the snow-tops of distant hills; the streak
   Of sufferance yet upon his forehead lay,
Where the blue veins looked shadowy, shrunk and weak;
   And his black curls were dewy with the spray
Which weighed upon them yet, all damp and salt,
Mixed with the stony vapours of the vault.

148
And she bent o'er him, and he lay beneath
   Hushed as the babe upon its mother's breast,
Drooped as the willow when no winds can breathe,
   Lulled like the depth of ocean when at rest,

Fair as the crowning rose of the whole wreath,
   Soft as the callow cygnet in its nest –
In short, he was a very pretty fellow,
Although his woes had turned him rather yellow!

149

He woke and gazed, and would have slept again,
   But the fair face which met his eyes forbade
Those eyes to close (though weariness and pain
   Had further sleep a further pleasure made),
For woman's face was never formed in vain
   For Juan, so that even when he prayed
He turned from grisly saints, and martyrs hairy,
To the sweet portraits of the Virgin Mary.

150

And thus upon his elbow he arose
   And looked upon the lady, in whose cheek
The pale contended with the purple rose,
   As with an effort she began to speak –
Her eyes were eloquent, her words would pose,
   Although she told him, in good modern Greek,
With an Ionian accent, low and sweet,
That he was faint, and must not talk, but eat . . .

168

And every day by daybreak – rather early
   For Juan, who was somewhat fond of rest –
She came into the cave, but it was merely
   To see her bird reposing in his nest;
And she would softly stir his locks so curly,
   Without disturbing her yet slumbering guest,
Breathing all gently o'er his cheek and mouth,
As o'er a bed of roses the sweet south.

169

And every morn his colour freshlier came,
   And every day helped on his convalescence.
'Twas well, because health in the human frame
   Is pleasant, besides being true love's essence,
For health and idleness to passion's flame
   Are oil and gunpowder – and some good lessons
Are also learnt from Ceres and from Bacchus,
Without whom Venus will not long attack us.

170

While Venus fills the heart (without heart really
   Love, though good always, is not quite so good)
Ceres presents a plate of vermicelli –
   For love must be sustained like flesh and blood –
While Bacchus pours out wine, or hands a jelly:
   Eggs, oysters too, are amatory food;
But who is their purveyor from above
Heaven knows – it may be Neptune, Pan, or Jove.

171

When Juan woke he found some good things ready:
   A bath, a breakfast, and the finest eyes
That ever made a youthful heart less steady –
   Besides her maid's, as pretty for their size –
But I have spoken of all this already
   (And repetition's tiresome and unwise),
Well – Juan, after bathing in the sea,
Came always back to coffee and Haidee.

172

Both were so young, and one so innocent,
   That bathing passed for nothing: Juan seemed
To her (as 'twere) the kind of being sent,
   Of whom these two years she had nightly dreamed,
A something to be loved, a creature meant
   To be her happiness, and whom she deemed
To render happy. All who joy would win,
Must share it – happiness was born a twin!

173

It was such pleasure to behold him, such
   Enlargement of existence to partake
Nature with him, to thrill beneath his touch,
   To watch him slumbering, and to see him wake.
To live with him for ever were too much;
   But then the thought of parting made her quake!
He was her own, her ocean-treasure, cast
Like a rich wreck – her first love, and her last.

174

And thus a moon rolled on, and fair Haidee
   Paid daily visits to her boy, and took
Such plentiful precautions, that still he
   Remained unknown within his craggy nook;

At last her father's prows put out to sea,
For certain merchantmen upon the look,
Not as of yore to carry off an Io,
But three Ragusan vessels, bound for Scio.

175

Then came her freedom, for she had no mother,
So that, her father being at sea, she was
Free as a married woman, or such other
Female, as where she likes may freely pass,
Without even the incumbrance of a brother –
The freest she that ever gazed on glass
(I speak of Christian lands in this comparison,
Where wives, at least, are seldom kept in garrison.)

176

Now she prolonged her visits and her talk
(For they must talk), and he had learnt to say
So much as to propose to take a walk –
For little had he wandered since the day
On which, like a young flower snapped from the stalk,
Drooping and dewy on the beach he lay –
And thus they walked out in the afternoon,
And saw the sun set opposite the moon . . .

185

They looked up to the sky, whose floating glow
Spread like a rosy ocean, vast and bright;
They gazed upon the glittering sea below,
Whence the broad moon rose circling into sight;
They heard the wave's splash, and the wind so low,
And saw each other's dark eyes darting light
Into each other, and, beholding this,
Their lips drew near, and clung into a kiss –

186

A long, long kiss, a kiss of youth and love
And beauty, all concentrating like rays
Into one focus, kindled from above –
Such kisses as belong to early days,
Where heart, and soul, and sense, in concert move,
And the blood's lava, and the pulse a blaze,
Each kiss a heart-quake (for a kiss's strength,
I think, it must be reckoned by its length).

187

By length I mean duration; theirs endured
Heaven knows how long – no doubt they never reckoned;
And if they had, they could not have secured
The sum of their sensations to a second.
They had not spoken; but they felt allured,
As if their souls and lips each other beckoned,
Which, being joined, like swarming bees they clung –
Their hearts the flowers from whence the honey sprung.

188

They were alone, but not alone as they
Who shut in chambers think it loneliness:
The silent ocean, and the starlight bay,
The twilight glow, which momently grew less,
The voiceless sands, and dropping caves, that lay
Around them, made them to each other press,
As if there were no life beneath the sky
Save theirs, and that their life could never die.

189

They feared no eyes nor ears on that lone beach,
They felt no terrors from the night, they were
All in all to each other: though their speech
Was broken words, they thought a language there –
And all the burning tongues the passions teach
Found in one sigh the best interpreter
Of Nature's oracle – first love – that all
Which Eve has left her daughters since her fall.

190

Haidee spoke not of scruples, asked no vows,
Nor offered any; she had never heard
Of plight and promises to be a spouse,
Or perils by a loving maid incurred;
She was all which pure ignorance allows,
And flew to her young mate like a young bird –
And, never having dreamt of falsehood, she
Had not one word to say of constancy.

191

She loved, and was beloved – she adored,
And she was worshipped; after Nature's fashion
Their intense souls, into each other poured,
If souls could die, had perished in that passion;

But by degrees their senses were restored,
   Again to be o'ercome, again to dash on –
And, beating 'gainst his bosom, Haidee's heart
Felt as if never more to beat apart.

192

Alas! they were so young, so beautiful,
   So lonely, loving, helpless, and the hour
Was that in which the heart is always full,
   And, having o'er itself no further power,
Prompts deeds eternity can not annul,
   But pays off moments in an endless shower
Of hell-fire – all prepared for people giving
Pleasure or pain to one another living.

193

Alas! for Juan and Haidee! they were
   So loving and so lovely – till then never,
Excepting our first parents, such a pair
   Had run the risk of being damned for ever;
And Haidee, being devout as well as fair,
   Had, doubtless heard about the Stygian river,
And Hell and Purgatory – but forgot
Just in the very crisis she should not.

194

They look upon each other, and their eyes
   Gleam in the moonlight; and her white arm clasps
Round Juan's head, and his around hers lies
   Half buried in the tresses which it grasps;
She sits upon his knee, and drinks his sighs,
   He hers, until they end in broken gasps;
And thus they form a group that's quite antique,
Half naked, loving, natural, and Greek.

195

And when those deep and burning moments passed,
   And Juan sunk to sleep within her arms,
She slept not, but all tenderly, though fast,
   Sustained his head upon her bosom's charms;
And now and then her eye to heaven is cast,
   And then on the pale cheek her breast now warms,
Pillowed on her o'erflowing heart, which pants
With all it granted, and with all it grants . . .

Canto III

12

Haidee and Juan were not married, but
   The fault was theirs, not mine. It is not fair,
Chaste reader, then, in any way to put
   The blame on me, unless you wish they were –
Then, if you'd have them wedded, please to shut
   The book which treats of this erroneous pair,
Before the consequences grow too awful!
'Tis dangerous to read of loves unlawful.

13

Yet they were happy, happy in the illicit
   Indulgence of their innocent desires;
But more imprudent grown with every visit,
   Haidee forgot the island was her sire's
(When we have what we like, 'tis hard to miss it,
   At least in the beginning, ere one tires),
Thus she came often, not a moment losing,
Whilst her piratical papa was cruising . . .

Canto IV

29

Now pillowed cheek to cheek, in loving sleep,
   Haidee and Juan their siesta took,
A gentle slumber, but it was not deep,
   For ever and anon a something shook
Juan, and shuddering o'er his frame would creep;
   And Haidee's sweet lips murmured like a brook
A wordless music, and her face so fair
Stirred with her dream as rose-leaves with the air;

30

Or as the stirring of a deep clear stream
   Within an Alpine hollow, when the wind
Walks o'er it, was she shaken by the dream,
   The mystical usurper of the mind –
O'erpowering us to be whate'er may seem
   Good to the soul which we no more can bind.
Strange state of being (for 'tis still to be),
Senseless to feel, and with sealed eyes to see!

31

She dreamed of being alone on the sea-shore,
   Chained to a rock; she knew not how, but stir
She could not from the spot, and the loud roar
   Grew, and each wave rose roughly, threatening her;
And o'er her upper lip they seemed to pour
   Until she sobbed for breath, and soon they were
Foaming o'er her lone head, so fierce and high
Each broke to drown her, yet she could not die.

32

Anon she was released, and then she strayed
   O'er the sharp shingles with her bleeding feet,
And stumbled almost every step she made;
   And something rolled before her in a sheet,
Which she must still pursue howe'er afraid –
   'Twas white and indistinct, nor stopped to meet
Her glance nor grasp, for still she gazed and grasped
And ran, but it escaped her as she clasped.

33

The dream changed: in a cave she stood, its walls
   Were hung with marble icicles (the work
Of ages on its water-fretted halls,
   Where waves might wash, and seals might breed and lurk),
Her hair was dripping, and the very balls
   Of her black eyes seemed turned to tears, and murk
The sharp rocks looked below each drop they caught,
Which froze to marble as it fell, she thought.

34

And wet, and cold, and lifeless at her feet,
   Pale as the foam that frothed on his dead brow,
Which she essayed in vain to clear (how sweet
   Were once her cares, how idle seemed they now!)
Lay Juan, nor could aught renew the beat
   Of his quenched heart; and the sea dirges low
Rang in her sad ears like a mermaid's song –
And that brief dream appeared a life too long.

35

And gazing on the dead, she thought his face
   Faded, or altered into something new,
Like to her father's features, till each trace
   More like and like to Lambro's aspect grew,

With all his keen worn look and Grecian grace –
    And starting, she awoke. And what to view?
Oh, Powers of Heaven! what dark eye meets she there?
'Tis – 'tis her father's – fixed upon the pair!

36

Then shrieking she arose, and shrieking fell,
    With joy and sorrow, hope and fear, to see
Him whom she deemed a habitant where dwell
    The ocean-buried, risen from death, to be
Perchance the death of one she loved too well:
    Dear as her father had been to Haidee,
It was a moment of that awful kind –
I have seen such, but must not call to mind!

37

Up Juan sprung to Haidee's bitter shriek,
    And caught her falling, and from off the wall
Snatched down his sabre, in hot haste to wreak
    Vengeance on him who was the cause of all:
Then Lambro, who till now forbore to speak,
    Smiled scornfully, and said, 'Within my call,
A thousand scimitars await the word –
Put up, young man, put up your silly sword!'

38

And Haidee clung around him: 'Juan, 'tis –
    'Tis Lambro – 'tis my father! Kneel with me –
He will forgive us – yes – it must be – yes!
    Oh dearest father! in this agony
Of pleasure and of pain – even while I kiss
    Thy garment's hem with transport, can it be
That doubt should mingle with my filial joy?
Deal with me as thou wilt, but spare this boy!'

39

High and inscrutable the old man stood,
    Calm in his voice, and calm within his eye
(Not always signs with him of calmest mood);
    He looked upon her, but gave no reply,
Then turned to Juan, in whose cheek the blood
    Oft came and went, as there resolved to die –
In arms at least he stood, in act to spring
On the first foe whom Lambro's call might bring.

40

'Young man, your sword!' so Lambro once more said:
   Juan replied, 'Not while this arm is free!'
The old man's cheek grew pale, but not with dread,
   And drawing from his belt a pistol, he
Replied, 'Your blood be then on your own head!'
   Then looked close at the flint, as if to see
'Twas fresh (for he had lately used the lock),
And next proceeded quietly to cock.

41

It has a strange quick jar upon the ear,
   That cocking of a pistol, when you know
A moment more will bring the sight to bear
   Upon your person, twelve yards off, or so
(A gentlemanly distance, not too near,
   If you have got a former friend for foe),
But after being fired at once or twice,
The ear becomes more Irish, and less nice.

42

Lambro presented, and one instant more
   Had stopped this Canto, and Don Juan's breath,
When Haidee threw herself her boy before;
   Stern as her sire, 'On me', she cried, 'let death
Descend! The fault is mine. This fatal shore
   He found – but sought not. I have pledged my faith;
I love him – I will die with him. I knew
Your nature's firmness – know your daughter's too!'

43

A minute past, and she had been all tears,
   And tenderness, and infancy; but now
She stood as one who championed human fears –
   Pale, statue-like, and stern, she wooed the blow;
And tall beyond her sex, and their compeers,
   She drew up to her height, as if to show
A fairer mark, and with a fixed eye scanned
Her father's face – but never stopped his hand!

44

He gazed on her, and she on him – 'twas strange
   How like they looked! The expression was the same:
Serenely savage, with a little change
   In the large dark eye's mutual-darted flame;

For she too was as one who could avenge,
  If cause should be – a lioness, though tame!
Her father's blood before her father's face
Boiled up, and proved her truly of his race.

45

I said they were alike, their features and
  Their stature differing but in sex and years;
Even to the delicacy of their hand
  There was resemblance, such as true blood wears;
And now to see them, thus divided, stand
  In fixed ferocity (when joyous tears,
And sweet sensations, should have welcomed both)
Shows what the passions are in their full growth!

46

The father paused a moment, then withdrew
  His weapon, and replaced it; but stood still,
And looking on her, as to look her through,
  'Not I', he said, 'have sought this stranger's ill –
Not I have made this desolation. Few
  Would bear such outrage, and forbear to kill –
But I must do my duty. How thou hast
Done thine, the present vouches for the past!

47

'Let him disarm; or, by my father's head,
  His own shall roll before you like a ball!'
He raised his whistle, as the word he said,
  And blew; another answered to the call,
And, rushing in, disorderly, though led
  (And armed from boot to turban, one and all),
Some twenty of his train came, rank on rank.
He gave the word, 'Arrest or slay the Frank!'

48

Then, with a sudden movement, he withdrew
  His daughter; while compressed within his clasp,
'Twixt her and Juan interposed the crew –
  In vain she struggled in her father's grasp,
His arms were like a serpent's coil! Then flew
  Upon their prey, as darts an angry asp,
The file of pirates – save the foremost, who
Had fallen, with his right shoulder half cut through.

49

The second had his cheek laid open; but
The third (a wary, cool old sworder) took
The blows upon his cutlass, and then put
His own well in – so well, ere you could look,
His man was floored, and helpless at his foot,
With the blood running like a little brook
From two smart sabre gashes, deep and red,
One on the arm, the other on the head.

50

And then they bound him where he fell, and bore
Juan from the apartment: with a sign
Old Lambro bade them take him to the shore,
Where lay some ships which were to sail at nine.
They laid him in a boat, and plied the oar
Until they reached some galliots, placed in line;
On board of one of these, and under hatches,
They stowed him, with strict orders to the watches.

51

The world is full of strange vicissitudes,
And here was one exceedingly unpleasant:
A gentleman, so rich in the world's goods,
Handsome and young, enjoying all the present,
Just at the very time when he least broods
On such a thing, is suddenly to sea sent,
Wounded and chained, so that he cannot move –
And all because a lady fell in love! . . .

58

The last sight which she saw was Juan's gore,
And he himself o'ermastered and cut down
(His blood was running on the very floor
Where late he trod, her beautiful, her own) –
Thus much she viewed an instant and no more –
Her struggles ceased with one convulsive groan.
On her sire's arm, which until now scarce held
Her writhing, fell she like a cedar felled.

59

A vein had burst, and her sweet lips' pure dyes
Were dabbled with the deep blood which ran o'er;
And her head drooped as when the lily lies
O'ercharged with rain. Her summoned handmaids bore

Their lady to her couch with gushing eyes;
Of herbs and cordials they produced their store,
But she defied all means they could employ,
Like one life could not hold, nor death destroy.

60

Days lay she in that state unchanged (though chill,
With nothing livid – still her lips were red);
She had no pulse, but death seemed absent still.
No hideous sign proclaimed her surely dead –
Corruption came not, in each mind to kill
All hope – to look upon her sweet face bred
New thoughts of life, for it seemed full of soul:
She had so much, earth could not claim the whole . . .

69

Twelve days and nights she withered thus. At last,
Without a groan, or sigh, or glance, to show
A parting pang, the spirit from her past;
And they who watched her nearest could not know
The very instant, till the change that cast
Her sweet face into shadow, dull and slow,
Glazed o'er her eyes – the beautiful, the black –
Oh, to possess such lustre – and then lack!

70

She died, but not alone: she held within
A second principle of life, which might
Have dawned a fair and sinless child of sin,
But closed its little being without light,
And went down to the grave unborn, wherein
Blossom and bough lie withered with one blight;
In vain the dews of heaven descend above
The bleeding flower, and blasted fruit, of love.

71

Thus lived, thus died, she. Never more on her
Shall sorrow light, or shame. She was not made
Through years, or moons, the inner weight to bear
Which colder hearts endure till they are laid
By age in earth; her days and pleasures were
Brief, but delightful – such as had not stayed
Long with her destiny; but she sleeps well
By the sea-shore, whereon she loved to dwell.

72

That isle is now all desolate and bare,
   Its dwellings down, its tenants past away.
None but her own and father's grave is there,
   And nothing outward tells of human clay:
Ye could not know where lies a thing so fair –
   No stone is there to show, no tongue to say,
What was – no dirge, except the hollow sea's,
Mourns o'er the Beauty of the Cyclades.

13. LETITIA ELIZABETH LANDON

The Indian Bride (*Improvisatrice* 1823)

She has lighted her lamp, and crowned it with flowers,
The sweetest that breathed of the summer hours,
Red and white roses linked in a band
Like a maiden's blush, or a maiden's hand;
Jasmines – some like silver spray,
Some like gold in the morning ray –
Fragrant stars, and favourites they,
When Indian girls on a festival-day
Braid their dark tresses, and all over weaves
The rosy-bower of lotus leaves –
Canopy suiting the lamp-lighted bark,
Love's own flowers, and Love's own ark.
   She watched the sky, the sunset grew dim;
She raised to Camdeo her evening hymn.
The scent of the night-flowers came on the air;
And then, like a bird escaped from the snare,
She flew to the river (no moon was bright,
But the stars and the fire-flies gave her their light);
She stood beneath the mangos' shade,
Half delighted and half afraid;
She trimmed her lamp, and breathed on each bloom
(Oh, that breath was sweeter than all their perfume!)
Threw spices and oil on the spire of flame,
Called thrice on her absent lover's name –
And every pulse throbbed as she gave
Her little boat to the Ganges' wave . . .
   Zaide watched her flower-built vessel glide,
Mirrored beneath on the deep-blue tide;

Lovely and lonely, scented and bright,
Like Hope's own bark, all bloom and light.
There's not one breath of wind on the air,
The heavens are cloudless, the waters are fair,
No dew is falling, yet woe to that shade –
The maiden is weeping, her lamp has decayed!
   Hark to the ring of the scimitar –
It tells that the soldier returns from afar.
Down from the mountains the warriors come:
Hark to the thunder-roll of the drum!
To the startling voice of the trumpet's call!
To the cymbal's clash – to the atabal!
The banners of crimson float in the sun;
The warfare is ended, the battle is won.
The mother hath taken the child from her breast
And raised it to look on its father's crest.
The pathway is lined, as the bands pass along,
With maidens, who meet them with flowers and song.
And Zaide hath forgotten in Azim's arms
All her so false lamp's falser alarms.
   This looks not a bridal – the singers are mute,
Still is the mandore, and breathless the lute;
Yet there the bride sits. Her dark hair is bound,
And the robe of her marriage floats white on the ground.
Oh, where is her lover, the bridegroom – oh, where?
Look under yon black pall – the bridegroom is there!
Yet the guests are all bidden, the feast is the same,
The bride plights her troth amid smoke and mid flame!
They have raised the death-pyre of sweet scented wood,
And sprinkled it o'er with the sacred flood
Of the Ganges. The priests are assembled – their song
Sinks deep on the ear as they bear her along,
The bride of the dead. Aye, is this not love –
That one pure, wild feeling all others above,
Vowed to the living, and kept to the tomb –
The same in its blight as it was in its bloom!
With no tear in her eye, and no change in her smile,
Young Zaide had come nigh to the funeral pile.
The bells of the dancing ceased from their sound;
Silent they stood by that holiest mound.
From a crowd like the sea-waves there came not a breath,
When the maiden stood by the place of death!
One moment was given, the last she might spare,
To the mother who stood in her weeping there.

She took the jewels that shone on her hand;
She took from her dark hair its flowery band,
And scattered them round. At once they raise
The hymn of rejoicing and love in her praise.
A prayer is muttered, a blessing said,
Her torch is raised – she is by the dead.
She has fired the pile! At once there came
A mingled rush of smoke and flame,
Though the wind swept it off. They saw the bride –
Laid by her Azim, side by side.
The breeze had spread the long curls of her hair:
Like a banner of fire they played on the air.
The smoke and the flame gathered round as before,
Then cleared – but the bride was seen no more!

14. FELICIA HEMANS

Arabella Stuart (*Records of Woman* 1828)

The Lady Arabella, as she has been frequently entitled, was descended from Margaret, eldest daughter of Henry VII, and consequently allied by birth to Elizabeth, as well as James I. This affinity to the throne proved the misfortune of her life, as the jealousies which it constantly excited in her royal relatives, who were anxious to prevent her marrying, shut her out from the enjoyment of that domestic happiness which her heart appears to have so fervently desired. By a secret, but early discovered, union with William Seymour, son of Lord Beauchamp, she alarmed the cabinet of James, and the wedded lovers were immediately placed in separate confinement . . . The following poem, meant as some record of her fate, and the imagined fluctuations of her thoughts and feelings, is supposed to commence during the time of her first imprisonment, whilst her mind was yet buoyed up by the consciousness of Seymour's affection, and the cherished hope of eventual deliverance.

(Hemans' headnote)

1

'Twas but a dream! – I saw the stag leap free
   Under the boughs where early birds were singing,
I stood o'ershadowed by the greenwood-tree,
   And heard, it seemed, a sudden bugle ringing
Far through a royal forest: then the fawn
Shot, like a gleam of light, from grassy lawn

To secret covert; and the smooth turf shook
And lilies quivered by the glade's lone brook,
And young leaves trembled, as, in fleet career,
A princely band, with horn, and hound, and spear,
Like a rich masque swept forth. I saw the dance
Of their white plumes, that bore a silvery glance
Into the deep wood's heart; and all passed by,
Save one – I met the smile of *one* clear eye,
Flashing out joy to mine. Yes, *thou* wert there.
Seymour, a soft wind blew the clustering hair
Back from thy gallant brow, as thou didst rein
Thy courser, turning from that gorgeous train,
And fling, methought, thy hunting-spear away,
And, lightly graceful in thy green array,
Bound to my side; and we, that met and parted,
   Ever in dread of some dark watchful power,
Won back to childhood's trust, and fearless-hearted,
   Blent the glad fullness of our thoughts that hour,
Even like the mingling of sweet streams, beneath
Dim woven leaves, and midst the floating breath
Of hidden forest-flowers.

2

'Tis past! – I wake,
   A captive, and alone, and far from thee,
My love and friend – yet fostering for thy sake
   A quenchless hope of happiness to be,
And feeling still my woman-spirit strong,
In the deep faith which lifts from earthly wrong
A Heavenward glance. I know, I know our love
Shall yet call gentle angels from above,
By its undying fervour, and prevail –
Sending a breath, as of the spring's first gale,
Through hearts now cold; and, raising its bright face
With a free gush of sunny tears, erase
The characters of anguish. In this trust
I bear, I strive, I bow not to the dust,
That I may bring thee back no faded form,
No bosom chilled and blighted by the storm,
But all my youth's first treasures, when we meet,
Making past sorrow, by communion, sweet.

3

And thou too art in bonds! – yet droop thou not,
Oh my beloved – there is *one* hopeless lot,
But one, and that not ours. Beside the dead
There sits the grief that mantles up its head,
Loathing the laughter and proud pomp of light,
When darkness, from the vainly doting sight
Covers its beautiful! If thou wert gone
   To the grave's bosom, with thy radiant brow;
If thy deep-thrilling voice, with that low tone
   Of earnest tenderness, which now, even now
Seems floating through my soul, were music taken
For ever from this world – oh! thus forsaken,
Could I bear on? Thou livest, thou livest, thou'rt mine!
With this glad thought I make my heart a shrine,
And by the lamp which quenchless there shall burn,
Sit a lone watcher for the day's return.

4

And lo, the joy that cometh with the morning,
   Brightly victorious o'er the hours of care!
I have not watched in vain, serenely scorning
   The wild and busy whispers of despair!
Thou hast sent tidings, as of Heaven – I wait
   The hour, the sign, for blesséd flight to thee.
Oh for the skylark's wing that seeks its mate
   As a star shoots! – but on the breezy sea
We shall meet soon. To think of such an hour!
   Will not my heart, o'erburdened by its bliss,
Faint and give way within me, as a flower
   Borne down and perishing by noontide's kiss?
Yet shall I *fear* that lot – the perfect rest,
The full deep joy of dying on thy breast,
After long suffering won? So rich a close
Too seldom crowns with peace affection's woes.

5

Sunset! – I tell each moment – from the skies
   The last red splendour floats along my wall,
Like a king's banner! Now it melts, it dies!
   I see one star – I hear – 'twas not the call,

The expected voice; my quick heart throbbed too soon.
I must keep vigil till yon rising moon
Shower down less golden light. Beneath her beam
Through my lone lattice poured, I sit and dream
Of summer-lands afar, where holy love,
Under the vine or in the citron grove,
May breathe from terror.
                                        Now the night grows deep,
And silent as its clouds, and full of sleep.
I hear my veins beat. Hark! a bell's slow chime!
My heart strikes with it. Yet again – 'tis time!
A step! – a voice! – or but a rising breeze?
Hark! – haste! – I come, to meet thee on the seas.

*   *   *

6

Now never more, oh! never, in the worth
Of its pure cause, let sorrowing love on earth
Trust fondly – never more! The hope is crushed
That lit my life, the voice within me hushed
That spoke sweet oracles; and I return
To lay my youth, as in a burial urn,
Where sunshine may not find it. All is lost!
No tempest met our barks – no billow tossed –
Yet were they severed, even as we must be,
That so have loved, so striven our hearts to free
From their close-coiling fate! In vain – in vain!
The dark links meet, and clasp themselves again,
And press out life. Upon the deck I stood,
And a white sail came gliding o'er the flood,
Like some proud bird of ocean; then mine eye
Strained out, one moment earlier to descry
The form it ached for, and the bark's career
Seemed slow to that fond yearning. It drew near,
Fraught with our foes! What boots it to recall
The strife, the tears? Once more a prison-wall
Shuts the green hills and woodlands from my sight,
And joyous glance of waters to the light,
And thee, my Seymour, thee!
                                                            I will not sink!
   Thou, *thou* hast rent the heavy chain that bound thee!
And this shall be my strength – the joy to think
   That thou mayst wander with heaven's breath around thee,

And all the laughing sky! This thought shall yet
Shine o'er my heart a radiant amulet,
Guarding it from despair. Thy bonds are broken,
And unto me, I know, thy true love's token
Shall one day be deliverance, though the years
Lie dim between, o'erhung with mists of tears.

7

My friend! my friend! where art thou? Day by day,
Gliding like some dark mournful stream away,
My silent youth flows from me. Spring, the while,
Comes and rains beauty on the kindling boughs
Round hall and hamlet; Summer with her smile,
Fills the green forest; young hearts breathe their vows;
Brothers long parted meet; fair children rise
Round the glad board; Hope laughs from loving eyes –
All this is in the world! These joys lie sown,
The dew of every path. On *one* alone
Their freshness may not fall – the stricken deer
Dying of thirst with all the waters near.

8

Ye are (from dingle and fresh glade) ye flowers
By some kind hand to cheer my dungeon sent;
O'er you the oak shed down the summer showers,
And the lark's nest was where your bright cups bent,
Quivering to breeze and raindrop, like the sheen
Of twilight stars. On you heaven's eye hath been,
Through the leaves, pouring its dark sultry blue
Into your glowing hearts; the bee to you
Hath murmured, and the rill. My soul grows faint
With passionate yearning, as its quick dreams paint
Your haunts by dell and stream – the green, the free,
The full of all sweet sound – the shut from me!

9

There went a swift bird singing past my cell –
Oh love and freedom, ye are lovely things!
With you the peasant on the hills may dwell,
And by the streams; but I – the blood of kings,
A proud unmingling river, through my veins
Flows in lone brightness, and its gifts are chains!

Kings! – I had silent visions of deep bliss,
Leaving their thrones far distant, and for this
I am cast under their triumphal car,
An insect to be crushed! Oh! Heaven is far –
Earth pitiless!

Dost thou forget me, Seymour? I am proved
So long, so sternly! Seymour, my beloved!
There are such tales of holy marvels done
By strong affection, of deliverance won
Through its prevailing power! Are these things told
Till the young weep with rapture, and the old
Wonder, yet dare not doubt; and thou! oh, thou!
   Dost thou forget me in my hope's decay? –
Thou canst not! – through the silent night, even now,
   I, that need prayer so much, awake and pray
Still first for thee. Oh gentle, gentle friend!
How shall I bear this anguish to the end?

Aid! – comes there yet no aid? The voice of blood
Passes Heaven's gate, even ere the crimson flood
Sinks through the greensward! Is there not a cry
From the wrung heart, of power, through agony,
To pierce the clouds? Hear, Mercy! – hear me! None
That bleed and weep beneath the smiling sun
Have heavier cause! – yet hear! – my soul grows dark –
Who hears the last shriek from the sinking bark
On the mid-seas, and with the storm alone,
And bearing to the abyss, unseen, unknown,
Its freight of human hearts? The o'ermastering wave –
Who shall tell how it rushed – and none to save?

Thou hast forsaken me! I feel, I know,
There would be rescue if this were not so.
Thou'rt at the chase, thou'rt at the festive board,
Thou'rt where the red wine free and high is poured,
Thou'rt where the dancers meet! – a magic glass
Is set within my soul, and proud shapes pass,
Flushing it o'er with pomp from bower and hall;
I see one shadow, stateliest there of all –
Thine! What dost thou amidst the bright and fair,
Whispering light words, and mocking my despair?

It is not well of thee! My love was more
Than fiery song may breathe, deep thought explore –
And there thou smilest, while my heart is dying,
With all its blighted hopes around it lying;
Even thou, on whom they hung their last green leaf.
Yet smile, smile on! Too bright art thou for grief.

Death – what? Is death a locked and treasured thing,
Guarded by swords of fire – a hidden spring,
A fabled fruit – that I should thus endure,
As if the world within me held no cure?
Wherefore not spread free wings? Heaven, Heaven control
These thoughts – they rush – I look into my soul
As down a gulf, and tremble at the array
Of fierce forms crowding it! Give strength to pray,
So shall their dark host pass.

The storm is stilled.
  Father in Heaven! thou, only thou, canst sound
The heart's great deep, with floods of anguish filled,
  For human line too fearfully profound.
Therefore forgive, my Father! if thy child,
Rocked on its heaving darkness, hath grown wild
And sinned in her despair! It well may be,
That thou wouldst lead my spirit back to thee –
By the crushed hope too long on this world poured,
The stricken love which hath perchance adored
A mortal in thy place! Now let me strive
With thy strong arm no more! Forgive, forgive!
Take me to peace!

And peace at last is nigh.
  A sign is on my brow, a token sent
The o'erwearied dust from home; no breeze flits by
  But calls me with a strange sweet whisper, blent
Of many mysteries.

Hark! the warning tone
Deepens – its word is Death! Alone, alone,
And sad in youth, but chastened, I depart,
Bowing to Heaven. Yet, yet my woman's heart
Shall wake a spirit and a power to bless,

Even in this hour's o'ershadowing fearfulness,
Thee, its first love! Oh! tender still, and true –
Be it forgotten if mine anguish threw
Drops from its bitter fountain on thy name,
Though but a moment.

Now, with fainting frame,
With soul just lingering on the flight begun,
To bind for thee its last dim thoughts in one,
I bless thee! Peace be on thy noble head,
Years of bright fame, when I am with the dead!
I bid this prayer survive me, and retain
Its might, again to bless thee, and again!
Thou hast been gathered into my dark fate
Too much; too long, for my sake, desolate
Hath been thine exiled youth; but now take back,
From dying hands, thy freedom, and retrack
(After a few kind tears for her whose days
Went out in dreams of thee) the sunny ways
Of hope, and find thou happiness! Yet send,
Even then, in silent hours, a thought, dear friend!
Down to my voiceless chamber; for thy love
Hath been to me all gifts of earth above,
Though bought with burning tears! It is the sting
Of death to leave that vainly-precious thing
In this cold world! What were it then, if thou,
With thy fond eyes, wert gazing on me now?
Too keen a pang! Farewell! and yet once more,
Farewell! – the passion of long years I pour
Into that word. Thou hearest not, but the woe
And fervour of its tones may one day flow
To thy heart's holy place – there let them dwell.
We shall o'ersweep the grave to meet – Farewell!

15. CAROLINE NORTON

The Faithless Knight (1830)

The lady she sat in her bower alone,
And she gazed from the lattice-window high
Where a white steed's hoofs were ringing on,
With a beating heart, and a smothered sigh.

Why doth she gaze through the sunset-rays?
Why doth she watch that white steed's track,
While a quivering smile on her red lip plays?
'Tis her own dear knight – will he not look back?

The steed flew fast, and the rider passed –
Nor paused he to gaze at the lady's bower –
The smile from her lip is gone at last!
There are tears on her cheek, like the dew on a flower!
And 'Plague on these foolish tears', she said,
'Which have dimmed the view of my young love's track!
For oh, I am sure, while I bent my head,
It was then – it was then – that my knight looked back!'

On flew that steed with an arrow's speed –
He is gone, and the green boughs wave between –
And she sighs, as the sweet breeze sighs through a reed,
As she watches the spot where he last has been.
Oh, many a sun shall rise and set,
And many an hour may she watch in vain,
And many a tear shall that soft cheek wet,
Ere that steed and its rider return again!

III. Romantic Solitude, Suffering and Endurance

A glance at Romantic poetry of solitude, suffering and endurance shows two things: first that this is a poetry of predicament – a poetry of the mind, as opposed to narrative, incident, plot; second, that, whether poets themselves are male or female, women sufferers vastly outnumber men in their writing. Cowper's Crazy Kate, anthologized again and again through the Romantic period, is the forerunner of numerous women raped, seduced or abandoned: Baillie's Storm-Beat Maid, Blake's Oothoon, Southey's Mary the Maid, Wordsworth's Mad Mother and Forsaken Indian Woman (with Margaret of *The Ruined Cottage* and Martha of *The Thorn*), all belong to the 1790s. Bryan's Kattern is knowingly based on the Wordsworth *Lyrical Ballads*. Shelley's Beatrice Cenci, Landon's and Hemans' heroic Indian women ('My warrior's eye hath looked upon another's face') show a similar pattern in the later period, though the impulse behind the poetry is so different.

Not all, but many, of these rejected women go mad, suggesting that the poets' interest is engaged with psychology, rather than protest at male behaviour and social injustice. In some way, however, all seem above their predicaments: even where it treats of suffering, Romantic poetry is at an important level optimistic. It looks for 'soothing thoughts that spring / Out of human suffering', asking our sympathy for pain, but not concerned with the merely downtrodden. Raped by Bromion, rejected (more painfully still) by her lover Theotormon, Oothoon towers imaginatively above them in Blake's *Visions of the Daughters of Albion*; awaiting execution for the murder of the father who has raped her, Shelley's Beatrice achieves a tragic nobility; Wordsworth's Mad Mother, and even Bryan's Kattern, crashing through the undergrowth, have a stature that rises above circumstance and setting.

If women in Romantic poetry of suffering seem to be marked out by maltreatment, men seem characterized rather by their otherness: the Ancient Mariner by his glittering eye and obsessional story; Wordsworth's beggars and Leech-Gatherer by an emphasis on the 'self-sufficing power of solitude'; Bonnivard in Byron's *Prisoner of Chillon* by a stoic philosophy that 'learns to love despair'. Here too there is an implication of the heroic. Byron it is who in The Shipwreck chooses to remind us that the human mind may sink to an opposite extreme.

1. WILLIAM COWPER

Crazy Kate (*Task* I, 534–56) 1785

There often wanders one, whom better days
Saw better clad, in cloak of satin trimmed
With lace, and hat with splendid ribband bound.
A serving-maid was she, and fell in love
With one who left her, went to sea and died.
Her fancy followed him through foaming waves

To distant shores, and she would sit and weep
At what a sailor suffers; fancy too,
Delusive most where warmest wishes are,
Would oft anticipate his glad return,
And dream of transports she was not to know.
She heard the doleful tidings of his death,
And never smiled again. And now she roams
The dreary waste – there spends the livelong day,
And there (unless when charity forbids)
The livelong night. A tattered apron hides,
Worn as a cloak – and hardly hides – a gown
More tattered still! And both but ill conceal
A bosom heaved with never-ceasing sighs.
She begs an idle pin of all she meets,
And hoards them in her sleeve; but needful food,
Though pressed with hunger oft, or comelier clothes,
Though pinched with cold, asks never – Kate is crazed.

2. JOANNA BAILLIE

The Storm-Beat Maid: Somewhat after the Style of Our Old English Ballads (1790)

All shrouded in the winter snow
   The maiden held her way;
Nor chilly winds that roughly blow,
   Nor dark night could her stay.

O'er hill and dale, through bush and briar,
   She on her journey kept;
Save often, when she gan to tire,
   She stopped awhile and wept.

Wild creatures left their caverns drear,
   To raise their nightly yell;
But little does the bosom fear
   Where inward troubles dwell.

No watch-light from the distant spire
   To cheer the gloom so deep,
Nor twinkling star, nor cottage fire,
   Did through the darkness peep.

Yet heedless still she held her way,
   Nor feared she crag, nor dell,
Like ghost that through the gloom to stray
   Wakes with the midnight bell.

Now night through her dark watches ran,
   Which lock the peaceful mind,
And through the neighbouring hamlets 'gan
   To wake the yawning hind.

Yet bark of dog, nor village cock,
   That spoke the morning near,
Nor gray light trembling on the rock,
   Her 'nighted mind could cheer.

The whirling flail, and clacking mill,
   Wake early with the day;
And careless children, loud and shrill,
   With new-made snowballs play,

And as she passed each cottage-door
   They did their gambols cease;
And old men shook their locks so hoar
   And wished her spirit peace.

For sometimes slow, and sometimes fast,
   She held her wavering pace,
Like early spring's inconstant blast
   That ruffles evening's face.

At length with weary feet she came
   Where in a sheltering wood,
Whose master bore no humble name,
   A stately castle stood.

The open gate and smoking fires,
   Which cloud the air so thin,
And shrill bell tinkling from the spires,
   Bespoke a feast within.

With busy looks, and hasty tread,
   The servants cross the hall,
And many a page in buskins red
   Await the master's call.

Fair streaming bows of bridal white
   On every shoulder played,
And clean, in lily kerchief dight,
   Tripped every household maid.

She asked for neither lord nor dame,
   Nor who the mansion owned,
But straight into the hall she came
   And sat her on the ground.

The busy crew all crowded nigh,
   And round the stranger stared;
But still she rolled her wandering eye,
   Nor for their questions cared.

'What dost thou want, thou storm-beat maid,
   That thou these portals passed?
Ill suiteth here thy looks dismayed –
   Thou art no bidden guest.'

'Oh chide not', said a gentle page,
   And wiped his tear-wet cheek,
'Who would not shun the winter's rage? –
   The wind is cold and bleak!

Her robe is stiff with drizzly snow,
   And rent her mantle grey –
None ever bade the wretched go
   Upon his wedding-day!'

Then to his lord he hied him straight,
   (Where round on silken seat
Sat many a courteous dame and knight
   And made obeisance meet:

'There is a stranger in your hall
   Who wears no common mien;
Hard were the heart, as flinty wall,
   That would not take her in.

A fairer dame in hall or bower
   Mine eyes did ne'er behold;
Though sheltered in no father's tower,
   And turned out to the cold.

Her face is like an early morn,
   Dimmed with the nightly dew;
Her skin is like the sheeted thorn,
   Her eyes are watery blue.

And tall and slender is her form,
   Like willow o'er the brook;
But on her brow there broods a storm,
   And restless is her look.

And well her troubled motions show
   The tempest of her mind,
Like the unsheltered sapling-bough
   Vexed with the wintry wind.

Her head droops on her ungirt breast,
   And scattered is her hair;
Yet lady braced in courtly vest
   Was never half so fair!'

Reverse, and cold, the turning blood
   The bridegroom's cheek forsook:
He shook and staggered as he stood,
   And faltered as he spoke.

'So soft and fair I know a maid,
   There is but only she;
A wretched man her love betrayed –
   And wretched let him be!'

Deep frowning turned the bride's dark eye,
   For bridal morn unmeet:
With trembling steps her lord did hie
   The stranger fair to greet.

Though loose in scattered weeds arrayed,
   And ruffled by the storm,
Like lambkin from its fellows strayed
   He knew her graceful form.

But when he spied her sunken eye,
   And features sharp and wan,
He heaved a deep and heavy sigh
   And down the big tears ran.

'Why droops thy head, thou lovely maid,
Upon thy hand of snow?
Is it because thy love's betrayed
That thou art brought so low?'

Quick from her eye the keen glance came,
Who questioned her to see,
And oft she muttered o'er his name –
And wist not it was he.

Full hard against his writhing brows
His clenchéd hands he prest;
Full high his labouring bosom rose,
And rent its silken vest.

'Oh curséd be the golden price
That did my baseness prove!
And curséd be my friends' advice,
That willed me from thy love!

And curséd be the woman's art
That lured me to her snare!
And curséd be the faithless heart
That left thee to despair!

Yet now I'll hold thee to my side,
Though worthless I have been:
Nor friends, nor wealth, nor dizened bride,
Shall ever stand between.

When thou art weary and depressed
I'll lull thee to thy sleep,
And when dark fancies vex thy breast
I'll sit by thee and weep.

I'll tend thee like a restless child
Where'er thy rovings be;
Nor gesture keen, nor eyeball wild,
Shall turn my love from thee.

Night shall not hang cold o'er thy head,
And I securely lie;
Nor drizzly clouds upon thee shed,
And I in covert dry.

I'll share the cold blast on the heath,
  I'll share thy wants and pain:
Nor friend nor foe, nor life nor death,
  Shall ever make us twain.'

3. CHARLOTTE SMITH

The Female Exile (Nov. 1792; publ. 1797)

November's chill blast on the rough beach is howling,
  The surge breaks afar, and then foams to the shore,
Dark clouds o'er the sea gather heavy and scowling,
  And the white cliffs re-echo the wild wintry roar.

Beneath that chalk rock, a fair stranger reclining,
  Has found on damp sea-weed a cold lonely seat;
Her eyes filled with tears, and her heart with repining,
  She starts at the billows that burst at her feet.

There, day after day, with an anxious heart heaving,
  She watches the waves where they mingle with air;
For the sail which, alas! all her fond hopes deceiving,
  May bring only tidings to add to her care.

Loose stream to wild winds those fair flowing tresses,
  Once woven with garlands of gay summer flowers;
Her dress unregarded bespeaks her distresses,
  And beauty is blighted by grief's heavy hours.

Her innocent children, unconscious of sorrow,
  To seek the glossed shell, or the crimson weed stray;
Amused with the present, they heed not tomorrow,
  Nor think of the storm that is gathering today.

The gilt, fairy ship, with its ribbon-sail spreading,
  They launch on the salt pool the tide left behind;
Ah victims – for whom their sad mother is dreading
  The multiplied miseries that wait on mankind!

To fair fortune born, she beholds them with anguish,
  Now wanderers with her on a once hostile soil,
Perhaps doomed for life in chill penury to languish,
  Or abject dependence, or soul-crushing toil.

But the sea-boat, her hopes and her terrors renewing,
   O'er the dim grey horizon now faintly appears;
She flies to the quay, dreading tidings of ruin,
   All breathless with haste, half expiring with fears.

Poor mourner – I would that my fortune had left me
   The means to alleviate the woes I deplore;
But like thine my hard fate has of affluence bereft me,
   I can warm the cold heart of the wretched no more.

4. WILLIAM BLAKE

Visions of the Daughters of Albion (1793)

The eye sees more than the heart knows.

The Argument

I loved Theotormon
And I was not ashamed,
I trembled in my virgin fears
And I hid in Leutha's vale –

I plucked Leutha's flower,
And I rose up from the vale;
But the terrible thunders tore
My virgin mantle in twain!

Visions

Enslaved, the Daughters of Albion weep – a trembling lamentation
Upon their mountains, in their valleys sighs toward America.
For the soft soul of America, Oothoon, wandered in woe
Along the vales of Leutha, seeking flowers to comfort her,
And thus she spoke to the bright Marygold of Leutha's vale:
'Art thou a flower? Art thou a nymph? I see thee now a flower,
Now a nymph! I dare not pluck thee from thy dewy bed.'
The golden nymph replied: 'Pluck thou my flower, Oothoon the
      mild.
Another flower shall spring, because the soul of sweet delight
Can never pass away.' She ceased and closed her golden shrine.

Then Oothoon plucked the flower saying, 'I pluck thee from thy
bed,
Sweet flower, and put thee here to glow between my breasts,
And thus I turn my face to where my whole soul seeks.'
Over the waves she went in winged exulting swift delight,
And over Theotormon's reign, took her impetuous course.
Bromion rent her with his thunders. On his stormy bed
Lay the faint maid, and soon her woes appalled his thunders hoarse.
Bromion spoke: 'Behold this harlot here on Bromion's bed,
And let the jealous dolphins sport around the lovely maid!
Thy soft American plains are mine, and mine thy north and south.
Stamped with my signet are the swarthy children of the sun –
They are obedient, they resist not, they obey the scourge,
Their daughters worship terrors and obey the violent!
Now thou mayst marry Bromion's harlot and protect the child
Of Bromion's rage that Oothoon shall put forth in nine moons time.'
Then storms rent Theotormon's limbs; he rolled his waves around
And folded his black jealous waters round the adulterate pair.
Bound back to back in Bromion's caves, terror and meekness dwell;
At entrance Theotormon sits, wearing the threshold hard
With secret tears. Beneath him sound like waves on a desert-shore
The voice of slaves beneath the sun, and children bought with
money
That shiver in religious caves beneath the burning fires
Of lust that belch incessant, from the summits of the earth.
Oothoon weeps not. She cannot weep – her tears are locked up –
But she can howl incessant writhing her soft snowy limbs
And calling Theotormon's eagles to prey upon her flesh:
'I call with holy voice, kings of the sounding air!
Rend away this defiled bosom that I may reflect
The image of Theotormon on my pure transparent breast.'
The eagles at her call descend and rend their bleeding prey;
Theotormon severely smiles. Her soul reflects the smile,
As the clear spring, muddied with feet of beasts, grows pure and
smiles.
The Daughters of Albion hear her woes, and echo back her sighs.
'Why does my Theotormon sit weeping upon the threshold
And Oothoon hovers by his side, persuading him in vain?
I cry "arise", oh Theotormon, for the village dog
Barks at the breaking day, the nightingale has done lamenting,
The lark does rustle in the ripe corn, and the eagle returns
From nightly prey and lifts his golden beak to the pure east,
Shaking the dust from his immortal pinions to awake
The sun that sleeps too long. Arise, my Theotormon, I am pure –

Because the night is gone that closed me in its deadly black.
They told me that the night and day were all that I could see,
They told me that I had five senses to inclose me up,
And they inclosed my infinite brain into a narrow circle
And sunk my heart into the abyss, a red round globe hot burning –
Till all from life I was obliterated and erased.
Instead of morn arises a bright shadow like an eye
In the eastern cloud, instead of night a sickly charnel-house,
That Theotormon hears me not! To him the night and morn
Are both alike – a night of sighs, a morning of fresh tears –
And none but Bromion can hear my lamentations.
   With what sense is it that the chicken shuns the ravenous hawk?
With what sense does the tame pigeon measure out the expanse?
With what sense does the bee form cells? Have not the mouse and
      frog
Eyes and ears and sense of touch – yet are their habitations
And their pursuits as different as their forms and as their joys?
Ask the wild ass why he refuses burdens, and the meek camel
Why he loves man. Is it because of eye, ear, mouth, or skin,
Or breathing nostrils? No, for these the wolf and tiger have.
Ask the blind worm the secrets of the grave, and why her spires
Love to curl round the bones of death, and ask the ravenous snake
Where she gets poison, and the winged eagle why he loves the sun –
And then tell me the thoughts of man, that have been hid of old.
   Silent I hover all the night, and all day could be silent
If Theotormon once would turn his loved eyes upon me.
How can I be defiled when I reflect thy image pure?
Sweetest the fruit that the worm feeds on, and the soul preyed on by
      woe,
The new-washed lamb tinged with the village smoke, and the bright
      swan
By the red earth of our immortal river. I bathe my wings,
And I am white and pure to hover round Theotormon's breast.'
   Then Theotormon broke his silence, and he answered:
'Tell me what is the night or day to one o'erflowed with woe!
Tell me what is a thought, and of what substance is it made!
Tell me what is a joy, and in what gardens do joys grow!
And in what rivers swim the sorrows, and upon what mountains
Wave shadows of discontent, and in what houses dwell the wretched
Drunken with woe, forgotten and shut up from cold despair?
Tell me where dwell the thoughts forgotten till thou call them forth!
Tell me where dwell the joys of old, and where the ancient loves,
And when will they renew again, and the night of oblivion past –
That I might traverse times and spaces far remote and bring

Comforts into a present sorrow, and a night of pain.
Where goest thou, oh thought, to what remote land is thy flight?
If thou returnest to the present moment of affliction
Wilt thou bring comforts on thy wings, and dews and honey and balm,
Or poison from the desert wilds, from the eyes of the envier?'
Then Bromion said, and shook the cavern with his lamentation:
'Thou knowest that the ancient trees seen by thine eyes have fruit,
But knowest thou that trees and fruits flourish upon the earth
To gratify senses unknown – trees, beasts and birds, unknown –
Unknown not unperceived, spread in the infinite microscope
In places yet unvisited by the voyager, and in worlds
Over another kind of seas, and in atmospheres unknown?
Ah, are there other wars beside the wars of sword and fire?
And are there other sorrows beside the sorrows of poverty?
And are there other joys beside the joys of riches and ease?
And is there not one law for both the lion and the ox?
And is there not eternal fire, and eternal chains,
To bind the phantoms of existence from eternal life?'
Then Oothoon waited silent all the day and all the night,
But when the morn arose, her lamentation renewed.
The Daughters of Albion hear her woes, and echo back her sighs.
'Oh Urizen, creator of men, mistaken demon of Heaven,
Thy joys are tears, thy labour vain to form men to thine image!
How can one joy absorb another? Are not different joys
Holy, eternal, infinite? – and each joy is a love.
Does not the great mouth laugh at a gift, and the narrow eyelids mock
At the labour that is above payment – and wilt thou take the ape
For thy councilor, or the dog for a schoolmaster to thy children?
Does he who condemns poverty, and he who turns with abhorrence
From usury, feel the same passion, or are they moved alike?
How can the giver of gifts experience the delights of the merchant,
How the industrious citizen the pains of the husbandman?
How different far the fat-fed hireling with hollow drum,
Who buys whole cornfields into wastes, and sings upon the heath –
How different their eye and ear, how different the world to them!
With what sense does the parson claim the labour of the farmer?
What are his nets and gins and traps, and how does he surround him
With cold floods of abstraction and with forests of solitude,
To build him castles and high spires where kings and priests may dwell,
Till she who burns with youth and knows no fixed lot is bound

In spells of law to one she loathes? And must she drag the chain
Of life in weary lust? Must chilling murderous thoughts obscure
The clear heaven of her eternal spring – to bear the wintry rage
Of a harsh terror, driven to madness, bound to hold a rod
Over her shrinking shoulders all the day, and all the night
To turn the wheel of false desire, and longings that wake her womb
To the abhorréd birth of cherubs in the human form
That live a pestilence, and die a meteor, and are no more –
Till the child dwell with one he hates, and do the deed he loathes,
And the impure scourge force his seed into its unripe birth
E'er yet his eyelids can behold the arrows of the day.
　Does the whale worship at thy footsteps as the hungry dog,
Or does he scent the mountain prey because his nostrils wide
Draw in the ocean? Does his eye discern the flying cloud
As the raven's eye, or does he measure the expanse like the vulture?
Does the still spider view the cliffs where eagles hide their young,
Or does the fly rejoice because the harvest is brought in?
Does not the eagle scorn the earth and despise the treasures
　　　beneath –
But the mole knoweth what is there, and the worm shall tell it thee.
Does not the worm erect a pillar in the mouldering churchyard,
And a place of eternity in the jaws of the hungry grave?
Over his porch these words are written: "Take thy bliss oh man,
And sweet shall be thy taste and sweet thy infant joys renew."
　Infancy, fearless, lustful, happy, nestling for delight
In laps of pleasure! Innocence, honest, open, seeking
The vigorous joys of morning-light, open to virgin bliss!
Who taught thee modesty, subtle modesty, child of night and sleep?
When thou awakest wilt thou dissemble all thy secret joys,
Or wert thou not awake when all this mystery was disclosed?
Then comest thou forth a modest virgin, knowing to dissemble,
With nets found under thy night-pillow to catch virgin joy,
And brand it with the name of whore and sell it in the night
In silence, even without a whisper, and in seeming sleep.
Religious dreams and holy vespers light thy smoky fires:
Once were thy fires lighted by the eyes of honest morn.
And does my Theotormon seek this hypocrite modesty –
This knowing, artful, secret, fearful, cautious, trembling hypocrite?
Then is Oothoon a whore indeed, and all the virgin joys
Of life are harlots, and Theotormon is a sick man's dream,
And Oothoon is the crafty slave of selfish holiness!
But Oothoon is not so – a virgin filled with virgin fancies
Open to joy and to delight wherever beauty appears!

If in the morning sun I find it, there my eyes are fixed
In happy copulation; if in evening mild, wearied with work,
Sit on a bank and draw the pleasures of this free-born joy.
  The moment of desire! The moment of desire! The virgin
That pines for man shall awaken her womb to enormous joys
In the secret shadows of her chamber. The youth shut up from
The lustful joy shall forget to generate, and create an amorous image
In the shadows of his curtains, and in the folds of his silent pillow.
Are not these the places of religion, the rewards of continence,
The self-enjoyings of self-denial? Why dost thou seek religion?
Is it because acts are not lovely that thou seekest solitude,
Where the horrible darkness is impressed with reflections of desire?
Father of Jealousy, be thou accursèd from the earth!
Why hast thou taught my Theotormon this accursèd thing?
Till beauty fades from off my shoulders, darkened and cast out,
A solitary shadow wailing on the margin of non-entity.
  I cry, love! love! love! Happy, happy love, free as the mountain wind!
Can that be love that drinks another as a sponge drinks water –
That clouds with jealousy his nights, with weepings all the day,
To spin a web of age around him, grey and hoary, dark,
Till his eyes sicken at the fruit that hangs before his sight?
Such is self-love that envies all, a creeping skeleton
With lamplike eyes watching around the frozen marriage-bed.
But silken nets and traps of adamant will Oothoon spread,
And catch for thee girls of mild silver, or of furious gold!
I'll lie beside thee on a bank and view their wanton play
In lovely copulation, bliss on bliss with Theotormon.
Red as the rosy morning, lustful as the first-born beam,
Oothoon shall view his dear delight, nor e'er with jealous cloud
Come in the heaven of generous love, nor selfish blightings bring.
  Does the sun walk in glorious raiment on the secret floor
Where the cold miser spreads his gold? Or does the bright cloud drop
On his stone threshold? Does his eye behold the beam that brings
Expansion to the eye of pity? Or will he bind himself
Beside the ox to thy hard furrow? Does not that mild beam blot
The bat, the owl, the glowing tiger, and the king of night?
The sea-fowl takes the wintry blast for a covering to her limbs,
And the wild snake the pestilence to adorn him with gems and gold –
And trees and birds and beasts and men behold their eternal joy.
Arise you little glancing wings, and sing your infant joy!

Arise and drink your bliss, for every thing that lives is holy!'
  Thus every morning wails Oothoon. But Theotormon sits
Upon the margined ocean conversing with shadows dire.
The Daughters of Albion hear her woes, and echo back her sighs.

5. ROBERT SOUTHEY

Mary the Maid of the Inn (1797)

Who is she, the poor maniac, whose wildly-fixed eyes
  Seem a heart overcharged to express?
She weeps not, yet often and deeply she sighs;
She never complains, but her silence implies
  The composure of settled distress.

No aid, no compassion, the maniac will seek –
  Cold and hunger awake not her care.
Through her rags do the winds of the winter blow bleak
On her poor withered bosom, half bare, and her cheek
  Hath the deathy pale hue of despair.

Yet cheerful and happy – nor distant the day –
  Poor Mary the Maniac has been:
The traveller remembers, who journeyed this way,
No damsel so lovely, no damsel so gay,
  As Mary the Maid of the Inn!

Her cheerful address filled the guests with delight
  As she welcomed them in with a smile;
Her heart was a stranger to childish affright,
And Mary would walk by the Abbey at night
  When the wind whistled down the dark aisle.

She loved – and young Richard had settled the day,
  And she hoped to be happy for life –
But Richard was idle, and worthless, and they
Who knew him would pity poor Mary, and say
  That she was too good for his wife.

'Twas in autumn, and stormy and dark was the night,
And fast were the windows and door;
Two guests sat enjoying the fire that burnt bright,
And, smoking in silence with tranquil delight,
They listened to hear the wind roar.

''Tis pleasant', cried one, 'seated by the fireside,
To hear the wind whistle without.'
'A fine night for the Abbey!' his comrade replied,
'Methinks a man's courage would now be well tried
Who should wander the ruins about.

I myself, like a schoolboy, should tremble to hear
The hoarse ivy shake over my head,
And could fancy I saw, half persuaded by fear,
Some ugly old Abbot's white spirit appear –
For this wind might awaken the dead!'

'I'll wager a dinner', the other one cried,
'That Mary would venture there now!'
'Then wager, and lose!' with a sneer he replied,
'I'll warrant she'd fancy a ghost by her side,
And faint if she saw a white cow!'

'Will Mary this charge on her courage allow?'
His companion exclaimed with a smile –
'I shall win, for I know she will venture there now,
And earn a new bonnet by bringing a bough
From the elder that grows in the aisle.'

With fearless good humour did Mary comply,
And her way to the Abbey she bent;
The night was dark, and the wind was high,
And as hollowly howling it swept through the sky
She shivered with cold as she went,

O'er the path so well-known still proceeded the Maid
Where the Abbey rose dim on the sight;
Through the gateway she entered – she felt not afraid,
Yet the ruins were lonely and wild, and their shade
Seemed to deepen the gloom of the night.

All around her was silent, save when the rude blast
   Howled dismally round the old pile;
Over weed-covered fragments still fearless she passed,
And arrived in the innermost ruin at last
   Where the elder-tree grew in the aisle.

Well pleased did she reach it, and quickly drew near,
   And hastily gathered the bough –
When the sound of a voice seemed to rise on her ear;
She paused, and she listened, all eager to hear,
   And her heart panted painfully now.

The wind blew, the hoarse ivy shook over her head;
   She listened – nought else could she hear!
The wind ceased – her heart sunk in her bosom with dread,
For she heard in the ruins distinctly the tread
   Of footsteps approaching her near.

Behind a wide column, half breathless with fear
   She crept to conceal herself there;
That instant the moon o'er a dark cloud shone clear,
And she saw in the moonlight two ruffians appear,
   And between them a corpse did they bear.

Then Mary could feel her heart-blood curdle cold;
   Again the rough wind hurried by:
It blew off the hat of the one – and behold
Even close to the feet of poor Mary it rolled!
   She felt, and expected to die.

'Curse the hat!' he exclaims. 'Nay, come on and first hide
   The dead body', his comrade replies.
She beheld them in safety pass on by her side,
She seizes the hat – fear her courage supplied –
   And fast through the Abbey she flies.

She ran with wild speed, she rushed in at the door,
   She gazed horribly eager around;
Then her limbs could support their faint burden no more,
And exhausted and breathless she sunk on the floor,
   Unable to utter a sound.

Ere yet her pale lips could the story impart,
  For a moment the hat met her view;
Her eyes from that object convulsively start,
For – oh God – what cold horror then thrilled through her heart
  When the name of her Richard she knew!

Where the old Abbey stands, on the common hard by,
  His gibbet is now to be seen –
Not far from the road it engages the eye –
The traveller beholds it, and thinks with a sigh
  Of poor Mary, the Maid of the Inn.

6. WILLIAM WORDSWORTH

Wordsworthian Solitaries

(i) *Old Man Travelling*

(May 1797; *Lyrical Ballads* 1798)

The little hedgerow-birds
That peck along the road, regard him not;
He travels on, and in his face, his step,
His gait, is one expression. Every limb,
His look and bending figure, all bespeak
A man who does not move with pain, but moves
With thought. He is insensibly subdued
To settled quiet, he is one by whom
All effort seems forgotten – one to whom
Long patience hath such mild composure given
That patience now doth seem a thing of which
He hath no need. He is by Nature led
To peace so perfect that the young behold
With envy what the old man hardly feels.

(ii) *The Discharged Soldier*

(Feb. 1798; *The Prelude* 1850/from MS 1970)

I love to walk
Along the public way when, for the night
Deserted in its silence, it assumes
A character of deeper quietness

Than pathless solitudes. At such a time
I slowly mounted up a steep ascent
Where the road's watery surface to the ridge
Of that sharp rising glittered in the moon,
And seemed before my eyes another stream
Stealing with silent lapse to join the brook
That murmured in the valley. On I passed
Tranquil, receiving in my own despite
Amusement, as I slowly passed along,
From such near objects as from time to time
Perforce disturbed the slumber of the sense
Quiescent and disposed to sympathy –
With an exhausted mind worn out by toil
And all unworthy of the deeper joy
Which waits on distant prospect, cliff or sea,
The dark blue vault, and universe of stars.
   Thus did I steal along that silent road,
My body from the stillness drinking in
A restoration like the calm of sleep
But sweeter far. Above, before, behind,
Around me, all was peace and solitude:
I looked not round, nor did the solitude
Speak to my eye, but it was heard and felt.
Oh happy state – what beauteous pictures now
Rose in harmonious imagery! They rose
As from some distant region of my soul
And came along like dreams – yet such as left
Obscurely mingled with their passing forms
A consciousness of animal delight,
A self-possession felt in every pause
And every gentle movement of my frame.
   While thus I wandered, step by step led on,
It chanced a sudden turning of the road
Presented to my view an uncouth shape
So near that, stepping back into the shade
Of a thick hawthorn, I could mark him well,
Myself unseen. He was of stature tall,
A foot above man's common measure tall,
And lank, and upright. There was in his form
A meagre stiffness – you might almost think
That his bones wounded him. His legs were long,
So long and shapeless that I looked at them
Forgetful of the body they sustained.
His arms were long and lean; his hands were bare;

His visage, wasted though it seemed, was large
In feature; his cheeks sunken; and his mouth
Showed ghastly in the moonlight. From behind,
A milestone propped him, and his figure seemed
Half-sitting and half-standing. I could mark
That he was clad in military garb,
Though faded yet entire. His face was turned
Towards the road, yet not as if he sought
For any living thing. He appeared
Forlorn and desolate, a man cut off
From all his kind, and more than half-detached
From his own nature.
He was alone,
Had no attendant, neither dog, nor staff,
Nor knapsack – in his very dress appeared
A desolation, a simplicity,
That appertained to solitude: I think
If but a glove had dangled in his hand
It would have made him more akin to man.
Long time I scanned him, with a mingled sense
Of fear and sorrow. From his lips meanwhile
There issued murmuring sounds as if of pain
Or of uneasy thought; yet still his form
Kept the same fearful steadiness. His shadow
Lay at his feet and moved not.
In a glen
Hard by, a village stood, whose silent doors
Were visible among the scattered trees,
Scarce distant from the spot an arrow's flight.
I wished to see him move, but he remained
Fixed to his place, and still from time to time
Sent forth a murmuring voice of dead complaint,
A groan scarce audible. Yet all the while
The chained mastiff in his wooden house
Was vexed, and from among the village trees
Howled never ceasing. Not without reproach
Had I prolonged my watch, and now confirmed,
And my heart's specious cowardice subdued,
I left the shady nook where I had stood
And hailed the stranger.
From his resting-place
He rose, and, with his lean and wasted arm
In measured gesture lifted to his head,
Returned my salutation. A short while

I held discourse on things indifferent
And casual matter. He meanwhile had ceased
From all complaint – his station had resumed,
Propped by the milestone as before. And when erelong
I asked his history, he in reply
Was neither slow nor eager, but unmoved,
And with a quiet uncomplaining voice,
A stately air of mild indifference,
He told a simple fact: that he had been
A soldier, to the Tropic Isles had gone,
Whence he had landed now some ten days past;
That on his landing he had been dismissed,
And with the little strength he yet had left
Was travelling to regain his native home.
   At this I turned, and through the trees looked down
Into the village – all were gone to rest:
Nor smoke nor any taper-light appeared,
But every silent window to the moon
Shone with a yellow glitter. 'No one there',
Said I, 'is waking; we must measure back
The way which we have come. Behind yon wood
A labourer dwells, an honest man and kind;
He will not murmur should we break his rest,
And he will give you food if food you need,
And lodging for the night.' At this he stooped,
And from the ground took up an oaken staff
By me yet unobserved, a traveller's staff,
Which I suppose from his slack hand had dropped,
And (such the languor of the weary man)
Had lain till now neglected in the grass,
But not forgotten.
                        Back we turned and shaped
Our course toward the cottage. He appeared
To travel without pain, and I beheld
With ill-suppressed astonishment his tall
And ghostly figure moving at my side.
As we advanced I asked him for what cause
He tarried there, nor had demanded rest
At inn or cottage. He replied, 'In truth
My weakness made me loath to move, and here
I felt myself at ease and much relieved –
But that the village mastiff fretted me,
And every second moment rang a peal
Felt at my very heart. There was no noise,

Nor any foot abroad; I do not know
What ailed him, but it seemed as if the dog
Were howling to the murmur of the stream.'
   While thus we travelled on I did not fail
To question him of what he had endured
From war and battle and the pestilence.
He all the while was in demeanour calm,
Concise in answer: solemn and sublime
He might have seemed, but that in all he said
There was a strange half-absence and a tone
Of weakness and indifference, as of one
Remembering the importance of his theme,
But feeling it no longer. We advanced
Slowly, and ere we to the wood were come
Discourse had ceased. Together on we passed
In silence through the shades gloomy and dark,
Then turning up along an open field
We gained the cottage.
                                        At the door I knocked,
And called aloud, 'My friend, here is a man
By sickness overcome; beneath your roof
This night let him find rest, and give him food –
The service if need be I will requite.'
Assured that now my comrade would repose
In comfort, I entreated that henceforth
He would not linger in the public ways
But at the door of cottage or of inn
Demand the succour which his state required,
And told him, feeble as he was, 'twere fit
He asked relief or alms. At this reproof,
With the same ghastly mildness in his look,
He said, 'My trust is in the God of Heaven,
And in the eye of him that passes me.'
   By this the labourer had unlocked the door,
And now my comrade touched his hat again
With his lean hand, and, in a voice that seemed
To speak with a reviving interest
Till then unfelt, he thanked me. I returned
The blessing of the poor unhappy man,
And so we parted.

(iii) *The Mad Mother* (*Lyrical Ballads* 1798)

Her eyes are wild, her head is bare,
The sun has burnt her coal-black hair,
Her eyebrows have a rusty stain,
And she came far from over the main.
She has a baby on her arm,
Or else she were alone;
And underneath the haystack warm,
And on the greenwood stone,
She talked and sung the woods among,
And it was in the English tongue.

'Sweet babe, they say that I am mad,
But nay, my heart is far too glad,
And I am happy when I sing
Full many a sad and doleful thing!
Then, lovely baby, do not fear –
I pray thee have no fear of me –
But, safe as in a cradle, here,
My lovely baby, thou shalt be.
To thee I know too much I owe;
I cannot work thee any woe.

A fire was once within my brain,
And in my head a dull dull pain,
And fiendish faces one, two, three,
Hung at my breasts, and pulled at me.
But then there came a sight of joy
(It came at once to do me good),
I waked and saw my little boy,
My little boy of flesh and blood –
Oh joy for me that sight to see
For he was here, and only he!

Suck, little babe, oh suck again –
It cools my blood, it cools my brain!
Thy lips I feel them, baby, they
Draw from my heart the pain away.

Oh press me with thy little hand,
It loosens something at my chest –
About that tight and deadly band
I feel thy little fingers pressed.
The breeze I see is in the tree;
It comes to cool my babe and me.

Oh love me, love me, little boy,
Thou art thy mother's only joy,
And do not dread the waves below,
When o'er the sea-rock's edge we go.
The high crag cannot work me harm,
Nor leaping torrents when they howl:
The babe I carry on my arm,
He saves for me my precious soul!
Then happy lie, for blest am I –
Without me my sweet babe would die.

Then do not fear, my boy, for thee
Bold as a lion I will be;
And I will always be thy guide,
Through hollow snows and rivers wide.
I'll build an Indian bower, I know
The leaves that make the softest bed;
And if from me thou wilt not go,
But still be true till I am dead,
My pretty thing, then thou shalt sing,
As merry as the birds in spring.

Thy father cares not for my breast –
'Tis thine, sweet baby, there to rest,
'Tis all thy own, and if its hue
Be changed, that was so fair to view,
'Tis fair enough for thee, my dove!
My beauty, little child, is flown,
But thou wilt live with me in love –
And what if my poor cheek be brown?
'Tis well for me: thou canst not see
How pale and wan it else would be.

Dread not their taunts, my little life,
I am thy father's wedded wife,
And underneath the spreading tree
We two will live in honesty.
If his sweet boy he could forsake,
With me he never would have stayed.
From him no harm my babe can take;
But he, poor man, is wretched made,
And every day we two will pray
For him that's gone and far away.

I'll teach my boy the sweetest things;
I'll teach him how the owlet sings.
My little babe, thy lips are still,
And thou hast almost sucked thy fill –
Where art thou gone, my own dear child?
What wicked looks are those I see?
Alas, alas, that look so wild,
It never, never came from me!
If thou art mad, my pretty lad,
Then I must be for ever sad.

Oh smile on me, my little lamb,
For I thy own dear mother am!
My love for thee has well been tried –
I've sought thy father far and wide.
I know the poisons of the shade,
I know the earth-nuts fit for food;
Then, pretty dear, be not afraid;
We'll find thy father in the wood.
Now laugh and be gay, to the woods away,
And there, my babe, we'll live for aye!'

(iv) *Complaint of a Forsaken Indian Woman* (*Lyrical Ballads* 1798)

When a Northern Indian, from sickness, is unable to continue his journey with his companions, he is left behind, covered over with deer-skins, and is supplied with water, food, and fuel if the situation of the place will afford it. He is informed of the track which his companions intend to pursue, and if he is unable to follow, or overtake them, he perishes alone in the desert – unless he should have the good fortune to fall in with some other tribes of Indians. It is unnecessary to add that the females are equally, or still more, exposed to the same fate. See that very interesting work, Hearne's *Journey from Hudson's Bay to the Northern Ocean.* Wordsworth

Before I see another day,
Oh let my body die away!
In sleep I heard the northern gleams,
The stars they were among my dreams;
In sleep did I behold the skies –
I saw the crackling flashes drive,
And yet they are upon my eyes,
And yet I am alive.
Before I see another day,
Oh let my body die away!

My fire is dead – it knew no pain;
Yet is it dead, and I remain.
All stiff with ice the ashes lie;
And they are dead, and I will die.
When I was well I wished to live,
For clothes, for warmth, for food, and fire;
But they to me no joy can give,
No pleasure now, and no desire.
Then here contented will I lie –
Alone I cannot fear to die.

Alas, you might have dragged me on
Another day, a single one!
Too soon despair o'er me prevailed,
Too soon my heartless spirit failed;
When you were gone my limbs were stronger,
And oh how grievously I rue
That afterwards, a little longer,
My friends, I did not follow you!
For strong and without pain I lay,
My friends, when you were gone away.

My child, they gave thee to another,
A woman who was not thy mother!
When from my arms my babe they took,
On me how strangely did he look:

Through his whole body something ran,
A most strange something did I see,
As if he strove to be a man
That he might pull the sledge for me!
And then he stretched his arms, how wild –
Oh mercy, like a little child!

My little joy! my little pride!
In two days more I must have died –
Then do not weep and grieve for me,
I feel I must have died with thee!
Oh wind that o'er my head art flying
The way my friends their course did bend,
I should not feel the pain of dying
Could I with thee a message send.
Too soon, my friends, you went away,
For I had many things to say.

I'll follow you across the snow –
You travel heavily and slow –
In spite of all my weary pain,
I'll look upon your tents again!
My fire is dead, and snowy white
The water which beside it stood;
The wolf has come to me tonight,
And he has stolen away my food –
For ever left alone am I,
Then wherefore should I fear to die?

My journey will be shortly run,
I shall not see another sun –
I cannot lift my limbs to know
If they have any life or no.
My poor forsaken child, if I
For once could have thee close to me,
With happy heart I then would die,
And my last thoughts would happy be!
I feel my body die away,
I shall not see another day.

(v) *Michael* (lines 217–490) *Lyrical Ballads* 1800

While this good household thus were living on
From day to day, to Michael's ear there came
Distressful tidings. Long before the time
Of which I speak, the shepherd had been bound
In surety for his brother's son, a man
Of an industrious life and ample means,
But unforeseen misfortunes suddenly
Had pressed upon him, and old Michael now
Was summoned to discharge the forfeiture –
A grievous penalty, but little less
Than half his substance. This unlooked-for claim,
At the first hearing, for a moment took
More hope out of his life than he supposed
That any old man ever could have lost.
As soon as he had gathered so much strength
That he could look his trouble in the face,
It seemed that his sole refuge was to sell
A portion of his patrimonial fields.
Such was his first resolve; he thought again,
And his heart failed him.
'Isabel', said he,
Two evenings after he had heard the news,
'I have been toiling more than seventy years,
And in the open sunshine of God's love
Have we all lived, yet if these fields of ours
Should pass into a stranger's hands, I think
That I could not lie quiet in my grave.
Our lot is a hard lot; the sun itself
Has scarcely been more diligent than I,
And I have lived to be a fool at last
To my own family. An evil man
That was, and made an evil choice, if he
Were false to us; and if he were not false,
There are ten thousand to whom loss like this
Had been no sorrow. I forgive him – but
'Twere better to be dumb than to talk thus!
When I began, my purpose was to speak
Of remedies and of a cheerful hope.
Our Luke shall leave us, Isabel; the land
Shall not go from us, and it shall be free –
He shall possess it, free as is the wind

That passes over it. We have, thou knowest,
Another kinsman; he will be our friend
In this distress. He is a prosperous man,
Thriving in trade, and Luke to him shall go
And with his kinsman's help and his own thrift
He quickly will repair this loss, and then
May come again to us. If here he stay,
What can be gained?'
At this the old man paused,
And Isabel sat silent, for her mind
Was busy looking back into past times:
'There's Richard Bateman', thought she to herself,
'He was a parish-boy – at the church-door
They made a gathering for him, shillings, pence
And halfpennies, wherewith the neighbours bought
A basket, which they filled with pedlar's wares,
And with this basket on his arm the lad
Went up to London, found a master there,
Who out of many chose the trusty boy
To go and overlook his merchandise
Beyond the seas, where he grew wondrous rich
And left estates and moneys to the poor,
And at his birthplace built a chapel, floored
With marble which he sent from foreign lands.'
These thoughts, and many others of like sort,
Passed quickly through the mind of Isabel,
And her face brightened. The old man was glad,
And thus resumed: 'Well, Isabel, this scheme
These two days has been meat and drink to me:
Far more than we have lost is left us yet.
We have enough – I wish indeed that I
Were younger, but this hope is a good hope.
Make ready Luke's best garments; of the best
Buy for him more, and let us send him forth
Tomorrow, or the next day, or tonight –
If he could go, the boy should go tonight!'
Here Michael ceased, and to the fields went forth
With a light heart. The housewife for five days
Was restless morn and night, and all day long
Wrought on with her best fingers to prepare
Things needful for the journey of her son.
But Isabel was glad when Sunday came
To stop her in her work; for when she lay
By Michael's side, she for the two last nights

Heard him, how he was troubled in his sleep;
And when they rose at morning she could see
That all his hopes were gone. That day at noon
She said to Luke, while they two by themselves
Were sitting at the door: 'Thou must not go,
We have no other child but thee to lose,
None to remember – do not go away,
For if thou leave thy father he will die.'
The lad made answer with a jocund voice,
And Isabel, when she had told her fears,
Recovered heart. That evening her best fare
Did she bring forth, and all together sat
Like happy people round a Christmas fire.
   Next morning Isabel resumed her work,
And all the ensuing week the house appeared
As cheerful as a grove in spring. At length
The expected letter from their kinsman came,
With kind assurances that he would do
His utmost for the welfare of the boy –
To which requests were added that forthwith
He might be sent to him. Ten times or more
The letter was read over; Isabel
Went forth to show it to the neighbours round;
Nor was there at that time on English land
A prouder heart than Luke's. When Isabel
Had to her house returned the old man said,
'He shall depart tomorrow.' To this word
The housewife answered, talking much of things
Which, if at such short notice he should go,
Would surely be forgotten – but at length
She gave consent, and Michael was at ease.
   Near the tumultuous brook of Greenhead Gill
In that deep valley, Michael had designed
To build a sheepfold, and before he heard
The tidings of his melancholy loss
For this same purpose he had gathered up
A heap of stones, which close to the brook-side
Lay thrown together, ready for the work.
With Luke that evening thitherward he walked,
And soon as they had reached the place he stopped,
And thus the old man spake to him: 'My son,
Tomorrow thou wilt leave me. With full heart
I look upon thee, for thou art the same
That wert a promise to me ere thy birth,

And all thy life hast been my daily joy.
I will relate to thee some little part
Of our two histories – 'twill do thee good
When thou art from me, even if I should speak
Of things thou canst not know of.
                                                                After thou
First camest into the world, as it befalls
To newborn infants, thou didst sleep away
Two days, and blessings from thy father's tongue
Then fell upon thee. Day by day passed on,
And still I loved thee with increasing love.
Never to living ear came sweeter sounds
Than when I heard thee by our own fireside
First uttering without words a natural tune –
When thou, a feeding babe, didst in thy joy
Sing at thy mother's breast. Month followed month,
And in the open fields my life was passed,
And in the mountains, else I think that thou
Hadst been brought up upon thy father's knees!
But we were playmates, Luke: among these hills,
As well thou knowest, in us the old and young
Have played together! – nor with me didst thou
Lack any pleasure which a boy can know.'
   Luke had a manly heart; but at these words
He sobbed aloud. The old man grasped his hand,
And said, 'Nay, do not take it so – I see
That these are things of which I need not speak.
Even to the utmost have I been to thee
A kind and a good father; and herein
I but repay a gift which I myself
Received at others' hands, for though now old
Beyond the common life of man I still
Remember them who loved me in my youth.
Both of them sleep together – here they lived
As all their forefathers had done; and when
At length their time was come, they were not loath
To give their bodies to the family mould.
   I wished that thou shouldst live the life they lived;
But 'tis a long time to look back, my son,
And see so little gain from sixty years.
These fields were burdened when they came to me:
Till I was forty years of age, not more
Than half of my inheritance was mine.
I toiled and toiled – God blest me in my work,

And till these three weeks past the land was free.
It looks as if it never could endure
Another master! Heaven forgive me, Luke,
If I judge ill for thee, but it seems good
That thou shouldst go.'
At this the old man paused,
Then, pointing to the stones near which they stood,
Thus after a short silence he resumed:
'This was a work for us, and now, my son,
It is a work for me! But, lay one stone –
Here, lay it for me, Luke, with thine own hands –
I for the purpose brought thee to this place.
Nay, boy, be of good hope, we both may live
To see a better day! At eighty-four
I still am strong and stout: do thou thy part,
I will do mine. I will begin again
With many tasks that were resigned to thee:
Up to the heights, and in among the storms,
Will I without thee go again, and do
All works which I was wont to do alone
Before I knew thy face.
Heaven bless thee,
Thy heart these two weeks has been beating fast
With many hopes. It should be so – yes, yes –
I knew that thou couldst never have a wish
To leave me, Luke. Thou hast been bound to me
Only by links of love! When thou art gone
What will be left to us? – but I forget
My purposes. Lay now the corner-stone
As I requested, and hereafter, Luke,
When thou art gone away, should evil men
Be thy companions, let this sheepfold be
Thy anchor and thy shield. Amid all fear,
And all temptation, let it be to thee
An emblem of the life thy fathers lived,
Who, being innocent, did for that cause
Bestir them in good deeds. Now, fare thee well.
When thou returnst, thou in this place wilt see
A work which is not here. A covenant
'Twill be between us – but whatever fate
Befall thee, I shall love thee to the last,
And bear thy memory with me to the grave.'
The shepherd ended here, and Luke stooped down
And, as his father had requested, laid

The first stone of the sheepfold. At the sight
The old man's grief broke from him. To his heart
He pressed his son; he kissed him and he wept,
And to the house together they returned.
Next morning, as had been resolved, the boy
Began his journey; and when he had reached
The public way he put on a bold face,
And all the neighbours as he passed their doors
Came forth with wishes and with farewell prayers
That followed him till he was out of sight.
    A good report did from their kinsman come
Of Luke and his well-doing; and the boy
Wrote loving letters, full of wondrous news,
Which, as the housewife phrased it, were throughout
The prettiest letters that were ever seen!
Both parents read them with rejoicing hearts.
So many months passed on, and once again
The shepherd went about his daily work
With confident and cheerful thoughts; and now
Sometimes when he could find a leisure hour
He to that valley took his way, and there
Wrought at the sheepfold. Meantime Luke began
To slacken in his duty, and at length
He in the dissolute city gave himself
To evil courses. Ignominy and shame
Fell on him, so that he was driven at last
To seek a hiding-place beyond the seas.
    There is a comfort in the strength of love,
'Twill make a thing endurable which else
Would break the heart – old Michael found it so.
I have conversed with more than one who well
Remember the old man, and what he was
Years after he had heard this heavy news.
His bodily frame had been from youth to age
Of an unusual strength. Among the rocks
He went, and still looked up upon the sun
And listened to the wind, and, as before,
Performed all kinds of labour for his sheep
And for the land, his small inheritance.
And to that hollow dell from time to time
Did he repair, to build the fold of which
His flock had need. 'Tis not forgotten yet
The pity which was then in every heart

For the old man, and 'tis believed by all
That many and many a day he thither went,
And never lifted up a single stone.
   There by the sheepfold sometimes was he seen
Sitting alone, with that his faithful dog
(Then old) beside him, lying at his feet.
The length of full seven years from time to time
He at the building of this sheepfold wrought,
And left the work unfinished when he died.
Three years, or little more, did Isabel
Survive her husband; at her death the estate
Was sold, and went into a stranger's hand.
The cottage which was named the Evening Star
Is gone; the ploughshare has been through the ground
On which it stood. Great changes have been wrought
In all the neighbourhood; yet the oak is left
That grew beside their door, and the remains
Of the unfinished sheepfold may be seen
Beside the boisterous brook of Greenhead Gill.

(vi) *The Leech-Gatherer* (spring 1802; publ. 1807)

There was a roaring in the wind all night,
The rain came heavily and fell in floods,
But now the sun is rising calm and bright,
The birds are singing in the distant woods,
Over his own sweet voice the stock-dove broods,
The jay makes answer as the magpie chatters,
And all the air is filled with pleasant noise of waters.

All things that love the sun are out of doors,
The sky rejoices in the morning's birth,
The grass is bright with raindrops; on the moors
The hare is running races in her mirth,
And with her feet she from the plashy earth
Raises a mist which, glittering in the sun,
Runs with her all the way, wherever she doth run.

I was a traveller then upon the moor:
I saw the hare that raced about with joy,
I heard the woods and distant waters roar –
Or heard them not – as happy as a boy;

The pleasant season did my heart employ;
My old remembrances went from me wholly,
And all the ways of men, so vain and melancholy.

But, as it sometimes chanceth – from the might
Of joy in minds that can no farther go –
As high as we have mounted in delight
In our dejection do we sink as low.
To me that morning did it happen so,
And fears and fancies thick upon me came:
Dim sadness, and blind thoughts I knew not, nor could name.

I heard the skylark singing in the sky
And I bethought me of the playful hare:
'Even such a happy child of earth am I –
Even as these blissful creatures do I fare!
Far from the world I walk, and from all care;
But there may come another day to me
Solitude, pain of heart, distress and poverty.

My whole life have I lived in pleasant thought
As if life's business were a summer mood,
As if all needful things would come unsought
To genial faith, still rich in genial good –
But how can he expect that others should
Build for him, sow for him, and at his call
Love him, who for himself will take no heed at all?'

I thought of Chatterton – the marvellous boy,
The sleepless soul that perished in its pride –
Of him who walked in glory and in joy
Behind his plough upon the mountain's side.
By our own spirits are we deified!
We poets in our youth begin in gladness,
But thereof comes in the end despondency and madness.

Now, whether it were by peculiar grace
(A leading from above, a something given),
Yet it befell that in this lonely place
When up and down my fancy thus was driven,
And I with these untoward thoughts had striven,
I saw a man before me unawares;
The oldest man he seemed that ever wore grey hairs.

My course I stopped as soon as I espied
The old man in that naked wilderness;
Close by a pond – upon the further side –
He stood alone a minute's space, I guess.
I watched him, he continuing motionless;
To the pool's further margin then I drew,
He being all the while before me full in view.

As a huge stone is sometimes seen to lie
Couched on the bald top of an eminence
(Wonder to all who do the same espy
By what means it could thither come, and whence)
So that it seems a thing endued with sense,
Like a sea-beast crawled forth, which on a shelf
Of rock or sand reposeth, there to sun itself –

Such seemed this man, not all alive nor dead,
Nor all asleep, in his extreme old age.
His body was bent double, feet and head
Coming together in their pilgrimage
As if some dire constraint of pain, or rage
Of sickness, felt by him in times long past,
A more than human weight upon his frame had cast.

Himself he propped – his body, limbs, and face –
Upon a long grey staff of shaven wood;
And still, as I drew near with gentle pace,
Beside the little pond or moorish flood
Motionless as a cloud the old man stood,
That heareth not the loud winds when they call,
And moveth altogether, if it move at all.

At length – himself unsettling – he the pond
Stirred with his staff, and fixedly did look
Upon the muddy water which he conned
As if he had been reading in a book;
And now such freedom as I could I took
And, drawing to his side, to him did say,
'This morning gives us promise of a glorious day.'

A gentle answer did the old man make
In courteous speech which forth he slowly drew,
And him with further words I thus bespake:
'What kind of work is that which you pursue? –

This is a lonesome place for one like you.'
He answered me with pleasure and surprise,
And there was, while he spake, a fire about his eyes.

His words came feebly from a feeble chest,
Yet each in solemn order followed each
With something of a lofty utterance dressed –
Choice word and measured phrase, above the reach
Of ordinary men – a stately speech
Such as grave livers do in Scotland use,
Religious men, who give to God and man their dues.

He told me that he to this pond had come
To gather leeches, being old and poor
(Employment hazardous and wearisome!)
And he had many hardships to endure.
From pond to pond he roamed, from moor to moor,
Housing, with God's good help, by choice or chance;
And in this way he gained an honest maintenance.

The old man still stood talking at my side,
But now his voice to me was like a stream
Scarce heard – nor word from word could I divide –
And the whole body of the man did seem
Like one whom I had met with in a dream,
Or like a man from some far region sent
To give me human strength, and strong admonishment.

My former thoughts returned: the fear that kills,
The hope that is unwilling to be fed –
Cold, pain, and labour, and all fleshly ills,
And mighty poets in their misery dead.
And now, not knowing what the old man had said,
My question eagerly did I renew:
'How is it that you live, and what is it you do?'

He with a smile did then his words repeat,
And said that, gathering leeches far and wide
He travelled, stirring thus about his feet
The waters of the ponds where they abide:
'Once I could meet with them on every side,
But they have dwindled long by slow decay;
Yet still I persevere, and find them where I may.'

While he was talking thus, the lonely place,
The old man's shape and speech, all troubled me;
In my mind's eye I seemed to see him pace
About the weary moors continually,
Wandering about alone and silently.
While I these thoughts within myself pursued,
He, having made a pause, the same discourse renewed,

And soon with this he other matter blended –
Cheerfully uttered, with demeanour kind,
But stately in the main – and when he ended
I could have laughed myself to scorn to find
In that decrepit man so firm a mind.
'God', said I, 'be my help and stay secure,
I'll think of the leech-gatherer on the lonely moor!'

(vii) The London Beggar

(1805 *Prelude* VII, 594–622) publ. 1850/from MS 1926

How often in the overflowing streets
Have I gone forwards with the crowd, and said
Unto myself 'The face of everyone
That passes by me is a mystery!'
Thus have I looked, nor ceased to look, oppressed
By thoughts of what and whither, when and how,
Until the shapes before my eyes became
A second-sight procession such as glides
Over still mountains, or appears in dreams,
And all the ballast of familiar life
(The present and the past, hope, fear, all stays –
All laws – of acting, thinking, speaking man)
Went from me, neither knowing me, nor known.
And once, far travelled in such mood, beyond
The reach of common indications, lost
Amid the moving pageant, 'twas my chance
Abruptly to be smitten with the view
Of a blind beggar, who, with upright face,
Stood propped against a wall, upon his chest
Wearing a written paper to explain
The story of the man, and who he was.
My mind did at this spectacle turn round
As with the might of waters, and it seemed
To me that in this label was a type

Or emblem of the utmost that we know
Both of ourselves and of the universe.
And on the shape of this unmoving man,
His fixéd face and sightless eyes, I looked
As if admonished from another world.

7. SAMUEL TAYLOR COLERIDGE

'Alone, Alone'

(i) *The Rime of the Ancyent Marinere, In Seven Parts* (*Lyrical Ballads* 1798)

Argument: How a Ship having passed the Line was driven by Storms to the cold Country towards the South Pole; and how from thence she made her course to the tropical Latitude of the Great Pacific Ocean; and of the strange things that befell; and in what manner the Ancyent Marinere came back to his own Country.

I

It is an ancyent Marinere,
   And he stoppeth one of three:
'By thy long grey beard and thy glittering eye
   Now wherefore stoppest me?

The Bridegroom's doors are opened wide
   And I am next of kin;
The Guests are met, the Feast is set –
   May'st hear the merry din.'

But still he holds the wedding-guest –
   'There was a Ship', quoth he –
'Nay, if thou'st got a laughsome tale,
   Marinere! come with me.'

He holds him with his skinny hand,
   Quoth he, 'There was a Ship' –
'Now get thee hence, thou grey-beard Loon!
   Or my Staff shall make thee skip.'

He holds him with his glittering eye –
   The wedding guest stood still
And listens like a three year's child;
   The Marinere hath his will.

The wedding-guest sate on a stone,
   He cannot chuse but hear –
And thus spake on that ancyent man,
   The bright-eyed Marinere:

'The Ship was cheered, the Harbour cleared –
   Merrily did we drop
Below the Kirk, below the Hill,
   Below the Light-house top.

The Sun came up upon the left,
   Out of the Sea came he;
And he shone bright, and on the right
   Went down into the Sea.

Higher and higher every day,
   Till over the mast at noon' –
The wedding-guest here beat his breast,
   For he heard the loud bassoon.

The Bride hath paced into the Hall,
   Red as a rose is she;
Nodding their heads before her goes
   The merry Minstralsy.

The wedding-guest he beat his breast,
   Yet he cannot chuse but hear –
And thus spake on that ancyent Man,
   The bright-eyed Marinere:

'Listen, Stranger! Storm and Wind,
   A Wind and Tempest strong!
For days and weeks it played us freaks –
   Like Chaff we drove along.

Listen, Stranger! Mist and Snow,
   And it grew wondrous cauld:
And Ice mast-high came floating by
   As green as Emerauld.

And through the drifts the snowy clifts
   Did send a dismal sheen;
Ne shapes of men ne beasts we ken –
   The Ice was all between.

The Ice was here, the Ice was there,
   The Ice was all around:
It cracked and growled, and roared and howled –
   Like noises of a swound.

At length did cross an Albatross,
   Thorough the Fog it came;
And an it were a Christian Soul,
   We hailed it in God's name.

The Marineres gave it biscuit-worms,
   And round and round it flew;
The Ice did split with a Thunder-fit,
   The Helmsman steered us through.

And a good south wind sprung up behind,
   The Albatross did follow,
And every day for food or play
   Came to the Marinere's hollo!

In mist or cloud on mast or shroud
   It perched for vespers nine,
Whiles all the night through fog smoke-white
   Glimmered the white moon-shine.'

'God save thee, ancyent Marinere!
   From the fiends that plague thee thus –
Why look'st thou so?' 'With my cross-bow
   I shot the Albatross.

II

The Sun came up upon the right,
   Out of the Sea came he;
And broad as a weft upon the left
   Went down into the Sea.

And the good south wind still blew behind,
   But no sweet Bird did follow
Ne any day for food or play
   Came to the Marinere's hollo!

And I had done an hellish thing
   And it would work 'em woe:
For all averred, I had killed the Bird
   That made the Breeze to blow.

Ne dim ne red, like God's own head,
   The glorious Sun uprist;
Then all averred, I had killed the Bird
   That brought the fog and mist.
'Twas right, said they, such birds to slay
   That bring the fog and mist.

The breezes blew, the white foam flew,
   The furrow followed free:
We were the first that ever burst
   Into that silent Sea.

Down dropt the breeze, the Sails dropt down,
   'Twas sad as sad could be
And we did speak only to break
   The silence of the Sea.

All in a hot and copper sky
   The bloody sun at noon,
Right up above the mast did stand,
   No bigger than the moon.

Day after day, day after day,
   We stuck, ne breath ne motion,
As idle as a painted Ship
   Upon a painted Ocean.

Water, water, every where
   And all the boards did shrink;
Water, water, every where,
   Ne any drop to drink.

The very deeps did rot: O Christ!
   That ever this should be!
Yea, slimy things did crawl with legs
   Upon the slimy Sea.

About, about, in reel and rout
   The Death-fires danced at night;
The water, like a witch's oils,
   Burnt green and blue and white.

And some in dreams assuréd were
   Of the Spirit that plagued us so:
Nine fathom deep he had followed us
   From the Land of Mist and Snow.

And every tongue through utter drouth
   Was withered at the root;
We could not speak – no more than if
   We had been choked with soot.

Ah wel-a-day! what evil looks
   Had I from old and young;
Instead of the Cross the Albatross
   About my neck was hung.

III

I saw a something in the Sky
   No bigger than my fist;
At first it seemed a little speck
   And then it seemed a mist:
It moved and moved, and took at last
   A certain shape, I wist.

A speck, a mist, a shape, I wist!
   And still it nered and nered;
And, an it dodged a water-sprite,
   It plunged and tacked and veered.

With throat unslacked with black lips baked
   Ne could we laugh, ne wail:
Then while through drouth all dumb they stood
I bit my arm and sucked the blood
   And cryed, "A sail! a sail!"

With throat unslacked, with black lips baked
   Agape they heared me call:
Gramercy! they for joy did grin
And all at once their breath drew in
   As they were drinking all.

She doth not tack from side to side –
   Hither to work us weal
Withouten wind, withouten tide
   She steddies with upright keel.

The western wave was all a flame,
   The day was well nigh done!
Almost upon the western wave
   Rested the broad bright Sun,
When that strange shape drove suddenly
   Betwixt us and the Sun.

And strait the Sun was flecked with bars
   (Heaven's mother send us grace)
As if through a dungeon grate he peered
   With broad and burning face.

Alas! (thought I, and my heart beat loud)
   How fast she neres and neres!
Are those her Sails that glance in the Sun
   Like restless gossameres?

Are these her naked ribs, which flecked
   The sun that did behind them peer?
And are these two all, all the crew,
   That woman and her fleshless *Pheere*?

His bones were black with many a crack,
   All black and bare, I ween;
Jet-black and bare, save where with rust
Of mouldy damps and charnel crust
   They're patched with purple and green.

Her lips are red, *her* looks are free,
   Her locks are yellow as gold:
Her skin is as white as leprosy,
And she is far liker Death than he;
   Her flesh makes the still air cold.

The naked Hulk alongside came
   And the Twain were playing dice;
"The Game is done! I've won, I've won!"
   Quoth she, and whistled thrice.

A gust of wind sterte up behind
   And whistled through his bones –
Through the holes of his eyes and the hole of his mouth
   Half-whistles and half-groans.

With never a whisper in the Sea
   Off darts the Spectre-ship;
While clombe above the Eastern bar
The hornéd Moon, with one bright Star
   Almost atween the tips.

One after one by the hornéd Moon
   (Listen, O Stranger! to me)
Each turned his face with a ghastly pang
   And cursed me with his ee.

Four times fifty living men,
   With never a sigh or groan,
With heavy thump, a lifeless lump
   They dropped down one by one.

Their souls did from their bodies fly –
   They fled to bliss or woe –
And every soul it passed me by,
   Like the whiz of my Cross-bow.'

IV

'I fear thee, ancyent Marinere!
   I fear thy skinny hand;
And thou art long and lank and brown
   As is the ribbed Sea-sand.

I fear thee and thy glittering eye
   And thy skinny hand so brown' –
'Fear not, fear not, thou wedding guest!
   This body dropt not down.

Alone, alone, all all alone
   Alone on the wide wide Sea;
And Christ would take no pity on
   My soul in agony.

The many men so beautiful,
   And they all dead did lie!
And a million million slimy things
   Lived on – and so did I.

I looked upon the rotting Sea,
   And drew my eyes away;
I looked upon the eldritch deck,
   And there the dead men lay.

I looked to Heaven, and tryed to pray;
   But or ever a prayer had gusht,
A wicked whisper came and made
   My heart as dry as dust.

I closed my lids and kept them close,
   Till the balls like pulses beat;
For the sky and the sea, and the sea and the sky
Lay like a load on my weary eye,
   And the dead were at my feet.

The cold sweat melted from their limbs,
   Ne rot, ne reek did they;
The look with which they looked on me,
   Had never passed away.

An orphan's curse would drag to Hell
   A spirit from on high:
But O! more horrible than that
   Is the curse in a dead man's eye!
Seven days, seven nights I saw that curse,
   And yet I could not die.

The moving Moon went up the sky
   And no where did abide:
Softly she was going up
   And a star or two beside –

Her beams bemocked the sultry main
   Like morning frosts yspread;
But where the ship's huge shadow lay,
The charméd water burnt alway
   A still and awful red.

Beyond the shadow of the ship
   I watched the water-snakes:
They moved in tracks of shining white;
And when they reared, the elfish light
   Fell off in hoary flakes.

Within the shadow of the ship
   I watched their rich attire:
Blue, glossy green, and velvet black
They coiled and swam; and every track
   Was a flash of golden fire.

O happy living things! no tongue
   Their beauty might declare:
A spring of love gusht from my heart,
   And I blest them unaware!
Sure my kind saint took pity on me,
   And I blest them unaware.

The self-same moment I could pray;
   And from my neck so free
The Albatross fell off, and sank
   Like lead into the sea.

V

O sleep, it is a gentle thing
   Beloved from pole to pole!
To Mary-queen the praise be yeven
She sent the gentle sleep from heaven
   That slid into my soul.

The silly buckets on the deck
   That had so long remained,
I dreamt that they were filled with dew
   And when I awoke it rained.

My lips were wet, my throat was cold,
   My garments all were dank;
Sure I had drunken in my dreams
   And still my body drank.

I moved and could not feel my limbs,
   I was so light, almost
I thought that I had died in sleep,
   And was a blesséd Ghost.

The roaring wind! it roared far off,
   It did not come anear;
But with its sound it shook the sails
   That were so thin and sere.

The upper air bursts into life,
   And a hundred fire-flags sheen
To and fro they are hurried about;
And to and fro, and in and out
   The stars dance on between.

The coming wind doth roar more loud;
   The sails do sigh, like sedge:
The rain pours down from one black cloud
   And the Moon is at its edge.

Hark! hark! the thick black cloud is cleft,
   And the Moon is at its side:
Like waters shot from some high crag,
The lightning falls with never a jag,
   A river steep and wide.

The strong wind reached the ship: it roared
   And dropped down, like a stone!
Beneath the lightning and the moon
   The dead men gave a groan.

They groaned, they stirred, they all uprose,
   Ne spake, ne moved their eyes:
It had been strange, even in a dream
   To have seen those dead men rise.

The helmsman steered, the ship moved on;
   Yet never a breeze up-blew;
The Marineres all 'gan work the ropes,
   Where they were wont to do:
They raised their limbs like lifeless tools –
   We were a ghastly crew.

The body of my brother's son
   Stood by me knee to knee:
The body and I pulled at one rope,
   But he said nought to me –
And I quaked to think of my own voice
   How frightful it would be!

The day-light dawned – they dropped their arms,
   And clustered round the mast:
Sweet sounds rose slowly through their mouths
   And from their bodies passed.

Around, around, flew each sweet sound,
   Then darted to the sun:
Slowly the sounds came back again
   Now mixed, now one by one.

Sometimes a-dropping from the sky
   I heard the Lavrock sing;
Sometimes all little birds that are
How they seemed to fill the sea and air
   With their sweet jargoning,

And now 'twas like all instruments,
   Now like a lonely flute;
And now it is an angel's song
   That makes the heavens be mute.

It ceased: yet still the sails made on
   A pleasant noise till noon,
A noise like of a hidden brook
   In the leafy month of June,
That to the sleeping woods all night
   Singeth a quiet tune.

Listen, O listen, thou Wedding-guest!'
  'Marinere! thou hast thy will;
For that, which comes out of thine eye, doth make
  My body and soul to be still.'

'Never sadder tale was told
  To a man of woman born:
Sadder and wiser thou wedding-guest!
  Thou'lt rise to morrow morn.

Never sadder tale was heard
  By a man of woman born:
The Marineres all returned to work
  As silent as beforne.

The Marineres all 'gan pull the ropes,
  But look at me they n'old:
Thought I, I am as thin as air –
  They cannot me behold.

Till noon we silently sailed on
  Yet never a breeze did breathe:
Slowly and smoothly went the ship
  Moved onward from beneath.

Under the keel nine fathom deep
  From the land of mist and snow
The spirit slid: and it was He
  That made the Ship to go.
The sails at noon left off their tune
  And the Ship stood still also.

The sun right up above the mast
  Had fixed her to the ocean:
But in a minute she 'gan stir
  With a short uneasy motion –
Backwards and forwards half her length
  With a short uneasy motion.

Then, like a pawing horse let go,
  She made a sudden bound;
It flung the blood into my head,
  And I fell into a swound.

How long in that same fit I lay,
   I have not to declare;
But ere my living life returned,
I heard and in my soul discerned
   Two voices in the air,

"Is it he?" quoth one, "Is this the man?
   By him who died on cross,
With his cruel bow he layed full low
   The harmless Albatross.

The spirit who bideth by himself
   In the land of mist and snow,
He loved the bird that loved the man
   Who shot him with his bow."

The other was a softer voice,
   As soft as honey-dew;
Quoth he, "The man hath penance done,
   And penance more will do."

VI

First Voice.
"But tell me, tell me! speak again,
   Thy soft response renewing –
What makes that ship drive on so fast?
   What is the Ocean doing?"

Second Voice.
"Still as a Slave before his Lord,
   The Ocean hath no blast:
His great bright eye most silently
   Up to the moon is cast

If he may know which way to go,
   For she guides him smooth or grim.
See, brother, see! how graciously
   She looketh down on him."

First Voice.
"But why drives on that ship so fast
   Withouten wave or wind?"
Second Voice.
"The air is cut away before,

And closes from behind.
Fly, brother, fly! more high, more high,
Or we shall be belated;
For slow and slow that ship will go,
When the Marinere's trance is abated."

I woke, and we were sailing on
As in a gentle weather:
'Twas night, calm night, the moon was high;
The dead men stood together.

All stood together on the deck,
For a charnel-dungeon fitter;
All fixed on me their stony eyes
That in the moon did glitter.

The pang, the curse, with which they died,
Had never passed away:
I could not draw my een from theirs
Ne turn them up to pray.

And in its time the spell was snapt,
And I could move my een:
I looked far-forth, but little saw
Of what might else be seen,

Like one that on a lonely road
Doth walk in fear and dread,
And having once turned round, walks on
And turns no more his head
Because he knows, a frightful fiend
Doth close behind him tread.

But soon there breathed a wind on me,
Ne sound ne motion made:
Its path was not upon the sea
In ripple or in shade.

It raised my hair, it fanned my cheek,
Like a meadow-gale of spring –
It mingled strangely with my fears,
Yet it felt like a welcoming.

Swiftly, swiftly flew the ship,
   Yet she sailed softly too:
Sweetly, sweetly blew the breeze –
   On me alone it blew.

O dream of joy! is this indeed
   The light-house top I see?
Is this the Hill? Is this the Kirk?
   Is this mine own countree?

We drifted o'er the Harbour-bar,
   And I with sobs did pray –
"O let me be awake, my God!
   Or let me sleep alway!"

The harbour-bay was clear as glass,
   So smoothly it was strewn!
And on the bay the moonlight lay,
   And the shadow of the moon.

The moonlight bay was white all o'er,
   Till rising from the same,
Full many shapes, that shadows were,
   Like as of torches came.

A little distance from the prow
   Those dark-red shadows were;
But soon I saw that my own flesh
   Was red as in a glare.

I turned my head in fear and dread,
   And by the holy rood,
The bodies had advanced, and now
   Before the mast they stood.

They lifted up their stiff right arms,
   They held them strait and tight;
And each right-arm burnt like a torch,
   A torch that's borne upright.
Their stony eye-balls glittered on
   In the red and smoky light.

I prayed and turned my head away
   Forth looking as before.
There was no breeze upon the bay,
   No wave against the shore.

The rock shone bright, the kirk no less
   That stands above the rock;
The moonlight steeped in silentness
   The steady weathercock.

And the bay was white with silent light,
   Till rising from the same
Full many shapes, that shadows were,
   In crimson colours came.

A little distance from the prow
   Those crimson shadows were:
I turned my eyes upon the deck –
   O Christ! what saw I there?

Each corse lay flat, lifeless and flat;
   And by the Holy rood
A man all light, a seraph-man,
   On every corse there stood.

This seraph-band, each waved his hand –
   It was a heavenly sight –
They stood as signals to the land,
   Each one a lovely light:

This seraph-band, each waved his hand,
   No voice did they impart –
No voice; but O! the silence sank,
   Like music on my heart.

Eftsones I heard the dash of oars,
   I heard the pilot's cheer;
My head was turned perforce away
   And I saw a boat appear.

Then vanished all the lovely lights;
   The bodies rose anew:
With silent pace, each to his place,
   Came back the ghastly crew.
The wind, that shade nor motion made,
   On me alone it blew.

The pilot, and the pilot's boy
   I heard them coming fast:
Dear Lord in Heaven! it was a joy,
   The dead men could not blast.

I saw a third – I heard his voice:
   It is the Hermit good!
He singeth loud his godly hymns
   That he makes in the wood.
He'll shrieve my soul, he'll wash away
   The Albatross's blood.

VII

This Hermit good lives in that wood
   Which slopes down to the Sea.
How loudly his sweet voice he rears!
He loves to talk with Marineres
   That come from a far Countree.

He kneels at morn and noon and eve –
   He hath a cushion plump:
It is the moss, that wholly hides
   The rotted old Oak-stump.

The Skiff-boat neerd, I heard them talk:
   "Why, this is strange, I trow!
Where are those lights so many and fair
   That signal made but now?"

"Strange, by my faith!" the Hermit said –
   "And they answered not our cheer.
The planks look warped, and see those sails
   How thin they are and sere!
I never saw aught like to them
   Unless perchance it were

The skeletons of leaves that lag
   My forest brook along:
When the Ivy-tod is heavy with snow,
And the Owlet whoops to the wolf below
   That eats the she-wolf's young."

"Dear Lord! it has a fiendish look",
   The Pilot made reply,
"I am a-feared." "Push on, push on!"
   Said the Hermit cheerily.

The Boat came closer to the Ship,
   But I ne spake ne stirred!
The Boat came close beneath the Ship,
   And strait a sound was heard!

Under the water it rumbled on,
   Still louder and more dread:
It reached the Ship, it split the bay;
   The Ship went down like lead.

Stunned by that loud and dreadful sound,
   Which sky and ocean smote,
Like one that hath been seven days drowned
   My body lay afloat,
But, swift as dreams, myself I found
   Within the Pilot's boat.

Upon the whirl, where sank the Ship,
   The boat spun round and round;
And all was still, save that the hill
   Was telling of the sound.

I moved my lips; the Pilot shrieked
   And fell down in a fit;
The Holy Hermit raised his eyes
   And prayed where he did sit.

I took the oars – the Pilot's boy,
   Who now doth crazy go,
Laughed loud and long, and all the while
   His eyes went to and fro:
"Ha! ha!" quoth he "full plain I see
   The devil knows how to row."

And now all in mine own Countree
   I stood on the firm land!
The Hermit stepped forth from the boat,
   And scarcely he could stand.

"O shrieve me, shrieve me, holy Man!"
   The Hermit crossed his brow –
"Say quick", quoth he, "I bid thee say
   What manner of man art thou?"

Forthwith this frame of mine was wrenched
   With a woeful agony,
Which forced me to begin my tale
   And then it left me free.

Since then at an uncertain hour,
   Now oftimes and now fewer,
That anguish comes and makes me tell
   My ghastly aventure.

I pass, like night, from land to land;
   I have strange power of speech;
The moment that his face I see
I know the man that must hear me –
   To him my tale I teach.

What loud uproar bursts from that door!
   The Wedding-guests are there,
But in the Garden-bower the Bride
   And Bride-maids singing are –
And hark the little Vesper-bell
   Which biddeth me to prayer.

O Wedding-guest! this soul hath been
   Alone on a wide wide sea:
So lonely 'twas, that God himself
   Scarce seemėd there to be.

O sweeter than the Marriage-feast,
   'Tis sweeter far to me
To walk together to the Kirk
   With a goodly company.

To walk together to the Kirk
   And all together pray,
While each to his great father bends,
Old men, and babes, and loving friends,
   And Youths, and Maidens gay.

Farewell, farewell! but this I tell
   To thee, thou Wedding-guest!
He prayeth well who loveth well
   Both man and bird and beast.

He prayeth best who loveth best,
   All things both great and small:
For the dear God, who loveth us,
   He made and loveth all.'

The Marinere, whose eye is bright,
   Whose beard with age is hoar,
Is gone; and now the Wedding-guest
   Turned from the bridegroom's door.

He went, like one that hath been stunned
   And is of sense forlorn:
A sadder and a wiser man
   He rose the morrow morn.

(ii) *Pains of Sleep* (Sept. 1803; publ. 1816)

Ere on my bed my limbs I lay,
It hath not been my use to pray
With moving lips or bended knees;
But silently, by slow degrees,
My spirit I to love compose,
In humble trust mine eyelids close
With reverential resignation,
No wish conceived, no thought expressed,
Only a sense of supplication –
A sense o'er all my soul impressed
That I am weak, yet not unblest,
Since in me, round me, everywhere
Eternal Strength and Wisdom are.

But yester-night I prayed aloud
In anguish and in agony,
Upstarting from the fiendish crowd
Of shapes and thoughts that tortured me:
A lurid light, a trampling throng,
Sense of intolerable wrong,
And whom I scorned, those only strong –
Thirst of revenge, the powerless will
Still baffled, and yet burning still!
Desire with loathing strangely mixed
On wild or hateful objects fixed!
Fantastic passions! maddening brawl!
And shame and terror over all!
Deeds to be hid which were not hid,
Which all confused I could not know
Whether I suffered, or I did;
For all seemed guilt, remorse or woe –
My own or others' – still the same
Life-stifling fear, soul-stifling shame!
So two nights passed. The night's dismay
Saddened and stunned the coming day:
Sleep, the wide blessing, seemed to me
Distemper's worst calamity.
The third night, when my own loud scream
Had waked me from the fiendish dream,
O'ercome with sufferings strange and wild
I wept as I had been a child;
And having thus by tears subdued
My anguish to a milder mood,
Such punishments, I said, were due
To natures deepliest stained with sin
(For aye entempesting anew
The unfathomable Hell within),
The horror of their deeds to view,
To know and loathe, yet wish and do!
Such griefs with such men well agree,
But wherefore, wherefore fall on me?
To be beloved is all I need,
And whom I love, I love indeed.

8. THOMAS CAMPBELL

Lord Ullin's Daughter (1809)

A chieftain to the Highlands bound
  Cries, 'Boatman, do not tarry!
And I'll give thee a silver pound
  To row us o'er the ferry.'

'Now who be ye would cross Lochgyle,
  This dark and stormy water?'
'Oh, I'm the chief of Ulva's isle,
  And this Lord Ullin's daughter.

'And fast before her father's men
  Three days we've fled together,
For should he find us in the glen
  My blood would stain the heather!

His horsemen hard behind us ride;
  Should they our steps discover,
Then who will cheer my bonny bride
  When they have slain her lover?'

Outspoke the hardy Highland wight,
  'I'll go, my chief! I'm ready –
It is not for your silver bright,
  But for your winsome lady!

And, by my word! the bonny bird
  In danger shall not tarry;
So, though the waves are raging white,
  I'll row you o'er the ferry!'

By this the storm grew loud apace,
  The water-wraith was shrieking;
And in the scowl of heaven each face
  Grew dark as they were speaking.

But still, as wilder blew the wind,
  And as the night grew drearer,
Adown the glen rode armèd men,
  Their trampling sounded nearer.

'O haste thee, haste!' the lady cries,
'Though tempests round us gather,
I'll meet the raging of the skies
But not an angry father!'

The boat has left a stormy land,
A stormy sea before her,
When, oh! too strong for human hand,
The tempest gathered o'er her.

And still they rowed amidst the roar
Of waters fast prevailing:
Lord Ullin reached that fatal shore,
His wrath was changed to wailing!

For sore dismayed, through storm and shade,
His child he did discover:
One lovely hand she stretched for aid,
And one was round her lover.

'Come back! come back!' he cried in grief
Across the stormy water,
'And I'll forgive your Highland chief,
My daughter! oh my daughter!'

'Twas vain – the loud waves lashed the shore,
Return or aid preventing;
The waters wild went o'er his child,
And he was left lamenting.

9. MARY BRYAN

The Visit (lines 45–126) 1815

'Here', said my guide,
'The poor crazed inmates of yon mansion stray;
Their keepers watch their moody wanderings,
Yet oft in these wild heights unseen they lurk
Eluding all research.' I trembled at the tale –
Oh frightful haunts! – lest a strange form,
With sudden rage and demon strength possessed,
Swift from yon jutting crag with fell intent

And horrid yell might rush, and hurl me down
The immense below. Urged by these terrors, soon
We gained the sullen dwelling – drear retreat!
The massy doors, the iron-grated lights,
Appalled with very strength – I trembled there
E'en in the terrible security.
    Then fearful wrecks of storms I ill endured
Unmeet to greet a sympathizing guest:
The shriek, the long loud laugh, the desperate din
I scarce forbore to join. I clasped my dewy brows
Insensate of the pressure, chilling cold.
I thought, 'Or death, or madness, soon will seize
My trembling frame, and I shall never more
Behold aught fair, or good, or blest, or dear.'
Instant I clasped them all! Oh, what a change
To love, and hope, and joy, one tender look –
One precious word of recognition – gave!
    Now, all her own sweet self in loveliness
(Restored by kindest care, and medicinal aid),
I saw my gentle friend – mutual surprise
Of unexpected bliss! Enquiry o'er,
And calmed the sudden joy, ' 'Tis years', she said,
'Dark years, since we have met – dark years of grief –
And dark the future too – but these will pass,
These too will pass, and so we'll meet in Heaven.
Nay, here we'll meet if, kind, my soon return
Thou'lt wait amongst our native bowers – shelters
From many a storm, when, rambling far, we saw
The gathering clouds with fear – fond maids! – nor shunned
The darker storms that early whelmed us o'er.
One more request, and we will say farewell
Lest night o'ertake thee.
                                        Dost thou remember,
Six years ago (past a few warmer suns
To give the summer ripeness) one evening
We lingered in the copse, plucking wild flowers
To weave us wreathes beseeming more, we said,
The brows of simple maids, than garden flowers
Flaunting so proud in artificial hues.
Capricious idlers! so we moralized,
'And this, for one afar!' you cried, bending
A pliant branch, on whose high top you hung
A varied garland. Withdrawn the gentle force,
Upsprung in air it waved its modest tints

So prettily, we, smiling, marked the while
'Till, roused by distant sounds threatening and rude,
We turned, and, through the mazy thicket
(Every repelling branch or bent, or torn),
Heedless of hurt, a tattered creature, wild,
Haggard and wan, pressed on to where we stood
Silent and still with fear – nor time for flight!
   In wrathful mood mad Kattern hailed us loud,
Then you, with feigned composure, forward stepped:
"This to Kate – sweet flowers for her! Does any
Harm poor Kate – aught ail her?" Relenting, pleased,
She took the fragrant gift, muttered and passed.
Poor Kate, rude boys had worried her to rage –
Harmless else, and sometimes happy too, for
Kate had long forgotten him who wronged her.
Blest forgetfulness! Oh falsest man,
Forgetting thee!'
                                        Then in those softest eyes
Gleamed wandering fires – fires not their own – but soon
To tears they changed. 'How much', she said, 'in fond
And idle talk I, wandering, lose myself,
Detaining thee. Tomorrow at this hour
Cross that low copse, and climb the ascent beyond,
So gay with yellow broom and purple heath;
I to yon sullen heights will bend my way,
And, if the day is fair, I have a glass
Will show thee there – thy white kerchief waving.
Though indistinct thy form I see, this sign
Will mark it thine – sweet consciousness! Again
Each day, return – the dearest hour I'll know
Till that I meet thee there! Farewell, farewell!'
'Each word of thine is treasured – oh, farewell!'

10. LORD BYRON

The Prisoner of Chillon (1816)

My hair is grey, but not with years –
      Nor grew it white
      In a single night,
As men's have grown from sudden fears;

My limbs are bowed, though not with toil
  But rusted with a vile repose,
For they have been a dungeon's spoil,
  And mine has been the fate of those
To whom the goodly earth and air
Are banned, and barred – forbidden fare!
But this was for my father's faith
I suffered chains and courted death –
That father perished at the stake
For tenets he would not forsake,
And for the same his lineal race
In darkness found a dwelling place!
We were seven, who now are one:
  Six in youth, and one in age,
Finished as they had begun,
  Proud of Persecution's rage.
One in fire, and two in field,
Their belief with blood have sealed,
Dying as their father died,
For the God their foes denied;
Three were in a dungeon cast,
Of whom this wreck is left the last!

There are seven pillars of gothic mould
In Chillon's dungeons deep and old,
There are seven columns, massy and grey,
Dim with a dull imprisoned ray
(A sunbeam which hath lost its way,
And through the crevice and the cleft
Of the thick wall is fallen and left,
Creeping o'er the floor so damp,
Like a marsh's meteor lamp),
And in each pillar there is a ring,
  And in each ring there is a chain –
That iron is a cankering thing,
  For in these limbs its teeth remain,
With marks that will not wear away,
Till I have done with this new day,
Which now is painful to these eyes
Which have not seen the sun so rise
For years – I cannot count them o'er,
I lost their long and heavy score
When my last brother drooped and died,
And I lay living by his side.

They chained us each to a column-stone,
And we were three – yet, each alone!
We could not move a single pace,
We could not see each other's face
But with that pale and livid light
That made us strangers in our sight:
And thus together – yet apart –
Fettered in hand but joined in heart,
'Twas still some solace in the dearth
Of the pure elements of earth,
To hearken to each other's speech,
And each turn comforter to each
With some new hope, or legend old,
Or song heroically bold –
But even these at length grew cold.
Our voices took a dreary tone,
An echo of the dungeon-stone,
   A grating sound, not full and free
   As they of yore were wont to be –
   It might be fancy, but to me
They never sounded like our own!

I was the eldest of the three,
   And to uphold and cheer the rest
   I ought to do – and did my best –
And each did well in his degree.
   The youngest, whom my father loved,
Because our mother's brow was given
To him, with eyes as blue as heaven –
   For him my soul was sorely moved.
And truly might it be distressed
To see such bird in such a nest;
For he was beautiful as day –
   When day was beautiful to me
   As to young eagles, being free –
   A polar day, which will not see
A sunset till its summer's gone,
   Its sleepless summer of long light,
The snow-clad offspring of the sun!
   And thus he was as pure and bright,
And in his natural spirit gay,

With tears for nought but others' ills –
And then they flowed like mountain-rills,
Unless he could assuage the woe
Which he abhorred to view below.

The other was as pure of mind,
But formed to combat with his kind:
Strong in his frame, and of a mood
Which 'gainst the world in war had stood,
And perished in the foremost rank
   With joy – but not in chains to pine!
His spirit withered with their clank,
   I saw it silently decline
   (And so perchance in sooth did mine,
But yet I forced it on to cheer
Those relics of a home so dear).
He was a hunter of the hills,
   Had followed there the deer and wolf;
   To him this dungeon was a gulf,
And fettered feet the worst of ills.

   Lake Leman lies by Chillon's walls:
A thousand feet in depth below
Its massy waters meet and flow –
Thus much the fathom-line was sent
From Chillon's snow-white battlement,
   Which round about the wave enthralls!
A double dungeon wall and wave
Have made – and like a living grave.
Below the surface of the lake
The dark vault lies wherein we lay –
We heard it ripple night and day –
   Sounding o'er our heads it knocked,
And I have felt the winter's spray
Wash through the bars when winds were high
And wanton in the happy sky;
   And then the very rock hath rocked,
   And I have felt it shake, unshocked,
Because I could have smiled to see
The death that would have set me free.

I said my nearer brother pined,
I said his mighty heart declined,
He loathed and put away his food –
It was not that 'twas coarse and rude,
For we were used to hunter's fare
And for the like had little care:
The milk drawn from the mountain-goat
Was changed for water from the moat,
Our bread was such as captives' tears
Have moistened many a thousand years
Since man first pent his fellow men
Like brutes within an iron den –
But what were these to us or him?
These wasted not his heart or limb!
My brother's soul was of that mould
Which in a palace had grown cold
Had his free breathing been denied
The range of the steep mountain's side –
But why delay the truth? He died.
I saw, and could not hold his head,
Nor reach his dying hand – nor dead,
Though hard I strove (but strove in vain)
To rend and gnash my bonds in twain.
He died – and they unlocked his chain
And scooped for him a shallow grave
Even from the cold earth of our cave.
I begged them, as a boon, to lay
His corse in dust whereon the day
Might shine – it was a foolish thought,
But then within my brain it wrought
That even in death his freeborn breast
In such a dungeon could not rest.
I might have spared my idle prayer –
They coldly laughed, and laid him there:
The flat and turfless earth above
The being we so much did love.
His empty chain above it leant –
Such murder's fitting monument!

But he, the favourite and the flower,
Most cherished since his natal hour,
His mother's image in fair face,
The infant love of all his race,

His martyred father's dearest thought,
My latest care (for whom I sought
To hoard my life, that his might be
Less wretched now, and one day free) –
He, too, who yet had held untired
A spirit natural or inspired –
He, too, was struck, and day by day
Was withered on the stalk away.
Oh, God! it is a fearful thing
To see the human soul take wing
In any shape, in any mood:
I've seen it rushing forth in blood,
I've seen it on the breaking ocean
Strive with a swoln convulsive motion,
I've seen the sick and ghastly bed
Of sin, delirious with its dread.
But these were horrors – this was woe
Unmixed with such – but sure and slow.
He faded, and so calm and meek,
So softly worn, so sweetly weak,
So tearless, yet so tender – kind,
And grieved for those he left behind;
With all the while a cheek whose bloom
Was as a mockery of the tomb,
Whose tints as gently sunk away
As a departing rainbow's ray;
An eye of most transparent light,
That almost made the dungeon bright;
And not a word of murmur, not
A groan o'er his untimely lot –
A little talk of better days,
A little hope my own to raise,
For I was sunk in silence, lost
In this last loss, of all the most.
And then the sighs he would suppress
Of fainting Nature's feebleness,
More slowly drawn, grew less and less:
I listened, but I could not hear;
I called, for I was wild with fear;
I knew 'twas hopeless, but my dread
Would not be thus admonishéd.
I called, and thought I heard a sound –
I burst my chain with one strong bound,

And rushed to him! I found him not!
I only stirred in this black spot,
I only lived, I only drew
The accurséd breath of dungeon-dew –
The last, the sole, the dearest link
Between me and the eternal brink,
Which bound me to my failing race,
Was broken in this fatal place.
One on the earth, and one beneath –
My brothers – both had ceased to breathe.
I took that hand which lay so still
(Alas, my own was full as chill),
I had not strength to stir, or strive,
But felt that I was still alive –
A frantic feeling, when we know
That what we love shall ne'er be so.
        I know not why
        I could not die;
I had no earthly hope – but faith,
And that forbade a selfish death.

What next befell me then and there
    I know not well – I never knew –
First came the loss of light, and air,
    And then of darkness too!
I had no thought, no feeling – none –
Among the stones I stood a stone,
And was (scarce conscious what I wist)
As shrubless crags within the mist.
For all was blank, and bleak, and grey:
It was not night – it was not day,
It was not even the dungeon-light,
So hateful to my heavy sight,
But vacancy absorbing space,
And fixédness, without a place!
There were no stars, no earth, no time,
No check, no change, no good, no crime –
But silence, and a stirless breath
Which neither was of life nor death:
A sea of stagnant idleness,
Blind, boundless, mute, and motionless!

A light broke in upon my brain,
   It was the carol of a bird –
It ceased, and then it came again,
   The sweetest song ear ever heard,
And mine was thankful till my eyes
Ran over with the glad surprise,
And they that moment could not see
I was the mate of misery!
But then by dull degrees came back
My senses to their wonted track;
I saw the dungeon-walls and floor
Close slowly round me as before;
I saw the glimmer of the sun
Creeping as it before had done,
But through the crevice where it came
That bird was perched, as fond and tame,
   And tamer than upon the tree –
A lovely bird, with azure wings
And song that said a thousand things,
   And seemed to say them all for me!
I never saw its like before,
I ne'er shall see its likeness more:
It seemed like me to want a mate,
But was not half so desolate,
And it was come to love me when
None lived to love me so again,
And cheering from my dungeon's brink,
Had brought me back to feel and think.
I know not if it late were free,
   Or broke its cage to perch on mine,
But knowing well captivity,
   Sweet bird, I could not wish for thine!
Or if it were, in wingéd guise,
A visitant from Paradise;
For (Heaven forgive that thought, the while
Which made me both to weep and smile)
I sometimes deemed that it might be
My brother's soul come down to me!
But then at last away it flew,
And then 'twas mortal well I knew,
For he would never thus have flown
And left me twice so doubly lone –

Lone as the corse within its shroud,
Lone as a solitary cloud,
   A single cloud on a sunny day,
While all the rest of heaven is clear,
A frown upon the atmosphere
That hath no business to appear
   When skies are blue, and earth is gay.

A kind of change came in my fate,
My keepers grew compassionate;
I know not what had made them so
(They were inured to sights of woe),
But so it was – my broken chain
With links unfastened did remain,
And it was liberty to stride
Along my cell from side to side,
And up and down, and then athwart,
And tread it over every part;
And round the pillars one by one,
Returning where my walk begun,
Avoiding only, as I trod,
My brothers' graves without a sod;
For if I thought with heedless tread
My step profaned their lowly bed,
My breath came gaspingly and thick,
And my crushed heart felt blind and sick.

I made a footing in the wall –
   It was not therefrom to escape,
For I had buried one and all
   Who loved me in a human shape,
And the whole earth would henceforth be
A wider prison unto me!
No child, no sire, no kin had I,
No partner in my misery;
I thought of this, and I was glad,
For thought of them had made me mad;
But I was curious to ascend
To my barred windows, and to bend
Once more, upon the mountains high,
The quiet of a loving eye.

I saw them – and they were the same,
They were not changed like me in frame;
I saw their thousand years of snow
On high – their wide long lake below,
And the blue Rhone in fullest flow!
I heard the torrents leap and gush
O'er channelled rock and broken bush;
I saw the white-walled distant town,
And whiter sails go skimming down;
And then there was a little isle,
Which in my very face did smile,
   The only one in view –
A small green isle, it seemed no more,
Scarce broader than my dungeon floor,
But in it there were three tall trees,
And o'er it blew the mountain-breeze,
And by it there were waters flowing,
And on it there were young flowers growing,
   Of gentle breath and hue.
The fish swam by the castle wall,
And they seemed joyous each and all;
The eagle rode the rising blast,
Methought he never flew so fast
As then to me he seemed to fly!
And then new tears came in my eye,
And I felt troubled – and would fain
I had not left my recent chain;
And when I did descend again,
The darkness of my dim abode
Fell on me as a heavy load.
It was as is a new-dug grave,
Closing o'er one we sought to save –
And yet my glance, too much opprest,
Had almost need of such a rest.

It might be months, or years, or days
   (I kept no count, I took no note,
I had no hope my eyes to raise,
   And clear them of their dreary mote),
At last men came to set me free.
   I asked not why, and recked not where;
It was at length the same to me,
Fettered or fetterless to be –
   I learned to love despair!

And thus when they appeared at last,
And all my bonds aside were cast,
These heavy walls to me had grown
A hermitage – and all my own!
And half I felt as they were come
To tear me from a second home:
With spiders I had friendship made,
And watched them in their sullen trade,
Had seen the mice by moonlight play,
And why should I feel less than they?
We were all inmates of one place,
And I, the monarch of each race,
Had power to kill – yet, strange to tell
In quiet we had learned to dwell.
My very chains and I grew friends,
So much a long communion tends
To make us what we are – even, I
Regained my freedom with a sigh.

11. JOHN KEATS

Isabella, or The Pot of Basil

(stanzas 32–63) April 1818; publ. 1820

32

In the mid-days of autumn, on their eves,
   The breath of Winter comes from far away,
And the sick west continually bereaves
   Of some bold tinge, and plays a roundelay
Of death among the bushes and the leaves,
   To make all bare before he dares to stray
From his north cavern. So sweet Isabel
By gradual decay from beauty fell,

33

Because Lorenzo came not. Oftentimes
   She asked her brothers, with an eye all pale,
Striving to be itself, what dungeon-climes
   Could keep him off so long? They spake a tale

Time after time, to quiet her. Their crimes
   Came on them, like a smoke from Hinnom's vale;
And every night in dreams they groaned aloud,
To see their sister in her snowy shroud.

34

And she had died in drowsy ignorance,
   But for a thing more deadly dark than all –
It came like a fierce potion, drunk by chance,
   Which saves a sick man from the feathered pall
For some few gasping moments – like a lance,
   Waking an Indian from his cloudy hall
With cruel pierce, and bringing him again
Sense of the gnawing fire at heart and brain.

35

It was a vision: in the drowsy gloom,
   The dull of midnight, at her couch's foot
Lorenzo stood, and wept. The forest tomb
   Had marred his glossy hair which once could shoot
Lustre into the sun, and put cold doom
   Upon his lips, and taken the soft lute
From his lorn voice, and past his loaméd ears
Had made a miry channel for his tears.

36

Strange sound it was when the pale shadow spake,
   For there was striving in its piteous tongue
To speak as when on earth it was awake –
   And Isabella on its music hung.
Languor there was in it, and tremulous shake,
   As in a palsied Druid's harp unstrung;
And through it moaned a ghostly under-song,
Like hoarse night-gusts sepulchral briars among.

37

Its eyes, though wild, were still all dewy bright
   With love, and kept all phantom fear aloof
From the poor girl by magic of their light,
   The while it did unthread the horrid woof
Of the late darkened time – the murderous spite
   Of pride and avarice – the dark pine roof
In the forest – and the sodden turféd-dell,
Where, without any word, from stabs he fell –

38

Saying moreover, 'Isabel, my sweet!
   Red whortle-berries droop above my head,
And a large flint-stone weighs upon my feet;
   Around me beeches and high chestnuts shed
Their leaves and prickly nuts; a sheepfold-bleat
   Comes from beyond the river to my bed –
Go, shed one tear upon my heather-bloom,
And it shall comfort me within the tomb.

39

I am a shadow now, alas! alas!
   Upon the skirts of human-nature dwelling
Alone. I chant alone the holy mass,
   While little sounds of life are round me knelling,
And glossy bees at noon do fieldward pass,
   And many a chapel-bell the hour is telling,
Paining me through! Those sounds grow strange to me,
And thou art distant in humanity.

40

I know what was, I feel full well what is –
   And I should rage, if spirits could go mad!
Though I forget the taste of earthly bliss,
   That paleness warms my grave, as though I had
A seraph chosen from the bright abyss
   To be my spouse. Thy paleness makes me glad;
Thy beauty grows upon me, and I feel
A greater love through all my essence steal.'

41

The spirit mourned 'Adieu', dissolved, and left
   The atom-darkness in a slow turmoil –
As when, of healthful midnight-sleep bereft,
   Thinking on ruggéd hours and fruitless toil,
We put our eyes into a pillowy cleft,
   And see the spangly gloom froth up and boil!
It made sad Isabella's eyelids ache,
And in the dawn she started up awake –

42

'Ha! ha!' said she, 'I knew not this hard life,
   I thought the worst was simple misery;
I thought some fate with pleasure or with strife
   Portioned us – happy days, or else to die.
But there is crime: a brother's bloody knife!
   Sweet spirit, thou hast schooled my infancy:
I'll visit thee for this, and kiss thine eyes,
And greet thee morn and even in the skies.'

43

When the full morning came, she had devised
   How she might secret to the forest hie;
How she might find the clay, so dearly prized,
   And sing to it one latest lullaby;
How her short absence might be unsurmised,
   While she the inmost of the dream would try.
Resolved, she took with her an agéd nurse,
And went into that dismal forest-hearse.

44

See, as they creep along the river-side,
   How she doth whisper to that agéd dame,
And, after looking round the champaign wide,
   Shows her a knife. 'What feverous hectic flame
Burns in thee, child? What good can thee betide,
   That thou shouldst smile again?' The evening came,
And they had found Lorenzo's earthy bed:
The flint was there, the berries at his head.

45

Who hath not loitered in a green churchyard,
   And let his spirit, like a demon-mole,
Work through the clayey soil and gravel hard,
   To see skull, coffined bones, and funeral-stole;
Pitying each form that hungry Death hath marred,
   And filling it once more with human soul?
Ah, this is holiday to what was felt
When Isabella by Lorenzo knelt!

46

She gazed into the fresh-thrown mould, as though
   One glance did fully all its secrets tell.
Clearly she saw, as other eyes would know
   Pale limbs at bottom of a crystal well.
Upon the murderous spot she seemed to grow,
   Like to a native lily of the dell –
Then with her knife, all sudden, she began
To dig more fervently than misers can.

47

Soon she turned up a soiléd glove, whereon
   Her silk had played in purple fantasies –
She kissed it with a lip more chill than stone,
   And put it in her bosom, where it dries
And freezes utterly unto the bone
   Those dainties made to still an infant's cries!
Then 'gan she work again – nor stayed her care,
But to throw back at times her veiling hair.

48

That old nurse stood beside her wondering,
   Until her heart felt pity to the core
At sight of such a dismal labouring,
   And so she kneeléd, with her locks all hoar,
And put her lean hands to the horrid thing.
   Three hours they laboured at this travail sore;
At last they felt the kernel of the grave,
And Isabella did not stamp and rave.

49

Ah, wherefore all this wormy circumstance?
   Why linger at the yawning tomb so long?
Oh for the gentleness of old romance,
   The simple plaining of a minstrel's song!
Fair reader, at the old tale take a glance,
   For here, in truth, it doth not well belong
To speak – oh turn thee to the very tale,
And taste the music of that vision pale.

50

With duller steel than the Perséan sword
They cut away no formless monster's head,
But one whose gentleness did well accord
With death, as life. The ancient harps have said
Love never dies, but lives, immortal Lord.
If Love impersonate was ever dead,
Pale Isabella kissed it, and low moaned.
'Twas Love, cold – dead indeed – but not dethroned.

51

In anxious secrecy they took it home,
And then the prize was all for Isabel!
She calmed its wild hair with a golden comb,
And all around each eye's sepulchral cell
Pointed each fringéd lash. The smearéd loam
With tears as chilly as a dripping well
She drenched away – and still she combed, and kept
Sighing all day – and still she kissed, and wept.

52

Then in a silken scarf – sweet with the dews
Of precious flowers plucked in Araby,
And divine liquids come with odorous ooze
Through the cold serpent-pipe refreshfully –
She wrapped it up, and for its tomb did choose
A garden-pot, wherein she laid it by
And covered it with mould, and o'er it set
Sweet basil, which her tears kept ever wet.

53

And she forgot the stars, the moon, and sun,
And she forgot the blue above the trees,
And she forgot the dells where waters run,
And she forgot the chilly autumn breeze –
She had no knowledge when the day was done,
And the new morn she saw not, but in peace
Hung over her sweet basil evermore,
And moistened it with tears unto the core.

54
And so she ever fed it with thin tears,
   Whence thick, and green, and beautiful it grew,
So that it smelt more balmy than its peers
   Of basil-tufts in Florence; for it drew
Nurture besides, and life, from human fears –
   From the fast-mouldering head there shut from view –
So that the jewel, safely casketed,
Came forth, and in perfuméd leafits spread.

55
Oh Melancholy, linger here awhile!
   Oh Music, Music, breathe despondingly!
Oh Echo, Echo, from some sombre isle
   Unknown, Lethean, sigh to us, oh sigh!
Spirits in grief, lift up your heads, and smile –
   Lift up your heads, sweet spirits, heavily,
And make a pale light in your cypress-glooms,
Tinting with silver wan your marble tombs.

56
Moan hither, all ye syllables of woe,
   From the deep throat of sad Melpomene!
Through bronzéd lyre in tragic order go,
   And touch the strings into a mystery!
Sound mournfully upon the winds and low,
   For simple Isabel is soon to be
Among the dead. She withers, like a palm
Cut by an Indian for its juicy balm.

57
Oh leave the palm to wither by itself,
   Let not quick winter chill its dying hour!
It may not be – those Baälites of pelf,
   Her brethren, noted the continual shower
From her dead eyes; and many a curious elf,
   Among her kindred, wondered that such dower
Of youth and beauty should be thrown aside
By one marked out to be a noble's bride.

58

And, furthermore, her brethren wondered much
   Why she sat drooping by the basil green,
And why it flourished, as by magic touch –
   Greatly they wondered what the thing might mean.
They could not surely give belief that such
   A very nothing would have power to wean
Her from her own fair youth and pleasures gay –
And even remembrance of her love's delay.

59

Therefore they watched a time when they might sift
   This hidden whim – and long they watched in vain,
For seldom did she go to chapel-shrift,
   And seldom felt she any hunger-pain;
And when she left, she hurried back, as swift
   As bird on wing to breast its eggs again,
And, patient as a hen-bird, sat her there
Beside her basil, weeping through her hair.

60

Yet they contrived to steal the basil-pot,
   And to examine it in secret place.
The thing was vile with green and livid spot,
   And yet they knew it was Lorenzo's face –
The guerdon of their murder they had got,
   And so left Florence in a moment's space,
Never to turn again. Away they went,
With blood upon their heads, to banishment!

61

Oh Melancholy, turn thine eyes away!
   Oh Music, Music, breathe despondingly!
Oh Echo, Echo, on some other day,
   From isles Lethean, sigh to us, oh sigh!
Spirits of grief, sing not your 'Well-a-way!'
   For Isabel, sweet Isabel, will die –
Will die a death too lone and incomplete,
Now they have ta'en away her basil sweet.

62

Piteous, she looked on dead and senseless things,
   Asking for her lost basil amorously;
And with melodious chuckle in the strings
   Of her lorn voice, she oftentimes would cry
After the pilgrim in his wanderings
   To ask him where her basil was, and why
'Twas hid from her. 'For cruel 'tis', said she,
'To steal my basil-pot away from me!'

63

And so she pined, and so she died forlorn,
   Imploring for her basil to the last.
No heart was there in Florence but did mourn
   In pity of her love, so overcast;
And a sad ditty, of this story born,
   From mouth to mouth through all the country passed.
Still is the burden sung: 'Oh cruelty,
To steal my basil-pot away from me!'

12. PERCY BYSSHE SHELLEY

Final Moments (*The Cenci* V, scenes iii–iv) 1819

Act V, scene iii. *The cell of a prison. Beatrice is discovered asleep on a couch.*

Enter Bernardo: How gently slumber rests upon her face,
   Like the last thoughts of some day sweetly spent
   Closing in night and dreams, and so prolonged.
   After such torments as she bore last night,
   How light and soft her breathing comes. Aye me,
   Methinks that I shall never sleep again.
   But I must shake the heavenly dew of rest
   From this sweet folded flower, thus – wake! awake!
   What, sister, canst thou sleep?
Beatrice (awaking): I was just dreaming
   That we were all in Paradise. Thou knowest
   This cell seems like a kind of Paradise
   After our father's presence.
Bernardo: Dear, dear sister,
   Would that thy dream were not a dream! Oh God!

How shall I tell?
Beatrice: What wouldst thou tell, sweet brother?
Bernardo: Look not so calm and happy, or even whilst
I stand considering what I have to say
My heart will break.
Beatrice: See now, thou makest me weep!
How very friendless thou wouldst be, dear child,
If I were dead. Say what thou hast to say.
Bernardo: They have confessed; they could endure no more
The tortures . . .
Beatrice: Ha! What was there to confess?
They must have told some weak and wicked lie
To flatter their tormentors. Have they said
That they were guilty? Oh white innocence,
That thou shouldst wear the mask of guilt to hide
Thine awful and serenest countenance
From those who know thee not!
(*Enter Judge with Lucretia and Giacomo, guarded.*)
Ignoble hearts!
For some brief spasms of pain, which are at least
As mortal as the limbs through which they pass,
Are centuries of high splendour laid in dust?
And that eternal honour which should live
Sunlike, above the reek of mortal fame,
Changed to a mockery and a byword? What!
Will you give up these bodies to be dragged
At horses' heels, so that our hair should sweep
The footsteps of the vain and senseless crowd,
Who (that they may make our calamity
Their worship and their spectacle) will leave
The churches and the theatres as void
As their own hearts? Shall the light multitude
Fling, at their choice, curses or faded pity,
Sad funeral flowers to deck a living corpse,
Upon us as we pass to pass away,
And leave – what memory of our having been?
Infamy, blood, terror, despair? Oh thou,
Who wert a mother to the parentless,
Kill not thy child! Let not her wrongs kill thee!
Brother, lie down with me upon the rack,
And let us each be silent as a corpse –
It soon will be as soft as any grave.
'Tis but the falsehood it can wring from fear
Makes the rack cruel.

Giacomo: They will tear the truth
Even from thee at last, those cruel pains –
For pity's sake say thou art guilty now.
Lucretia: Oh, speak the truth! Let us all quickly die –
And after death, God is our judge, not they!
He will have mercy on us.
Bernardo: If indeed
It can be true, say so, dear sister mine,
And then the Pope will surely pardon you,
And all be well.
Judge: Confess, or I will warp
Your limbs with such keen tortures –
Beatrice: Tortures! Turn
The rack henceforth into a spinning-wheel!
Torture your dog, that he may tell when last
He lapped the blood his master shed! Not me –
My pangs are of the mind, and of the heart,
And of the soul; aye, of the inmost soul,
Which weeps within tears as of burning gall
To see, in this ill world where none are true,
My kindred false to their deserted selves.
And with considering all the wretched life
Which I have lived, and its now wretched end,
And the small justice shown by Heaven and Earth
To me or mine; and what a tyrant thou art,
And what slaves these; and what a world we make,
The oppressor and the oppressed – such pangs compel
My answer. What is it thou wouldst with me?
Judge: Art thou not guilty of thy father's death?
Beatrice: Or wilt thou rather tax high-judging God
That He permitted such an act as that
Which I have suffered, and which He beheld –
Made it unutterable, and took from it
All refuge, all revenge, all consequence,
But that which thou hast called my father's death? –
Which is, or is not, what men call a crime;
Which either I have done, or have not done!
Say what ye will, I shall deny no more.
If ye desire it thus, thus let it be,
And so an end of all. Now do your will –
No other pains shall force another word!
Judge: She is convicted, but has not confessed.
Be it enough. Until their final sentence

Let none have converse with them. You, young Lord,
Linger not here!
Beatrice: Oh, tear him not away!
Judge: Guards, do your duty.
Bernardo (*embracing Beatrice*): Oh! would ye divide
Body from soul?
Officer: That is the headsman's business.
(*Exeunt all but Lucretia, Beatrice, and Giacomo.*)
Giacomo: Have I confessed? Is it all over now?
No hope! No refuge! Oh weak, wicked tongue
Which hast destroyed me, would that thou hadst been
Cut out and thrown to dogs first! To have killed
My father first, and then betrayed my sister –
Aye, thee! the one thing innocent and pure
In this black guilty world – to that which I
So well deserve. My wife! My little ones!
Destitute, helpless, and I – Father! God!
Canst Thou forgive even the unforgiving,
When their full hearts break thus, thus?
(*Covers his face and weeps.*)
Lucretia: Oh my child!
To what a dreadful end are we all come!
Why did I yield? Why did I not sustain
Those torments? Oh, that I were all dissolved
Into these fast and unavailing tears,
Which flow and feel not!
Beatrice: What 'twas weak to do,
'Tis weaker to lament, once being done.
Take cheer! The God who knew my wrong, and made
Our speedy act the angel of His wrath,
Seems, and but seems, to have abandoned us.
Let us not think that we shall die for this.
Brother, sit near me; give me your firm hand –
You had a manly heart. Bear up! Bear up!
Oh dearest Lady, put your gentle head
Upon my lap, and try to sleep awhile:
Your eyes look pale, hollow and overworn,
With heaviness of watching and slow grief.
Come, I will sing you some low, sleepy tune,
Not cheerful, nor yet sad – some dull old thing,
Some outworn and unused monotony,
Such as our country gossips sing and spin,
Till they almost forget they live! Lie down –

So, that will do. Have I forgot the words?
Faith! They are sadder than I thought they were:
Song:
False friend, wilt thou smile or weep
When my life is laid asleep?
Little cares for a smile or a tear,
The clay-cold corpse upon the bier!
Farewell! Heigho!
What is this whispers low?
There is a snake in thy smile, my dear,
And bitter poison within thy tear.

Sweet sleep, were death like to thee,
Or if thou couldst mortal be,
I would close these eyes of pain –
When to wake? Never again.
Oh world, farewell!
Listen to the passing bell!
It says, thou and I must part,
With a light and a heavy heart.
(*The scene closes.*)

Scene iv. *A hall of the prison. Enter Camillo and Bernardo.*

Camillo: The Pope is stern, not to be moved or bent.
He looked as calm and keen as is the engine
Which tortures and which kills, exempt itself
From aught that it inflicts – a marble form,
A rite, a law, a custom, not a man!
He frowned, as if to frown had been the trick
Of his machinery, on the advocates
Presenting the defenses, which he tore
And threw behind, muttering with hoarse, harsh voice:
'Which among ye defended their old father
Killed in his sleep?' Then to another: 'Thou
Dost this in virtue of thy place. 'Tis well.'
He turned to me then, looking deprecation,
And said these three words, coldly: 'They must die.'
Bernardo: And yet you left him not?
Camillo: I urged him still;
Pleading, as I could guess, the devilish wrong
Which prompted your unnatural parent's death.
And he replied: 'Paolo Santa Croce
Murdered his mother yester-evening,

And he is fled. Parricide grows so rife
That soon, for some just cause no doubt, the young
Will strangle us all, dozing in our chairs.
Authority, and power, and hoary hair
Are grown crimes capital. You are my nephew,
You come to ask their pardon – stay a moment –
Here is their sentence! Never see me more
Till, to the letter, it be all fulfilled.'
Bernardo: Oh God, not so! I did believe indeed
That all you said was but sad preparation
For happy news. Oh, there are words and looks
To bend the sternest purpose! Once I knew them,
Now I forget them at my dearest need.
What think you if I seek him out, and bathe
His feet and robe with hot and bitter tears,
Importune him with prayers, vexing his brain
With my perpetual cries, until in rage
He strike me with his pastoral cross, and trample
Upon my prostrate head, so that my blood
May stain the senseless dust on which he treads,
And remorse waken mercy? I will do it!
Oh, wait till I return! (*Rushes out*)
Camillo: Alas, poor boy!
A wreck-devoted seaman thus might pray
To the deaf sea.
Enter Lucretia, Beatrice, and Giacomo, guarded.
Beatrice: I hardly dare to fear
That thou bringst other news than a just pardon.
Camillo: May God in heaven be less inexorable
To the Pope's prayers, than he has been to mine.
Here is the sentence and the warrant.
Beatrice (wildly): Oh,
My God! Can it be possible I have
To die so suddenly? So young to go
Under the obscure, cold, rotting, wormy ground!
To be nailed down into a narrow place;
To see no more sweet sunshine; hear no more
Blithe voice of living thing; muse not again
Upon familiar thoughts, sad, yet thus lost.
How fearful! – to be nothing! Or to be –
What? Oh, where am I? Let me not go mad!
Sweet Heaven, forgive weak thoughts! If there should be
No God, no Heaven, no Earth, in the void world –
The wide, gray, lampless, deep, unpeopled world!

If all things then should be – my father's spirit,
His eye, his voice, his touch surrounding me,
The atmosphere and breath of my dead life!
If sometimes, as a shape more like himself,
Even the form which tortured me on earth,
Masked in gray hairs and wrinkles, he should come
And wind me in his hellish arms, and fix
His eyes on mine, and drag me down, down, down!
For was he not alone omnipotent
On earth, and ever-present? Even though dead,
Does not his spirit live in all that breathe,
And work for me and mine still the same ruin,
Scorn, pain, despair? Whoever yet returned
To teach the laws of Death's untrodden realm –
Unjust perhaps as those which drive us now,
Oh, whither, whither?

Lucretia: Trust in God's sweet love,
The tender promises of Christ! Ere night,
Think, we shall be in Paradise.

Beatrice: 'Tis past!
Whatever comes my heart shall sink no more.
And yet, I know not why, your words strike chill.
How tedious, false and cold seem all things! I
Have met with much injustice in this world:
No difference has been made by God or man,
Or any power moulding my wretched lot,
Twixt good or evil, as regarded me.
I am cut off from the only world I know –
From light, and life, and love, in youth's sweet prime.
You do well telling me to trust in God,
I hope I do trust in Him. In whom else
Can any trust? And yet my heart is cold.
(*During the latter speeches Giacomo has retired conversing with Camillo, who now goes out; Giacomo advances.*)

Giacomo: Know you not, Mother – Sister, know you not?
Bernardo even now is gone to implore
The Pope to grant our pardon.

Lucretia: Child, perhaps
It will be granted. We may all then live
To make these woes a tale for distant years:
Oh, what a thought! It gushes to my heart
Like the warm blood.

Beatrice: Yet both will soon be cold.
Oh, trample out that thought! Worse than despair,

Worse than the bitterness of death, is hope!
It is the only ill which can find place
Upon the giddy, sharp and narrow hour
Tottering beneath us. Plead with the swift frost
That it should spare the eldest flower of spring;
Plead with awakening earthquake, o'er whose couch
Even now a city stands, strong, fair, and free –
Now stench and blackness yawn, like death! Oh, plead
With famine, or wind-walking pestilence,
Blind lightning, or the deaf sea, not with man –
Cruel, cold, formal man; righteous in words,
In deeds a Cain! No, Mother, we must die;
Since such is the reward of innocent lives,
Such the alleviation of worst wrongs.
And whilst our murderers live, and hard, cold men,
Smiling and slow, walk through a world of tears
To death as to life's sleep, 'twere just the grave
Were some strange joy for us. Come, obscure Death,
And wind me in thine all-embracing arms!
Like a fond mother hide me in thy bosom,
And rock me to the sleep from which none wake.
Live ye, who live, subject to one another
As we were once, who now –
Bernardo rushes in. Oh, horrible!
That tears, that looks, that hope poured forth in prayer
Even till the heart is vacant and despairs,
Should all be vain! The ministers of death
Are waiting round the doors. I thought I saw
Blood on the face of one! What if 'twere fancy –
Soon the heart's blood of all I love on earth
Will sprinkle him, and he will wipe it off
As if 'twere only rain. Oh life! Oh world!
Cover me! Let me be no more! To see
That perfect mirror of pure innocence
Wherein I gazed, and grew happy and good,
Shivered to dust! To see thee, Beatrice,
Who made all lovely thou didst look upon –
Thee, light of life – dead, dark! While I say 'Sister',
To hear I have no sister! And thou, Mother,
Whose love was as a bond to all our loves –
Dead! The sweet bond broken! (*Enter Camillo and guards.*) They come! Let me
Kiss those warm lips before their crimson leaves
Are blighted, white, cold – say farewell before

Death chokes that gentle voice! Oh, let me hear
You speak!
Beatrice: Farewell, my tender brother. Think
Of our sad fate with gentleness, as now,
And let mild, pitying thoughts lighten for thee
Thy sorrow's load. Err not in harsh despair,
But tears and patience. One thing more, my child:
For thine own sake be constant to the love
Thou bearest us – and to the faith that I,
Though wrapped in a strange cloud of crime and shame,
Lived ever holy and unstained. And though
Ill tongues shall wound me, and our common name
Be as a mark stamped on thine innocent brow
For men to point at as they pass, do thou
Forbear, and never think a thought unkind
Of those who perhaps love thee in their graves.
So mayst thou die as I do, fear and pain
Being subdued. Farewell! Farewell! Farewell!
Bernardo: I cannot say, farewell!
Camillo: Oh, Lady Beatrice!
Beatrice: Give yourself no unnecessary pain,
My dear Lord Cardinal. Here, Mother, tie
My girdle for me, and bind up this hair
In any simple knot – aye, that does well.
And yours I see is coming down. How often
Have we done this for one another; now
We shall not do it any more. My Lord,
We are quite ready. Well – 'tis very well.

13. LORD BYRON

The Shipwreck (from *Don Juan* II) 1819

51

At half-past eight o'clock, booms, hencoops, spars,
And all things, for a chance, had been cast loose
That still could keep afloat the struggling tars –
For yet they strove, although of no great use:
There was no light in heaven but a few stars,
The boats put off o'ercrowded with their crews;
She gave a heel, and then a lurch to port,
And, going down head foremost – sunk, in short.

52

Then rose from sea to sky the wild farewell,
   Then shrieked the timid, and stood still the brave;
Then some leaped overboard with dreadful yell,
   As eager to anticipate their grave;
And the sea yawned around her like a hell,
   And down she sucked with her the whirling wave,
Like one who grapples with his enemy,
And strives to strangle him before he die . . .

56

Juan got into the long-boat, and there
   Contrived to help Pedrillo to a place.
It seemed as if they had exchanged their care,
   For Juan wore the magisterial face
Which courage gives, while poor Pedrillo's pair
   Of eyes were crying for their owner's case:
Battista, though (a name called shortly 'Tita')
Was lost by getting at some aqua-vita.

57

Pedro, his valet, too, he tried to save,
   But the same cause, conducive to his loss,
Left him so drunk, he jumped into the wave
   As o'er the cutter's edge he tried to cross,
And so he found a wine-and-watery grave;
   They could not rescue him although so close,
Because the sea ran higher every minute,
And for the boat – the crew kept crowding in it.

58

A small old spaniel, which had been Don Jóse's
   (His father's), whom he loved, as ye may think,
For on such things the memory reposes
   With tenderness, stood howling on the brink,
Knowing – dogs have such intellectual noses! –
   No doubt, the vessel was about to sink,
And Juan caught him up, and ere he stepped
Off, threw him in, then after him he leapt . . .

65

'Tis said that persons living on annuities
   Are longer-lived than others – God knows why,
Unless to plague the grantors – yet so true it is
   That some, I really think, do never die!

Of any creditors the worst a Jew it is,
   And that's their mode of furnishing supply:
In my young days they lent me cash that way,
Which I found very troublesome to pay.

66

'Tis thus with people in an open boat,
   They live upon the love of life, and bear
More than can be believed, or even thought,
   And stand like rocks the tempest's wear and tear;
And hardship still has been the sailor's lot,
   Since Noah's ark went cruising here and there –
She had a curious crew as well as cargo,
Like the first old Greek privateer, the *Argo*.

67

But man is a carnivorous production
   And must have meals, at least one meal a day;
He cannot live, like woodcocks, upon suction,
   But, like the shark and tiger, must have prey –
Although his anatomical construction
   Bears vegetables in a grumbling way,
Your labouring-people think beyond all question,
Beef, veal, and mutton, better for digestion.

68

And thus it was with this our hapless crew,
   For on the third day there came on a calm,
And though at first their strength it might renew
   (And lying on their weariness like balm,
Lulled them like turtles sleeping on the blue
   Of ocean), when they woke they felt a qualm
And fell all ravenously on their provision,
Instead of hoarding it with due precision.

69

The consequence was easily foreseen –
   They ate up all they had, and drank their wine,
In spite of all remonstrances, and then
   On what, in fact, next day were they to dine?
They hoped the wind would rise, these foolish men!
   And carry them to shore – these hopes were fine,
But as they had but one oar, and that brittle,
It would have been more wise to save their victual!

70
The fourth day came, but not a breath of air,
   And Ocean slumbered like an unweaned child:
The fifth day, and their boat lay floating there –
   The sea and sky were blue, and clear, and mild –
With their one oar (I wish they had had a pair)
   What could they do? And hunger's rage grew wild!
So Juan's spaniel, spite of his entreating,
Was killed, and portioned out for present eating.

71
On the sixth day they fed upon his hide,
   And Juan, who had still refused, because
The creature was his father's dog that died,
   Now feeling all the vulture in his jaws,
With some remorse received (though first denied)
   As a great favour one of the forepaws,
Which he divided with Pedrillo, who
Devoured it, longing for the other too.

72
The seventh day, and no wind – the burning sun
   Blistered and scorched, and, stagnant on the sea,
They lay like carcasses; and hope was none,
   Save in the breeze that came not! Savagely
They glared upon each other – all was done,
   Water, and wine, and food – and you might see
The longings of the cannibal arise
(Although they spoke not) in their wolfish eyes.

73
At length one whispered his companion, who
   Whispered another, and thus it went round,
And then into a hoarser murmur grew
   (An ominous, and wild, and desperate sound),
And when his comrade's thought each sufferer knew,
'Twas but his own, suppressed till now, he found –
And out they spoke of lots for flesh and blood,
And who should die to be his fellow's food.

74

But ere they came to this, they that day shared
  Some leathern caps, and what remained of shoes;
And then they looked around them, and despaired,
  And none to be the sacrifice would choose:
At length the lots were torn up, and prepared,
  But of materials that much shock the Muse –
Having no paper, for the want of better,
They took by force from Juan, Julia's letter.

75

The lots were made, and marked, and mixed, and handed,
  In silent horror, and their distribution
Lulled even the savage hunger which demanded,
  Like the Promethean vulture, this pollution.
None in particular had sought or planned it,
  'Twas Nature gnawed them to this resolution,
By which none were permitted to be neuter –
And the lot fell on Juan's luckless tutor.

76

He but requested to be bled to death:
  The surgeon had his instruments, and bled
Pedrillo, and so gently ebbed his breath
  You hardly could perceive when he was dead.
He died as born, a Catholic in faith,
  Like most in the belief in which they're bred,
And first a little crucifix he kissed,
And then held out his jugular and wrist.

77

The surgeon, as there was no other fee,
  Had his first choice of morsels for his pains;
But being thirstiest at the moment, he
  Preferred a draught from the fast-flowing veins.
Part was divided, part thrown in the sea,
  And such things as the entrails and the brains
Regaled two sharks, who followed o'er the billow –
The sailors ate the rest of poor Pedrillo.

78

The sailors ate him, all save three or four
   Who were not quite so fond of animal food;
To these was added Juan who, before,
   Refusing his own spaniel, hardly could
Feel now his appetite increased much more –
   'Twas not to be expected that he should,
Even in extremity of their disaster,
Dine with them on his pastor and his master.

79

'Twas better that he did not; for, in fact,
   The consequence was awful in the extreme:
For they, who were most ravenous in the act,
   Went raging mad. Lord! how they did blaspheme,
And foam and roll, with strange convulsions racked,
   Drinking salt-water like a mountain-stream,
Tearing, and grinning, howling, screeching, swearing,
And, with hyaena-laughter, died despairing.

80

Their numbers were much thinned by this infliction,
   And all the rest were thin enough, Heaven knows;
And some of them had lost their recollection,
   Happier than they who still perceived their woes;
But others pondered on a new dissection,
   As if not warned sufficiently by those
Who had already perished, suffering madly,
For having used their appetites so sadly.

81

And next they thought upon the master's mate,
   As fattest; but he saved himself, because,
Besides being much averse from such a fate,
   There were some other reasons: the first was,
He had been rather indisposed of late –
   And that which chiefly proved his saving clause,
Was a small present made to him at Cadiz,
By general subscription of the ladies.

82

Of poor Pedrillo something still remained,
   But was used sparingly – some were afraid,
And others still their appetites constrained,
   Or but at times a little supper made –
All except Juan, who throughout abstained,
   Chewing a piece of bamboo, and some lead
At length they caught two boobies, and a noddy,
And then they left off eating the dead body.

83

And if Pedrillo's fate should shocking be,
   Remember Ugolino condescends
To eat the head of his arch-enemy
   The moment after he politely ends
His tale; if foes be food in Hell, at sea
   'Tis surely fair to dine upon our friends,
When shipwreck's short allowance grows too scanty,
Without being much more horrible than Dante.

14. THOMAS HOOD

The Dream of Eugene Aram (1826)

'Twas in the prime of summer-time,
   An evening calm and cool,
And four-and-twenty happy boys
   Came bounding out of school:
There were some that ran, and some that leapt
   Like troutlets in a pool.

Away they sped with gamesome minds,
   And souls untouched by sin –
To a level mead they came, and there
   They drove the wickets in;
Pleasantly shone the setting sun
   Over the town of Lynn.

Like sportive deer they coursed about,
   And shouted as they ran –
Turning to mirth all things of earth,
   As only boyhood can;
But the Usher sat remote from all,
   A melancholy man.

His hat was off, his vest apart,
   To catch Heaven's blessèd breeze,
For a burning thought was in his brow,
   And his bosom ill at ease –
So he leaned his head on his hands, and read
   The book between his knees.

Leaf after leaf he turned it o'er,
   Nor ever glanced aside;
For the peace of his soul he read that book
   In the golden eventide –
Much study had made him very lean,
   And pale, and leaden-eyed.

At last he shut the ponderous tome –
   With a fast and fervent grasp
He strained the dusky covers close,
   And fixed the brazen hasp:
'Oh God, could I so close my mind,
   And clasp it with a clasp!'

Then leaping on his feet upright,
   Some moody turns he took –
Now up the mead, then down the mead,
   And past a shady nook –
And lo, he saw a little boy
   That pored upon a book.

'My gentle lad, what is't you read –
   Romance or fairy-fable?
Or is it some historic page
   Of kings and crowns unstable?'
The young boy gave an upward glance:
   'It is *The Death of Abel.*'

The Usher took six hasty strides,
As smit with sudden pain –
Six hasty strides beyond the place,
Then slowly back again –
And down he sat beside the lad,
And talked with him of Cain,

And (long since then) of bloody men
Whose deeds tradition saves:
Of lonely folk cut off unseen,
And hid in sudden graves;
Of horrid stabs, in groves forlorn,
And murders done in caves;

And how the sprites of injured men
Shriek upward from the sod,
Aye, how the ghostly hand will point
To show the burial-clod,
And unknown facts of guilty acts
Are seen in dreams from God!

He told how murderers walk the earth
Beneath the curse of Cain,
With crimson clouds before their eyes,
And flames about their brain –
For blood has left upon their souls
Its everlasting stain!

'And well' quoth he, 'I know, for truth,
Their pangs must be extreme –
Woe, woe, unutterable woe –
Who spill life's sacred stream!
For why? Methought, last night, I wrought
A murder in a dream:

One that had never done me wrong
(A feeble man, and old),
I led him to a lonely field –
The moon shone clear and cold –
Now here, said I, this man shall die,
And I will have his gold!

Two sudden blows with a ragged stick,
   And one with a heavy stone,
One hurried gash with a hasty knife –
   And then the deed was done!
There was nothing lying at my foot
   But lifeless flesh and bone –

Nothing but lifeless flesh and bone,
   That could not do me ill,
And yet I feared him all the more
   For lying there so still:
There was a manhood in his look
   That murder could not kill.

And lo, the universal air
   Seemed lit with ghastly flame –
Ten thousand, thousand dreadful eyes
   Were looking down in blame:
I took the dead man by his hand,
   And called upon his name!

Oh God, it made me quake to see
   Such sense within the slain;
But when I touched the lifeless clay
   The blood gushed out amain –
For every clot, a burning spot
   Was scorching in my brain!

My head was like an ardent coal,
   My heart as solid ice;
My wretched, wretched soul, I knew,
   Was at the Devil's price!
A dozen times I groaned –the Dead
   Had never groaned but twice.

And now, from forth the frowning sky,
   From the Heaven's topmost height,
I heard a voice – the awful voice
   Of the blood-avenging sprite:
"Thou guilty man, take up thy dead
   And hide it from my sight!"

I took the dreary body up,
   And cast it in a stream,
A sluggish water, black as ink,
   Its depth was so extreme –
My dearest boy, remember this
   Is nothing but a dream!

Down went the corse with hollow plunge
   And vanished in the pool;
Anon I cleansed my bloody hands,
   And washed my forehead cool –
And sat among the urchins young
   That evening in the School!

Oh Heaven, to think of their white souls,
   And mine so black and grim!
I could not share in childish prayer,
   Nor join in evening hymn –
Like a devil of the pit I seemed,
   Mid holy cherubim!

And peace went with them, one and all,
   And each calm pillow spread,
But Guilt was my grim chamberlain
   That lighted me to bed,
And drew my midnight-curtains round
   With fingers bloody red!

All night I lay in agony,
   In anguish dark and deep;
My fevered eyes I dared not close,
   But stared aghast at Sleep –
For Sin had rendered unto her
   The keys of Hell to keep!

All night I lay in agony,
   From weary chime to chime,
With one besetting horrid hint
   That racked me all the time –
A mighty yearning, like the first
   Fierce impulse unto crime!

One stern tyrannic thought, that made
All other thoughts its slave –
Stronger and stronger every pulse
Did that temptation crave,
Still urging me to go and see
The dead man in his grave!

Heavily I rose up, as soon
As light was in the sky,
And sought the black accursed pool
With a wild misgiving eye –
And saw the Dead in the river bed,
For the faithless stream was dry!

Merrily rose the lark, and shook
The dewdrop from its wing –
But I never marked its morning-flight,
I never heard it sing,
For I was stooping once again
Under the horrid thing!

With breathless speed, like a soul in chase,
I took him up and ran –
There was no time to dig a grave
Before the day began:
In a lonesome wood, with heaps of leaves,
I hid the murdered man.

And all that day I read in school,
But my thought was other-where –
As soon as the midday task was done,
In secret I was there:
And a mighty wind had swept the leaves,
And still the corse was bare!

Then down I cast me on my face,
And first began to weep,
For I knew my secret then was one
The earth refused to keep –
Or land or sea, though he should be
Ten thousand fathoms deep!

So wills the fierce avenging sprite,
   Till blood for blood atones!
Aye, though he's buried in a cave,
   And trodden down with stones,
And years have rotted off his flesh –
   The world shall see his bones!

Oh God, that horrid, horrid dream
   Besets me, now awake:
Again, again, with dizzy brain,
   The human life I take –
And my red right hand grows raging hot
   Like Cranmer's at the stake.

And still no peace for the restless clay
   Will wave or mound allow;
The horrid thing pursues my soul –
   It stands before me now!'
The fearful boy looked up and saw
   Huge drops upon his brow.

That very night, while gentle sleep
   The urchin's eyelids kissed,
Two stern-faced men set out from Lynn
   Through the cold and heavy mist;
And Eugene Aram walked between,
   With gyves upon his wrist.

15. FELICIA HEMANS

Indian Woman's Death Song

(*Records of Woman* 1828)

An Indian woman, driven to despair by her husband's desertion of her for another wife, entered a canoe with her children, and rowed it down the Mississippi towards a cataract. Her voice was heard from the shore singing a mournful death-song, until overpowered by the sound of the waters in which she perished. The tale is related in Long's *Expedition to the Source of St Peter's River*. (Hemans)

'Let not my child be a girl, for very sad is the life of a woman.'
(Cooper: *The Prairie*)

Down a broad river of the western wilds,
Piercing thick forest-glooms, a light canoe
Swept with the current. Fearful was the speed
Of the frail bark, as by a tempest's wing
Borne leaf-like on to where the mist of spray
Rose with the cataract's thunder. Yet within,
Proudly, and dauntlessly, and all alone,
Save that a babe lay sleeping at her breast,
A woman stood. Upon her Indian brow
Sat a strange gladness, and her dark hair waved
As if triumphantly! She pressed her child
In its bright slumber to her beating heart,
And lifted her sweet voice, that rose awhile
Above the sound of waters, high and clear,
Wafting a wild proud strain – a song of death:

'Roll swiftly to the spirit's land, thou mighty stream and free!
Father of ancient waters, roll – and bear our lives with thee!
The weary bird that storms have tossed would seek the sunshine's
calm,
And the deer that hath the arrow's hurt flies to the woods of balm.

Roll on! My warrior's eye hath looked upon another's face,
And mine hath faded from his soul, as fades a moonbeam's trace:
My shadow comes not o'er his path, my whisper to his dream,
He flings away the broken reed – roll swifter yet, thou stream!

The voice that spoke of other days is hushed within his breast,
But mine its lonely music haunts, and will not let me rest:
It sings a low and mournful song of gladness that is gone,
I cannot live without that light – father of waves, roll on!

Will he not miss the bounding step that met him from the chase,
The heart of love that made his home an ever-sunny place,
The hand that spread the hunter's board, and decked his couch of
yore?
He will not! Roll, dark foaming stream, on to the better shore!

Some blessèd fount amidst the woods of that bright land must flow,
Whose waters from my soul may lave the memory of this woe;
Some gentle wind must whisper there, whose breath may waft away
The burden of the heavy night, the sadness of the day.

And thou, my babe! though born like me for woman's weary lot,
Smile! To that wasting of the heart, my own! I leave thee not –
Too bright a thing art thou to pine in aching love away –
Thy mother bears thee far, young fawn! from sorrow and decay.

She bears thee to the glorious bowers where none are heard to
weep,
And where the unkind one hath no power again to trouble sleep,
And where the soul shall find its youth, as wakening from a dream –
One moment, and that realm is ours! On, on, dark rolling stream!'

16. LETITIA ELIZABETH LANDON

She Sat Alone Beside Her Hearth

(c. 1835; publ. 1839)

She sat alone beside her hearth –
For many nights alone –
She slept not on the pleasant couch
Where fragrant herbs were strown.

At first she bound her raven hair
With feather and with shell –
But then she hoped! – at length, like night,
Around her neck it fell.

They saw her wandering mid the woods,
Lone, with the cheerless dawn,
And then they said, 'Can this be her
We called the Startled Fawn?'

Her heart was in her large sad eyes,
Half sunshine and half shade,
And love – as love first springs to life –
Of every thing afraid.

The red leaf far more heavily
Fell down to autumn earth
Than her light feet, which seemed to move
To music and to mirth.

With the light feet of early youth,
  What hopes and joys depart –
Ah, nothing like the heavy step
  Betrays the heavy heart.

It is a usual history
  That Indian girl could tell:
Fate sets apart one common doom
  For all who love too well.

The proud, the shy, the sensitive –
  Life has not many such –
They dearly buy their happiness,
  By feeling it too much.

A stranger to her forest home,
  That fair young stranger came;
They raised for him the funeral song –
  For him the funeral flame.

Love sprang from pity, and her arms
  Around his arms she threw;
She told her father, 'If he dies,
  Your daughter dieth too!'

For her sweet sake they set him free –
  He lingered at her side;
And many a native song yet tells
  Of that pale stranger's bride.

Two years have passed – how much two years
  Have taken in their flight!
They've taken from the lip its smile,
  And from the eye its light.

Poor child! – she was a child in years,
  So timid and so young –
With what a fond and earnest faith
  To desperate hope she clung!

His eyes grew cold, his voice grew strange
  (They only grew more dear)
She served him meekly, anxiously,
  With love – half faith, half fear.

And can a fond and faithful heart
   Be worthless in those eyes
For which it beats? Ah, woe to those
   Who such a heart despise!

Poor child! what lonely days she passed,
   With nothing to recall
But bitter taunts, and careless words,
   And looks more cold than all.

Alas for love that sits at home,
   Forsaken, and yet fond –
The grief that sits beside the hearth,
   Life has no grief beyond!

He left her, but she followed him –
   She thought he could not bear,
When she had left her home for him,
   To look on her despair.

Adown the strange and mighty stream
   She took her lonely way:
The stars at night her pilots were,
   As was the sun by day.

Yet mournfully – how mournfully –
   The Indian looked behind
When the last sound of voice or step
   Died on the midnight wind.

Yet still adown the gloomy stream
   She plied her weary oar –
Her husband, he had left their home,
   And it was home no more.

She found him – but she found in vain –
   He spurned her from his side;
He said her brow was all too dark
   For her to be his bride.

She grasped his hands – her own were cold –
   And silent turned away,
As she had not a tear to shed
   And not a word to say.

And pale as death she reached her boat,
   And guided it along;
With broken voice she strove to raise
   A melancholy song.

None watched the lonely Indian girl –
   She passed unmarked of all –
Until they saw her slight canoe
   Approach the mighty Fall!

Upright within that slender boat
   They saw the pale girl stand,
Her dark hair streaming far behind,
   Upraised her desperate hand.

The air is filled with shriek and shout:
   They call, but call in vain!
The boat amid the waters dashed –
   'Twas never seen again.

IV. Ennobling Interchange: Man and Nature

Wordsworth's sense of 'A balance, an ennobling interchange / Of action from within and from without' assumes a reciprocal relationship between man and Nature. It is the aspect of Romantic thinking that can most obviously be regarded as a tradition, and it is the area in which forerunners are of greatest importance. Speaking in the guise of a mouse, trapped by Joseph Priestley (discoverer of oxygen, founder of the Unitarian faith as preached by Coleridge), Barbauld speculates in 1773 that

> mind, as ancient sages taught,
> A never-dying flame,
> Still shifts through matter's varying forms,
> In every form the same.

Cowper, eighteen years later, sits before the fire in his Georgian drawing-room, in a 'waking dream' such as Keats will later experience. Seeing in his fantasy trees, towers, faces, in the embers, he is aware of the outgoing of the mind – 'myself creating what I saw' is the way he puts it.

Already influenced by Cowper's blank-verse meditations, Coleridge in 1798 uses the *Winter Evening* reverie as the basis for *Frost at Midnight*, his major Conversation Poem and most impressive early definition of imagination's power. Nature is the language 'uttered' by God – the means by which he, as the 'Great Universal Teacher, reveals 'Himself in all, and all things in himself'. Imagination is the godlike human faculty that reads the language. Taking up the thread, Wordsworth in *Tintern Abbey* (written a mere six months later) perceives a life-force, present at once in external Nature ('the light of setting suns') and 'in the mind of man'. 'Dosed' with Wordsworth by Shelley in 1816, Byron will write,

> I live not for myself, but I become
> Portion of that around me, and to me
> High mountains are a feeling . . .

Within weeks, Shelley himself (while claiming to be an atheist) will write in *Mont Blanc* of the 'everlasting universe of things', flowing through the mind, and of a mysterious 'Secret Strength of Things' who inhabits the mountain and 'governs' human thought.

Keats, though (like Byron) not usually a poet who thinks in such terms, will add in 1818 the numinous lines of *Endymion*:

> Wherein lies happiness? In that which becks
> Our ready minds to fellowship divine,
> A fellowship with essence . . .

Meanwhile, unpublished (and therefore not a part of this known progression), are the great visionary scenes of Wordsworth's 1805 *Prelude*, above all the Climbing of Snowdon, where mist on the slopes of the mountain images the mind in its transforming power, and the poet

> is exalted by an underpresence,
> The sense of God, or whatso'er is dim
> Or vast in [his] own being.

Not all Romantic poetry of Nature tends to this sublime (Clare's for instance doesn't very often), but little is merely descriptive. Response is felt, almost always, to be more important than description.

1. ANNA LAETITIA BARBAULD

(i) *The Mouse's Petition to Dr Priestley, Found in the Trap where he had been Confined all Night* (1773)

Oh, hear a pensive captive's prayer,
For liberty that sighs,
And never let thine heart be shut
Against the prisoner's cries!

For here forlorn and sad I sit,
Within the wiry grate,
And tremble at the approaching morn
Which brings impending fate.

If e'er thy breast with freedom glowed,
And spurned a tyrant's chain,
Let not thy strong oppressive force
A free-born mouse detain!

Oh, do not stain with guiltless blood
Thy hospitable hearth,
Nor triumph that thy wiles betrayed
A prize so little worth.

The scattered gleanings of a feast
My scanty meals supply –
But if thine unrelenting heart
That slender boon deny,

The cheerful light, the vital air,
Are blessings widely given;
Let Nature's commoners enjoy
The common gifts of Heaven.

The well-taught philosophic mind
To all compassion gives;
Casts round the world an equal eye,
And feels for all that lives.

If mind, as ancient sages taught,
A never-dying flame,
Still shifts through matter's varying forms,
In every form the same,

Beware, lest in the worm you crush
A brother's soul you find;
And tremble lest thy luckless hand
Dislodge a kindred mind.

Or, if this transient gleam of day
Be *all* of life we share,
Let pity plead within thy breast
That little *all* to spare.

So may thy hospitable board
With health and peace be crowned,
And every charm of heartfelt ease
Beneath thy roof be found.

So, when unseen destruction lurks,
Which mice like men may share,
May some kind angel clear thy path,
And break the hidden snare.

(ii) *A Summer's Evening's Meditation*

(lines 17–98) 1773

'Tis now the hour
When Contemplation from her sunless haunts
(The cool damp grotto or the lonely depth
Of unpierced woods), where, wrapped in solid shade,
She mused away the gaudy hours of noon
And fed on thoughts unripened by the sun,
Moves forward, and with radiant finger points
To yon blue concave swelled by breath divine,
Where, one by one, the living eyes of Heaven
Awake, quick-kindling o'er the face of ether
One boundless blaze – ten thousand trembling fires
And dancing lustres – where the unsteady eye,
Restless and dazzled, wanders unconfined
O'er all this field of glories! Spacious field,
And worthy of the Master – he whose hand
With hieroglyphics older than the Nile
Inscribed the mystic tablet hung on high
To public gaze, and said, 'Adore, oh man,
The finger of thy God!'
From what pure wells
Of milky light, what soft o'erflowing urn,
Are all these lamps so filled – these friendly lamps
For ever streaming o'er the azure deep
To point our path and light us to our home?
How soft they slide along their lucid spheres,
And, silent as the foot of time, fulfil
Their destined courses! Nature's self is hushed
And, but a scattered leaf which rustles through
The thick-wove foliage, not a sound is heard
To break the midnight air – though the raised ear,
Intensely listening, drinks in every breath.
How deep the silence, yet how loud the praise!
But are they silent all? Or is there not
A tongue in every star that talks with man
And woos him to be wise – nor woos in vain?
This dead of midnight is the noon of thought,
And wisdom mounts her zenith with the stars.
At this still hour the self-collected soul

Turns inward, and beholds a stranger there
Of high descent, and more than mortal rank:
An embryo God, a spark of fire divine
Which must burn on for ages, when the sun
(Fair transitory creature of a day)
Has closed his golden eye and, wrapped in shades,
Forgets his wonted journey through the east.
Ye citadels of light and seats of gods –
Perhaps my future home! – from whence the soul,
Revolving periods past, may oft look back
With recollected tenderness on all
The various busy scenes she left below
(Its deep-laid projects and its strange events),
As on some fond and doting tale that soothed
Her infant hours. Oh be it lawful now
To tread the hallowed circle of your courts,
And with mute wonder and delighted awe
Approach your burning confines!
Seized in thought,
On fancy's wild and roving wing I sail,
From the green borders of the peopled earth
And the pale moon, her duteous fair attendant;
From solitary Mars; from the vast orb
Of Jupiter, whose huge gigantic bulk
Dances in ether like the lightest leaf –
To the dim verge, the suburbs of the system,
Where cheerless Saturn midst her watery moons,
Girt with a lucid zone, majestic sits
In gloomy grandeur, like an exiled queen
Amongst her weeping handmaids.
Fearless thence
I launch into the trackless deeps of space
Where, burning round, ten thousand suns appear
Of elder beam, which ask no leave to shine
Of our terrestrial star, nor borrow light
From the proud regent of our scanty day –
Sons of the morning, first-born of Creation,
And only less than Him who marks their track
And guides their fiery wheels. Here must I stop,
Or is there aught beyond? What hand unseen
Impels me onward through the glowing orbs
Of habitable Nature far remote,

To the dread confines of eternal night,
To solitudes of vast unpeopled space,
The deserts of Creation, wide and wild,
Where embryo systems and unkindled suns
Sleep in the womb of chaos?

2. WILLIAM COWPER

The Winter Evening (*Task* IV, 267–332) 1785

Just when our drawing-rooms begin to blaze
With lights, by clear reflection multiplied
From many a mirror – in which he of Gath,
Goliath, might have seen his giant bulk
Whole, without stooping, towering crest and all –
My pleasures, too, begin. But me perhaps,
The glowing hearth may satisfy awhile
With faint illumination, that uplifts
The shadow to the ceiling, there by fits
Dancing uncouthly to the quivering flame.
Not undelightful is an hour to me
So spent in parlour-twilight: such a gloom
Suits well the thoughtful or unthinking mind,
The mind contemplative, with some new theme
Pregnant, or indisposed alike to all.
Laugh ye, who boast your more mercurial powers –
That never feel a stupor, know no pause,
Nor need one – I am conscious, and confess,
Fearless, a soul that does not always think.
Me oft has fancy, ludicrous and wild,
Soothed with a waking dream of houses, towers,
Trees, churches, and strange visages, expressed
In the red cinders, while with poring eye
I gazed, myself creating what I saw.
Nor less amused have I quiescent watched
The sooty films that play upon the bars,
Pendulous, and foreboding, in the view
Of superstition – prophesying still,
Though still deceived – some stranger's near approach.
'Tis thus the understanding takes repose

In indolent vacuity of thought,
And sleeps and is refreshed. Meanwhile the face
Conceals the mood lethargic with a mask
Of deep deliberation, as the man
Were tasked to his full strength, absorbed and lost.
Thus oft, reclined at ease, I lose an hour
At evening, till at length the freezing blast,
That sweeps the bolted shutter, summons home
The recollected powers, and, snapping short
The glassy threads with which the fancy weaves
Her brittle toys, restores me to myself.
How calm is my recess – and how the frost,
Raging abroad, and the rough wind, endear
The silence and the warmth within!
  I saw the woods and fields, at close of day,
A variegated show: the meadows green,
Though faded; and the lands where lately waved
The golden harvest, of a mellow brown,
Upturned so lately by the forceful share.
I saw far off the weedy fallows smile
With verdure not unprofitable, grazed
By flocks, fast feeding and selecting each
His favourite herb – while all the leafless groves
That skirt the horizon wore a sable hue,
Scarce noticed in the kindred dusk of eve.
Tomorrow brings a change, a total change!
Which even now – though silently performed,
And slowly, and by most unfelt – the face
Of universal Nature undergoes.
Fast falls a fleecy shower: the downy flakes,
Descending, and with never-ceasing lapse
Softly alighting upon all below,
Assimilate all objects. Earth receives
Gladly the thickening mantle, and the green
And tender blade that feared the chilling blast
Escapes unhurt beneath so warm a veil.

3. ROBERT BURNS

To a Mouse, On Turning Her Up in Her Nest with the Plough, November 1785 (1786)

Wee, sleeket, cowran', tim'rous beastie,
O, what a panic's in thy breastie!
Thou need na start awa sae hasty
Wi' bickering brattle –
I wad be laith to rin an' chase thee
Wi' murd'ring pattle!

I'm truly sorry man's dominion
Has broken Nature's social union,
An' justifies that ill opinion
Which makes thee startle
At me, thy poor earth-born companion
An' fellow-mortal!

I doubt na, whyles, but thou may thieve –
What then? poor beastie, thou maun live!
A daimen-icker in a thrave
'S a sma' request;
I'll get a blessin' wi' the lave,
An' never miss't!

Thy wee-bit housie, too, in ruin –
Its silly wa's the win's are strewin' –
An' naething, now, to big a new ane
O' foggage green!
An' bleak December's winds ensuin',
Baith snell an' keen!

1 *sleeket* glossy (sleeked). *cowran* cowering.
4 *bickering brattle* hurry and clatter. 5 *rin* run.
6 *pattle* spade (paddle). 13 *whyles* at times.
15 *A daimen-icker in a thrave* the odd ear of corn in a load.
17 *a blessin'* my reward. *the lave* the rest.
20 *silly wa's* feeble walls. *win's* winds. 21 *big* build.
22 *foggage* coarse grass. 24 *snell* bitter.

Thou saw the fields laid bare an' wast,
An' weary winter comin' fast,
An' cozie here, beneath the blast,
Thou thought to dwell –
Till crash! the cruel coulter past
Out thro' thy cell.

That wee-bit heap o' leaves an' stibble,
Has cost thee monie a weary nibble!
Now thou's turn'd out, for a' thy trouble,
But house or hald,
To thole the winter's sleety dribble
An' cranreuch cauld!

But Mousie, thou art no thy-lane
In proving foresight may be vain:
The best laid schemes o' mice an' men
Gang aft agley,
An' lea'e us nought but grief an' pain,
For promis'd joy!

Still, thou art blest compar'd wi' me:
The present only toucheth thee,
But och! I backward cast my e'e
On prospects drear –
An' forward, though I canna see,
I guess an' fear!

4. SAMUEL TAYLOR COLERIDGE

Conversation Poems

(i) *The Eolian Harp* (20 Aug. 1795; publ. 1796)

My pensive Sara! – thy soft cheek reclined
Thus on mine arm, most soothing sweet it is
To sit beside our cot, our cot o'ergrown
With white-flowered jasmine and the broad-leaved myrtle

29 *coulter* iron blade in front of a plough. **34** *hald* defence (hold).
36 *cranreuch* frost. **37** *thy-lane* on your own.
40 *Gang aft agley* go often astray.

(Meet emblems they of innocence and love),
And watch the clouds, that late were rich with light,
Slow saddening round, and mark the Star of Eve
Serenely brilliant (such should wisdom be)
Shine opposite. How exquisite the scents
Snatched from yon bean-field – and the world so hushed!
The stilly murmur of the distant sea
Tells us of silence.
                                        And that simplest lute,
Placed lengthways in the clasping casement – hark
How, by the desultory breeze caressed
Like some coy maid half yielding to her lover,
It pours such sweet upbraiding as must needs
Tempt to repeat the wrong! And now, its strings
Boldlier swept, the long sequacious notes
Over delicious surges sink and rise –
Such a soft floating witchery of sound
As twilight elfins make, when they at eve
Voyage on gentle gales from Faery Land,
Where *melodies* round honey-dropping flowers
(Footless and wild, like birds of Paradise)
Nor pause, nor perch, hovering on untamed wing!
        And thus, my love, as on the midway slope
Of yonder hill I stretch my limbs at noon,
Whilst through my half-closed eyelids I behold
The sunbeams dance like diamonds on the main,
And tranquil muse upon tranquillity,
Full many a thought uncalled and undetained,
And many idle flitting fantasies,
Traverse my indolent and passive brain –
As wild and various as the random gales
That swell and flutter on this subject lute!
And what if all of animated Nature
Be but organic harps, diversely framed,
That tremble into thought as o'er them sweeps,
Plastic and vast, one intellectual breeze,
At once the soul of each, and God of all?
But thy more serious eye a mild reproof
Darts, oh belovéd woman – nor such thoughts,
Dim and unhallowed, dost thou not reject –
And biddest me walk humbly with my God.
        Meek daughter in the family of Christ,
Well hast thou said – and holily dispraised
These shapings of the unregenerate mind,

Bubbles that glitter as they rise and break
On vain Philosophy's aye-babbling spring!
For never guiltless may I speak of him,
The Incomprehensible, save when with awe
I praise him, and with faith that inly *feels*,
Who with his saving mercies healéd me,
A sinful and most miserable man,
Wildered and dark, and gave me to possess
Peace, and this cot, and thee, heart-honoured maid!

(ii) *This Lime-Tree Bower, My Prison: A Poem Addressed to Charles Lamb of the India-House, London* (July 1797; publ. 1800)

In the June of 1797 some long-expected friends paid a visit to the author's cottage, and on the morning of their arrival he met with an accident which disabled him from walking during the whole time of their stay. One evening, when they had left him for a few hours, he composed the following lines in the garden bower.

Well, they are gone, and here must I remain,
This lime-tree bower my prison! I have lost
Such beauties and such feelings as had been
Most sweet to have remembered, even when age
Had dimmed my eyes to blindness! They, meanwhile,
My friends, whom I may never meet again,
On springy heath along the hilltop edge
Wander in gladness, and wind down, perchance,
To that still roaring dell of which I told
(The roaring dell, o'erwooded, narrow, deep,
And only speckled by the mid-day sun),
Where its slim trunk the ash from rock to rock
Flings arching like a bridge – that branchless ash,
Unsunned and damp, whose few poor yellow leaves
Ne'er tremble in the gale, yet tremble still,
Fanned by the waterfall! And there my friends
Behold the dark-green file of long lank weeds,
That all at once – a most fantastic sight! –
Still nod and drip beneath the dripping edge
Of the dim clay-stone.
                                        Now my friends emerge
Beneath the wide wide heaven, and view again

The many-steepled tract magnificent
Of hilly fields and meadows, and the sea,
With some fair bark, perhaps, which lightly touches
The slip of smooth clear blue betwixt two isles
Of purple shadow! Yes, they wander on
In gladness all; but thou, methinks, most glad,
My gentle-hearted Charles! For thou hast pined
And hungered after Nature many a year
In the great city pent, winning thy way
With sad yet patient soul, through evil and pain
And strange calamity! Ah, slowly sink
Behind the western ridge, thou glorious sun!
Shine in the slant beams of the sinking orb,
Ye purple heath-flowers! Richlier burn, ye clouds!
Live in the yellow light, ye distant groves!
And kindle, thou blue ocean! So my friend
Struck with deep joy may stand, as I have stood,
Silent with swimming sense; yea, gazing round
On the wide landscape, gaze till all doth seem
Less gross than bodily; a living thing
Which *acts* upon the mind – and with such hues
As clothe the Almighty Spirit when he makes
Spirits perceive his presence.
A delight
Comes sudden on my heart, and I am glad
As I myself were there! Nor in this bower,
This little lime-tree bower, have I not marked
Much that has soothed me. Pale beneath the blaze
Hung the transparent foliage, and I watched
Some broad and sunny leaf, and loved to see
The shadow of the leaf and stem above
Dappling its sunshine! And that walnut-tree
Was richly tinged, and a deep radiance lay
Full on the ancient ivy, which *usurps*
Those fronting elms – and now, with blackest mass,
Makes their dark branches gleam a lighter hue
Through the late twilight. And though now the bat
Wheels silent by, and not a swallow twitters,
Yet still the solitary humble-bee
Sings in the bean-flower!
Henceforth I shall know
That Nature ne'er deserts the wise and pure –
No scene so narrow but may well employ
Each faculty of sense, and keep the heart

Awake to love and beauty! And sometimes
'Tis well to be bereft of promised good,
That we may lift the soul, and contemplate
With lively joy the joys we cannot share.
My gentle-hearted Charles, when the last rook
Beat its straight path along the dusky air
Homewards, I blest it! – deeming its black wing
(Now a dim speck, now vanishing in light)
Had crossed the mighty orb's dilated glory
While thou stoodst gazing; or, when all was still,
Flew creeking o'er thy head, and had a charm
For thee, my gentle-hearted Charles, to whom
No sound is dissonant which tells of life.

(iii) *Frost at Midnight* (Feb. 1798; publ. 1798)

The frost performs its secret ministry,
Unhelped by any wind. The owlet's cry
Came loud – and hark, again – loud as before!
The inmates of my cottage, all at rest,
Have left me to that solitude which suits
Abstruser musings – save that at my side
My cradled infant slumbers peacefully.
'Tis calm indeed – so calm that it disturbs
And vexes meditation with its strange
And extreme silentness. Sea, hill, and wood,
This populous village – sea, and hill, and wood,
With all the numberless goings-on of life,
Inaudible as dreams! The thin blue flame
Lies on my low-burnt fire, and quivers not.
Only that film, which fluttered on the grate,
Still flutters there, the sole unquiet thing!
   Methinks, its motion in this hush of Nature
Gives it dim sympathies with me who live,
Making it a companionable form,
With which I can hold commune. Idle thought!
But still the living spirit in our frame,
That loves not to behold a lifeless thing,
Transfuses into all its own delights,
Its own volition, sometimes with deep faith,
And sometimes with fantastic playfulness.
Ah me! amused by no such curious toys,
How often in my early schoolboy days,

With most believing superstitious wish
Presageful, have I gazed upon the bars
To watch the *stranger* there!
And oft, belike,
With unclosed lids, already had I dreamt
Of my sweet birth-place, and the old church-tower,
Whose bells, the poor man's only music, rang
From morn to evening, all the hot Fair-day,
So sweetly, that they stirred and haunted me
With a wild pleasure, falling on mine ear
Most like articulate sounds of things to come.
So gazed I, till the soothing things I dreamt
Lulled me to sleep, and sleep prolonged my dreams!
And so I brooded all the following morn,
Awed by the stern preceptor's face, mine eye
Fixed with mock study on my swimming book;
Save if the door half opened, and I snatched
A hasty glance – and still my heart leapt up,
For still I hoped to see the *stranger's* face,
Townsman, or aunt, or sister more beloved,
My play-mate when we both were clothed alike!
Dear babe, that sleepest cradled by my side,
Whose gentle breathings, heard in this dead calm,
Fill up the interspersèd vacancies
And momentary pauses of the thought!
My babe so beautiful, it thrills my heart
With tender gladness, thus to look at thee,
And think that thou shalt learn far other lore,
And in far other scenes! For I was reared
In the great city, pent mid cloisters dim,
And saw nought lovely but the sky and stars.
But thou, my babe, shalt wander like a breeze
By lakes and sandy shores, beneath the crags
Of ancient mountain, and beneath the clouds,
Which image in their bulk both lakes and shores
And mountain-crags. So shalt thou see and hear
The lovely shapes and sounds intelligible
Of that eternal language which thy God
Utters, who from eternity doth teach
Himself in all, and all things in himself.
Great universal Teacher – he shall mould
Thy spirit, and by giving make it ask!

Therefore all seasons shall be sweet to thee,
Whether the summer clothe the general earth
With greenness, or the redbreast sit and sing
Betwixt the tufts of snow on the bare branch
Of mossy apple-tree, while all the thatch
Smokes in the sun-thaw; whether the eave-drops fall
Heard only in the trances of the blast,
Or whether the secret ministry of cold
Shall hang them up in silent icicles,
Quietly shining to the quiet moon –
Like those, my babe, which, ere tomorrow's warmth
Have capped their sharp keen points with pendulous drops,
Will catch thine eye, and with their novelty
Suspend thy little soul, then make thee shout
And stretch and flutter from thy mother's arms
As thou wouldst fly for very eagerness.

(iv) *The Nightingale*

(May 1798; publ. *Lyrical Ballads*)

No cloud, no relic of the sunken day,
Distinguishes the west, no long thin slip
Of sullen light, no obscure trembling hues.
Come, we will rest on this old mossy bridge!
You see the glimmer of the stream beneath,
But hear no murmuring: it flows silently
O'er its soft bed of verdure. All is still,
A balmy night! And though the stars be dim,
Yet let us think upon the vernal showers
That gladden the green earth, and we shall find
A pleasure in the dimness of the stars.
And hark, the nightingale begins its song,
'Most musical, most melancholy'!
A melancholy bird? Oh idle thought:
In Nature there is nothing melancholy.
But some night-wandering man, whose heart was pierced
With the remembrance of a grievous wrong,
Or slow distemper, or neglected love,
And so, poor wretch! filled all things with himself
And made all gentle sounds tell back the tale
Of his own sorrows – he, and such as he,

First named these notes a melancholy strain,
And many a poet echoes the conceit,
Poet, who hath been building up the rhyme
When he had better far have stretched his limbs
Beside a brook in mossy forest-dell
By sun or moonlight, to the influxes
Of shapes and sounds and shifting elements
Surrendering his whole spirit, of his song
And of his fame forgetful! So his fame
Should share in Nature's immortality –
A venerable thing – and so his song
Should make all Nature lovelier, and itself
Be loved, like Nature. But 'twill not be so;
And youths and maidens most poetical
Who lose the deepening twilights of the spring
In ball-rooms and hot theatres, they still
(Full of meek sympathy) must heave their sighs
O'er Philomela's pity-pleading strains!
My friend, and my friend's sister! we have learnt
A different lore: we may not thus profane
Nature's sweet voices, always full of love
And joyance! 'Tis the merry nightingale
That crowds, and hurries, and precipitates,
With fast thick warble, his delicious notes,
As he were fearful, that an April night
Would be too short for him to utter forth
His love-chant, and disburden his full soul
Of all its music! And I know a grove
Of large extent, hard by a castle huge
Which the great lord inhabits not; and so
This grove is wild with tangling underwood,
And the trim walks are broken up, and grass,
Thin grass and king-cups, grow within the paths –
But never elsewhere in one place I knew
So many nightingales! And far and near,
In wood and thicket, over the wide grove
They answer and provoke each other's songs
With skirmish and capricious passagings,
And murmurs musical, and swift jug jug,
And one low piping sound more sweet than all,
Stirring the air with such an harmony
That, should you close your eyes, you might almost
Forget it was not day! On moonlight bushes,
Whose dewy leafits are but half disclosed,

You may perchance behold them on the twigs,
Their bright, bright eyes – their eyes both bright and full –
Glistening, while many a glow-worm in the shade
Lights up her love-torch.
                                        A most gentle maid
Who dwelleth in her hospitable home
Hard by the Castle, and at latest eve
(Even like a lady vowed and dedicate
To something more than Nature in the grove)
Glides through the pathways. She knows all their notes,
That gentle maid! and oft, a moment's space,
What time the moon was lost behind a cloud,
Hath heard a pause of silence – till the moon,
Emerging, hath awakened earth and sky
With one sensation, and those wakeful birds
Have all burst forth in choral minstrelsy,
As if one quick and sudden gale had swept
An hundred airy harps! And she hath watched
Many a nightingale perch giddily
On blossomy twig still swinging from the breeze,
And to that motion tune his wanton song
Like tipsy joy that reels with tossing head.
   Farewell, oh warbler, till tomorrow eve!
And you, my friends, farewell – a short farewell!
We have been loitering long and pleasantly,
And now for our dear homes. That strain again –
Full fain it would delay me! My dear babe,
Who, capable of no articulate sound,
Mars all things with his imitative lisp,
How he would place his hand beside his ear
(His little hand), the small forefinger up,
And bid us listen! And I deem it wise
To make him Nature's playmate. He knows well
The evening star – and once when he awoke
In most distressful mood (some inward pain
Had made up that strange thing, an infant's dream)
I hurried with him to our orchard-plot,
And he beholds the moon, and, hushed at once,
Suspends his sobs, and laughs most silently,
While his fair eyes that swam with undropt tears
Did glitter in the yellow moon-beam!
                                                    Well,
It is a father's tale. But if that Heaven
Should give me life, his childhood shall grow up

Familiar with these songs, that with the night
He may associate joy! Once more farewell,
Sweet nightingale! Once more, my friends, farewell!

5. WILLIAM WORDSWORTH

'Images of a Mighty Mind'

(i) *Tintern Abbey* (13 July 1798; publ. *Lyrical Ballads*)

Five years have passed, five summers, with the length
Of five long winters, and again I hear
These waters, rolling from their mountain-springs
With a sweet inland murmur. Once again
Do I behold these steep and lofty cliffs,
Which on a wild secluded scene impress
Thoughts of more deep seclusion, and connect
The landscape with the quiet of the sky.
The day is come when I again repose
Here, under this dark sycamore, and view
These plots of cottage-ground, these orchard-tufts
Which at this season, with their unripe fruits,
Among the woods and copses lose themselves,
Nor with their green and simple hue disturb
The wild green landscape. Once again I see
These hedgerows – hardly hedgerows, little lines
Of sportive wood run wild – these pastoral farms
Green to the very door, and wreaths of smoke
Sent up, in silence, from among the trees
With some uncertain notice, as might seem
Of vagrant dwellers in the houseless woods,
Or of some hermit's cave, where by his fire
The hermit sits alone.
Though absent long,
These forms of beauty have not been to me
As is a landscape to a blind man's eye;
But oft, in lonely rooms, and mid the din
Of towns and cities, I have owed to them,
In hours of weariness, sensations sweet
Felt in the blood, and felt along the heart,
And passing even into my purer mind

With tranquil restoration – feelings too
Of unremembered pleasure; such, perhaps,
As may have had no trivial influence
On that best portion of a good man's life,
His little nameless unremembered acts
Of kindness and of love. Nor less, I trust,
To them I may have owed another gift,
Of aspect more sublime: that blessèd mood
In which the burden of the mystery,
In which the heavy and the weary weight
Of all this unintelligible world,
Is lightened – that serene and blessèd mood
In which the affections gently lead us on,
Until, the breath of this corporeal frame
And even the motion of our human blood
Almost suspended, we are laid asleep
In body, and become a living soul,
While, with an eye made quiet by the power
Of harmony, and the deep power of joy,
We see into the life of things.
                                                  If this
Be but a vain belief, yet oh, how oft,
In darkness, and amid the many shapes
Of joyless daylight, when the fretful stir
Unprofitable and the fever of the world
Have hung upon the beatings of my heart,
How oft in spirit have I turned to thee
Oh sylvan Wye, thou wanderer through the woods –
How often has my spirit turned to thee!
   And now, with gleams of half-extinguished thought,
With many recognitions dim and faint,
And somewhat of a sad perplexity,
The picture of the mind revives again,
While here I stand, not only with the sense
Of present pleasure, but with pleasing thoughts
That in this moment there is life and food
For future years. And so I dare to hope
Though changed, no doubt, from what I was when first
I came among these hills, when like a roe
I bounded o'er the mountains, by the sides
Of the deep rivers and the lonely streams,
Wherever Nature led – more like a man
Flying from something that he dreads, than one

Who sought the thing he loved. For Nature then
(The coarser pleasures of my boyish days,
And their glad animal movements, all gone by)
To me was all in all. I cannot paint
What then I was. The sounding cataract
Haunted me like a passion; the tall rock,
The mountain, and the deep and gloomy wood,
Their colours and their forms, were then to me
An appetite – a feeling and a love
That had no need of a remoter charm
By thought supplied, or any interest
Unborrowed from the eye.
                                        That time is past,
And all its aching joys are now no more,
And all its dizzy raptures. Not for this
Faint I, nor mourn, nor murmur: other gifts
Have followed, for such loss, I would believe,
Abundant recompense. For I have learned
To look on Nature, not as in the hour
Of thoughtless youth, but hearing oftentimes
The still, sad music of humanity,
Nor harsh, nor grating, though of ample power
To chasten and subdue. And I have felt
A presence that disturbs me with the joy
Of elevated thoughts, a sense sublime
Of something far more deeply interfused,
Whose dwelling is the light of setting suns,
And the round ocean, and the living air,
And the blue sky, and in the mind of man –
A motion and a spirit that impels
All thinking things, all objects of all thought,
And rolls through all things. Therefore am I still
A lover of the meadows and the woods
And mountains, and of all that we behold
From this green earth – of all the mighty world
Of eye and ear, both what they half-create,
And what perceive – well pleased to recognize
In Nature and the language of the sense
The anchor of my purest thoughts, the nurse,
The guide, the guardian of my heart, and soul
Of all my moral being.
                                    Nor perchance

If I were not thus taught, should I the more
Suffer my genial spirits to decay;
For thou art with me, here, upon the banks
Of this fair river – thou, my dearest friend,
My dear, dear friend – and in thy voice I catch
The language of my former heart, and read
My former pleasures in the shooting lights
Of thy wild eyes. Oh, yet a little while
May I behold in thee what I was once,
My dear, dear sister. And this prayer I make,
Knowing that Nature never did betray
The heart that loved her: 'tis her privilege
Through all the years of this our life to lead
From joy to joy. For she can so inform
The mind that is within us, so impress
With quietness and beauty, and so feed
With lofty thoughts, that neither evil tongues,
Rash judgments, nor the sneers of selfish men,
Nor greetings where no kindness is, nor all
The dreary intercourse of daily life,
Shall e'er prevail against us, or disturb
Our cheerful faith that all which we behold
Is full of blessings. Therefore let the moon
Shine on thee in thy solitary walk,
And let the misty mountain winds be free
To blow against thee; and in after years,
When these wild ecstasies shall be matured
Into a sober pleasure, when thy mind
Shall be a mansion for all lovely forms,
Thy memory be as a dwelling-place
For all sweet sounds and harmonies – oh, then
If solitude, or fear, or pain, or grief,
Should be thy portion, with what healing thoughts
Of tender joy wilt thou remember me
And these my exhortations!
                                        Nor perchance
If I should be where I no more can hear
Thy voice, nor catch from thy wild eyes these gleams
Of past existence, wilt thou then forget
That on the banks of this delightful stream
We stood together, and that I, so long
A worshipper of Nature, hither came

Unwearied in that service – rather say
With warmer love, oh, with far deeper zeal
Of holier love! Nor wilt thou then forget
That after many wanderings, many years
Of absence, these steep woods and lofty cliffs,
And this green pastoral landscape, were to me
More dear, both for themselves, and for thy sake.

(ii) *There Was a Boy*

(Oct. 1798; publ. *Lyrical Ballads* 1800)

There was a boy – ye knew him well, ye cliffs
And islands of Winander – many a time
At evening, when the stars had just begun
To move along the edges of the hills,
Rising or setting, would he stand alone
Beneath the trees or by the glimmering lake,
And there, with fingers interwoven, both hands
Pressed closely palm to palm and to his mouth
Uplifted, he, as through an instrument,
Blew mimic hootings to the silent owls,
That they might answer him. And they would shout
Across the watery vale, and shout again,
Responsive to his call, with quivering peals,
And long halloos, and screams, and echoes loud,
Redoubled and redoubled – a wild scene
Of mirth and jocund din. And when it chanced
That pauses of deep silence mocked his skill,
Then sometimes in that silence, while he hung
Listening, a gentle shock of mild surprise
Has carried far into his heart the voice
Of mountain torrents; or the visible scene
Would enter unawares into his mind
With all its solemn imagery – its rocks,
Its woods, and that uncertain heaven – received
Into the bosom of the steady lake.

(iii) *The Two-Part Prelude*

(Oct. 1798–Dec. 1799; publ. 1850/from MS 1972)

First Part

Was it for this
That one, the fairest of all rivers, loved
To blend his murmurs with my nurse's song,
And from his alder shades and rocky falls,
And from his fords and shallows, sent a voice
That flowed along my dreams? For this didst thou,
Oh Derwent, travelling over the green plains
Near my 'sweet birthplace', didst thou, beauteous stream,
Make ceaseless music through the night and day,
Which with its steady cadence tempering
Our human waywardness, composed my thoughts
To more than infant softness, giving me
Among the fretful dwellings of mankind
A knowledge, a dim earnest, of the calm
Which Nature breathes among the fields and groves?
Belovéd Derwent, fairest of all streams,
Was it for this that I, a four years' child,
A naked boy, among thy silent pools
Made one long bathing of a summer's day,
Basked in the sun, or plunged into thy streams,
Alternate, all a summer's day, or coursed
Over the sandy fields, and dashed the flowers
Of yellow groundsel – or, when crag and hill,
The woods, and distant Skiddaw's lofty height,
Were bronzed with a deep radiance, stood alone
A naked savage in the thunder-shower?
And afterwards ('twas in a later day,
Though early), when upon the mountain-slope
The frost and breath of frosty wind had snapped
The last autumnal crocus, 'twas my joy
To wander half the night among the cliffs
And the smooth hollows where the woodcocks ran
Along the moonlight turf. In thought and wish
That time, my shoulder all with springes hung,
I was a fell destroyer. Gentle powers,
Who give us happiness and call it peace,
When scudding on from snare to snare I plied
My anxious visitation, hurrying on,

Still hurrying, hurrying onward, how my heart
Panted! – among the scattered yew-trees and the crags
That looked upon me, how my bosom beat
With expectation! Sometimes strong desire
Resistless overpowered me, and the bird
Which was the captive of another's toils
Became my prey; and when the deed was done
I heard among the solitary hills
Low breathings coming after me, and sounds
Of undistinguishable motion, steps
Almost as silent as the turf they trod.
   Nor less in springtime, when on southern banks
The shining sun had from his knot of leaves
Decoyed the primrose flower, and when the vales
And woods were warm, was I a rover then
In the high places, on the lonesome peaks,
Among the mountains and the winds. Though mean
And though inglorious were my views, the end
Was not ignoble. Oh, when I have hung
Above the raven's nest, by knots of grass
Or half-inch fissures in the slippery rock
But ill sustained, and almost, as it seemed,
Suspended by the blast which blew amain
Shouldering the naked crag, oh, at that time,
While on the perilous ridge I hung alone,
With what strange utterance did the loud dry wind
Blow through my ears; the sky seemed not a sky
Of earth, and with what motion moved the clouds!
   The mind of man is fashioned and built up
Even as a strain of music. I believe
That there are spirits which, when they would form
A favoured being, from his very dawn
Of infancy do open out the clouds
As at the touch of lightning, seeking him
With gentle visitation – quiet powers,
Retired, and seldom recognized, yet kind,
And to the very meanest not unknown –
With me, though, rarely in my boyish days
They communed. Others too there are, who use,
Yet haply aiming at the self-same end,
Severer interventions, ministry
More palpable – and of their school was I.
   They guided me: one evening led by them
I went alone into a shepherd's boat,

A skiff, that to a willow-tree was tied
Within a rocky cave, its usual home.
The moon was up, the lake was shining clear
Among the hoary mountains; from the shore
I pushed, and struck the oars, and struck again
In cadence, and my little boat moved on
Just like a man who walks with stately step
Though bent on speed. It was an act of stealth
And troubled pleasure. Not without the voice
Of mountain echoes did my boat move on,
Leaving behind her still on either side
Small circles glittering idly in the moon,
Until they melted all into one track
Of sparkling light.
A rocky steep uprose
Above the cavern of the willow-tree,
And now, as suited one who proudly rowed
With his best skill, I fixed a steady view
Upon the top of that same craggy ridge,
The bound of the horizon – for behind
Was nothing but the stars and the grey sky.
She was an elfin pinnace; twenty times
I dipped my oars into the silent lake,
And as I rose upon the stroke my boat
Went heaving through the water like a swan –
When from behind that rocky steep, till then
The bound of the horizon, a huge cliff,
As if with voluntary power instinct,
Upreared its head. I struck, and struck again,
And, growing still in stature, the huge cliff
Rose up between me and the stars, and still,
With measured motion, like a living thing
Strode after me. With trembling hands I turned,
And through the silent water stole my way
Back to the cavern of the willow-tree.
There in her mooring-place I left my bark,
And through the meadows homeward went with grave
And serious thoughts; and after I had seen
That spectacle, for many days my brain
Worked with a dim and undetermined sense
Of unknown modes of being. In my thoughts
There was a darkness – call it solitude,
Or blank desertion – no familiar shapes
Of hourly objects, images of trees,

Of sea or sky, no colours of green fields,
But huge and mighty forms that do not live
Like living men moved slowly through my mind
By day, and were the trouble of my dreams.
   Ah, not in vain ye beings of the hills,
And ye that walk the woods and open heaths
By moon or starlight, thus, from my first dawn
Of childhood, did ye love to intertwine
The passions that build up our human soul
Not with the mean and vulgar works of man,
But with high objects, with eternal things,
With life and Nature, purifying thus
The elements of feeling and of thought,
And sanctifying by such discipline
Both pain and fear, until we recognize
A grandeur in the beatings of the heart.
   Nor was this fellowship vouchsafed to me
With stinted kindness. In November days,
When vapours rolling down the valleys made
A lonely scene more lonesome, among woods
At noon, and mid the calm of summer nights
When by the margin of the trembling lake
Beneath the gloomy hills I homeward went
In solitude, such intercourse was mine.
   And in the frosty season, when the sun
Was set, and visible for many a mile
The cottage windows through the twilight blazed,
I heeded not the summons. Clear and loud
The village-clock tolled six; I wheeled about
Proud and exulting, like an untired horse
That cares not for its home. All shod with steel
We hissed along the polished ice in games
Confederate, imitative of the chase
And woodland pleasures, the resounding horn,
The pack loud bellowing, and the hunted hare.
So through the darkness and the cold we flew,
And not a voice was idle. With the din,
Meanwhile, the precipices rang aloud;
The leafless trees and every icy crag
Tinkled like iron; while the distant hills
Into the tumult sent an alien sound
Of melancholy, not unnoticed; while the stars,
Eastward, were sparkling clear, and in the west
The orange sky of evening died away.

Not seldom from the uproar I retired
Into a silent bay, or sportively
Glanced sideway, leaving the tumultuous throng,
To cut across the shadow of a star
That gleamed upon the ice. And oftentimes
When we had given our bodies to the wind
And all the shadowy banks on either side
Came sweeping through the darkness, spinning still
The rapid line of motion, then at once
Have I, reclining back upon my heels,
Stopped short – yet still the solitary cliffs
Wheeled by me, even as if the earth had rolled
With visible motion her diurnal round.
Behind me did they stretch in solemn train,
Feebler and feebler, and I stood and watched
Till all was tranquil as a summer sea.
Ye powers of earth, ye genii of the springs,
And ye that have your voices in the clouds,
And ye that are familiars of the lakes
And of the standing pools, I may not think
A vulgar hope was yours when ye employed
Such ministry – when ye through many a year
Thus by the agency of boyish sports,
On caves and trees, upon the woods and hills,
Impressed upon all forms the characters
Of danger or desire, and thus did make
The surface of the universal earth
With meanings of delight, of hope and fear,
Work like a sea.
Not uselessly employed,
I might pursue this theme through every change
Of exercise and sport to which the year
Did summon us in its delightful round.
We were a noisy crew; the sun in heaven
Beheld not vales more beautiful than ours,
Nor saw a race in happiness and joy
More worthy of the fields where they were sown.
I would record with no reluctant voice
Our home amusements by the warm peat fire
At evening, when with pencil and with slate,
In square divisions parcelled out, and all
With crosses and with cyphers scribbled o'er,
We schemed and puzzled, head opposed to head,
In strife too humble to be named in verse;

Or round the naked table, snow-white deal,
Cherry, or maple, sat in close array,
And to the combat – loo or whist – led on
A thick-ribbed army, not as in the world
Discarded and ungratefully thrown by
Even for the very service they had wrought,
But husbanded through many a long campaign.
   Oh, with what echoes on the board they fell –
Ironic diamonds, hearts of sable hue,
Queens gleaming through their splendour's last decay,
Knaves wrapped in one assimilating gloom,
And kings indignant at the shame incurred
By royal visages. Meanwhile abroad
The heavy rain was falling, or the frost
Raged bitterly with keen and silent tooth,
And, interrupting the impassioned game,
Oft from the neighbouring lake the splitting ice,
While it sank down towards the water, sent
Among the meadows and the hills its long
And frequent yellings, imitative some
Of wolves that howl along the Bothnic main.
   Nor with less willing heart would I rehearse
The woods of autumn, and their hidden bowers
With milk-white clusters hung; the rod and line –
True symbol of the foolishness of hope –
Which with its strong enchantment led me on
By rocks and pools, where never summer star
Impressed its shadow, to forlorn cascades
Among the windings of the mountain-brooks;
The kite in sultry calms from some high hill
Sent up, ascending thence till it was lost
Among the fleecy clouds – in gusty days
Launched from the lower grounds, and suddenly
Dashed headlong and rejected by the storm.
All these, and more, with rival claims demand
Grateful acknowledgement. It were a song
Venial, and such as (if I rightly judge)
I might protract unblamed, but I perceive
That much is overlooked, and we should ill
Attain our object if, from delicate fears
Of breaking in upon the unity
Of this my argument, I should omit
To speak of such effects as cannot here
Be regularly classed, yet tend no less

To the same point – the growth of mental power
And love of Nature's works.
                                        Ere I had seen
Eight summers (and 'twas in the very week
When I was first transplanted to thy vale,
Belovéd Hawkshead! – when thy paths, thy shores
And brooks, were like a dream of novelty
To my half-infant mind), I chanced to cross
One of those open fields which, shaped like ears,
Make green peninsulas on Esthwaite's lake.
Twilight was coming on, yet through the gloom
I saw distinctly on the opposite shore,
Beneath a tree and close by the lake side,
A heap of garments, as if left by one
Who there was bathing. Half an hour I watched
And no one owned them; meanwhile the calm lake
Grew dark with all the shadows on its breast,
And now and then a leaping fish disturbed
The breathless stillness.
                                    The succeeding day
There came a company, and in their boat
Sounded with iron hooks and with long poles.
At length the dead man, mid that beauteous scene
Of trees and hills and water, bolt upright
Rose with his ghastly face. I might advert
To numerous accidents in flood or field,
Quarry or moor, or mid the winter snows,
Distresses and disasters, tragic facts
Of rural history that impressed my mind
With images to which in following years
Far other feelings were attached – with forms
That yet exist with independent life,
And, like their archetypes, know no decay.
   There are in our existence spots of time
Which with distinct preeminence retain
A fructifying virtue, whence, depressed
By trivial occupations and the round
Of ordinary intercourse, our minds –
Especially the imaginative power –
Are nourished and invisibly repaired.
Such moments chiefly seem to have their date
In our first childhood.
                                  I remember well
('Tis of an early season that I speak,

The twilight of rememberable life),
While I was yet an urchin, one who scarce
Could hold a bridle, with ambitious hopes
I mounted, and we rode towards the hills.
We were a pair of horsemen: honest James
Was with me, my encourager and guide.
We had not travelled long ere some mischance
Disjoined me from my comrade, and, through fear
Dismounting, down the rough and stony moor
I led my horse, and stumbling on, at length
Came to a bottom where in former times
A man, the murderer of his wife, was hung
In irons. Mouldered was the gibbet-mast;
The bones were gone, the iron and the wood;
Only a long green ridge of turf remained
Whose shape was like a grave. I left the spot,
And reascending the bare slope I saw
A naked pool that lay beneath the hills,
The beacon on the summit, and more near
A girl who bore a pitcher on her head
And seemed with difficult steps to force her way
Against the blowing wind. It was in truth
An ordinary sight, but I should need
Colours and words that are unknown to man
To paint the visionary dreariness
Which, while I looked all round for my lost guide,
Did at that time invest the naked pool,
The beacon on the lonely eminence,
The woman and her garments vexed and tossed
By the strong wind.
Nor less I recollect –
Long after, though my childhood had not ceased –
Another scene which left a kindred power
Implanted in my mind. One Christmas-time,
The day before the holidays began,
Feverish, and tired, and restless, I went forth
Into the fields, impatient for the sight
Of those three horses which should bear us home,
My brothers and myself. There was a crag,
An eminence, which from the meeting-point
Of two highways ascending overlooked
At least a long half-mile of those two roads,
By each of which the expected steeds might come –
The choice uncertain. Thither I repaired

Up to the highest summit. 'Twas a day
Stormy, and rough, and wild, and on the grass
I sat half sheltered by a naked wall.
Upon my right hand was a single sheep,
A whistling hawthorn on my left, and there,
Those two companions at my side, I watched
With eyes intensely straining, as the mist
Gave intermitting prospects of the wood
And plain beneath.
                                        Ere I to school returned
That dreary time, ere I had been ten days
A dweller in my father's house, he died,
And I and my two brothers, orphans then,
Followed his body to the grave. The event,
With all the sorrow which it brought, appeared
A chastisement; and when I called to mind
That day so lately passed, when from the crag
I looked in such anxiety of hope,
With trite reflections of morality,
Yet with the deepest passion, I bowed low
To God who thus corrected my desires.
And afterwards the wind and sleety rain,
And all the business of the elements,
The single sheep, and the one blasted tree,
And the bleak music of that old stone wall,
The noise of wood and water, and the mist
Which on the line of each of those two roads
Advanced in such indisputable shapes –
All these were spectacles and sounds to which
I often would repair, and thence would drink
As at a fountain. And I do not doubt
That in this later time, when storm and rain
Beat on my roof at midnight, or by day
When I am in the woods, unknown to me
The workings of my spirit thence are brought.
   Nor, sedulous as I have been to trace
How Nature by collateral interest,
And by extrinsic passion, peopled first
My mind with forms or beautiful or grand
And made me love them, may I well forget
How other pleasures have been mine, and joys
Of subtler origin – how I have felt
Not seldom, even in that tempestuous time,
Those hallowed and pure motions of the sense

Which seem in their simplicity to own
An intellectual charm, that calm delight
Which, if I err not, surely must belong
To those first-born affinities that fit
Our new existence to existing things,
And, in our dawn of being, constitute
The bond of union betwixt life and joy.
   Yes, I remember when the changeful earth
And twice five seasons on my mind had stamped
The faces of the moving year, even then,
A child, I held unconscious intercourse
With the eternal beauty, drinking in
A pure organic pleasure from the lines
Of curling mist, or from the level plain
Of waters coloured by the steady clouds.
The sands of Westmorland, the creeks and bays
Of Cumbria's rocky limits, they can tell
How when the sea threw off his evening shade
And to the shepherd's hut beneath the crags
Did send sweet notice of the rising moon,
How I have stood, to images like these
A stranger, linking with the spectacle
No body of associated forms,
And bringing with me no peculiar sense
Of quietness or peace – yet I have stood
Even while my eye has moved o'er three long leagues
Of shining water, gathering, as it seemed,
Through the wide surface of that field of light
New pleasure, like a bee among the flowers.
   Thus often in those fits of vulgar joy
Which through all seasons on a child's pursuits
Are prompt attendants, mid that giddy bliss
Which like a tempest works along the blood
And is forgotten, even then I felt
Gleams like the flashing of a shield. The earth
And common face of Nature spake to me
Rememberable things – sometimes, 'tis true,
By quaint associations, yet not vain
Nor profitless, if haply they impressed
Collateral objects and appearances,
Albeit lifeless then, and doomed to sleep
Until maturer seasons called them forth
To impregnate and to elevate the mind.
And if the vulgar joy by its own weight

Wearied itself out of the memory,
The scenes which were a witness of that joy
Remained, in their substantial lineaments
Depicted on the brain, and to the eye
Were visible, a daily sight. And thus
By the impressive agency of fear,
By pleasure and repeated happiness –
So frequently repeated – and by force
Of obscure feelings representative
Of joys that were forgotten, these same scenes,
So beauteous and majestic in themselves,
Though yet the day was distant, did at length
Become habitually dear, and all
Their hues and forms were by invisible links
Allied to the affections.
I began
My story early, feeling, as I fear,
The weakness of a human love for days
Disowned by memory – ere the birth of spring
Planting my snowdrops among winter snows.
Nor will it seem to thee, my friend, so prompt
In sympathy, that I have lengthened out
With fond and feeble tongue a tedious tale.
Meanwhile my hope has been that I might fetch
Reproaches from my former years, whose power
May spur me on, in manhood now mature,
To honourable toil. Yet should it be
That this is but an impotent desire –
That I by such inquiry am not taught
To understand myself, nor thou to know
With better knowledge how the heart was framed
Of him thou lovest – need I dread from thee
Harsh judgements if I am so loath to quit
Those recollected hours that have the charm
Of visionary things, and lovely forms
And sweet sensations, that throw back our life
And make our infancy a visible scene
On which the sun is shining?

Second Part

Thus far, my friend, have we retraced the way
Through which I travelled when I first began
To love the woods and fields. The passion yet

Was in its birth, sustained, as might befall,
By nourishment that came unsought – for still
From week to week, from month to month, we lived
A round of tumult. Duly were our games
Prolonged in summer till the daylight failed:
No chair remained before the doors, the bench
And threshold-steps were empty, fast asleep
The labourer and the old man who had sat
A later lingerer, yet the revelry
Continued and the loud uproar. At last,
When all the ground was dark and the huge clouds
Were edged with twinkling stars, to bed we went
With weary joints and with a beating mind.
Ah, is there one, who ever has been young
And needs a monitory voice to tame
The pride of virtue and of intellect?
And is there one, the wisest and the best
Of all mankind, who does not sometimes wish
For things which cannot be, who would not give,
If so he might, to duty and to truth
The eagerness of infantine desire?
A tranquillizing spirit presses now
On my corporeal frame, so wide appears
The vacancy between me and those days,
Which yet have such self-presence in my heart
That sometimes when I think of them I seem
Two consciousnesses – conscious of myself,
And of some other being.
A grey stone
Of native rock, left midway in the square
Of our small market-village, was the home
And centre of these joys; and when, returned
After long absence, thither I repaired,
I found that it was split and gone to build
A smart assembly-room that perked and flared
With wash and rough-cast, elbowing the ground
Which had been ours. But let the fiddle scream,
And be ye happy! Yet I know, my friends,
That more than one of you will think with me
Of those soft starry nights, and that old dame
From whom the stone was named, who there had sat
And watched her table with its huckster's wares,
Assiduous, for the length of sixty years.
We ran a boisterous race, the year spun round

With giddy motion; but the time approached
That brought with it a regular desire
For calmer pleasures – when the beauteous scenes
Of Nature were collaterally attached
To every scheme of holiday delight,
And every boyish sport, less grateful else
And languidly pursued. When summer came
It was the pastime of our afternoons
To beat along the plain of Windermere
With rival oars; and the selected bourne
Was now an island musical with birds
That sang for ever, now a sister isle
Beneath the oak's umbrageous covert, sown
With lilies-of-the-valley like a field,
And now a third small island where remained
An old stone table and one mouldered cave –
A hermit's history. In such a race,
So ended, disappointment could be none,
Uneasiness, or pain, or jealousy;
We rested in the shade, all pleased alike,
Conquered or conqueror. Thus our selfishness
Was mellowed down, and thus the pride of strength
And the vainglory of superior skill
Were interfused with objects which subdued
And tempered them, and gradually produced
A quiet independence of the heart.
And to my friend who knows me I may add,
Unapprehensive of reproof, that hence
Ensued a diffidence and modesty,
And I was taught to feel – perhaps too much –
The self-sufficing power of solitude.
   No delicate viands sapped our bodily strength:
More than we wished we knew the blessing then
Of vigorous hunger, for our daily meals
Were frugal, Sabine fare – and then, exclude
A little weekly stipend, and we lived
Through three divisions of the quartered year
In penniless poverty. But now, to school
Returned from the half-yearly holidays,
We came with purses more profusely filled,
Allowance which abundantly sufficed
To gratify the palate with repasts
More costly than the dame of whom I spake,
That ancient woman, and her board, supplied.

Hence inroads into distant vales, and long
Excursions far away among the hills,
Hence rustic dinners on the cool green ground –
Or in the woods, or by a river-side
Or fountain – festive banquets, that provoked
The languid action of a natural scene
By pleasure of corporeal appetite.
   Nor is my aim neglected if I tell
How twice in the long length of those half-years
We from our funds perhaps with bolder hand
Drew largely, anxious for one day at least
To feel the motion of the galloping steed;
And with the good old innkeeper, in truth,
I needs must say that sometimes we have used
Sly subterfuge, for the intended bound
Of the day's journey was too distant far
For any cautious man: a structure famed
Beyond its neighbourhood, the antique walls
Of a large abbey, with its fractured arch,
Belfry, and images, and living trees –
A holy scene. Along the smooth green turf
Our horses grazed. In more than inland peace,
Left by the winds that overpass the vale,
In that sequestered ruin trees and towers –
Both silent and both motionless alike –
Hear all day long the murmuring sea that beats
Incessantly upon a craggy shore.
   Our steeds remounted, and the summons given,
With whip and spur we by the chantry flew
In uncouth race, and left the cross-legged knight
And the stone abbot, and that single wren
Which one day sang so sweetly in the nave
Of the old church that, though from recent showers
The earth was comfortless, and, touched by faint
Internal breezes, from the roofless walls
The shuddering ivy dripped large drops, yet still
So sweetly mid the gloom the invisible bird
Sang to itself that there I could have made
My dwelling-place, and lived for ever there,
To hear such music. Through the walls we flew
And down the valley, and, a circuit made
In wantonness of heart, through rough and smooth
We scampered homeward. Oh, ye rocks and streams,
And that still spirit of the evening air,

Even in this joyous time I sometimes felt
Your presence, when, with slackened step, we breathed
Along the sides of the steep hills, or when,
Lightened by gleams of moonlight from the sea,
We beat with thundering hoofs the level sand.
There was a row of ancient trees, since fallen,
That on the margin of a jutting land
Stood near the lake of Coniston, and made,
With its long boughs above the water stretched,
A gloom through which a boat might sail along
As in a cloister. An old hall was near,
Grotesque and beautiful, its gavel-end
And huge round chimneys to the top o'ergrown
With fields of ivy. Thither we repaired –
'Twas even a custom with us – to the shore,
And to that cool piazza. They who dwelt
In the neglected mansion-house supplied
Fresh butter, tea-kettle and earthenware,
And chafing-dish with smoking coals; and so
Beneath the trees we sat in our small boat,
And in the covert ate our delicate meal
Upon the calm smooth lake.
It was a joy
Worthy the heart of one who is full-grown
To rest beneath those horizontal boughs
And mark the radiance of the setting sun,
Himself unseen, reposing on the top
Of the high eastern hills. And there I said,
That beauteous sight before me, there I said
(Then first beginning in my thoughts to mark
That sense of dim similitude which links
Our moral feelings with external forms)
That in whatever region I should close
My mortal life I would remember you,
Fair scenes – that dying I would think on you,
My soul would send a longing look to you,
Even as that setting sun, while all the vale
Could nowhere catch one faint memorial gleam,
Yet with the last remains of his last light
Still lingered, and a farewell lustre threw
On the dear mountain-tops where first he rose.
'Twas then my fourteenth summer, and these words
Were uttered in a casual access
Of sentiment, a momentary trance

That far outran the habit of my mind.
    Upon the eastern shore of Windermere
Above the crescent of a pleasant bay
There was an inn, no homely-featured shed,
Brother of the surrounding cottages,
But 'twas a splendid place, the door beset
With chaises, grooms, and liveries, and within
Decanters, glasses and the blood-red wine.
In ancient times, or ere the hall was built
On the large island, had the dwelling been
More worthy of a poet's love, a hut
Proud of its one bright fire and sycamore shade;
But though the rhymes were gone which once inscribed
The threshold, and large golden characters
On the blue-frosted signboard had usurped
The place of the old lion, in contempt
And mockery of the rustic painter's hand,
Yet to this hour the spot to me is dear
With all its foolish pomp. The garden lay
Upon a slope surmounted by the plain
Of a small bowling-green; beneath us stood
A grove, with gleams of water through the trees
And over the tree-tops – nor did we want
Refreshment, strawberries and mellow cream –
And there through half an afternoon we played
On the smooth platform, and the shouts we sent
Made all the mountains ring.
                                        But ere the fall
Of night, when in our pinnace we returned
Over the dusky lake, and to the beach
Of some small island steered our course, with one,
The minstrel of our troop, and left him there,
And rowed off gently, while he blew his flute
Alone upon the rock, oh, then the calm
And dead still water lay upon my mind
Even with a weight of pleasure, and the sky,
Never before so beautiful, sank down
Into my heart and held me like a dream.
    Thus day by day my sympathies increased,
And thus the common range of visible things
Grew dear to me. Already I began
To love the sun – a boy I loved the sun
Not as I since have loved him (as a pledge
And surety of my earthly life, a light

Which while I view I feel I am alive),
But for this cause, that I had seen him lay
His beauty on the morning hills, had seen
The western mountain touch his setting orb
In many a thoughtless hour, when from excess
Of happiness my blood appeared to flow
With its own pleasure, and I breathed with joy.
And from like feelings, humble though intense,
To patriotic and domestic love
Analogous, the moon to me was dear:
For I would dream away my purposes
Standing to look upon her, while she hung
Midway between the hills as if she knew
No other region but belonged to thee,
Yea appertained by a peculiar right
To thee and thy grey huts, my native vale.
   Those incidental charms which first attached
My heart to rural objects, day by day
Grew weaker, and I hasten on to tell
How Nature, intervenient till this time
And secondary, now at length was sought
For her own sake. But who shall parcel out
His intellect by geometric rules
Split like a province into round and square?
Who knows the individual hour in which
His habits were first sown even as a seed?
Who that shall point as with a wand, and say
'This portion of the river of my mind
Came from yon fountain'? Thou, my friend, art one
More deeply read in thy own thoughts, no slave
Of that false secondary power by which
In weakness we create distinctions, then
Believe our puny boundaries are things
Which we perceive, and not which we have made.
To thee, unblinded by these outward shows,
The unity of all has been revealed;
And thou wilt doubt with me, less aptly skilled
Than many are to class the cabinet
Of their sensations, and in voluble phrase
Run through the history and birth of each
As of a single independent thing.
Hard task to analyze a soul, in which
Not only general habits and desires,
But each most obvious and particular thought –

Not in a mystical and idle sense,
But in the words of reason deeply weighed –
Hath no beginning.
Blest the infant babe –
For with my best conjectures I would trace
The progress of our being – blest the babe
Nursed in his mother's arms, the babe who sleeps
Upon his mother's breast, who, when his soul
Claims manifest kindred with an earthly soul,
Doth gather passion from his mother's eye.
Such feelings pass into his torpid life
Like an awakening breeze, and hence his mind,
Even in the first trial of its powers,
Is prompt and watchful, eager to combine
In one appearance all the elements
And parts of the same object, else detached
And loath to coalesce. Thus day by day,
Subjected to the discipline of love,
His organs and recipient faculties
Are quickened, are more vigorous; his mind spreads,
Tenacious of the forms which it receives.
In one belovéd presence – nay and more,
In that most apprehensive habitude
And those sensations which have been derived
From this belovéd presence – there exists
A virtue which irradiates and exalts
All objects through all intercourse of sense.
No outcast he, bewildered and depressed;
Along his infant veins are interfused
The gravitation and the filial bond
Of Nature that connect him with the world.
Emphatically such a being lives,
An inmate of this *active* universe.
From Nature largely he receives, nor so
Is satisfied, but largely gives again;
For feeling has to him imparted strength,
And – powerful in all sentiments of grief,
Of exultation, fear and joy – his mind,
Even as an agent of the one great mind,
Creates, creator and receiver both,
Working but in alliance with the works
Which it beholds. Such, verily, is the first
Poetic spirit of our human life –
By uniform control of after-years

In most abated and suppressed, in some
Through every change of growth or of decay
Pre-eminent till death.
From early days,
Beginning not long after that first time
In which, a babe, by intercourse of touch
I held mute dialogues with my mother's heart,
I have endeavoured to display the means
Whereby this infant sensibility,
Great birthright of our being, was in me
Augmented and sustained. Yet is a path
More difficult before me, and I fear
That in its broken windings we shall need
The chamois' sinews and the eagle's wing.
For now a trouble came into my mind
From obscure causes. I was left alone
Seeking this visible world, nor knowing why:
The props of my affections were removed,
And yet the building stood, as if sustained
By its own spirit. All that I beheld
Was dear to me, and from this cause it came
That now to Nature's finer influxes
My mind lay open – to that more exact
And intimate communion which our hearts
Maintain with the minuter properties
Of objects which already are beloved,
And of those only.
Many are the joys
Of youth, but oh, what happiness to live
When every hour brings palpable access
Of knowledge, when all knowledge is delight,
And sorrow is not there. The seasons came,
And every season brought a countless store
Of modes and temporary qualities
Which but for this most watchful power of love
Had been neglected – left a register
Of permanent relations, else unknown.
Hence life and change and beauty, solitude
More active even than 'best society',
Society made sweet as solitude
By silent inobtrusive sympathies,
And gentle agitations of the mind
From manifold distinctions (difference
Perceived in things where to the common eye

No difference is) – and hence, from the same source,
Sublimer joy.
For I would walk alone
In storm and tempest, or in starlight nights
Beneath the quiet heavens, and at that time
Would feel whate'er there is of power in sound
To breathe an elevated mood, by form
Or image unprofaned; and I would stand
Beneath some rock, listening to sounds that are
The ghostly language of the ancient earth,
Or make their dim abode in distant winds.
Thence did I drink the visionary power.
I deem not profitless these fleeting moods
Of shadowy exaltation; not for this,
That they are kindred to our purer mind
And intellectual life, but that the soul –
Remembering how she felt, but what she felt
Remembering not – retains an obscure sense
Of possible sublimity, to which
With growing faculties she doth aspire,
With faculties still growing, feeling still
That whatsoever point they gain they still
Have something to pursue.
And not alone
In grandeur and in tumult, but no less
In tranquil scenes, that universal power
And fitness in the latent qualities
And essences of things, by which the mind
Is moved with feelings of delight, to me
Came strengthened with a superadded soul,
A virtue not its own. My morning walks
Were early: oft before the hours of school
I travelled round our little lake, five miles
Of pleasant wandering – happy time, more dear
For this, that one was by my side, a friend
Then passionately loved. With heart how full
Will he peruse these lines, this page (perhaps
A blank to other men); for many years
Have since flowed in between us, and, our minds
Both silent to each other, at this time
We live as if those hours had never been.
Nor seldom did I lift our cottage latch
Far earlier, and before the vernal thrush
Was audible, among the hills I sat

Alone upon some jutting eminence
At the first hour of morning, when the vale
Lay quiet in an utter solitude.
How shall I trace the history, where seek
The origin of what I then have felt?
Oft in those moments such a holy calm
Did overspread my soul that I forgot
The agency of sight, and what I saw
Appeared like something in myself, a dream,
A prospect in my mind.
'Twere long to tell
What spring and autumn, what the winter snows,
And what the summer shade, what day and night,
The evening and the morning, what my dreams
And what my waking thoughts, supplied to nurse
That spirit of religious love in which
I walked with Nature. But let this at least
Be not forgotten, that I still retained
My first creative sensibility,
That by the regular action of the world
My soul was unsubdued. A plastic power
Abode with me, a forming hand, at times
Rebellious, acting in a devious mood,
A local spirit of its own, at war
With general tendency, but for the most
Subservient strictly to the external things
With which it communed. An auxiliar light
Came from my mind, which on the setting sun
Bestowed new splendour; the melodious birds,
The gentle breezes, fountains that ran on
Murmuring so sweetly in themselves, obeyed
A like dominion, and the midnight storm
Grew darker in the presence of my eye.
Hence my obeisance, my devotion hence,
And *hence* my transport.
Nor should this, perchance,
Pass unrecorded, that I still had loved
The exercise and produce of a toil
Than analytic industry to me
More pleasing, and whose character I deem
Is more poetic, as resembling more
Creative agency – I mean to speak
Of that interminable building reared
By observation of affinities

In objects where no brotherhood exists
To common minds. My seventeenth year was come,
And, whether (from this habit rooted now
So deeply in my mind, or from excess
Of the great social principle of life
Coercing all things into sympathy)
To unorganic natures I transferred
My own enjoyments, or (the power of truth
Coming in revelation) I conversed
With things that really are, I at this time
Saw blessings spread around me like a sea.
Thus did my days pass on, and now at length
From Nature and her overflowing soul
I had received so much that all my thoughts
Were steeped in feeling.
                                        I was only then
Contented when with bliss ineffable
I felt the sentiment of being, spread
O'er all that moves and all that seemeth still,
O'er all that, lost beyond the reach of thought
And human knowledge, to the human eye
Invisible, yet liveth to the heart,
O'er all that leaps, and runs, and shouts, and sings,
Or beats the gladsome air, o'er all that glides
Beneath the wave, yea, in the wave itself
And mighty depth of waters. Wonder not
If such my transports were, for in all things
I saw one life, and felt that it was joy;
One song they sang and it was audible –
Most audible then when the fleshly ear,
O'ercome by grosser prelude of that strain,
Forgot its functions and slept undisturbed.
    If this be error, and another faith
Find easier access to the pious mind,
Yet were I grossly destitute of all
Those human sentiments which make this earth
So dear if I should fail with grateful voice
To speak of you, ye mountains, and ye lakes
And sounding cataracts, ye mists and winds
That dwell among the hills where I was born.
If in my youth I have been pure in heart,
If, mingling with the world, I am content
With my own modest pleasures, and have lived
With God and Nature communing, removed

From little enmities and low desires,
The gift is yours! If, in these times of fear,
This melancholy waste of hopes overthrown,
If, mid indifference and apathy
And wicked exultation, when good men
On every side fall off we know not how
To selfishness (disguised in gentle names
Of peace and quiet and domestic love,
Yet mingled, not unwillingly, with sneers
On visionary minds) – if, in this time
Of dereliction and dismay, I yet
Despair not of our nature, but retain
A more than Roman confidence, a faith
That fails not, in all sorrow my support,
The blessing of my life, the gift is yours
Ye mountains, thine oh Nature! Thou hast fed
My lofty speculations, and in thee,
For this uneasy heart of ours, I find
A never-failing principle of joy
And purest passion.
Thou, my friend, wast reared
In the great city, mid far other scenes,
But we by different roads at length have gained
The self-same bourne. And from this cause to thee
I speak unapprehensive of contempt,
The insinuated scoff of coward tongues,
And all that silent language which so oft
In conversation betwixt man and man
Blots from the human countenance all trace
Of beauty and of love. For thou hast sought
The truth in solitude, and thou art one
The most intense of Nature's worshippers,
In many things my brother, chiefly here
In this my deep devotion.
Fare thee well!
Health and the quiet of a healthful mind
Attend thee, seeking oft the haunts of men –
But yet more often living with thyself,
And for thyself – so haply shall thy days
Be many, and a blessing to mankind.

(iv) Statue Horse (Feb. 1804; from MS 1969)

One evening, walking in the public way,
A peasant of the valley where I dwelt
Being my chance companion, he stopped short
And pointed to an object full in view
At a small distance. 'Twas a horse, that stood
Alone upon a little breast of ground
With a clear silver moonlight sky behind.
With one leg from the ground the creature stood,
Insensible and still: breath, motion, gone –
Hairs, colour, all but shape and substance, gone –
Mane, ears, and tail, as lifeless as the trunk
That had no stir of breath! We paused awhile
In pleasure of the sight, and left him there,
With all his functions silently sealed up,
Like an amphibious work of Nature's hand,
A borderer dwelling betwixt life and death,
A living statue or a statued life.

(v) Climbing of Snowdon

(1805 *Prelude* XIII, 10–73) Feb. 1804; publ. 1850/from MS 1926

It was a summer's night, a close warm night,
Wan, dull and glaring, with a dripping mist
Low-hung and thick that covered all the sky
Half threatening storm and rain; but on we went
Unchecked, being full of heart and having faith
In our tried pilot. Little could we see
Hemmed round on every side with fog and damp,
And, after ordinary travellers' chat
With our conductor, silently we sank
Each into commerce with his private thoughts.
Thus did we breast the ascent, and by myself
Was nothing either seen or heard the while
Which took me from my musings, save that once
The shepherd's cur did to his own great joy
Unearth a hedgehog in the mountain crags
Round which he made a barking turbulent.
This small adventure (for even such it seemed
In that wild place and at the dead of night)

Being over and forgotten, on we wound
In silence as before.
With forehead bent
Earthward, as if in opposition set
Against an enemy, I panted up
With eager pace, and no less eager thoughts.
Thus might we wear perhaps an hour away,
Ascending at loose distance each from each,
And I, as chanced, the foremost of the band –
When at my feet the ground appeared to brighten,
And with a step or two seemed brighter still;
Nor had I time to ask the cause of this,
For instantly a light upon the turf
Fell like a flash! I looked about, and lo,
The moon stood naked in the heavens at height
Immense above my head, and on the shore
I found myself of a huge sea of mist,
Which meek and silent rested at my feet.
A hundred hills their dusky backs upheaved
All over this still ocean; and beyond,
Far, far beyond, the vapours shot themselves
In headlands, tongues, and promontory shapes,
Into the sea – the real sea, that seemed
To dwindle and give up its majesty,
Usurped upon as far as sight could reach.
Meanwhile, the moon looked down upon this show
In single glory, and we stood, the mist
Touching our very feet.
And from the shore
At distance not the third part of a mile
Was a blue chasm, a fracture in the vapour,
A deep and gloomy breathing-place through which
Mounted the roar of waters, torrents, streams
Innumerable, roaring with one voice!
The universal spectacle throughout
Was shaped for admiration and delight,
Grand in itself alone, but in that breach
Through which the homeless voice of waters rose,
That dark deep thoroughfare, had Nature lodged
The soul, the imagination of the whole.
A meditation rose in me that night
Upon the lonely mountain when the scene
Had passed away, and it appeared to me
The perfect image of a mighty mind,

Of one that feeds upon infinity,
That is exalted by an underpresence,
The sense of God, or whatso'er is dim
Or vast in its own being.

(vi) Crossing the Alps

(1805 *Prelude* VI, 494–572) March 1804; publ. 1850/from MS 1926

Upturning with a band
Of travellers, from the Valais we had clomb
Along the road that leads to Italy;
A length of hours, making of these our guides
Did we advance, and having reached an inn
Among the mountains, we together ate
Our noon's repast, from which the travellers rose
Leaving us at the board. Erelong we followed,
Descending by the beaten road that led
Right to a rivulet's edge, and there broke off.
The only track now visible was one
Upon the further side, right opposite,
And up a lofty mountain. This we took
After a little scruple, and short pause,
And climbed with eagerness, though not at length
Without surprise and some anxiety
On finding that we did not overtake
Our comrades gone before. By fortunate chance,
While every moment now increased our doubts,
A peasant met us, and from him we learned
That to the place which had perplexed us first
We must descend, and there should find the road,
Which in the stony channel of the stream
Lay a few steps, and then along its banks –
And further, that thenceforward all our course
Was downwards with the current of that stream.
Hard of belief, we questioned him again,
And all the answers which the man returned
To our inquiries – in their sense and substance,
Translated by the feelings which we had –
Ended in this, that we had crossed the Alps!
Imagination – lifting up itself
Before the eye and progress of my song

Like an unfathered vapour, here that power,
In all the might of its endowments, came
Athwart me! I was lost as in a cloud,
Halted without a struggle to break through;
And now, recovering, to my soul I say
'I recognize thy glory.' In such strength
Of usurpation, in such visitings
Of awful promise, when the light of sense
Goes out in flashes that have shown to us
The invisible world, does greatness make abode –
There harbours whether we be young or old.
Our destiny, our nature, and our home,
Is with infinitude, and only there –
With hope it is, hope that can never die,
Effort, and expectation, and desire,
And something evermore about to be.
The mind beneath such banners militant
Thinks not of spoils or trophies, nor of aught
That may attest its prowess, blest in thoughts
That are their own perfection and reward –
Strong in itself, and in the access of joy
Which hides it like the overflowing Nile.

The dull and heavy slackening which ensued
Upon those tidings by the peasant given
Was soon dislodged. Downwards we hurried fast,
And entered with the road which we had missed
Into a narrow chasm. The brook and road
Were fellow-travellers in this gloomy pass,
And with them did we journey several hours
At a slow step. The immeasurable height
Of woods decaying, never to be decayed,
The stationary blasts of waterfalls,
And everywhere along the hollow rent
Winds thwarting winds, bewildered and forlorn,
The torrents shooting from the clear blue sky,
The rocks that muttered close upon our ears,
Black drizzling crags that spake by the wayside
As if a voice were in them, the sick sight
And giddy prospect of the raving stream,
The unfettered clouds and region of the heavens,
Tumult and peace, the darkness and the light –
Were all like workings of one mind, the features

Of the same face, blossoms upon one tree,
Characters of the great apocalypse,
The types and symbols of eternity,
Of first, and last, and midst, and without end.

6. WILLIAM LISLE BOWLES

from *Coombe Ellen* (1798)

Call the strange spirit that abides unseen
In wilds and wastes and shaggy solitudes,
And bid his dim hand lead thee through these scenes
That burst immense around – by mountains, glens,
And solitary cataracts that dash
Through dark ravines, and trees whose wreathéd roots
O'erhang the torrent's channelled course, and streams
That far below, along the narrow vale,
Upon their rocky way wind musical!
  Stranger, if Nature charm thee – if thou lovest
To trace her awful steps, in glade or glen,
Or under covert of the rocking wood
That sways its murmuring and mossy boughs
Above thy head – now, when the wind at times
Stirs its deep silence round thee, and the shower
Falls on the sighing foliage, hail her here
In these her haunts, and, wrapt in musings high,
Think that thou holdest converse with some power
Invisible and strange . . .
Here Melancholy, on the pale crags laid,
Might muse herself to sleep; or Fancy come,
Witching the mind with tender cozenage,
And shaping things that are not – here all day
Might Meditation listen to the lapse
Of the white waters flashing through the cleft,
And, gazing on the many shadowing trees,
Mingle a pensive moral as she gazed.
  High o'er thy head, amidst the shivered slate,
Behold (a sapling yet) the wild ash bend,
Its dark red berries clustering, as if it wished
In the clear liquid mirror, ere it fell,
To trace its beauties. O'er the prone cascade,
Airy, and light, and elegant, the birch

Displays its glossy stem amidst the gloom
Of alders and jagg'd fern, as she wooed
The passing gale to whisper flatteries!
Upon the adverse bank, withered, and stripped
Of all its pleasant leaves, a scathéd oak
Hangs desolate . . .
Now wind we up the glen, and hear below
The dashing torrent, in deep woods concealed –
And now, again, white water flashing on the view
O'er the huge craggy fragments! Ancient stream,
That murmurest through the mountain-solitudes,
The time has been when no eye marked thy course
Save his who made the world. Fancy might dream
She saw thee thus bound on from age to age
Unseen of man, whilst awful Nature sat
On the rent rocks, and said: 'These haunts be mine!'
Now Taste has marked thy features, here and there
Touching with tender hand, but injuring not,
Thy beauties – whilst along thy woody verge
Ascends the winding pathway, and the eye
Catches at intervals thy varied falls.

7. CHARLOTTE SMITH

Beachy Head (lines 346–506) c. 1805; publ. 1807

An early worshipper at Nature's shrine,
I loved her rudest scenes – warrens, and heaths,
And yellow commons, and birch-shaded hollows,
And hedgerows bordering unfrequented lanes,
Bowered with wild roses and the clasping woodbine,
Where purple tassels of the tangling vetch
With bittersweet and bryony inweave,
And the dew fills the silver bindweed's cups.
I loved to trace the brooks whose humid banks
Nourish the harebell and the freckled pagil,
And stroll among o'ershadowing woods of beech,
Lending in summer from the heats of noon
A whispering shade; while haply there reclines
Some pensive lover of uncultured flowers
Who, from the tumps with bright green mosses clad,
Plucks the wood-sorrel with its light thin leaves,

Heart-shaped and triply-folded, and its root
Creeping like beaded coral – or who there
Gathers (the copse's pride) anemones,
With rays like golden studs on ivory laid
Most delicate, but touched with purple clouds,
Fit crown for April's fair but changeful brow.
    Ah, hills so early loved! In fancy still
I breathe your pure keen air and still behold
Those widely spreading views, mocking alike
The poet and the painter's utmost art –
And still (observing objects more minute)
Wondering remark the strange and foreign forms
Of seashells, with the pale calcareous soil
Mingled, and seeming of resembling substance –
Though surely the blue ocean (from the heights
Where the downs westward tend, but dimly seen)
Here never rolled its surge? Does Nature then
Mimic, in wanton mood, fantastic shapes
Of bivalves, and inwreathed volutes, that cling
To the dark sea-rock of the watery world?
Or did this range of chalky mountains once
Form a vast basin, where the ocean-waves
Swelled fathomless, what time these fossil shells,
Buoyed on their native element, were thrown
Among the imbedding calx when the huge hill
Its giant bulk heaved, and in strange ferment
Grew up a guardian-barrier 'twixt the sea
And the green level of the sylvan weald?
    Ah, very vain is Science' proudest boast,
And but a little light its flame yet lends
To its most ardent votaries; since from whence
These fossil forms are seen is but conjecture,
Food for vague theories, or vain dispute –
While to his daily task the peasant goes
Unheeding such inquiry, with no care
But that kindly change of sun and shower
Fit for his toil the earth he cultivates.
As little recks the herdsman of the hill
(Who on some turfy knoll, idly reclined,
Watches his wether-flock) that deep beneath
Rest the remains of men of whom is left
No traces in the records of mankind,
Save what these half-obliterated mounds
And half-filled trenches doubtfully impart . . .

Near where a richer tract of cultured land
Slopes to the south, and (burnished by the sun)
Bend in the gale of August floods of corn;
The guardian of the flock, with watchful care,
Repels by voice and dog the encroaching sheep –
While his boy visits every wiréd trap
That scars the turf; and from the pit-falls takes
The timid migrants, who, from distant wilds,
Warrens and stone-quarries, are destined thus
To lose their short existence. But unsought
By Luxury yet, the shepherd still protects
The social bird, who from his native haunts
Of willowy current, or the rushy pool,
Follows the fleecy crowd, and flirts and skims,
In fellowship among them.
Where the knoll
More elevated takes the changeful winds,
The windmill rears its vanes; and thitherward
With his white load, the master travelling
Scares the rooks rising slow on whispering wings,
While o'er his head (before the summer sun
Lights up the blue expanse), heard more than seen,
The lark sings matins, and, above the clouds
Floating, embathes his spotted breast in dew.
Beneath the shadow of a gnarléd thorn
Bent by the sea blast, from a seat of turf
With fairy nosegays strewn, how wide the view!
Till in the distant north it melts away
And mingles indiscriminate with clouds –
But if the eye could reach so far, the mart
Of England's capital, its domes and spires,
Might be perceived! Yet hence the distant range
Of Kentish hills appear in purple haze,
And nearer, undulate the wooded heights
And airy summits that above the mole
Rise in green beauty, and the beaconed ridge
Of Black Down shagged with heath, and, swelling rude
Like a dark island from the vale, its brow
Catching the last rays of the evening sun
That gleam between the nearer park's old oaks,
Then lighten up the river, and make prominent
The portal, and the ruined battlements
Of that dismantled fortress, raised what time
The Conqueror's successors fiercely fought,

Tearing with civil feuds the desolate land.
But now a tiller of the soil dwells there,
And of the turret's looped and raftered halls
Has made an humbler homestead – where he sees,
Instead of arméd foemen, herds that graze
Along his yellow meadows, or his flocks
At evening from the upland driven to fold.

8. AMELIA OPIE

Stanzas Written Under Aeolus' Harp (1808)

Come ye, whose hearts the tyrant sorrows wound,
Come ye, whose breasts the tyrant passions tear,
And seek this harp in whose still varying sound
Each woe its own appropriate plaint may hear.

Solemn and slow yon murmuring cadence rolls
Till on the attentive ear it dies away,
To your fond griefs responsive – ye whose souls,
O'er loved lost friends, regret's sad tribute pay!

But hark, in regular progression move
Yon silver sounds, and mingle as they fall!
Do they not wake thy trembling nerves, oh Love,
And into warmer life thy feelings call?

Again it speaks, but, shrill and swift, the tones
In wild disorder strike upon the ear!
Pale Frenzy listens, kindred wildness owns,
And starts – appalled the well-known sounds to hear!

Lo, e'en the gay, the giddy and the vain,
In deep delight these vocal wires attend –
Silent and breathless watch the varying strain
And, pleased, the vacant toils of mirth suspend.

So when the lute on Memnon's statue hung
(At day's first rising) strains melodious poured
Untouched by mortal hands, the gathering throng
In silent wonder listened and adored.

But the wild cadence of these trembling strings
The enchantress Fancy with most rapture hears –
At the sweet sound to grasp her wand she springs,
And lo, her band of airy shapes appears!

She (rapt enthusiast) thinks the melting strains
A choir of angels breathe, in bright array
Bearing on radiant clouds to yon blue plains
A soul just parted from its silent clay.

And oft at eve her wild creative eye
Sees to the gale their silken pinions stream,
While in the quivering trees soft zephyrs sigh,
And through the leaves disclose the moon's pale beam.

Oh, breathing instrument, be ever near
While to the pensive muse my vows I pay;
Thy softest call the inmost soul can hear,
Thy faintest breath can Fancy's pinions play.

And when art's laboured strains my feelings tire,
To seek thy simple music shall be mine;
I'll strive to win its graces to my lyre,
And make my plaintive lays enchant like thine!

9. ISABELLA LICKBARROW

On Esthwaite Water (1814)

O'er Esthwaite's lake, serene and still,
  At sunset's silent peaceful hour
Scarce moved the zephyr's softest breath,
  Or sighed along its reedy shore.

The lovely landscape on its sides,
  With evening's softening hues impressed,
Shared in the general calm, and gave
  Sweet visions of repose and rest.

Inverted on the waveless flood,
   A spotless mirror smooth and clear,
Each fair surrounding object shone
   In softer beauty imaged there.

Brown hills and woods of various shades,
   Orchards and sloping meadows green,
Sweet rural seats and sheltered farms,
   Were in the bright reflector seen.

E'en lofty Tilberthwaite from far
   His giant shadow boldly threw,
His ruggéd, dark, high-towering head
   On Esthwaite's tranquil breast to view.

Struck with the beauty of the scene,
   I cried, 'Oh may my yielding breast
Retain but images of peace
   Like those, sweet lake, on thine impressed!

Ne'er may it feel a ruder gale
   Than that which o'er thy surface spreads,
When sportive zephyrs briskly play,
   And whisper through thy bordering reeds –

When, dancing in the solar beam,
   Thy silvery waves the margin seek
With gently undulating flow,
   And there in softest murmurs break.'

Vain wish – o'er Esthwaite's tranquil lake
   A stronger gale full frequent blows,
The soothing prospect disappears,
   The lovely visions of repose!

10. LORD BYRON

'Concentred in a Life Intense'

(i) Lake Leman

(from *Childe Harold* III) June 1816; publ. Dec. 1817

68

Lake Leman woos me with its crystal face,
The mirror where the stars and mountains view
The stillness of their aspect in each trace
Its clear depth yields of their far height and hue.
There is too much of man here, to look through
With a fit mind the might which I behold;
But soon in me shall loneliness renew
Thoughts hid, but not less cherished than of old,
Ere mingling with the herd had penned me in their fold.

69

To fly from, need not be to hate, mankind:
All are not fit with them to stir and toil,
Nor is it discontent to keep the mind
Deep in its fountain, lest it over-boil
In the hot throng, where we become the spoil
Of our infection, till too late and long
We may deplore and struggle with the coil,
In wretched interchange of wrong for wrong
Midst a contentious world, striving where none are strong.

70

There, in a moment, we may plunge our years
In fatal penitence, and in the blight
Of our own soul turn all our blood to tears,
And colour things to come with hues of night!
The race of life becomes a hopeless flight
To those that walk in darkness – on the sea
The boldest steer but where their ports invite –
But there are wanderers o'er eternity
Whose bark drives on and on, and anchored ne'er shall be.

71

Is it not better, then, to be alone,
And love Earth only for its earthly sake –
By the blue rushing of the arrowy Rhone,
Or the pure bosom of its nursing Lake
Which feeds it as a mother who doth make
A fair but froward infant her own care,
Kissing its cries away as these awake –
Is it not better thus our lives to wear,
Than join the crushing crowd, doomed to inflict or bear?

72

I live not in myself, but I become
Portion of that around me, and to me
High mountains are a feeling, but the hum
Of human cities torture! I can see
Nothing to loathe in Nature, save to be
A link reluctant in a fleshly chain,
Classed among creatures, when the soul can flee,
And with the sky, the peak, the heaving plain
Of ocean, or the stars, mingle – and not in vain.

73

And thus I am absorbed, and this is life:
I look upon the peopled desert past,
As on a place of agony and strife,
Where, for some sin, to sorrow I was cast,
To act and suffer, but remount at last
With a fresh pinion – which I feel to spring,
Though young, yet waxing vigorous as the blast
Which it would cope with, on delighted wing
Spurning the clay-cold bonds which round our being cling.

74

And when, at length, the mind shall be all free
From what it hates in this degraded form,
Reft of its carnal life, save what shall be
Existent happier in the fly and worm –
When elements to elements conform
And dust is as it should be, shall I not
Feel all I see less dazzling but more warm?
The bodiless thought? The spirit of each spot,
Of which, even now, I share at times the immortal lot?

75

Are not the mountains, waves, and skies, a part
Of me and of my soul, as I of them?
Is not the love of these deep in my heart
With a pure passion? Should I not contemn
All objects, if compared with these – and stem
A tide of suffering, rather than forego
Such feelings for the hard and worldly phlegm
Of those whose eyes are only turned below,
Gazing upon the ground with thoughts which dare not glow? . . .

85

Clear, placid Leman! thy contrasted lake,
With the wild world I dwelt in, is a thing
Which warns me, with its stillness, to forsake
Earth's troubled waters for a purer spring.
This quiet sail is as a noiseless wing
To waft me from distraction. Once I loved
Torn ocean's roar, but thy soft murmuring
Sounds sweet as if a sister's voice reproved
That I with stern delights should e'er have been so moved.

86

It is the hush of night, and all between
Thy margin and the mountains, dusk, yet clear
(Mellowed and mingling, yet distinctly seen),
Save darkened Jura, whose capped heights appear
Precipitously steep – and drawing near,
There breathes a living fragrance from the shore,
Of flowers yet fresh with childhood; on the ear
Drops the light drip of the suspended oar,
Or chirps the grasshopper one good-night carol more.

87

He is an evening reveller, who makes
His life an infancy, and sings his fill!
At intervals, some bird from out the brakes
Starts into voice a moment, then is still.
There seems a floating whisper on the hill –
But that is fancy! – for the starlight-dews
All silently their tears of love instill,
Weeping themselves away, till they infuse
Deep into Nature's breast the spirit of her hues.

88

Ye stars, which are the poetry of Heaven!
If in your bright leaves we would read the fate
Of men and empires, 'tis to be forgiven
That in our aspirations to be great,
Our destinies o'erleap their mortal state,
And claim a kindred with you – for ye are
A beauty and a mystery, and create
In us such love and reverence from afar
That fortune, fame, power, life, have named themselves a star.

89

All Heaven and Earth are still – though not in sleep,
But breathless, as we grow when feeling most,
And silent, as we stand in thoughts too deep –
All Heaven and Earth are still! From the high host
Of stars, to the lulled lake and mountain-coast,
All is concentred in a life intense
Where not a beam, nor air, nor leaf is lost,
But hath a part of being, and a sense
Of that which is of all creator and defense.

90

Then stirs the feeling infinite, so felt
In solitude, where we are least alone –
A truth which through our being then doth melt,
And purifies from self: it is a tone,
The soul and source of music, which makes known
Eternal harmony . . .

(ii) *Epistle to Augusta* (July 1816; publ. 1830)

My sister! my sweet sister! if a name
Dearer and purer were, it should be thine.
Mountains and seas divide us, but I claim
No tears but tenderness to answer mine:
Go where I will, to me thou art the same –
A loved regret which I would not resign!
There yet are two things in my destiny:
A world to roam through, and a home with thee.

The first were nothing, had I still the last!
It were the haven of my happiness –
But other claims and other ties thou hast,
And mine is not the wish to make them less.
A strange doom is thy father's son's, and past
Recalling, as it lies beyond redress –
Reversed for him our grandsire's fate of yore:
He had no rest at sea, nor I on shore!

If my inheritance of storms hath been
In other elements, and on the rocks
Of perils, overlooked or unforeseen,
I have sustained my share of worldly shocks,
The fault was mine – nor do I seek to screen
My errors with defensive paradox –
I have been cunning in mine overthrow,
The careful pilot of my proper woe!

Mine were my faults, and mine be their reward.
My whole life was a contest, since the day
That gave me being gave me that which marred
The gift – a fate, or will – that walked astray!
And I at times have found the struggle hard,
And thought of shaking off my bonds of clay,
But now I fain would for a time survive,
If but to see what next can well arrive.

Kingdoms and Empires in my little day
I have outlived, and yet I am not old!
And when I look on this, the petty spray
Of my own years of troubles (which have rolled
Like a wild bay of breakers) melts away.
Something – I know not what – does still uphold
A spirit of slight patience: not in vain,
Even for its own sake, do we purchase pain.

Perhaps the workings of defiance stir
Within me – or, perhaps, a cold despair
Brought on when ills habitually recur –
Perhaps a kinder clime, or purer air
(For even to this may change of soul refer,
And with light armour we may learn to bear),
Have taught me a strange quiet, which was not
The chief companion of a calmer lot.

I feel almost at times as I have felt
In happy childhood: trees, and flowers, and brooks,
Which do remember me of where I dwelt
Ere my young mind was sacrificed to books,
Come as of yore upon me, and can melt
My heart with recognition of their looks –
And even at moments I could think I see
Some living thing to love – but none like thee!

Here are the Alpine landscapes which create
A fund for contemplation – to admire
Is a brief feeling of a trivial date,
But something worthier do such scenes inspire.
Here to be lonely is not desolate,
For much I view which I could most desire,
And (above all) a lake I can behold,
Lovelier – not dearer – than our own of old!

Oh that thou wert but with me – but I grow
The fool of my own wishes, and forget
The solitude which I have vaunted so
Has lost its praise in this but one regret.
There may be others which I less may show:
I am not of the plaintive mood, and yet
I feel an ebb in my philosophy,
And the tide rising in my altered eye.

I did remind thee of our own dear Lake,
By the old Hall which may be mine no more.
Leman's is fair, but think not I forsake
The sweet remembrance of a dearer shore –
Sad havoc time must with my memory make
Ere that or thou can fade these eyes before,
Though (like all things which I have loved) they are
Resigned for ever, or divided far.

The world is all before me! I but ask
Of Nature that with which she will comply –
It is but in her summer's sun to bask,
To mingle with the quiet of her sky,
To see her gentle face without a mask,
And never gaze on it with apathy.
She was my early friend, and now shall be
My sister – till I look again on thee.

I can reduce all feelings but this one –
And that I would not! For at length I see
Such scenes as those wherein my life begun:
The earliest – even the only – paths for me.
Had I but sooner learnt the crowd to shun,
I had been better than I now can be –
The passions which have torn me would have slept:
I had not suffered, and thou hadst not wept!

With false ambition what had I to do?
Little with love, and least of all with fame!
And yet they came unsought, and with me grew,
And made me all which they can make, a name!
Yet this was not the end I did pursue –
Surely I once beheld a nobler aim –
But all is over. I am one the more
To baffled millions which have gone before.

And for the future, this world's future may
From me demand but little of my care –
I have outlived myself by many a day,
Having survived so many things that were!
My years have been no slumber, but the prey
Of ceaseless vigils; for I had the share
Of life which might have filled a century,
Before its fourth in time had passed me by.

And for the remnant which may be to come
I am content – and for the past I feel
Not thankless – for within the crowded sum
Of struggles, happiness at times would steal!
And for the present, I would not benumb
My feelings farther – nor shall I conceal
That with all this I still can look around,
And worship Nature with a thought profound.

For thee, my own sweet sister, in thy heart
I know myself secure, as thou in mine.
We were and are – I am, even as thou art –
Beings who ne'er each other can resign.
It is the same, together or apart!
From life's commencement to its slow decline
We are entwined – let death come slow or fast,
The tie which bound the first endures the last!

11. PERCY BYSSHE SHELLEY

'The Secret Strength of Things'

(i) *Mont Blanc: Lines Written in the Vale of Chamouni* (July 1816; publ. 1817)

I

The everlasting universe of things
Flows through the mind, and rolls its rapid waves,
Now dark, now glittering, now reflecting gloom,
Now lending splendour, where from secret springs
The source of human thought its tribute brings
Of waters – with a sound but half its own,
Such as a feeble brook will oft assume
In the wild woods, among the mountains lone,
Where waterfalls around it leap for ever,
Where woods and winds contend, and a vast river
Over its rocks ceaselessly bursts and raves.

II

Thus thou, Ravine of Arve – dark, deep Ravine –
Thou many-coloured, many-voicéd vale,
Over whose pines, and crags, and caverns sail
Fast cloud-shadows and sunbeams. Awful scene,
Where Power in likeness of the Arve comes down
From the ice-gulfs that gird his secret throne,
Bursting through these dark mountains like the flame
Of lightning through the tempest! Thou dost lie,
Thy giant brood of pines around thee clinging
(Children of elder time, in whose devotion
The chainless winds still come and ever came
To drink their odours, and their mighty swinging
To hear: an old and solemn harmony),
Thine earthly rainbows stretched across the sweep
Of the aethereal waterfall, whose veil
Robes some unsculptured image – the strange sleep
Which when the voices of the desert fail
Wraps all in its own deep eternity –
Thy caverns echoing to the Arve's commotion,
A loud, lone sound no other sound can tame!
Thou art pervaded with that ceaseless motion,

Thou art the path of that unresting sound,
Dizzy Ravine! and when I gaze on thee
I seem as in a trance sublime and strange
To muse on my own separate fantasy,
My own, my human mind, which passively
Now renders and receives fast influencings,
Holding an unremitting interchange
With the clear universe of things around –
One legion of wild thoughts, whose wandering wings
Now float above thy darkness, and now rest
Where that, or thou, art no unbidden guest,
In the still cave of the witch Poesy,
Seeking among the shadows that pass by
(Ghosts of all things that are) some shade of thee,
Some phantom, some faint image. Till the breast
From which they fled recalls them, thou art there!

III

Some say that gleams of a remoter world
Visit the soul in sleep – that death is slumber,
And that its shapes the busy thoughts outnumber
Of those who wake and live. I look on high:
Has some unknown omnipotence unfurled
The veil of life and death? Or do I lie
In dream, and does the mightier world of sleep
Spread far around and inaccessibly
Its circles? For the very spirit fails,
Driven like a homeless cloud from steep to steep
That vanishes among the viewless gales!
Far, far above, piercing the infinite sky,
Mont Blanc appears, still, snowy, and serene.
Its subject mountains their unearthly forms
Pile around it, ice and rock – broad vales between
Of frozen floods, unfathomable deeps,
Blue as the overhanging heaven, that spread
And wind among the accumulated steeps –
A desert peopled by the storms alone,
Save when the eagle brings some hunter's bone,
And the wolf tracks her there! How hideously
Its shapes are heaped around – rude, bare, and high,
Ghastly, and scarred, and riven! Is this the scene
Where the old Earthquake-Demon taught her young
Ruin? Were these their toys? Or did a sea
Of fire envelop once this silent snow?

None can reply – all seems eternal now.
The wilderness has a mysterious tongue
Which teaches awful doubt, or faith so mild,
So solemn, so serene, that man may be,
But for such faith, with Nature reconciled.
Thou hast a voice, great Mountain, to repeal
Large codes of fraud and woe – not understood
By all, but which the wise, and great, and good
Interpret, or make felt, or deeply feel.

IV

The fields, the lakes, the forests, and the streams,
Ocean, and all the living things that dwell
Within the daedal earth; lightning and rain,
Earthquake and fiery flood, and hurricane;
The torpor of the year when feeble dreams
Visit the hidden buds, or dreamless sleep
Holds every future leaf and flower; the bound
With which from that detested trance they leap;
The works and ways of man, their death and birth,
And that of him and all that his may be;
All things that move and breathe with toil and sound
Are born and die; revolve, subside, and swell.
Power dwells apart in its tranquillity,
Remote, serene and inaccessible,
And this the naked countenance of earth
On which I gaze, even these primeval mountains,
Teach the adverting mind. The glaciers creep
Like snakes that watch their prey, from their far fountains
Slow rolling on. There, many a precipice
Frost and the sun, in scorn of mortal power,
Have piled: dome, pyramid, and pinnacle –
A city of death, distinct with many a tower
And wall impregnable of beaming ice.
Yet not a city, but a flood of ruin
Is there, that from the boundaries of the sky
Rolls its perpetual stream: Vast pines are strewing
Its destined path, or in the mangled soil
Branchless and shattered stand.
The rocks, drawn down
From yon remotest waste, have overthrown
The limits of the dead and living world,
Never to be reclaimed. The dwelling-place
Of insects, beasts and birds, becomes its spoil;

Their food and their retreat for ever gone,
So much of life and joy is lost. The race
Of man flies far in dread; his work and dwelling
Vanish like smoke before the tempest's stream,
And their place is not known. Below, vast caves
Shine in the rushing torrents' restless gleam,
Which from those secret chasms in tumult welling
Meet in the vale, and one majestic river,
The breath and blood of distant lands, for ever
Rolls its loud waters to the ocean-waves,
Breathes its swift vapours to the circling air.

V

Mont Blanc yet gleams on high – the power is there,
The still and solemn power of many sights,
And many sounds, and much of life and death.
In the calm darkness of the moonless nights,
In the lone glare of day, the snows descend
Upon that Mountain; none beholds them there,
Nor when the flakes burn in the sinking sun,
Or the star-beams dart through them. Winds contend
Silently there, and heap the snow with breath
Rapid and strong, but silently! Its home
The voiceless lightning in these solitudes
Keeps innocently, and like vapour broods
Over the snow. The secret Strength of Things
Which governs thought, and to the infinite dome
Of heaven is as a law, inhabits thee!
And what were thou, and earth, and stars, and sea,
If to the human mind's imaginings
Silence and solitude were vacancy?

(ii) *To Jane: The Invitation*

(2 Feb. 1822; publ. 1824)

Best and brightest, come away –
Fairer far than this fair day,
Which, like thee to those in sorrow,
Comes to bid a sweet good-morrow
To the rough year just awake
In its cradle on the brake.
The brightest hour of unborn spring,
Through the winter wandering,

Found, it seems, this halcyon morn
To hoar February born –
Bending from heaven, in azure mirth,
It kissed the forehead of the Earth,
And smiled upon the silent sea,
And bade the frozen streams be free,
And waked to music all their fountains,
And breathed upon the frozen mountains,
And like a prophetess of May
Strewed flowers upon the barren way,
Making the wintry world appear
Like one on whom thou smilest, dear.
   Away, away, from men and towns
To the wild wood and the downs,
To the silent wilderness
Where the soul need not repress
Its music lest it should not find
An echo in another's mind,
While the touch of Nature's art
Harmonizes heart to heart.
I leave this notice on my door
For each accustomed visitor:
   'I am gone into the fields
To take what this sweet hour yields!
Reflection, you may come tomorrow,
Sit by the fireside with Sorrow –
You with the unpaid bill, Despair,
You, tiresome verse-reciter, Care!
I will pay you in the grave –
Death will listen to your stave!
Expectation too, be off –
Today is for itself enough!
Hope, in pity mock not Woe
With smiles, nor follow where I go.
Long having lived on thy sweet food,
At length I find one moment's good
After long pain – with all your love,
This you never told me of!'
   Radiant sister of the day,
Awake, arise, and come away!
To the wild woods and the plains,
And the pools where winter-rains
Image all their roof of leaves,
Where the pine its garland weaves

Of sapless green and ivy dun
Round stems that never kiss the sun –
Where the lawns and pastures be,
And the sandhills of the sea –
Where the melting hoar-frost wets
The daisy-star that never sets,
And wind-flowers, and violets,
Which yet join not scent to hue,
Crown the pale year weak and new;
When the night is left behind
In the deep east, dun and blind,
And the blue noon is over us,
And the multitudinous
Billows murmur at our feet,
Where the earth and ocean meet,
And all things seem only one
In the universal sun.

(iii) *To Jane: A Recollection*

(Feb. 1822; publ. 1824)

Now the last day of many days,
All beautiful and bright as thou,
The loveliest and the last, is dead –
Rise, Memory, and write its praise!
Up, to thy wonted work! Come, trace
The epitaph of glory fled;
For now the Earth has changed its face,
A frown is on the Heaven's brow.
We wandered to the pine forest
That skirts the ocean-foam,
The lightest wind was in its nest,
   The tempest in its home.
The whispering waves were half asleep,
   The clouds were gone to play,
And on the bosom of the deep
   The smile of Heaven lay –
It seemed as if the hour were one
   Sent from beyond the skies,
Which scattered from above the sun
   A light of Paradise!

We paused amid the pines that stood
The giants of the waste,
Tortured by storms to shapes as rude
   As serpents interlaced,
And soothed by every azure breath,
   That under Heaven is blown,
To harmonies and hues beneath,
   As tender as its own –
Now all the tree-tops lay asleep,
   Like green waves on the sea,
As still as in the silent deep
   The ocean-woods may be.

How calm it was – the silence there
   By such a chain was bound
That even the busy woodpecker
   Made stiller by her sound
The inviolable quietness!
   The breath of peace we drew,
With its soft motion, made not less
   The calm that round us grew.
There seemed from the remotest seat
   Of the white mountain-waste,
To the soft flower beneath our feet,
   A magic circle traced –
A spirit interfused around,
   A thrilling, silent life!
To momentary peace it bound
   Our mortal nature's strife –
And still I felt the centre of
   The magic circle there
Was one fair form that filled with love
   The lifeless atmosphere.

We paused beside the pools that lie
   Under the forest bough:
Each seemed as 'twere a little sky
   Gulfed in a world below –
A firmament of purple light
   Which in the dark earth lay,
More boundless than the depth of night,
   And purer than the day!

In which the lovely forests grew,
   As in the upper air,
More perfect both in shape and hue
   Than any spreading there.
There lay the glade and neighbouring lawn,
   And through the dark green wood
The white sun twinkling like the dawn
   Out of a speckled cloud.
Sweet views, which in our world above
   Can never well be seen,
Were imaged by the water's love
   Of that fair forest green.
And all was interfused beneath
   With an Elysian glow,
An atmosphere without a breath,
   A softer day below.
Like one beloved the scene had lent
   To the dark water's breast,
Its every leaf and lineament
   With more than truth exprest –
Until an envious wind crept by,
   Like an unwelcome thought,
Which from the mind's too faithful eye
   Blots one dear image out.
Though thou art ever fair and kind,
   The forests ever green,
Less oft is peace in Shelley's mind,
   Than calm in waters, seen!

12. JOHN KEATS

'A Sort of Oneness'

(i) *Endymion* (I, 777–802) c. April 1817; publ. 1818

Wherein lies happiness? In that which becks
Our ready minds to fellowship divine,
A fellowship with essence, till we shine
Full alchemized, and free of space. Behold
The clear religion of Heaven! Fold
A roseleaf round thy finger's taperness
And soothe thy lips. Hist, when the airy stress

Of music's kiss impregnates the free winds,
And with a sympathetic touch unbinds
Eolian magic from their lucid wombs –
Then old songs waken from enclouded tombs,
Old ditties sigh above their father's grave,
Ghosts of melodious prophesyings rave
Round every spot where trod Apollo's foot;
Bronze clarions awake and faintly bruit
Where long ago a giant-battle was;
And, from the turf, a lullaby doth pass
In every place where infant Orpheus slept.
   Feel we these things? That moment have we stepped
Into a sort of oneness, and our state
Is like a floating spirit's. But there are
Richer entanglements, enthralments far
More self-destroying, leading, by degrees,
To the chief intensity: the crown of these
Is made of love and friendship, and sits high
Upon the forehead of humanity.

(ii) *Epistle to J. H. Reynolds*

(lines 82–105) March 1818; publ. 1848

                                    It is a flaw
In happiness to see beyond our bourne –
It forces us in summer skies to mourn;
It spoils the singing of the nightingale.
Dear Reynolds, I have a mysterious tale
And cannot speak it. The first page I read
Upon a limpit-rock of green sea-weed
Among the breakers. 'Twas a quiet eve;
The rocks were silent; the wide sea did weave
An untumultuous fringe of silver foam
Along the flat brown sand. I was at home,
And should have been most happy, but I saw
Too far into the sea, where every maw,
The greater on the less, feeds evermore –
But I saw too distinct into the core
Of an eternal fierce destruction,
And so from happiness I far was gone.
Still am I sick of it; and though today
I've gathered young spring-leaves, and flowers gay

Of periwinkle and wild strawberry,
Still do I that most fierce destruction see:
The shark at savage prey, the hawk at pounce,
The gentle robin, like a pard or ounce,
Ravening a worm.

13. SAMUEL PALMER

Twilight Time (lines 1–24) c. 1827; from MS 1942

And now the trembling light
Glimmers behind the little hills and corn,
Lingering as loath to part. Yet part thou must,
And though than open day far pleasing more
(Ere yet the fields, and pearlèd cups of flowers
        Twinkle in the parting light),
Thee night shall hide, sweet visionary gleam
That softly lookest through the rising dew –
        Till, all like silver bright,
    The Faithful Witness, pure and white,
    Shall look o'er yonder grassy hill
    At this village, safe, and still.
        All is safe, and all is still,
    Save what noise the watch-dog makes
    Or the shrill cock the silence breaks
        Now and then –
        And now and then.
        Hark! once again,
        The wether's bell to us doth tell
        Some little stirring in the fold.
        Methinks the lingering, dying ray
        Of twilight time doth seem more fair,
    And lights the soul up more than day,
        When wide-spread, sultry sunshines are . . .

14. JOHN CLARE

This Leaning Tree with Ivy Overhung

(early 1830s; from MS 3 1979)

This leaning tree with ivy overhung,
This crooked brook o'er which is rudely flung
A slender plank that bends beneath the feet,
And that small hill the shepherd's summer seat,
Make up a picture to the mind and wear
A nobler gild than palace-walls can heir.
To me the wild wind dashes o'er the scene
Enchantment's shades of vivifying green:
I see her, sketchy pencil in her hand,
Painting the moving scene to fairy land!
That blackbird's music from the hazel bower
Turns into golden drops this summer shower –
To think the rain that wets his sooty wing
Should wake the gushes of his soul to sing!
Hark at the melody, how rich and loud
(Like daylight breaking through the morning cloud),
How luscious through that sea of green it floats!
Knowst thou of music breathed from sweeter notes
Than that wild minstrel of the summer shower
Breathes at this moment from that hazel-bower?
To me the anthem of a thousand tongues
Were poor and idle to the simple songs
Of that high-toned and edifying bird
That sings to Nature, by itself, unheard.
   There is a language wrote on earth and sky
By God's own pen in silent majesty;
There is a voice that's heard and felt and seen
In spring's young shades and summer's endless green;
There is a book of poesy and spells
In which that voice in sunny splendour dwells;
There is a page in which that voice aloud
Speaks music to the few, and not the crowd!
Though no romantic scenes my feet hath trod,
The voice of Nature, as the voice of God,
Appeals to me in every tree and flower,
Breathing his glory, magnitude and power.

In Nature's open book I read, and see
Beauty's rich lesson in this seeming pea.
Crowds see no magic in this trifling thing –
'Pshaw, 'tis a weed, and millions come with spring!'
I hear rich music whereso'er I look,
But heedless worldlings chide the brawling brook.
And that small lark between me and the sky
Breathes sweetest strains of morning's melody –
Yet by the heedless crowd 'tis only heard
As the small warbling of a common bird
That o'er the plough-teams hails the morning-sun.
They see no music from such magic won;
Yet I see melody in Nature's laws –
Or do I dream? Still wonder bids me pause.
  I pause and hear a voice that speaks aloud:
' 'Tis not on earth, nor in the thunder-cloud!
The many look for sound, 'tis silence speaks –
And song, like sunshine, from her rapture breaks.'
I hear it in my bosom, ever near,
'Tis in these winds, and they are everywhere –
It casts around my vision magic spells,
And makes earth Heaven, where poor fancy dwells!
I read its speech, and its speech is joy!
So, without teaching, when a lonely boy,
Each weed to me did happy tidings bring
(Plain as the daisy wrote the name of spring),
And God's own language, unto Nature given,
Seemed universal as the light of Heaven
And common as the grass upon the plain
That all may read and meet with joy again –
Save the unheeding heart, who, like the tomb,
Shuts joy in darkness, and forbids its bloom.

15. FELICIA HEMANS

Remembrance of Nature (1835; publ. 1838)

Oh Nature thou didst rear me for thine own,
With thy free singing-birds and mountain-brooks,
Feeding my thoughts in primrose-haunted nooks
With fairy fantasies and wood-dreams lone;

And thou didst teach me every wandering tone
Drawn from thy many-whispering trees and waves,
And guide my steps to founts and sparry caves,
And where bright mosses wove thee a rich throne
Midst the green hills. And now that, far estranged
From all sweet sounds and odours of thy breath,
Fading I lie, within my heart unchanged
So glows the love of thee that not for death
Seems that pure passion's fervour, but ordained
To meet on brighter shores thy majesty unstained.

16. LETITIA ELIZABETH LANDON

(i) *Scale Force, Cumberland* (c. 1836; publ. 1839)

It sweeps, as sweeps an army
Adown the mountain-side,
With the voice of many thunders
Like the battle's sounding tide.

Yet the sky is blue above it,
And the dashing of the spray
Wears the colour of the rainbow
Upon an April day.

It rejoices in the sunshine
When after heavy rain
It gathers the far waters
To dash upon the plain.

It is terrible yet lovely
Beneath the morning rays,
Like a dream of strength and beauty
It haunted those who gaze.

We feel that it is glorious –
Its power is on the soul –
And lofty thoughts within us
Acknowledge its control.

A generous inspiration
Is on the outward world –
It waketh thoughts and feelings
In careless coldness furled.

To love and to admire
Seems natural to the heart;
Life's small and selfish interests
From such a scene depart!

(ii) *Fountains Abbey* (c. 1836; publ. 1839)

Never more, when the day is o'er,
Will the lonely vespers sound;
No bells are ringing – no monks are singing –
When the moonlight falls around.

A few pale flowers, which in other hours
May have cheered the dreary mood;
When the votary turned to the world he had spurned,
And repined at the solitude.

Still do they blow mid the ruins below,
For fallen are fane and shrine,
And the moss has grown o'er the sculptured stone
Of an altar no more divine.

Still on the walls where the sunshine falls,
The ancient fruit-tree grows;
And o'er tablet and tomb, extends the bloom
Of many a wilding rose.

Fair though they be, yet they seemed to me
To mock the wreck below;
For mighty the tower, where the fragile flower
May now as in triumph blow.

Oh, foolish the thought, that my fancy brought;
More true and more wise to say,
That still thus doth spring, some gentle thing,
With its beauty to cheer decay.

V. Romantic Odes

The Romantic period is the period of the ode at its grandest – not that many are written at this level, but those that are, are of a power and beauty unmatched since Milton's *Ode on the Morning of Christ's Nativity* and the Pindaric (irregular) *Lycidas*. Neither Blake nor Byron is represented, but Burns, Wordsworth, Coleridge, Shelley and Keats are felt in this idiom to have achieved their highest lyrical effects. By definition the ode is a poem of exalted subject-matter and a certain complexity of musical structure. Wordsworth saw *Tintern Abbey* (despite its being in blank verse) as having the form's 'principle requisites' in 'the impassioned music of its versification'. The great odes presented below have also important similarities of theme and subject-matter. To read them in sequence is to experience at its most impressive the grandeur and the pathos of high Romantic art.

1. ROBERT BURNS

Despondency, An Ode (1786)

I

Oppressed with grief, oppressed with care,
A burden more than I can bear,
I set me down and sigh;
Oh life! thou art a galling load,
Along a rough, a weary road,
To wretches such as I!
Dim-backward as I cast my view,
What sickening scenes appear –
What sorrows *yet* may pierce me through,
Too justly I may fear!
Still caring, despairing,
Must be my bitter doom;
My woes here shall close ne'er
But with the closing tomb!

II

Happy ye sons of busy life
Who, equal to the bustling strife,
No other view regard
(Even when the wishéd end's denied,
Yet while the busy means are plied,
They bring their own reward);
Whilst I, a hope-abandoned wight,
Unfitted with an aim,
Meet every sad returning night
And joyless morn the same.
You, bustling and justling,
Forget each grief and pain;
I, listless yet restless,
Find every prospect vain!

III

How blest the solitary's lot,
Who, all-forgetting, all-forgot,
Within his humble cell –
The cavern wild with tangling roots –

21 *wight* man. **29** *the solitary's lot* the hermit's way of life.

Sits o'er his newly-gathered fruits,
   Beside his crystal well!
Or haply to his evening thought,
   By unfrequented stream,
The ways of men are distant brought,
   A faint-collected dream;
      While praising, and raising
         His thoughts to Heaven on high,
      As wandering, meandering,
         He views the solemn sky.

IV

Than I, no lonely hermit, placed
Where never human footstep traced,
   Less fit to play the part:
The lucky moment to improve,
And just to stop, and just to move,
   With self-respecting art.
But ah, those pleasures, loves, and joys,
   Which I too keenly taste,
The solitary can despise –
   Can want and yet be blest!
      He needs not, he heeds not
         Or human love, or hate;
      Whilst I here must cry here
         At perfidy ingrate!

V

Oh enviable early days,
When dancing thoughtless pleasure's maze,
   To care, to guilt unknown –
How ill exchanged for riper times,
To feel the follies or the crimes
   Of others, or my own!
Ye tiny elves that guiltless sport,
   Like linnets in the bush,
Ye little know the ills ye court,
   When manhood is your wish!

52 *want* lack, be without. **56** *perfidy ingrate* treachery and ingratitude.

The losses, the crosses
That active man engage;
The fears all, the tears all
Of dim declining age!

2. WILLIAM WORDSWORTH

The Immortality Ode

(spring 1802/Feb. 1804; publ. 1807)

I

There was a time when meadow, grove, and stream,
The earth and every common sight
To me did seem
Apparelled in celestial light –
The glory and the freshness of a dream.
It is not now as it has been of yore;
Turn wheresoe'er I may,
By night or day,
The things which I have seen I now can see no more.

II

The rainbow comes and goes,
And lovely is the rose;
The moon doth with delight
Look round her when the heavens are bare;
Waters on a starry night
Are beautiful and fair;
The sunshine is a glorious birth –
But yet I know, where'er I go,
That there hath passed away a glory from the earth.

III

Now, while the birds thus sing a joyous song,
And while the young lambs bound
As to the tabor's sound,
To me alone there came a thought of grief.
A timely utterance gave that thought relief,
And I again am strong!
The cataracts blow their trumpets from the steep

67 *crosses* trials, annoyances.

(No more shall grief of mine the season wrong),
I hear the echoes through the mountains throng;
The winds come to me from the fields of sleep,
　　　　And all the earth is gay;
　　　　　　Land and sea
　　　　Give themselves up to jollity,
　　　　　　And with the heart of May
　　　　Doth every beast keep holiday;
　　　　　　Thou child of joy,
Shout round me – let me hear thy shouts, thou happy
　shepherd-boy!

IV

Ye blesséd creatures I have heard the call
　　Ye to each other make; I see
The heavens laugh with you in your jubilee;
　　My heart is at your festival,
　　　　My head hath its coronal,
The fullness of your bliss, I feel – I feel it all!
　　　　Oh evil day, if I were sullen
　　　　While the Earth herself is adorning
　　　　　　This sweet May-morning,
　　　　And the children are pulling
　　　　　　On every side
　　　　In a thousand valleys far and wide
　　　　Fresh flowers; while the sun shines warm,
And the babe leaps up on his mother's arm.
　　　　I hear, I hear, with joy I hear!
　　　　But there's a tree, of many one,
A single field which I have looked upon –
Both of them speak of something that is gone.
　　　　　　The pansy at my feet
　　　　　　Doth the same tale repeat:
Whither is fled the visionary gleam?
Where is it gone, the glory and the dream?

V

Our birth is but a sleep and a forgetting:
The soul that rises with us, our life's star,
　　　　Hath had elsewhere its setting
　　　　　　And cometh from afar.
　　　　Not in entire forgetfulness,
　　　　And not in utter nakedness,

But trailing clouds of glory do we come
From God who is our home.
Heaven lies about us in our infancy –
Shades of the prison-house begin to close
Upon the growing boy,
But he beholds the light and whence it flows,
He sees it in his joy.
The youth, who daily farther from the east
Must travel, still is Nature's priest
And by the vision splendid
Is on his way attended;
At length the man perceives it die away
And fade into the light of common day.

VI

Earth fills her lap with pleasures of her own:
Yearnings she hath in her own natural kind,
And even with something of a mother's mind
And no unworthy aim
The homely nurse doth all she can
To make her foster-child, her inmate, man,
Forget the glories he hath known,
And that imperial palace whence he came.

VII

Behold the child among his new-born blisses,
A four years' darling of a pigmy size –
See where, mid work of his own hand, he lies,
Fretted by sallies of his mother's kisses,
With light upon him from his father's eyes!
See at his feet some little plan or chart,
Some fragment from his dream of human life
Shaped by himself with newly-learnéd art
(A wedding or a festival,
A mourning or a funeral),
And this hath now his heart,
And unto this he frames his song.
Then he will fit his tongue
To dialogues of business, love or strife;
But it will not be long
Ere this be thrown aside,
And with new joy and pride
The little actor cons another part,

Filling from time to time his 'humourous stage'
With all the persons down to palsied age
That life brings with her in her equipage–
As if his whole vocation
Were endless imitation.

VIII

Thou whose exterior semblance doth belie
Thy soul's immensity,
Thou best philosopher, who yet dost keep
Thy heritage – thou eye among the blind
That, deaf and silent, readst the eternal deep,
Haunted for ever by the eternal mind;
Mighty prophet, seer blest,
On whom those truths do rest
Which we are toiling all our lives to find!
Thou over whom thy immortality
Broods like the day, a master o'er a slave –
A presence which is not to be put by –
To whom the grave
Is but a lonely bed without the sense or sight
Of day or the warm light,
A place of thought where we in waiting lie;
Thou little child, yet glorious in the might
Of untamed pleasures, on thy being's height
Why with such earnest pains dost thou provoke
The years to bring the inevitable yoke,
Thus blindly with thy blessedness at strife?
Full soon thy soul shall have her earthly freight,
And custom lie upon thee with a weight
Heavy as frost and deep almost as life!

IX

Oh joy that in our embers
Is something that doth live,
That nature yet remembers
What was so fugitive!
The thought of our past years in me doth breed
Perpetual benedictions; not indeed
For that which is most worthy to be blest –
Delight and liberty, the simple creed
Of childhood, whether fluttering or at rest,
With new-born hope for ever in his breast –

Not for these I raise
The song of thanks and praise,
But for those obstinate questionings
Of sense and outward things,
Fallings from us, vanishings,
Blank misgivings of a creature
Moving about in worlds not realized,
High instincts, before which our mortal nature
Did tremble like a guilty thing surprised –
But for those first affections,
Those shadowy recollections
Which be they what they may
Are yet the fountain-light of all our day,
Are yet the master-light of all our seeing;
Uphold us, cherish us, and make
Our noisy years seem moments in the being
Of the eternal silence – truths that wake
To perish never,
Which neither listlessness, nor mad endeavour,
Nor man nor boy,
Nor all that is at enmity with joy,
Can utterly abolish or destroy!
Hence in a season of calm weather,
Though inland far we be,
Our souls have sight of that immortal sea
Which brought us hither,
Can in a moment travel thither
And see the children sport upon the shore,
And hear the mighty waters rolling evermore.

X

Then sing ye birds, sing, sing a joyous song,
And let the young lambs bound
As to the tabor's sound!
We in thought will join your throng –
Ye that pipe and ye that play,
Ye that through your hearts today
Feel the gladness of the May!
What though the radiance which was once so bright
Be now forever taken from my sight,
Though nothing can bring back the hour
Of splendour in the grass, of glory in the flower,
We will grieve not, rather find
Strength in what remains behind:

In the primal sympathy
Which having been must ever be,
In the soothing thoughts that spring
Out of human suffering,
In the faith that looks through death,
In years that bring the philosophic mind.

XI

And oh ye fountains, meadows, hills, and groves,
Think not of any severing of our loves;
Yet in my heart of hearts I feel your might –
I only have relinquished one delight
To live beneath your more habitual sway!
I love the brooks which down their channels fret,
Even more than when I tripped lightly as they;
The innocent brightness of a new-born day
Is lovely yet;
The clouds that gather round the setting sun
Do take a sober colouring from an eye
That hath kept watch o'er man's mortality;
Another race hath been, and other palms are won.
Thanks to the human heart by which we live –
Thanks to its tenderness, its joys, and fears –
To me the meanest flower that blows can give
Thoughts that do often lie too deep for tears.

3. SAMUEL TAYLOR COLERIDGE

Dejection: An Ode (summer 1802; publ. 4 Oct.)

Late, late yestreen I saw the new moon,
With the old moon in her arms,
And I fear, I fear, my Master dear,
We shall have a deadly storm.
(*Ballad of Sir Patrick Spens*)

I

Well, if the bard was weather-wise, who made
The grand old ballad of Sir Patrick Spens,
This night, so tranquil now, will not go hence
Unroused by winds, that ply a busier trade

Than those which mould yon cloud in lazy flakes,
Or the dull sobbing draught, that drones and rakes
Upon the strings of this Eolian lute,
    Which better far were mute.
  For lo! the new moon, winter-bright
  And overspread with phantom light –
  With swimming phantom light o'erspread,
  But rimmed and circled by a silver thread –
I see the old moon in her lap, foretelling
  The coming-on of rain and squally blast.
And oh, that even now the gust were swelling,
  And the slant night-shower driving loud and fast!
Those sounds which oft have raised me, while they awed,
    And sent my soul abroad,
Might now perhaps their wonted impulse give,
Might startle this dull pain, and make it move and live!

II

A grief without a pang, void, dark, and drear,
  A stifled, drowsy, unimpassioned grief,
  Which finds no natural outlet, no relief,
    In word, or sigh, or tear –
Oh Edmund, in this wan and heartless mood,
To other thoughts by yonder throstle wooed,
  All this long eve, so balmy and serene,
Have I been gazing on the western sky,
  And its peculiar tint of yellow-green –
And still I gaze – and with how blank an eye!
And those thin clouds above, in flakes and bars,
That give away their motion to the stars;
Those stars, that glide behind them or between,
Now sparkling, now bedimmed, but always seen;
Yon crescent moon, as fixed as if it grew
In its own cloudless, starless lake of blue –
A boat becalmed, a lovely sky-canoe!
I see them all, so excellently fair,
I *see*, not *feel*, how beautiful they are!

III

  My genial spirits fail;
  And what can these avail
To lift the smothering weight from off my breast?

It were a vain endeavour,
Though I should gaze for ever
On that green light that lingers in the west:
I may not hope from outward forms to win
The passion and the life, whose fountains are within.

IV

Oh Edmund, we receive but what we give,
And in *our* life alone does Nature live:
Ours is her wedding garment, ours her shroud!
And would we aught behold of higher worth
Than that inanimate cold world allowed
To the poor loveless ever-anxious crowd,
Ah! from the soul itself must issue forth
A light, a glory, a fair luminous cloud
Enveloping the earth –
And from the soul itself must there be sent
A sweet and potent voice, of its own birth,
Of all sweet sounds the life and element.

Oh pure of heart, thou needst not ask of me
What this strong music in the soul may be –
What, and wherein it doth exist,
This light, this glory, this fair luminous mist,
This beautiful and beauty-making power.
Joy, virtuous Edmund – joy that ne'er was given,
Save to the pure, and in their purest hour –
Joy, Edmund, is the spirit and the power
Which, wedding Nature to us, gives in dower
A new Earth and new Heaven,
Undreamt of by the sensual and the proud!
Joy is the sweet voice, joy the luminous cloud –
We, we ourselves, rejoice!
And thence flows all that charms or ear or sight –
All melodies the echoes of that voice,
All colours a suffusion from that light.

V

Yes, dearest Edmund, yes,
There was a time when, though my path was rough,
This joy within me dallied with distress,
And all misfortunes were but as the stuff
Whence fancy made me dreams of happiness;

For hope grew round me like the twining vine,
And fruits and foliage not my own, seemed mine!
But now afflictions bow me down to earth –
Nor care I that they rob me of my mirth,
    But oh, each visitation
Suspends what Nature gave me at my birth,
  My shaping spirit of imagination!

VI

Oh, wherefore did I let it haunt my mind,
  This dark distressful dream?
I turn from it and listen to the wind,
  Which long has raved unnoticed. What a scream
Of agony, by torture lengthened out,
That lute sent forth! Thou wind, that ravest without!
  Bare crag, or mountain-tairn, or blasted tree,
Or pine-grove whither woodman never clomb,
Or lonely house, long held the witches' home,
  Methinks were fitter instruments for thee,
Mad lutanist, who in this month of showers,
Of dark-brown gardens, and of peeping flowers,
Makest devils' yule, with worse than wintry song
The blossoms, buds, and timorous leaves among.
  Thou actor, perfect in all tragic sounds!
    Thou mighty poet, even to frenzy bold!
What tellest thou now about?
'Tis of the rushing of an host in rout,
    With many groans of men with smarting wounds –
      At once they groan with pain, and shudder with the cold!
But hush, there is a pause of deepest silence!
  And all that noise, as of a rushing crowd,
    With groans and tremulous shudderings – all is over!
  It tells another tale, with sounds less deep and loud,
      A tale of less affright
    And tempered with delight,
As Edmund's self had framed the tender lay.
    'Tis of a little child
    Upon a lonesome wild
Not far from home, but she has lost her way
And now moans low in utter grief and fear,
And now screams loud, and hopes to make her mother hear!

VII

'Tis midnight, and small thoughts have I of sleep –
Full seldom may my friend such vigils keep!
Visit him, gentle sleep, with wings of healing,
   And may this storm be but a mountain-birth,
May all the stars hang bright above his dwelling,
   Silent as though they watched the sleeping Earth!
      With light heart may he rise,
      Gay fancy, cheerful eyes,
And sing his lofty song, and teach me to rejoice!
Oh Edmund, friend of my devoutest choice,
Oh, raised from anxious dread and busy care
By the immenseness of the good and fair
Which thou seest everywhere –
Joy lifts thy spirit, joy attunes thy voice;
To thee do all things live, from pole to pole,
Their life the eddying of thy living soul!
Oh simple spirit, guided from above;
Oh lofty poet, full of light and love;
Brother and friend of my devoutest of my choice,
Thus mayst thou ever, evermore rejoice!

4. PERCY BYSSHE SHELLEY

Hymn to Intellectual Beauty

(July 1816; publ. 1817)

I

The awful shadow of some unseen power
   Floats, though unseen, among us – visiting
   This various world with as inconstant wing
As summer winds that creep from flower to flower.
Like moonbeams that behind some piny mountain-shower,
      It visits with inconstant glance
      Each human heart and countenance:
Like hues and harmonies of evening,
      Like clouds in starlight widely spread,
      Like memory of music fled –
      Like aught that for its grace may be
Dear, and yet dearer for its mystery.

II

Spirit of Beauty – that dost consecrate
With thine own hues all thou dost shine upon
Of human thought or form – where art thou gone?
Why dost thou pass away and leave our state,
This dim vast vale of tears, vacant and desolate?
Ask why the sunlight not for ever
Weaves rainbows o'er yon mountain-river,
Why aught should fail and fade that once is shown,
Why fear and dream and death and birth
Cast on the daylight of this earth
Such gloom – why man has such a scope
For love and hate, despondency and hope?

III

No voice from some sublimer world hath ever
To sage or poet these responses given,
Therefore the names of Demon, Ghost, and Heaven,
Remain the records of their vain endeavour –
Frail spells, whose uttered charm might not avail to sever,
From all we hear and all we see,
Doubt, chance, and mutability.
Thy light alone – like mist o'er mountains driven,
Or music by the night-wind sent
Through strings of some still instrument,
Or moonlight on a midnight stream –
Gives grace and truth to life's unquiet dream.

IV

Love, hope, and self-esteem, like clouds depart
And come, for some uncertain moments lent.
Man were immortal, and omnipotent,
Didst thou, unknown and awful as thou art,
Keep with thy glorious train firm state within his heart!
Thou messenger of sympathies,
That wax and wane in lovers' eyes,
Thou that to human thought art nourishment
Like darkness to a dying flame,
Depart not as thy shadow came –
Depart not, lest the grave should be,
Like life and fear, a dark reality.

V

While yet a boy I sought for ghosts, and sped
Through many a listening chamber, cave and ruin,
And starlight wood, with fearful steps pursuing
Hopes of high talk with the departed dead.
I called on poisonous names with which our youth is fed –
I was not heard! I saw them not!
When musing deeply on the lot
Of life, at that sweet time when winds are wooing
All vital things that wake to bring
News of birds and blossoming,
Sudden thy shadow fell on me –
I shrieked, and clasped my hands in ecstasy!

VI

I vowed that I would dedicate my powers
To thee and thine – have I not kept the vow?
With beating heart and streaming eyes, even now
I call the phantoms of a thousand hours
Each from his voiceless grave! They have in visioned bowers
Of studious zeal, or love's delight,
Outwatched with me the envious night –
They know that never joy illumed my brow
Unlinked with hope that thou wouldst free
This world from its dark slavery,
That thou, oh awful Loveliness,
Wouldst give whate'er these words cannot express.

VII

The day becomes more solemn and serene
When noon is past; there is a harmony
In autumn, and a lustre in its sky,
Which through the summer is not heard or seen –
As if it could not be, as if it had not been!
Thus let thy power, which like the truth
Of Nature on my passive youth
Descended, to my onward life supply
Its calm – to one who worships thee,
And every form containing thee,
Whom, Spirit fair, thy spells did bind
To fear himself, and love all human kind.

5. JOHN KEATS

Odes of Spring 1819 (publ. 1820)

(i) *Ode to Psyche* (late April)

I

Oh Goddess, hear these tuneless numbers, wrung
   By sweet enforcement and remembrance dear,
And pardon that thy secrets should be sung
   Even into thine own soft-conchéd ear!
Surely I dreamt to-day, or did I see
   The wingéd Psyche with awakened eyes?
I wandered in a forest thoughtlessly,
   And, on the sudden, fainting with surprise,
Saw two fair creatures, couchéd side by side
   In deepest grass, beneath the whispering roof
   Of leaves and trembled blossoms, where there ran
      A brooklet, scarce espied.

II

Mid hushed, cool-rooted flowers, fragrant-eyed,
   Blue, silver-white, and budded Tyrian,
They lay calm-breathing on the bedded grass.
   Their arms embracéd, and their pinions too;
   Their lips touched not, but had not bade adieu,
As if disjoinéd by soft-handed slumber,
And ready still past kisses to outnumber
   At tender eye-dawn of aurorean love:
      The wingéd boy I knew –
   But who wast thou, oh happy, happy dove?
      His Psyche true!

III

Oh latest born and loveliest vision far
   Of all Olympus' faded hierarchy!
Fairer than Phoebe's sapphire-regioned star,
   Or Vesper, amorous glow-worm of the sky –
Fairer than these, though temple thou hast none,
      Nor altar heaped with flowers;
Nor virgin-choir to make delicious moan
      Upon the midnight hours –

No voice, no lute, no pipe, no incense sweet
From chain-swung censer teeming;
No shrine, no grove, no oracle, no heat
Of pale-mouthed prophet dreaming.

IV

Oh brightest, though too late for antique vows!
Too, too late for the fond believing lyre,
When holy were the haunted forest-boughs,
Holy the air, the water, and the fire.
Yet even in these days, so far retired
From happy pieties, thy lucent fans,
Fluttering among the faint Olympians,
I see, and sing, by my own eyes inspired.
So let me be thy choir, and make a moan
Upon the midnight hours –
Thy voice, thy lute, thy pipe, thy incense sweet
From swingéd censer teeming;
Thy shrine, thy grove, thy oracle, thy heat
Of pale-mouthed prophet dreaming.

V

Yes, I will be thy priest, and build a fane
In some untrodden region of my mind,
Where branchéd thoughts, new grown with pleasant pain,
Instead of pines shall murmur in the wind.
Far, far around shall those dark-clustered trees
Fledge the wild-ridgéd mountains steep by steep;
And there by zephyrs, streams, and birds, and bees,
The moss-lain dryads shall be lulled to sleep.
And in the midst of this wide quietness
A rosy sanctuary will I dress
With the wreathed trellis of a working brain,
With buds, and bells, and stars without a name –
With all the gardener Fancy e'er could feign,
Who, breeding flowers, will never breed the same.
And there shall be for thee all soft delight
That shadowy thought can win,
A bright torch, and a casement ope at night,
To let the warm Love in!

(ii) *Ode to a Nightingale* (early May)

I

My heart aches, and a drowsy numbness pains
   My sense, as though of hemlock I had drunk,
Or emptied some dull opiate to the drains
   One minute past, and Lethe-wards had sunk.
'Tis not through envy of thy happy lot,
   But being too happy in thine happiness –
      That thou, light-wingéd dryad of the trees,
         In some melodious plot
      Of beechen green, and shadows numberless,
         Singest of summer in full-throated ease.

II

Oh, for a draught of vintage that hath been
   Cooled a long age in the deep-delvéd earth,
Tasting of Flora and the country green,
   Dance, and Provençal song, and sunburnt mirth!
Oh for a beaker full of the warm South,
   Full of the true, the blushful Hippocrene,
      With beaded bubbles winking at the brim,
         And purple-stainéd mouth;
   That I might drink, and leave the world unseen,
      And with thee fade away into the forest dim –

III

Fade far away, dissolve, and quite forget
   What thou among the leaves hast never known,
The weariness, the fever, and the fret
   Here, where men sit and hear each other groan –
Where palsy shakes a few, sad, last, grey hairs,
   Where youth grows pale, and spectre-thin, and dies;
      Where but to think is to be full of sorrow
         And leaden-eyed despairs,
   Where beauty cannot keep her lustrous eyes
      Or new love pine at them beyond tomorrow.

IV

Away! Away! For I will fly to thee,
   Not charioted by Bacchus and his pards,
But on the viewless wings of poesy,
   Though the dull brain perplexes and retards.

Already with thee! Tender is the night,
   And haply the Queen-Moon is on her throne,
      Clustered around by all her starry fays;
         But here there is no light,
   Save what from heaven is with the breezes blown
      Through verdurous glooms and winding mossy ways.

V

I cannot see what flowers are at my feet,
   Nor what soft incense hangs upon the boughs,
But, in embalméd darkness, guess each sweet
   Wherewith the seasonable month endows
The grass, the thicket, and the fruit-tree wild;
   White hawthorn, and the pastoral eglantine;
      Fast fading violets covered up in leaves;
         And mid-May's eldest child,
   The coming musk-rose, full of dewy wine,
      The murmurous haunt of flies on summer eves.

VI

Darkling I listen, and for many a time
   I have been half in love with easeful death,
Called him soft names in many a muséd rhyme,
   To take into the air my quiet breath.
Now more than ever seems it rich to die,
   To cease upon the midnight with no pain,
      While thou art pouring forth thy soul abroad
         In such an ecstasy!
   Still wouldst thou sing, and I have ears in vain –
      To thy high requiem become a sod.

VII

Thou wast not born for death, immortal bird!
   No hungry generations tread thee down;
The voice I hear this passing night was heard
   In ancient days by emperor and clown –
Perhaps the self-same song that found a path
   Through the sad heart of Ruth, when, sick for home,
      She stood in tears amid the alien corn;
         The same that oft-times hath
   Charmed magic casements, opening on the foam
      Of perilous seas, in fairy lands forlorn.

VIII

Forlorn – the very word is like a bell
To toll me back from thee to my sole self!
Adieu! The fancy cannot cheat so well
As she is famed to do, deceiving elf!
Adieu! adieu! Thy plaintive anthem fades
Past the near meadows, over the still stream,
Up the hillside; and now 'tis buried deep
In the next valley-glades:
Was it a vision, or a waking dream?
Fled is that music! Do I wake or sleep?

(iii) *Ode on a Grecian Urn* (May)

I

Thou still unravished bride of quietness,
Thou foster-child of silence and slow time,
Sylvan historian, who canst thus express
A flowery tale more sweetly than our rhyme!
What leaf-fringed legend haunts about thy shape,
Of deities or mortals, or of both,
In Tempe or the dales of Arcady?
What men or gods are these? What maidens loath?
What mad pursuit? What struggle to escape?
What pipes and timbrels? What wild ecstasy?

II

Heard melodies are sweet, but those unheard
Are sweeter; therefore, ye soft pipes, play on –
Not to the sensual ear, but, more endeared,
Pipe to the spirit ditties of no tone.
Fair youth, beneath the trees, thou canst not leave
Thy song, nor ever can those trees be bare;
Bold lover, never, never canst thou kiss,
Though winning near the goal – yet, do not grieve:
She cannot fade, though thou hast not thy bliss,
For ever wilt thou love, and she be fair!

III

Ah, happy, happy boughs! that cannot shed
Your leaves, nor ever bid the spring adieu;
And, happy melodist, unwearièd,
For ever piping songs for ever new!

More happy love! more happy, happy love!
  For ever warm and still to be enjoyed,
    For ever panting, and for ever young –
All breathing human passion far above,
  That leaves a heart high-sorrowful and cloyed,
    A burning forehead, and a parching tongue.

IV

Who are these coming to the sacrifice?
  To what green altar, oh mysterious priest,
Leadst thou that heifer lowing at the skies,
  And all her silken flanks with garlands drest?
What little town by river or sea shore,
  Or mountain-built with peaceful citadel,
    Is emptied of this folk, this pious morn?
And, little town, thy streets for evermore
  Will silent be; and not a soul to tell
    Why thou art desolate, can e'er return.

V

Oh Attic shape! Fair attitude! with brede
  Of marble men and maidens overwrought,
With forest branches and the trodden weed –
  Thou, silent form, dost tease us out of thought
As doth eternity. Cold pastoral!
  When old age shall this generation waste
    Thou shalt remain, in midst of other woe
Than ours, a friend to man, to whom thou sayst,
  'Beauty is truth, truth beauty – that is all
    Ye know on earth, and all ye need to know.'

(iv) *Ode on Melancholy* (May)

I

No, no, go not to Lethe, neither twist
  Wolf's-bane, tight-rooted, for its poisonous wine;
Nor suffer thy pale forehead to be kissed
  By nightshade, ruby grape of Proserpine.

Make not your rosary of yew-berries,
   Nor let the beetle, nor the death-moth, be
      Your mournful Psyche, nor the downy owl
A partner in your sorrow's mysteries;
   For shade to shade will come too drowsily,
      And drown the wakeful anguish of the soul.

II
But when the melancholy fit shall fall
   Sudden from heaven like a weeping cloud
That fosters the droop-headed flowers all
   And hides the green hill in an April shroud,
Then glut thy sorrow on a morning rose,
   Or on the rainbow of the salt sand-wave,
      Or on the wealth of globéd peonies –
Or, if thy mistress some rich anger shows,
   Emprison her soft hand and let her rave,
      And feed deep, deep upon her peerless eyes.

III
She dwells with Beauty – Beauty that must die;
   And Joy, whose hand is ever at his lips
Bidding adieu; and aching Pleasure, nigh,
   Turning to poison while the bee-mouth sips.
Ay, in the very temple of Delight
   Veiled Melancholy has her sovran shrine,
      Though seen of none save him whose strenuous tongue
Can burst Joy's grape against his palate fine –
   His soul shall taste the sadness of her might,
      And be among her cloudy trophies hung.

(v) *Ode on Indolence* (late May)

'They toil not, neither do they spin.'

I
One morn before me were three figures seen,
   With bowéd necks and joinéd hands, side-faced,
And one behind the other stepped serene,
   In placid sandals and in white robes graced.

They passed, like figures on a marble urn
When shifted round to see the other side;
They came again – as when the urn once more
Is shifted round the first-seen shades return –
And they were strange to me, as may betide
With vases, to one deep in Phidian lore.

II

'How is it, Shadows, that I knew ye not?
How came ye muffled in so hush a masque?
Was it a silent deep-disguiséd plot
To steal away, and leave without a task
My idle days? Ripe was the drowsy hour;
The blissful cloud of summer-indolence
Benumbed my eyes; my pulse grew less and less;
Pain had no sting, and pleasure's wreath no flower!
Oh, why did ye not melt, and leave my sense
Unhaunted quite of all, but – nothingness?'

III

A third time passed they by – and, passing, turned
Each one the face a moment-whiles to me –
Then faded, and to follow them I burned,
And ached for wings, because I knew the three.
The first was a fair maid, and Love her name;
The second was Ambition, pale of cheek,
And ever watchful with fatigued eye;
The last, whom I love more, the more of blame
Is heaped upon her (maiden most unmeek),
I knew to be my demon Poesy.

IV

They faded, and, forsooth, I wanted wings!
Oh folly! What is love, and where is it? –
And, for that poor ambition! It springs
From a man's little heart's short fever-fit!
For Poesy! No, she has not a joy
(At least for me) so sweet as drowsy noons,
And evenings steeped in honeyed indolence!
Oh, for an age so sheltered from annoy,
That I may never know how change the moons,
Or hear the voice of busy common-sense!

V

And once more came they by. Alas, wherefore?
My sleep had been embroidered with dim dreams;
My soul had been a lawn besprinkled o'er
With flowers, and stirring shades, and baffled beams.
The morn was clouded, but no shower fell,
Though in her lids hung the sweet tears of May;
The open casement pressed a new-leaved vine,
Let in the budding warmth and throstle's lay:
'Oh Shadows, 'twas a time to bid farewell!
Upon your skirts had fallen no tears of mine.

VI

So, ye three Ghosts, adieu! Ye cannot raise
My head cool-bedded in the flowery grass;
For I would not be dieted with praise –
A pet-lamb in a sentimental farce!
Fade softly from my eyes, and be once more
In masque-like figures on the dreamy urn.
Farewell! I yet have visions for the night,
And for the day faint visions there is store –
Vanish, ye Phantoms, from my idle sprite
Into the clouds, and never more return!'

6. PERCY BYSSHE SHELLEY

Ode to the West Wind (Oct. 1819; publ. 1820)

This poem was conceived and chiefly written in a wood that skirts the Arno, near Florence, and on a day when that tempestuous wind, whose temperature is at once mild and animating, was collecting the vapours which pour down the autumnal rains. They began, as I foresaw, at sunset, with a violent tempest of hail and rain, attended by that magnificent thunder and lightning peculiar to the cisalpine regions.

(Shelley)

I

Oh wild West Wind, thou breath of autumn's being,
Thou, from whose unseen presence the leaves dead
Are driven, like ghosts from an enchanter fleeing,

Yellow, and black, and pale, and hectic red –
Pestilence-stricken multitudes! Oh thou,
Who chariotest to their dark wintry bed

The wingéd seeds, where they lie cold and low,
Each like a corpse within its grave, until
Thine azure sister of the spring shall blow

Her clarion o'er the dreaming earth, and fill
(Driving sweet buds like flocks to feed in air)
With living hues and odours plain and hill:

Wild Spirit, which art moving everywhere –
Destroyer and preserver – hear, oh, hear!

II

Thou on whose stream, mid the steep sky's commotion,
Loose clouds like earth's decaying leaves are shed,
Shook from the tangled boughs of Heaven and Ocean,

Angels of rain and lightning – there are spread
On the blue surface of thine airy surge,
Like the bright hair uplifted from the head

Of some fierce Maenad, even from the dim verge
Of the horizon to the zenith's height,
The locks of the approaching storm. Thou dirge

Of the dying year, to which this closing night
Will be the dome of a vast sepulchre,
Vaulted with all thy congregated might

Of vapours, from whose solid atmosphere
Black rain, and fire, and hail will burst – oh, hear!

III

Thou who didst waken from his summer dreams
The blue Mediterranean, where he lay,
Lulled by the coil of his crystalline streams,

Beside a pumice isle in Baiae's bay,
And saw in sleep old palaces and towers
Quivering within the wave's intenser day,

All overgrown with azure moss and flowers
So sweet, the sense faints picturing them! Thou
For whose path the Atlantic's level powers

Cleave themselves into chasms, while far below
The sea-blooms and the oozy woods which wear
The sapless foliage of the ocean, know

Thy voice, and suddenly grow grey with fear,
And tremble and despoil themselves – oh, hear!

IV

If I were a dead leaf thou mightest bear,
If I were a swift cloud to fly with thee,
A wave to pant beneath thy power, and share

The impulse of thy strength, only less free
Than thou, oh uncontrollable! – if even
I were as in my boyhood, and could be

The comrade of thy wanderings over heaven,
As then, when to outstrip thy skiey speed
Scarce seemed a vision – I would ne'er have striven

As thus with thee in prayer in my sore need.
Oh, lift me as a wave, a leaf, a cloud!
I fall upon the thorns of life! I bleed!

A heavy weight of hours has chained and bowed
One too like thee, tameless, and swift, and proud.

V

Make me thy lyre, even as the forest is –
What if my leaves are falling like its own? –
The tumult of thy mighty harmonies

Will take from both a deep autumnal tone,
Sweet though in sadness. Be thou, Spirit fierce,
My spirit! Be thou me, impetuous one!

Drive my dead thoughts over the universe
Like withered leaves to quicken a new birth!
And, by the incantation of this verse,

Scatter, as from an unextinguished hearth
Ashes and sparks, my words among mankind!
Be through my lips to unawakened earth

The trumpet of a prophecy! Oh, Wind,
If winter comes, can spring be far behind?

VI. Romantic Lyric and Song

It seems inevitable that the Romantic period, with its emphasis on individuality and its belief in personal emotion, should be a great age of the lyric. At its outset we have the astonishing achievements of Burns and Blake as writers of song. Though usually at work on longer poems, Wordsworth is a lyric-poet of many voices, all of them distinctive. Coleridge, by contrast, wrote few major lyrics, and (surprisingly) the same is true of Keats, if one excludes the odes and sonnets. Despite his many longer poems, Shelley is among the greatest of lyric-poets. And Byron, though he is prompted to lyric writing only from time to time, has perhaps the purest lyricism of them all:

> There be none of Beauty's daughters
>   With a magic like to thee,
> And like music on the waters
>   Is thy sweet voice to me . . .

With no formal constraints, no cramping tradition, the lyric is a mode that lends itself to the big poet off duty, to the part-time poet, to the poet with an ear for popular song, or a love that has to find expression. It is also a mode in which women poets come to the front. Blamire, early in the period, is a natural song writer, in Cumbrian and Scottish as well as southern English; Smith is mainly a sonneteer, but Robinson (at one moment a Della Cruscan, at the next writing a plain style of passionate intensity) is always ready to explore; Hemans, Landon and Norton, at the end of the period, are endlessly inventive, producing so many good lyrics that it is hard to make a selection.

1. WILLIAM BLAKE

Song ('How sweet I roamed') *Poetical Sketches* 1783

How sweet I roamed from field to field
    And tasted all the summer's pride,
Till I the Prince of Love beheld,
    Who in the sunny beams did glide.

He showed me lilies for my hair,
    And blushing roses for my brow;
He led me through his gardens fair,
    Where all his golden pleasures grow.

With sweet May dews my wings were wet,
    And Phoebus fired my vocal rage.
He caught me in his silken net,
    And shut me in his golden cage.

He loves to sit and hear me sing,
    Then laughing sports and plays with me –
Then stretches out my golden wing,
      And mocks my loss of liberty.

2. ROBERT BURNS

Songs 1786–93

(i) *It Was upon a Lammas Night* (1786)

It was upon a Lammas night
  When corn rigs are bonnie,
Beneath the moon's unclouded light,
  I held awa to Annie;
The time flew by wi' tentless heed,
  Till, 'tween the late and early,
Wi' sma' persuasion she agreed,
  To see me thro' the barley.

Corn rigs, an' barley rigs,
  An' corn rigs are bonnie
I'll ne'er forget that happy night,
  Amang the rigs wi' Annie!

The sky was blue, the wind was still,
  The moon was shining clearly,
I set her down, wi' right good will,
  Amang the rigs o' barley.
I ken't her heart was a' my ain,
  I loved her most sincerely,
I kissed her owre and owre again
  Amang the rigs o' barley.

Corn rigs, an' barley rigs,
  An' corn rigs are bonnie
I'll ne'er forget that happy night,
  Amang the rigs wi' Annie!

I locked her in my fond embrace
  (Her heart was beating rarely),
My blessings on that happy place
  Amang the rigs o' barley –

4 *held awa* took my way. 5 *tentless heed* no consideration.
17 *ken't* knew.

But by the moon and stars so bright,
She ay shall bless that happy night,
   Amang the rigs o' barley!

Corn rigs, an' barley rigs,
   An' corn rigs are bonnie
I'll ne'er forget that happy night,
   Amang the rigs wi' Annie!

I hae been blythe wi' comrades dear,
   I hae been merry drinking,
I hae been joyfu' gath'rin gear,
   I hae been happy thinking –
But a' the pleasures e'er I saw,
   Tho' three times doubl'd fairly,
That happy night was worth them a',
   Amang the rigs o' barley.

Corn rigs, an' barley rigs,
   An' corn rigs are bonnie
I'll ne'er forget that happy night,
   Amang the rigs wi' Annie!

(ii) *The Banks o' Doon* (March 1791; publ. 1808)

Ye flowery banks o' bonnie Doon
   How can ye blume sae fair,
How can ye chant, ye little birds,
   And I sae fu' o'care?

Thou'll break my heart, thou bonnie bird
   That sings upon the bough,
Thou minds me o' the happy days
   When my fause luve was true.

Thou'll break my heart, thou bonnie bird
   That sings beside thy mate,
For sae I sat, and sae I sang,
   And wist na o' my fate.

38 *gath'rin gear* making money (not something that happened often with Burns).

Aft hae I roved by bonnie Doon
To see the woodbine twine,
And ilka bird sang o' its love,
And sae did I o' mine.

Wi' lightsome heart I pu'd a rose
Frae aff its thorny tree,
And my fause luver staw the rose,
But left the thorn wi' me!

Wi' lightsome heart I pu'd a rose
Upon a morn in June,
And sae I flourished on the morn,
And sae was pu'd or noon!

(iii) *A Red Red Rose* (collected 1793; publ. 1794)

O my luve's like a red, red rose,
That's newly sprung in June;
O my luve's like the melodie
That's sweetly played in tune:

As fair art thou, my bonnie lass,
So deep in luve am I;
And I will love thee still, my dear,
Till a' the seas gang dry –

Till a' the seas gang dry, my dear,
And the rocks melt wi' the sun –
I will love thee still, my dear,
While the sands o' life shall run!

And fare thee weel, my only luve,
And fare thee weel, a while –
And I will come again, my luve,
Tho' it were ten thousand mile!

19 *staw* stole. **24** *or* ere, before.

3. WILLIAM BLAKE

from *Songs of Innocence* (1784–9; engraved 1789)

(i) *Introduction*

Piping down the valleys wild,
Piping songs of pleasant glee,
On a cloud I saw a child
And he laughing said to me:

'Pipe a song about a lamb.'
So I piped with merry cheer –
'Piper, pipe that song again!'
So I piped; he wept to hear.

'Drop thy pipe, thy happy pipe,
Sing thy songs of happy cheer.'
So I sung the same again,
While he wept with joy to hear.

'Piper, sit thee down and write,
In a book that all may read.'
So he vanished from my sight,
And I plucked a hollow reed,

And I made a rural pen,
And I stained the water clear,
And I wrote my happy songs
Every child may joy to hear.

(ii) *The Shepherd*

How sweet is the shepherd's sweet lot,
From the morn to the evening he strays:
He shall follow his sheep all the day
And his tongue shall be filled with praise.

For he hears the lamb's innocent call,
And he hears the ewe's tender reply;
He is watchful while they are in peace,
For they know when their shepherd is nigh.

(iii) *Infant Joy*

'I have no name,
I am but two days old!'
'What shall I call thee?'
'I happy am,
Joy is my name –
Sweet joy befall thee!'

'Pretty joy,
Sweet joy but two days old –
Sweet joy I call thee!
Thou dost smile,
I sing the while –
Sweet joy befall thee!'

(iv) *The Echoing Green*

The sun does arise,
And make happy the skies.
The merry bells ring
To welcome the spring.
The skylark and thrush,
The birds of the bush,
Sing louder around
To the bells' cheerful sound,
While our sports shall be seen
On the echoing green.

Old John with white hair
Does laugh away care,
Sitting under the oak
Among the old folk.
They laugh at our play,
And soon they all say:
'Such, such were the joys
When we all, girls and boys,
In our youth-time were seen
On the echoing green.'

Till the little ones weary
No more can be merry,
The sun does descend
And our sports have an end.
Round the laps of their mothers
Many sisters and brothers,
Like birds in their nest,
Are ready for rest,
And sport no more seen,
On the darkening green.

(v) *Laughing Song* (May 1784)

When the green woods laugh with the voice of joy
And the dimpling stream runs laughing by,
When the air does laugh with our merry wit
And the green hill laughs with the noise of it,

When the meadows laugh with lively green
And the grasshopper laughs in the merry scene,
When Mary and Susan and Emily
With their sweet round mouths sing 'ha, ha, he!'

When the painted birds laugh in the shade
Where our table with cherries and nuts is spread,
Come live and be merry and join with me,
To sing the sweet chorus of 'ha, ha, he!'

(vi) *Nurse's Song* (c. 1784)

When the voices of children are heard on the green
And laughing is heard on the hill,
My heart is at rest within my breast
And everything else is still.

'Then come home my children, the sun is gone down
And the dews of night arise;
Come, come, leave off play, and let us away
Till the morning appears in the skies!'

'No, no, let us play, for it is yet day,
And we cannot go to sleep;
Besides, in the sky the little birds fly,
And the hills are all covered with sheep!'

'Well, well, go and play, till the light fades away,
And then go home to bed.'
The little ones leaped and shouted and laughed,
And all the hills echoéd.

(vii) *Holy Thursday* (c. 1784)

'Twas on a Holy Thursday – their innocent faces clean –
The children walking two and two in red and blue and green;
Grey-headed beadles walked before with wands as white as snow
Till into the high dome of Paul's they like Thames waters flow.

Oh what a multitude they seemed, these flowers of London town!
Seated in companies they sit, with radiance all their own!
The hum of multitudes was there, but multitudes of lambs –
Thousands of little boys and girls raising their innocent hands.

Now, like a mighty wind they raise to Heaven the voice of song,
Or like harmonious thunderings the seats of Heaven among.
Beneath them sit the agéd men, wise guardians of the poor –
Then cherish pity, lest you drive an angel from your door.

(viii) *The Lamb*

Little lamb who made thee?
Dost thou know who made thee,
Gave thee life and bid thee feed
By the stream and o'er the mead,
Gave thee clothing of delight,
Softest clothing woolly bright,
Gave thee such a tender voice,
Making all the vales rejoice!
Little lamb who made thee,
Dost thou know who made thee?

Little lamb I'll tell thee,
Little lamb I'll tell thee!
He is callèd by thy name,
For He calls himself a lamb;
He is meek and He is mild,
He became a little child.
I a child and thou a lamb,
We are callèd by his name –
Little lamb God bless thee,
Little lamb God bless thee!

(ix) *The Chimney Sweeper*

When my mother died I was very young,
And my father sold me while yet my tongue
Could scarcely cry 'weep, weep, weep, weep!'
So your chimneys I sweep and in soot I sleep.

There's little Tom Dacre, who cried when his head
That curled like a lamb's back was shaved, so I said,
'Hush Tom never mind it, for when your head's bare,
You know that the soot cannot spoil your white hair.'

And so he was quiet, and that very night
As Tom was a-sleeping he had such a sight,
That thousands of sweepers Dick, Joe, Ned, and Jack,
Were all of them locked up in coffins of black,

And by came an angel who had a bright key,
And he opened the coffins and set them all free.
Then down a green plain leaping, laughing they run
And wash in a river and shine in the sun.

Then naked and white, all their bags left behind,
They rise upon clouds, and sport in the wind.
And the angel told Tom if he'd be a good boy,
He'd have God for his father and never want joy.

And so Tom awoke and we rose in the dark
And got with our bags and our brushes to work.
Though the morning was cold, Tom was happy and warm –
So if all do their duty, they need not fear harm.

(x) *The Divine Image*

To Mercy, Pity, Peace, and Love,
All pray in their distress,
And to these virtues of delight
Return their thankfulness.

For Mercy, Pity, Peace, and Love,
Is God our father dear,
And Mercy, Pity, Peace, and Love,
Is man, his child and care.

For Mercy has a human heart,
Pity, a human face,
And Love, the human form divine,
And Peace, the human dress.

Then every man of every clime
That prays in his distress,
Prays to the human form divine
Love, Mercy, Pity, Peace.

And all must love the human form,
In heathen, Turk or Jew:
Where Mercy, Love, and Pity dwell
There God is dwelling too.

4. SUSANNA BLAMIRE

(i) *The Siller Croun* (1790; publ. 1842)

'And ye shall walk in silk attire,
   And siller hae to spare,
Gin ye'll consent to be his bride,
   Nor think o' Donald mair.'
'O wha wad buy a silken goun
   Wi' a poor broken heart!
Or what's to me a siller croun,
   Gin frae my love I part!

The mind wha's every wish is pure
   Far dearer is to me;
And ere I'm forced to break my faith
   I'll lay me doun an' dee!
For I hae pledged my virgin troth
   Brave Donald's fate to share;
And he has gi'en to me his heart,
   Wi' a' its virtues rare.

His gentle manners wan my heart,
   He gratefu' took the gift;
Could I but think to seek it back
   It wad be waur than theft!
For langest life can ne'er repay
   The love he bears to me;
And ere I'm forced to break my troth
   I'll lay me doun an' dee.'

(ii) *Oh Bid Me Not to Wander*

(c. 1792; publ. 1842)

Written when earnestly entreated to go the South of France for the recovery of her health.

Oh urge me not to wander,
   And quit my pleasant native shore;
Oh let me still meander
   On those sweet banks I loved before!
The heart when filled with sorrow
   Can find no joy in change of scene,
Nor can that cheat, tomorrow,
   Be aught but what today has been.

If pleasure e'er o'ertakes me,
   'Tis when I tread the wonted round
Where former joy awakes me,
   And strews its relics o'er the ground.
There's not a shrub or flower
   But tells some dear loved tale to me,
And paints some happy hour
   Which I, alas, no more shall see.

5. WILLIAM BLAKE

from *Songs of Experience* (1791–2; engraved 1794)

(i) *Introduction* (c. 1794)

Hear the voice of the bard
Who present, past, and future sees,
Whose ears have heard
The Holy Word
That walked among the ancient trees

Calling the lapséd soul,
And weeping in the evening dew –
That might control
The starry pole,
And fallen, fallen, light renew!

Oh Earth, oh Earth return,
Arise from out the dewy grass!
Night is worn,
And the morn
Rises from the slumberous mass.

Turn away no more –
Why wilt thou turn away?
The starry floor,
The watery shore,
Is given thee till the break of day.

(ii) *Earth's Answer* (c. 1794)

Earth raised up her head
From the darkness dread and drear:
Her light fled,
Stony dread!
And her locks covered with grey despair.

'Prisoned on watery shore,
Starry Jealousy does keep my den;
Cold and hoar,
Weeping o'er,
I hear the father of the ancient men,

Selfish father of men –
Cruel, jealous, selfish fear!
Can delight
Chained in night
The virgins of youth and morning bear?

Does spring hide its joy
When buds and blossoms grow?
Does the sower
Sow by night,
Or the ploughman in darkness plough?

Break this heavy chain
That does freeze my bones around –
Selfish, vain,
Eternal bane,
That free Love with bondage bound!'

(iii) *My Pretty Rose Tree*

A flower was offered to me –
Such a flower as May never bore –
But I said, 'I've a pretty rose-tree',
And I passed the sweet flower o'er.

Then I went to my pretty rose-tree,
To tend her by day and by night;
But my rose turned away with jealousy
And her thorns were my only delight!

(iv) *The Clod and the Pebble*

'Love seeketh not itself to please,
Nor for itself hath any care,
But for another gives its ease,
And builds a Heaven in Hell's despair.'

So sang a little clod of clay,
Trodden with the cattle's feet,
But a pebble of the brook
Warbled out these metres meet:

'Love seeketh only self to please,
To bind another to its delight –
Joys in another's loss of ease,
And builds a Hell in Heaven's despite.'

(v) *The Garden of Love*

I went to the Garden of Love,
And saw what I never had seen:
A chapel was built in the midst
Where I used to play on the green.

And the gates of this chapel were shut,
And 'Thou shalt not' writ over the door;
So I turned to the Garden of Love
That so many sweet flowers bore,

And I saw it was filled with graves,
And tomb-stones where flowers should be,
And priests in black gowns, were walking their rounds,
And binding with briars my joys and desires.

(vi) *A Poison Tree*

I was angry with my friend –
I told my wrath, my wrath did end.
I was angry with my foe –
I told it not, my wrath did grow.

And I watered it in fears,
Night and morning with my tears;
And I sunnéd it with smiles,
And with soft deceitful wiles.

And it grew both day and night
Till it bore an apple bright,
And my foe beheld it shine,
And he knew that it was mine,

And into my garden stole,
When the night had veiled the pole;
In the morning glad I see
My foe outstretched beneath the tree.

(vii) *Infant Sorrow*

My mother groaned, my father wept,
Into the dangerous world I leapt –
Helpless, naked, piping loud,
Like a fiend hid in a cloud!

Struggling in my father's hands,
Striving against my swadling bands,
Bound and weary I thought best
To sulk upon my mother's breast.

(viii) *London*

I wander through each chartered street,
Near where the chartered Thames does flow,
And mark in every face I meet
Marks of weakness, marks of woe.

In every cry of every man,
In every infant's cry of fear,
In every voice, in every ban,
The mind-forged manacles I hear:

How the chimney-sweeper's cry
Every blackening church appals,
And the hapless soldier's sigh
Runs in blood down palace walls;

But most through midnight streets I hear
How the youthful harlot's curse
Blasts the new-born infant's tear
And blights with plagues the marriage-hearse.

(ix) *Nurse's Song*

When the voices of children are heard on the green
And whisperings are in the dale
The days of my youth rise fresh in my mind,
My face turns green and pale.

'Then come home my children, the sun is gone down
And the dews of night arise.
Your spring and your day are wasted in play
And your winter and night in disguise.'

(x) *The Tyger*

Tyger, tyger, burning bright
In the forests of the night,
What immortal hand or eye
Could frame thy fearful symmetry?

In what distant deeps or skies
Burnt the fire of thine eyes?
On what wings dare he aspire?
What the hand dare seize the fire?

And what shoulder, and what art,
Could twist the sinews of thy heart?
And when thy heart began to beat,
What dread hand? And what dread feet?

What the hammer? What the chain?
In what furnace was thy brain?
What the anvil? What dread grasp
Dare its deadly terrors clasp?

When the stars threw down their spears,
And watered heaven with their tears,
Did he smile his work to see?
Did he who made the lamb make thee?

Tyger, tyger burning bright
In the forests of the night,
What immortal hand or eye
Dare frame thy fearful symmetry?

(xi) *The Human Abstract*

Pity would be no more
If we did not make somebody poor;
And mercy no more could be,
If all were as happy as we;

And mutual fear brings peace
Till the selfish loves increase,
Then Cruelty knits a snare
And spreads his baits with care.

He sits down with holy fears
And waters the ground with tears,
Then Humility takes its root
Underneath his foot.

Soon spreads the dismal shade
Of mystery over his head;
And the caterpillar and fly
Feed on the mystery,

And it bears the fruit of deceit,
Ruddy and sweet to eat;
And the raven his nest has made
In its thickest shade.

The gods of the earth and sea
Sought through nature to find this tree,
But their search was all in vain –
There grows one in the human brain!

(xii) *The Sick Rose*

Oh rose thou art sick!
The invisible worm
That flies in the night
In the howling storm

Has found out thy bed
Of crimson joy
And his dark secret love
Does thy life destroy.

(xiii) *The Chimney Sweeper*

A little black thing among the snow
Crying 'weep, weep', in notes of woe!
'Where are thy father and mother, say?'
'They are both gone up to the church to pray.

Because I was happy upon the heath
And smiled among the winter's snow,
They clothed me in the clothes of death
And taught me to sing the notes of woe.

And because I am happy, and dance, and sing,
They think they have done me no injury,
And are gone to praise God and his priest and king,
Who make up a Heaven of our misery!'

(xiv) *Holy Thursday*

Is this a holy thing to see,
In a rich and fruitful land,
Babes reduced to misery,
Fed with cold and usurous hand?

Is that trembling cry a song?
Can it be a song of joy?
And so many children poor?
It is a land of poverty!

And their sun does never shine.
And their fields are bleak and bare.
And their ways are filled with thorns.
It is eternal winter there.

For where'er the sun does shine,
And where'er the rain does fall,
Babe can never hunger there,
Nor poverty the mind appal.

(xv) *The Fly*

Little fly,
Thy summer's play
My thoughtless hand
Has brushed away.

Am not I
A fly like thee?
Or art not thou
A man like me?

For I dance
And drink and sing;
Till some blind hand
Shall brush my wing.

If thought is life
And strength and breath;
And the want
Of thought is death;

Then am I
A happy fly,
If I live,
Or if I die!

(xvi) *Ah! Sun-Flower* (written c. 1794)

Ah! sun-flower, weary of time,
Who countest the steps of the sun,
Seeking after that sweet golden clime
Where the traveller's journey is done,

Where the youth pined away with desire,
And the pale virgin shrouded in snow,
Arise from their graves and aspire,
Where my sun-flower wishes to go.

6. ANN BATTEN CRISTALL

Through Springtime Walks (1795)

Through springtime walks, with flowers perfumed,
   I chased a wild capricious fair,
Where hyacinths and jonquils bloomed,
   Chanting gay sonnets through the air;
      Hid amid a briary dell
         Or 'neath a hawthorn-tree,
      Her sweet enchantments led me on
         And still deluded me.

While summer's 'splendent glory smiles
   My ardent love in vain essayed,
I strove to win her heart by wiles,
   But still a thousand pranks she played;
Still o'er each sunburnt furzy hill,
   Wild, playful, gay, and free,
She laughed and scorned; I chased her still,
   And still she bantered me.

When autumn waves her golden ears
   And wafts o'er fruits her pregnant breath,
The sprightly lark its pinions rears;
   I chased her o'er the daisied heath,
And all around was glee –
Still, wanton as the timid hart,
   She swiftly flew from me.

Now winter lights its cheerful fire,
While jests with frolic mirth resound
And draws the wandering beauty nigher,
'Tis now too cold to rove around;
The Christmas-game, the playful dance,
Incline her heart to glee –
Mutual we glow, and kindling love
Draws every wish to me.

7. MARY ROBINSON

A Thousand Torments (1797)

A thousand torments wait on love –
The sigh, the tear, the anguished groan –
But he who never learnt to prove
A jealous pang has nothing known!

For jealousy, supreme of woe,
Nursed by distorted fancy's power,
Can round the heart bid misery grow,
Which darkens with the lingering hour,

While shadows, blanks to reason's orb,
In dread succession haunt the brain,
And pangs, that every pang absorb,
In wild, convulsive tumults reign.

At morn, at eve, the fever burns,
While phantoms tear the aching breast;
Day brings no calm, and night returns
To mark no soothing hour of rest.

Nor, when the bosom's wasted fires
Are all extinct, is anguish o'er;
For *jealousy*, that ne'er expires,
Still wounds, when *passion* lives no more.

8. THOMAS CAMPBELL

Written on Visiting a Scene in Argyleshire

(c. 1793; publ. 1800)

At the silence of twilight's contemplative hour
  I have mused in a sorrowful mood
On the wind-shaken reeds that embosom the bower
  Where the home of my forefathers stood.
All ruined and wild is their roofless abode,
  And lonely the dark raven's sheltering tree –
And travelled by few is the grass-covered road
Where the hunter of deer and the warrior trod
    To his hills that encircle the sea.

Yet, wandering, I found on my ruinous walk,
  By the dial-stone agéd and green,
One rose of the wilderness left on its stalk
  To mark where a garden had been.
Like a brotherless hermit, the last of his race,
  All wild in the silence of Nature it drew
From each wandering sunbeam a lonely embrace –
For the night-weed and thorn overshadowed the place
  Where the flower of my forefathers grew.

Sweet bud of the wilderness, emblem of all
  That remains in this desolate heart!
The fabric of bliss to its centre may fall,
  But patience shall never depart
Though the wilds of enchantment, all vernal and bright
  In the days of delusion, by fancy combined
With the vanishing phantoms of love and delight,
Abandon my soul like a dream of the night
  And leave but a desert behind.

Be hushed, my dark spirit, for wisdom condemns
  When the faint and the feeble deplore –
Be strong as the rock of the ocean, that stems
  A thousand wild waves on the shore!

Through the perils of chance and the scowl of disdain
   May thy front be unaltered, thy courage elate!
Yea, even the name I have worshipped in vain
Shall awake not the sigh of remembrance again:
   To bear is to conquer our fate.

9. WILLIAM WORDSWORTH

1. Alfoxden Lyric (1798; publ. *Lyrical Ballads*)

Lines Written in Early Spring

I heard a thousand blended notes
While in a grove I sat reclined,
In that sweet mood when pleasant thoughts
Bring sad thoughts to the mind.

To her fair works did Nature link
The human soul that through me ran,
And much it grieved my heart to think
What man has made of man.

Through primrose-tufts, in that sweet bower,
The periwinkle trailed its wreathes;
And 'tis my faith that every flower
Enjoys the air it breathes.

The birds around me hopped and played,
Their thoughts I cannot measure,
But the least motion which they made,
It seemed a thrill of pleasure.

The budding twigs spread out their fan,
To catch the breezy air;
And I must think – do all I can –
That there was pleasure there.

If I these thoughts may not prevent,
If such be of my creed the plan,
Have I not reason to lament
What man has made of man?

11. Goslar Lyrics (1798–9; publ. *Lyrical Ballads* 1800)

(i) *Two April Mornings*

We walked along while bright and red
Uprose the morning sun,
And Matthew stopped – he looked, and said
'The will of God be done!'

A village schoolmaster was he
With hair of glittering grey,
As blithe a man as you could see
On a spring holiday.

And on that morning, through the grass
And by the steaming rills,
We travelled merrily to pass
A day among the hills.

'Our work', said I, 'was well begun –
Then, from thy breast what thought,
Beneath so beautiful a sun ,
So sad a sigh has brought?'

A second time did Matthew stop
And, fixing still his eye
Upon the eastern mountain-top,
To me he made reply:

'Yon cloud with that long purple cleft
Brings fresh into my mind
A day like this which I have left
Full thirty years behind.

And on that slope of springing corn
The self-same crimson hue
Fell from the sky that April morn –
The same which now I view.

With rod and line my silent sport
I plied by Derwent's wave,
And, coming to the church, stopped short
Beside my daughter's grave.

Nine summers had she scarcely seen,
The pride of all the vale!
And then she sang – she would have been
A very nightingale!

Six feet in earth my Emma lay,
And yet I loved her more
(For so it seemed) than till that day
I e'er had loved before.

And, turning from her grave, I met
Beside the churchyard-yew
A blooming girl, whose hair was wet
With points of morning dew.

A basket on her head she bare,
Her brow was smooth and white;
To see a child so very fair,
It was a pure delight!

No fountain from its rocky cave
E'er tripped with foot so free;
She seemed as happy as a wave
That dances on the sea.

There came from me a sigh of pain
Which I could ill confine;
I looked at her, and looked again –
And did not wish her mine.'

Matthew is in his grave, yet now
Methinks I see him stand,
As at that moment, with his bough
Of wilding in his hand.

(ii) *The Fountain*

We talked with open heart, and tongue
Affectionate and true –
A pair of friends, though I was young,
And Matthew seventy-two.

We lay beneath a spreading oak,
Beside a mossy seat,
And from the turf a fountain broke
And gurgled at our feet.

'Now, Matthew, let us try to match
This water's pleasant tune
With some old Border song or catch
That suits a summer's noon.

Or of the church-clock and the chimes
Sing here beneath the shade
That half-mad thing of witty rhymes
Which you last April made!'

In silence Matthew lay, and eyed
The spring beneath the tree;
And thus the dear old man replied,
The grey-haired man of glee:

'Down to the vale this water steers –
How merrily it goes! –
'Twill murmur on a thousand years,
And flow as now it flows.

And here, on this delightful day,
I cannot choose but think
How oft, a vigorous man, I lay
Beside this fountain's brink.

My eyes are dim with childish tears,
My heart is idly stirred,
For the same sound is in my ears
Which in those days I heard.

Thus fares it still in our decay;
And yet the wiser mind
Mourns less for what age takes away
Than what it leaves behind.

The blackbird in the summer trees,
The lark upon the hill,
Let loose their carols when they please,
Are quiet when they will.

With Nature never do *they* wage
A foolish strife; they see
A happy youth, and their old age
Is beautiful and free.

But we are pressed by heavy laws,
And often – glad no more –
We wear a face of joy, because
We have been glad of yore.

If there is one who need bemoan
His kindred laid in earth,
The household-hearts that were his own,
It is the man of mirth.

My days, my friend, are almost gone,
My life has been approved,
And many love me, but by none
Am I enough beloved.'

'Now both himself and me he wrongs,
The man who thus complains!
I live and sing my idle songs
Upon these happy plains –

And, Matthew, for thy children dead
I'll be a son to thee!'
At this he grasped his hands, and said
'Alas, that cannot be!'

We rose up from the fountain-side,
And down the smooth descent
Of the green sheep-track did we glide,
And through the wood we went,

And, ere we came to Leonard's Rock,
He sang those witty rhymes
About the crazy old church-clock
And the bewildered chimes.

III. Grasmere Lyrics

(spring 1802; publ. *Poems* 1807)

(i) *To the Cuckoo*

Oh blithe new-comer, I have heard,
I hear, thee and rejoice –
Oh cuckoo, shall I call thee bird,
Or but a wandering voice?

While I am lying on the grass
I hear thy restless shout;
From hill to hill it seems to pass
About and all about.

To me, no babbler with a tale
Of sunshine and of showers,
Thou tellest – cuckoo in the vale –
Of visionary hours.

Thrice welcome darling of the spring!
Even yet thou art to me
No bird, but an invisible thing,
A voice, a mystery,

The same whom in my schoolboy days,
I listened to – that cry
Which made me look a thousand ways
In bush, and tree, and sky.

To seek thee did I often rove
Through woods and on the green,
And thou wert still a hope, a love –
Still longed for, never seen.

And I can listen to thee yet,
Can lie upon the plain,
And listen till I do beget
That golden time again.

Oh blessèd bird, the earth we pace
Again appears to be
An unsubstantial fairy place
That is fit home for thee!

(ii) *The Rainbow*

My heart leaps up when I behold
        A rainbow in the sky:
So was it when my life began,
So is it now I am a man,
So be it when I shall grow old,
        Or let me die!
The child is father of the man;
And I could wish my days to be
Bound each to each by natural piety.

(iii) *To H. C., Six Years Old*

Oh thou whose fancies from afar are brought,
Who of thy words dost make a mock apparel,
And fittest to unutterable thought
The breeze-like motion and the self-born carol;
Thou fairy voyager, that dost float
In such clear water, that thy boat
May rather seem
To brood on air that on an earthly stream –
Suspended in a stream as clear as sky,
Where earth and heaven do make one imagery.
Oh blessèd vision, happy child,
That art so exquisitely wild,
I think of thee with many fears
For what may be thy lot in future years.

I thought of times when Pain might be thy guest,
Lord of thy house and hospitality;
And Grief – uneasy Lover – never rest
But when she sat within the touch of thee.
Oh too industrious folly!
Oh vain and causeless melancholy!
Nature will either end thee quite,
Or, lengthening out thy season of delight,

Preserve for thee, by individual right,
A young lamb's heart among the full-grown flocks.
What hast thou to do with sorrow,
Or the injuries of tomorrow?
Thou art a dew-drop which the morn brings forth,
Not doomed to jostle with unkindly shocks
Or to be trailed along the soiling earth –
A gem that glitters while it lives,
And no forewarning gives,
But, at the touch of wrong, without a strife,
Slips in a moment out of life.

(iv) *The Cock Is Crowing*

The cock is crowing,
The stream is flowing,
The small birds twitter,
The lake doth glitter,
The green field sleeps in the sun;
The oldest and youngest
Are at work with the strongest;
The cattle are grazing,
Their heads never raising –
There are forty feeding like one!

Like an army defeated
The snow hath retreated
And now doth fare ill
On the top of the bare hill;
The ploughboy is whooping, anon, anon –
There's joy in the mountains,
There's life in the fountains,
Small clouds are sailing,
Blue sky prevailing,
The rain is over and gone!

(v) *To a Butterfly* ('I've watched you')

I've watched you now a full half-hour
Self-poised upon that yellow flower,
And little butterfly indeed
I know not if you sleep or feed.

How motionless! Not frozen seas
More motionless – and then,
What joy awaits you, when the breeze
Hath found you out among the trees
And calls you forth again!

This plot of orchard ground is ours
(My trees they are, my sister's flowers),
Stop here whenever you are weary
And rest as in a sanctuary.
Come often to us – fear no wrong –
Sit near us on the bough!
We'll talk of sunshine and of song,
And summer days when we were young –
Sweet childish days that were as long
As twenty days are now.

(vi) *I Have Thoughts that Are Fed by the Sun* (from MS 1947)

I have thoughts that are fed by the sun:
  The things which I see
  Are welcome to me,
  Welcome every one –
  I do not wish to lie
    Dead, dead,
Dead, without any company.
  Here alone on my bed
With thoughts that are fed by the sun,
And hopes that are welcome every one,
  Happy am I.

Oh life there is about thee
A deep delicious peace;
I would not be without thee,
  Stay, oh stay!
Yet be thou ever as now –
Sweetness and breath, with the quiet of death –
Be but thou ever as now,
  Peace, peace, peace.

(vii) *The Sun Has Long Been Set*

The sun has long been set:
The stars are out by twos and threes;
The little birds are piping yet
Among the bushes and trees;
There's a cuckoo, and one or two thrushes,
And a noise of wind that rushes,
With a noise of water that gushes,
And the cuckoo's sovereign cry
Fills all the hollow of the sky!
Who would go 'parading'
In London, and 'masquerading',
On such a night of June,
With that beautiful soft half-moon
And all those innocent blisses –
On such a night as this is?

IV. Grasmere Lyrics (1804–5; publ. *Poems* 1807)

(i) *Daffodils* (Feb. 1804, expanded c. 1815)

I wandered lonely as a cloud
That floats on high o'er vales and hills,
When all at once I saw a crowd,
A host, of golden daffodils;
Beside the lake, beneath the trees,
Fluttering and dancing in the breeze.

Continuous as the stars that shine
And twinkle on the Milky Way,
They stretched in never-ending line
Along the margin of a bay:
Ten thousand saw I at a glance,
Tossing their heads in sprightly dance.

The waves beside them danced; but they
Out-did the sparkling waves in glee:
A poet could not but be gay,
In such a jocund company:
I gazed, and gazed, but little thought
What wealth the show to me had brought –

For oft, when on my couch I lie
In vacant or in pensive mood,
They flash upon that inward eye
Which is the bliss of solitude;
And then my heart with pleasure fills,
And dances with the daffodils.

(ii) *Stepping Westward*

'What, you are stepping westward?' 'Yea.'
'Twould be a wildish destiny
If we, who thus together roam
In a strange land, and far from home,
Were in this place the guests of Chance.
Yet who would stop, or fear to advance,
Though home or shelter he had none,
With such a sky to lead him on?

The dewy ground was dark and cold –
Behind, all gloomy to behold –
And stepping westward seemed to be
A kind of *heavenly* destiny.
I liked the greeting! 'Twas a sound
Of something without place or bound,
And seemed to give me spiritual right
To travel through that region bright.

The voice was soft, and she who spake
Was walking by her native lake;
The salutation had to me
The very sound of courtesy.
Its power was felt – and while my eye
Was fixed upon the glowing sky,
The echo of the voice inwrought
A human sweetness with the thought
Of travelling through the world that lay
Before me in my endless way.

(iii) *The Solitary Reaper*

Behold her, single in the field,
Yon solitary highland lass,
Reaping and singing by herself –
Stop here, or gently pass!
Alone she cuts and binds the grain,
And sings a melancholy strain:
Oh listen, for the vale profound
Is overflowing with the sound!

No nightingale did ever chant
So sweetly to reposing bands
Of travellers in some shady haunt
Among Arabian sands;
No sweeter voice was ever heard
In springtime from the cuckoo-bird,
Breaking the silence of the seas
Among the farthest Hebrides.

Will no one tell me what she sings?
Perhaps the plaintive numbers flow
For old, unhappy, far-off things,
And battles long ago;
Or is it some more humble lay,
Familiar matter of today –
Some natural sorrow, loss, or pain,
That has been, and may be again?

Whate'er the theme, the maiden sang
As if her song could have no ending;
I saw her singing at her work
And o'er the sickle bending;
I listened till I had my fill,
And as I mounted up the hill
The music in my heart I bore
Long after it was heard no more.

10. SAMUEL TAYLOR COLERIDGE

Lyrics 1798–1803

(i) *Something Childish, but Very Natural*

(April 1799; publ. 1800)

If I had but two little wings,
  And were a little feathery bird,
    To you I'd fly, my dear!
But thoughts like these are idle things,
    And I stay here.

But in my sleep to you I fly –
  I'm always with you in my sleep –
    The world is all one's own!
But then one wakes, and where am I?
    All, all alone.

Sleep stays not, though a monarch bids,
  So I love to wake ere break of day;
    For though my sleep be gone,
Yet while 'tis dark one shuts one's lids –
    And still dreams on.

(ii) *The Keepsake* (1802)

The tedded hay, the first fruits of the soil –
The tedded hay and corn-sheaves in one field –
Show summer gone, ere come. The foxglove tall
Sheds its loose purple bells, or in the gust,
Or when it bends beneath the up-springing lark
Or mountain-finch alighting. And the rose
(In vain the darling of successful love)
Stands, like some boasted beauty of past years,
The thorns remaining, and the flowers all gone.
Nor can I find, amid my lonely walk
By rivulet, or spring, or wet roadside,
That blue and bright-eyed floweret of the brook,
Hope's gentle gem, the sweet forget-me-not!
So will not fade the flowers which Emmeline

With delicate fingers on the snow-white silk
Has worked (the flowers which most she knew I loved),
And, more beloved than they, her auburn hair.
    In the cool morning twilight, early waked
By her full bosom's joyous restlessness,
Softly she rose, and lightly stole along
Down the slope-coppice to the woodbine-bower,
Whose rich flowers, swinging in the morning breeze,
Over their dim fast-moving shadows hung,
Making a quiet image of disquiet
In the smooth, scarcely moving river-pool.
There, in that bower where first she owned her love
And let me kiss my own warm tear of joy
From off her glowing cheek, she sat and stretched
The silk upon the frame, and worked her name
Between the moss-rose and forget-me-not –
Her own dear name, with her own auburn hair! –
That, forced to wander till sweet spring return,
I yet might ne'er forget her smile, her look,
Her voice (that even in her mirthful mood
Has made me wish to steal away and weep),
Nor yet the entrancement of that maiden-kiss
With which she promised that, when spring returned,
She would resign one half of that dear name,
And own thenceforth no other name but mine!

(iii) *Answer to a Child's Question* (1802)

Do you ask what the birds say? The sparrow, the dove,
The linnet and thrush, say, 'I love and I love!'
In the winter they're silent, the wind is so strong –
What it says, I don't know, but it sings a loud song –
But green leaves, and blossoms, and sunny warm weather,
And singing, and loving, all come back together!
But the lark is so brimful of gladness and love
(The green fields below him, the blue sky above)
That he sings, and he sings, and forever sings he:
'I love my love, and my love loves me!'

11. THOMAS MOORE

Away with this Pouting (1801)

Away with this pouting and sadness!
   Sweet girl, will you never give o'er?
I love you, by Heaven, to madness –
   And what can I swear to you more?
Believe not the old women's fable
   That oaths are as short as a kiss,
I'll love you as long as I'm able,
   And swear for no longer than this.

Then waste not the time with professions,
   For *not* to be blest when we can
Is one of the darkest trangressions
   That happen 'twixt woman and man.
Pretty moralist, why thus beginning
   My innocent warmth to reprove?
Heaven knows that I never loved sinning,
   Except little sinnings of love!

If swearing, however, will do it,
   Come, bring me the calendar, pray –
I vow, by that lip, I'll go through it,
   And not miss a saint on my way!
The angels shall help me to wheedle,
   I'll swear upon every one
That e'er danced on the point of a needle,
   Or rode on a beam of the sun!

Oh! why should Platonic control, love,
   Enchain an emotion so free?
Your soul, though a very sweet soul, love,
   Will ne'er by sufficient for me.
If you think by this coldness and scorning
   To seem more angelic and bright,
Be an angel, my love, in the morning,
   But, oh, *be a woman tonight*!

12. CHARLOTTE SMITH

A Walk by the Water (1804)

Let us walk where reeds are growing,
By the alders in the mead;
Where the crystal streams are flowing,
In whose waves the fishes feed.

There the golden carp is laving,
With the trout, the perch, and bream;
Mark! their flexile fins are waving,
As they glance along the stream.

Now they sink in deeper billows,
Now upon the surface rise;
Or from under roots of willows,
Dart to catch the water-flies.

Midst the reeds and pebbles hiding,
See the minnow and the roach –
Or by water-lilies gliding,
Shun with fear our near approach.

Do not dread us, timid fishes,
We have neither net nor hook;
Wanderers we, whose only wishes
Are to read in Nature's book.

13. MARY TIGHE

Address to My Harp (c. 1804; publ. 1811)

Oh, my loved harp! companion dear!
Sweet soother of my secret grief,
No more thy sounds my soul must cheer,
No more afford a soft relief.

When anxious cares my heart oppressed,
When doubts distracting tore my soul,
The pains which heaved my swelling breast
Thy gentle sway could oft control.

Each well remembered, practised strain,
The cheerful dance, the tender song,
Recalled with pensive, pleasing pain
Some image loved and cherished long.

Where joy sat smiling o'er my fate,
And marked each bright and happy day,
When partial friends around me sat,
And taught my lips the simple lay;

And when by disappointment grieved
I saw some darling hope o'erthrown,
Thou hast my secret pain relieved;
O'er thee I wept, unseen, alone.

Oh! must I leave thee, must we part,
Dear partner of my happiest days?
I may forget thy much-loved art,
Unused thy melody to raise,

But ne'er can memory cease to love
Those scenes where I thy charms have felt,
Though I no more thy power may prove,
Which taught my softened heart to melt.

Forced to forego with thee this spot,
Endeared by many a tender tie,
When rosy pleasure blessed my lot,
And sparkled in my cheated eye.

Yet still thy strings, in Fancy's ear,
With soothing melody shall play;
Thy silver sounds I oft shall hear,
To pensive gloom a silent prey.

14. DOROTHY WORDSWORTH

A Cottage in Grasmere Vale

(c. 1805; from MS 1882)

Peaceful our valley, fair and green,
And beautiful her cottages,
Each in its nook, its sheltered hold,
Or guarded by its tuft of trees.

Many and beautiful they are,
But there is *one* that I love best,
A lowly shed in truth it is,
A brother of the rest.

Yet when I sit on rock or hill,
Down-looking on the valley fair,
That cottage with its clustering trees
Summons my heart – it settles there.

Others there are whose small domain
Of fertile fields and hedgerows green
Might more entice a wanderer's mind
To wish that *there* his home had been.

Such wish be his, I blame him not –
My fancy is unfettered, wild –
I love that house because it is
The very mountains' child!

Fields hath it of its own, green fields,
But they are craggy, steep and bare;
Their fence is of the mountain-stone
And moss and lichen flourish there.

And when the storm comes from the north
It lingers near that pastoral spot,
And piping through the mossy walls,
It seems delighted with its lot.

And let it take its own delight,
And let it range the pastures bare,
Until it reach that group of trees –
It may not enter there!

A green unfading grove it is,
Skirted with many a lesser tree –
Hazel and holly, beech and oak –
A bright and flourishing company!

Precious the shelter of those trees,
They screen the cottage that I love;
The sunshine pierces to the roof
And the tall pine-trees tower above.

15. JANE TAYLOR

The Star (1806)

Twinkle, twinkle, little star,
How I wonder what you are!
Up above the world so high,
Like a diamond in the sky.

When the blazing sun is gone,
When he nothing shines upon,
Then you show your little light,
Twinkle, twinkle, all the night.

Then the traveller in the dark,
Thanks you for your tiny spark!
He could not see which way to go,
If you did not twinkle so.

In the dark blue sky you keep,
And often through my curtains peep,
For you never shut your eye
Till the sun is in the sky.

As your bright and tiny spark
Lights the traveller in the dark,
Though I know not what you are,
Twinkle, twinkle, little star.

16. LORD BYRON

Lyrics Early and Late

(i) *The Maid of Athens* (c. Jan. 1810; publ. 1812)

Maid of Athens, ere we part,
Give, oh give me back, my heart!
Or, since that has left my breast,
Keep it now – and take the rest!
Hear my vow, before I go:
My life, I love you.

By those tresses unconfined,
Wooed by each Aegean wind;
By those lids whose jetty fringe
Kiss thy soft cheeks' blooming tinge;
By those wild eyes like the roe –
My life, I love you.

By that lip I long to taste;
By that zone-encircled waist;
By all the token-flowers that tell
What words can never speak so well;
By love's alternate joy and woe –
My life, I love you.

Maid of Athens, I am gone!
Think of me, sweet, when alone –
Though I fly to Istamboul,
Athens holds my heart and soul!
Can I cease to love thee? No!
My life, I love you.

(ii) *She Walks in Beauty* (June 1814; publ. 1815)

She walks in beauty, like the night
Of cloudless climes and starry skies,
And all that's best of dark and bright
Meet in her aspect and her eyes –
Thus mellowed to that tender light
Which Heaven to gaudy day denies.

One shade the more, one ray the less,
Had half impaired the nameless grace
Which waves in every raven tress,
Or softly lightens o'er her face,
Where thoughts serenely sweet express
How pure, how dear, their dwelling-place.

And on that cheek, and o'er that brow,
So soft, so calm, yet eloquent,
The smiles that win, the tints that glow,
But tell of days in goodness spent,
A mind at peace with all below,
A heart whose love is innocent.

(iii) *Stanzas for Music*

('There be none of Beauty's daughters') 1816

There be none of Beauty's daughters
With a magic like to thee,
And like music on the waters
Is thy sweet voice to me,
When, as if its sound were causing
The charmèd ocean's pausing,
The waves lie still and gleaming,
And the lulled winds seem dreaming,

And the midnight-moon is weaving
Her bright chain o'er the deep,
Whose breast is gently heaving
Like an infant's asleep –
So the spirit bows before thee
To listen and adore thee,
With a full but soft emotion
Like the swell of summer's ocean.

(iv) *Stanzas for Music* ('There's not a joy') 1816

There's not a joy the world can give like that it takes away
   When the glow of early thought declines in feeling's dull decay:
'Tis not on youth's smooth cheek the blush alone which fades so fast,
   But the tender bloom of heart is gone ere youth itself be past.

Then the few whose spirits float above the wreck of happiness
   Are driven o'er the shores of guilt, or ocean of excess –
The magnet of their course is gone, or only points in vain
   The shore to which their shivered sail shall never stretch again.

Then the mortal coldness of the soul like death itself comes down
   (It cannot feel for others' woes, it dare not dream its own):
That heavy chill has frozen o'er the fountain of our tears –
   And though the eye may sparkle still, 'tis where the ice appears!

Though wit may flash from fluent lips, and mirth distract the breast,
   Through midnight hours that yield no more their former hope of rest,
'Tis but as ivy-leaves around the ruined turret wreathe,
   All green and wildly fresh without, but worn and grey beneath.

Oh could I feel what I have felt, or be what I have been,
   Or weep as I could once have wept o'er many a vanished scene –
As springs in desert found seem sweet, all brackish though they be,
   So, midst the withered waste of life, those tears would flow for me!

(v) *We'll Go No More A-Roving*

(28 Feb. 1817; publ. 1830)

So we'll go no more a-roving
   So late into the night,
Though the heart be still as loving,
   And the moon be still as bright.

For the sword outwears its sheath,
   And the soul wears out the breast,
And the heart must pause to breathe,
   And love itself have rest.

Though the night was made for loving,
  And the day returns too soon,
Yet we'll go no more a-roving
  By the light of the moon.

(vi) *The Isles of Greece*

(*Don Juan*, Canto III, 86–7) 1821

The isles of Greece, the isles of Greece!
    Where burning Sappho loved and sung,
Where grew the arts of war and peace,
    Where Delos rose, and Phoebus sprung –
Eternal summer gilds them yet,
But all, except their sun, is set.

The Scian and the Telan muse –
    The hero's harp, the lover's lute –
Have found the fame your shores refuse;
    Their place of birth alone is mute
To sounds which echo further west
Than your sires' Islands of the Blest.

The mountains look on Marathon,
    And Marathon looks on the sea;
And musing there an hour alone,
    I dreamed that Greece might still be free –
For, standing on the Persians' grave,
I could not deem myself a slave.

A King sat on the rocky brow
    Which looks o'er sea-born Salamis;
And ships, by thousands, lay below,
    And men in nations – all were his!
He counted them at break of day –
And when the sun set, where were they?

And where are they? And where art thou,
    My country? On thy voiceless shore
The heroic lay is tuneless now,
    The heroic bosom beats no more!
And must thy lyre, so long divine,
Degenerate into hands like mine?

'Tis something, in the dearth of fame,
    Though linked among a fettered race,
To feel at least a patriot's shame,
    Even as I sing, suffuse my face.
For what is left the poet here?
For Greeks a blush – for Greece a tear!

Must *we* but weep o'er days more blest?
    Must *we* but blush? Our fathers bled!
Earth, render back from out thy breast
    A remnant of our Spartan dead!
Of the three hundred grant but three,
To make a new Thermopylae!

What, silent still – and silent all?
    Ah, no! The voices of the dead
Sound like a distant torrent's fall,
    And answer, 'Let one living head,
But one, arise – we come, we come!'
'Tis but the living who are dumb.

In vain – in vain! Strike other chords –
    Fill high the cup with Samian wine!
Leave battles to the Turkish hordes,
    And shed the blood of Scio's vine!
Hark – rising to the ignoble call,
How answers each bold Bacchanal!

You have the Pyrrhic dance as yet,
    Where is the Pyrrhic phalanx gone?
Of two such lessons, why forget
    The nobler and the manlier one?
You have the letters Cadmus gave –
Think ye he meant them for a slave?

Fill high the bowl with Samian wine –
    We will not think of themes like these!
It made Anacreon's song divine:
    He served, but served Polycrates,
A tyrant – but our masters then
Were still, at least, our countrymen!

The Tyrant of the Chersonese
	Was freedom's best and bravest friend;
That tyrant was Miltiades!
	Oh, that the present hour would lend
Another despot of the kind –
Such chains as his were sure to bind!

Fill high the bowl with Samian wine!
	On Suli's rock, and Parga's shore,
Exists the remnants of a line
	Such as the Doric mothers bore;
And there, perhaps, some seed is sown,
The Heracleidan blood might own.

Trust not for freedom to the Franks,
	They have a King who buys and sells!
In native swords, and native ranks,
	The only hope of courage dwells –
But Turkish force, and Latin fraud,
Would break your shield, however broad.

Fill high the bowl with Samian wine!
	Our virgins dance beneath the shade –
I see their glorious black eyes shine –
	But gazing on each glowing maid,
My own the burning tear-drop laves,
To think such breasts must suckle slaves!

Place me on Sunium's marbled steep,
	Where nothing, save the waves and I,
May hear our mutual murmurs sweep;
	There, swan-like, let me sing and die!
A land of slaves shall ne'er be mine –
Dash down yon cup of Samian wine!

(vii) *On This Day I Complete My Thirty-Sixth Year* (22 Jan. 1824; publ. 1824)

'Tis time this heart should be unmoved,
	Since others it hath ceased to move –
Yet, though I cannot be beloved,
	Still let me love!

My days are in the yellow leaf;
The flowers and fruits of love are gone;
The worm, the canker, and the grief
Are mine alone!

The fire that on my bosom preys
Is lone as some volcanic isle;
No torch is kindled at its blaze –
A funeral pile!

The hope, the fear, the jealous care,
The exalted portion of the pain
And power of love, I cannot share,
But wear the chain.

But 'tis not *thus* – and 'tis not *here* –
Such thoughts should shake my soul – nor *now*,
Where glory decks the hero's bier,
Or binds his brow.

The sword, the banner, and the field,
Glory and Greece, around me see!
The Spartan, borne upon his shield,
Was not more free.

Awake! – not Greece, she is awake! –
Awake, my spirit! Think through whom
Thy life-blood tracks its parent lake,
And then strike home!

Tread those reviving passions down,
Unworthy manhood! Unto thee
Indifferent should the smile or frown
Of Beauty be.

If thou regretst thy youth, why live?
The land of honourable death
Is here! Up to the field, and give
Away thy breath!

Seek out – less often sought than found –
A soldier's grave (for thee the best);
Then look around, and choose thy ground,
And take thy rest

17. PERCY BYSSHE SHELLEY

Lyric Poetry, 1817–21

(i) *To Constantia, Singing*

(late 1817; publ. Jan. 1818)

Thy voice, slow rising like a spirit, lingers
O'ershadowing me with soft and lulling wings;
The blood and life within thy snowy fingers
Teach witchcraft to the instrumental strings!
My brain is wild, my breath comes quick,
The blood is listening in my frame,
And thronging shadows fast and thick
Fall on my overflowing eyes,
My heart is quivering like a flame –
As morning-dew that in the sunbeam dies
I am dissolved in these consuming ecstasies.

I have no life, Constantia, but in thee,
Whilst, like the world-surrounding air, thy song
Flows on, and fills all things with melody!
Now is thy voice a tempest swift and strong
On which, as one in trance upborne,
Secure o'er woods and waves I sweep
Rejoicing like a cloud of morn –
Now 'tis the breath of summer's night
Which, where the starry waters sleep
Round western isles with incense-blossoms bright,
Lingering suspends my soul in its voluptuous flight.

A deep and breathless awe (like the swift change
Of dreams unseen, but felt, in youthful slumbers),
Wild, sweet, yet incommunicably strange,
Thou breathest now, in fast-ascending numbers.
The cope of Heaven seems rent and cloven
By the enchantment of thy strain,
And o'er my shoulders wings are woven
To follow its sublime career
Beyond the mighty moons that wane
Upon the verge of Nature's utmost sphere,
Till the world's shadowy walls are past, and disappear.

Cease, cease, for such wild lessons madmen learn!
Long thus to sink, thus to be lost and die,
Perhaps is death indeed – Constantia turn!
Yes, in thine eyes a power like light doth lie
        Even though the sounds – its voice – that were
        Between thy lips are laid to sleep,
        Within thy breath and on thy hair
        Like odour it is lingering yet,
        And from thy touch like fire doth leap!
Even while I write my burning cheeks are wet –
Such things the heart can feel and learn, but not forget!

(ii) *Stanzas Written in Dejection, December 1818, Near Naples* (publ. 1824)

  The sun is warm, the sky is clear,
    The waves are dancing fast and bright,
  Blue isles and snowy mountains wear
    The purple noon's transparent might,
    The breath of the moist earth is light,
  Around its unexpanded buds;
    Like many a voice of one delight,
  The winds, the birds, the ocean floods,
The City's voice itself, is soft like solitude's.

  I see the deep's untrampled floor
    With green and purple seaweeds strown;
  I see the waves upon the shore,
    Like light dissolved in star-showers, thrown;
    I sit upon the sands alone.
  The lightning of the noontide ocean
    Is flashing round me, and a tone
  Arises from its measured motion,
How sweet – did any heart now share in my emotion!

  Alas, I have nor hope, nor health,
    Nor peace within, nor calm around,
  Nor that content surpassing wealth
    The sage in meditation found,

And walked with inward glory crowned –
Nor fame, nor power, nor love, nor leisure.
Others I see whom these surround,
Smiling they live, and call life pleasure –
To me that cup has been dealt in another measure.

Yet now despair itself is mild,
Even as the winds and waters are;
I could lie down like a tired child,
And weep away the life of care
Which I have borne and yet must bear,
Till death like sleep might steal on me
And I might feel in the warm air
My cheek grow cold, and hear the sea
Breathe o'er my dying brain its last monotony.

Some might lament that I were cold –
As I, when this sweet day is gone
(Which my lost heart, too soon grown old,
Insults with this untimely moan),
They might lament – for I am one
Whom men love not, and yet regret;
Unlike this day, which, when the sun
Shall on its stainless glory set,
Will linger, though enjoyed, like joy in memory yet.

(iii) *The Cloud* (1820)

I bring fresh showers for the thirsting flowers
From the seas and the streams,
I bear light shade for the leaves when laid
In their noonday dreams.
From my wings are shaken the dews that waken
The sweet buds every one,
When rocked to rest on their Mother's breast,
As she dances about the sun.
I wield the flail of the lashing hail,
And whiten the green plains under,
And then again I dissolve it in rain,
And laugh as I pass in thunder.

I sift the snow on the mountains below,
   And their great pines groan aghast;
And all the night 'tis my pillow white,
   While I sleep in the arms of the blast.
Sublime on the towers of my skiey bowers,
   Lightning my pilot sits;
In a cavern under is fettered the thunder,
   It struggles and howls at fits;
Over earth and ocean, with gentle motion,
   This pilot is guiding me,
Lured by the love of the genii that move
   In the depths of the purple sea;
Over the rills, and the crags, and the hills,
   Over the lakes and the plains,
Wherever he dream, under mountain or stream,
   The spirit he loves remains;
And I all the while bask in Heaven's blue smile,
   Whilst he is dissolving in rains.

The sanguine Sunrise, with his meteor-eyes,
   And his burning plumes outspread,
Leaps on the back of my sailing rack
   When the morning-star shines dead –
As on the jag of a mountain-crag,
   Which an earthquake rocks and swings,
An eagle alit one moment may sit
   In the light of its golden wings.
And when Sunset may breathe, from the lit sea beneath,
   Its ardours of rest and of love,
And the crimson pall of eve may fall
   From the depth of Heaven above,
With wings folded I rest, on mine airy nest,
   As still as a brooding dove.

That orbéd maiden with white fire laden,
   Whom mortals call the Moon,
Glides glimmering o'er my fleece-like floor,
   By the midnight breezes strewn;
And wherever the beat of her unseen feet,
   Which only the angels hear,
May have broken the woof of my tent's thin roof,
   The stars peep behind her and peer.

And I laugh to see them whirl and flee,
   Like a swarm of golden bees,
When I widen the rent in my wind-built tent,
   Till the calm rivers, lakes, and seas,
Like strips of the sky fallen through me on high,
   Are each paved with the moon and these.

I bind the Sun's throne with a burning zone,
   And the Moon's with a girdle of pearl;
The volcanoes are dim, and the stars reel and swim,
   When the whirlwinds my banner unfurl.
From cape to cape, with a bridge-like shape,
   Over a torrent sea,
Sunbeam-proof, I hang like a roof –
   The mountains its columns be!
The triumphal arch through which I march
   With hurricane, fire, and snow,
When the Powers of the Air are chained to my chair,
   Is the million-coloured bow;
The sphere-fire above its soft colours wove,
   While the moist Earth was laughing below.

I am the daughter of Earth and Water,
   And the nursling of the Sky;
I pass through the pores of the ocean and shores;
   I change, but I cannot die.
For after the rain when with never a stain
   The pavilion of Heaven is bare,
And the winds and sunbeams with their convex gleams
   Build up the blue dome of air,
I silently laugh at my own cenotaph,
   And out of the caverns of rain,
Like a child from the womb, like a ghost from the tomb,
   I arise and unbuild it again.

(iv) *Hellas: The Last Chorus*

(Oct. 1821; publ. 1822)

The world's great age begins anew,
   The golden years return,
The earth doth like a snake renew

Her winter weeds outworn;
Heaven smiles, and faiths and empires gleam
Like wrecks of a dissolving dream.

A brighter Hellas rears its mountains
From waves serener far,
A new Peneus rolls his fountains
Against the morning-star
Where fairer Tempes bloom; there sleep
Young Cycladson a sunnier deep.

A loftier Argo cleaves the main,
Fraught with a later prize;
Another Orpheus sings again,
And loves, and weeps, and dies;
A new Ulysses leaves once more
Calypso for his native shore.

Oh write no more the tale of Troy,
If earth Death's scroll must be!
Nor mix with Laian rage the joy
Which dawns upon the free;
Although a subtler Sphinx renew
Riddles of death Thebes never knew.

Another Athens shall arise,
And to remoter time
Bequeath, like sunset to the skies,
The splendour of its prime,
And leave, if nought so bright may live,
All earth can take or Heaven give.

Saturn and Love their long repose
Shall burst, more bright and good
Than all who fell, than one who rose,
Than many unsubdued;
Not gold, not blood their altar dowers
But votive tears and symbol flowers.

Oh cease! must hate and death return?
Cease! must men kill and die?
Cease! drain not to its dregs the urn
Of bitter prophecy.
The world is weary of the past,
Oh might it die or rest and last!

(v) *Music, When Soft Voices Die*

(c. 1821; publ. 1824)

Music, when soft voices die,
Vibrates in the memory;
Odours, when sweet violets sicken,
Live within the sense they quicken.

Rose leaves, when the rose is dead,
Are heaped for the belovéd's bed;
And so thy thoughts, when thou art gone,
Love itself shall slumber on.

18. JOHN KEATS

Lyrics 1817–19

(i) *Where Be Ye Going* (21 March 1818; publ. 1848)

Where be ye going, you Devon maid?
    And what have you there in the basket?
Ye tight little fairy, just fresh from the dairy,
    Will ye give me some cream if I ask it?

I love your meads, and I love your flowers,
    And I love your junkets mainly,
But 'hind the door I love kissing more,
    Oh look not so disdainly!

I love your hills and I love your dales,
    And I love your flocks a-bleating –
But oh, on the heather to lie together
    With both our hearts a-beating!

I'll put your basket all safe in a nook,
    Your shawl I hang on this willow,
And we will sigh in the daisy's eye
    And kiss on a grass-green pillow.

(ii) *The Witching Time* (14 Oct. 1818; publ. 1848)

'Tis the 'witching time of night',
Orbéd is the moon and bright,
And the stars, they glisten, glisten,
Seeming with bright eyes to listen!
For what listen they?
For a song and for a charm –
See they glisten in alarm,
And the moon is waxing warm
To hear what I shall say!
Moon, keep wide thy golden ears!
Hearken stars, and hearken spheres!
Hearken thou eternal sky!
I sing an infant's lullaby,
A pretty lullaby.
Listen, listen, listen, listen,
Glisten, glisten, glisten, glisten,
And hear my lullaby!
   Though the rushes that will make
Its cradle still are in the lake;
Though the linen that will make
Its swathe is on the cotton-tree;
Though the woollen that will keep
It warm is on the silly sheep;
Listen stars-light, listen, listen,
Glisten, glisten, glisten, glisten,
And hear my lullaby.
Child, I see thee! Child, I've found thee
Midst of the quiet all around thee!
Child, I see thee! Child, I spy thee!
And thy mother sweet is nigh thee!
Child, I know thee – child no more,
But a poet evermore!
See, see, the lyre, the lyre
In a flame of fire,
Upon the little cradle's top
Flaring, flaring, flaring,
Past the eyesight's bearing –
Awake it from its sleep,
And see if it can keep
Its eyes upon the blaze.
   Amaze, amaze!

It stares, it stares, it stares –
It dares what no one dares!
It lifts its little hand into the flame
Unharmed, and on the strings
Paddles a little tune, and sings
With dumb endeavour, sweetly!
Bard art thou completely,
Little child
O' the western wild,
Bard art thou completely:
Sweetly, with dumb endeavour,
A poet now or never!
Little child
O' the western wild,
A poet now or never!

(iii) *I Had a Dove* (c. Dec. 1818; publ. 1848)

I had a dove, and the sweet dove died,
   And I have thought it died of grieving.
Oh, what could it grieve for? Its feet were tied
   With a silken thread of my own hand's weaving.
Sweet little red feet! Why should you die –
Why would you leave me, sweet dove, why?
You lived alone on the forest-tree,
Why, pretty thing, could you not live with me?
I kissed you oft, and gave you white peas –
Why not live sweetly, as in the green trees?

(iv) *Hush, Hush! Tread Softly*

(c. Dec. 1818; publ. 1845)

Hush, hush! Tread softly! Hush, hush, my dear!
      All the house is asleep, but we know very well
That the jealous, the jealous old bald-pate may hear –
      Though you've padded his nightcap, oh sweet Isabel!
            Though your feet are more light than a fairy's feet,
            Who dances on bubbles where brooklets meet.
Hush, hush! Soft tiptoe! Hush, hush, my dear!
For less than a nothing the jealous can hear.

No leaf doth tremble, no ripple is there
    On the river; all's still, and the night's sleepy eye
Closes up and forgets all its Lethean care,
    Charmed to death by the drone of the humming mayfly –
        And the moon, whether prudish or complaisant,
        Has fled to her bower, well knowing I want
No light in the dusk, no torch in the gloom,
Than my Isabel's eyes, and her lips pulped with bloom.

Lift the latch! Ah, gently! Ah, tenderly, sweet!
    We are dead if that latchet gives one little clink –
Well done – now those lips, and a flowery seat!
    The old man may sleep and the planets may wink,
        The shut rose shall dream of our loves, and awake
        Full-blown, and such warmth for the morning's take;
The stock-dove shall hatch her soft brace, and shall coo,
While I kiss to the melody, aching all through.

(v) *This Living Hand*

(c. Nov. 1819; from MS 1898)

This living hand, now warm and capable
Of earnest grasping, would, if it were cold
And in the icy silence of the tomb,
So haunt thy days and chill thy dreaming nights
That thou wouldst wish thine own heart dry of blood
So in my veins red life might stream again,
And thou be conscience-calmed. See, here it is –
I hold it towards you.

19. JOHN CLARE

Song ('Sad was the day') 1820

Sad was the day when my Willie did leave me,
  Sad was the moments that winged him away,
And oh most distressing and most it did grieve me
  To witness his looks when I pressed him to stay!

It hurt him to think that in vain was my crying,
Which I couldn't help though I knew it so too –
The trumpets all sounding the colours all flying
A soldier my Willie he couldn't but go.

The youths never heeding tomorrow and danger
Were laughing and toasting their girls o'er their beer,
But oh my poor Willie just like a lost stranger
Stood speechless among them half-dead as it were!
He kissed me – 'twas all – not a word when he started,
And oh in his silence too much I could see:
He knew for a truth, and he knew broken-hearted,
That kiss was the last he should ever give me!

20. THOMAS HOOD

(i) *Ruth* (1827)

She stood breast high amid the corn
Clasped by the golden light of morn,
Like the sweetheart of the sun
Who many a glowing kiss had won.

On her cheek an autumn flush
Deeply ripened – such a blush
In the midst of brown was born,
Like red poppies grown with corn.

Round her eyes her tresses fell,
Which were blackest none could tell,
But long lashes veiled a light
That had else been all too bright.

And her hat, with shady brim,
Made her tressy forehead dim;
Thus she stood amid the stooks
Praising God with sweetest looks –

Sure, I said, Heaven did not mean
Where I reap thou shouldst but glean,
Lay thy sheaf adown and come,
Share my harvest and my home.

21. CHARLES LAMB

(i) *To Louisa Martin, Whom I Used to Call 'Monkey'* (1827)

Louisa, serious grown and mild,
I knew you once a romping child,
Obstreperous much and very wild.
Then you would clamber up my knees,
And strive with every art to tease,
When every art of yours could please.
Those things would scarce be proper now.
But they are gone, I know not how,
And *woman*'s written on your brow.
Time draws his finger o'er the scene,
But I cannot forget between
The thing to me you once have been:
Each sportive sally, wild escape –
The scoff, the banter, and the jape –
And antics of my gamesome Ape.

(ii) *In My Own Album* (1829)

Fresh clad from Heaven in robes of white,
A young probationer of light,
Thou wert, my soul, an album bright –

A spotless leaf! But thought, and care,
And friends, and foes, in foul or fair,
Have 'written strange defeature' there;

And Time, with heaviest hand of all,
Like that fierce writing on the wall,
Hath stamped sad dates, he can't recall;

And Error, gilding worst designs
(Like speckled snake that strays and shines),
Betrays his path by crooked lines;

And Vice hath left his ugly blot,
And good resolves, a moment hot –
Fairly begun, but finished not;

And fruitless Late Remorse doth trace
(Like Hebrew lore) a backward pace,
Her irrecoverable race.

Disjointed numbers, sense unknit,
Huge reams of folly, shreds of wit,
Compose the mingled mass of it.

My scalded eyes no longer brook
Upon this ink-blurred thing to look –
Go, shut the leaves, and clasp the book.

22. LETITIA ELIZABETH LANDON

(i) *Song* ('My heart is like the failing hearth') 1827

My heart is like the failing hearth
        Now by my side,
One by one its bursts of flame
        Have burnt and died;
There are none to watch the sinking blaze,
        And none to care,
Or if it kindle into strength,
        Or waste in air.
My fate is as yon faded wreath
        Of summer flowers:
They've spent their store of fragrant health
        In sunny hours,
Which recked them not, which heeded not
        When they were dead –
Other flowers, unwarned by them,
        Will spring instead.
And my own heart is as the lute
        I am now waking;
Wound to too fine and high a pitch,
        They both are breaking.

And of their song what memory
Will stay behind?
An echo, like a passing thought,
Upon the wind.
Silence, forgetfulness, and rust,
Lute, are for thee –
And such my lot – neglect, the grave,
These are for me.

23. FELICIA HEMANS

(i) *The Graves of a Household* (1828)

They grew in beauty, side by side,
They filled one home with glee –
Their graves are severed, far and wide,
By mount, and stream, and sea.

The same fond mother bent at night
O'er each fair sleeping brow;
She had each folded flower in sight –
Where are those dreamers now?
One, midst the forests of the west,

By a dark stream is laid –
The Indian knows his place of rest,
Far in the cedar-shade.
The sea, the blue lone sea, hath one,
He lies where pearls lie deep:

He was the loved of all, yet none
O'er his low bed may weep!
One sleeps where southern vines are dressed
Above the noble slain:
He wrapped his colours round his breast,

On a blood-red field of Spain.
And one – o'er *her* the myrtle showers
Its leaves, by soft winds fanned –
She faded midst Italian flowers
The last of that bright band.

And parted thus they rest, who played
    Beneath the same green tree;
Whose voices mingled as they prayed
    Around one parent knee!

They that with smiles lit up the hall,
    And cheered with song the hearth –
Alas for love, if *thou* wert all,
    And nought beyond, oh Earth!

(ii) *A Parting Song* (1828)

'O mes amis! rapellez-vous quelquefois mes vers! mon ame y est empreinté.' (Madame de Staël)

When will ye think of me, my friends?
    When will ye think of me?
When the last red light, the farewell of day,
From the rock and the river is passing away –
When the air with a deepening hush is fraught,
And the heart grows tender with burdened thought –
        Then let it be!

When will ye think of me, kind friends?
    When will ye think of me?
When the rose of the rich midsummer-time
Is filled with the hues of its glorious prime –
When ye gather its bloom, as in bright hours fled,
From the walks where my footsteps no more may tread –
        Then let it be!

When will ye think of me, sweet friends?
    When will ye think of me?
When the sudden tears o'erflow your eye
At the sound of some olden melody –
When ye hear the voice of a mountain-stream,
When ye feel the charm of a poet's dream –
        Then let it be!

Thus let my memory be with you, friends!
    Thus ever think of me!
Kindly and gently, but as of one
For whom 'tis well to be fled and gone –

As of a bird from a chain unbound,
As of a wanderer whose home is found –
        So let it be.

24. CAROLINE NORTON

Dreams (1830)

Surely I heard a voice – surely my name
Was breathed in tones familiar to my heart?
I listened, and the low wind stealing came,
In darkness and in silence to depart.

Surely I saw a form, a proud bright form,
Standing beside my couch? I raised mine eyes –
'Twas but a dim cloud, herald of a storm,
That floated through the grey and twilight skies.

Surely the brightness of the summer-hour
Hath suddenly burst upon the circling gloom?
I dream – 'twas but the perfume of a flower,
Which the breeze wafted through the silent room.

Surely a hand clasped mine with greetings fond?
A name is murmured by my lips with pain!
Woe for that sound – woe for love's broken bond!
I start, I wake, I am alone again!

25. JAMES HOGG

When Maggy Gangs Away (1831)

Oh what will a' the lads do
   When Maggy gangs away?
Oh what will a' the lads do
   When Maggy gangs away?
There's no a heart in a' the glen
   That disna dread the day!
Oh what will a' the lads do
   When Maggy gangs away?

Young Jock has ta'en the hill for't –
A waefu' wight is he –
Poor Harry's ta'en the bed for't,
An' laid him down to dee;
An' Sandy's gane unto the kirk,
An learnin' fast to pray!
And, oh, what will the lads do
When Maggy gangs away?

The young laird o' the Lang-Shaw
Has drunk her health in wine;
The priest has said (in confidence)
The lassie was divine –
And that is mair in maiden's praise
Than ony priest should say!
But, oh, what will the lads do
When Maggy gangs away?

The wailing in our green glen
That day will quaver high,
'Twill draw the redbreast frae the wood,
The laverock frae the sky;
The fairies frae their beds o' dew
Will rise an' join the lay:
An' hey, what a day will be
When Maggy gangs away!

9 *has ta'en the hill for't* taken to the heather, gone native.
28 *laverock* lark.

VII. The Romantic Sonnet

The sonnet, so important to the sixteenth century and Shakespeare, and (though he in fact wrote few) used with the greatest power and flexibility by Milton, went out of fashion for 150 years after the Civil War. Among those who brought it back, and made it available to the Romantics, Smith (*Elegiac Sonnets* 1784, many times augmented) was immensely influential, having the field almost to herself until the publication of Bowles' *Fourteen Sonnets* coincided with her expanded fifth edition, 1789. Robinson's sonnet-sequence, *Sappho and Phaon* 1796, opted for the fluid Petrarchan (and Miltonic) form, as opposed to the stiff Shakespearean, with its too conclusive final couplet. Among the major Romantics, Wordsworth proved by far the most prolific sonneteer – too prolific, one might think, looking at the sequences of his later years: the *Duddon Sonnets* (powerful only in the wonderful *Afterthought*), *Ecclesiastical Sketches*, the unmentionable *Sonnets on Capital Punishment*. In his early years, Wordsworth had been an admirer of Smith, but significantly it was Dorothy Wordsworth's reading of Milton to her brother that inspired his burst of creativity, 1802–3, producing in a matter of months so many of the greatest English sonnets: *Westminster Bridge*, *The World Is Too Much With Us*, *Milton, Thou Shouldst Be Living at this Hour*.

Unexpectedly it may be Clare who comes second to Wordsworth in terms of numbers of sonnets written, constraining his natural style and natural observation with apparent ease:

> The evening o'er the meadow seems to stoop,
> More distant lessens the diminished spire –
> Mists in the hollows reaks and curdles up
> Like fallen clouds . . .

The bulk of Coleridge's sonnet writing belongs to his time as disciple of the lugubrious Bowles in the 1790s, before Wordsworth's going back to Milton had given the form its new freedom. Byron could have written great sonnets, but didn't bother; Shelley wrote few, but these include *Ozymandias* and *Lift Not the Painted Veil*. Keats was more attracted to the form, writing at the height of his powers in *On First Looking into Chapman's Homer*, *On Sitting Down to Read 'King Lear' Once Again* and *Bright Star*. Hunt, Hood, Hemans, Landon and Norton – especially the latter – were all distinguished sonneteers. And at the end of the period, Hartley Coleridge wrote, in *Long*

Time a Child, one of the great Romantic sonnets, in this sole respect proving himself able to distance, and improve upon, his father.

1. THOMAS WARTON

To the River Loden (1777)

Ah! what a weary race my feet have run
Since first I trod thy banks with alders crowned,
And thought my way was all through fairy-ground
Beneath thy azure sky and golden sun,

Where first my Muse to lisp her notes begun!
While pensive Memory traces back the round
Which fills the varied interval between,
Much pleasure – more of sorrow – marks the scene.
Sweet native stream, those skies and suns so pure
No more return to cheer my evening road!
Yet still one joy remains: that not obscure,
Nor useless, all my vacant days have flowed,
From youth's gay dawn to manhood's prime mature –
Nor with the Muse's laurel unbestowed.

2. CHARLOTTE SMITH

from *Elegiac Sonnets*, 1784

(i) *The Partial Muse* (I)

The partial Muse has from my earliest hours
Smiled on the ruggéd path I'm doomed to tread,
And still, with sportive hand, has snatched wild flowers
To weave fantastic garlands for my head;
But far, far happier is the lot of those
Who never learned her dear delusive art,
Which, while it decks the head with many a rose,
Reserves the thorn to fester in the heart.
For still she bids soft Pity's melting eye
Stream o'er the hills she knows not to remove –
Points every pang, and deepens every sigh
Of mourning friendship, or unhappy love.
Ah, then how dear the Muse's favours cost
If those paint sorrow best, who feel it most!

(ii) *Should the Lone Wanderer* (XXXVI)

Should the lone wanderer, fainting on his way,
Rest for a moment of the sultry hours,
And though his path through thorns and roughness lay,
Pluck the wild rose, or woodbine's gadding flowers,

Weaving gay wreaths beneath some sheltering tree,
  The sense of sorrow he awhile may lose;
So have I sought thy flowers, fair Poesy!
  So charmed my way with Friendship and the Muse.
But darker now grows life's unhappy day,
  Dark with new clouds of evil yet to come,
Her pencil sickening Fancy throws away,
  And weary Hope reclines upon the tomb;
And points my wishes to that tranquil shore,
Where the pale spectre Care pursues no more.

3. WILLIAM LISLE BOWLES

from *Fourteen Sonnets*, 1789

(i) *At a Village in Scotland* (VII)

Oh North, as thy romantic vales I leave,
  And bid farewell to each retiring hill
  Where thoughtful fancy seems to linger still
Tracing the broad bright landscape, much I grieve
  That (mingled with the toiling crowd) no more
I shall return, your varied views to mark –
Of rocks, amid the sunshine towering dark,
  Of rivers winding wild, and mountains hoar,
Or castle gleaming on the distant steep.
  Yet not the less I pray your charms may last,
  And many a softened image of the past
Pensive combine, and bid remembrance keep
  To cheer me with the thought of pleasure flown
  When I am wandering on my way alone.

(ii) *To the River Itchin* (VIII)

Itchin, when I behold thy banks again,
  Thy crumbling margin, and thy silver breast
  On which the self-same tints still seem to rest,
Why feels my heart the shivering sense of pain?

Is it that many a summer's day has past
Since in life's morn I carolled on thy side?
Is it that oft since then my heart has sighed
As youth, and hope's delusive gleams, flew fast?
Is it that those who circled on thy shore,
Companions of my youth, now meet no more?
Whate'er the cause, upon thy banks I bend
Sorrowing, yet feel such solace at my heart
As at the meeting of some long-lost friend
From whom, in happier hours, we wept to part.

4. SAMUEL TAYLOR COLERIDGE

(i) *Pantisocracy* (1794)

No more my visionary soul shall dwell
On joys that were! No more endure to weigh
The shame and anguish of the evil day,
Wisely forgetful! O'er the ocean swell
Sublime of hope I seek the cottaged dell,
Where virtue calm with careless step may stray,
And dancing to the moonlight roundelay
The wizard passions weave an holy spell.
Eyes that have ached with sorrow! Ye shall weep
Tears of doubt-mingled joy, like theirs who start
From precipices of distempered sleep
On which the fierce-eyed fiends their revels keep,
And see the rising sun, and feel it dart
New rays of pleasance trembling to the heart.

(ii) *To the River Otter* (1796)

Dear native brook! wild streamlet of the west!
How many various-fated years have past,
What blissful and what anguished hours, since last
I skimmed the smooth thin stone along thy breast,
Numbering its light leaps! Yet so deep impressed
Sink the sweet scenes of childhood, that mine eyes
I never shut amid the sunny blaze,
But straight with all their tints thy waters rise –

Thy crossing-plank, thy margin's willowy maze,
And bedded sand that veined with various dyes
Gleamed through thy bright transparence to the gaze!
Visions of childhood! oft have ye beguiled
Lone manhood's cares, yet waking fondest sighs:
Ah, that I were once more a careless child!

5. MARY ROBINSON

from *Sappho and Phaon* (1796)

It must strike every admirer of poetical composition that the [Shakespearean] sonnet, concluding with two lines winding up the sentiment of the whole, confines the poet's fancy, and frequently occasions an abrupt termination of a beautiful and interesting picture, and that the [Petrarchan] may be carried on in a series of sketches . . . forming in the whole a complete and connected story. (Robinson)

(i) *Sappho's Conjectures* (XXIII)

To Etna's scorching sands my Phaon flies!
False youth, can other charms attractive prove?
Say, can Sicilian loves thy passions move,
Play round thy heart and fix thy fickle eyes,
While in despair the Lesbian Sappho dies?
Has spring for thee a crown of poppies wove,
Or dost thou languish in the Idalian grove,
Whose altar kindles, fanned by lovers' sighs?
Ah, think that while on Etna's shores you stray,
A fire, more fierce than Etna's, fills my breast;
Nor deck Sicilian nymphs with garlands gay
While Sappho's brows with cypress wreaths are dressed –
Let one kind word my weary woes repay,
Or, in eternal slumbers bid them rest.

(ii) *Her Address to the Moon* (XXIV)

Oh thou, meek orb, that stealing o'er the dale
   Cheerest with thy modest beams the noon of night,
   On the smooth lake diffusing silvery light,
Sublimely still, and beautifully pale!
What can thy cool and placid eye avail,
   Where fierce despair absorbs the mental sight,
   While inbred glooms the vagrant thoughts invite
To tempt the gulf where howling fiends assail?
   Oh Night, all nature owns thy tempered power,
Thy solemn pause, thy dews, thy pensive beam;
   Thy sweet breath whispering in the moonlight bower
While fainting flowerets kiss the wandering stream!
   Yet, vain is every charm, and vain the hour,
That brings to madding love no soothing dream!

(iii) *To Phaon* (XXV)

Canst thou forget, oh idol of my soul,
   Thy Sappho's voice, her form, her dulcet lyre
   That melting every thought to fond desire
Bade sweet delirium o'er thy senses roll?
Canst thou so soon renounce the blest control
   That calmed with pity's tears love's raging fire,
   While hope, slow breathing on the trembling wire,
In every note with soft persuasion stole?
   Oh, sovereign of my heart – return, return!
For me no spring appears, no summers bloom,
   No sun-beams glitter, and no altars burn!
The mind's dark winter of eternal gloom
   Shows midst the waste a solitary urn,
A blighted laurel, and a mouldering tomb!

6. CHARLES LAMB

When Last I Roved (1797)

When last I roved these winding wood-walks green,
   Green winding walks, and shady pathways sweet,
Oft-times would Anna seek the silent scene,
   Shrouding her beauties in the lone retreat.
No more I hear her footsteps in the shade:
   Her image only in these pleasant ways
   Meets me self-wandering, where in happier days
I held free converse with the fair-haired maid.
I passed the little cottage which she loved,
   The cottage which did once my all contain!
   It spake of days which ne'er must come again –
Spake to my heart, and much my heart was moved:
'Now fair befall thee, gentle maid!' said I,
And from the cottage turned me with a sigh.

7. ROBERT SOUTHEY

To a Brook Near the Village of Corston (1797)

As thus I bend me o'er thy babbling stream
   And watch thy current, Memory's hand portrays
   The faint-formed scenes of the departed days,
Like the far forest by the moon's pale beam
Dimly descried, yet lovely. I have worn
   Upon thy banks the live-long hour away
   When sportive childhood wantoned through the day,
Joyed at the opening splendour of the morn,
Or, as the twilight darkened, heaved the sigh
   Thinking of distant home, as down my cheek
   (At the fond thought slow stealing on) would speak
The silent eloquence of the full eye.
Dim are the long-past days, yet still they please
As thy soft sounds, half-heard, borne on the inconstant breeze.

8. CHARLES LLOYD

On the Death of Priscilla Farmer (1797)

As o'er the dying embers oft I cower
When my tired spirits rest, and my heart swells
Lulled by domestic quiet, Memory dwells
On that blest tide, when thou the evening hour
Didst gladden. While upon the accustomed chair
I look, it seems as if thou still wert there;
Kirtled in snowy apron, thy dear knees,
Propt on the fendered hearth, my fancy sees,
O'er which – exchanging souls – we wont to bend!
And as I lift my head, thy features send
A cheering smile to me – but, in its flight
O'er my rain-pelted sash, a blast of night
Sweeps surlily! I start, and fain would creep
To the bleak dwelling where thy cold limbs sleep!

9. ANNA SEWARD

By Derwent's Rapid Stream (1799)

By Derwent's rapid stream as oft I strayed
With infancy's light step and glances wild,
And saw vast rocks on steepy mountains piled
Frown o'er the umbrageous glen, or pleased surveyed
The cloudy moonshine in the shadowy glade,
Romantic Nature to the enthusiast child
Grew dearer far than when serene she smiled
In uncontrasted loveliness arrayed.
But oh! in every scene, with sacred sway
Her graces fire me; from the bloom that spreads
Resplendent in the lucid morn of May,
To the green light the little glow-worm sheds
On mossy banks when midnight glooms prevail,
And softest silence broods o'er all the dale.

10. MARY TIGHE

Written at Scarborough (1799)

As musing pensive in my silent home
  I hear far off the sullen ocean's roar,
  Where the rude wave just sweeps the level shore
Or bursts upon the rocks with whitening foam,
I think upon the scenes my life has known –
  On days of sorrow, and some hours of joy;
  Both which alike Time could so soon destroy!
And now they seem a busy dream alone;
While on the earth exists no single trace
  Of all that shook my agitated soul,
  As on the beach new waves for ever roll
And fill their past forgotten brother's place;
  But I, like the worn sand, exposed remain
  To each new storm which frets the angry main.

11. CHARLOTTE SMITH

from *Elegiac Sonnets*, 1799

(i) *Written at the Close of Spring* (II)

The garlands fade that Spring so lately wove,
  Each simple flower, which she had nursed in dew,
Anemones, that spangled every grove,
  The primrose wan, and hare-bell, mildly blue.
No more shall violets linger in the dell,
  Or purple orchis variegate the plain,
Till Spring again shall call forth every bell,
  And dress with humid hands her wreaths again.
Ah, poor humanity! so frail, so fair,
  Are the fond visions of thy early day,
Till tyrant passion, and corrosive care,
  Bid all thy fairy colours fade away!
Another May new buds and flowers shall bring:
Ah! why has happiness – no second Spring?

(ii) *From the Thirteenth Cantata of Metastasio* (XVII)

On thy grey bark, in witness of my flame,
I carve Miranda's cypher – beauteous tree!
Graced with the lovely letters of her name,
Henceforth be sacred to my love and me!
Though the tall elm, the oak, and darker pine,
With broader arms, may noon's fierce ardours break,
To shelter me, and her I love, be thine;
And thine to see her smile and hear her speak.
No bird, ill-omened, round thy graceful head
Shall clamour harsh, or wave his heavy wing,
But fern and flowers arise beneath thy shade,
Where the wild bees their lullabies shall sing.
And in thy boughs the murmuring ring-dove rest;
And there the nightingale shall build her nest.

(iii) *To the Earl of Egremont* (XVIII)

Wyndham! 'tis not thy blood, though pure it runs
Through a long line of glorious ancestry,
Percys and Seymours, Britain's boasted sons,
Who trust the honours of their race to thee.

'Tis not thy splendid domes (where Science loves
To touch the canvas, and the bust to raise),
Thy rich domains, fair fields, and spreading groves –
'Tis not all these the Muse delights to praise:

In birth, and wealth, and honours, great thou art!
But nobler in thy independent mind,
And in that liberal hand and feeling heart
Given thee by Heaven – a blessing to mankind!
Unworthy oft may titled fortune be:
A soul like thine – is true Nobility!

12. WILLIAM WORDSWORTH

Sonnets of 1802 (publ. 1807)

(i) *I Grieved for Bonaparté* (21 May)

I grieved for Bonaparté with a vain
And an unthinking grief – the vital blood
Of that man's mind, what can it be? What food
Fed his first hopes? What knowledge could he gain?
'Tis not in battles that from youth we train
The governor who must be wise and good
And temper with the sternness of the brain
Thoughts motherly and meek as womanhood.
Wisdom doth live with children round her knees:
Books, leisure, perfect freedom, and the talk
Man holds with weekday man in the hourly walk
Of the mind's business. These are the degrees
By which true sway doth mount; this is the stalk
True power doth grow on – and her rights are these.

(ii) *With Ships the Sea Was Sprinkled*

With ships the sea was sprinkled far and nigh
Like stars in heaven, and joyously it showed;
Some lying fast at anchor in the road,
Some veering up and down, one knew not why.
A goodly vessel did I then espy
Come like a giant from a haven broad,
And lustily along the bay she strode,
Her tackling rich, and of apparel high.
This ship was nought to me, nor I to her,
Yet I pursued her with a lover's look –
This ship to all the rest did I prefer!
When will she turn, and whither? She will brook
No tarrying – where she comes the winds must stir! –
On went she, and due north her journey took.

(iii) *Westminster Bridge* (3 Sept.)

Earth hath not anything to show more fair!
Dull would he be of soul who could pass by
A sight so touching in its majesty.
This city now doth like a garment wear
The beauty of the morning: silent, bare,
Ships, towers, domes, theatres, and temples lie
Open unto the fields and to the sky,
All bright and glittering in the smokeless air.
Never did sun more beautifully steep
In his first splendour valley, rock or hill;
Ne'er saw I, never felt, a calm so deep –
The river glideth at his own sweet will –
Dear God, the very houses seem asleep,
And all that mighty heart is lying still!

(iv) *Milton, Thou Shouldst Be Living at this Hour*

Milton, thou shouldst be living at this hour,
England hath need of thee! She is a fen
Of stagnant waters! Altar, sword, and pen,
Fireside, the heroic wealth of hall and bower,
Have forfeited their ancient English dower
Of inward happiness. We are selfish men –
Oh raise us up, return to us again,
And give us manners, virtue, freedom, power!
Thy soul was like a star and dwelt apart;
Thou hadst a voice whose sound was like the sea –
Pure as the naked heavens, majestic, free –
So didst thou travel on life's common way
In cheerful godliness. And yet thy heart
The lowliest duties on itself did lay.

(v) *The World Is Too Much with Us*

The world is too much with us: late and soon,
Getting and spending, we lay waste our powers –
Little we see in Nature that is ours –
We have given our hearts away, a sordid boon!

This sea that bares her bosom to the moon,
The winds that will be howling at all hours
And are up-gathered now like sleeping flowers;
For this, for every thing, we are out of tune:
It moves us not. Great God! I'd rather be
A pagan suckled in a creed outworn
So might I, standing on this pleasant lea,
Have glimpses that would make me less forlorn –
Have sight of Proteus coming from the sea,
Or hear old Triton blow his wreathéd horn.

(vi) *Ere We Had Reached the Wished-for Place* (4 Oct.)

Ere we had reached the wished-for place, night fell;
We were too late at least by one dark hour,
And nothing could we see of all that power
Of prospect whereof many thousands tell.
The western sky did recompense us well
With Grecian temple, minaret, and bower,
And in one part a minster with its tower
Substantially distinct – a place for bell
Or clock to toll from! Many a glorious pile
Did we behold, sights that might well repay
All disappointment – and, as such, the eye
Delighted in them – but we felt, the while,
We should forget them. They are of the sky
And from our earthly memory fade away.

(vii) *Nuns Fret Not*

Nuns fret not at their convent's narrow room,
And hermits are contented with their cells,
And students with their pensive citadels;
Maids at the wheel, the weaver at his loom,
Sit blithe and happy; bees that soar for bloom
High as the highest peak of Furness Fells
Will murmur by the hour in foxglove bells.
In truth, the prison unto which we doom
Ourselves, no prison is; and hence to me,

In sundry moods, 'twas pastime to be bound
Within the sonnet's scanty plot of ground –
Pleased if some souls (for such there needs must be)
Who have felt the weight of too much liberty,
Should find short solace there, as I have found.

(viii) *Scorn Not the Sonnet* (c. 1802; publ. 1827)

Scorn not the sonnet! Critic, you have frowned
Mindless of its just honours. With this key
Shakespeare unlocked his heart, the melody
Of this small lute gave ease to Petrarch's wound;
A thousand times this pipe did Tasso sound;
With it Camöens soothed an exile's grief.
The sonnet glittered a gay myrtle-leaf
Amid the cypress with which Dante crowned
His visionary brow – a glow-worm lamp.
It cheered mild Spenser, called from Faery-land
To struggle through dark ways, and, when a damp
Fell round the path of Milton, in his hand
The thing became a trumpet, whence he blew
Soul-animating strains – alas, too few!

13. MARY TIGHE

To Death (c. 1805; publ. 1811)

Oh thou most terrible, most dreaded power,
   In whatsoever form thou meetst the eye –
   Whether thou biddest thy sudden arrow fly
In the dread silence of the midnight-hour;
Or whether, hovering o'er the lingering wretch
   Thy sad cold javelin hangs suspended long,
   While round the couch the weeping kindred throng
With hope and fear alternately on stretch –
Oh, say, for me what horrors are prepared?
   Am I now doomed to meet thy fatal arm?
   Or wilt thou first from life steal every charm,
And bear away each good my soul would guard,
That thus, deprived of all it loved, my heart
From life itself contentedly may part?

14. JAMES LEIGH HUNT

Sonnets, 1814–18

(i) *Written During the Author's Imprisonment, November 1814* (*Examiner*)

Winter has reached thee once again at last,
And now the rambler, whom thy groves yet please,
Feels on his house-warm lips the thin air freeze,
While in his shrugging neck the resolute blast
Comes edging; and the leaves, in heaps down cast,
He shuffles with his hastening foot, and sees
The cold sky whitening through the wiry trees,
And sighs to think his loitering noons have passed.

And do I love thee less, to paint thee so?
No. This the season is of beauty still,
Doubled at heart; of smoke, with whirling glee
Uptumbling ever from the blaze below,
And home remembered most – and oh, loved hill,
The second, and the last, away from thee!

(ii) *Written in the Spring that Succeeded Imprisonment, May 1815* (*Examiner*)

As one who after long and far-spent years
Comes on his mistress in an hour of sleep,
And (wondering half that he can silence keep)
Stands smiling o'er her through a flash of tears
To see how sweet and self-same she appears,
Till, at his touch, with little moving creep
Of joy, she wakes from out her calmness deep,
And then his heart finds voice, and dances round her ears –

So I, first coming on my haunts again,
In pause and stillness of the early prime,
Stood thinking of the past and present time
With earnest eyesight, scarcely crossed with pain,
Till the fresh-moving leaves, and startling birds,
Loosened my long-suspended breath in words!

(iii) *On a Lock of Milton's Hair*

(Jan. 1818; *Examiner*)

It lies before me there, and my own breath
Stirs its thin outer threads, as though beside
The living head I stood in honoured pride
Talking of lovely things that conquer death.
Perhaps he pressed it once, or underneath
Ran his fine fingers when he leant, blank-eyed,
And saw in fancy Adam and his bride
With their rich locks – or his own Delphic wreath!

There seems a love in hair, though it be dead:
It is the gentlest, yet the strongest thread
Of our frail plant – a blossom from the tree
Surviving the proud trunk – as though it said
'Patience and gentleness is power. In me
Behold affectionate eternity!'

15. MARY BRYAN

To My Brother (1815)

Oh transient sorrows, light as morning dews
Chased with soon-rising beams –
Yet oft sick fancy deems
Portents of ill they came, since care's worn hues
O'ercast thy sister's cheek, where stands a tear
Unheeded or forgotten now
Like cold drops on the pallid brow
Of pain or fear.
When, when wilt thou return?
Since thou art far away,
Each desolated day
Has brought me much to mourn –
And oh, my brother, if thou long shouldst roam,
To her who loves thee best thou never wilt come home!

16. LORD BYRON

Sonnets Written at the Villa Diodati, July 1816 (1816)

(i) *Sonnet on Chillon*

Eternal spirit of the chainless mind!
Brightest in dungeons, Liberty, thou art,
For there thy habitation is the heart –
The heart which love of thee alone can bind!
And when thy sons to fetters are consigned –
To fetters, and the damp vault's dayless gloom –
Their country conquers with their martyrdom,
And Freedom's fame finds wings on every wind.
Chillon! thy prison is a holy place,
And thy sad floor an altar – for 'twas trod,
Until his very steps have left a trace,
Worn (as if thy cold pavement were a sod)
By Bonnivard! May none those marks efface –
For they appeal from tyranny to God!

(ii) *Sonnet to Lake Leman* (1816)

Rousseau, Voltaire, our Gibbon, and De Staël!
Leman, these names are worthy of thy shore –
Thy shore of names like these! Wert thou no more,
Their memory thy remembrance would recall!
To them thy banks were lovely, as to all,
But they have made them lovelier, for the lore
Of mighty minds doth hallow in the core
Of human hearts the ruin of a wall
Where dwelt the wise and wondrous – but by thee
How much more, Lake of Beauty, do we feel,
In sweetly gliding o'er thy crystal sea,
The wild glow of that not ungentle zeal,
Which of the heirs of immortality
Is proud, and makes the breath of glory real!

17. JOHN KEATS

Sonnets of 1816–19

(i) *On First Looking into Chapman's Homer* (Oct. 1816; publ. Dec.)

Much have I travelled in the realms of gold,
And many goodly states and kingdoms seen;
Round many western islands have I been
Which bards in fealty to Apollo hold.
Oft of one wide expanse had I been told
That deep-browed Homer ruled as his demesne;
Yet did I never breathe its pure serene
Till I heard Chapman speak out loud and bold!
Then felt I like some watcher of the skies
When a new planet swims into his ken;
Or like stout Cortez when with eagle eyes
He stared at the Pacific – and all his men
Looked at each other with a wild surmise,
Silent, upon a peak in Darien.

(ii) *Great Spirits Now on Earth are Sojourning* (19–20 Nov. 1816; publ. 1817)

Great spirits now on earth are sojourning –
He of the cloud, the cataract, the lake,
Who on Helvellyn's summit, wide awake,
Catches his freshness from Archangel's wing;
He of the rose, the violet, the spring,
The social smile, the chain for freedom's sake;
And lo! – whose steadfastness would never take
A meaner sound than Raphael's whispering.
And other spirits there are, standing apart
Upon the forehead of the age to come.
These, these will give the world another heart
And other pulses. Hear ye not the hum
Of mighty workings? –
Listen awhile ye nations, and be dumb!

(iii) *To Mrs Reynolds' Cat*

(16 Jan. 1818; publ. 1830)

Cat, who has past thy grand climacteric,
How many mice and rats hast in thy days
Destroyed? How many titbits stolen? Gaze
With those bright languid segments green, and prick
Those velvet ears – but prithee do not stick
Thy latent talons in me, and upraise
Thy gentle mew, and tell me all the frays
Of fish and mice, and rats and tender chick.
Nay, look not down, nor lick thy dainty wrists –
For all the wheezy asthma, and for all
Thy tail's tip is nicked off, and though the fists
Of many a maid have given thee many a maul,
Still is that fur as soft as when the lists
In youth thou enteredst on glass-bottled wall!

(iv) *On Sitting Down to Read 'King Lear' Once Again* (22 Jan. 1818; publ. 1838)

Oh golden-tongued Romance, with serene lute!
Fair plumèd syren, Queen of far-away!
Leave melodizing on this wintry day –
Shut up thine olden pages, and be mute.
Adieu, for, once again, the fierce dispute
Betwixt damnation and impassioned clay
Must I burn through – once more humbly assay
The bitter-sweet of this Shakespearean fruit.
Chief poet! and ye clouds of Albion
(Begetters of our deep eternal theme),
When through the old oak forest I am gone,
Let me not wander in a barren dream,
But, when I am consumèd in the fire,
Give me new phoenix-wings to fly at my desire.

(v) *When I Have Fears that I May Cease to Be* (late Jan. 1818; publ. 1848)

When I have fears that I may cease to be
   Before my pen has gleaned my teeming brain,
Before high-pilèd books, in charactery,
   Hold like rich garners the full ripened grain;
When I behold, upon the night's starred face,
   Huge cloudy symbols of a high romance,
And think that I may never live to trace
   Their shadows, with the magic hand of chance;
And when I feel, fair creature of an hour,
   That I shall never look upon thee more,
Never have relish in the fairy power
   Of unreflecting love – then on the shore
Of the wide world I stand alone, and think
Till love and fame to nothingness do sink.

(vi) *Bright Star* (autumn 1819; publ. 1838)

Bright star, would I were steadfast as thou art!
   Not in lone splendour hung aloft the night
And watching with eternal lids apart,
   Like Nature's patient sleepless eremite,
The moving waters at their priestlike task
   Of pure ablution round earth's human shores;
Or gazing on the new soft-fallen mask
   Of snow upon the mountains and the moors.
No! Yet still steadfast, still unchangeable,
   Pillowed upon my fair Love's ripening breast
To feel for ever its soft fall and swell,
   Awake for ever in a sweet unrest –
Still, still to hear her tender-taken breath,
And so live ever: or else swoon to death.

18. HORACE SMITH

In Egypt's Sandy Silence

(Dec. 1817; publ. 1 Feb. 1818)

In Egypt's sandy silence, all alone,
Stands a gigantic leg, which far off throws
The only shadows that the desert knows.
'I am great Ozymandias', saith the stone,
'The King of Kings – This mighty city shows
The wonders of my hand!' The city's gone,
Nought but the leg remaining to disclose
The site of this forgotten Babylon.
We wonder, and some hunter may express
Wonder like ours, when through the wilderness
Where London stood, holding the wolf in chase,
He meets some fragment huge, and stops to guess
What powerful but unrecorded race
Once dwelt in that annihilated place.

19. PERCY BYSSHE SHELLEY

(i) *Ozymandias* (Dec. 1817; publ. 11 Jan. 1818)

I met a traveller from an antique land
Who said: 'Two vast and trunkless legs of stone
Stand in the desert. Near them on the sand,
Half sunk, a shattered visage lies, whose frown,
And wrinkled lip, and sneer of cold command,
Tell that its sculptor well those passions read
Which yet survive (stamped on these lifeless things)
The hand that mocked them and the heart that fed.
And on the pedestal these words appear:
"My name is Ozymandias, King of Kings;
Look on my works, ye Mighty, and despair!"
Nothing beside remains. Round the decay
Of that colossal wreck, boundless and bare
The lone and level sands stretch far away.'

(ii) *Lift Not the Painted Veil*

(late 1819; publ. 1824)

Lift not the painted veil which those who live
Call life! Though unreal shapes be pictured there,
And it but mimic all we would believe
With colours idly spread, behind, lurk Fear
And Hope, twin destinies, who ever weave
Their shadows o'er the chasm, sightless and drear.
I knew one who had lifted it: he sought
(For his lost heart was tender) things to love,
But found them not, alas – nor was there aught
The world contains, the which he could approve.
Through the unheeding many he did move,
A splendour among shadows, a bright blot
Upon this gloomy scene, a spirit that strove
For truth, and like the Preacher found it not.

20. JOHN CLARE

(i) *Give Me the Gloomy Walk*

(1819–20; publ. 1820)

Give me the gloomy walk in summer-time
That intersects the woods where Nature weaves
Her bowers at will (that, close-encumbered, climb
Dark overhead their many-mingling leaves),
While curious anxiousness the bosom heaves
The hidden beauties of the shade to find
That in the negligence of summer lives;
Each herb, leaf, noting of peculiar kind,
And many a flower and many a nameless weed,
Where eye scarce marks 'em ere they're run to seed –
And where the mossy stump invites to rest,
And woodbines up the hazel's stem proceed,
Drop down and muse within one's sheltered nest
Or from one's pocket take a book and read.

(ii) *A Wish* (1819–20; publ. 1828)

Be where I may when death brings in his bill
Demanding payment for life's lingering debt –
Or in my native village nestling still,
Or tracing scenes I've never known as yet –
Oh let one wish (go where it will) be mine:
To turn me back and wander home to die,
'Mong nearest friends my latest breath resign,
And in my churchyard wi' my kindred lie,
Neath the thick shade's sycamores decay –
Its broad leaves trembling to the breeze of day –
To see its shadow o'er my ashes wave!
How soothing will it be, while, hovering near,
My unseen spirit haunts its daisied grave
Pausing on scenes that life once loved so dear.

21. WILLIAM WORDSWORTH

The River Duddon: Afterthought (1820)

I thought of thee, my partner and my guide,
As being past away. Vain sympathies –
For backward, Duddon, as I cast my eyes,
I see what was, and is, and will abide.
Still glides the stream, and shall forever glide
(The form remains, the function never dies),
While we, the brave, the mighty, and the wise –
We men, who in our morn of youth defied
The elements – must vanish. Be it so!
Enough if something from our hands have power
To live, and act, and serve the future hour;
And if, as toward the silent tomb we go,
Through love, through hope, and faith's transcendent dower
We feel that we are greater than we know.

22. SAMUEL TAYLOR COLERIDGE

To Nature (1820)

It may indeed be fantasy, when I
Essay to draw from all created things
Deep, heartfelt, inward joy that closely clings,
And trace in leaves and flowers that round me lie
Lessons of love and earnest piety.
So let it be! And if the wide world rings
In mock of this belief, it brings
Nor fear, nor grief, nor vain perplexity.
So will I build my altar in the fields,
And the blue sky my fretted dome shall be,
And the sweet fragrance that the wild-flower yields
Shall be the incense I will yield to thee –
Thee only, God! and thou shall not despise
Even me, the priest of this poor sacrifice.

23. THOMAS HOOD

Written in Keats' 'Endymion'

(*London Magazine* 1823)

I saw pale Dian, sitting by the brink
Of silver falls, the overflow of fountains
From cloudy steeps; and I grew sad to think
Endymion's foot was silent on those mountains,
And he but a hushed name, that Silence keeps
In dear remembrance – lonely, and forlorn,
Singing it to herself until she weeps
Tears that perchance still glisten in the morn!
And as I mused, in dull imaginings,
There came a flash of garments, and I knew
The awful Muse by her harmonious wings
Charming the air to music as she flew.
Anon there rose an echo through the vale
Gave back Endymion in a dreamlike tale!

24. HARTLEY COLERIDGE

Long Time a Child (1833)

Long time a child, and still a child when years
Had painted manhood on my cheek, was I;
For yet I lived like one not born to die –
A thriftless prodigal of smiles and tears,
No hope I needed, and I knew no fears.
But sleep, though sweet, is only sleep; and waking,
I waked to sleep no more, at once o'ertaking
The vanguard of my age, with all arrears
Of duty on my back. Nor child, nor man,
Nor youth, nor sage, I find my head is grey,
For I have lost the race I never ran!
A rathe December blights my lagging May,
And still I am a child, though I be old –
Time is my debtor for my years untold.

25. FELICIA HEMANS

To a Distant Scene (1834)

Still are the cowslips from thy bosom springing,
Oh far-off, grassy dell? And dost thou see,
When southern winds first wake their vernal singing,
The star-gleam of the wood anemone?
Doth the shy ring-dove haunt thee yet, the bee
Hang on thy flowers as when I breathed farewell
To their wild blooms? And, round my beechen tree,
Still, in green softness, doth the moss-bank swell?
   Oh, strange illusion! by the fond heart wrought,
Whose own warm life suffuses Nature's.
   My being's tide of many-coloured thought
Hath passed from thee; and now, rich, leafy place,
I paint thee oft, scarce consciously, a scene
Silent, forsaken, dim, shadowed by what hath been.

26. CAROLINE NORTON

Be Frank with Me (1830)

Be frank with me, and I accept my lot;
But deal not with me as a grieving child,
Who for the loss of that which he hath not
Is by a show of kindness thus beguiled!
Raise not for me, from its enshrouded tomb,
The ghostly likeness of a hope deceased;
Nor think to cheat the darkness of my doom
By wavering doubts how far thou art released.
This dressing pity in the garb of love,
This effort of the heart to seem the same,
These sighs and lingerings (which nothing prove
But that thou leavest me with a kind of shame),
Remind me more, by their most vain deceit,
Of the dear loss of all which thou dost counterfeit.

27. LETITIA ELIZABETH LANDON

The Castle of Chillon (1835)

Fair lake, thy lovely and thy haunted shore
Hath only echoes for the poet's lute;
None may tread there save with unsandalled foot,
Submissive to the great who went before,
Filled with the mighty memories of yore.
And yet how mournful are the records there –
Captivity, and exile, and despair,
Did they endure who now endure no more.
The patriot, the woman, and the bard,
Whose names thy winds and waters bear along;
What did the world bestow for their reward
But suffering, sorrow, bitterness, and wrong?
Genius, a hard and weary lot is thine –
Thy heart thy fuel, and the grave thy shrine.

VIII. The Gothic and Surreal

Normally thought of in terms of the novel (Radcliffe's *Mysteries of Udolpho*, Lewis' *Monk*, Mary Shelley's *Frankenstein*, Maturin's *Melmoth the Wanderer*), the Gothic impulse produced in the Romantic period verse that puts these prose achievements into perspective: *Tam O'Shanter*, *The Ancient Mariner* (here placed under Romantic Solitude, Suffering and Endurance), *Christabel* and *The Thorn*, *Peter Grimes* and *La Belle Dame Sans Merci* – not to mention the eccentric power of Byron's *Darkness* and Hood's *Last Man*.

The origins of the Gothic novel are commonly traced to Walpole's *Castle of Otranto* (1764); those of Gothic verse go back to Warton's *The Pleasures of Melancholy* almost twenty years before: 'In hollow charnel let me watch the flame / Of taper dim . . .' Radcliffe's *Sicilian Romance* (1790) marks the beginning of the Romantic vogue for Gothic in the novel, but Blake's *Poetical Sketches* (1983) had included *Fair Elenor*, and Helen Maria Williams' *Part of an Irregular Fragment Found in a Dark Passage of the Tower* (*Poems* 1786) is Gothic in all particulars:

> But whence arose that solemn call?
> Yon bloody phantom waves his hand
> And beckons me to deeper gloom –
> Rest, troubled form, I come . . .

Aged sixteen, Wordsworth based his *Vale of Esthwaite* on the *Irregular Fragment*, but as it turned out, this kind of self-conscious early Gothicism persisted longer in prose than in verse.

Tam O'Shanter (1790) emerges from a native Scots folk-tradition of witches and warlocks; English Romanticism, meanwhile, in its Gothic phase, borrows the impulse from Germany. Behind *The Ancient Mariner*, *The Thorn*, Southey's *Old Woman of Berkeley* and Robinson's *Haunted Beach*, lies Gottfried Bürger's horror-ballad, *Lenora*, that came suddenly into fashion (and was five times translated) in 1796. *Lenora* offered a story that was crudely supernatural in its plot, and black and white in its morality: make the mistake of wishing yourself dead, and God will send your ghostly lover on the stroke of midnight to accompany you to the grave! Yet *The Ancient Mariner* would never have been written without *Lenora*, and *The Thorn* is a queasy reworking of Bürger's no more acceptable *Lass of Fair Wone*.

Bürger's influence was as brief as it was sudden, lasting into Lewis' *Tales of Wonder* (1800) and *Tales of Terror* (1801), but hardly further. To a large extent the surreal, in its various forms – Crabbe's *Peter Grimes*, Byron's *Darkness* and Hood's *Last Man* – takes over from the Gothic at this stage. One aspect of the surreal, as one might expect, derives from the pleasure in magic. In place of the earlier crudities we have Scott's adventure of Deloraine in *The Lay of the Last Minstrel*, and the plangency of Keats' *Belle Dame Sans Merci*.

1. WILLIAM BLAKE

Fair Elenor (*Poetical Sketches* 1783)

The bell struck one and shook the silent tower;
The graves gave up their dead – fair Elenor
Walked by the castle gate, and lookéd in.
A hollow groan ran through the dreary vaults!

She shrieked aloud, and sunk upon the steps
On the cold stone her pale cheek. Sickly smells
Of death issue as from a sepulchre,
And all is silent but the sighing vaults.

Chill death withdraws his hand, and she revives!
Amazed, she finds herself upon her feet,
And, like a ghost, through narrow passages
Walking, feeling the cold walls with her hands.

Fancy returns, and now she thinks of bones,
And grinning skulls, and corruptible death,
Wrapped in his shroud; and now fancies she hears
Deep sighs and sees pale sickly ghosts gliding.

At length, no fancy – but reality –
Distracts her. A rushing sound, and the feet
Of one that fled, approaches! Ellen stood
Like a dumb statue, froze to stone with fear.

The wretch approaches, crying: 'The deed is done!
Take this, and send it by whom thou wilt send.
It is my life – send it to Elenor –
He's dead, and howling after me for blood!

Take this!' he cried, and thrust into her arms
A wet napkin, wrapped about – then rushed
Past, howling. She received into her arms
Pale death, and followed on the wings of fear!

They passed swift through the outer gate. The wretch,
Howling, leaped o'er the wall into the moat,
Stifling in mud. Fair Ellen passed the bridge,
And heard a gloomy voice cry, 'Is it done?'

As the deer wounded, Ellen flew over
The pathless plain! As the arrows that fly
By night, destruction flies and strikes in darkness!
She fled from fear, till at her house arrived.

Her maids await her. On her bed she falls –
That bed of joy, where erst her lord hath pressed.
'Ah, woman's fear!' she cried: 'Ah, curséd duke!
Ah, my dear lord! Ah, wretched Elenor!

My lord was like a flower upon the brows
Of lusty May! Ah, life as frail as a flower!
Oh ghastly Death, withdraw thy cruel hand –
Seekest thou that flower to deck thy horrid temples?

My lord was like a star in the highest heaven,
Drawn down to earth by spells and wickedness;
My lord was like the opening eyes of day,
When western winds creep softly o'er the flowers.

But he is darkened – like the summer's noon,
Clouded – fallen like the stately tree cut down!
The breath of heaven dwelt among his leaves.
Oh Elenor, weak woman, filled with woe!'

Thus having spoke, she raised up her head
And saw the bloody napkin by her side,
Which in her arms she brought – and now, tenfold
More terrified, saw it unfold itself!

Her eyes were fixed. The bloody cloth unfolds,
Disclosing to her sight the murdered head
Of her dear lord, all ghastly pale, clotted
With gory blood. It groaned, and thus it spake:

'O Elenor, behold thy husband's head,
Who, sleeping on the stones of yonder tower,
Was reft of life by the accurséd Duke!
A hiréd villain turned my sleep to death.

'Oh Elenor, beware the curséd Duke –
Oh give him not thy hand, now I am dead.
He seeks thy love, who (coward in the night)
Hiréd a villain to bereave my life.'

She sat with dead cold limbs, stiffened to stone;
She took the gory head up in her arms;
She kisséd the pale lips; she had no tears to shed;
She hugged it to her breast – and groaned her last!

2. HELEN MARIA WILLIAMS

Part of an Irregular Fragment Found in a Dark Passage of the Tower (1786)

Rise, winds of night! Relentless tempests rise!
   Rush from the troubled clouds, and o'er me roll –
In this chill pause a deeper horror lies,
   A wilder fear appals my shuddering soul!
'Twas on this day, this hour accurst,
   That Nature, starting from repose,
Heard the dire shrieks of murder burst –
   From infant innocence they rose,
      And shook these solemn towers!
I shuddering pass that fatal room,
For ages wrapped in central gloom –
I shuddering pass that iron door
Which Fate perchance unlocks no more:
Death, smeared with blood, o'er the dark portal lowers.

   How fearfully my step resounds
   Along these onely bounds!
Spare, savage blast, the taper's quivering fires –
Deep in these gathering shades its flame expires.
   Ye host of Heaven! the door recedes –
   It mocks my grasp – what unseen hands
      Have burst its iron bands!
   No mortal force this gate unbarred
   (Where danger lives, which terrors guard) –
   Dread powers! its screaming hinges close
      On this dread scene of impious deeds –
   My feet are fixed! Dismay has bound
   My step on this polluted ground –
But lo! the pitying moon a line of light
Athwart the horrid darkness dimly throws,
And from yon grated window chases night.

   Ye visions that before me roll,
That freeze my blood, that shake my soul!
   Are ye the phantoms of a dream?
Pale spectres! are ye what ye seem?

They glide more near –
Their forms unfold!
Fixed are their eyes, on me they bend –
Their glaring look is cold!
And hark! I hear
Sounds that the throbbing pulse of life suspend . . .

But whence arose yon solemn call?
Yon bloody phantom waves his hand,
And beckons me to deeper gloom –
Rest, troubled form, I come!
Some unknown power my step impels
To Horror's secret cells . . .

3. ROBERT BURNS

Tam O' Shanter (late 1790; publ. 1791)

Of Brownyis and of Bogillis full is this Buke.
(Gavin Douglas, *Eneados*)

When chapman billies leave the street,
And drouthy neebors neebors meet;
As market-days are wearing late,
An' folk begin to tak the gate;
While we sit bousing at the nappy,
An' getting fou and unco happy,
We think na on the lang Scots miles,
The mosses, waters, slaps, and styles,
That lie between us and our hame,
Whare sits our sulky, sullen dame,
Gathering her brows like gathering storm,
Nursing her wrath to keep it warm!
This truth fand honest Tam o' Shanter,
As he frae Ayr ae night did canter –

1 *chapman billies* hawkers, street-traders. 2 *drouthy* thirsty.
4 *tak the gate* take their way. 5 *bousing at the nappy* boozing ale.
6 *fou and unco happy* full and strangely happy.
8 *mosses, waters, slaps* bogs, ponds, wall-gaps.
9 *hame* home. 13 *fand* found.

Auld Ayr, wham ne'er a town surpasses,
For honest men and bonnie lasses.
  Oh Tam, hadst thou but been sae wise
As taen thy ain wife Kate's advice!
She tauld thee weel thou was a skellum,
A blethering, blustering, drunken blellum –
That frae November till October,
Ae market-day thou was nae sober;
That ilka melder wi' the miller,
Thou sat as lang as thou had siller;
That ev'ry naig was caed a shoe on,
The smith and thee gat roaring fou on;
That at the Lord's house, even on Sunday,
Thou drank wi' Kirkton Jean till Monday.
She prophesied, that, late or soon,
Thou would be found deep drowned in Doon,
Or catched wi' warlocks in the mirk
By Alloway's auld, haunted kirk.
Ah! gentle dames, it gars me greet
To think how monie counsels sweet,
How monie lengthened, sage advices
The husband frae the wife despises!
  But to our tale! Ae market-night,
Tam had got planted unco right,
Fast by an ingle, bleezing finely,
Wi' reaming swats, that drank divinely
And at his elbow Souter Johnie,
His ancient, trusty, drouthy cronie:
(Tam loved him like a very brither –
They had been fou for weeks thegither).
The night drave on wi' sangs and clatter,
And ay the ale was growing better!
The landlady and Tam grew gracious
Wi' secret favours, sweet and precious;
The Souter tauld his queerest stories;
The landlord's laugh was ready chorus;

19 *skellum* scoundrel, layabout. **20** *blellum* windbag.
23 *melder* corn-grinding session. **24** *siller* silver.
25 *ev'ry naig was caed a shoe on* every horse that was shoed.
31 *warlocks* male witches. **33** *gars me greet* makes me cry. **39** *ingle* fire.
40 *reaming swats* frothing mugs of beer. **41** *Souter* Cobbler.

The storm without might rair and rustle,
Tam did na mind the storm a whistle.
Care, mad to see a man sae happy,
E'en drowned himsel amang the nappy!
As bees flee hame wi' lades o' treasure,
The minutes winged their way wi' pleasure –
Kings may be blest, but Tam was glorious,
O'er a' the ills o' life victorious!
  But pleasures are like poppies spread –
You seize the flower, its bloom is shed –
Or like the snow falls in the river,
A moment white, then melts for ever;
Or like the borealis race,
That flit ere you can point their place;
Or like the rainbow's lovely form
Evanishing amid the storm.
Nae man can tether time or tide –
The hour approaches Tam maun ride –
That hour, o' night's black arch the key-stane,
That dreary hour Tam mounts his beast in,
And sic a night he taks the road in
As ne'er poor sinner was abroad in.
The wind blew as 'twad blawn its last;
The rattling showers rose on the blast;
The speedy gleams the darkness swallowed;
Loud, deep, and lang the thunder bellowed –
That night, a child might understand,
The Deil had business on his hand!
Weel mounted on his grey mare Meg
(Better never lifted leg)
Tam skelpit on through dub and mire,
Despising wind, and rain, and fire;
Whiles holding fast his guid blue bonnet,
Whiles crooning o'er some auld Scots sonnet,
Whiles glow'ring round wi' prudent cares,
Lest bogles catch him unawares!
Kirk-Alloway was drawing nigh,
Whare ghaists and houlets nightly cry.

51 *rair* roar. **55** *lades* loads.
65 *That hour . . . the key-stane* The darkest hour (keystone) in the black arch of night. **73** *as 'twad blawn* as if it would have blown.
81 *skelpit on through dub and mire* hurried on through pool and bog.
83 *Whiles* At times. **84** *sonnet* song. **88** *houlets* owls.

By this time he was cross the ford,
Whare in the snaw the chapman smoored;
And past the birks and meikle stane,
Whare drunken Charlie brak's neck-bane;
And through the whins, and by the cairn,
Whare hunters fand the murdered bairn;
And near the thorn, aboon the well,
Whare Mungo's mither hanged hersel.
Before him Doon pours all his floods;
The doubling storm roars through the woods;
The lightning's flash from pole to pole;
Near and more near the thunders roll –
When, glimmering through the groaning trees,
Kirk-Alloway seemed in a bleeze:
Through ilka bore the beams were glancing,
And loud resounded mirth and dancing.
Inspiring bold John Barleycorn,
What dangers thou canst make us scorn!
Wi' tippenny, we fear nae evil;
Wi' usquabae, we'll face the Devil!
The swats sae reamed in Tammie's noddle,
Fair play, he cared na deils a boddle.
But Maggie stood, right sair astonished,
Till, by the heel and hand admonished,
She ventured forward on the light,
And, wow, Tam saw an unco sight! –
Warlocks and witches in a dance –
Nae cotillion, brent new frae France,
But hornpipes, jigs, strathspeys and reels,
Put life and mettle in their heels.
A winnock-bunker in the east,
There sat Auld Nick, in shape o' beast
(A tousie tyke, black, grim, and large) –
To gie them music was his charge.
He screwed the pipes and gart them skirl,
Till roof and rafters a' did dirl.

90 *smoored* smothered. **92** *brak's neck-bane* broke his neck-bone.
93 *whins* gorse bushes. **95** *aboon* above. **103** *ilka bore* every chink.
107 *tippenny* tuppenny ale. **108** *usquabae* whisky.
110 *Fair play . . . a boddle* To be fair to him, he didn't care a farthing for devils.
116 *brent new* brand new.
119 *A winnock-bunker in the east* On a window-seat at the east end of the church.
121 *tyke* dog. **123** *screwed* tuned. **124** *dirl* ring.

Coffins stood round, like open presses,
That shawed the dead in their last dresses;
And, by some devilish cantraip sleight,
Each in its cauld hand held a light –
By which heroic Tam was able
To note upon the haly table,
A murderer's banes, in gibbet-airns;
Twa span-lang, wee, unchristened bairns;
A thief new-cutted frae a rape
(Wi' his last gasp his gab did gape);
Five tomahawks wi' bluid red-rusted;
Five scymitars wi' murder crusted;
A garter which a babe had strangled;
A knife a father's throat had mangled,
Whom his ain son o' life bereft –
The grey-hairs yet stack to the heft! –
Wi' mair of horrible and awefu',
Which even to name wad be unlawfu'.
As Tammie glowred, amazed and curious,
The mirth and fun grew fast and furious;
The piper loud and louder blew,
The dancers quick and quicker flew,
They reeled, they set, they crossed, they cleekit.
Till ilka carlin swat and reekit,
And coost her duddies to the wark,
And linket at it in her sark!
Now Tam, oh Tam – had thae been queans,
A' plump and strapping in their teens –
Their sarks, instead o' creeshie flannen,
Been snaw-white seventeen-hunder linen,
Thir breeks o' mine (my only pair
That ance were plush, o' guid blue hair),
I wad hae gi'en them off my hurdies
For ae blink o' the bonnie burdies!

125 *presses* cupboards. **127** *cantraip* magic. **130** *haly table* altar.
131 *gibbet-airns* gibbet-irons (used to hold the body together as it decomposed).
143 *glowred* gazed. **147** *cleekit* linked.
148 *Till ilka carlin swat and reekit* Till every witch sweated and steamed.
149 *And coost . . . the wark* And cast off her outer clothing in the process.
150 *sark* shift. **153** *creeshie flanners* greasy flannel.
154 *seventeen-hunder linen* fine linen (with 1,700 threads to the width).
156 *ance were plush* once were velvet. **157** *hurdies* buttocks.
158 *bonie burdies* bonny lasses.

But withered beldams, auld and droll,
Rigwoodie hags wad spean a foal,
Louping and flinging on a crummock,
I wonder did na turn thy stomach!
  But Tam kend what was what fu' brawlie:
There was ae winsome wench and wawlie
That night enlisted in the core,
Lang after kend on Carrick shore –
For monie a beast to dead she shot,
An' perished monie a bonnie boat,
And shook baith meikle corn and bear,
And kept the country-side in fear!
Her cutty sark, o' Paisley harn,
That while a lassie she had worn,
In longitude though sorely scanty,
It was her best, and she was vauntie.
Ah, little kend thy reverend grannie,
That sark she coft for her wee Nannie,
Wi' twa pund Scots ('twas a' her riches),
Wad ever graced a dance of witches!
  But here my Muse her wing maun cour,
Sic flights are far beyond her power –
To sing how Nannie lap and flang
(A souple jade she was and strang),
And how Tam stood like ane bewitched,
And thought his very een enriched!
Even Satan glowred, and fidged fu' fain,
And hotched and blew wi' might and main;
Till – first ae caper, syne anither –
Tam tint his reason a' thegither,
And roars out: 'Weel done, Cutty-sark!'
And in an instant all was dark;
And scarcely had he Maggie rallied,
When out the hellish legion sallied.
As bees bizz out wi' angry fyke,
When plundering herds assail their byke;

160 *Rigwoodie hags wad spean a foal* Withered hags who would put a foal off its food. **161** *crummock* crook. **164** *wawlie* plump. **165** *core* dance.
168 *perished* sank. **169** *corn and bear* oats and barley.
171 *Her cutty sark, o' Paisley harn* Her scanty shift of Paisley linen.
172 *while* since. **174** *vauntie* proud of it. **176** *coft* bought.
179 *maun cour* must stoop (cower). **181** *lap* leaped. **184** *een* eyes.
185 *fidged fu' fain* twitched with excitement. **186** *hotched* jerked.
194 *herds assail their byke* shepherds attack their hive.

As open pussie's mortal foes,
When, pop! she starts before their nose;
As eager runs the market-crowd,
When 'Catch the thief!' resounds aloud –
So Maggie runs; the witches follow,
Wi' monie an eldritch skriech and hollo!
   Ah, Tam! Ah, Tam! thou'll get thy fairin –
In hell they'll roast thee like a herrin!
In vain thy Kate awaits thy comin –
Kate soon will be a woefu' woman!
Now, do thy speedy utmost, Meg,
And win the key-stane of the brig;
There, at them thou thy tail may toss,
A running stream they dare na cross!
But ere the key-stane she could make,
The fient a tail she had to shake –
For Nannie, far before the rest,
Hard upon noble Maggie prest,
And flew at Tam wi' furious ettle!
But little wist she Maggie's mettle –
Ae spring brought off her master hale,
But left behind her ain grey tail:
The carlin claught her by the rump,
And left poor Maggie scarce a stump!
   Now, wha this tale o' truth shall read,
Ilk man, and mother's son, take heed:
Whene'er to drink you are inclined,
Or cutty sarks run in your mind,
Think, ye may buy the joys o'er dear –
Remember Tam o' Shanter's mare!

195 *As open pussie's mortal foes* As the hare's (pussy's) enemies give tongue ('open'). **201** *fairin* reward.
206 *key-stane of the brig* the centre (keystone) of the bridge.
210 *The fient . . . to shake* The devil a tail she has left to shake.
213 *ettle* intent. **215** *hale* whole. **217** *claught* clutched.

4. GOTTFRIED BÜRGER (trans. WILLIAM TAYLOR, 1796)

(i) *Lenora*

At break of day, with frightful dreams
   Lenora struggled sore:
'My William, art thou slaine', say'd she,
   'Or dost thou love no more?'

He went abroade with Richard's host,
   The Paynim foes to quell;
But he no word to her had writt,
   An he were sick or well.

With sowne of trump, and beat of drum,
   His fellow-soldyers come –
Their helmes bydeckt with oaken boughs,
   They seeke their long'd-for home.

And ev'ry roade and ev'ry lane
   Was full of old and young,
To gaze at the rejoicing band,
   To hail with gladsome toung.

'Thank God!' their wives and children saide,
   'Welcome!' the brides did saye;
But greete or kiss Lenora gave
   To none upon that daye!

She askte of all the passing traine
   For him she wisht to see,
But none of all the passing traine
   Could tell if livéd hee.

And when the soldyers all were bye
   She tore her raven haire,
And cast herself upon the growne
   In furious despaire.

Her mother ran and lyfte her up,
   And claspéd in her arme:
'My child, my child, what dost thou ail?
   God shield thy life from harm!'

'O mother, mother, William's gone!
   What's all besyde to me?
There is no mercye, sure, above –
   All, all were spar'd but hee!'

'Kneel downe, thy paternoster saye,
   'Twill calm thy troubled spright!
The Lord is wyse, the Lord is good;
   What hee hath done is right.'

'O mother, mother, say not so!
   Most cruel is my fate –
I prayde, and prayde, but watte avayl'd?
   'Tis now, alas! too late.'

'Our Heavenly Father, if we praye,
   Will help a suff'ring childe –
Go take the holy sacrament,
   So shall thy grief grow milde.'

'O mother, what I feel within
   No sacrament can staye –
No sacrament can teche the dead
   To bear the sight of daye!'

'May be, among the heathen folk
   Thy William false doth prove,
And puts away his faith and troth,
   And takes another love.

Then wherefore sorrow for his loss?
   Thy moans are all in vain:
And when his soul and body parte,
   His falsehode brings him paine.'

'O mother, mother! gone is gone –
   My hope is all forlorne –
The grave mie onlye safeguarde is:
   O, had I ne'er been borne!

Go out, go out, my lampe of life –
   In grislie darkness die!
There is no mercye, sure, above –
   For ever let me die.'

'Almighty God! O do not judge
   My poor unhappy childe;
She knows not what her lips pronounce,
   Her anguish makes her wilde.

My girl, forget thine earthly woe,
   And think on God and bliss;
For so, at least, shall not thy soule
   Its heavenly bridegroom miss.'

'O mother, mother! what is blisse,
   And what the fiendis celle?
With him 'tis Heaven any where,
   Without my William, Helle.

'Go out, go out, my lamp of life –
   In endless darkness die!
Without him I must loathe the earth,
   Without him scorne the skye.'

And so despaire did rave and rage
   Athwarte her boiling veins;
Against the providence of Heaven
   She hurlde her impious strains.

She beet her breaste, and wrung her hands,
   And rollde her tearlesse eye,
From rise of morne, till the pale stars
   Again did freeke the skye.

When harke! abroade she hearde the trampe
   Of nimble-hoofèd steed;
She hearde a knighte with clank alighte,
   And climb the staire in speede.

And soon she herde a tinkling hande,
   That twirlèd at the pin;
And thro' her door, that open'd not,
   These words were breathed in:

'What ho! what ho! thy dore undoe –
   Art watching or asleepe?
My love, dost yet remember mee,
   And dost thou laugh or weep?'

'Ah! William here so late at night!
   Oh! I have watchte and wak'd –
Whence dost thou come? For thy return
   My herte has sorely ak'd!'

'At midnight only we may ride –
   I come o'er land and sea –
I mounted late, but soone I go!
   Aryse, and come with me.'

'O William, enter first my bowre,
   And give me one embrace!
The blasts athwarte the hawthorne hiss –
   Awayte a little space.'

'The blasts athwarte the hawthorn hiss,
   I may not harboure here –
My spurre is sharpe, my courser pawes,
   My houre of flighte is nere.

All as thou lyest upon thy couch,
   Aryse, and mounte behinde –
To-night we'le ride a thousand miles,
   The bridal bed to finde!'

'How, ride to-night a thousand miles?
   Thy love thou dost bemocke –
Eleven is the stroke that still
   Rings on within the clocke.'

'Looke up! the moone is bright, and we
   Outstride the earthlie men –
I'll take thee to the bridal bed
   And night shall end but then.'

'And where is, then, thy house and home,
   And where thy bridal bed?'
' 'Tis narrow, silent, chilly, dark –
   Far hence I rest my head!'

'And is there any room for mee,
   Wherein that I may creepe?'
'There's room enough for thee and mee,
   Wherein that wee may sleepe.

All as thou ly'st upon thy couch,
   Aryse, no longer stop –
The wedding-guests thy coming waite,
   The chamber dore is ope!'

All in her sarke, as there she lay,
   Upon his horse she sprung;
And with her lily hands so pale
   About her William clung.

And hurry-skurry forth they go,
   Unheeding wet or dry;
And horse and rider snort and blow,
   And sparkling pebbles fly.

How swift the flood, the mead, the wood,
   Aright, aleft, are gone!
The bridges thunder as they pass,
   But earthlie sowne is none.

Tramp, tramp, across the land they speede;
   Splash, splash, across the see –
'Hurrah! the dead can ride apace;
   Dost feare to ride with mee?

The moone is bryghte, and blue the nyghte –
   Dost quake the blast to stem?
Dost shudder, mayde, to seeke the dead?'
'No, no, but what of them?

How glumlie sownes yon dirgye song!
   Night-ravens flappe the wing!
What knell doth slowlie toll ding-dong –
   The psalmes of death who sing?

It creeps, the swarthie funeral-traine,
   The corse is onn the beere;
Like croke of todes from lonely moores,
   The chaunte doth meet the eere.'

'Go, bear her corse when midnight's past,
With song, and fear, and wayle;
I've gott my wife, I take her home,
My howre of wedlocke hayl!

Lead forth, O clarke, the chaunting quire,
To swell our nuptial song:
Come, preaste, and reade the blessing soone –
For bed, for bed we long!'

They heede his calle, and husht the sowne –
The biere was seene no more –
And followde him ore feeld and flood
Yet faster than before.

Halloo! halloo! away they goe,
Unheeding wet or drye;
And horse and rider snort and blowe,
And sparkling pebbles flye.

How swifte the hill, how swifte the dale,
Aright, aleft, are gone!
By hedge and tree, by thorpe and towne,
They gallop, gallop on.

Tramp, tramp, across the land they speede,
Splash, splash, across the see –
'Hurrah! the dead can ride apace,
Dost fear to ride with mee?

Look up, look up, an airy crewe
In roundel daunces reele;
The moone is bryghte, and blue the nyghte,
Mayst dimlie see them wheele.

Come to, come to, ye gostlie crew,
Come to, and follow mee,
And daunce for us the wedding-daunce,
When we in bed shall be!'

And brush, brush, brush, the ghostlie crew
Come wheeling ore their heads,
All rustling like the wither'd leaves
That wyde the wirlwind spreads.

Halloo! halloo away they go,
   Unheeding wet or dry;
And horse and rider snort and blowe,
   And sparkling pebbles flye.

And all that in the moonshyne lay,
   Behynde them fled afar;
And backwarde scudded overhead
   The sky and every star.

Tramp, tramp, across the lande they speede,
   Splash, splash, across the see:
'Hurrah! the dead can ride apace –
   Dost fear to ride with mee?

I weene the cock prepares to crowe,
   The sand will soone be runne,
I snuffe the earlye morning aire –
   Downe, downe, our work is done!

The dead, the dead, can ryde apace
   (Oure wed-bed here is fit),
Oure race is ridde, oure journey ore,
   Oure endlesse union knit!'

And lo! an yren-grated gate
   Soon biggens to their viewe –
He crackte his whyppe: the clangynge boltes,
   The doores asunder flewe.

They pass, and 'twas on graves they trode –
   ''Tis hither we are bounde!' –
And many a tombstone gostlie white
   Lay inn the moonshyne round.

And when hee from his steede alytte,
   His armour, black as cinder,
Did moulder, moulder all awaye,
   As were it made of tinder.

His head became a naked scull –
   Nor haire nor eyne had hee –
His body grew a skeleton,
   Whylome so blythe of blee.

And att his drye and boney heele
   No spur was left to be;
And inn his witherde hande you might
   The scythe and houre-glasse see.

And lo! his steede did thin to smoke,
   And charnel fires outbreathe;
And pal'd, and bleach'd, then vanish'd quite
   The mayde from underneathe.

And hollow howlings hung in aire,
   And shrekes from vaults arose –.
Then knew the mayde she mighte no more
   Her living eyes unclose!

But onwarde to the Judgement-seat,
   Thro' myste and moonlighte dreare,
The gostlie crewe their flyghte persewe,
   And hollow inn her eare:

'Be patient! tho' thyne herte should breke,
   Arrayne not Heven's decree –
Thou nowe art of thie bodie refte,
   Thie soule forgiven bee!'

(ii) *The Lass of Fair Wone*

Beside the parson's bower of yew
   Why strays a troubled spright,
That peaks and pines, and dimly shines
   Thro' curtains of the night?

Why steals along the pond of toads
   A gliding fire so blue,
That lights a spot where grows no grass,
   Where falls no rain nor dew?

The parson's daughter once was good,
   And gentle as the dove,
And young and fair – and many came
   To win the damsel's love.

High o'er the hamlet, from the hill
   Beyond the winding stream,
The windows of a stately house
   In sheen of evening gleam.

There dwelt, in riot, rout, and roar,
   A lord so frank and free,
That oft, with inward joy of heart,
   The maid beheld his glee –

Whether he met the dawning day
   In hunting trim so fine,
Or tapers, sparkling from his hall,
   Beshone the midnight wine.

He sent the maid his picture, girt
   With diamond, pearl, and gold,
And silken-paper, sweet with musk,
   This gentle message told:

'Let go thy sweethearts, one and all!
   Shalt thou be basely woo'd,
That worthy art to gain the heart
   Of youths of noble blood?

The tale I would to thee bewray,
   In secret must be said:
At midnight-hour I'll seek thy bower –
   Fair lass, be not afraid!

And when the amorous nightingale
   Sings sweetly to his mate,
I'll pipe my quail-call from the field –
   Be kind, nor make me wait.'

In cap and mantle clad he came,
   At night, with lonely tread,
Unseen, and silent as a mist,
   And hush'd the dogs with bread.

And when the amorous nightingale
   Sung sweetly to his mate,
She heard his quail-call in the field,
   And, ah, ne'er made him wait!

The words he whisper'd were so soft
   They won her ear and heart –
How soon will she who loves believe!
   How deep a lover's art!

No lure, no soothing guise, he spar'd,
   To banish virtuous shame;
He call'd on holy God above,
   As witness to his flame.

He clasp'd her to his breast, and swore
   To be for ever true:
'O yield thee to my wishful arms,
   Thy choice thou shalt not rue!'

And while she strove, he drew her on,
   And led her to the bower,
So still, so dim – and round about
   Sweet smelt the beans in flower.

There beat her heart, and heav'd her breast,
   And pleaded every sense –
And there the glowing breath of lust
   Did blast her innocence!

But when the fragrant beans began
   Their sallow blooms to shed,
Her sparkling eyes their lustre lost;
   Her cheek, its roses fled:

And when she saw the pods increase,
   The ruddier cherries strain,
She felt her silken robe grow tight,
   Her waist new weight sustain.

And when the mowers went afield,
   The yellow corn to ted,
She felt her burden stir within,
   And shook with tender dread.

And when the winds of autumn hist
   Along the stubble-field;
Then could the damsel's piteous plight
   No longer be conceal'd.

Her sire, a harsh and angry man,
With furious voice revil'd:
'Hence from my sight! I'll none of thee –
I harbour not thy child!'

And fast, amid her fluttering hair,
With clenchéd fist he gripes,
And seiz'd a leathern thong, and lash'd
Her side with sounding stripes.

Her lily skin, so soft and white,
He ribb'd with bloody wales,
And thrust her out – tho' black the night,
Tho' sleet and storm assails.

Up the harsh rock, on flinty paths,
The maiden had to roam –
On tottering feet she grop'd her way,
And sought her lover's home.

'A mother thou has made of me,
Before thou mad'st a wife:
For this, upon my tender breast,
These livid stripes are rife –

Behold!' And then, with bitter sobs,
She sank upon the floor:
'Make good the evil thou has wrought –
My injur'd name restore!'

'Poor soul! I'll have thee hous'd and nurs'd!
Thy terrors I lament,
Stay here – we'll have some further talk –
The old one shall repent.

'I have no time to rest and wait –
That saves not my good name –
If thou with honest soul hast sworn,
O leave me not to shame;

But at the holy altar be
Our union sanctified:
Before the people and the priest
Receive me for thy bride.'

'Unequal matches must not blot
   The honours of my line –
Art thou of wealth or rank for me
   To harbour thee as mine?

What's fit and fair I'll do for thee:
   Shalt yet retain my love –
Shalt wed my huntsman – and we'll then
   Our former transports prove.'

'Thy wicked soul, hard-hearted man,
   May pangs in Hell await –
Sure, if not suited for thy bride,
   I was not for thy mate!

Go, seek a spouse of nobler blood,
   Nor God's just judgements dread!
So shall, ere long, some base-born wretch
   Defile thy marriage-bed –

Then, traitor, feel how wretched they
   In hopeless shame immerst –
Then smite thy forehead on the wall,
   While horrid curses burst!

Roll thy dry eyes in wild despair –
   Unsooth'd thy grinning woe!'
Thro' thy pale temples fire the ball,
   And sink to fiends below.

Collected then she started up
   And thro' the hissing sleet,
Thro' thorn and briar, thro' flood and mire,
   She fled with bleeding feet.

'Where now', she cry'd, 'my gracious God!
   What refuge have I left?'
And reach'd the garden of her home,
   Of hope in man bereft.

On hand and foot she feebly crawl'd
   Beneath the bower unblest,
Where withering leaves and gathering snow
   Prepar'd her only rest.

There rending pains and darting throes
   Assail'd her shuddering frame;
And from her womb a lovely boy
   With wail and weeping came.

Forth from her hair a silver pin
   With hasty hand she drew,
And prest against its tender heart,
   And the sweet babe she slew.

Erst when the act of blood was done,
   Her soul its guilt abhorr'd:
'My Jesus! what has been my deed?
   Have mercy on me, Lord!'

With bloody nails, beside the pond,
   Its shallow grave she tore:
'There rest in God – there shame and want
   Thou can'st not suffer more!

Me vengeance waits! My poor, poor child,
   Thy wound shall bleed afresh,
When ravens from the gallows tear
   Thy mother's mould'ring flesh!'

Hard by the bower her gibbet stands;
   Her skull is still to show –
It seems to eye the barren grave,
   Three spans in length below.

That is the spot where grows no grass,
   Where falls no rain nor dew,
Whence steals along the pond of toads
   A hovering fire so blue!

And nightly, when the ravens come,
   Her ghost is seen to glide;
Pursues and tries to quench the flame,
   And pines the pool beside.

5. MATTHEW 'MONK' LEWIS

Alonzo the Brave and the Fair Imogine

(1796)

A warrior so bold and a virgin so bright
  Conversed, as they sat on the green;
They gazed on each other with tender delight –
Alonzo the Brave was the name of the knight,
  The maid's was the Fair Imogine.

'And, oh!' said the youth, 'since to-morrow I go
  To fight in a far-distant land,
Your tears for my absence soon leaving to flow,
Some other will court you, and you will bestow
  On a wealthier suitor your hand!'

'Oh hush these suspicions', Fair Imogine said,
  'Offensive to love and to me!
For, if you be living, or if you be dead,
I swear by the Virgin, that none in your stead
  Shall husband of Imogine be.

And if e'er for another my heart should decide,
  Forgetting Alonzo the Brave,
God grant that, to punish my falsehood and pride,
Your ghost at the marriage may sit by my side –
May tax me with perjury, claim me as bride,
  And bear me away to the grave!'

To Palestine hastened the hero so bold,
  His love she lamented him sore –
But scarce had a twelvemonth elapsed when, behold,
A Baron all covered with jewels and gold
  Arrived at Fair Imogine's door.

His treasure, his presents, his spacious domain,
  Soon made her untrue to her vows:
He dazzled her eyes, he bewildered her brain,
He caught her affections so light and so vain –
  And carried her home as his spouse,

And now had the marriage been blest by the priest;
  The revelry now was begun;
The tables they groaned with the weight of the feast –
Nor yet had the laughter and merriment ceased,
  When the bell of the Castle tolled one!

Then first with amazement Fair Imogine found
  That a stranger was placed by her side:
His air was terrific; he uttered no sound;
He spoke not, he moved not, he looked not around,
  But earnestly gazed on the bride.

His vizor was closed, and gigantic his height;
  His armour was sable to view;
All pleasure and laughter were hushed at his sight;
The dogs, as they eyed him, drew back in affright;
  The lights in the chamber burnt blue!

His presence all bosoms appeared to dismay;
  The guests sat in silence and fear;
At length spoke the bride, while she trembled: 'I pray
Sir Knight, that your helmet aside you would lay,
  And deign to partake of our cheer.'

The lady is silent, the stranger complies –
  His vizor he slowly unclosed –
Oh, then what a sight met Fair Imogine's eyes!
What words can express her dismay and surprise
  When a skeleton's head was exposed!

All present then uttered a terrified shout –
  All turned with disgust from the scene –
The worms they crept in, and the worms they crept out,
And sported his eyes and his temples about,
  While the spectre addressed Imogine:

'Behold me, thou false one! Behold me!' he cried,
  'Remember Alonzo the Brave!
God grants that, to punish thy falsehood and pride,
My ghost at thy marriage should sit by thy side –
Should tax thee with perjury, claim thee as bride,
  And bear thee away to the grave!'

Thus saying, his arms round the lady he wound,
While loudly she shrieked in dismay,
Then sank with his prey through the wide-yawning ground –
Nor ever again was Fair Imogine found,
Or the spectre who bore her away.

Not long lived the Baron, and none since that time
To inhabit the Castle presume;
For chronicles tell that, by order sublime,
There Imogine suffers the pain of her crime,
And mourns her deplorable doom.

At midnight four times in each year does her sprite,
When mortals in slumber are bound,
Arrayed in her bridal apparel of white,
Appear in the hall with that skeleton-knight,
And shriek as he whirls her around.

While they drink out of skulls newly torn from the grave,
Dancing round them pale spectres are seen!
Their liquor is blood, and this horrible stave
They howl: 'To the health of Alonzo the Brave,
And his consort, the False Imogine!'

6. WILLIAM WORDSWORTH

The Thorn (March 1798; publ. *Lyrical Ballads*)

'There is a thorn, it looks so old
In truth you'd find it hard to say
How it could ever have been young,
It looks so old and grey.
Not higher than a two years' child
It stands erect, this agéd thorn.
No leaves it has, no thorny points;
It is a mass of knotted joints,
A wretched thing forlorn.
It stands erect, and like a stone
With lichens it is overgrown.

Like rock or stone, it is o'ergrown
With lichens to the very top,
And hung with heavy tufts of moss,
A melancholy crop.
Up from the earth these mosses creep,
And this poor thorn they clasp it round
So close you'd say that they were bent
With plain and manifest intent
To drag it to the ground,
And all had joined in one endeavour
To bury this poor thorn for ever.

High on a mountain's highest ridge
(Where oft the stormy winter gale
Cuts like a scythe, while through the clouds
It sweeps from vale to vale),
Not five yards from the mountain-path
This thorn you on your left espy;
And to the left, three yards beyond,
You see a little muddy pond
Of water, never dry.
I've measured it from side to side:
'Tis three feet long and two feet wide.

And close beside this agéd thorn
There is a fresh and lovely sight
A beauteous heap, a hill of moss,
Just half a foot in height.
All lovely colours there you see,
All colours that were ever seen,
And mossy network too is there,
As if by hand of lady fair
The work had woven been –
And cups, the darlings of the eye,
So deep is their vermilion dye.

Ah me, what lovely tints are there
Of olive-green and scarlet bright,
In spikes, in branches, and in stars,
Green, red, and pearly white!
This heap of earth o'ergrown with moss,
Which close beside the thorn you see
So fresh in all its beauteous dyes,
Is like an infant's grave in size –

As like as like can be –
But never, never, anywhere
An infant's grave was half so fair!

Now would you see this agéd thorn,
This pond and beauteous hill of moss,
You must take care and choose your time
The mountain when to cross.
For oft there sits, between the heap
That's like an infant's grave in size
And that same pond of which I spoke,
A woman in a scarlet cloak,
And to herself she cries,
"Oh misery! Oh misery!
Oh woe is me, oh misery!"

At all times of the day and night
This wretched woman thither goes,
And she is known to every star,
And every wind that blows.
And there beside the thorn she sits
When the blue daylight's in the skies,
And when the whirlwind's on the hill,
Or frosty air is keen and still,
And to herself she cries,
"Oh misery! Oh misery!
Oh woe is me, oh misery!"'

'Now wherefore thus, by day and night,
In rain, in tempest, and in snow,
Thus to the dreary mountain-top
Does this poor woman go?
And why sits she beside the thorn
When the blue daylight's in the sky,
Or when the whirlwind's on the hill,
Or frosty air is keen and still,
And wherefore does she cry –
Oh wherefore, wherefore, tell me why,
Does she repeat that doleful cry?'

'I cannot tell, I wish I could,
For the true reason no one knows;
But if you'd gladly view the spot,
The spot to which she goes –

The heap that's like an infant's grave,
The pond and thorn, so old and grey –
Pass by her door ('tis seldom shut)
And if you see her in her hut,
Then to the spot away!
I never heard of such as dare
Approach the spot when she is there!'

'But wherefore to the mountain-top
Can this unhappy woman go,
Whatever star is in the skies,
Whatever wind may blow?'
'Nay, rack your brain, 'tis all in vain!
I'll tell you everything I know –
But to the thorn, and to the pond
Which is a little step beyond,
I wish that you would go:
Perhaps when you are at the place
You something of her tale may trace.

I'll give you the best help I can:
Before you up the mountain go,
Up to the dreary mountain-top,
I'll tell you all I know.
'Tis now some two-and-twenty years
Since she (her name is Martha Ray)
Gave with a maiden's true good will
Her company to Stephen Hill,
And she was blithe and gay –
And she was happy, happy still
Whene'er she thought of Stephen Hill.

And they had fixed the wedding-day –
The morning that must wed them both –
But Stephen to another maid
Had sworn another oath,
And with this other maid to church
Unthinking Stephen went.
Poor Martha, on that woeful day
A cruel, cruel fire, they say,
Into her bones was sent –
It dried her body like a cinder,
And almost turned her brain to tinder!

They say, full six months after this,
While yet the summer-leaves were green,
She to the mountain-top would go,
And there was often seen.
'Tis said a child was in her womb,
As now to any eye was plain:
She was with child and she was mad –
Yet often she was sober sad
From her exceeding pain.
Oh me, ten thousand times I'd rather
That he had died, that cruel father!

Sad case for such a brain to hold
Communion with a stirring child –
Sad case, as you may think, for one
Who had a brain so wild!
Last Christmas when we talked of this,
Old Farmer Simpson did maintain
That in her womb the infant wrought
About its mother's heart, and brought
Her senses back again;
And when at last her time drew near,
Her looks were calm, her senses clear.

No more I know, I wish I did,
And I would tell it all to you –
For what became of this poor child
There's none that ever knew;
And if a child was born or no,
There's no one that could ever tell;
And if 'twas born alive or dead,
There's no one knows, as I have said –
But some remember well
That Martha Ray about this time
Would up the mountain often climb.

And all that winter, when at night
The wind blew from the mountain-peak,
'Twas worth your while, though in the dark,
The churchyard-path to seek;
For many a time and oft were heard
Cries coming from the mountain-head.
Some plainly living voices were,
And others (I've heard many swear)

Were voices of the dead –
I cannot think, whate'er they say,
They had to do with Martha Ray.

But that she goes to this old thorn,
The thorn which I've described to you,
And there sits in a scarlet cloak,
I will be sworn is true.
For one day with my telescope,
To view the ocean wide and bright
(When to this country first I came,
Ere I had heard of Martha's name),
I climbed the mountain's height;
A storm came on, and I could see
No object higher than my knee.

'Twas mist and rain, and storm and rain!
No screen, no fence, could I discover –
And then the wind, in faith it was
A wind full ten times over!
I looked around, I thought I saw
A jutting crag, and off I ran
Head-foremost through the driving rain
The shelter of the crag to gain,
And, as I am a man,
Instead of jutting crag I found
A woman seated on the ground.

I did not speak – I saw her face –
Her face it was enough for me!
I turned about and heard her cry,
"Oh misery! Oh misery!"
And there she sits, until the moon
Through half the clear blue sky will go;
And when the little breezes make
The waters of the pond to shake
(As all the country know),
She shudders, and you hear her cry,
"Oh misery! Oh misery!"'

'But what's the thorn, and what's the pond,
And what's the hill of moss to her?
And what's the creeping breeze that comes
The little pond to stir?'

'I cannot tell, but some will say
She hanged her baby on the tree;
Some say she drowned it in the pond,
Which is a little step beyond;
But all and each agree
The little babe was buried there,
Beneath that hill of moss so fair.

I've heard the scarlet moss is red
With drops of that poor infant's blood –
But kill a new-born infant thus,
I do not think she could!
Some say, if to the pond you go
And fix on it a steady view,
The shadow of a babe you trace,
A baby and a baby's face,
And that it looks at you –
Whene'er you look on it, 'tis plain
The baby looks at you again.

And some had sworn an oath that she
Should be to public justice brought;
And for the little infant's bones
With spades they would have sought.
But then the beauteous hill of moss
Before their eyes began to stir,
And for full fifty yards around
The grass it shook upon the ground –
But all do still aver
The little babe is buried there,
Beneath that hill of moss so fair.

I cannot tell how this may be,
But plain it is the thorn is bound
With heavy tufts of moss that strive
To drag it to the ground.
And this I know, full many a time
When she was on the mountain high,
By day, and in the silent night
When all the stars shone clear and bright,
That I have heard her cry,
"Oh misery! Oh misery!
Oh woe is me, oh misery!"'

7. SAMUEL TAYLOR COLERIDGE

Christabel, Part I (April 1798; publ. 1816)

'Tis the middle of night by the Castle-clock,
And the owls have awakened the crowing cock:
Tu-whit! Tu-whoo!
And hark, again! the crowing cock,
How drowsily it crew.

Sir Leoline, the Baron rich,
Hath a toothless mastiff bitch;
From her kennel beneath the rock
She makes answer to the clock,
Four for the quarters, and twelve for the hour –
Ever and aye, moonshine or shower,
Sixteen short howls, not over loud
(Some say, she sees my Lady's shroud).

Is the night chilly and dark?
The night is chilly, but not dark.
The thin grey cloud is spread on high –
It covers but not hides the sky.
The moon is behind, and at the full,
And yet she looks both small and dull.
The night is chill, the cloud is grey –
'Tis a month before the month of May,
And the spring comes slowly up this way.

The lovely lady, Christabel,
Whom her father loves so well,
What makes her in the wood so late,
A furlong from the Castle-gate?
She had dreams all yesternight
Of her own betrothéd knight –
Dreams that made her moan and leap
As on her bed she lay in sleep –
And she in the midnight-wood will pray
For the weal of her lover that's far away.

She stole along, she nothing spoke,
The breezes they were still also,
And naught was green upon the oak
But moss and rarest mistletoe;

She kneels beneath the huge oak-tree,
And in silence prayeth she.

The lady leaps up suddenly,
The lovely lady, Christabel!
It moaned as near, as near can be,
But what it is she cannot tell –
On the other side it seems to be,
Of the huge, broad-breasted, old oak-tree!

The night is chill; the forest bare;
Is it the wind that moaneth bleak?
There is not wind enough in the air
To move away the ringlet-curl
From the lovely lady's cheek –
There is not wind enough to twirl
The one red leaf, the last of its clan,
That dances as often as dance it can,
Hanging so light, and hanging so high,
On the topmost twig that looks up at the sky.

Hush, beating heart of Christabel –
Jesu, Maria, shield her well!
She folded her arms beneath her cloak,
And stole to the other side of the oak.
What sees she there?

There she sees a damsel bright,
Drest in a silken robe of white;
Her neck, her feet, her arms, bare,
And the jewels disordered in her hair.
I guess, 'twas frightful there to see
A lady so richly clad as she –
Beautiful exceedingly!

'Mary mother, save me now!'
Said Christabel, 'and who art thou?'

The lady strange made answer meet,
And her voice was faint and sweet:
'Have pity on my sore distress –
I scarce can speak for weariness –

Stretch forth thy hand, and have no fear!'
Said Christabel, 'How camest thou here?'
And the lady, whose voice was faint and sweet,
Did thus pursue her answer meet:

'My sire is of a noble line,
And my name is Geraldine;
Five warriors seized me yestermorn,
Me, even me, a maid forlorn –
They choked my cries with force and fright,
And tied me on a palfrey white.
The palfrey was as fleet as wind,
And they rode furiously behind.
They spurred amain, their steeds were white –
And once we crossed the shade of night.
As sure as Heaven shall rescue me,
I have no thought what men they be;
Nor do I know how long it is
(For I have lain in fits, I wis)
Since one, the tallest of the five,
Took me from the palfrey's back,
A weary woman, scarce alive.
Some muttered words his comrades spoke:
He placed me underneath this oak,
He swore they would return with haste –
Whither they went I cannot tell.
I thought I heard, some minutes past,
Sounds as of a castle-bell.
Stretch forth thy hand (thus ended she),
And help a wretched maid to flee.'

Then Christabel stretched forth her hand,
And comforted fair Geraldine,
Saying that she should command
The service of Sir Leoline,
And straight be convoyed, free from thrall,
Back to her noble father's hall.

So up she rose, and forth they passed
With hurrying steps, yet nothing fast.
Her lucky stars the lady blest,
And Christabel she sweetly said:

'All our household are at rest,
Each one sleeping in his bed;
Sir Leoline is weak in health,
And may not well awakened be,
So to my room we'll creep in stealth,
And you tonight must sleep with me.'

They crossed the moat, and Christabel
Took the key that fitted well;
A little door she opened straight,
All in the middle of the gate –
The gate that was ironed within and without,
Where an army in battle-array had marched out.
The lady sank, belike through pain,
And Christabel with might and main
Lifted her up, a weary weight,
Over the threshold of the gate –
Then the lady rose again,
And moved as she were not in pain.

So free from danger, free from fear,
They crossed the court – right glad they were!
And Christabel devoutly cried
To the lady by her side,
'Praise we the Virgin all divine
Who hath rescued thee from thy distress!'
'Alas, alas!' said Geraldine,
'I cannot speak for weariness.'
So free from danger, free from fear,
They crossed the court – right glad they were!

Outside her kennel, the mastiff old
Lay fast asleep, in moonshine cold.
The mastiff old did not awake,
Yet she an angry moan did make!
And what can ail the mastiff bitch?
Never till now she uttered yell
Beneath the eye of Christabel –
Perhaps it is the owlet's scritch,
For what can ail the mastiff bitch?

They passed the hall, that echoes still,
Pass as lightly as you will!
The brands were flat, the brands were dying,
Amid their own white ashes lying;

But when the lady passed there came
A tongue of light, a fit of flame,
And Christabel saw the lady's eye –
And nothing else saw she thereby,
Save the boss of the shield of Sir Leoline tall,
Which hung in a murky old niche in the wall.
'Oh softly tread', said Christabel,
'My father seldom sleepeth well.'

Sweet Christabel her feet she bares,
And they are creeping up the stairs
(Now in glimmer, and now in gloom),
And now they pass the Baron's room,
As still as death, with stifled breath!
And now have reached her chamber-door,
And now with eager feet press down
The rushes of her chamber-floor.

The moon shines dim in the open air,
And not a moonbeam enters here;
But they without its light can see
The chamber carved so curiously –
Carved with figures strange and sweet,
All made out of the carver's brain,
For a lady's chamber meet:
The lamp with twofold silver chain
Is fastened to an angel's feet.

The silver lamp burns dead and dim;
But Christabel the lamp will trim –
She trimmed the lamp, and made it bright,
And left it swinging to and fro,
While Geraldine, in wretched plight,
Sank down upon the floor below.

'Oh weary lady, Geraldine,
I pray you, drink this cordial wine!
It is a wine of virtuous powers –
My mother made it of wild flowers.'

'And will your mother pity me,
Who am a maiden most forlorn?'
Christabel answered: 'Woe is me!
She died the hour that I was born.

I have heard the gray-haired friar tell
How on her deathbed she did say
That she should hear the Castle-bell
Strike twelve upon my wedding-day –
Oh mother dear, that thou wert here!'
'I would', said Geraldine, 'she were!'

But soon with altered voice, said she,
'Off, wandering mother! Peak and pine!
I have power to bid thee flee.'
Alas, what ails poor Geraldine?
Why stares she with unsettled eye?
Can she the bodiless dead espy?
And why with hollow voice cries she,
'Off, woman, off! This hour is mine –
Though thou her guardian spirit be,
Off, woman, off! – 'tis given to me.'

Then Christabel knelt by the lady's side,
And raised to Heaven her eyes so blue –
'Alas!' said she, 'this ghastly ride,
Dear lady, it hath wildered you!'
The lady wiped her moist cold brow,
And faintly said, ' 'Tis over now!'

Again the wild-flower wine she drank:
Her fair large eyes 'gan glitter bright,
And from the floor whereon she sank
The lofty lady stood upright –
She was most beautiful to see,
Like a lady of a far countree!

And thus the lofty lady spake –
'All they who live in the upper sky,
Do love you, holy Christabel!
And you love them, and for their sake
And for the good which me befel,
Even I in my degree will try,
Fair maiden, to requite you well.
But now unrobe yourself, for I
Must pray, ere yet in bed I lie.'

Quoth Christabel, 'So let it be!
And as the lady bade, did she.
Her gentle limbs did she undress,
And lay down in her loveliness.

But through her brain, of weal and woe
So many thoughts moved to and fro
That vain it were her lids to close;
So half-way from the bed she rose,
And on her elbow did recline
To look at the lady Geraldine.

Beneath the lamp the lady bowed,
And slowly rolled her eyes around;
Then, drawing in her breath aloud
Like one that shuddered, she unbound
The cincture from beneath her breast.
Her silken robe and inner vest
Dropt to her feet, and, full in view,
Behold her bosom and half her side –
A sight to dream of, not to tell!
And she is to sleep with Christabel.

[Yet Geraldine nor speaks nor stirs;
Ah! what a stricken look was hers!
Deep from within she seems half-way
To lift some weight with sick assay,
And eyes the maid and seeks delay –
Then suddenly, as one defied,
Collects herself in scorn and pride,]
And lay down by the maiden's side!
And in her arms the maid she took,
        Ah wel-a-day!
And with low voice and doleful look
These words did say:
'In the touch of this bosom there worketh a spell,
Which is lord of thy utterance, Christabel!
Thou knowest to-night, and wilt know to-morrow,
This mark of my shame, this seal of my sorrow;
        But vainly thou warrest,
          For this is alone in
        Thy power to declare,

That in the dim forest
Thou heardst a low moaning,
And foundst a bright lady, surpassingly fair;
And didst bring her home with thee in love and in charity,
To shield her and shelter her from the damp air.'

8. ROBERT SOUTHEY

The Old Woman of Berkeley (1799)

The raven croaked as she sat at her meal
And the Old Woman knew what she said,
And she grew pale at the raven's tale
And sickened and went to her bed!

'Now fetch me my children, and fetch them with speed',
The Old Woman of Berkeley said –
'The Monk, my son, and my daughter the Nun,
Bid them hasten, or I shall be dead.'

The Monk, her son, and her daughter the Nun
Their way to Berkeley went,
And they have brought, with pious thought,
The holy sacrament.

The Old Woman shrieked as they entered the door,
And she cried with a voice of despair:
'Now take away the sacrament,
For its presence I cannot bear!'

Her lip it trembled with agony,
The sweat ran down her brow:
'I have tortures in store for evermore,
But spare me, my children, now!'

Away they sent the sacrament,
The fit it left her weak,
She looked at her children with ghastly eyes
And faintly struggled to speak:

'All kinds of sin I have rioted in,
And the Judgment now must be –
But I secured my children's souls,
Oh, pray, my children, for me!

I have 'nointed myself with infants' fat –
The fiends have been my slaves –
From sleeping babes I have sucked the breath,
And, breaking by charms the sleep of death,
I have called the dead from their graves.

And the Devil will fetch me now in fire,
My witchcrafts to atone;
And I who have troubled the dead man's grave
Shall never have rest in my own.

Bless, I entreat, my winding-sheet,
My children, I beg of you;
And with holy water sprinkle my shroud –
And sprinkle my coffin too!

And let me be chained in my coffin of stone,
And fasten it strong, I implore,
With iron bars – and with three chains
Chain it to the church-floor!

And bless the chains, and sprinkle them,
And let fifty priests stand round,
Who night and day the mass may say
When I lie on the ground.

And see that fifty choristers
Beside the bier attend me,
And day and night by the taper's light
With holy hymns defend me.

Let the church-bells all, both great and small,
Be tolled by night and day,
To drive from thence the fiends who come
To bear my body away.

And ever have the church-door barred,
   After the Evensong –
And I beseech you, children dear,
   Let the bars and bolts be strong.

And let this be three days and nights,
   My wretched corpse to save –
Till the fourth morning keep me safe,
   And then I may rest in my grave.'

The Old Woman of Berkeley laid her down,
   And her eyes grew deadly dim;
Short came her breath, and the struggle of death
   Did loosen every limb.

They blessed the Old Woman's winding-sheet
   With rites and prayers due;
With holy water they sprinkled her shroud,
   And they sprinkled her coffin too.

And they chained her in her coffin of stone,
   And with iron barred it down,
And in the church with three strong chains
   They chained it to the ground.

And they blessed the chains and sprinkled them,
   And fifty priests stood round
By night and day the mass to say
   Where she lay on the ground.

And fifty sacred choristers
   Beside the bier attend her,
Who day and night, by tapers' light,
   Should with holy hymns defend her.

To see the priests and choristers
   It was a goodly sight,
Each holding (as it were a staff)
   A taper burning bright.

And the church-bells all, both loud and small,
   Did toll so loud and long;
And they have barred the church-door hard,
   After the Evensong.

And the first night, the tapers' light
   Burnt steadily and clear;
But they, without, an hideous rout
   Of angry fiends could hear –

A hideous roar at the church-door
   Like a long thunder-peal –
And the priests they prayed, and the choristers sung,
   Louder in fearful zeal!

Loud tolled the bell, the priests prayed well,
   The tapers they burnt bright;
The Monk her son, and her daughter the Nun,
   They told their beads all night.

The cock he crew, the fiends they flew
   From the voice of the morning away;
Then undisturbed the choristers sing,
   And the fifty priests they pray:
As they had sung and prayed all night,
   They prayed and sung all day.

The second night the taper's light
   Burnt dismally and blue,
And everyone saw his neighbour's face
   Like a dead man's face to view.

And yells and cries, without, arise
   That the stoutest heart might shock,
And a deafening roaring, like a cataract pouring
   Over a mountain-rock.

The Monk and Nun they told their beads
   As fast as they could tell,
And aye as louder grew the noise
   The faster went the bell!

Louder and louder the choristers sung
   As they trembled more and more;
And the priests, as they prayed to Heaven for aid,
   They smote their breasts full sore.

The cock he crew, the fiends they flew
   From the voice of the morning away;
Then undisturbed the choristers sing,
   And the fifty priests they pray:
As they had sung and prayed all night,
   They prayed and sung all day.

The third night came, and the tapers' flame
   A frightful stench did make,
And they burnt as though they had been dipped
   In the burning brimstone lake!

And the loud commotion, like the rushing of ocean,
   Grew momently more and more;
And strokes as of a battering-ram
   Did shake the strong church-door.

The bellmen, they for very fear
   Could toll the bell no longer;
And still as louder grew the strokes,
   Their fear it grew the stronger.

The Monk and Nun forgot their beads –
   They fell on the ground in dismay –
There was not a single saint in Heaven
   To whom they did not pray!

And the choristers' song, which late was so strong,
Faltered with consternation,
For the church did rock as an earthquake-shock
   Uplifted its foundation.

And a sound was heard like the trumpet-blast
   That shall one day wake the dead;
The strong church-door could bear no more,
   And the bolts and the bars they fled;

And the tapers' light was extinguished quite
   And the choristers faintly sung;
And the priests dismayed, panted and prayed,
And on all saints in Heaven for aid
   They called with trembling tongue!

And in He came with eyes of flame,
  The Devil to fetch the dead,
And all the church with his presence glowed
  Like a fiery furnace red.

He laid his hand on the iron chains,
  And like flax they mouldered asunder,
And the coffin-lid, which was barred so firm,
  He burst with his voice of thunder.

And he bade the old Woman of Berkeley rise,
  And come with her master away –
A cold sweat started on that cold corpse
  At the voice she was forced to obey!

She rose on her feet in her winding-sheet,
  Her dead flesh quivered with fear,
And a groan like that which the Old Woman gave
  Never did mortal hear!

She followed her Master to the church-door –
  There stood a black horse there,
His breath was red like furnace-smoke,
  His eyes like a meteor's glare.

The Devil he flung her on the horse,
  And he leapt up before,
And away like the lightning's speed they went,
  And she was seen no more.

They saw her no more, but her cries
  For four miles round they could hear,
And children at rest at their mother's breast
  Started, and screamed with fear!

9. MARY ROBINSON

The Haunted Beach (1800)

Upon a lonely desert beach
  Where the white foam was scattered,
A little shed upreared its head
  Though lofty barks were shattered.

The sea-weeds gathering near the door
  A sombre path displayed;
And, all around, the deafening roar
Re-echoed on the chalky shore,
  By the green billows made.

Above a jutting cliff was seen
  Where sea-birds hovered, craving;
And all around the crags were bound
  With weeds – for ever waving.
And here and there, a cavern wide
  Its shadowy jaws displayed;
And near the sands, at ebb of tide,
A shivered mast was seen to ride
  Where the green billows strayed.

And often, while the moaning wind
  Stole o'er the summer ocean,
The moonlight scene was all serene,
  The waters scarce in motion;
Then, while the smoothly slanting sand
  The tall cliff wrapped in shade,
The fisherman beheld a band
Of spectres gliding hand in hand –
  Where the green billows played.

And pale their faces were as snow,
  And sullenly they wandered;
And to the skies with hollow eyes
  They looked as though they pondered.
And sometimes, from their hammock-shroud,
  They dismal howlings made,
And while the blast blew strong and loud
The clear moon marked the ghastly crowd,
  Where the green billows played!

And then above the haunted hut
  The curlews screaming hovered;
And the low door, with furious roar,
  The frothy breakers covered.
For in the fisherman's lone shed

A murdered man was laid,
With ten wide gashes in his head,
And deep was made his sandy bed
Where the green billows played.

A shipwrecked mariner was he,
Doomed from his home to sever,
Who swore to be through wind and sea
Firm and undaunted ever!
And when the wave resistless rolled,
About his arm he made
A packet rich of Spanish gold,
And, like a British sailor bold,
Plunged where the billows played!

The spectre band, his messmates brave,
Sunk in the yawning ocean,
While to the mast he lashed him fast,
And braved the storm's commotion.
The winter moon upon the sand
A silvery carpet made,
And marked the sailor reach the land,
And marked his murderer wash his hand
Where the green billows played.

And since that hour the fisherman
Has toiled and toiled in vain;
For all the night the moony light
Gleams on the spectered main!
And when the skies are veiled in gloom,
The murderer's liquid way
Bounds o'er the deeply yawning tomb,
And flashing fires the sands illume,
Where the green billows play!

Full thirty years his task has been,
Day after day more weary;
For Heaven designed his guilty mind
Should dwell on prospects dreary.
Bound by a strong and mystic chain,
He has not power to stray;
But destined misery to sustain,
He wastes, in solitude and pain,
A loathsome life away.

10. WALTER SCOTT

The Lay of the Last Minstrel

(Canto II, stanzas 1–23) 1805

1

If thou wouldst view fair Melrose aright,
Go visit it by the pale moon-light;
For the gay beams of lightsome day
Gild, but to flout, the ruins grey.
When the broken arches are black in night,
And each shafted oriel glimmers white;
When the cold light's uncertain shower
Streams on the ruined central tower;
When buttress and buttress, alternately,
Seem framed of ebon and ivory;
When silver edges the imagery,
And the scrolls that teach thee to live and die;
When distant Tweed is heard to rave,
And the owlet to hoot o'er the dead man's grave;
Then go – but go alone the while –
Then view St David's ruined pile;
And, home returning, soothly swear,
Was never scene so sad and fair!

2

Short halt did Deloraine make there;
Little recked he of the scene so fair.
With dagger's hilt, on the wicket strong,
He struck full loud, and struck full long.
The porter hurried to the gate –
'Who knocks so loud, and knocks so late?'
'From Branksome I', the warrior cried;
And strait the wicket opened wide:
For Branksome's chiefs had in battle stood,
        To fence the rights of fair Melrose;
And lands and livings, many a rood,
        Had gifted the shrine for their souls' repose.

3

Bold Deloraine his errand said;
The porter bent his humble head;
With torch in hand, and foot unshod,
And noiseless step, the path he trod;

The archéd cloisters, far and wide,
Rang to the warrior's clanking stride;
Till, stooping low his lofty crest,
He entered the cell of the ancient priest,
And lifted his barréd aventayle,
To hail the Monk of St Mary's aisle.

4

'The Ladye of Branksome greets thee by me –
    Says that the fated hour is come,
And that to-night I shall watch with thee,
    To win the treasure of the tomb.'
From sackcloth couch the Monk arose,
    With toil his stiffened limbs he reared
(A hundred years had flung their snows
    On his thin locks and floating beard),

5

And strangely on the knight looked he,
    And his blue eyes gleamed wild and wide:
'And, darest thou, warrior, seek to see
    What Heaven and Hell alike would hide ?
My breast, in belt of iron pent,
    With shirt of hair and scourge of thorn,
For threescore years, in penance spent,
    My knees those flinty stones have worn –
Yet all too little to atone
For knowing what should ne'er be known.
Wouldst thou thy every future year
    In ceaseless prayer and penance drie,
Yet wait thy latter end with fear? –
    Then, daring warrior, follow me !'

6

'Penance, father, will I none!
Prayer know I hardly one –
For mass or prayer can I rarely tarry,
Save to patter an Avé Mary
When I ride on a Border foray –
Other prayer can I none
So speed me my errand, and let me be gone.'

7

Again on the Knight looked the Churchman old
        And again he sighed heavily;
For he had himself been a warrior bold,
        And fought in Spain and Italy.
And he thought on the days that were long since bye,
When his limbs were strong, and his courage was high;
Now, slow and faint, he led the way,
Where, cloistered round, the garden lay;
The pillared arches were over their head,
And beneath their feet were the bones of the dead.

8

Spreading herbs and flowerets bright,
Glistened with the dew of night;
Nor herb nor floweret glistened there,
But was carved in the cloister arches as fair.
        The Monk gazed long on the lovely moon,
Then into the night he lookéd forth;
        And red and bright the streamers light
            Were dancing in the glowing north.
        So had he seen, in fair Castile,
            The youth in glittering squadrons start;
        Sudden the flying jennet wheel,
            And hurl the unexpected dart.
He knew, by the streamers that shot so bright,
That spirits were riding the northern light.

9

By a steel-clenchéd postern-door,
        They entered now the chancel tall;
The darkened roof rose high aloof
        On pillars lofty, and light, and small;
The keystone, that locked each ribbéd aisle,
Was a fleur-de-lys, or a quatre-feuille;
The corbells were carved grotesque and grim;
And the pillars, with clustered shafts so trim,
With plinth and with capital flourished around,
Seemed bundles of lances which garlands had bound.

10

Full many a scutcheon and banner riven
Shook to the cold night-wind of heaven,
        Around the screenéd altar's pale;
And there the dying lamps did burn,

Before thy low and lonely urn,
Oh gallant chief of Otterburne,
And thine, dark knight of Liddesdale!
Oh fading honours of the dead!
Oh high ambition, lowly laid!

11

The moon on the east oriel shone,
Through slender shafts of shapely stone,
By foliaged tracery combined;
Thou wouldst have thought some fairy's hand,
'Twixt poplars straight, the osier wand,
In many a freakish knot, had twined –
Then framed a spell, when the work was done,
And changed the willow-wreaths to stone.
The silver light, so pale and faint,
Shewed many a prophet and many a saint,
Whose image on the glass was dyed;
Full in the midst, his cross of red
Triumphant Michael brandishéd,
And trampled the apostate's pride.
The moonbeam kissed the holy pane,
And threw on the pavement a bloody stain.

12

They sate them down on a marble stone
(A Scottish monarch slept below);
Thus spoke the Monk, in solemn tone:
'I was not always a man of woe,
For Paynim countries I have trod
And fought beneath the cross of God –
Now, strange to my eyes thine arms appear,
And their iron clang sounds strange to my ear.

13

In these far climes, it was my lot
To meet the wondrous Michael Scott;
A wizard of such dreaded fame,
That when, in Salamanca's cave,
Him listed his magic wand to wave,
The bells would ring in Notre Dame!
Some of his skill he taught to me;
And, warrior, I could say to thee
The words that clove Eildon hills in three,

And bridled the Tweed with a curb of stone;
But to speak them were a deadly sin;
And for having but thought them my heart within,
A treble penance must be done.

14

When Michael lay on his dying-bed,
His conscience was awakenéd;
He bethought him of his sinful deed,
And he gave me a sign to come with speed:
I was in Spain when the morning rose,
But I stood by his bed ere evening close!
The words may not again be said
That he spoke to me, on death-bed laid;
They would rend this Abbaye's massy nave,
And pile it in heaps above his grave.

15

I swore to bury his mighty book,
That never mortal might therein look;
And never to tell where it was hid,
Save at his chief of Branksome's need –
And when that need was past and o'er,
Again the volume to restore.
I buried him on St Michael's night,
When the bell tolled one, and the moon was bright;
And I dug his chamber among the dead,
Where the floor of the chancel was stainéd red,
That his patron's cross might over him wave,
And scare the fiends from the wizard's grave.

16

It was a night of woe and dread,
When Michael in the tomb I laid!
Strange sounds along the chancel past;
The banners waved without a blast!'
(Still spoke the Monk, when the bell tolled one –
I tell you, that a braver man
Than William of Deloraine, good at need,
Against a foe ne'er spurred a steed;
Yet somewhat was he chilled with dread,
And his hair did bristle upon his head.)

17

'Lo, warrior, now the cross of red
Points to the grave of the mighty dead;
Within it burns a wondrous light,
To chase the spirits that love the night:
That lamp shall burn unquenchably,
Until the eternal doom shall be.'
Slow moved the Monk to the broad flagstone,
Which the bloody cross was traced upon:
He pointed to a secret nook;
A bar from thence the warrior took;
And the Monk made a sign with his withered hand,
The grave's huge portal to expand.

18

With beating heart to the task he went
(His sinewy frame o'er the gravestone bent),
With bar of iron heaved amain,
Till the toil-drops fell from his brows like rain!
It was by dint of passing strength
That he moved the massy stone at length.
I would you had been there to see
How the light broke forth so gloriously –
Streamed upward to the chancel roof,
And through the galleries far aloof!
No earthly flame blazed e'er so bright:
It shone like Heaven's own blessḗd light,
        And, issuing from the tomb,
Shewed the Monk's cowl and visage pale,
Danced on the dark-browed Warrior's mail,
        And kissed his waving plume.

19

Before their eyes the wizard lay
As if he had not been dead a day,
His hoary beard in silver rolled
(He seemed some seventy winters old),
A palmer's amice wrapped him round,
With a wrought Spanish baldric bound,
        Like a pilgrim from beyond the sea;
His left hand held his book of might,
A silver cross was in his right;
        The lamp was placed beside his knee.

High and majestic was his look,
At which the fellest fiends had shook,
And all unruffled was his face –
They trusted his soul had gotten grace!

20

Often had William of Deloraine
Rode through the battle's bloody plain,
And trampled down the warriors slain,
    And neither known remorse or awe;
Yet now remorse and awe he owned:
His breath came thick, his head swam round,
    When this strange scene of death he saw!
Bewildered and unnerved he stood,
And the priest prayed fervently and loud –
With eyes averted prayéd he,
He might not endure the sight to see
Of the man he had loved so brotherly.

21

And when the priest his death-prayer had prayed,
Thus unto Deloraine he said:
'Now speed thee what thou hast to do,
Or, warrior, we may dearly rue;
For those thou mayest not look upon
Are gathering fast round the yawning stone!'
Then Deloraine, in terror, took
From the cold hand the mighty book,
With iron clasped and with iron bound –
He thought as he took it the dead man frowned,
But the glare of the sepulchral light
Perchance had dazzled the warrior's sight.

22

When the huge stone sunk o'er the tomb
The night returned, in double gloom,
For the moon had gone down and the stars were few,
And, as the Knight and Priest withdrew,
With wavering steps and dizzy brain,
They hardly might the postern gain.
'Tis said, as through the aisles they passed
They heard strange noises on the blast;

And through the cloister-galleries small,
Which at mid-height thread the chancel-wall,
Loud sobs, and laughter louder, ran –
And voices unlike the voice of man,
As if the fiends kept holiday
Because these spells were brought today.
I cannot tell how the truth may be,
I say the tale as ’twas said to me!

23

‘Now hie thee hence’, the father said,
‘And when we are on death-bed laid,
O may our dear Ladye, and sweet St John,
Forgive our souls for the deed we have done!’
The Monk returned him to his cell,
And many a prayer and penance sped –
When the Convent met at the noontide-bell,
The Monk of St Mary’s aisle was dead . . .

11. JAMES HOGG

The Wife of Crowle (1807)

And aye she sat by the cheek of the grate,
Pretending to shape and to sew;
But she looked at all that entered the hall
As if she would look them through.

Her hands she rung, and at times she sung
Some wild airs for the dead;
Then ’gan to tell a crazy tale –
She told it for a meed:

‘I once had a son, but now he is gone –
They tore my son from me –
His life-blood streamed where the cormorant screamed,
On the wild rocks girt by the sea.

So hard his lone bed, and unpillowed his head,
For the dark-sea cave is his urn;
The cliff-flowers weep o’er his slumbers so deep,
And the dead-lights over him burn.

Say what can restore the form that's no more,
  Or illumine the death-set eye?
Yes, a wild mother's tears, and a wild mother's prayers,
  A spirit may force from the sky!

When the sun had rose high, and the season gone by,
  My yearnings continued the same:
I prayed to Heaven both morning and even
  To send me my son – till he came!

One evening late by the chimney I sate:
  I dreamed of the times that were gone –
Of its chirrup so eerie the cricket was weary,
  All silent I sate and alone.

The fire burnt bright, and I saw by the light
  My own son enter the hall;
A white birchen wand he held in his hand,
  But no shadow had he on the wall.

He looked at the flame, as forward he came,
  All steadfast, and looked not away;
His motion was still as mist on the hill,
  And his colour like cold-white clay.

I knew him full well – but the tones of the bell
  Which quavered as midnight it rung
So stunned me I strove, but I could not move
  My hand, my foot, nor my tongue.

Blood-drops in a shower then fell on the floor
  From the roof, and they fell upon me:
No water their stain could wash out again –
  Those blood-drops still may you see!

His form still grew, and the flame burnt blue,
  I stretched out my arms to embrace;
But he turned his dead eye, so hollow and dry,
  And so wistfully gazed in my face,

That my head whirled round, and the walls and the ground
  All darkened – no more could I see –
But each finger's point, and each finger's joint,
  Grew thick as the joint of my knee.

I wakened ere day, but my son was away,
No word to me had he said;
Though my blood was boiling, and my heart recoiling,
To see him again still I prayed –

And often he has come to my lonely home,
In guise that might adamant melt:
He has offered his hand with expression so bland,
But that hand could never be felt.

I've oft seen him glide so close by my side,
On his grave-cloth the seams I could trace:
The blood from a wound trickled down to the ground,
And a napkin was over his face.

So oft have I seen that death-like mien
It has somewhat bewildered my brain;
Yet though chilled with affright at the terrible sight,
I long still to see it again!

12. GEORGE CRABBE

Peter Grimes (1810)

Methought the souls of all that I had murdered
Came to my tent, and every one did threat . . .
(Shakespeare, *Richard III*, V iii)

The times have been
That, when the brains were out, the man would die,
And there an end: but now they rise again,
With twenty mortal murders on their crowns,
And push us from our stools.
(Shakespeare, *Macbeth* III iv)

Old Peter Grimes made fishing his employ
(His wife he cabined with him and his boy)
And seemed that life laborious to enjoy:
To town came quiet Peter with his fish,
And had of all a civil word and wish.
He left his trade upon the Sabbath-day,
And took young Peter in his hand to pray;

But soon the stubborn boy from care broke loose,
At first refused, then added his abuse.
His father's love he scorned, his power defied,
But being drunk, wept sorely when he died.
   Yes, then he wept, and to his mind there came
Much of his conduct, and he felt the shame –
How he had oft the good old man reviled,
And never paid the duty of a child;
How, when the father in his Bible read,
He in contempt and anger left the shed.
'It is the word of life', the parent cried!
'This is the life itself', the boy replied.
And, while old Peter in amazement stood,
Gave the hot spirit to his boiling blood;
How he, with oath and furious speech, began
To prove his freedom and assert the man;
And when the parent checked his impious rage,
How he had cursed the tyranny of age –
Nay, once had dealt the sacrilegious blow
On his bare head, and laid his parent low.
The father groaned, 'If thou art old', said he,
And hast a son, thou wilt remember me:
Thy mother left me in a happy time,
Thou killedst not her! Heaven spares the double crime.'
On an inn-settle, in his maudlin grief,
This he revolved, and drank for his relief.
   Now lived the youth in freedom, but debarred
From constant pleasure, and he thought it hard –
Hard that he could not every wish obey,
But must awhile relinquish ale and play –
Hard that he could not to his cards attend,
But must acquire the money he would spend!
With greedy eye he looked on all he saw
(He knew not justice, and he laughed at law),
On all he marked he stretched his ready hand –
He fished by water and he filched by land!
Oft in the night has Peter dropped his oar,
Fled from his boat, and sought for prey on shore;
Oft up the hedgerow glided, on his back
Bearing the orchard's produce in a sack,
Or farm-yard load, tugged fiercely from the stack.
And as these wrongs to greater numbers rose,
The more he looked on all men as his foes.

He built a mud-walled hovel, where he kept
His various wealth, and there he oft-times slept;
But no success could please his cruel soul:
He wished for one to trouble and control –
He wanted some obedient boy to stand
And bear the blow of his outrageous hand,
And hoped to find in some propitious hour
A feeling creature subject to his power.
Peter had heard there were in London then
(Still have they being!) workhouse clearing-men,
Who, undisturbed by feelings just or kind,
Would parish-boys to needy tradesmen bind:
They in their want a trifling sum would take,
And toiling slaves of piteous orphans make.
   Such Peter sought, and when a lad was found,
The sum was dealt him, and the slave was bound.
Some few in town observed in Peter's trap
A boy, with jacket blue and woollen cap;
But none enquired how Peter used the rope,
Or what the bruise that made the stripling stoop;
None could the ridges on his back behold,
None sought him shivering in the winter's cold;
None put the question, 'Peter, dost thou give
The boy his food? What, man, the lad must live!
Consider, Peter, let the child have bread,
He'll serve thee better if he's stroked and fed.'
None reasoned thus, and some, on hearing cries,
Said calmly, 'Grimes is at his exercise.'
   Pinned, beaten, cold, pinched, threatened and abused,
His efforts punished and his food refused,
Awake tormented (soon aroused from sleep),
Struck if he wept, and yet compelled to weep,
The trembling boy dropped down and strove to pray,
Received a blow, and trembling turned away,
Or sobbed and hid his piteous face – while he,
The savage master, grinned in horrid glee!
He'd now the power he ever loved to show,
A feeling being subject to his blow.
Thus lived the lad, in hunger, peril, pain,
His tears despised, his supplications vain.
Compelled by fear to lie, by need to steal,
His bed uneasy and unblest his meal,

For three sad years the boy his tortures bore,
And then his pains and trials were no more.
'How died he, Peter?' when the people said,
He growled, 'I found him lifeless in his bed' –
Then tried for softer tone, and sighed, 'Poor Sam is dead.'
Yet murmurs were there, and some questions asked –
How he was fed, how punished, and how tasked?
Much they suspected, but they little proved,
And Peter passed untroubled and unmoved.
Another boy with equal ease was found,
The money granted, and the victim bound –
And what his fate? One night it chanced he fell
From the boat's mast and perished in her well,
Where fish were living kept, and where the boy,
So reasoned men, could not himself destroy.
'Yes, so it was', said Peter. 'In his play
(For he was idle both by night and day)
He climbed the mainmast and then fell below' –
Then showed his corpse, and pointed to the blow.
What said the jury? They were long in doubt,
But sturdy Peter faced the matter out;
So they dismissed him, saying at the time,
'Keep fast your hatchway when you've boys who climb.'
This hit the conscience, and he coloured more
Than for the closest questions put before.
Thus all his fears the verdict set aside,
And at the slave-shop Peter still applied.
Then came a boy of manners soft and mild –
Our seamen's wives with grief beheld the child;
All thought (the poor themselves) that he was one
Of gentle blood, some noble sinner's son,
Who had, belike, deceived some humble maid,
Whom he had first seduced and then betrayed.
However this, he seemed a gracious lad,
In grief submissive and with patience sad.
Passive he laboured, till his slender frame
Bent with his loads, and he at length was lame –
Strange that a frame so weak could bear so long
The grossest insult and the foulest wrong,
But there were causes: in the town they gave
Fire, food, and comfort, to the gentle slave;
And though stern Peter, with a cruel hand
And knotted rope, enforced the rude command,

Yet he considered what he'd lately felt,
And his vile blows with selfish pity dealt.
  One day such draughts the cruel fisher made,
He could not vend them in his borough-trade,
But sailed for London-mart. The boy was ill,
But ever humbled to his master's will,
And on the river, where they smoothly sailed,
He strove with terror and awhile prevailed –
But new to danger on the angry sea,
He clung affrightened to his master's knee.
The boat grew leaky and the wind was strong,
Rough was the passage and the time was long;
His liquor failed, and Peter's wrath arose –
No more is known, the rest we must suppose
Or learn of Peter. Peter says he spied
The stripling's danger and for harbour tried –
Meantime the fish, and then the apprentice, died.'
The pitying women raised a clamour round
And weeping said, 'Thou hast thy 'prentice drowned.'
  Now the stern man was summoned to the hall
To tell his tale before the burghers all –
He gave the account, professed the lad he loved,
And kept his brazen features all unmoved.
The mayor himself with tone severe replied:
'Henceforth with thee shall never boy abide.
Hire thee a freeman, whom thou durst not beat,
But who in thy despite will sleep and eat!
Free thou art now – again shouldst thou appear,
Thou'lt find thy sentence, like thy soul, severe.'
  Alas for Peter! Not a helping hand
(So was he hated) could he now command –
Alone he rowed his boat, alone he cast
His nets beside, or made his anchor fast.
To hold a rope, or hear a curse, was none –
He toiled and railed, he groaned and swore, alone.
Thus by himself compelled to live each day,
To wait for certain hours the tide's delay,
At the same time the same dull views to see:
The bounding marsh-bank and the blighted tree;
The water only, when the tides were high,
When low, the mud half-covered and half-dry;
The sun-burnt tar that blisters on the planks,
And bank-side stakes in their uneven ranks;

Heaps of entangled weeds that slowly float,
As the tide rolls by the impeded boat.
When tides were neap, and, in the sultry day,
Through the tall bounding mud-banks made their way,
Which on each side rose swelling, and below
The dark warm flood ran silently and slow,
There anchoring, Peter chose from man to hide,
There hang his head, and view the lazy tide
In its hot slimy channel slowly glide.
Where the small eels, that left the deeper way
For the warm shore, within the shallows play –
Where gaping mussels, left upon the mud,
Slope their slow passage to the fallen flood –
Here dull and hopeless he'd lie down and trace
How sidelong crabs had scrawled their crooked race,
Or sadly listen to the tuneless cry
Of fishing gull or clanging golden-eye.
What time the sea-birds to the marsh would come,
And the loud bittern, from the bullrush home,
Gave from the salt-ditch side the bellowing boom,
He nursed the feelings these dull scenes produce
And loved to stop beside the opening sluice
Where the small stream, confined in narrow bound,
Ran with a dull, unvaried, saddening sound –
Where all presented to the eye or ear
Oppressed the soul with misery, grief, and fear.
Besides these objects, there were places three
Which Peter seemed with certain dread to see:
When he drew near them he would turn from each,
And loudly whistle till he passed the reach.
A change of scene to him brought no relief:
In town, 'twas plain, men took him for a thief;
The sailors' wives would stop him in the street
And say, 'Now, Peter, thou'st no boy to beat!'
Infants at play, when they perceived him, ran,
Warning each other – 'That's the wicked man!'
He growled an oath, and in an angry tone
Cursed the whole place, and wished to be alone.
Alone he was, the same dull scenes in view,
And still more gloomy in his sight they grew.
Though man he hated, yet, employed alone
At bootless labour, he would swear and groan,
Cursing the shoals that glided by the spot
And gulls that caught them when his arts could not.

Cold nervous tremblings shook his sturdy frame,
And strange disease (he couldn't say the name);
Wild were his dreams, and oft he rose in fright,
Waked by his view of horrors in the night –
Horrors that would the sternest minds amaze,
Horrors that demons might be proud to raise.
And though he felt forsaken, grieved at heart
To think he lived from all mankind apart,
Yet, if a man approached, in terrors he would start.
   A winter passed since Peter saw the town,
And summer lodgers were again come down;
These, idly curious, with their glasses spied
The ships in bay (as anchored for the tide
The river's craft) the bustle of the quay –
And seaport views, which landsmen love to see.
One, up the river, had a man and boat
Seen day by day, now anchored, now afloat.
Fisher he seemed, yet used no net nor hook;
Of sea-fowl swimming by no heed he took,
But on the gliding waves still fixed his lazy look.
At certain stations he would view the stream,
As if he stood bewildered in a dream,
Or that some power had chained him for a time
To feel a curse or meditate on crime.
This known, some curious, some in pity, went,
And others questioned: 'Wretch, dost thou repent?'
He heard, he trembled, and in fear resigned
His boat. New terror filled his restless mind;
Furious he grew, and up the country ran,
And there they seized him – a distempered man.
   Him we received, and to a parish-bed,
Followed and cursed, the groaning man was led.
Here when they saw him, whom they used to shun –
A lost, lone man, so harassed and undone –
Our gentle females (ever prompt to feel)
Perceived compassion on their anger steal.
His crimes they could not from their memories blot,
But they were grieved, and trembled at his lot.
A priest too came, to whom his words are told –
And all the signs they shuddered to behold.
'Look! look!' they cried 'his limbs with horror shake,
And as he grinds his teeth, what noise they make!
How glare his angry eyes, and yet he's not awake!

See what cold drops upon his forehead stand,
And how he clenches that broad bony hand!'
  The priest attending found he spoke at times
As one alluding to his fears and crimes:
'It was the fall', he muttered, 'I can show
The manner how – I never struck a blow.'
And then aloud, 'Unhand me, free my chain.
On oath he fell – it struck him to the brain.
Why ask my father? That old man will swear
Against my life – besides, he wasn't there.
What, all agreed? Am I to die to-day?
My Lord, in mercy give me time to pray.'
Then as they watched him, calmer he became,
And grew so weak he couldn't move his frame,
But murmuring spake–while they could see and hear
The start of terror and the groan of fear –
See the large dew-beads on his forehead rise,
And the cold death-drop glaze his sunken eyes.
  Nor yet he died, but with unwonted force
Seemed with some fancied being to discourse.
He knew not us, or with accustomed art
He hid the knowledge, yet exposed his heart –
'Twas part confession and the rest defence,
A madman's tale, with gleams of waking sense.
'I'll tell you all', he said, 'the very day
When the old man first placed them in my way –
My father's spirit – he who always tried
To give me trouble, when he lived and died:
When he was gone he could not be content
To see my days in painful labour spent,
But would appoint his meetings, and he made
Me watch at these, and so neglect my trade.
  'Twas one hot noon, all silent, still, serene,
No living being had I lately seen;
I paddled up and down and dipped my net,
But (such his pleasure) I could nothing get –
A father's pleasure, when his toil was done,
To plague and torture thus an only son!
And so I sat and looked upon the stream,
How it ran on, and felt as in a dream –
But dream it was not. No! I fixed my eyes
On the mid stream and saw the spirits rise –
I saw my father on the water stand
And hold a thin pale boy in either hand,

And there they glided ghastly on the top
Of the salt flood, and never touched a drop.
I would have struck them, but they knew the intent
And smiled upon the oar, and down they went.
   Now, from that day, whenever I began
To dip my net, there stood the hard old man –
He and those boys! I humbled me and prayed
They would be gone – they heeded not, but stayed.
Nor could I turn, nor would the boat go by,
But, gazing on the spirits, there was I –
They bade me leap to death, but I was loath to die.
And every day, as sure as day arose,
Would these three spirits meet me ere the close;
To hear and mark them daily was my doom,
And "Come" they said, with weak sad voices, "Come!"
To row away, with all my strength I tried,
But there were they, hard by me in the tide,
The three unbodied forms – and "Come", still "Come" they cried!
   Fathers should pity – but this old man shook
His hoary locks, and froze me by a look!
Thrice, when I struck them, through the water came
A hollow groan, that weakened all my frame:
"Father", said I, "have mercy!" He replied
I know not what – the angry spirit lied!
"Didst thou not draw thy knife?" said he. 'Twas true,
But I had pity and my arm withdrew –
He cried for mercy, which I kindly gave,
But he has no compassion in his grave.
   There were three places, where they ever rose
(The whole long river has not such as those),
Places accurst, where if a man remain
He'll see the things which strike him to the brain –
And there they made me on my paddle lean
And look at them for hours. Accurséd scene,
When they would glide to that smooth eddy-space,
Then bid me leap and join them in the place –
And at my groans each little villain-sprite
Enjoyed my pains and vanished in delight!
   In one fierce summer-day, when my poor brain
Was burning hot, and cruel was my pain,
Then came this father-foe – and there he stood
With his two boys again, upon the flood.
There was more mischief in their eyes, more glee
In their pale faces when they glared at me!

Still did they force me on the oar to rest,
And when they saw me fainting and oppressed,
He, with his hand – the old man – scooped the flood,
And there came flame about him mixed with blood!
He bade me stoop and look upon the place,
Then flung the hot-red liquor in my face!
Burning it blazed, and then I roared for pain –
I thought the demons would have turned my brain.
   Still there they stood, and forced me to behold
A place of horrors (they cannot be told) –
Where the flood opened, there I heard the shriek
Of tortured guilt, no earthly tongue can speak:
"All days alike, for ever!" did they say,
"And unremitted torments every day!"
Yes, so they said.' But here he ceased, and gazed
On all around, affrightened and amazed.
And still he tried to speak, and looked in dread
Of frightened females gathering round his bed –
Then dropped exhausted, and appeared at rest,
Till the strong foe the vital powers possessed;
Then with an inward, broken voice he cried,
'Again they come!' and muttered as he died.

13. LORD BYRON

Darkness (1816)

I had a dream, which was not all a dream:
The bright sun was extinguished, and the stars
Did wander darkling in the eternal space,
Rayless and pathless, and the icy Earth
Swung blind and blackening in the moonless air!
Morn came, and went, and came – and brought no day.
And men forgot their passions in the dread
Of this their desolation; and all hearts
Were chilled into a selfish prayer for light.
And they did live by watchfires – and the thrones,
The palaces of crownéd kings, the huts,
The habitations of all things which dwell,
Were burnt for beacons. Cities were consumed,
And men were gathered round their blazing homes
To look once more into each other's face.

Happy were those who dwelt within the eye
Of the volcanos, and their mountain-torch!
A fearful hope was all the World contained –
Forests were set on fire, but hour by hour
They fell and faded, and the crackling trunks
Extinguished with a crash, and all was black.
    The brows of men by the despairing light
Wore an unearthly aspect, as by fits
The flashes fell upon them. Some lay down
And hid their eyes and wept; and some did rest
Their chins upon their clenchéd hands, and smiled;
And others hurried to and fro, and fed
Their funeral-piles with fuel, and lookéd up
With mad disquietude on the dull sky,
The pall of a past World – and then again
With curses cast them down upon the dust,
And gnashed their teeth and howled. The wild birds shrieked
And, terrified, did flutter on the ground,
And flap their useless wings; the wildest brutes
Came tame and tremulous; and vipers crawled
And twined themselves among the multitude,
Hissing, but stingless – they were slain for food!
And War, which for a moment was no more,
Did glut himself again: a meal was bought
With blood, and each sat sullenly apart
Gorging himself in gloom. No love was left.
All earth was but one thought, and that was death,
Immediate and inglorious – and the pang
Of famine fed upon all entrails! Men
Died, and their bones were tombless as their flesh.
The meagre by the meagre were devoured.
Even dogs assailed their masters – all save one,
And he was faithful to a corse, and kept
The birds and beasts and famished men at bay,
Till hunger clung them, or the dropping dead
Lured their lank jaws – himself sought out no food,
But with a piteous and perpetual moan,
And a quick desolate cry, licking the hand
Which answered not with a caress, he died.
    The crowd was famished by degrees; but two
Of an enormous city did survive,
And they were enemies. They met beside
The dying embers of an altar-place
Where had been heaped a mass of holy things

For an unholy usage; they raked up,
And shivering scraped with their cold skeleton hands,
The feeble ashes, and their feeble breath
Blew for a little life, and made a flame
Which was a mockery. Then they lifted up
Their eyes as it grew lighter, and beheld
Each other's aspects – saw, and shrieked, and died –
Even of their mutual hideousness they died,
Unknowing who he was upon whose brow
Famine had written fiend!
                                        The world was void:
The populous and the powerful was a lump,
Seasonless, herbless, treeless, manless, lifeless –
A lump of death – a chaos of hard clay!
The rivers, lakes, and ocean all stood still,
And nothing stirred within their silent depths.
Ships, sailorless, lay rotting on the sea,
And their masts fell down piecemeal – as they dropped
They slept on the abyss without a surge.
The waves were dead; the tides were in their grave
(The Moon, their mistress, had expired before);
The winds were withered in the stagnant air,
And the clouds perished – Darkness had no need
Of aid from them – She was the Universe!

14. JOHN KEATS

La Belle Dame Sans Merci

(21 April 1819; *Indicator*, May 1820)

'Oh, what can ail thee, knight-at-arms,
   Alone and palely loitering?
The sedge is withered from the lake,
   And no birds sing!

Oh, what can ail thee, knight-at-arms,
   So haggard and so woe-begone?
The squirrel's granary is full,
   And the harvest's done.

I see a lily on thy brow,
With anguish moist and fever-dew,
And on thy cheek a fading rose
Fast withereth too.'

'I met a lady in the meads
Full beautiful, a fairy's child;
Her hair was long, her foot was light,
And her eyes were wild.

I made a garland for her head,
And bracelets too, and fragrant zone;
She looked at me as she did love,
And made sweet moan.

I set her on my pacing steed,
And nothing else saw all day long;
For sidelong would she bend, and sing
A fairy's song.

She found me roots of relish sweet,
And honey wild, and manna-dew;
And sure in language strange she said,
'I love thee true.'

She took me to her elfin grot,
And there she wept, and sighed full sore,
And there I shut her wild wild eyes
With kisses four.

And there she lulléd me asleep
And there I dreamed, ah woe betide!
The latest dream I ever dreamed
On the cold hill side.

I saw pale kings, and princes too,
Pale warriors – death-pale were they all –
Who cried: 'La belle Dame sans merci
Thee hath in thrall!'

I saw their starved lips in the gloam
With horrid warning gapéd wide,
And I awoke, and found me here
On the cold hill's side.

And this is why I sojourn here
  Alone and palely loitering,
Though the sedge is withered from the lake,
  And no birds sing.'

15. JOHN CLARE

Superstition's Dream (lines 13–68) 1822

That time was come, or seemed as it was come,
When death no longer makes the grave its home,
When waking spirits leave their earthly rest
To mix forever with the damned or blest,
When years in drowsy thousands counted by
Then hung on minutes with their destiny,
When life in terror drops its draining glass
And all that's mortal like to shadows pass
As 'neath approaching tempests sinks the sun,
When time shall leave eternity begun.
Life swooned in terror at that hour's dread birth
And as in ague, shook the fearful earth,
And shuddering Nature seemed herself to shun
While trembling conscience felt the deed was done!
  A gloomy sadness round the sky was cast,
And clouds seemed hurrying with unusual haste –
Winds urged them forward like to restless ships,
And light dim faded with its last eclipse,
While Agitation turned a straining eye,
And Hope stood watching like a bird to fly,
And cringing Nature (like a child in dread)
Clung to her fading garments till she fled,
And awful sights began to be revealed
Which Death's dark dungeons had so long concealed!
Each grave its doomsday prisoner resigned,
And burst in noises like an hollow wind,
And spirits (mingling with the living then)
Thrilled fearful voices with the cries of men,
And, flying furious, grinning deep despair
Shaped dismal shadows on the troubled air,
And lightning shot its flashes as they came
And passing clouds seemed kindling into flame
And strong, and, stronger came the sulphury smell

While demons followed in the breath of Hell,
Grinning in mockery as the doomed complained –
Losing their pains in seeing others pained!
  Fierce raged destruction sweeping o'er the land
And the last counted moment seemed at hand;
As scales near equal hang the earnest eyes
In doubtful balance which shall fall or rise,
So in the moment of that crashing blast
Eyes hearts and hopes paused trembling for the last,
And sudden thunder-claps with yawing rents
Gashed the frail garment of the elements
And bursting whirlwinds, winged in purple flame,
And lightning's flash in stronger terrors came
Burning all life and Nature where they fell
And leaving earth as desolate as Hell.
The pleasant hues of fields and woods was past
And Nature's beauties had enjoyed their last:
The coloured flower, the green of field and tree,
What they had been forever ceased to be;
Grass shriveled brown in miserable hues
And showers of fire dried up the hissing dews;
Leaves crumbled ashes to the air's hot breath,
And all awaited universal death . . .

16. THOMAS LOVELL BEDDOES

The Bride's Tragedy (1822)

Act II, scene iv. *A tapestried Chamber: Hesperus (starting from his couch)*

Who speaks? Who whispers there? A light! A light!
I'll search the room! Something hath called me thrice
With a low muttering voice of toadish hisses –
And thrice I slept again. But still it came
Nearer and nearer – plucked my mantle from me,
And made mine heart an ear, in which it poured
Its loathed enticing courtship. Ho! A light!
(Enter attendant with a torch.)
Thou drowsy snail, thy footsteps are asleep –
Hold up thy torch!
Attendant: My lord, you are disturbed.

Have you seen aught?
Hesperus: I lay upon my bed,
And something in the air, out-jetting night,
Converting feeling to intenser vision,
Featured its ghastly self upon my soul
Deeper than night.
Attendant: This is delusion surely!
She's busy with men's thoughts at all night hours;
And to the waking subtle apprehension
The darkling chamber's still and sleepy air
Hath breath and motion oft.
Hesperus: Lift up the hangings, mark the doors, the corners –
Seest nothing yet? No face of fiendlike mirth
More frightful than the fixed and doggish grin
Of a dead madman?
Attendant: Nought I see, my lord,
Save the long, varied crowd of warlike shapes
Set in the stitched picture.
Hesperus:
Heard ye then?
There was a sound, as though some marble tongue
Moved on its rusty hinge, syllabling harshly
The hoarse death-rattle into speech.
Attendant: The wind is high, and through the silent rooms
Murmurs his burden, to an heedless ear
Almost articulate.
Hesperus: Thou sleepest, fool!
A voice has been at my bedside tonight
Its breath is burning on my forehead still –
Still o'er my brain its accents, wildly sweet,
Hover and fall. Away, and dream again!
I'll watch, myself. (*He takes the torch, and turns to the hangings. Exit Attendant.*)
Aye, these are living colours:
Those cheeks have worn their youth these hundred years,
Those flowers are verdant in their worsted spring,
And blooming still –
While she, whose needle limned so cunningly,
Sleeps and dreams not. It is a goodly state,
And there is one I wish had ta'en her bed
In the stone dormitory.
Blindfold moth!
Thou shalt not burn thy life – there, I have saved thee –
If thou art grateful, mingle with the air

That feeds the lips of her I thought of once –
Choke her, moth, choke her! I could be content
If she were safe in Heaven.
                                        Yon stout dagger
Is fairly fashioned for a blade of stitches,
And shines, methinks, most grimly! Well, thou art
An useful tool sometimes – thy tooth works quickly,
And if thou gnawest a secret from the heart,
Thou tellest it not again! Ha, the feigned steel
Doth blush and steam: there is a snuff of blood! (*Grasps his dagger convulsively.*)
Who placed this iron aspic in my hand?
Speak – who is at my ear?
(*He turns, and addresses his shadow.*)
                                        I know thee now,
I know the hideous laughter of thy face!
'Tis Malice's eldest imp – the heir of Hell,
Red-handed Murder. Slow it whispers me,
Coaxingly with serpent voice. Well sung,
Syren of Acheron!
                                I'll not look on thee –
Why does thy frantic weapon dig the air
With such most frightful vehemence? Back! Back!
Tell the dark grave I will not give it food . . .

17. THOMAS CAMPBELL

The Last Man (1823)

All worldly shapes shall melt in gloom,
   The Sun himself die,
Before this mortal shall assume
   Its Immortality!
I saw a vision in my sleep
That gave my spirit strength to sweep
   Adown the gulf of Time!
I saw the last of human mould
That shall Creations's death behold.
   As Adam saw her prime!

The Sun's eye had a sickly glare,
  The Earth with age was wan,
The skeletons of nations were
  Around that lonely man!
Some had expired in fight – the brands
Still rusted in their bony hands;
  In plague and famine some!
Earth's cities had no sound nor tread;
And ships were drifting with the dead
  To shores where all was dumb!

Yet, prophet-like, that lone one stood
  With dauntless words and high,
That shook the sere leaves from the wood
  As if a storm passed by,
Saying, 'We are twins in death, proud Sun!
Thy face is cold, thy race is run,
  'Tis Mercy bids thee go;
For thou ten thousand thousand years
Hast seen the tide of human tears,
  That shall no longer flow.

What though beneath thee man put forth
  His pomp, his pride, his skill,
And arts that made fire, flood, and earth
  The vassals of his will?
Yet mourn I not thy parted sway,
Thou dim discrownéd king of day:
  For all those trophied arts
And triumphs that beneath thee sprang
Healed not a passion or a pang
  Entailed on human hearts.

Go, let oblivion's curtain fall
  Upon the stage of men,
Nor with thy rising beams recall
  Life's tragedy again.
Its piteous pageants bring not back,
Nor waken flesh upon the rack
  Of pain anew to writhe –
Stretched in disease's shapes abhorred,
Or mown in battle by the sword
  Like grass beneath the scythe.

Even I am weary in yon skies
   To watch thy fading fire;
Test of all sumless agonies,
   Behold not me expire!
My lips that speak thy dirge of death –
Their rounded gasp and gargling breath
   To see thou shalt not boast;
The eclipse of Nature spreads my pall –
The majesty of Darkness shall
   Receive my parting ghost!

This spirit shall return to Him
   That gave its heavenly spark;
Yet think not, Sun, it shall be dim
   When thou thyself are dark!
No! it shall live again, and shine
In bliss unknown to beams of thine,
   By Him recalled to breath
Who captive led captivity,
Who robbed the grave of Victory,
   And took the sting from Death!

Go, Sun, while Mercy holds me up
   On Nature's awful waste
To drink this last and bitter cup
   Of grief that man shall taste –
Go, tell the night that hides thy face
Thou saw'st the last of Adam's race
   On Earth's sepulchral clod
The darkening universe defy
To quench his immortality
   Or shake his trust in God!'

18. THOMAS HOOD

The Last Man (1826; publ. 1829)

'Twas in the year two thousand and one,
A pleasant morning of May,
I sat on the gallows-tree all alone,

A chanting a merry lay –
To think how the pest had spared my life
To sing with the larks that day!

When up the heath came a jolly knave,
Like a scarecrow all in rags;
It made me crow to see his old duds
All abroad in the winds like flags –
So up he came to the timbers' foot
And pitched down his greasy bags.

Good Lord, how blithe the old beggar was
At pulling out his scraps –
The very sight of his broken orts
Made a work in his wrinkled chaps!
'Come down', says he, 'you Newgate-bird,
And have a taste of my snaps!'

Then down the rope, like a tar from the mast,
I slided, and by him stood;
But I wished myself on the gallows again
When I smelt that beggar's food –
A foul beef-bone, and a mouldy crust –
'Oh', quoth he, 'the Heavens are good!'

Then, after this grace, he cast him down:
Says I, 'You'll get sweeter air
A pace or two off, on the windward side' –
For the felons' bones lay there!
But he only laughed at the empty skulls,
And offered them part of his fare.

'I never harmed *them*, and they won't harm me –
Let the proud and the rich be cravens!'
I did not like that strange beggar-man,
He looked up so at the Heaven –
Anon he shook out his empty old poke:
'There's the crumbs', saith he, 'for the ravens!'

It made me angry to see his face,
It had such a jesting look;
But while I made up my mind to speak,
A small case-bottle he took:
Quoth he, 'Though I gather the green watercress,
My drink is not of the brook!'

Full manners-like he tendered the dram –
Oh it came of a dainty cask –
But whenever it came to his turn to pull:
'Your leave, good sir, I must ask;
But I always wipe the brim with my sleeve
When a hangman sups at my flask!'

And then he laughed so loudly and long,
The churl was quite out of breath –
I thought the very Old One was come
To mock me before my death,
And wished I had buried the dead men's bones
That were lying about the heath.

But the beggar gave me a jolly clap:
'Come, let us pledge each other,
For all the wide world is dead beside'
And we are brother and brother –
I've a yearning for thee in my heart
As if we had come from one mother.

I've a yearning for thee in my heart
That almost makes me weep,
For as I passed from town to town
The folks were all stone-asleep,
But when I saw thee sitting aloft
It made me both laugh and leap!'

Now a curse (I thought) be on his love,
And a curse be on his mirth,
An' it were not for that beggar-man
I'd be the King of the Earth –
But I promised myself an hour should come
To make him rue his birth.

So down we sat and boused again
Till the sun was in mid-sky,
When, just as the gentle west wind came,
We hearkened a dismal cry:
'Up, up on the tree', quoth the beggar-man,
'Till those horrible dogs go by!'

And lo, from the forest's far-off skirts
They came all yelling for gore,
A hundred hounds all yelling at once,
And a panting hart before –
Till he sunk down at the gallows' foot,
And there his haunches they tore!

His haunches they tore, without a horn
To tell when the chase was done,
And there was not a scarlet coat
To flaunt it in the sun –
I turned and looked at the beggar-man,
And his tears dropped one by one.

And with curses sore he chid the hounds,
Till the last dropped out of sight –
Anon saith he, 'Let's down again,
And ramble for our delight,
For the world's all free, and we may choose
A right cozy barn for tonight!'

With that he set up his staff on end
And it fell with the point due west;
So we fared that way to a city great
Where the folks had died of the pest –
It was fine to enter in house and hall
Wherever it liked me best!

For the porters all were stiff and cold,
And could not lift their heads;
And when we came where their masters lay,
The rats leapt out of the beds –
The grandest palaces in the land
Were as free as workhouse-sheds.

But the beggar-man made a mumping face,
And knocked at every gate:
It made me curse to hear how he whined,
So our fellowship turned to hate,
And I bade him walk the world by himself,
For I scorned so humble a mate.

So *he* turned right, and *I* turned left,
As if we had never met,
And I chose a fair stone-house for myself,
For the city was all to let –
And for three brave holydays drank my fill
Of the choicest I could get!

And because my jerkin was coarse and worn
I got me a properer vest;
It was purple velvet, stitched over with gold,
And a shining star at the breast –
'Twas enough to fetch old Joan from her grave,
To see me so purely dressed!

But Joan was dead, and under the mould,
And every buxom lass –
In vane I watched at the window-pane
For a Christian soul to pass,
But sheep and kine wandered up the street
And browsed on the new-come grass.

When lo, I spied the old beggar-man,
And lustily he did sing;
His rags were lapped in a scarlet cloak,
And a crown he had, like a king –
So he stepped right up before my gate
And danced me a saucy fling!

Heaven mend us all – but within my mind
I had killed him then and there
To see him lording so braggart-like
That was born to his beggar's fare –
And now he had stolen the royal crown
His betters were meant to wear!

But God forbid that a thief should die
Without his share of the laws!
So I nimbly whipped my tackle out
And soon tied up his claws –
I was judge myself, and jury, and all,
And solemnly tried the cause.

But the beggar-man would not plead, but cried
Like a babe without its corals,
For he knew how hard it is apt to go
When the law and a thief have quarrels –
There was not a Christian soul alive
To speak a word for his morals!

Oh how gaily I doffed my costly gear
And put on my workday clothes –
I was tired of such long Sunday life,
And was never one of the sloths;
But the beggar-man grumbled a weary deal,
And made many crooked mouths.

So I hauled him off to the gallows' foot,
And blinded him in his bags;
'Twas a weary job to heave him up
(For a doomed man always lags),
But by ten of the clock he was off his legs
In the wind and airing his rags!

So there he hung, and there I stood
The LAST MAN left alive,
To have my own will of all the earth:
Quoth I, 'Now I shall thrive!'
But when was ever honey made
With one bee in a hive?

My conscience began to gnaw my heart
Before the day was done,
For other men's lives had all gone out
Like candles in the sun –
But it seemed as if I had broke at last
A thousand necks in one!

So I went and cut his body down
To bury it decently
(God send there were any soul alive
To do the same by me),
But the wild dogs came with a terrible speed,
And bayed me up the tree.

My sight was like a drunkard's sight,
And my head began to swim,
To see their jaws all white with foam
Like the ravenous ocean's brim –
But when the wild dogs trotted away
Their jaws were bloody and grim!

Their jaws were bloody and grim, good Lord,
But the beggar-man, where was he?
There was nought of him but some ribbons of rags
Below the gallows-tree –
I know the Devil, when I am dead,
Will send his hounds for me!

I've buried my babies one by one,
And dug the deep hole for Joan,
And covered the faces of kith and kin,
And felt the old churchyard-stone
Go cold to my heart, full many a time –
But I never felt so lone!

For the lion and Adam were company,
And the tiger him beguiled;
But the simple kind are foes to my life,
And the household brutes are wild.
If the veriest cur would lick my hand,
I could love it like a child!

And the beggar-man's ghost besets my dreams
At night, to make me madder,
And my wretched conscience within my breast
Is stinging like an adder –
I sigh when I pass the gallows' foot,
And look at the rope and ladder!

For hanging looks sweet – but alas, in vain
My desperate fancy begs;
I must turn my cup of sorrows quite up,
And drink it to the dregs,
For there is not another man alive
In the world, to pull my legs!

IX. Romantic Comedy and Satire

As a writer of comic genius Byron towers over his period – funny, serious, subversive, romantic, a beautiful observer of man- (and woman-) kind, able to hold our attention over hundreds of pages through wit, personality and rightness of judgement. Alongside *Don Juan* among comic poems of the Romantic period one thinks of Frere's exuberant *Whistlecraft* (much scoffed at, little read), which provided Byron's metre, and Crabbe's *Procrastination* (showing a Byronic love of Pope and distaste for contemporary poetic trends). But *The Idiot Boy* too is a comic masterpiece, written in the tradition of Sterne, and celebrating the love it tenderly mocks. Shelley's satire of Wordsworth in *Peter Bell the Third* is mingled with respect that it quietly appropriate:

> He had as much imagination
>   As a pint-pot. He never could
> Fancy another situation
> From which to dart his contemplation
>   Than that wherein he stood.
>
> Yet his was individual mind
>   And new created all he saw . . .

Parody – certain to exist in a period that takes so seriously its styles and values, but often facile – offers delightful comedy in *The Rovers* (taking off the sublime of Schiller's *Robbers*), and is at its height in Hogg's mimicry of *Excursion* blank verse in *The Poetic Mirror*. Burns, in *Holy Willie's Prayer* attacks not a style, but an Elder of the Kirk, creating at once a magnificent lampoon and a brilliant study of self-deception. Blake, in his songs from *An Island in the Moon* (1785), ridicules Dr Johnson in tipsy verses, but also shows his power to shock, in *Old Corruption*, a version of the Orc cycle ten years ahead of its time. The Augustans might have a tradition of comedy – for the Romantics it is personal, a vivid expression of individuality. Whether it takes the form of parody, or comic narrative or monologue, it is a matter chiefly of voice – nowhere more so than in Norton's beautifully controlled *First Love*:

> Yes, I know that you once were my lover,
> But that sort of thing has an end,
> And though love and its transports are over,
> You know you can still be – my friend!

1. WILLIAM BLAKE

Songs from *An Island in the Moon*

(c. 1784; from MS 1907)

(i) *Old Corruption*

'Ah', said Sipsop, I only wish Jack Tearguts had had the cutting of Plutarch, he understands anatomy better than any of the Ancients. He'll plunge his knife up to the hilt in a single drive, and thrust his fist in – and all in the space of a quarter of an hour! He does not mind their crying – though they cry everso, he'll swear at them, and keep them down with his fist, and tell them that he'll scrape their bones if they don't lay still and be quiet . . .' 'Hang that!' said Suction, 'let us have a song.' Then the Cynic sang:

When Old Corruption first begun,
Adorned in yellow vest,
He committed on Flesh a whoredom –
Oh, what a wicked beast!

From them a callow babe did spring,
And Old Corruption smiled
To think his race could never end,
For now he had a child.

He called him Surgery, and fed
The babe with his own milk,
For Flesh and he could ne'er agree –
She would not let him suck.

And this he always kept in mind,
And formed a crooked knife,
And ran about with bloody hands
To seek his mother's life;

And as he ran to seek his mother
He met with a dead woman –
He fell in love, and married her:
A deed which is not common.

She soon grew pregnant, and brought forth
Scurvy and Spotted Fever;
The father grinned and skipped about,
And said, 'I'm made for ever –

For now I have procured these imps,
I'll try experiments!'
With that he tied poor Scurvy down
And stopped up all its vents,

And when the child began to swell
He shouted out aloud,
'I've found the dropsy out – and soon
Shall do the world more good!'

He took up Fever by the neck,
And cut out all its spots –
And through the holes which he had made
He first discovered guts!

(ii) *Lo, the Bat*

'I say, this evening we'll all get drunk! I say, dash! – an anthem, an anthem' said Suction:

Lo, the bat with leathern wing,
Winking and blinking,
Winking and blinking,
Winking and blinking
Like Doctor Johnson.

[*Quid*] 'Oh ho!' said Doctor Johnson
To Scipio Africanus,
'If you don't own me a philosopher
I'll kick your Roman anus!'

[*Suction*] 'Ah ha!' to Doctor Johnson
Said Scipio Africanus,
'Lift up my Roman petticoat,
And kiss my Roman anus!'

(iii) *Village Cricket*

Here nobody could sing any longer, till Tilly Lally plucked up spirit and he sung:

Oh I say, you Joe,
Throw us the ball!
I've a good mind to go
And leave you all.
I never saw such a bowler –
To bowl the ball in a tansey,
And to clean it with my handkercher
Without saying a word!

That Bill's a foolish fellow –
He has given me a black eye!
He does not know how to handle a bat
Any more than a dog or a cat:
He has knocked down the wicket
And broke the stumps,
And runs without shoes to save his pumps!

2. ROBERT BURNS

Holy Willie's Prayer (1786)

'And send the godly in a pet to pray' (Pope, *Rape of the Lock*)

Argument

Holy Willie was a rather oldish bachelor Elder in the parish of Mauchline, and much and justly famed for that polemical chattering which ends in tippling orthodoxy – and for that spiritualized bawdry which refines to liquorish devotion. In a Sessional process with a gentleman in Mauchline, a Mr Gavin Hamilton, Holy Willie and his Priest, Father Auld, after full hearing in the Presbytery of Ayr, came off but second best – owing partly to the oratorical powers of Mr Robert Aiken, Mr Hamilton's Counsel, but chiefly to Mr Hamilton's being one of the most irreproachable and truly respectable characters in the country. On losing his Process, the Muse overheard him at his devotions, as follows:

Oh thou that in the heavens does dwell,
Wha, as it pleases best thysel,
Sends ane to Heaven and ten to Hell,
A' for thy glory –
And no for ony gude or ill
They've done before thee!

I bless and praise thy matchless might,
When thousands thou hast left in night,
That I am here before thy sight,
For gifts and grace,
A burning and a shining light
To a' this place!

What was I, or my generation,
That should get such exaltation?
I, wha deserved most just damnation
For broken laws
Sax thousand years ere my creation,
Through Adam's cause!

When from my mother's womb I fell,
Thou might hae plunged me deep in Hell,
To gnash my gooms, and weep, and wail,
In burning lakes,
Where damnéd devils roar and yell
Chained to their stakes.

Yet I am here, a chosen sample,
To show thy grace is green and ample:
I'm here, a pillar of thy temple
Strong as a rock,
A guide, a ruler and example
To a' thy flock!

Oh Lord thou kens what zeal I bear,
When drinkers drink, and swearers swear,
And singin' there and dancin' here,

6 *before thee* in thy sight. **13** *generation* breeding, birthright. **21** *gooms* gums; Matthew 13.42 predicts 'wailing and gnashing of teeth' for those who have failed to recognize Christ. **25** *sample* example.

Wi' great an' sma';
For I am keepet by thy fear,
Free frae them a'.

But yet, oh Lord (confess I must),
At times I'm fashed wi' fleshly lust;
And sometimes too, in warldly trust
Vile self gets in!
But thou remembers we are dust,
Defiled wi' sin!

Oh Lord – yestreen – thou kens – wi' Meg –
Thy pardon I sincerely beg!
Oh may't ne'er be a living plague,
To my dishonour,
And I'll never lift a lawless leg
Again upon her!

Besides, I farther maun avow,
Wi' Leezi's lass, three times – I trow –
But Lord, that friday I was fou
When I cam near her;
Or else, thou kens, thy servant true
Wad never steer her.

Maybe thou lets this fleshly thorn
Buffet thy servant even and morn,
Lest he over proud and high should turn,
That he's sae gifted;
If sae, thy hand maun even be borne
Until thou lift it.

Lord bless thy chosen in this place –
For here thou has a chosen race –
But God, confound their stubborn face,
And blast their name,
Wha bring thy rulers to disgrace
And open shame!

35–6 *I am keepet . . . them a'* I am preserved by fear of thee from all these sins.
38 *fashed worried.* **51** *fou* drunk.

Lord mind Gaun Hamilton's deserts!
He drinks, and swears, and plays at cartes,
Yet has sae mony taking arts
Wi' great and sma',
Frae God's ain priest the people's hearts
He steals awa.

And when we chastened him therefore,
Thou kens how he bred sic a splore,
And set the warld in a roar
O' laughin' at us:
Curse thou his basket and his store,
Kail and potatoes!

Lord hear my earnest cry and prayer
Against that Presbytry of Ayr!
Thy strong right hand, Lord, make it bare
Upon their heads!
Lord visit them, and dinna spare,
For their misdeeds!

Oh Lord my God, that glib-tongued Aiken!
My very heart and flesh are quaking
To think how I sat, sweating, shaking,
And pissed wi' dread,
While Auld wi' hingin lip gaed sneaking
And hid his head!

Lord, in thy day o' vengeance try him!
Lord visit him that did employ him!
And pass not in thy mercy by them,
Nor hear their prayer;
But for thy people's sake destroy them,
And dinna spare!

But Lord, remember me and mine
Wi' mercies temporal and divine!
That I for grace and gear may shine,
Excelled by nane!
And a' the glory shall be thine!
Amen! Amen!

74 *sic a splore* such a fuss.

3. MARY ROBINSON

January, 1795 (publ. 1796)

Pavement slippery, people sneezing;
Lords in ermine, beggars freezing;
Titled gluttons dainties carving,
Genius in a garret starving!

Lofty mansions, warm and spacious;
Courtiers cringing and voracious;
Misers scarce the wretched heeding;
Gallant soldiers fighting, bleeding.

Wives who laugh at passive spouses;
Theatres and meeting-houses;
Balls, where simpering misses languish;
Hospitals, and groans of anguish.

Arts and sciences bewailing;
Commerce drooping, credit failing;
Placemen mocking subjects loyal;
Separations, weddings royal.

Authors who can't earn a dinner;
Many a subtle rogue a winner;
Fugitives for shelter seeking;
Misers hoarding, tradesmen breaking.

Taste and talents quite deserted;
All the laws of truth perverted;
Arrogance o'er merit soaring –
Merit silently deploring.

Ladies gambling night and morning;
Fools the works of genius scorning;
Ancient dames for girls mistaken,
Youthful damsels quite forsaken.

Some in luxury, delighting
More in talking than in fighting;
Lovers old, and beaux decrepid,
Lordlings empty and insipid.

Poets, painters and musicians;
Lawyers, doctors, politicians;
Pamphlets, newspapers and odes,
Seeking fame by different roads.

Gallant souls with empty purses;
Generals only fit for nurses;
Schoolboys smit with martial spirit
Taking place of martial merit.

Honest men who can't get places,
Knaves who show unblushing faces –
Ruin hastened, peace retarded,
Candour spurned and art rewarded.

4. WILLIAM WORDSWORTH

Ballad Comedies, spring 1798

(i) *The Idiot Boy* (late March; publ. *Lyrical Ballads*)

'Tis eight o'clock, a clear March night,
The moon is up, the sky is blue,
The owlet in the moonlight air
He shouts from nobody knows where,
He lengthens out his lonely shout,
Halloo! Halloo! A long halloo!

Why bustle thus about your door,
What means this bustle, Betty Foy?
Why are you in this mighty fret?
And why on horseback have you set
Him whom you love, your idiot boy?

Beneath the moon that shines so bright,
Till she is tired, let Betty Foy
With girth and stirrup fiddle-faddle –
But wherefore set upon a saddle
Him whom she loves, her idiot boy?

There's scarce a soul that's out of bed;
Good Betty, put him down again!
His lips with joy they burr at you,
But Betty, what has he to do
With stirrup, saddle, or with rein?

The world will say 'tis very idle,
Bethink you of the time of night!
There's not a mother, no not one,
But when she hears what you have done,
Oh Betty she'll be in a fright!

But Betty's bent on her intent,
For her good neighbour, Susan Gale
(Old Susan, she who dwells alone)
Is sick, and makes a piteous moan
As if her very life would fail.

There's not a house within a mile,
No hand to help them in distress;
Old Susan lies abed in pain,
And sorely puzzled are the twain,
For what she ails they cannot guess.

And Betty's husband's at the wood
Where by the week he doth abide,
A woodman in the distant vale;
There's none to help poor Susan Gale –
What must be done, what will betide?

And Betty from the lane has fetched
Her pony that is mild and good
Whether he be in joy or pain,
Feeding at will along the lane
Or bringing faggots from the wood.

And he is all in travelling trim,
And by the moonlight Betty Foy
Has up upon the saddle set –
The like was never heard of yet –
Him whom she loves, her idiot boy.

And he must post without delay
Across the bridge that's in the dale,
And by the church, and o'er the down,
To bring a doctor from the town,
Or she will die, old Susan Gale.

There is no need of boot or spur,
There is no need of whip or wand,
For Johnny has his holly-bough,
And with a hurly-burly now
He shakes the green bough in his hand.

And Betty o'er and o'er has told
The boy who is her best delight,
Both what to follow, what to shun,
What do, and what to leave undone,
How turn to left, and how to right.

And Betty's most especial charge
Was, 'Johnny! Johnny! mind that you
Come home again, nor stop at all,
Come home again, whate'er befall,
My Johnny do, I pray you do.'

To this did Johnny answer make
Both with his head and with his hand,
And proudly shook the bridle too;
And then, his words were not a few,
Which Betty well could understand!

And now that Johnny is just going,
Though Betty's in a mighty flurry,
She gently pats the pony's side
On which her idiot boy must ride,
And seems no longer in a hurry.

But when the pony moved his legs,
Oh, then for the poor idiot boy! –
For joy he cannot hold the bridle,
For joy his head and heels are idle,
He's idle all for very joy!

And while the pony moves his legs,
In Johnny's left hand you may see
The green bough's motionless and dead;
The moon that shines above his head
Is not more still and mute than he.

His heart it was so full of glee
That till full fifty yards were gone
He quite forgot his holly whip
And all his skill in horsemanship –
Oh happy, happy, happy John!

And Betty's standing at the door,
And Betty's face with joy o'erflows –
Proud of herself, and proud of him,
She sees him in his travelling trim,
How quietly her Johnny goes.

The silence of her idiot boy,
What hopes it sends to Betty's heart!
He's at the guide-post – he turns right,
She watches till he's out of sight,
And Betty will not then depart.

Burr, burr – now Johnny's lips they burr,
As loud as any mill, or near it!
Meek as a lamb the pony moves,
And Johnny makes the noise he loves,
And Betty listens, glad to hear it.

Away she hies to Susan Gale,
And Johnny's in a merry tune;
The owlets hoot, the owlets curr,
And Johnny's lips they burr, burr, burr,
And on he goes beneath the moon.

His steed and he right well agree,
For of this pony there's a rumour
That should he lose his eyes and ears,
And should he live a thousand years,
He never will be out of humour.

But then he is a horse that thinks,
And when he thinks his pace is slack!
Now, though he knows poor Johnny well,
Yet for his life he cannot tell
What he has got upon his back.

So through the moonlight lanes they go,
And far into the moonlight dale,
And by the church, and o'er the down,
To bring a doctor from the town,
To comfort poor old Susan Gale.

And Betty, now at Susan's side,
Is in the middle of her story,
What comfort Johnny soon will bring–
With many a most diverting thing
Of Johnny's wit and Johnny's glory.

And Betty's still at Susan's side –
By this time she's not quite so flurried;
Demure with porringer and plate
She sits, as if in Susan's fate
Her life and soul were buried.

But Betty, poor good woman, she
(You plainly in her face may read it)
Could lend out of that moment's store
Five years of happiness or more,
To any that might need it!

But yet I guess that now and then
With Betty all was not so well;
And to the road she turns her ears,
And thence full many a sound she hears
Which she to Susan will not tell.

Poor Susan moans, poor Susan groans,
'As sure as there's a moon in heaven',
Cries Betty, 'he'll be back again!
They'll both be here, 'tis almost ten –
They'll both be here before eleven.'

Poor Susan moans, poor Susan groans,
The clock gives warning for eleven –
'Tis on the stroke! 'If Johnny's near',
Quoth Betty, 'he will soon be here,
As sure as there's a moon in heaven.'

The clock is on the stroke of twelve
And Johnny is not yet in sight;
The moon's in heaven, as Betty sees,
But Betty is not quite at ease –
And Susan has a dreadful night!

And Betty, half an hour ago,
On Johnny vile reflections cast,
'A little idle sauntering thing!'
With other names, an endless string,
But now that time is gone and past.

And Betty's drooping at the heart,
That happy time all past and gone,
'How can it be he is so late?
The doctor he has made him wait –
Susan, they'll both be here anon.'

And Susan's growing worse and worse,
And Betty's in a sad quandary –
And then there's nobody to say
If she must go or she must stay;
She's in a sad quandary.

The clock is on the stroke of one,
But neither doctor nor his guide
Appear along the moonlight road;
There's neither horse nor man abroad,
And Betty's still at Susan's side.

And Susan she begins to fear
Of sad mischances not a few:
That Johnny may perhaps be drowned,
Or lost perhaps, and never found –
Which they must both forever rue.

She prefaced half a hint of this
With, 'God forbid it should be true!'
At the first word that Susan said
Cried Betty, rising from the bed,
'Susan, I'd gladly stay with you!

I must be gone, I must away!
Consider, Johnny's but half-wise;
Susan, we must take care of him.
If he is hurt in life or limb' –
'Oh God forbid!' poor Susan cries.

'What can I do?' says Betty, going,
'What can I do to ease your pain?
Good Susan tell me, and I'll stay;
I fear you're in a dreadful way,
But I shall soon be back again.'

'Good Betty go, good Betty go,
There's nothing that can ease my pain'
Then off she hies, but with a prayer
That God poor Susan's life would spare,
Till she comes back again.

So through the moonlight lane she goes,
And far into the moonlight dale;
And how she ran, and how she walked,
And all that to herself she talked,
Would surely be a tedious tale.

In high and low, above, below,
In great and small, in round and square,
In tree and tower, was Johnny seen –
In bush and brake, in black and green,
'Twas Johnny, Johnny, everywhere.

She's past the bridge that's in the dale,
And now the thought torments her sore,
Johnny perhaps his horse forsook
To hunt the moon that's in the brook,
And never will be heard of more.

And now she's high upon the down,
Alone amid a prospect wide;
There's neither Johnny nor his horse
Among the fern or in the gorse;
There's neither doctor nor his guide.

'Oh saints, what is become of him?
Perhaps he's climbed into an oak,
Where he will stay till he is dead;
Or sadly he has been misled,
And joined the wandering gypsy-folk.

Or him that wicked pony's carried
To the dark cave, the goblins' hall,
Or in the castle he's pursuing,
Among the ghosts, his own undoing;
Or playing with the waterfall.'

At poor old Susan then she railed
While to the town she posts away,
'If Susan had not been so ill,
Alas, I should have had him still,
My Johnny, till my dying day.'

Poor Betty, in this sad distemper,
The doctor's self would hardly spare;
Unworthy things she talked and wild –
Even he, of cattle the most mild,
The pony had his share.

And now she's got into the town,
And to the doctor's door she hies;
'Tis silence all on every side –
The town so long, the town so wide,
Is silent as the skies.

And now she's at the doctor's door,
She lifts the knocker, rap, rap, rap;
The doctor at the casement shows
His glimmering eyes that peep and doze,
And one hand rubs his old nightcap.

'Oh doctor, doctor, where's my Johnny?'
'I'm here, what is't you want with me?'
'Oh sir, you know I'm Betty Foy,
And I have lost my poor dear boy!
You know him, him you often see –

He's not so wise as some folks be.'
'The Devil take his wisdom!' said
The doctor, looking somewhat grim;
'What, woman, should I know of him?'
And, grumbling, he went back to bed.

'Oh woe is me! Oh woe is me!
Here will I die, here will I die;
I thought to find my Johnny here,
But he is neither far nor near –
Oh what a wretched mother I!'

She stops, she stands, she looks about,
Which way to turn she cannot tell.
Poor Betty! It would ease her pain
If she had heart to knock again;
The clock strikes three – a dismal knell!

Then up along the town she hies,
No wonder if her senses fail,
This piteous news so much it shocked her,
She quite forgot to send the doctor,
To comfort poor old Susan Gale.

And now she's high upon the down,
And she can see a mile of road,
'Oh cruel! I'm almost three-score –
Such night as this was ne'er before,
There's not a single soul abroad.'

She listens, but she cannot hear
The foot of horse, the voice of man;
The streams with softest sound are flowing,
The grass you almost hear it growing –
You hear it now if e'er you can.

The owlets through the long blue night
Are shouting to each other still –
Fond lovers, yet not quite hob-nob,
They lengthen out the tremulous sob
That echoes far from hill to hill.

Poor Betty now has lost all hope,
Her thoughts are bent on deadly sin;
A green-grown pond she just has passed,
And from the brink she hurries fast,
Lest she should drown herself therein.

And now she sits her down and weeps –
Such tears she never shed before –
'Oh dear, dear pony! My sweet joy!
Oh carry back my idiot boy,
And we will ne'er o'erload thee more!'

A thought is come into her head:
'The pony he is mild and good,
And we have always used him well;
Perhaps he's gone along the dell
And carried Johnny to the wood.'

Then up she springs as if on wings,
She thinks no more of deadly sin –
If Betty fifty ponds should see,
The last of all her thoughts would be
To drown herself therein.

Oh reader, now that I might tell
What Johnny and his horse are doing!
What they've been doing all this time –
Oh could I put it into rhyme,
A most delightful tale pursuing!

Perhaps (and no unlikely thought!)
He with his pony now doth roam
The cliffs and peaks so high that are,
To lay his hands upon a star,
And in his pocket bring it home.

Perhaps he's turned himself about,
His face unto his horse's tail,
And still and mute, in wonder lost,
All like a silent horseman-ghost
He travels on along the vale.

And now perhaps he's hunting sheep,
A fierce and dreadful hunter he!
Yon valley, that's so trim and green,
In five months' time, should he be seen,
A desert wilderness will be.

Perhaps, with head and heels on fire
And like the very soul of evil,
He's galloping away, away,
And so he'll gallop on for aye,
The bane of all that dread the Devil.

I to the Muses have been bound,
These fourteen years, by strong indentures;
Oh gentle Muses, let me tell
But half of what to him befell,
For sure he met with strange adventures!

Oh gentle Muses, is this kind?
Why will ye thus my suit repel?
Why of your further aid bereave me?
And can ye thus unfriended leave me,
Ye Muses, whom I love so well?

Who's yon, that near the waterfall
Which thunders down with headlong force
Beneath the moon, yet shining fair,
As careless as if nothing were,
Sits upright on a feeding horse?

Unto his horse, that's feeding free,
He seems, I think, the rein to give;
Of moon or stars he takes no heed
(Of such we in romances read) –
'Tis Johnny, Johnny, as I live!

And that's the very pony too!
Where is she, where is Betty Foy?
She hardly can sustain her fears –
The roaring waterfall she hears,
And cannot find her idiot boy.

Your pony's worth his weight in gold;
Then calm your terrors, Betty Foy!
She's coming from among the trees,
And now, all full in view, she sees
Him whom she loves, her idiot boy.

And Betty sees the pony too!
Why stand you thus good Betty Foy?
It is no goblin, 'tis no ghost,
'Tis he whom you so long have lost,
He whom you love, your idiot boy.

She looks again – her arms are up –
She screams – she cannot move for joy!
She darts as with a torrent's force,
She almost has o'erturned the horse,
And fast she holds her idiot boy.

And Johnny burrs and laughs aloud –
Whether in cunning or in joy
I cannot tell, but while he laughs
Betty a drunken pleasure quaffs
To hear again her idiot boy.

And now she's at the pony's tail,
And now she's at the pony's head,
On that side now, and now on this;
And, almost stifled with her bliss,
A few sad tears does Betty shed.

She kisses o'er and o'er again
Him whom she loves, her idiot boy;
She's happy here, she's happy there,
She is uneasy everywhere –
Her limbs are all alive with joy.

She pats the pony, where or when
She knows not, happy Betty Foy!
The little pony glad may be,
But he is milder far than she,
You hardly can perceive his joy.

'Oh Johnny, never mind the doctor!
You've done your best, and that is all.'
She took the reins, when this was said,
And gently turned the pony's head
From the loud waterfall.

By this the stars were almost gone;
The moon was setting on the hill,
So pale you scarcely looked at her;
The little birds began to stir,
Though yet their tongues were still.

The pony, Betty, and her boy,
Wind slowly through the woody dale:
And who is she, betimes abroad,
That hobbles up the steep rough road –
Who is it, but old Susan Gale?

Long Susan lay deep lost in thought,
And many dreadful fears beset her,
Both for her messenger and nurse;
And as her mind grew worse and worse,
Her body it grew better.

She turned, she tossed herself, in bed –
On all sides doubts and terrors met her;
Point after point did she discuss,
And while her mind was fighting thus,
Her body still grew better.

'Alas, what is become of them?
These fears can never be endured –
I'll to the wood.' The word scarce said,
Did Susan rise up from her bed,
As if by magic cured.

Away she posts up hill and down,
And to the wood at length is come;
She spies her friends, she shouts a greeting –
Oh me, it is a merry meeting
As ever was in Christendom!

The owls have hardly sung their last
While our four travellers homeward wend;
The owls have hooted all night long –
And with the owls began my song,
And with the owls must end.

For while they all were travelling home,
Cried Betty, 'Tell us Johnny, do,
Where all this long night you have been,
What you have heard, what you have seen,
And Johnny, mind you tell us true.'

Now Johnny all night long had heard
The owls in tuneful concert strive;
No doubt too he the moon had seen,
For in the moonlight he had been
From eight o'clock till five.

And thus to Betty's question, he
Made answer, like a traveller bold
(His very words I give to you):
'The cocks did crow to-whoo, to-whoo,
And the sun did shine so cold.'
Thus answered Johnny in his glory,
And that was all his travel's story.

(ii) from *Peter Bell* (late April; publ. 1819)

Is it some party, in a parlour
Crammed (just as they on earth were crammed),
Some sipping punch, some sipping tea,
But as you by their faces see,
All silent and all damned?

'Tis no such thing, I do assure you,
Which Peter sees in the clear flood.
It is no ugly apprehension
Of eyes and ears, 'tis no invention –
It is a thing of flesh and blood . . .

And now poor Peter is convinced,
While still he holds the ass's head,
That 'tis a fiend with visage wan,
A live man-fiend, a living man,
That's lying in the river-bed.

He looks, he looks, he looks again,
He sees a motion, hears a groan;
His eyes will burst, his heart will break,
He gives a loud and dreadful shriek,
And back he falls just like a stone . . .

He lifts his head, he sees his staff,
He touches – 'tis to him a treasure!
To find that he is not in Hell,
As you'll suppose to Peter Bell
Doth give a sweet and languid pleasure.

And while upon his side he lies,
His head upon his elbow raised,
Almost you'd say as in a dream
His eyes are settling on the stream
Where he before had gazed.

No dimple now disturbs the stream;
In Peter's brain there is no riot;
His eye upon the stream he fixes,
And with the sight no terror mixes,
His heart is calm and quiet.

Quoth he, 'That is a dead man's face
Among the shadows of the trees!
Those are no doubt a dead man's knuckles,
And there you see his brass shoe-buckles.
And there his breeches' knees.'

At last he rises from his side,
And sits upright upon the ground,
And o'er the stream he hangs his nose
And points his staff as you'd suppose
The river's depth to sound.

This sees the ass, while on the grass
Close by the river's brink he lies,
And straight with a transition tragic,
That seems just like the touch of magic,
Up from the ground the ass doth rise.

At this friend Peter round him looks,
And sees the poor and patient creature
Close to him, in his uncouth way
Expressing all the joy he may
In every limb and feature.

His meagre bones all shake with joy,
And close by Peter's side he stands;
While Peter o'er the river bends,
The little ass his neck extends
And fondly licks his hands.

Such life is in the ass's eyes,
Such life is in his limbs and ears,
That Peter Bell, if he had been
The veriest coward ever seen,
Must now have thrown aside his fears.

With caution Peter eyes the stream
(The sapling deep and deeper goes);
'The body is no doubt', quoth he,
'The thing which it appears to be –
It moves not, neither limbs, nor clothes.'

The ass looks on, and to his work
Is Peter quietly resigned:
He touches here, he touches there,
And now among the dead man's hair
His sapling Peter has entwined.

He pulls, and pulls, and pulls again,
And he whom the poor ass had lost –
The man who had been four days dead –
Head-foremost from the river's bed
Uprises like a ghost!

(iii) *We Are Seven*

(late April/early May; publ. *Lyrical Ballads*)

A simple child, dear brother Jim,
That lightly draws its breath,
And feels its life in every limb,
What should it know of death?

I met a little cottage-girl–
She was eight years old, she said –
Her hair was thick with many a curl
That clustered round her head.

She had a rustic, woodland air,
And she was wildly clad;
Her eyes were fair, and very fair –
Her beauty made me glad.

'Sisters and brothers, little maid,
How many may you be?'
'How many? Seven in all', she said,
And wondering looked at me.

'And where are they, I pray you tell?'
She answered, 'Seven are we,
And two of us at Conway dwell,
And two are gone to sea;

Two of us in the churchyard lie,
My sister and my brother;
And in the churchyard-cottage, I
Dwell near them with my mother.'

'You say that two at Conway dwell,
And two are gone to sea,
Yet you are seven – I pray you tell,
Sweet maid, how this may be?'

Then did the little maid reply,
'Seven boys and girls are we –
Two of us in the churchyard lie,
Beneath the churchyard-tree.'

'You run about, my little maid,
Your limbs they are alive;
If two are in the churchyard laid,
Then ye are only five.'

'Their graves are green, they may be seen',
The little maid replied,
'Twelve steps or more from my mother's door,
And they are side by side.

My stockings there I often knit,
My kerchief there I hem,
And there upon the ground I sit,
I sit and sing to them.

And often after sunset, sir,
When it is light and fair,
I take my little porringer
And eat my supper there.

The first that died was little Jane;
In bed she moaning lay,
Till God released her of her pain,
And then she went away.

So in the churchyard she was laid,
And all the summer dry
Together round her grave we played,
My brother John and I.

And when the ground was white with snow
And I could run and slide,
My brother John was forced to go,
And he lies by her side.'

'How many are you then', said I,
'If they two are in Heaven?'
The little maiden did reply,
'Oh master, we are seven!'

'But they are dead, those two are dead –
Their spirits are in Heaven!'
'Twas throwing words away, for still
The little maid would have her will,
And said, 'Nay, we are seven!'

5. JOHN HOOKHAM FRERE AND GEORGE CANNING

from *The Rovers* (June 1798)

Scene: A subterranean vault in the Abbey of Quedlinburg, with coffins, scutcheons, death's-heads and cross-bones. Toads and other obscene reptiles are seen traversing the obscurer parts of the stage. Rogero appears in chains and a suit of rusty armour.

Rogero: Eleven years! It is now eleven years since I was first immured in this living sepulchre – the cruelty of a Minister, the perfidy of a Monk – yes Matilda, for thy sake alive amidst the dead – chained, coffined, confined . . . Eleven years and fifteen days! Hah! the twenty-eighth of August – how does the recollection of it vibrate on my heart! It was on this day that I took my last leave of my Matilda. It was a summer evening – her melting hand seemed to dissolve in mine . . . I stood gazing on the hated vehicle which was conveying her away for ever. The tears were petrified under my eyelids – my heart was crystallized with agony! . . . Soft, what air was that? It seemed a sound of more than human warblings? Again [*listens attentively for some minutes*] – Only the wind! It is well, however – it reminds me of that melancholy air which has so often solaced the hours of my captivity! Let me see whether the damps of this dungeon have not yet injured my guitar [*Takes his guitar, tunes it, and begins the following air, with a full accompaniment of violins from the orchestra.*]

Whene'er with haggard eyes I view
  This dungeon that I'm rotting in
I think of those companions true
  Who studied with me at the U
        niversity of Gottingen,
        niversity of Gottingen.

[*Weeps, and pulls out a blue kerchief, with which he wipes his eyes. Gazing tenderly at it, he proceeds.*]

Sweet kerchief, checked with heavenly blue,
   Which once my love sat knotting in –
Alas, Matilda *then was true*!
   At least I thought so at the U
         niversity of Gottingen,
         niversity of Gottingen.

[*At the repetition of this line, Rogero clanks his chains in cadence.*]

Barbs! barbs! Alas, how swift you flew,
   Her neat post-waggon trotting in!
Ye bore Matilda from my view –
   Forlorn I languished at the U
         niversity of Gottingen,
         niversity of Gottingen.

This faded form! This pallid hue!
   This blood my veins is clotting in!
My years are many – they were few
   When first I entered at the U
         niversity of Gottingen,
         niversity of Gottingen.

There first for thee my passions grew,
   Sweet! sweet Matilda Pottingen!
Thou wast the daughter of my Tu
   tor, Law Professor at the U
         niversity of Gottingen,
         niversity of Gottingen.

Sun, moon, and thou, vain world, adieu!
   That Kings and Priests are plotting in –
Here doomed to starve on water gru
   el, never shall I see the U
         niveristy of Gottingen,
         niversity of Gottingen!

[*During the last stanza Rogero dashes his head repeatedly against the walls of his prison . . . The curtain drops, the music continuing to play till it has wholly fallen.*]

6. ROBERT SOUTHEY AND SAMUEL TAYLOR COLERIDGE

The Devil's Thoughts (1799)

From his brimstone bed at break of day
A walking the Devil is gone,
To visit his snug little farm the Earth,
And see how his stock went on.

Over the hill and over the dale,
And he went over the plain,
And backward and forward he swished his long tail
As a gentleman swishes his cane.

He saw a lawyer killing a viper
On the dunghill beside his stable;
'Oh, oh!', quoth he, for it put him in mind
Of the story of Cain and Abel.

An apothecary on a white horse
   Rode by on his vocation,
And the Devil thought of his old friend
   Death in the *Revelation.*

He went into a rich bookseller's shop,
   Quoth he, 'We are both of one college!
For I sat myself, like a cormorant, once
   Upon the tree of knowledge.'

He saw a turnkey in a trice
   Hand-cuff a troublesome blade;
'Nimbly,' quoth he, 'the fingers move
   If a man is but used to his trade.'

He saw the same turnkey unfettering a man,
   With but little expedition,
And he laughed for he thought of the long debates
   On the Slave-trade abolition.

As he went through [Cold-Bath] fields he looked
    At a solitary cell;
And the Devil was pleased, for it gave him a hint
    For improving the prisons of Hell.

He past a cottage with a double coach-house,
    A cottage of gentility;
And he grinned at the sight, for his favourite vice
    Is pride that apes humility.

He saw a pig right rapidly
    Adown the river float,
The pig swam well, but every stroke
    Was cutting his own throat.

Old Nicholas grinned and swished his tail
    For joy and admiration;
And he thought of his daughter, Victory,
    And his darling babe, Taxation.

He met an old acquaintance
    Just by the Methodist meeting –
She held a consecrated flag,
    And the Devil nods a greeting.

She tipped him the wink, then frowned and cried,
    'Avaunt! my name's Religion',
And turned to Mr. W[ilberforce]
    And leered like a love-sick pigeon.

General [Gascoigne]'s burning face
    He saw with consternation,
And back to Hell his way did take,
For the Devil thought by a slight mistake
    It was general conflagration.

7. GEORGE CRABBE

Procrastination (1812)

Love will expire – the gay, the happy dream
Will turn to scorn, indifference, or esteem.
Some favoured pairs, in this exchange, are blest,
Nor sigh for raptures in a state of rest;
Others, ill-matched, with minds unpaired, repent
At once the deed, and know no more content –
From joy to anguish they in haste decline,
And, with their fondness, their esteem resign.
More luckless still their fate, who are the prey
Of long-protracted hope and dull delay:
Mid plans of bliss the heavy hours pass on,
Till love is withered, and till joy is gone.
   This gentle flame two youthful hearts possessed,
The sweet disturber of unenvied rest:
The prudent Dinah was the maid beloved,
And the kind Rupert was the swain approved.
A wealthy aunt her gentle niece sustained,
He, with a father, at his desk remained –
The youthful couple, to their vows sincere,
Thus loved expectant, year succeeding year,
With pleasant views and hopes, but not a prospect near.
Rupert some comfort in his station saw,
But the poor virgin lived in dread and awe;
Upon her anxious looks the widow smiled,
And bade her wait, 'for she was yet a child'.
She for her neighbour had a due respect,
Nor would his son encourage or reject;
And thus the pair, with expectations vain,
Beheld the seasons change and change again.
Meantime the nymph her tender tales perused,
Where cruel aunts impatient girls refused –
While hers, though teasing, boasted to be kind,
And she, resenting, to be all resigned!
   The dame was sick, and when the youth applied
For her consent, she groaned, and coughed, and cried,
Talked of departing, and again her breath
Drew hard, and coughed, and talked again of death:

'Here you may live, my Dinah – here the boy
And you together my estate enjoy!'
Thus to the lovers was her mind expressed,
Till they forbore to urge the fond request.
Servant, and nurse, and comforter, and friend,
Dinah had still some duty to attend –
But yet their walk, when Rupert's evening call
Obtained an hour, made sweet amends for all.
So long they now each other's thoughts had known,
That nothing seemed exclusively their own;
But with the common wish, the mutual fear,
They now had travelled to their thirtieth year.
   At length a prospect opened – but alas!
Long time must yet, before the union, pass:
Rupert was called, in other clime, to increase
Another's wealth, and toil for future peace.
Loath were the lovers; but the aunt declared
'Twas fortune's call, and they must be prepared:
'You now are young, and for this brief delay,
And Dinah's care, what I bequeath will pay –
All will be yours! Nay, love, suppress that sigh!
The kind must suffer, and the best must die!'
Then came the cough, and strong the signs it gave
Of holding long contention with the grave.
   The lovers parted with a gloomy view,
And little comfort, but that both were true;
He for uncertain duties doomed to steer,
While hers remained too certain and severe.
Letters arrived, and Rupert fairly told
His cares were many, and his hopes were cold:
The view more clouded, that was never fair,
And love alone preserved him from despair –
In other letters brighter hopes he drew,
His friends were kind, and he believed them true!
When the sage widow Dinah's grief descried,
She wondered much why one so happy sighed,
Then bade her see how her poor aunt sustained
The ills of life, nor murmured nor complained.
To vary pleasures, from the lady's chest
Were drawn the pearly string and tabby vest,
Beads, jewels, laces, all their value shown,
With the kind notice – 'They will be your own!'
   This hope, these comforts, cherished day by day,
To Dinah's bosom made a gradual way,

Till love of treasure had as large a part
As love of Rupert, in the virgin's heart.
Whether it be that tender passions fail,
From their own nature, while the strong prevail;
Or whether avarice, like the poison-tree,
Kills all beside it, and alone will be –
Whatever cause prevailed, the pleasure grew
In Dinah's soul: she loved the hoards to view;
With lively joy those comforts she surveyed,
And love grew languid in the careful maid.
Now the grave niece partook the widow's cares,
Looked to the great, and ruled the small affairs;
Saw cleaned the plate, arranged the china-show,
And felt her passion for a shilling grow:
The indulgent aunt increased the maid's delight,
By placing tokens of her wealth in sight;
She loved the value of her bonds to tell,
And spake of stocks, and how they rose and fell.
   This passion grew, and gained at length such sway
That other passions shrank to make it way;
Romantic notions now the heart forsook,
She read but seldom, and she changed her book;
And for the verses she was wont to send,
Short was her prose – and she was Rupert's friend.
Seldom she wrote, and then the widow's cough,
And constant call, excused her breaking off;
Who, now oppressed, no longer took the air,
But sat and dozed upon an easy chair.
The cautious doctor saw the case was clear,
But judged it best to have companions near;
They came, they reasoned, they prescribed – at last,
Like honest men, they said their hopes were past!
Then came a priest – 'tis comfort to reflect,
When all is over, there was no neglect!
   And all was over: by her husband's bones
The widow rests beneath the sculptured stones
That yet record their fondness and their fame;
While all they left, the virgin's care became –
Stock, bonds, and buildings! It disturbed her rest
To think what load of troubles she possessed;
Yet, if a trouble, she resolved to take
The important duty for the donor's sake!
She too was heiress to the widow's taste,
Her love of hoarding, and her dread of waste.

Sometimes the past would on her mind intrude,
And then a conflict full of care ensued:
The thoughts of Rupert on her mind would press –
His worth she knew, but doubted his success –
Of old she saw him heedless: what the boy
Forbore to save, the man would not enjoy.
Oft had he lost the chance that care would seize,
Willing to live, but more to live at ease –
Yet could she not a broken vow defend,
And Heaven, perhaps, might yet enrich her friend!
   Month after month was passed, and all were spent
In quiet comfort and in rich content:
Miseries there were, and woes the world around,
But these had not her pleasant dwelling found;
She knew that mothers grieved, and widows wept,
And she was sorry, said her prayers, and slept!
Thus passed the seasons, and to Dinah's board
Gave what the seasons to the rich afford;
For she indulged – nor was her heart so small,
That one strong passion should engross it all!
A love of splendour now with avarice strove,
And oft appeared to be the stronger love:
A secret pleasure filled the Widow's breast
When she reflected on the hoards possessed,
But livelier joy inspired the ambitious Maid
When she the purchase of those hoards displayed.
In small but splendid room she loved to see
That all was placed in view and harmony;
There, as with eager glance she looked around,
She much delight in every object found;
While books devout were near her – to destroy,
Should it arise, an overflow of joy!
   Within that fair apartment guests might see
The comforts culled for wealth by vanity:
Around the room an Indian paper blazed,
With lively tint and figures boldly raised;
Silky and soft upon the floor below,
The elastic carpet rose with crimson glow.
All things around implied both cost and care –
What met the eye was elegant or rare!
Some curious trifles round the room were laid,
By hope presented to the wealthy maid;
Within a costly case of varnished wood,
In level rows, her polished volumes stood

(Shown as a favour to a chosen few,
To prove what beauty for a book could do);
A silver urn with curious work was fraught,
A silver lamp from Grecian pattern wrought;
Above her head, all gorgeous to behold,
A timepiece stood on feet of burnished gold.
A stag's-head crest adorned the pictured case –
Through the pure crystal shone the enamelled face –
And while on brilliants moved the hands of steel,
It clicked from prayer to prayer, from meal to meal.
   Here as the lady sat, a friendly pair
Stepped in to admire the view, and took their chair –
They then related how the young and gay
Were thoughtless wandering in the broad highway,
How tender damsels sailed in tilted boats
And laughed with wicked men in scarlet coats,
And how we live in such degenerate times
That men conceal their wants, and show their crimes,
While vicious deeds are screened by fashion's name,
And what was once our pride is now our shame.
Dinah was musing, as her friends discoursed,
When these last words a sudden entrance forced
Upon her mind – and 'what was once her pride
And now her shame' some painful views supplied.
Thoughts of the past within her bosom pressed,
And there a change was felt, and was confessed.
While thus the virgin strove with secret pain,
Her mind was wandering o'er the troubled main –
Still she was silent, nothing seemed to see,
But sat and sighed in pensive reverie.
   The friends prepared new subjects to begin –
When tall Susannah, maiden starch, stalked in!
Not in her ancient mode, sedate and slow,
As when she came, the mind she knew, to know;
Nor as, when listening half an hour before,
She twice or thrice tapped gently at the door;
But, all decorum cast in wrath aside,
'I think the devil's in the man!' she cried –
'A huge tall sailor, with his tawny cheek,
And pitted face, will with my lady speak!
He grinned an ugly smile, and said he knew,
Please you, my lady, 'twould be joy to you –
What must I answer?' Trembling and distressed
Sank the pale Dinah by her fears oppressed,

When, thus alarmed, and brooking no delay,
Swift to her room the stranger made his way.
'Revive, my love', said he, 'I've done thee harm –
Give me thy pardon!' and he looked alarm.
Meantime the prudent Dinah had contrived
Her soul to question, and she then revived.
'See, my good friend' – and then she raised her head –
'The bloom of life, the strength of youth is fled!
Living we die – to us the world is dead!
We parted blest with health, and I am now
Age-struck and feeble – so I find art thou:
Thine eye is sunken, furrowed is thy face,
And downward lookst thou. So we run our race –
And happier they whose race is nearly run,
Their troubles over, and their duties done!'
'True, lady, true – we are not girl and boy,
But time has left us something to enjoy.'
'What! thou hast learned my fortune? Yes, I live
To feel how poor the comforts wealth can give!
Thou too perhaps art wealthy – but our fate
Still mocks our wishes! Wealth is come too late.'

'To me, nor late nor early! I am come
Poor as I left thee to my native home –
Nor yet', said Rupert, 'will I grieve. 'Tis mine
To share thy comforts, and the glory thine:
For thou wilt gladly take that generous part
That both exalts and gratifies the heart;
While mine rejoices –' 'Heavens!' returned the maid,
'This talk to one so withered and decayed?
No! all my care is now to fit my mind
For other spousal, and to die resigned.
As friend and neighbour, I shall hope to see
These noble views, this pious love, in thee –
That we together may the change await
(Guides and spectators in each other's fate),
When, fellow-pilgrims, we shall daily crave
The mutual prayer that arms us for the grave!'
Half angry, half in doubt, the lover gazed
On the meek maiden, by her speech amazed:
'Dinah', said he, 'dost thou respect thy vows?
What spousal meanest thou? Thou art Rupert's spouse!
The chance is mine to take, and thine to give –
But, trifling this, if we together live.

Can I believe that after all the past,
Our vows, our loves, thou wilt be false at last?
Something thou hast – I know not what – in view:
I find thee pious – let me find thee true!'
'Ah, cruel this – but do, my friend, depart,
And to its feelings leave my wounded heart!'
'Nay, speak at once – and Dinah, let me know,
Meanest thou to take me, now I'm wrecked, in tow?
Be fair; nor longer keep me in the dark –
Am I forsaken for a trimmer spark?
Heaven's spouse thou art not; nor can I believe
That God accepts her who will man deceive!
True I am shattered – I have service seen,
And service done, and have in trouble been!
My cheek (it shames me not) has lost its red,
And the brown buff is o'er my features spread.
Perchance my speech is rude, for I among
The untamed have been, in temper and in tongue –
Have been trepanned, have lived in toil and care,
And wrought for wealth I was not doomed to share.
It touched me deeply, for I felt a pride
In gaining riches for my destined bride!
Speak then my fate. For these my sorrows past,
Time lost, youth fled, hope wearied, and at last
This doubt of thee (a childish thing to tell,
But certain truth) – my very throat they swell;
They stop the breath, and but for shame could I
Give way to weakness, and with passion cry.
These are unmanly struggles, but I feel
This hour must end them – and perhaps will heal.'
   Here Dinah sighed, as if afraid to speak,
And then repeated – they were frail and weak;
His soul she loved, and hoped he had the grace
To fix his thoughts upon a better place.
She ceased. With steady glance, as if to see
The very root of this hypocrisy,
He her small fingers moulded in his hard
And bronzed broad hand – then told her his regard,
His best respect were gone, but love had still
Hold in his heart, and governed yet the will,
Or he would curse her. Saying this, he threw
The hand in scorn away, and bade adieu
To every lingering hope, with every care in view.

Proud and indignant, suffering, sick, and poor,
He grieved unseen, and spoke of love no more –
Till all he felt in indignation died,
As hers had sunk in avarice and pride.
In health declining, as in mind distressed,
To some in power his troubles he confessed,
And shares a parish-gift. At prayers he sees
The pious Dinah dropped upon her knees;
Thence as she walks the street with stately air
As chance directs, oft meet the parted pair.
When he, with thickset coat of badge-man's blue,
Moves near her shaded silk of changeful hue;
When his thin locks of gray approach her braid
(A costly purchase made in beauty's aid);
When his frank air, and his unstudied pace,
Are seen with her soft manner, air, and grace,
And his plain artless look with her sharp meaning face;
It might some wonder in a stranger move,
How these together could have talked of love.
Behold them now! See there a tradesman stands,
And humbly hearkens to some fresh commands.
He moves to speak, she interrupts him: 'Stay!'
Her air expresses – 'Hark to what I say!'
Ten paces off, poor Rupert on a seat
Has taken refuge from the noonday heat,
His eyes on her intent, as if to find
What were the movements of that subtle mind.
How still, how earnest is he! It appears
His thoughts are wandering through his earlier years –
Through years of fruitless labour, to the day
When all his earthly prospects died away:
'Had I', he thinks, 'been wealthier of the two,
Would she have found me so unkind, untrue?
Or knows not man when poor, what man when rich will do?
Yes, yes! I feel that I had faithful proved,
And should have soothed and raised her, blest and loved!'
But Dinah moves – she had observed before,
The pensive Rupert at an humble door.
Some thoughts of pity raised by his distress,
Some feeling touch of ancient tenderness;
Religion, duty, urged the maid to speak,
In terms of kindness to a man so weak;

But pride forbade – and to return would prove
She felt the shame of his neglected love.
Nor wrapped in silence could she pass, afraid
Each eye should see her, and each heart upbraid.
One way remained – the way the Levite took,
Who without mercy could on misery look
(A way perceived by craft, approved by pride),
She crossed and passed him on the other side.

8. JAMES SMITH

The Baby's Debut, by W. W.

(*Rejected Addresses*, 1812)

Spoken in the character of Nancy Lake, a girl eight years of age, who is drawn upon the stage in a child's chaise by Samuel Hughes, her uncle's porter.

'My brother Jack was nine in May,
And I was eight on New Year's Day;
   So in Kate Wilson's shop
Papa (he's my papa and Jack's)
Bought me, last week, a doll of wax,
   And brother Jack a top.

Jack's in the pouts, and this it is –
He thinks mine came to more than his;
   So to my drawer he goes,
Takes out the doll, and, O, my stars!
He pokes her head between the bars,
   And melts off half her nose!

Quite cross, a bit of string I beg,
And tie it to his peg-top's peg,
   And bang, with might and main,
Its head against the parlour-door:
Off flies the head, and hits the floor,
   And breaks a window-pane.

This made him cry with rage and spite:
Well, let him cry, it serves him right.
  A pretty thing, forsooth!
If he's to melt, all scalding hot,
Half my doll's nose, and I am not
  To draw his peg-top's tooth!

Aunt Hannah heard the window break,
And cried, "O naughty Nancy Lake,
  Thus to distress your aunt:
No Drury-Lane for you to-day!"
And while papa said, "Pooh, she may!"
  Mamma said, "No, she shan't!"

Well, after many a sad reproach,
They got into a hackney coach,
  And trotted down the street.
I saw them go: one horse was blind,
The tails of both hung down behind,
  Their shoes were on their feet.

The chaise in which poor brother Bill
Used to be drawn to Pentonville,
  Stood in the lumber-room:
I wiped the dust from off the top,
While Molly mopped it with a mop,
  And brushed it with a broom.

My uncle's porter, Samuel Hughes,
Came in at six to black the shoes
  (I always talk to Sam);
So what does he, but takes, and drags
Me in the chaise along the flags,
  And leaves me where I am.

My father's walls are made of brick,
But not so tall and not so thick
  As these; and, goodness me!
My father's beams are made of wood,
But never, never half so good
  As those that now I see.

What a large floor! 'tis like a town!
The carpet when they lay it down,
   Won't hide it, I'll be bound;
And there's a row of lamps! – my eye!
How they do blaze! I wonder why
   They keep them on the ground.

At first I caught hold of the wing,
And kept away; but Mr. Thing-
   umbob, the prompter man,
Gave with his hand my chaise a shove,
And said, "Go on, my pretty love;
   Speak to 'em, little Nan.

You've only got to curtsy, whisp-
er, hold your chin up, laugh, and lisp,
   And then you're sure to take:
I've known the day when brats, not quite
Thirteen, got fifty pounds a-night;
   Then why not Nancy Lake?"

But while I'm speaking, where's papa?
And where's my aunt? and where's mamma?
   Where's Jack? Oh, there they sit!
They smile, they nod; I'll go my ways,
And order round poor Billy's chaise,
   To join them in the pit.

And now, good gentle-folks, I go
To join mamma, and see the show;
   So, bidding you adieu,
I curtsy, like a pretty miss,
And if you'll blow to me,
I'll blow a kiss to you.'

[*Blows a kiss, and exit.*]

9. JAMES HOGG

from *The Poetic Mirror* (1816)

A number of years has elapsed since [the author] first conceived the idea of procuring something original from each of the principle living Bards of Britain, and publishing them together: Byron, Scott, Wordsworth, Hogg, Coleridge, Southey, Wilson.

(i) *James Rigg: Still Further Extract from 'The Recluse, A Poem'*

On Tuesday morn, at half past six o'clock,
I rose and dressed myself, and having shut
The door o' the bedroom still and leisurely,
I walked down stairs. When at the outer door
I firmly grasped the key, that ere night-fall
Had turned the lock into its wonted niche
Within the brazen implement, that shone
With no unseemly splendour – mellowed light
Elicited by touch of careful hand
On the brown lintel – and the obedient door
(As at a potent necromancer's touch)
Into the air receded suddenly,
And gave wide prospect of the sparkling lake,
Just then emerging from the snow-white mist
Like angel's veil slow-folded up to Heaven.
And lo! a vision bright and beautiful
Sheds a refulgent glory o'er the sand –
The sand and glory of my avenue,
For, standing silent by the kitchen-door
(Tinged by the morning sun, and in its own
Brown natural hide most lovely, two long ears
Upstretching perpendicularly, then
With the horizon levelled – to my gaze
Superb as horn of fabled unicorn –
Each in its own proportions grander far
Than the frontal glory of that wandering beast,
Child of the desert), lo! a beauteous ass,
With panniers hanging silent at each side,
Silent as cage of bird whose song is mute –
Though silent yet not empty – filled with bread,
The staff of life, the means by which the soul

(By fate obedient to the powers of sense)
Renews its faded vigour, and keeps up
A proud communion with the external heavens.
Fastened to a ring it stood, while at its head
A boy of six years old, an angel bright,
Patted its neck, and to its mouth applied
The harmless thistle that his hand had plucked
From the wild common, melancholy crop!
   Not undelightful was that simple sight,
For I at once did recognize that ass
To be the property of one James Rigg . . .

(ii) *Isabelle*

Can there be a moon in heaven tonight,
That the hill and gray cloud seem so light?
The air is whitened by some spell,
For there is no moon, I know it well;
On this third day the sages say –
'Tis wonderful how well they know! –
The moon is journeying far away,
Bright somewhere in a heaven below.

   It is a strange and lovely night,
A grayish pale, but not white!
Is it rain, or is it dew,
That falls so thick I see its hue?
In rays it follows, one, two, three,
Down the air so merrily;
Said Isabelle, 'So let it be!'

   Why does the Lady Isabelle
Sit in the damp and dewy dell
Counting the racks of drizzly rain?
And how often the rail cries over again,
For she's harping, harping, in the brake,
'Craik, craik, craik, craik' –
Ten times nine, and thrice eleven;
That last call was an hundred and seven!
'Craik, craik, the hour is near!'
Let it come, I have no fear –
Yet it is a dreadful work, I wis,
Such doings in a night like this!

Sounds the river harsh and loud?
The stream sounds harsh, but not loud.
There is a cloud that seems to hover
By western hill the churchyard over –
What is it like? 'Tis like a whale!
'Tis like a shark with half the tail –
Not half, but a third and more –
Now 'tis a wolf, and now a boar;
Its face is raised, it cometh here –
Let it come, there is no fear!
There's two for Heaven, and ten for Hell –
'Let it come, 'tis well, 'tis well!'
Said the Lady Isabelle.

10. JOHN HOOKHAM FRERE

'Irrational Gigantic Anger'

(*Whistlecraft*, Canto III, stanzas 1–7, 15–19) 1818

1

'I've a proposal here from Mr Murray –
He offers handsomely, the money down –
My dear, you might recover from your flurry
In a nice airy lodging out of town,
At Croyden, Epsom, anywhere in Surrey –
If every stanza brings us in a crown,
I think that I might venture to bespeak
A bedroom and front parlour for next week.

2

Tell me, my dear Thalia, what you think –
Your nerves have undergone a sudden shock,
Your poor dear spirits have begun to sink –
On Banstead Downs you'd muster a new stock,
And I'd be sure to keep away from drink
And always go to bed by twelve o'clock!
We'll travel down there in the morning stages:
Our verses shall go down to distant ages.

3

And here in town we'll breakfast on hot rolls,
  And you shall have a better shawl to wear –
These pantaloons of mine are chafed in holes,
  By Monday next I'll compass a new pair –
Come now, fling up the cinders, fetch the coals,
  And take away the things you hung to air;
Set out the tea-things, and bid Phoebe bring
The kettle up – *Arms and the Monks I sing*!

4

Some ten miles off an ancient Abbey stood
  Amidst the mountains, near a noble stream –
A level eminence, enshrined with wood,
  Sloped to the river's bank and southern beam.
Within were fifty friars fat and good,
  Of goodly persons, and of good esteem,
That passed an easy, exemplary life,
Remote from want and care and worldly strife.

5

Between the Monks and Giants there subsisted
  In the first Abbot's lifetime much respect;
The Giants let them settle where they listed –
  The Giants were a tolerating sect!
A poor lame Giant once the Monks assisted:
  Old and abandoned, dying with neglect,
The Prior found him, cured his broken bone,
And very kindly cut him for the stone.

6

This seemed a glorious, golden opportunity
  To civilize the whole gigantic race;
To draw them to pay tithes and dwell in unity;
  The Giant's valley was a fertile place,
And might have much enriched the whole community
  Had the old Giant lived a longer space –
But he relapsed, and though all means were tried,
They could but just baptize him – when he died.

7

And I believe the Giants never knew
  Of the kind treatment that befell their mate
(He broke down all at once, and all the crew
  Had taken leave, and left him to his fate),

And though the Monks exposed him full in view,
Propped on his crutches at the garden-gate
To prove their cure, and show that all was right,
It happened that no Giants came in sight . . .

15

In castles and in courts Ambition dwells,
But not in castles or in courts alone;
She breathed a wish, throughout those sacred cells,
For bells of larger size, and louder tone.
Giants abominate the sound of bells,
And soon the fierce antipathy was shown –
The tinkling and the jingling and the clangour
Roused their irrational gigantic anger!

16

Unhappy mortals, ever blind to fate!
Unhappy Monks, you see no danger nigh!
Exulting in their sound and size and weight,
From morn till noon the merry peal you ply:
The belfry rocks, your bosoms are elate,
Your spirits with the ropes and pulleys fly –
Tired, but transported, panting, pulling, hauling,
Ramping and stamping, overjoyed and bawling.

17

Meanwhile the solemn mountains that surrounded
The silent valley where the Convent lay,
With tintinabular uproar were astounded,
When the first peal burst forth at break of day:
Feeling their granite ears severely wounded,
They scarce knew what to think, or what to say,
And – though large mountains commonly conceal
Their sentiments, dissembling what they feel –

18

Yet Cader-Gibbrish from his cloudy throne
To huge Loblommon gave an intimation
Of this strange rumour, with an awful tone
Thundering his deep surprise and indignation.
The lesser hills, in language of their own,
Discussed the topic by reverberation,
Discoursing with their echoes all day long –
Their only conversation was, 'ding-dong'!

19

Those giant-mountains inwardly were moved,
   But never made an outward change of place:
Not so the mountain-giants – as behoved
   A more alert and locomotive race –
Hearing a clatter which they disapproved,
   They ran straight forward to besiege the place
With a discordant universal yell,
Like house-dog howling at a dinner-bell.

11. JOHN KEATS

Old Meg She Was a Gypsy

(2 July 1818; publ. 1838)

Old Meg she was a gypsy,
   And lived upon the moors,
Her bed it was the brown heath-turf,
   And her house was out-of-doors.

Her apples were swart blackberries,
   Her currants pods o' broom,
Her wine was dew of the white wild rose,
   Her book a churchyard tomb.

Her brothers were the craggy hills,
   Her sisters larchen trees –
Alone with her great family
   She lived as she did please.

No breakfast had she many a morn,
   No dinner many a noon,
And 'stead of supper she would stare
   Full hard against the moon.

For every morn, of woodbine fresh
   She made a garlanding,
And every night the dark glen yew
   She wove – and she would sing!

And with her fingers old and brown
   She plaited mats o' rushes,
And gave them to the cottagers
   She met among the bushes.

Old Meg she was brave as Margaret Queen
   And tall as Amazon,
An old red blanket-cloak she wore,
   A chip-hat had she on –
God rest her agéd bones somewhere,
   She died full long agone!

12. PERCY BYSSHE SHELLEY

Sin (*Peter Bell the Third* IV, 1–65) 1819; publ. 1839

Is it a party in a parlour –
Crammed just as they on earth were crammed,
Some sipping punch – some sipping tea;
But, as you by their faces see,
All silent and all – damned!
(*Peter Bell*, by W. Wordsworth)

Lo, Peter in Hell's Grosvenor Square,
   A footman in the Devil's service!
And the misjudging world would swear
That every man in service there
   To virtue would prefer vice.

But Peter, though now damned, was not
   What Peter was before damnation:
Men oftentimes prepare a lot
Which, ere it finds them, is not what
   Suits with their genuine station.

All things that Peter saw and felt
   Had a peculiar aspect to him;
And when they came within the belt
Of his own nature, seemed to melt,
   Like cloud to cloud, into him.

And so the outward world uniting
  To that within him, he became
Considerably uninviting
To those who, meditation slighting,
  Were moulded in a different frame.

And he scorned them, and they scorned him!
  And he scorned all they did – and they
Did all that men of their own trim
Are wont to do to please their whim,
  Drinking, lying, swearing, play.

Such were his fellow-servants – thus
  His virtue, like our own, was built
Too much on that indignant fuss
Hypocrite pride stirs up in us
  To bully one another's guilt.

He had a mind which was somehow
  At once circumference and centre
Of all he might or feel or know –
Nothing went ever out, although
  Something did ever enter.

He had as much imagination
  As a pint-pot – he never could
Fancy another situation,
From which to dart his contemplation,
  Than that wherein he stood!

Yet his was individual mind,
  And new created all he saw
In a new manner, and refined
Those new creations, and combined
  Them, by a master-spirit's law.

Thus, though unimaginative,
  An apprehension clear, intense,
Of his mind's work, had made alive
The things it wrought on – I believe
  Wakening a sort of thought in sense.

But from the first 'twas Peter's drift
To be a kind of moral eunuch,
He touched the hem of Nature's shift,
Felt faint – and never dared uplift
The closest, all-concealing tunic!

She laughed the while, with an arch smile,
And kissed him with a sister's kiss,
And said: 'My best Diogenes,
I love you well, but, if you please,
Tempt not again my deepest bliss!

'Tis you are cold – for I, not coy,
Yield love for love, frank, warm, and true;
And Burns, a Scottish peasant-boy –
His errors prove it – knew my joy
More, learnéd friend, than you . . .

13. LORD BYRON

Juan and Julia

(*Don Juan* I, stanzas 54–117, 133–87) 1819

54

Young Juan now was sixteen years of age,
Tall, handsome, slender, but well knit; he seemed
Active, though not so sprightly, as a page;
And everybody but his mother deemed
Him almost man; but she flew in a rage
And bit her lips (for else she might have screamed)
If any said so, for to be precocious
Was in her eyes a thing the most atrocious.

55

Amongst her numerous acquaintance, all
Selected for discretion and devotion,
There was the Donna Julia, whom to call
Pretty were but to give a feeble notion
Of many charms in her as natural
As sweetness to the flower, or salt to ocean,
Her zone to Venus, or his bow to Cupid
(But this last simile is trite and stupid).

56

The darkness of her oriental eye
    Accorded with her Moorish origin.
Her blood was not all Spanish, by the by
    (In Spain, you know, this is a sort of sin):
When proud Grenada fell, and, forced to fly,
    Boabdil wept, of Donna Julia's kin
Some went to Africa, some stayed in Spain –
Her great great grandmamma chose to remain.

57

She married (I forget the pedigree)
    With an hidalgo, who transmitted down
His blood less noble than such blood should be;
    At such alliances his sires would frown,
In that point so precise in each degree
    That they bred in and in, as might be shown,
Marrying their cousins – nay, their aunts and nieces,
Which always spoils the breed, if it increases.

58

This heathenish cross restored the breed again,
    Ruined its blood, but much improved its flesh;
For, from a root the ugliest in old Spain
    Sprung up a branch as beautiful as fresh;
The sons no more were short, the daughters plain –
    But there's a rumour which I fain would hush:
'Tis said that Donna Julia's grandmamma
Produced her Don more heirs at love than law.

59

However this might be, the race went on
    Improving still through every generation,
Until it centered in an only son,
    Who left an only daughter; my narration
May have suggested that this single one
    Could be but Julia (whom on this occasion
I shall have much to speak about), and she
Was married, charming, chaste, and twenty-three.

60

Her eye (I'm very fond of handsome eyes)
  Was large and dark, suppressing half its fire
Until she spoke, then through its soft disguise
  Flashed an expression more of pride than ire,
And love than either; and there would arise
  A something in them which was not desire,
But would have been, perhaps, but for the soul
Which struggled through and chastened down the whole.

61

Her glossy hair was clustered o'er a brow
  Bright with intelligence, and fair and smooth;
Her eyebrow's shape was like the aerial bow,
  Her cheek all purple with the beam of youth,
Mounting, at times, to a transparent glow,
  As if her veins ran lightning; she, in sooth,
Possessed an air and grace by no means common,
Her stature tall – I hate a dumpy woman.

62

Wedded she was some years, and to a man
  Of fifty – and such husbands are in plenty –
And yet, I think, instead of such a ONE
  'Twere better to have TWO of five and twenty,
Especially in countries near the sun:
  And now I think on't, *mi vien in mente*,
Ladies even of the most uneasy virtue
Prefer a spouse whose age is short of thirty.

63

'Tis a sad thing, I cannot choose but say,
  And all the fault of that indecent sun
Who cannot leave alone our helpless clay
  But will keep baking, broiling, burning on,
That howsoever people fast and pray
  The flesh is frail, and so the soul undone:
What men call gallantry, and gods adultery,
Is much more common where the climate's sultry.

64

Happy the nations of the moral north!
  Where all is virtue, and the winter season
Sends sin, without a rag on, shivering forth
  ('Twas snow that brought St Anthony to reason);

Where juries cast up what a wife is worth
   By laying whate'er sum, in mulct, they please on
The lover, who must pay a handsome price
Because it is a marketable vice.

65

Alfonso was the name of Julia's lord,
   A man well looking for his years, and who
Was neither much beloved, nor yet abhorred;
   They lived together as most people do,
Suffering each other's foibles by accord,
   And not exactly either one or two;
Yet he was jealous, though he did not show it,
For jealousy dislikes the world to know it.

66

Julia was – yet I never could see why –
   With Donna Inez quite a favourite friend;
Between their tastes there was small sympathy,
   For not a line had Julia ever penned.
Some people whisper (but, no doubt, they lie,
   For malice still imputes some private end)
That Inez had, ere Don Alfonso's marriage,
Forgot with him her very prudent carriage;

67

And that, still keeping up the old connection,
   Which time had lately rendered much more chaste,
She took his lady also in affection.
   And certainly this course was much the best:
She flattered Julia with her sage protection,
   And complimented Don Alfonso's taste;
And if she could not (who can?) silence scandal,
At least she left it a more slender handle.

68

I can't tell whether Julia saw the affair
   With other people's eyes, or if her own
Discoveries made, but none could be aware
   Of this, at least no symptom e'er was shown;
Perhaps she did not know, or did not care,
   Indifferent from the first, or callous grown:
I'm really puzzled what to think or say,
She kept her counsel in so close a way.

69

Juan she saw, and, as a pretty child,
   Caressed him often, such a thing might be
Quite innocently done, and harmless styled,
   When she had twenty years, and thirteen he;
But I am not so sure I should have smiled
   When he was sixteen, Julia twenty-three,
These few short years make wondrous alterations,
Particularly amongst sun-burnt nations.

70

Whate'er the cause might be, they had become
   Changed; for the dame grew distant, the youth shy,
Their looks cast down, their greetings almost dumb,
   And much embarrassment in either eye.
There surely will be little doubt with some
   That Donna Julia knew the reason why,
But as for Juan, he had no more notion
Than he who never saw the sea of ocean.

71

Yet Julia's very coldness still was kind,
   And tremulously gentle her small hand
Withdrew itself from his, but left behind
   A little pressure, thrilling, and so bland
And slight, so very slight, that to the mind
   'Twas but a doubt; but ne'er magician's wand
Wrought change with all Armida's fairy art
Like what this light touch left on Juan's heart.

72

And if she met him, though she smiled no more,
   She looked a sadness sweeter than her smile,
As if her heart had deeper thoughts in store
   She must not own, but cherished more the while
For that compression in its burning core.
   Even innocence itself has many a wile,
And will not dare to trust itself with truth –
And love is taught hypocrisy from youth.

73

But passion most dissembles yet betrays
   Even by its darkness; as the blackest sky
Foretells the heaviest tempest, it displays
   Its workings through the vainly guarded eye,

And in whatever aspect it arrays
Itself, 'tis still the same hypocrisy;
Coldness or anger, even disdain or hate,
Are masks it often wears, and still too late.

74

Then there were sighs, the deeper for suppression,
And stolen glances, sweeter for the theft,
And burning blushes, though for no transgression,
Tremblings when met, and restlessness when left;
All these are little preludes to possession,
Of which young passion cannot be bereft,
And merely tend to show how greatly love is
Embarrassed at first starting with a novice.

75

Poor Julia's heart was in an awkward state;
She felt it going, and resolved to make
The noblest efforts for herself and mate,
For honour's, pride's, religion's, virtue's sake;
Her resolutions were most truly great,
And almost might have made a Tarquin quake;
She prayed the Virgin Mary for her grace,
As being the best judge of a lady's case.

76

She vowed she never would see Juan more,
And next day paid a visit to his mother,
And looked extremely at the opening door,
Which, by the Virgin's grace, let in another;
Grateful she was, and yet a little sore –
Again it opens, it can be no other,
'Tis surely Juan now – No! I'm afraid
That night the Virgin was no further prayed.

77

She now determined that a virtuous woman
Should rather face and overcome temptation,
That flight was base and dastardly, and no man
Should ever give her heart the least sensation;
That is to say, a thought beyond the common
Preference that we must feel upon occasion
For people who are pleasanter than others –
But then they only seem so many brothers.

78

And even if by chance (and who can tell –
  The devil's so very sly) she should discover
That all within was not so very well,
  And, if still free, that such or such a lover
Might please perhaps, a virtuous wife can quell
  Such thoughts, and be the better when they're over.
And if the man should ask, 'tis but denial:
I recommend young ladies to make trial.

79

And then there are such things as love divine,
  Bright and immaculate, unmixed and pure,
Such as the angels think so very fine,
  And matrons, who would be no less secure,
Platonic, perfect, 'just such love as mine':
  Thus Julia said – and thought so, to be sure –
And so I'd have her think, were I the man
On whom her reveries celestial ran.

80

Such love is innocent, and may exist
  Between young persons without any danger –
A hand may first, and then a lip be kissed –
  For my part, to such doings I'm a stranger,
But hear these freedoms form the utmost list
  Of all o'er which such love may be a ranger:
If people go beyond, 'tis quite a crime,
But not my fault – I tell them all in time.

81

Love, then, but love within its proper limits,
  Was Julia's innocent determination
In young Don Juan's favour. And to him, its
  Exertion might be useful on occasion,
And (lighted at too pure a shrine to dim its
  Etherial lustre) with what sweet persuasion
He might be taught, by love and her together –
I really don't know what, nor Julia either!

82

Fraught with this fine intention, and well fenced
  In mail of proof (her purity of soul),
She, for the future, of her strength convinced,
  And that her honour was a rock, or mole,

Exceeding sagely from that hour dispensed
   With any kind of troublesome control –
   But whether Julia to the task was equal
Is that which must be mentioned in the sequel.

83

Her plan she deemed both innocent and feasible,
   And, surely, with a stripling of sixteen
Not scandal's fangs could fix on much that's seizable,
   Or if they did so, satisfied to mean
Nothing but what was good, her breast was peaceable –
   A quiet conscience makes one so serene!
Christians have burnt each other, quite persuaded
That all the Apostles would have done as they did.

84

And if in the mean time her husband died –
   But Heaven forbid that such a thought should cross
Her brain, though in a dream – and then she sighed –
   Never could she survive that common loss! –
But just suppose that moment should betide,
   I only say suppose it, *inter nos*
(This should be *entre nous*, for Julia thought
In French, but then the rhyme would go for nought),

85

I only say suppose this supposition:
   Juan being then grown up to man's estate
Would fully suit a widow of condition,
   Even seven years hence it would not be too late;
And in the interim (to pursue this vision)
   The mischief, after all, could not be great,
For he would learn the rudiments of love –
I mean the seraph way of those above.

86

So much for Julia. Now we'll turn to Juan,
   Poor little fellow, he had no idea
Of his own case, and never hit the true one;
   In feelings quick as Ovid's Miss Medea,
He puzzled over what he found a new one,
   But not as yet imagined it could be a
Thing quite in course, and not at all alarming,
Which, with a little patience, might grow charming.

87

Silent and pensive, idle, restless, slow,
His home deserted for the lonely wood,
Tormented with a wound he could not know,
His, like all deep grief, plunged in solitude:
I'm fond myself of solitude or so,
But then, I beg it may be understood,
By solitude I mean a sultan's, not
A hermit's, with a harem for a grot.

88

'Oh Love! in such a wilderness as this,
Where transport and security entwine,
Here is the empire of thy perfect bliss,
And here thou art a god indeed divine.'
The bard I quote from does not sing amiss,
With the exception of the second line,
For that same twining 'transport and security'
Are twisted to a phrase of some obscurity.

89

The poet meant, no doubt, and thus appeals
To the good sense and senses of mankind,
The very thing which everybody feels,
As all have found on trial, or may find,
That no one likes to be disturbed at meals
Or love! I won't say more about 'entwined'
Or 'transport', as we knew all that before,
But beg 'security' will bolt the door.

90

Young Juan wandered by the glassy brooks
Thinking unutterable things; he threw
Himself at length within the leafy nooks
Where the wild branch of the cork forest grew;
There poets find materials for their books,
And every now and then we read them through,
So that their plan and prosody are eligible,
Unless, like Wordsworth, they prove unintelligible.

91

He, Juan (and not Wordsworth) so pursued
His self-communion with his own high soul
Until his mighty heart, in its great mood,
Had mitigated part, though not the whole

Of its disease; he did the best he could
With things not very subject to control,
And turned, without perceiving his condition,
Like Coleridge, into a metaphysician.

92

He thought about himself, and the whole earth,
Of man the wonderful, and of the stars,
And how the deuce they ever could have birth;
And then he thought of earthquakes, and of wars,
How many miles the moon might have in girth,
Of air-balloons, and of the many bars
To perfect knowledge of the boundless skies –
And then he thought of Donna Julia's eyes.

93

In thoughts like these true wisdom may discern
Longings sublime, and aspirations high,
Which some are born with, but the most part learn
To plague themselves withal, they know not why:
'Twas strange that one so young should thus concern
His brain about the action of the sky;
If you think 'twas philosophy that this did,
I can't help thinking puberty assisted.

94

He pored upon the leaves, and on the flowers,
And heard a voice in all the winds; and then
He thought of wood nymphs and immortal bowers,
And how the goddesses came down to men:
He missed the pathway, he forgot the hours,
And when he looked upon his watch again,
He found how much old Time had been a winner –
He also found that he had lost his dinner.

95

Sometimes he turned to gaze upon his book,
Boscan, or Garcilasso – by the wind
Even as the page is rustled while we look,
So by the poesy of his own mind
Over the mystic leaf his soul was shook,
As if 'twere one whereon magicians bind
Their spells, and give them to the passing gale,
According to some good old woman's tale.

96

Thus would he while his lonely hours away
 Dissatisfied, nor knowing what he wanted;
Nor glowing reverie, nor poet's lay,
 Could yield his spirit that for which it panted,
A bosom whereon he his head might lay,
 And hear the heart beat with the love it granted,
With – several other things, which I forget,
Or which, at least, I need not mention yet.

97

Those lonely walks, and lengthening reveries,
 Could not escape the gentle Julia's eyes;
She saw that Juan was not at his ease;
 But that which chiefly may, and must, surprise
Is, that the Donna Inez did not tease
 Her only son with question or surmise;
Whether it was she did not see, or would not,
Or, like all very clever people, could not.

98

This may seem strange, but yet 'tis very common;
 For instance, gentlemen, whose ladies take
Leave to o'erstep the written rights of woman
 And break the – which commandment is't they break
(I have forgot the number, and think no man
 Should rashly quote, for fear of a mistake) –
I say, when these same gentlemen are jealous,
They make some blunder, which their ladies tell us.

99

A real husband always is suspicious,
 But still no less suspects in the wrong place,
Jealous of some one who had no such wishes,
 Or pandering blindly to his own disgrace
By harbouring some dear friend extremely vicious –
 The last indeed's infallibly the case:
And when the spouse and friend are gone off wholly,
He wonders at their vice, and not his folly.

100

Thus parents also are at times short-sighted;
 Though watchful as the lynx, they ne'er discover,
The while the wicked world beholds delighted,
 Young Hopeful's mistress, or Miss Fanny's lover,

Till some confounded escapade has blighted
   The plan of twenty years, and all is over;
And then the mother cries, the father swears,
And wonders why the devil he got heirs.

101

But Inez was so anxious, and so clear
   Of sight, that I must think, on this occasion,
She had some other motive much more near
   For leaving Juan to his new temptation;
But what that motive was, I shan't say here;
   Perhaps to finish Juan's education,
Perhaps to open Don Alfonso's eyes,
In case he thought his wife too great a prize.

102

It was upon a day, a summer's day –
   Summer's indeed a very dangerous season,
And so is spring about the end of May –
   The sun, no doubt, is the prevailing reason;
But whatsoe'er the cause is, one may say,
   And stand convicted of more truth than treason,
That there are months which nature grows more merry in:
March has its hares, and May must have its heroine.

103

'Twas on a summer's day – the sixth of June –
   I like to be particular in dates,
Not only of the age, and year, but moon;
   They are a sort of post-house, where the Fates
Change horses, making history change its tune,
   Then spur away o'er empires and o'er states,
Leaving at last not much besides chronology,
Excepting the post-obits of theology.

104

'Twas on the sixth of June, about the hour
   Of half-past six – perhaps still nearer seven –
When Julia sat within as pretty a bower
   As e'er held houri in that heathenish heaven
Described by Mahomet, and Anacreon Moore,
   To whom the lyre and laurels have been given,
With all the trophies of triumphant song –
He won them well, and may he wear them long!

105

She sat, but not alone; I know not well
How this same interview had taken place,
And even if I knew, I should not tell –
People should hold their tongues in any case –
No matter how or why the thing befell,
But there were she and Juan, face to face.
When two such faces are so, 'twould be wise,
But very difficult, to shut their eyes.

106

How beautiful she looked! Her conscious heart
Glowed in her cheek, and yet she felt no wrong.
Oh Love, how perfect is thy mystic art,
Strengthening the weak, and trampling on the strong,
How self-deceitful is the sagest part
Of mortals whom thy lure hath led along –
The precipice she stood on was immense,
So was her creed in her own innocence.

107

She thought of her own strength, and Juan's youth,
And of the folly of all prudish fears,
Victorious virtue, and domestic truth,
And then of Don Alfonso's fifty years:
I wish these last had not occurred, in sooth,
Because that number rarely much endears,
And through all climes, the snowy and the sunny,
Sounds ill in love, whate'er it may in money.

108

When people say, 'I've told you fifty times',
They mean to scold, and very often do;
When poets say, 'I've written fifty rhymes',
They make you dread that they'll recite them too;
In gangs of fifty, thieves commit their crimes;
At fifty love for love is rare, 'tis true,
But then, no doubt, it equally as true is,
A good deal may be bought for fifty Louis.

109

Julia had honour, virtue, truth, and love
For Don Alfonso; and she inly swore,
By all the vows below to powers above,
She never would disgrace the ring she wore,

Nor leave a wish which wisdom might reprove;
  And while she pondered this, besides much more,
One hand on Juan's carelessly was thrown,
Quite by mistake – she thought it was her own;

110

Unconsciously she leaned upon the other,
  Which played within the tangles of her hair;
And to contend with thoughts she could not smother,
  She seemed by the distraction of her air.
'Twas surely very wrong in Juan's mother
  To leave together this imprudent pair –
She who for many years had watched her son so:
I'm very certain mine would not have done so.

111

The hand which still held Juan's, by degrees
  Gently, but palpably confirmed its grasp,
As if it said 'Detain me, if you please';
  Yet there's no doubt she only meant to clasp
His fingers with a pure Platonic squeeze;
  She would have shrunk as from a toad, or asp,
Had she imagined such a thing could rouse
A feeling dangerous to a prudent spouse.

112

I cannot know what Juan thought of this,
  But what he did, is much what you would do;
His young lip thanked it with a grateful kiss,
  And then, abashed at its own joy, withdrew
In deep despair, lest he had done amiss,
  Love is so very timid when 'tis new:
She blushed, and frowned not, but she strove to speak,
And held her tongue, her voice was grown so weak.

113

The sun set, and up rose the yellow moon –
  The devil's in the moon for mischief – they
Who called her chaste, methinks, began too soon
  Their nomenclature; there is not a day,
The longest, not the twenty-first of June,
  Sees half the business in a wicked way
On which three single hours of moonshine smile.
And then she looks so modest all the while!

114

There is a dangerous silence in that hour,
   A stillness, which leaves room for the full soul
To open all itself, without the power
   Of calling wholly back its self-control;
The silver light which, hallowing tree and tower,
   Sheds beauty and deep softness o'er the whole,
Breathes also to the heart, and o'er it throws
A loving languor, which is not repose.

115

And Julia sat with Juan, half embraced
   And half retiring from the glowing arm,
Which trembled like the bosom where 'twas placed;
   Yet still she must have thought there was no harm,
Or else 'twere easy to withdraw her waist;
   But then the situation had its charm,
And then – God knows what next – I can't go on;
I'm almost sorry that I e'er begun.

116

Oh Plato! Plato! You have paved the way,
   With your confounded fantasies, to more
Immoral conduct by the fancied sway
   Your system feigns o'er the controlless core
Of human hearts, than all the long array
   Of poets and romancers. You're a bore,
A charlatan, a coxcomb – and have been,
At best, no better than a go-between!

117

And Julia's voice was lost, except in sighs,
   Until too late for useful conversation;
The tears were gushing from her gentle eyes,
   I wish, indeed, they had not had occasion,
But who, alas, can love, and then be wise?
   Not that remorse did not oppose temptation,
A little still she strove, and much repented,
And whispering 'I will ne'er consent' – consented . . .

133

Man's a phenomenon, one knows not what,
   And wonderful beyond all wondrous measure;
'Tis pity though, in this sublime world, that
   Pleasure's a sin, and sometimes sin's a pleasure!

Few mortals know what end they would be at,
But whether glory, power, or love, or treasure,
The path is through perplexing ways, and when
The goal is gained, we die, you know – and then?

134

What then? I do not know. No more do you –
And so good night! Return we to our story:
'Twas in November, when fine days are few,
And the far mountains wax a little hoary
And clap a white cape on their mantles blue,
And the sea dashes round the promontory,
And the wild breaker boils against the rock,
And sober suns must set at five o'clock.

135

'Twas, as the watchmen say, a cloudy night;
No moon, no stars, the wind was low or loud
By gusts, and many a sparkling hearth was bright
With the piled wood, round which the family crowd;
There's something cheerful in that sort of light,
Even as a summer sky's without a cloud:
I'm fond of fire, and crickets, and all that,
A lobster salad, and champagne, and chat.

136

'Twas midnight, Donna Julia was in bed
(Sleeping, most probably), when at her door
Arose a clatter might awake the dead,
If they had never been awoke before –
And that they have been so we all have read,
And are to be so, at the least, once more!
The door was fastened, but with voice and fist
First knocks were heard, then 'Madam – Madam – hist!

137

For God's sake, Madam – Madam – here's my master,
With more than half the city at his back –
Was ever heard of such a curst disaster!
'Tis not my fault – I kept good watch. Alack!
Do, pray undo the bolt a little faster –
They're on the stair just now, and in a crack
Will all be here! Perhaps he yet may fly –
Surely the window's not so very high?'

138

By this time Don Alfonso was arrived,
With torches, friends, and servants in great number;
The major part of them had long been wived,
And therefore paused not to disturb the slumber
Of any wicked woman, who contrived
By stealth her husband's temples to encumber:
Examples of this kind are so contagious,
Were one not punished, all would be outrageous!

139

I can't tell how, or why, or what suspicion
Could enter into Don Alfonso's head;
But for a cavalier of his condition
It surely was exceedingly ill-bred,
Without a word of previous admonition,
To hold a levée round his lady's bed,
And summon lackeys, armed with fire and sword,
To prove himself the thing he most abhorred.

140

Poor Donna Julia! starting as from sleep,
(Mind, that I do not say, she had not slept)
Began at once to scream, and yawn, and weep;
Her maid Antonia, who was an adept,
Contrived to fling the bedclothes in a heap,
As if she had just now from out them crept:
I can't tell why she should take all this trouble
To prove her mistress had been sleeping double.

141

But Julia mistress, and Antonia maid,
Appeared like two poor harmless women, who,
Of goblins, but still more of men, afraid,
Had thought one man might be deterred by two,
And therefore side by side were gently laid
Until the hours of absence should run through
And truant husband should return, and say
'My dear, I was the first who came away.'

142

Now Julia found at length a voice, and cried
'In heaven's name, Don Alfonso, what d'ye mean?
Has madness seized you? Would that I had died
Ere such a monster's victim I had been!

What may this midnight violence betide,
   A sudden fit of drunkenness or spleen?
Dare you suspect me, whom the thought would kill?
Search, then, the room!' Alfonso said, 'I will.'

143

He searched, they searched, and rummaged everywhere,
   Closet and clothes-press, chest and window-seat,
And found much linen, lace, and several pair
   Of stockings, slippers, brushes, combs, complete,
With other articles of ladies fair,
   To keep them beautiful, or leave them neat:
Arras they pricked, and curtains, with their swords,
And wounded several shutters, and some boards.

144

Under the bed they searched, and there they found –
   No matter what – it was not that they sought!
They opened windows, gazing if the ground
   Had signs or footmarks, but the earth said nought;
And then they stared each others' faces round:
   'Tis odd, not one of all these seekers thought
(And seems to me almost a sort of blunder),
Of looking in the bed as well as under.

145

During this inquisition Julia's tongue
   Was not asleep: 'Yes, search and search', she cried,
'Insult on insult heap, and wrong on wrong!
   It was for this that I became a bride!
For this in silence I have suffered long
   A husband like Alfonso at my side;
But now I'll bear no more, nor here remain,
If there be law, or lawyers, in all Spain.

146

'Yes, Don Alfonso! – husband now no more
   (If ever you indeed deserved the name),
Is't worthy of your years? You have threescore –
   Fifty, or sixty, it is all the same!
Is't wise or fitting causeless to explore
   For facts against a virtuous woman's fame?
Ungrateful, perjured, barbarous Don Alfonso,
How dare you think your lady would go on so?

147

Is it for this I have disdained to hold
   The common privileges of my sex? –
That I have chosen a confessor so old
   And deaf, that any other it would vex,
And never once he has had cause to scold,
   But found my very innocence perplex
So much, he always doubted I was married –
How sorry you will be when I've miscarried!

148

Was it for this that no cortejo ere
   I yet have chosen from out the youth of Seville?
Is it for this I scarce went anywhere,
   Except to bull-fights, mass, play, rout, and revel?
Is it for this, whate'er my suitors were,
   I favoured none–nay, was almost uncivil?
Is it for this that General Count O'Reilly,
Who took Algiers, declares I used him vilely?

149

Did not the Italian Musico Cazzani
   Sing at my heart six months at least in vain?
Did not his countryman, Count Corniani,
   Call me the only virtuous wife in Spain?
Were there not also Russians, English, many?
   The Count Strongstroganoff I put in pain,
And Lord Mount Coffeehouse, the Irish peer,
Who killed himself for love (with wine) last year.

150

Have I not had two bishops at my feet?
   The Duke of Ichar, and Don Fernan Nunez,
And is it thus a faithful wife you treat?
   I wonder in what quarter now the moon is!
I praise your vast forbearance not to beat
   Me also, since the time so opportune is –
Oh, valiant man! with sword drawn and cocked trigger,
Now, tell me, don't you cut a pretty figure?

151

Was it for this you took your sudden journey,
   Under pretence of business indispensable
With that sublime of rascals your attorney,
   Whom I see standing there, and looking sensible

Of having played the fool? Though both I spurn, he
   Deserves the worst, his conduct's less defensible,
Because, no doubt, 'twas for his dirty fee,
And not from any love to you nor me.

152

If he comes here to take a deposition,
   By all means let the gentleman proceed;
You've made the apartment in a fit condition –
   There's pen and ink for you, sir, when you need –
Let every thing be noted with precision,
   I would not you for nothing should be fee'd!
But, as my maid's undressed, pray turn your spies out.'
'Oh!' sobbed Antonia, 'I could tear their eyes out.'

153

'There is the closet, there the toilette, there
   The anti-chamber – search them under, over!
There is the sofa, there the great armchair,
   The chimney (which would really hold a lover).
I wish to sleep, and beg you will take care
   And make no further noise, till you discover
The secret cavern of this lurking treasure –
And when 'tis found, let me, too, have that pleasure.

154

And now, Hidalgo! now that you have thrown
   Doubt upon me, confusion over all,
Pray have the courtesy to make it known
   Who is the man you search for? How d'ye call
Him? What's his lineage? Let him but be shown!
   I hope he's young and handsome – is he tall?
Tell me – and be assured that since you stain
My honour thus, it shall not be in vain!

155

At least, perhaps, he has not sixty years!
   At that age he would be too old for slaughter,
Or for so young a husband's jealous fears–
   Antonia! let me have a glass of water –
I am ashamed of having shed these tears,
   They are unworthy of my father's daughter;
My mother dreamed not in my natal hour
That I should fall into a monster's power!

156

Perhaps 'tis of Antonia you are jealous,
You saw that she was sleeping by my side
When you broke in upon us with your fellows!
Look where you please – we've nothing, sir, to hide –
Only another time, I trust, you'll tell us,
Or for the sake of decency abide
A moment at the door, that we may be
Dressed to receive so much good company!

157

And now, sir, I have done, and say no more!
The little I have said may serve to show
The guileless heart in silence may grieve o'er
The wrongs to whose exposure it is slow –
I leave you to your conscience as before,
'Twill one day ask you why you used me so.
God grant you feel not then the bitterest grief –
Antonia! where's my pocket-handkerchief?'

158

She ceased, and turned upon her pillow. Pale
She lay, her dark eyes flashing through their tears,
Like skies that rain and lighten – as a veil,
Waved and o'ershading her wan cheek, appears
Her streaming hair. The black curls strive, but fail,
To hide the glossy shoulder, which uprears
Its snow through all – her soft lips lie apart,
And louder than her breathing beats her heart.

159

The Señor Don Alfonso stood confused;
Antonia bustled round the ransacked room,
And, turning up her nose, with looks abused
Her master, and his myrmidons, of whom
Not one, except the attorney, was amused –
He, like Achates, faithful to the tomb,
So there were quarrels, cared not for the cause,
Knowing they must be settled by the laws.

160

With prying snub-nose, and small eyes, he stood,
Following Antonia's motions here and there,
With much suspicion in his attitude.
For reputations he had little care –

So that a suit or action were made good –
   Small pity had he for the young and fair,
And ne'er believed in negatives, till these
Were proved by competent false witnesses.

161

But Don Alfonso stood with downcast looks,
   And, truth to say, he made a foolish figure;
When, after searching in five hundred nooks,
   And treating a young wife with so much rigour,
He gained no point, except some self-rebukes,
   Added to those his lady with such vigour
Had poured upon him for the last half-hour,
Quick, thick, and heavy – as a thunder-shower.

162

At first he tried to hammer an excuse,
   To which the sole reply were tears, and sobs,
And indications of hysterics, whose
   Prologue is always certain throes, and throbs,
Gasps, and whatever else the owners choose –
   Alfonso saw his wife, and thought of Job's!
He saw too, in perspective, her relations,
And then he tried to muster all his patience.

163

He stood in act to speak, or rather stammer,
   But sage Antonia cut him short before
The anvil of his speech received the hammer,
   With 'Pray sir, leave the room, and say no more,
Or madam dies!' Alfonso muttered 'Damn her',
   But nothing else, the time of words was o'er –
He cast a rueful look or two, and did
(He knew not wherefore) that which he was bid.

164

With him retired his *posse comitatus*,
   The attorney last, who lingered near the door
Reluctantly, still tarrying there as late as
   Antonia let him – not a little sore
At this most strange and unexplained 'hiatus'
   In Don Alfonso's facts, which just now wore
An awkward look. As he revolved the case
The door was fastened in his legal face.

165

No sooner was it bolted, than – oh shame!
Oh sin! oh sorrow! and oh womankind!
How can you do such things and keep your fame,
Unless this world, and t'other too, be blind?
Nothing so dear as an unfilched good name!
But to proceed (for there is more behind) –
With much heart-felt reluctance be it said,
Young Juan slipped, half-smothered, from the bed.

166

He had been hid – I don't pretend to say
How, nor can I indeed describe the where
(Young, slender, and packed easily, he lay,
No doubt, in little compass, round or square) –
But pity him I neither must nor may
His suffocation by that pretty pair:
'Twere better, sure, to die so, than be shut
With maudlin Clarence in his Malmsey butt.

167

And, secondly, I pity not, because
He had no business to commit a sin,
Forbid by heavenly, fined by human laws –
At least 'twas rather early to begin!
But at sixteen the conscience rarely gnaws
So much as when we call our old debts in
At sixty years, and draw the accounts of evil,
And find a deucéd balance with the Devil!

168

Of his position I can give no notion –
'Tis written in the Hebrew Chronicle,
How the physicians, leaving pill and potion,
Prescribed, by way of blister, a young belle,
When old King David's blood grew dull in motion,
And that the medicine answered very well.
Perhaps 'twas in a different way applied,
For David lived, but Juan nearly died!

169

What's to be done? Alfonso will be back
The moment he has sent his fools away.
Antonia's skill was put upon the rack,
But no device could be brought into play –

And how to parry the renewed attack?
    Besides, it wanted but few hours of day:
Antonia puzzled; Julia did not speak,
But pressed her bloodless lip to Juan's cheek.

170

He turned his lip to hers, and with his hand
    Called back the tangles of her wandering hair;
Even then their love they could not all command,
    And half forgot their danger and despair:
Antonia's patience now was at a stand –
    'Come, come, 'tis no time now for fooling there!'
She whispered, in great wrath –'I must deposit
This pretty gentleman within the closet.

171

Pray, keep your nonsense for some luckier night!
    Who can have put my master in this mood?
What will become on't? I'm in such a fright –
    The devil's in the urchin, and no good!
Is this a time for giggling – this a plight?
    Why, don't you know that it may end in blood?
You'll lose your life, and I shall lose my place,
My mistress, all – for that half-girlish face!

172

Had it but been for a stout cavalier
    Of twenty-five or thirty (come, make haste),
But for a child, what piece of work is here!
    I really, madam, wonder at your taste
(Come, sir, get in) – my Master must be near!
    There, for the present, at the least he's fast,
And, if we can but till the morning keep
Our counsel – Juan, mind, you must not sleep!'

173

Now, Don Alfonso entering, but alone,
    Closed the oration of the trusty maid:
She loitered, and he told her to be gone,
    An order somewhat sullenly obeyed;
However, present remedy was none,
    And no great good seemed answered if she stayed:
Regarding both with slow and sidelong view,
She snuffed the candle, curtsied, and withdrew.

174

Alfonso paused a minute, then begun
   Some strange excuses for his late proceeding –
He would not justify what he had done,
   To say the best, it was extreme ill-breeding;
But there were ample reasons for it (none
   Of which he specified in this his pleading) –
His speech was a fine sample, on the whole,
Of rhetoric, which the learn'd call *rigmarole*.

175

Julia said nought; though all the while there rose
   A ready answer, which at once enables
A matron who her husband's foible knows,
   By a few timely words to turn the tables,
Which if it does not silence still must pose –
   Even if it should comprise a pack of fables:
'Tis to retort with firmness, and when he
Suspects with one, do you reproach with three.

176

Julia, in fact, had tolerable grounds
   (Alfonso's loves with Inez were well known);
But whether 'twas that one's own guilt confounds –
   But that can't be, as has been often shown
A lady with apologies abounds –
   It might be that her silence sprang alone
From delicacy to Don Juan's ear,
To whom she knew his mother's fame was dear.

177

There might be one more motive (which makes two):
   Alfonso ne'er to Juan had alluded –
Mentioned his jealousy, but never who
   Had been the happy lover he concluded
Concealed amongst his premises ('tis true,
   His mind the more o'er this its mystery brooded) –
To speak of Inez now were, one may say,
Like throwing Juan in Alfonso's way!

178

A hint, in tender cases, is enough;
   Silence is best, besides there is a tact
(That modern phrase appears to me sad stuff,
   But it will serve to keep my verse compact)

Which keeps, when pushed by questions rather rough,
   A lady always distant from the fact –
The charming creatures lie with such a grace,
There's nothing so becoming to the face.

179

They blush, and we believe them; at least I
   Have always done so! 'Tis of no great use,
In any case, attempting a reply,
   For then their eloquence grows quite profuse –
And when at length they're out of breath, they sigh,
   And cast their languid eyes down, and let loose
A tear or two, and then we make it up:
And then – and then – and then – sit down and sup.

180

Alfonso closed his speech, and begged her pardon,
   Which Julia half withheld, and then half granted,
And laid conditions, he thought very hard, on –
   Denying several little things he wanted!
He stood like Adam lingering near his garden,
   With useless penitence perplexed and haunted,
Beseeching she no further would refuse –
When lo! he stumbled o'er a pair of shoes.

181

A pair of shoes – what then? Not much, if they
   Are such as fit with lady's feet – but these
(No one can tell how much I grieve to say)
   Were masculine! To see them, and to seize,
Was but a moment's act! Ah, well-a-day –
   My teeth begin to chatter, my veins freeze –
Alfonso first examined well their fashion,
And then flew out into another passion.

182

He left the room for his relinquished sword,
   And Julia instant to the closet flew.
'Fly, Juan, fly! for Heaven's sake! Not a word –
   The door is open – you may yet slip through
The passage you so often have explored –
   Here is the garden-key! Fly – fly – Adieu!
Haste – haste! – I hear Alfonso's hurrying feet!
Day has not broke – there's no one in the street.'

183

None can say that this was not good advice,
The only mischief was, it came too late
(Of all experience 'tis the usual price,
A sort of income-tax laid on by fate) –
Juan had reached the room-door in a trice,
And might have done so by the garden-gate,
But met Alfonso in his dressing-gown,
Who threatened death – so Juan knocked him down.

184

Dire was the scuffle, and out went the light,
Antonia cried out 'Rape!' and Julia 'Fire!'
But not a servant stirred to aid the fight.
Alfonso, pummelled to his heart's desire,
Swore lustily he'd be revenged this night –
And Juan, too, blasphemed an octave higher!
His blood was up – though young, he was a tartar,
And not at all disposed to prove a martyr!

185

Alfonso's sword had dropped ere he could draw it,
And they continued battling hand to hand,
For Juan very luckily ne'er saw it!
His temper not being under great command,
If at that moment he had chanced to claw it,
Alfonso's days had not been in the land
Much longer. Think of husbands', lovers', lives!
And how ye may be doubly widows–wives!

186

Alfonso grappled to detain the foe,
And Juan throttled him to get away,
And blood ('twas from the nose) began to flow;
At last, as they more faintly wrestling lay,
Juan contrived to give an awkward blow,
And then his only garment quite gave way –
He fled, like Joseph, leaving it! but there,
I doubt, all likeness ends between the pair.

187

Lights came at length, and men, and maids, who found
An awkward spectacle their eyes before:
Antonia in hysterics, Julia swooned,
Alfonso leaning, breathless, by the door;

Some half-torn drapery scattered on the ground,
Some blood, and several footsteps, but no more –
Juan the gate gained, turned the key about,
And liking not the inside, locked the out!

14. ROBERT SOUTHEY

The Cataract of Lodore (1823)

'How does the Water,
Come down at Lodore?'
My little boy asked me
Thus, once on a time;
And moreover he tasked me
To tell him in rhyme!
Anon at the word,
There first came one daughter
And then came another,
To second and third
The request of their brother,
And to hear how the Water
Comes down at Lodore,
With its rush and its roar,
As many a time
They had seen it before.
So I told them in rhyme,
For of rhymes I had store;
And 'twas in my vocation
For their recreation
That so I should sing;
Because I was Laureate
To them and the King.

From its sources which well
In the tarn on the fell;
From its fountains
In the mountains,
It's rills and it's gills;
Through moss and through brake,
It runs and it creeps
For awhile, till it sleeps

In its own little lake.
And thence at departing,
Awakening and starting,
It runs through the reeds
And away it proceeds,
Through meadow and glade,
In sun and in shade,
And through the wood-shelter,
Among crags in its flurry,
Helter-skelter,
Hurry-scurry!
Here it comes sparkling,
And there it lies darkling;
Now smoking and frothing
It's tumult and wrath in,
Till in this rapid race
On which it is bent,
It reaches the place
Of its steep descent.

The Cataract strong
Then plunges along,
Striking and raging
As if a war waging
Its caverns and rocks among:
Rising and leaping,
Sinking and creeping,
Swelling and sweeping,
Showering and springing,
Flying and flinging,
Writhing and ringing,
Eddying and whisking,
Spouting and frisking,
Turning and twisting,
Around and around
With endless rebound;
Smiting and fighting,
A sight to delight in;
Confounding, astounding,
Dizzying and deafening the ear with its sound!

Collecting, projecting,
Receding and speeding,
And shocking and rocking,

And darting and parting,
And threading and spreading,
And whizzing and hissing,
And dripping and skipping,
And hitting and splitting,
And shining and twining,
And rattling and battling,
And shaking and quaking,
And pouring and roaring,
And waving and raving,
And tossing and crossing,
And flowing and going,
And running and stunning,
And foaming and roaming,
And dinning and spinning,
And dropping and hopping,
And working and jerking,
And guggling and struggling,
And heaving and cleaving,
And moaning and groaning;
And glittering and frittering,
And gathering and feathering,
And whitening and brightening,
And quivering and shivering,
And hurrying and skurrying,
And thundering and floundering;

Dividing and gliding and sliding,
And falling and brawling and sprawling,
And driving and riving and striving,
And sprinkling and twinkling and wrinkling,
And sounding and bounding and rounding,
And bubbling and troubling and doubling,
And grumbling and rumbling and tumbling,
And clattering and battering and shattering;

Retreating and beating and meeting and sheeting,
Delaying and straying and playing and spraying,
Advancing and prancing and glancing and dancing,
Recoiling, turmoiling and toiling and boiling,
And gleaming and streaming and steaming and beaming,
And rushing and flushing and brushing and gushing,
And flapping and rapping and clapping and slapping
And curling and whirling and purling and twirling,

And thumping and plumping and bumping and jumping,
And dashing and flashing and splashing and clashing;
And so never ending, but always descending,
Sounds and motions for ever and ever are blending,
All at once and all o'er, with a mighty uproar –
And this way the Water comes down at Lodore.

15. THOMAS LOVE PEACOCK

The Legend of Manor Hall (c. 1824; publ. 1837)

Old Farmer Wall, of Manor Hall,
   To market drove his wain:
Along the road it went, well stowed
   With sacks of golden grain.

His station he took, but in vain did he look
   For a customer all the morn,
Though the farmers all, save Farmer Wall,
   They sold off all their corn.

Then home he went, sore discontent,
   And many an oath he swore,
And he kicked up rows with his children and spouse
   When they met him at the door!

Next market-day he drove away
   To the town his loaded wain:
The farmers all, save Farmer Wall,
   They sold off all their grain!

No bidder he found, and he stood astound
   At the close of the market-day,
When the market was done, and the chapmen were gone
   Each man his several way.

He stalked by his load along the road,
   His face with wrath was red;
His arms he tossed, like a good man crossed
   In seeking his daily bread.

His face was red, and fierce was his tread,
   And with lusty voice cried he,
'My corn I'll sell to the Devil of Hell,
   If he'll my chapman be!'

These words he spoke just under an oak
   Seven hundred winters old;
And he straight was aware of a man sitting there
   On the roots and grassy mould.

The roots rose high, o'er the greensward dry,
   And the grass around was green
Save just the space of the stranger's place,
   Where it seemed as a fire had been.

All scorched was the spot, as gypsy-pot
   Had swung and bubbled there:
The grass was marred, the roots were charred,
   And the ivy-stems were bare.

The stranger sprung up: to the farmer he flung
   A loud and friendly hail,
And he said, 'I see well thou hast corn to sell –
   And I'll buy it on the nail!'

The twain in a trice agreed on the price;
   The stranger his earnest paid,
And with horses and wain to come for the grain
   His own appointment made.

The farmer cracked his whip and tracked
   His way right merrily on;
He struck up a song as he trudged along
   For joy that his job was done.

His children fair he danced in the air –
   His heart with joy was big –
He kissed his wife, he seized a knife,
   He slew a sucking-pig!

The faggots burned, the porkling turned
   And crackled before the fire,
And an odour arose that was sweet in the nose
   Of a passing ghostly friar.

He tirled the pin, he entered in,
He sat down at the board;
The pig he blest, when he saw it well dressed,
And the humming ale outpoured.

The friar laughed, the friar quaffed,
He chirped like a bird in May;
The farmer told how his corn he had sold
As he journeyed home that day.

The friar he quaffed, but no longer he laughed,
He changed from red to pale;
'Oh hapless elf, 'tis the Fiend himself
To whom thou hast made thy sale!'

The friar he quaffed, he took a deep draught,
He crossed himself amain:
'Oh slave of pelf, 'tis the Devil himself
To whom thou has sold thy grain!

And sure as the day, he'll fetch thee away
With the corn which thou hast sold,
If thou let him pay o'er one tester more
Than thy settled price in gold.'

The farmer gave vent to a loud lament,
The wife to a long outcry;
Their relish for pig and ale had flown,
The friar alone picked every bone
And drained the flagon dry!

The friar was gone, the morning dawn
Appeared, and the stranger's wain
Came to the hour, with six-horse power,
To fetch the purchased grain.

The horses were black – on their dewy track
Light steam from the ground upcurled;
Long wreaths of smoke from their nostrils broke,
And their tails like torches whirled!

More dark and grim, in face and limb,
Seemed the stranger than before,
As his empty wain, with steeds thrice twain,
Drew up at the farmer's door.

On the stranger's face was a sly grimace
  As he seized the sacks of grain
And, one by one, till left were none,
  He tossed them on the wain.

And slyly he leered as his hand upreared
  A purse of costly mould,
Where bright and fresh through a silver mesh
  Shone forth the glittering gold.

The farmer held out his right hand stout,
  And drew it back with dread;
For in fancy he heard each warning word
  The supping friar had said.

His eye was set on the silver net,
  His thoughts were in fearful strife
When, sudden as fate, the glittering bait
  Was snatched by his loving wife!

And, swift as thought, the stranger caught
  The farmer his waist around,
And at once the twain and the loaded wain
  Sank through the rifted ground.

The gable-end wall of Manor Hall
  Fell in ruins on the place –
That stone-heap old the tale has told
  To each succeeding race.

The wife gave a cry that rent the sky
  At her goodman's downward flight;
But she held the purse fast, and a glance she cast
  To see that all was right!

'Twas the Fiend's full-pay for her goodman gray,
  And the gold was good and true;
Which made her declare that 'his dealings were fair,
  To give the Devil his due!'

She wore the black pall for Farmer Wall,
  From her fond embraces riven –
But she won the vows of a younger spouse
  With the gold which the Fiend had given!

Now, farmers, beware of the oaths you swear
   When you cannot sell your corn,
Lest to bid and buy a stranger be nigh,
   With hidden tail and horn!

And with good heed the moral a-read
   Which is of this tale the pith:
If your corn you sell to the Fiend of Hell
   You may sell yourself therewith.

And if by mishap you fall in the trap,
   Would you bring the fiend to shame,
Lest the tempting prize should dazzle her eyes,
   Lock up your frugal dame!

16. THOMAS HOOD

Mary's Ghost (1826)

'Twas in the middle of the night,
   To sleep young William tried,
When Mary's ghost came stealing in
   And stood at his bedside:

Oh William dear, oh William dear,
   My rest eternal ceases –
Alas, my everlasting peace
   Is broken into pieces!

I thought the last of all my cares
   Would end with my last minute;
But though I went to my long home,
   I didn't stay long in it.

The body-snatchers they have come,
   And made a snatch at me –
It's very hard them kind of men
   Won't let a body be!

You thought that I was buried deep,
   Quite decent like and chary,
But from her grave in Mary-bone
   They've come and boned your Mary!

The arm that used to take your arm
   Is took to Doctor Vyse;
And both my legs are gone to walk
   The hospital at Guy's.

I vowed that you should have my hand,
   But fate gives us denial;
You'll find it there at Doctor Bell's
   In spirits and a phial.

As for my feet, the little feet
   You used to call so pretty,
There's one, I know, in Bedford Row,
   The tother's in the City.

I can't tell where my head is gone,
   But Doctor Carpue can;
As for my trunk, it's all packed up
   To go by Pickford's van!

I wish you'd go to Mister P.
   And save me such a ride –
I don't half like the outside place
   They've took for my inside.

The cock it crows – I must be gone!
   My William I must part!
But I'll be yours in death, although
   Sir Astley has my heart.

Don't go to weep upon my grave,
   And think that there I be;
They haven't left an atom there
   Of my anatomy.

17. CAROLINE NORTON

First Love (1830)

Yes, I know that you once were my lover,
But that sort of thing has an end,
And though love and its transports are over,
You know you can still be – my friend:
I was young, too, and foolish, remember
(Did you ever hear John Hardy sing?) –
It was then the fifteenth of November,
And this is the end of the spring!

You complain that you are not well-treated
By my suddenly altering so;
Can I help it? – you're very conceited,
If you think yourself equal to Joe.
Don't kneel at my feet, I implore you;
Don't write on the drawings you bring;
Don't ask me to say, 'I adore you,'
For, indeed, it is now no such thing.

I confess, when at Bognor we parted,
I swore that I worshipped you then –
That I was a maid broken-hearted,
And you the most charming of men.
I confess, when I read your first letter,
I blotted your name with a tear –
But, oh! I was young – knew no better,
Could I tell that I'd meet Hardy here?

How dull you are grown! How you worry,
Repeating my vows to be true –
If I said so, I told you a story,
For I love Hardy better than you!
Yes! my fond heart has fixed on another
(I sigh so whenever he's gone),
I shall always love you – as a brother,
But my heart is John Hardy's alone.

X. Protest and Politics

The Romantic period begins with anti-slavery protests and the French Revolution; it sees a war lasting more than twenty years, 1793–1815, with working class unrest and government repression both in its early years and in its aftermath; and it concludes with the (not very radical) Reform Bill of 1832 and Coronation of Queen Victoria (1837). Much of the political verse it produced is ephemeral; but Cowper, More, Yearsley and Southey protest impressively against the slave trade; Southey writes an exquisite satire of war in *The Battle of Blenheim*; Bloomfield and Clare lament enclosures that have destroyed a landscape and a way of life; and at the end of the period Norton, Landon and Hood attack the exploitation that is reducing work-class children and their mothers to worse than slavery – and making Britain great.

The big Romantic poets show political involvement in distinctively different ways: Burns strikes a blow for equality in *For A' That, and A' That*; Coleridge magnificently denounces French imperialism in *France: An Ode*; Wordsworth in the unpublished *Prelude* gives to us (though not to his contemporaries) the great sympathetic account of the Revolution, and how it felt to live through its failure; Byron lampoons George III and his new Tory admirer, Southey, in the brilliantly funny *Vision of Judgment*; Shelley is at his most imaginative in advocating passive resistance in *The Mask of Anarchy*. Blake thinks of politics within the contexts of myth, and, it has to be said, writes confusedly when attempting to be straightforward in *The French Revolution*; Keats has no major political poem. Indeed, for a friend of Hunt and Hazlitt, he seems (whatever his critics might wish) to have little interest in politics. He held the right views, of course, but not very strongly.

1. WILLIAM COWPER

Sweet Meat Has Sour Sauce, or The Slave Trader in the Dumps (1788)

A trader I am to the African shore,
But since that my trading is like to be o'er
I'll sing you a song which you ne'er heard before,
Which nobody can deny, deny,
Which nobody can deny!

When I first heard the news it gave me a shock
Much like what they call an electrical knock,
And now I am going to sell off my stock
Which nobody can deny, deny,
Which nobody can deny!

'Tis a curious assortment of dainty regales
To tickle the negroes with when the ship sails –
Fine chains for the neck, and a cat with nine tails,
Which nobody can deny, deny,
Which nobody can deny!

Here's supple-jack plenty, and store of rattan
That will wind itself round the sides of a man
As close as a hoop round a bucket or can,
Which nobody can deny, deny,
Which nobody can deny!

Here's padlocks and bolts and screws for the thumbs
That squeeze them so lovingly till the blood comes,
They sweeten the temper like comfits or plums
Which nobody can deny, deny,
Which nobody can deny!

When a negro his head from his victuals withdraws
And clenches his teeth and thrusts out his paws,
Here's a notable engine to open his jaws –
Which nobody can deny, deny,
Which nobody can deny!

Thus, going to market, we kindly prepare
A pretty black cargo of African ware
For what they must meet with when they get there,
        Which nobody can deny, deny,
        Which nobody can deny!

'Twould do your heart good to see 'em below
Lie flat on their backs all the way as we go
Like sprats on a gridiron, scores in a row!
        Which nobody can deny, deny,
        Which nobody can deny!

But ah, if in vain I have studied an art
So gainful to me (all boasting apart),
I think it will break my compassionate heart –
        Which nobody can deny, deny,
        Which nobody can deny!

For oh, how it enters my soul like an awl:
This pity (which some people self-pity call)
Is sure the most heart-piercing pity of all!
        Which nobody can deny, deny,
        Which nobody can deny!

So this is my song – as I told you before –
Come buy off my stock, for I must no more
Carry Caesars and Pompeys to Sugar-cane Shore,
        Which nobody can deny, deny,
        Which nobody can deny!

2. HANNAH MORE

from *Slavery: A Poem* (1788)

  No; they have heads to think, and hearts to feel,
And souls to act, with firm though erring zeal;
For they have keen affections, kind desires,
Love strong as death, and active patriot fires;
All the rude energy, the fervid flame
Of high-souled passion and ingenuous shame –
Strong but luxuriant virtues boldly shoot
From the wild vigour of a savage root!

Nor weak their sense of honour's proud control
(For pride is virtue in a pagan soul):
A sense of worth, a conscience of desert,
A high, unbroken haughtiness of heart –
That self-same stuff which erst proud empires swayed,
Of which the conquerors of the world were made.
Capricious fate of man! That very pride
In Afric scourged, in Rome was deified . . .

Whene'er to Afric's shores I turn my eyes,
Horrors of deepest, deadliest guilt arise:
I see (by more than fancy's mirror shown)
The burning village and the blazing town –
See the dire victim torn from social life,
The shrieking babe, the agonizing wife!
She, wretch forlorn, is dragged by hostile hands,
To distant tyrants sold, in distant lands!
Transmitted miseries and successive chains
The sole sad heritage her child obtains!
Even this last wretched boon their foes deny:
To weep together, or together die.
By felon hands, by one relentless stroke,
See the fond links of feeling nature broke!
The fibres twisting round a parent's heart,
Torn from their grasp, and bleeding as they part.
Hold, murderers, hold! Nor aggravate distress –
Respect the passions you yourselves possess –
Even you, of ruffian heart and ruthless hand,
Love your own offspring, love your native land.
Ah, leave them holy Freedom's cheering smile,
The Heaven-taught fondness for the parent soil!
Revere affections mingled with our frame –
In every nature, every clime the same!
In all, these feelings equal sway maintain,
In all, the love of home and freedom reign,
And Tempe's vale and parched Angola's sand
One equal fondness of their sons command.
The unconquered savage laughs at pain and toil,
Basking in Freedom's beams which gild his native soil . . .

And thou, white savage, whether lust of gold
Or lust of conquest ruled thee uncontrolled –
Hero or robber – by whatever name
Thou plead thy impious claim to wealth or fame:

Whether inferior mischiefs be thy boast
(A petty tyrant rifling Gambia's coast),
Or bolder carnage track thy crimson way
(Kings dispossessed, and provinces thy prey),
Panting to tame wide Earth's remotest bound –
All Cortez murdered, all Columbus found –
O'er plundered realms to reign, detested lord,
Make millions wretched, and thyself abhorred;
In reason's eye, in wisdom's fair account,
Your sum of glory boasts a like amount –
The means may differ, but the end's the same:
Conquest is pillage with a nobler name!

3. ANN YEARSLEY

Death of Luco (from *On the Inhumanity of the Slave Trade*) 1788

The sun had reached
His zenith. Pausing faintly, Luco stood
Leaning upon his hoe, while memory brought,
In piteous imagery, his agéd father,
His poor fond mother, and his faithful maid.
The mental group in wildest motion set
Fruitless imagination – fury, grief,
Alternate shame, the sense of insult, all
Conspire to aid the inward storm! Yet words
Were no relief: he stood in silent woe.
Gorgon, remorseless Christian, saw the slave
Stand musing mid the ranks and, stealing soft
Behind the studious Luco, struck his cheek
With a too-heavy whip that reached his eye,
Making it dark for ever. Luco turned
In strongest agony, and with his hoe
Struck the rude Christian on the forehead. Pride,
With hateful malice, seized on Gorgon's soul
(By nature fierce), while Luco sought the beach
And plunged beneath the wave. But near him lay
A planter's barge, whose seamen grasped his hair,
Dragging to life a wretch who wished to die.

Rumour now spreads the tale, while Gorgon's breath
Envenomed aids her blast. Imputed crimes
Oppose the plea of Luco, till he scorns
Even a just defence, and stands prepared.
The planters, conscious that to fear alone
They owe their cruel power, resolve to blend
New torment with the pangs of death, and hold
Their victim high in dreadful view to fright
The wretched number left. Luco is chained
To a huge tree, his fellow-slaves are ranged
To share the horrid sight; fuel is placed
In an increasing train, some paces back,
To kindle slowly, and approach the youth,
With more than native terror.
See, it burns!
He gazes on the growing flame, and calls
For 'Water, water!' The small boon's denied.
E'en Christians throng each other to behold
The different alterations of his face
As the hot death approaches. (Oh shame, shame
Upon the followers of Jesus! Shame
On him that dares avow a God!) He writhes,
While down his breast glide the unpitied tears,
And in their sockets strain their scorchéd balls.
'Burn, burn me quick! I cannot die!' he cries,
'Bring fire more close!' The planters heed him not,
But still prolonging Luco's torture, threat
Their trembling slaves around . . .
Gracious God!
Why thus in mercy let thy whirlwinds sleep
O'er a vile race of Christians, who profane
Thy glorious attributes? Sweep them from Earth,
Or check their cruel power! The savage tribes
Are angels when compared to brutes like these.

4. ANNA LAETITIA BARBAULD

On the Expected General Rising of the French Nation in 1792 (publ. 1825)

Rise, mighty nation, in thy strength,
And deal thy dreadful vengeance round –
Let thy great spirit, roused at length,
Strike hordes of despots to the ground!

Devoted land, thy mangled breast
Eager the royal vultures tear!
By friends betrayed, by foes oppressed –
And Virtue struggles with Despair.

The tocsin sounds! Arise, arise!
Stern o'er each breast let Country reign –
Nor virgin's plighted hand, nor sighs,
Must now the ardent youth detain:

Nor must the hind who tills thy soil
The ripened vintage stay to press,
Till Rapture crown the flowing bowl,
And Freedom boast of full success.

Briareus-like extend thy hands,
That every hand may crush a foe –
In millions pour thy generous bands,
And end a warfare by a blow!

Then wash with sad repentant tears
Each deed that clouds thy glory's page,
Each frenzied start impelled by fears,
Each transient burst of headlong rage!

Then fold in thy relenting arms
Thy wretched outcasts where they roam;
From pining want and war's alarms,
Oh call the child of misery home!

Then build the tomb – oh not alone
Of him who bled in Freedom's cause:
With equal eye the martyr own
Of faith revered and ancient laws.

Then be thy tide of glory stayed!
Then be thy conquering banners furled!
Obey the laws thyself hast made,
And rise the model of the world!

5. HELEN MARIA WILLIAMS

France 1792 (from *To Dr Moore, in Answer to a Poetical Epistle Written by Him in Wales*) 1792

Delightful land – ah, now with general voice
Thy village sons and daughters may rejoice . . .
For now on Gallia's plains the peasant knows
Those equal rights impartial Heaven bestows.
He now, by Freedom's ray illumined, taught
Some self-respect, some energy of thought,
Discerns the blessings that to all belong,
And lives to guard his humble shed from wrong.
   Auspicious Liberty! in vain thy foes
Deride thy ardour, and thy force oppose;
In vain refuse to mark thy spreading light,
While, like the mole they hide their heads in night,
Or hope their eloquence with taper-ray
Can dim the blaze of philosophic day –
Those reasoners who pretend that each abuse,
Sanctioned by precedent, has some blest use!
Does then some chemic power to Time belong,
Extracting by some process right from wrong?
Must feudal governments for ever last
(Those gothic piles, the works of ages past) –
Nor may obtrusive Reason boldly scan,
Far less reform, the rude misshapen plan:
The winding labyrinths, the hostile towers
(Whence danger threatens, and where horror lowers),

The jealous drawbridge, and the moat profound,
The lonely dungeon in the caverned ground,
The sullen dome above those central caves
Where lives one despot, and a host of slaves?
   Ah, Freedom, on this renovated shore
That fabric frights the moral world no more!
Shook to its basis by thy powerful spell,
Its triple walls in massy fragments fell;
While, rising from the hideous wreck, appears
The temple thy firm arm sublimely rears –
Of fair proportions, and of simple grace,
A mansion worthy of the human race.
For me, the witness of those scenes, whose birth
Forms a new era in the storied earth,
Oft, while with glowing breast those scenes I view,
They lead, ah friend beloved, my thoughts to you!
Ah, still each fine emotion they impart
With your idea mingles in my heart –
You, whose warm bosom, whose expanded mind,
Have shared this glorious triumph of mankind –
You, whom I oft have heard, with generous zeal,
With all that truth can urge or pity feel,
Refute the pompous argument, that tried
The common cause of millions to deride . . .

6. WILLIAM WORDSWORTH

from *The Female Vagrant*

(1793–4; publ. *Lyrical Ballads* 1798)

33

'Four years each day with daily bread was blest,
By constant toil and constant prayer supplied.
Three lovely infants lay within my breast,
And often, viewing their sweet smiles, I sighed
And knew not why. My happy father died
Just as the children's meal began to fail,
For War the nations to the field defied:
The loom stood still unwatched, the idle gale
Wooed in deserted shrouds the unregarding sail.

34

How changed at once: for Labour's cheerful hum,
Silence and fears and Misery's weeping train.
But soon with proud parade the noisy drum
Beat round to sweep the streets of want and pain!
My husband's arms now only served to strain
Me and his children, hungering in his view.
He could not beg. My prayers and tears were vain!
To join those miserable men he flew –
We reached the western world a poor devoted crew.

35

Oh dreadful price of being – to resign
All that is dear in being! Better far
In Want's most lonely cave till death to pine
Unseen, unheard, unwatched by any star.
Better before proud Fortune's sumptuous car
Obvious our dying bodies to obtrude,
Than dog-like, wading at the heels of War,
Protract a curst existence with the brood
That lap, their very nourishment, their brother's blood!

36

The pains and plagues that on our heads came down
(Disease and famine, agony and fear,
In wood or wilderness, in camp or town),
It would thy brain unsettle even to hear!
All perished, all, in one remorseless year –
Husband and children, one by one, by sword
And scourge of fiery fever. Every tear
Dried up, despairing, desolate, on board
A British ship I waked, as from a trance restored . . .

40

Peaceful as this immeasurable plain
By these extended beams of dawn impressed,
In the calm sunshine slept the glittering main.
The very ocean has its hour of rest
Ungranted to the human mourner's breast.
Remote from man and storms of mortal care,
With wings which did the world of waves invest,
The spirit of God diffused through balmy air
Quiet that might have healed, if aught could heal, despair.

41

Ah, how unlike each smell, each sight and sound,
That late the stupor of my spirit broke!
Of noisome hospitals the groan profound,
The mine's dire earthquake, the bomb's thunder-stroke,
Heart-sickening Famine's grim despairing look;
The midnight flames in thundering deluge spread;
The stormèd town's expiring shriek that woke
Far round the grisly phantoms of the dead –
And, pale with ghastly light, the victor's human head!

42

Some mighty gulf of separation passed,
I seemed transported to another world –
A dream resigned with pain when from the mast
The impatient mariner the sail unfurled
And, whistling, called the wind that hardly curled
The silent seas. The pleasant thoughts of home
With tears his weather-beaten cheek impearled:
For me, farthest from earthly port to roam
Was best – my only wish to shun where man might come.

43

And oft, robbed of my perfect mind, I thought
At last my feet a resting-place had found.
"Here will I weep in peace", so Fancy wrought,
"Roaming the illimitable waters round –
Here gaze, of every friend but Death disowned,
All day my ready tomb the ocean-flood."
To break my dream the vessel reached its bound,
And homeless near a thousand homes I stood,
And near a thousand tables pined and wanted food.'

7. ROBERT BURNS

For A' That, and A' That (1795)

Is there, for honest Poverty
That hings his head, and a' that?
The coward-slave, we pass him by,
We dare be poor for a' that!
For a' that, and a' that
(Our toils obscure, and a' that),
The rank is but the guinea's stamp,
The Man's the gowd for a' that!

What though on hamely fare we dine,
Wear hoddin grey, and a' that –
Gie fools their silks and knaves their wine,
A man's a man for a' that!
For a' that, and a' that,
Their tinsel show, and a' that,
The honest man, though e'er sae poor,
Is king o' men for a' that.

Ye see yon birkie ca'd a lord,
Wha struts, and stares, and a' that,
Though hundreds worship at his word,
He's but a coof for a' that!
For a' that and a' that
(His ribband, star, and a' that),
The man of independent mind,
He looks and laughs at a' that!

A prince can mak a belted knight –
A marquis, duke, and a' that –
But an honest man's aboun his might:
Gude faith, he mauna fa' that!

1 *Is there, for* is there a place for. **2** *hings* hangs.
7–8 *The rank . . . a' that* Rank has as little to do with value as the face on a gold coin. **10** *hoddin* coarse homespun cloth of mixed black and white wool.
17 *birkie* whippersnapper. **17** *ca'd a lord* addressed as a nobleman.
19 *worship* bow down. **20** *coof* fool.
28 *mauna fa' that* must not claim that.

For a' that, and a' that
(Their dignities, and a' that),
The pith o' sense, and pride o' worth,

Are higher rank than a' that!
Then let us pray that come it may,
As come it will for a' that,
That sense and worth, o'er a' the earth
Shall bear the gree, and a' that –
For a' that, and a' that,
Its comin yet for a' that,
That man to man, the warld o'er,
Shall brothers be, for a' that!

8. ROBERT SOUTHEY

Poems on the Slave Trade (April 1798; publ. 1799)

High in the air exposed the slave is hung
To all the birds of heaven, their living food!
He groans not, though – awakened by that fierce sun –
New torturers live to drink their parent blood!
He groans not, though the gorging vulture tear
The quivering fibre! Hither gaze, oh ye
Who tore this man from peace and liberty –
Gaze hither, ye who weigh with scrupulous care
The right and prudent – for beyond the grave
There is another world! And call to mind,
Ere your decrees proclaim to all mankind
Murder is legalized, that there the slave
Before the Eternal, 'thunder-tongued shall plead
Against the deep damnation of your deed'!

36 *bear the gree* win the prize, come off best.

9. SAMUEL TAYLOR COLERIDGE

(i) *France: An Ode* (April 1798; publ. 1798)

1

Ye clouds, that far above me float and pause,
Whose pathless march no mortal may control!
Ye ocean-waves, that whereso'er ye roll,
Yield homage only to eternal laws!
Ye woods, that listen to the night-bird's singing,
Midway the smooth and perilous slope reclined,
Save where your own imperious branches swinging
Have made a solemn music of the wind,
Where (like a man beloved of God)
Through glooms which never woodman trod
How oft, pursuing fancies holy,
My moonlight way o'er flowering weeds I wound
Inspired, beyond the guess of folly,
By each rude shape and wild unconquerable sound!
Oh ye loud waves, and oh ye forests high,
And oh ye clouds that far above me soared –
Thou rising sun, thou blue rejoicing sky,
Yea, every thing that is, and will be, free –
Bear witness for me, whereso'er ye be,
With what deep worship I have still adored
The spirit of divinest Liberty!

2

When France in wrath her giant-limbs upreared,
And, with an oath which smote air, earth and sea,
Stamped her strong foot and said she would be free,
Bear witness for me how I hoped and feared –
With what a joy my lofty gratulation
Unawed I sang, amid a slavish band –
And when to whelm the disenchanted nation
(Like fiends embattled by a wizard's wand)
The Monarchs marched in evil day,
And Britain joined the dire array,
Though dear her shores and circling ocean;
Though many friendships, many youthful loves,
Had swoln the patriot emotion
And flung a magic light o'er all her hills and groves;
Yet still my voice, unaltered, sang defeat

To all that braved the tyrant-quelling lance –
And shame (too long delayed) and vain retreat!
For ne'er, oh Liberty, with partial aim
I dimmed thy light or damped thy holy flame,
But blest the paeans of delivered France,
And hung my head, and wept at Britain's name.

3

'And what', I said, 'though Blasphemy's loud scream
With that sweet music of deliverance strove –
Though all the fierce and drunken passions wove
A dance more wild that e'er was maniac's dream!
Ye storms that round the dawning East assembled,
The sun was rising, though ye hid his light!'
And when (to soothe my soul, that hoped and trembled)
The dissonance ceased, and all seemed calm and bright;
When France her front, deep-scarred and gory,
Concealed with clustering wreaths of glory;
When, insupportably advancing,
Her arm made mockery of the warrior's ramp;
While, timid looks of fury glancing,
Domestic treason (crushed beneath her fatal stamp)
Writhed like a wounded dragon in his gore;
Then I reproached my fears that would not flee –
'And soon', I said, 'shall Wisdom teach her lore
In the low huts of them that toil and groan!
And, conquering by her happiness alone,
Shall France compel the nations to be free.
Till Love and Joy look round, and call the Earth their own.'

4

Forgive me, Freedom – oh forgive those dreams!
I hear thy voice, I hear thy loud lament,
From bleak Helvetia's icy caverns sent –
I hear thy groans upon her bloodstained streams!
Heroes, that for thy peaceful country perished –
And ye that, fleeing, spot your mountain-snows
With bleeding wounds – forgive me that I cherished
One thought that ever blest your cruel foes!
To scatter rage, and traitorous guilt,
Where Peace her jealous home had built;
A patriot-race to disinherit
Of all that made their stormy wilds so dear;
And with inexpiable spirit

To taint the bloodless freedom of the mountaineer –
Oh France, that mockest Heaven, adulterous, blind,
And patriot only in pernicious toils!
Are these thy boasts, champion of human kind?
To mix with Kings in the low lust of sway,
Yell in the hunt, and share the murderous prey,
To insult the shrine of Liberty with spoils
From freemen torn – to tempt, and to betray?

5

The sensual and the dark rebel in vain,
Slaves by their own compulsion! In mad game
They burst their manacles, and wear the name
Of Freedom graven on a heavier chain!
Oh Liberty, with profitless endeavour
Have I pursued thee many a weary hour
But thou nor swellst the victor's strain, nor ever
Didst breathe thy soul in forms of human power.
Alike, from all, howe'er they praise thee
(Nor prayer, nor boastful name delays thee) –
Alike from Priestcraft's harpy minions
And factious Blasphemy's obscener slaves
Thou speedest on thy subtle pinions,
The guide of homeless winds, and playmate of the waves!
And there I felt thee – on the sea-cliff's verge,
Whose pines, scarce travelled by the breeze above,
Had made one murmur with the distant surge.
Yes, while I stood and gazed, my temples bare,
And shot my being through earth, sea and air,
Possessing all things with intensest love,
Oh Liberty, my spirit found thee there!

(ii) 'Dainty Terms for Fratricide'

(from *Fears in Solitude*, 90–93, 101–20) 1798

We, this whole people, have been clamorous
For war and bloodshed, animating sports
The which we pay for, as a thing to talk of,
Spectators and not combatants! . . .
Boys and girls,
And women, that would groan to see a child
Pull off an insect's leg, all read of war,

The best amusement for our morning meal!
The poor wretch, who has learnt his only prayers
From curses, who knows scarcely words enough
To ask a blessing of his heavenly Father,
Becomes a fluent phraseman, absolute
And technical in victories and defeats,
And all our dainty terms for fratricide,
Terms which we trundle smoothly o'er our tongues
Like mere abstractions, empty sounds to which
We join no feeling and attach no form –
As if the soldier died without a wound;
As if the fibres of this godlike frame
Were gored without a pang; as if the wretch,
Who fell in battle doing bloody deeds,
Passed off to Heaven, translated and not killed;
As though he had no wife to pine for him,
No God to judge him!

10. ROBERT SOUTHEY

The Battle of Blenheim (1799)

It was a summer evening,
   Old Kaspar's work was done,
And he before his cottage door
   Was sitting in the sun,
And by him sported on the green
His little grandchild Wilhelmine.

She saw her brother Peterkin
   Roll something large and round
That he beside the rivulet
   In playing there had found;
He came to ask what he had found
That was so large, and smooth, and round.

Old Kaspar took it from the boy
   Who stood expectant by,
And then the old man shook his head
   And with a natural sigh,
' 'Tis some poor fellow's skull', said he,
'Who fell in the great victory.

I find them in the garden for
   There's many here about,
And often when I go to plough
   The ploughshare turns them out –
For many thousand men', said he,
'Were slain in the great victory.'

'Now tell us what 'twas all about',
   Young Peterkin he cries,
And little Wilhelmine looks up
   With wonder-waiting eyes,
'Now tell us all about the war
And what they killed each other for.'

'It was the English', Kaspar cried,
   'That put the French to rout,
But what they killed each other for
   I could not well make out.
But everybody said', quoth he,
'That 'twas a famous victory.

My father lived at Blenheim then,
   Yon little stream hard by –
They burnt his dwelling to the ground
   And he was forced to fly;
So with his wife and child he fled,
Nor had he where to rest his head.

With fire and sword the country round
   Was wasted far and wide,
And many a childing mother then
   And new-born infant died.
But things like that, you know, must be
At every famous victory.

They say it was a shocking sight
   After the field was won,
For many thousand bodies here
   Lay rotting in the sun –
But things like that you know must be
After a famous victory.

Great praise the Duke of Marlborough won,
    And our good Prince Eugene.'
'Why 'twas a very wicked thing!'
    Said little Wilhelmine.
'Nay, nay, my little girl', quoth he,
'It was a famous victory,

And everybody praised the Duke
    Who such a fight did win.'
'But what good came of it at last?'
    Quoth little Peterkin.
'Why that I cannot tell', said he,
'But 'twas a famous victory!'

11. ROBERT BLOOMFIELD

The Farmer's Boy (from *Summer*) 1801

Now, ere sweet Summer bids its long adieu,
And winds blow keen where late the blossoms grew,
The bustling day and jovial night must come,
The long-accustomed feast of Harvest Home . . .
    Behold the round oak table's massy frame
Bestride the kitchen-floor! The careful dame
And generous host invite their friends around,
While all that cleared the crop, or tilled the ground,
Are guests by right of custom – old and young . . .
    Such were the days – of days long past I sing –
When pride gave place to mirth without a sting,
Ere tyrant customs strength sufficient bore
To violate the feelings of the poor,
To leave them distanced in the madding race
Where'er refinement shows its hated face –
Not causeless hated: 'tis the peasant's curse,
That hourly makes his wretched station worse,
Destroys life's intercourse, the social plan
That rank to rank cements, as man to man.
Wealth flows round him, Fashion lordly reigns;

Yet poverty is his, and mental pains.
Methinks I hear the mourner thus impart
The stifled murmurs of his wounded heart:

'Whence comes this change, ungracious, irksome, cold?
Whence the new grandeur that mine eyes behold,
The widening distance that I darkly see?
Has Wealth done this? Then Wealth's a foe to me,
Foe to our rights . . .
Our annual feast, when Earth her plenty yields,
When crowned with boughs the last load quits the fields
The aspect still of ancient joy puts on –
The aspect only, with the substance gone.
Where unaffected Freedom charmed the soul,
The *separate* table and the costly bowl,
Cool as the blast that checks the budding Spring,
A mockery of gladness round them fling . . .
Nor reigns that joy, when hand in hand they join,
That good old Master felt in shaking mine.
Heaven bless his memory – bless his honoured name! –
The poor will speak his lasting worthy fame.
To souls fair-purposed, strength and guidance give –
In pity to us, still let goodness live –
Let Labour have its due! My cot shall be
From chilling want and guilty murmurs free!
Let Labour have its due – then peace is mine,
And never, never shall my heart repine.

12. WILLIAM WORDSWORTH

1. Sonnets, 1802 (publ. 1807)

(i) *On the Extinction of the Venetian Republic*

Once did she hold the gorgeous East in fee,
And was the safeguard of the West – the worth
Of Venice did not fall below her birth,
Venice, the eldest child of Liberty!
She was a maiden-city, bright and free,
No guile seduced, no force could violate;
And when she took unto herself a mate,

She must espouse the everlasting sea.
And what if she had seen those glories fade,
Those titles vanish, and that strength decay?
Yet shall some tribute of regret be paid
When her long life hath reached its final day:
Men are we, and must grieve when even the shade
Of that which once was great is passed away.

(ii) *To Toussaint L'Ouverture*

Toussaint – the most unhappy man of men! –
Whether the rural milkmaid by her cow
Sing in thy hearing, or thou liest now
Alone in some deep dungeon's earless den,
Oh miserable chieftain, where and when
Wilt thou find patience? Yet die not! Do thou
Wear rather in thy bonds a cheerful brow;
Though fallen thyself, never to rise again,
Live, and take comfort! Thou hast left behind
Powers that will work for thee – air, earth, and skies –
There's not a breathing of the common wind
That will forget thee! Thou hast great allies:
Thy friends are exultations, agonies,
And love, and man's unconquerable mind.

(iii) *We Had a Fellow-Passenger*

We had a fellow-passenger who came
From Calais with us, gaudy in array –
A negro woman, like a lady gay,
Yet silent as a woman fearing blame.
Dejected, meek – yea, pitiably tame –
She sat, from notice turning not away,
But on our proffered kindness still did lay
A weight of languid speech, or at the same
Was silent, motionless in eyes and face.
She was a negro woman driven from France,
Rejected like all others of that race,
Not one of whom may now find footing there.
This the poor outcast did to us declare,
Nor murmured at the unfeeling ordinance.

11. 1805 *Prelude* Scenes from the French Revolution (1804; publ. 1850/from MS 1926)

(i) 'Golden Hours': Calais and the Rhone, July 1790 (VI, 352–69, 380–413)

'Twas a time when Europe was rejoiced,
France standing on the top of golden hours,
And human nature seeming born again.
Bound, as I said, to the Alps, it was our lot
To land at Calais on the very eve
Of that great Federal Day; and there we saw,
In a mean city and among a few,
How bright a face is worn when joy of one
Is joy of tens of millions!
Southward thence
We took our way, direct through hamlets, towns,
Gaudy with relics of that festival,
Flowers left to wither on triumphal arcs
And window-garlands. On the public roads
(And once three days successively through paths
By which our toilsome journey was abridged)
Among sequestered villages we walked,
And found benevolence and blessedness
Spread like a fragrance everywhere . . .
Unhoused beneath the evening star we saw
Dances of liberty, and in late hours
Of darkness, dances in the open air.
Among the vine-clad hills of Burgundy,
Upon the bosom of the gentle Soane
We glided forward with the flowing stream.
Swift Rhone, thou wert the wings on which we cut
Between thy lofty rocks! Enchanting show
Those woods and farms and orchards did present,
And single cottages and lurking towns –
Reach after reach, procession without end
Of deep and stately vales. A lonely pair
Of Englishmen we were, and sailed along
Clustered together with a merry crowd
Of those emancipated, with a host

Of travellers, chiefly delegates returning
From the great spousals newly solemnized
In their chief city, in the sight of Heaven.
   Like bees they swarmed – gaudy and gay as bees!
Some vapoured in the unruliness of joy,
And flourished with their swords as if to fight
The saucy air! In this blithe company
We landed, took with them our evening meal,
Guests welcome almost as the angels were
To Abraham of old. The supper done,
With flowing cups elate, and happy thoughts,
We rose at signal given, and formed a ring
And hand in hand danced round and round the board.
All hearts were open, every tongue was loud
With amity and glee. We bore a name
Honoured in France, the name of Englishmen,
And hospitably did they give us hail
As their forerunners in a glorious course –
And round and round the board they danced again!

(ii) A Tourist's Unconcern: Paris, Dec. 1791 (IX, 40–71)

Through Paris lay my readiest path, and there
I sojourned a few days and visited
In haste each spot of old and recent fame –
The latter chiefly – from the Field of Mars
Down to the suburbs of St Antony,
And from Mont Martyr southward to the Dome
Of Genevieve. In both her clamorous halls
(The National Synod and the Jacobins)
I saw the revolutionary power
Toss like a ship at anchor, rocked by storms;
The Arcades I traversed in the Palace huge
Of Orleans, coasted round and round the line
Of tavern, brothel, gaming-house and shop –
Great rendezvous of worst and best, the walk
Of all who had a purpose, or had not!
I stared, and listened with a stranger's ears
To hawkers and haranguers (hubbub wild!)
And hissing factionists with ardent eyes,
In knots, or pairs, or single – ant-like swarms

Of builders and subverters, every face
That hope or apprehension could put on:
Joy, anger and vexation, in the midst
Of gaiety and dissolute idleness.
   Where silent zephyrs sported with the dust
Of the Bastille I sat in the open sun
And from the rubbish gathered up a stone,
And pocketed the relic in the guise
Of an enthusiast; yet, in honest truth
Though not without some strong incumbencies,
And glad – could living man be otherwise? –
I looked for something which I could not find,
Affecting more emotion than I felt.

(iii) Among Royalists: Blois, spring 1792

(IX, 127–68)

A knot of military officers
That to a regiment appertained which then
Was stationed in the city were the chief
Of my associates; some of these wore swords
Which had been seasoned in the wars, and all
Were men well-born – at least, laid claim to such
Distinction, as the chivalry of France.
In age and temper differing, they had yet
One spirit ruling in them all – alike
(Save only one, hereafter to be named)
Were bent upon undoing what was done!
This was their rest, and only hope; therewith
No fear had they of bad becoming worse,
For worst to them had come – nor would have stirred,
Or deemed it worth a moment's while to stir,
In any thing, save only if the act
Looked thitherward.
                                        One, reckoning by years,
Was in the prime of manhood, and erewhile
He had sat lord in many tender hearts,
Though heedless of such honours now, and changed:
His temper was quite mastered by the times,
And they had blighted him, had eat away
The beauty of his person, doing wrong
Alike to body and to mind. His port,
Which once had been erect and open, now

Was stooping and contracted, and a face
By nature lovely in itself, expressed,
As much as any that was ever seen,
A ravage out of season, made by thoughts
Unhealthy and vexatious. At the hour,
The most important of each day, in which
The public news was read, the fever came,
A punctual visitant, to shake this man,
Disarmed his voice and fanned his yellow cheek
Into a thousand colours, While he read,
Or mused, his sword was haunted by his touch
Continually, like an uneasy place
In his own body.
'Twas in truth an hour
Of universal ferment – mildest men
Were agitated, and commotions, strife
Of passions and opinion, filled the walls
Of peaceful houses with unquiet sounds!

(iv) 'A Patriot': Blois, early summer 1792

(IX, 294–9, 511–34)

Among that band of officers was one,
Already hinted at, of other mould –
A patriot, thence rejected by the rest,
And with an oriental loathing spurned
As of a different caste. A meeker man
Than this lived never, or a more benign . . .
And when we chanced
One day to meet a hunger-bitten girl
Who crept along fitting her languid self
Unto a heifer's motion – by a cord
Tied to her arm, and picking thus from the lane
Its sustenance, while the girl with her two hands
Was busy knitting in a heartless mood
Of solitude – and at the sight my friend
In agitation said, ''Tis against *that*
Which we are fighting!' I with him believed
Devoutly that a spirit was abroad
Which could not be withstood; that poverty,
At least like this, would in a little time
Be found no more; that we should see the Earth

Unthwarted in her wish to recompense
The industrious and the lowly child of toil,
All institutes for ever blotted out
That legalized exclusion, empty pomp
Abolished, sensual state and cruel power
(Whether by edict of the one or few),
And finally, as sum and crown of all,
Should see the people having a strong hand
In making their own laws – whence better days
To all mankind!

(v) 'Sleep No More': Paris, Oct. 1792

(X, 24–82)

The state, as if to stamp the final seal
On her security, and to the world
Show what she was, a high and fearless soul –
Or rather in a spirit of thanks to those
Who had stirred up her slackening faculties
To a new transition – had assumed with joy
The body and the venerable name
Of a republic. Lamentable crimes,
'Tis true, had gone before this hour, the work
Of massacre, in which the senseless sword
Was prayed to as a judge. But these were past,
Earth free from them for ever (as was thought),
Ephemeral monsters, to be seen but once –
Things that could only show themselves, and die!
   This was the time in which, inflamed with hope,
To Paris I returned. Again I ranged,
More eagerly than I had done before,
Through the wide city – and in progress passed
The prison where the unhappy monarch lay,
Associate with his children and his wife
In bondage, and the Palace, lately stormed
With roar of canon and a numerous host.
I crossed (a black and empty area then)
The Square of the Carroussel, few weeks back
Heaped up with dead and dying – upon these
And other sights looking as doth a man
Upon a volume whose contents he knows
Are memorable but from him locked up,

Being written in a tongue he cannot read,
So that he questions the mute leaves with pain
And half upbraids their silence.
But that night,
When on my bed I lay, I was most moved
And felt most deeply in what world I was.
My room was high and lonely, near the roof
Of a large mansion or hotel, a spot
That would have pleased me in more quiet times –
Nor was it wholly without pleasure then.
With unextinguished taper I kept watch,
Reading at intervals. The fear gone by
Pressed on me almost like a fear to come.
I thought of those September massacres,
Divided from me by a little month,
And felt and touched them, a substantial dread
(The rest was conjured up from tragic fictions
And mournful calendars of true history,
Remembrances and dim admonishments):
'The horse is taught his manage, and the wind
Of heaven wheels round and treads in his own steps!
Year follows year, the tide returns again,
Day follows day: all things have second birth –
The earthquake is not satisfied at once!'
And in such way I wrought upon myself
Until I seemed to hear a voice that cried
To the whole city, 'Sleep no more!' To this
Add comments of a calmer mind, from which
I could not gather full security,
But at the best it seemed a place of fear
Unfit for the repose of night,
Defenceless as a place where tigers roam.

(vi) War and Alienation: London and Wales, 1793–4 (X, 201–74)

When to my native land
(After a whole year's absence) I returned
I found the air yet busy with the stir
Of a contention which had been raised up
Against the traffickers in negro blood –

An effort which, though baffled, nevertheless
Had called back old forgotten principles
Dismissed from service, had diffused some truths,
And more of virtuous feeling, through the heart
Of the English people . . .
For me that strife had ne'er
Fastened on my affections – nor did now
Its unsuccessful issue much excite
My sorrow, having laid this faith to heart
That if France prospered good men would not long
Pay fruitless worship to humanity,
And this most rotten branch of human shame
(Object, it seemed, of a superfluous pains)
Would fall together with its parent tree.
Such was my then belief – that there was one,
And only one, solicitude for all!
And now the strength of Britain was put forth
In league with the confederated host;
Not in my single self alone I found,
But in the minds of all ingenuous youth,
Change and subversion from that hour. No shock
Given to my moral nature had I known
Down to that moment – neither lapse,
Nor turn of sentiment, that might be named
A revolution, save at this one time!
All else was progress on the self-same path
On which, with a diversity of pace,
I had been travelling – this, a stride at once
Into another region.
True it is
'Twas not concealed with what ungracious eyes
Our native rulers from the very first
Had looked upon regenerated France,
Nor had I doubted that this day would come;
But in such contemplation I had thought
Of general interests only, beyond this
Had never once foretasted the event.
Now I had other business, for I felt
The ravage of this most unnatural strife
In my own heart. There it lay like a weight,
At enmity with all the tenderest springs
Of my enjoyments.
I who with the breeze

Had played, a green leaf on the blesséd tree
Of my beloved country (nor had wished
For happier fortune than to wither there),
Now from my pleasant station was cut off,
And tossed about in whirlwinds. I rejoiced –
Yea, afterwards, truth painful to record,
Exulted in the triumph of my soul,
When Englishmen by thousands were o'erthrown,
Left without glory on the field, or driven,
Brave hearts, to shameful flight.
It was a grief –
Grief call it not, 'twas anything but that –
A conflict of sensations without name,
Of which he only who may love the sight
Of a village-steeple as I do can judge,
When in the congregation, bending all
To their great Father, prayers were offered up
Or praises for our country's victories,
And, mid the simple worshippers perchance
I only, like an uninvited guest
Whom no one owned, sat silent – shall I add
Fed on the day of vengeance yet to come!

(vii) 'Eternal Justice': Morecambe Sands, Aug. 1794 (X, 466–76, 515–56)

Oh Friend, few happier moments have been mine
Through my whole life than that when first I heard
That this foul tribe of Moloch was o'erthrown
And their chief regent levelled with the dust!
The day was one which haply may deserve
A separate chronicle. Having gone abroad
From a small village where I tarried then,
To the same far-secluded privacy
I was returning. Over the smooth sands
Of Levens' ample estuary lay
My journey, and beneath a genial sun . . .
Without me and within as I advanced
All that I saw, or felt, or communed with,
Was gentleness and peace. Upon a small
And rocky island near, a fragment stood –

Itself like a sea-rock – of what had been
A Romish chapel, where in ancient times
Masses were said at the hour which suited those
Who crossed the sands with ebb of morning tide.
Not far from this still ruin all the plain
Was spotted with a variegated crowd
Of coaches, wains, and travellers (horse, and foot),
Wading beneath the conduct of their guide
In loose procession through the shallow stream
Of inland-water – the great sea meanwhile
Was at safe distance, far retired.
                                                I paused
Unwilling to proceed, the scene appeared
So gay and cheerful – when, a traveller
Chancing to pass, I carelessly enquired
If any news were stirring. He replied
(In the familiar language of the day)
That *Robespierre was dead.* Nor was a doubt,
On further question, left within my mind,
But that the tidings were substantial truth –
That he and his supporters all were fallen.
   Great was my glee of spirit, great my joy
In vengeance, and eternal justice, thus
Made manifest. 'Come now, ye golden times',
Said I, forth-breathing on those open sands
A hymn of triumph, 'as the morning comes
Out of the bosom of the night, come ye!
Thus far our trust is verified: behold,
They who with clumsy desperation brought
Rivers of blood, and preached that nothing else
Could cleanse the Augean stable, by the might
Of their own helper have been swept away!
Their madness is declared and visible –
Elsewhere will safety now be sought, and earth
March firmly towards righteousness and peace.'
Then schemes I framed more calmly when and how
The madding factions might be tranquillized,
And (through hardships manifold and long)
The mighty renovation would proceed.

13. JOHN CLARE

(i) *Helpstone* (lines 95–134) c. 1813; publ. 1820

Thou far-fled pasture, long evanished scene,
Where Nature's freedom spread the flowery green –
Where golden kingcups opened into view,
Where silver daisies charmed the raptured view,
And tottering (hid among those brighter gems)
Where silver grasses bent their tiny stems,
Where the pale lilac mean and lowly grew
Courting in vain each gazer's heedless view,
While cowslips, sweetest flowers upon the plain,
Seemingly bowed to shun the hand in vain,
Where lowing oxen roamed to feed at large
And bleating there the shepherd's woolly charge
Whose constant calls thy echoing valleys cheered,
Thy scenes adorned and rural life endeared –
No calls of hunger pity's feelings wound,
'Twas wanton plenty raised the joyful sound!
Thy grass in plenty gave the wished supply
Ere sultry suns had waked the troubling fly
Then blest retiring (by thy bounty fed)
They sought thy shades and found an easy bed.
    But now, alas, those scenes exist no more,
The pride of life with thee (like mine) is o'er:
Thy pleasing spots, to which fond memory clings,
Sweet cooling shades and soft refreshing springs –
And though Fate's pleased to lay their beauties by
In a dark corner of obscurity,
As fair and sweet they bloomed thy plains among
As blooms those Edens by the poets sung,
Now all laid waste by Desolation's hand
Whose curséd weapons levels half the land!
Oh who could see my dear green willows fall,
What feeling heart but dropped a tear for all!
Accurséd Wealth, o'erbounding human laws,
Of every evil thou remains the cause:
Victims of want, those wretches such as me,
Too truly lay their wretchedness to thee!
Thou art the bar that keeps from being fed,
And thine our loss of labour and of bread –
Thou art the cause that levels every tree,
And woods bow down to clear a way for thee!

(ii) *Lamentations of Round-Oak Waters*

(lines 157–96) 1818; publ. 1821

Look backward on the days of yore
   Upon my injured brook,
In fancy con its beauties o'er,
   How it had used to look –
Oh then what trees my banks did crown,
   What willows flourished here –
Hard as the axe that cut them down
   The senseless wretches were!

But sweating slaves I do not blame
   (Those slaves by wealth decreed),
No, I should hurt their harmless name
   To brand 'em with the deed:
Although their aching hands did wield
   The axe that gave the blow,
Yet 'twas not them that owned the field,
   Nor planned its overthrow.

No, no, the foes that hurt my field
   Hurts these poor moilers too,
And thy own bosom knows and feels
   Enough to prove it true –
And oh, poor souls, they may complain,
   But their complaining's all:
The injured worms that turn again,
   But turn again to fall!

Their foes and mine are lawless foes,
   And laws themselves they hold
Which clipt-winged Justice can't oppose,
   But forcéd yields to Gold!
These are the foes of mine and me,
   These all our ruin planned,
Although they never felled a tree
   Or took a tool in hand.

Ah cruel foes, with plenty blest,
   So hankering after more,
To lay the greens and pastures waste
   Which profited before –

Poor greedy souls, what would they have,
Beyond their plenty given?
Will riches keep 'em from the grave,
Or buy them rest in Heaven?

14. JAMES LEIGH HUNT

from *The St James's Phenomenon* (1814)

Good people all attend now,
And I'll tell ye of such a monster
As shall make your eyes
Be double their size
And the hats that ye have on stir!

I'm aware there've been before this
As pretty frights as may be –
Two sisters in one,
And babes like a tun,
And much worse things than they be.

For I've heard of an unlegged body
That went about on castors,
And a head that would come
Bolt into a room
And cry, 'How now, my masters?'

But Lord! all these were handsome
To the one I'm going to mention –
To whom a shark
Is a perfect spark,
And an ogre deserves a pension.

Hard by St James's Palace
You may see this Prince of Shockings;
But not before three,
For at one, d'ye see,
He begins to put on his stockings!

His head, or else what should be
In the place that's on his shoulders,
Is nothing but hair,
Frizzled here and there
To the terror of all beholders! . . .

Of his fingers a tailor tells me
(For one here and there the truth picks)
That the right, when they span,
Are a lady's fan,
And the left a start of toothpicks.

His organs of digestion
Make a noise like the wheels of mangles;
His tongue's a skin,
And hollow within,
And his teeth are dice at angles . . .

N.B. Behave respectful;
For if he thinks you flout him,
He's got a big
Old judges' wig
Wherewith he lays about him!

15. LORD BYRON

Napoleon's Farewell (1814; publ. 1816)

Farewell to the land where the gloom of my glory
Arose and o'ershadowed the Earth with her name –
She abandons me now, but the page of her story,
The brightest, or blackest, is filled with my fame!

I have warred with a world which vanquished me only
When the meteor of conquest allured me too far;
I have coped with the nations which dread me, thus lonely,
The last single captive to millions in war!

Farewell to thee, France! When thy diadem crowned me,
I made thee the gem and the wonder of Earth,
But thy weakness decrees I should leave as I found thee,
Decayed in thy glory, and sunk in thy worth.

Farewell to thee, France! But when Liberty rallies
Once more in thy regions, remember me then!
The violet still grows in the depth of thy valleys –
Though withered, thy tears will unfold it again.

Yet yet, I may baffle the hosts that surround us,
And yet may thy heart leap awake to my voice –
There are links which must break in the chain that has bound us,
Then turn thee and call on the Chief of thy choice!

16. PERCY BYSSHE SHELLEY

(i) *The Mask of Anarchy* (Sept. 1819; publ. 1832)

As I lay asleep in Italy
There came a voice from over the sea,
And with great power it forth led me
To walk in the visions of poesy.

I met Murder on the way –
He had a mask like Castlereagh –
Very smooth he looked, yet grim;
Seven blood-hounds followed him:

All were fat, and well they might
Be in admirable plight,
For one by one, and two by two,
He tossed them human hearts to chew
Which from his wide cloak he drew.

Next came Fraud, and he had on,
Like Eldon, an ermined gown –
His big tears (for he wept well)
Turned to millstones as they fell.

And the little children, who
Round his feet played to and fro,
Thinking every tear a gem,
Had their brains knocked out by them.

Clothed with the bible, as with light,
And the shadows of the night,
Like Sidmouth, next, Hypocrisy
On a crocodile rode by.

And many more Destructions played
In this ghastly masquerade,
All disguised, even to the eyes,
Like bishops, lawyers, peers, or spies.

Last came Anarchy: he rode
On a white horse, splashed with blood;
He was pale even to the lips,
Like Death in the Apocalypse.

And he wore a kingly crown;
And in his grasp a sceptre shone;
On his brow this mark I saw –
'I am God, and King, and Law!'

With a pace stately and fast,
Over English land he passed,
Trampling to a mire of blood
The adoring multitude.

And a mighty troop around,
With their trampling shook the ground,
Waving each a bloody sword
For the service of their Lord.

And with glorious triumph, they
Rode through England proud and gay,
Drunk as with intoxication
On the wine of desolation.

O'er fields and towns, from sea to sea,
Passed the Pageant swift and free,
Tearing up, and trampling down;
Till they came to London town.

And each dweller, panic-stricken,
Felt his heart with terror sicken
Hearing the tempestuous cry
Of the triumph of Anarchy.

For with pomp to meet him came
Clothed in arms like blood and flame
The hired murderers, who did sing
'Thou art God, and Law, and King!

We have waited, weak and lone,
For thy coming, Mighty One!
Our purses are empty, our swords are cold –
Give us glory, and blood, and gold.'

Lawyers and priests, a motley crowd,
To the earth their pale brows bowed;
Like a prayer not over loud
Whispering, 'Thou art Law and God!'

Then all cried with one accord,
'Thou art King, and God, and Lord!
Anarchy, to thee we bow,
Be thy name made holy now!'

And Anarchy, the skeleton,
Bowed and grinned to every one,
As well as if his education
Had cost ten millions to the nation.

For he knew the palaces
Of our Kings were rightly his;
His the sceptre, crown, and globe,
And the gold-inwoven robe.

So he sent his slaves before
To seize upon the Bank and Tower,
And was proceeding with intent
To meet his pensioned Parliament

When one fled past, a manic maid,
And her name was Hope, she said:
But she looked more like Despair,
And she cried out in the air:

'My father Time is weak and grey
With waiting for a better day;
See how idiot-like he stands,
Fumbling with his palsied hands!

'He has had child after child,
And the dust of death is piled
Over every one but me –
Misery, oh, misery!'

Then she lay down in the street,
Right before the horses' feet,
Expecting, with a patient eye,
Murder, Fraud, and Anarchy.

When between her and her foes
A mist, a light, an image rose,
Small at first, and weak, and frail
Like the vapour of a vale,

Till as clouds grow on the blast,
Like tower-crowned giants striding fast,
And glare with lightnings as they fly,
And speak in thunder to the sky,

It grew – a shape arrayed in mail
Brighter than the viper's scale,
And upborne on wings whose grain
Was as the light of sunny rain.

On its helm, seen far away,
A planet, like the morning's, lay;
And those plumes its light rained through
Like a shower of crimson dew.

With step as soft as wind it passed
O'er the heads of men – so fast
That they knew the presence there,
And looked – but all was empty air!

As flowers beneath May's footstep waken,
As stars from Night's loose hair are shaken,
As waves arise when loud winds call,
Thoughts sprung where'er that step did fall.

And the prostrate multitude
Looked, and ankle-deep in blood,
Hope, that maiden most serene,
Was walking with a quiet mien;

And Anarchy, the ghastly birth,
Lay, dead earth upon the earth –
The horse of Death, tameless as wind,
Fled, and with his hoofs did grind
To dust the murderers thronged behind.

A rushing light of clouds and splendour,
A sense awakening and yet tender,
Was heard and felt – and at its close
These words of joy and fear arose

As if their own indignant Earth
Which gave the sons of England birth
Had felt their blood upon her brow,
And, shuddering with a mother's throe,

Had turnéd every drop of blood
By which her face had been bedewed
To an accent unwithstood –
As if her heart had cried aloud:

'Men of England, heirs of glory,
Heroes of unwritten story,
Nurslings of one mighty Mother,
Hopes of her and one another,

Rise like Lions after slumber
In unvanquishable number,
Shake your chains to earth like dew
Which in sleep had fallen on you –
Ye are many, they are few!

What is Freedom? Ye can tell
That which slavery is, too well –
For its very name has grown
To an echo of your own.

'Tis to work and have such pay
As just keeps life from day to day
In your limbs – as in a cell
For the tyrants' use to dwell –

So that ye for them are made,
Loom, and plough, and sword, and spade,
With or without your own will bent
To their defence and nourishment!

'Tis to see your children weak,
With their mothers pine and peak
When the winter winds are bleak –
They are dying whilst I speak!

'Tis to hunger for such diet
As the rich man in his riot
Casts to the fat dogs that lie
Surfeiting beneath his eye!

'Tis to let the ghost of gold
Take from toil a thousandfold
More than e'er its substance could
In the tyrannies of old –

Paper coin! – that forgery
Of the title-deeds, which ye
Hold to something of the worth
Of the inheritance of Earth.

'Tis to be a slave in soul
And to hold no strong control
Over your own wills, but be
All that others make of ye –

And at length when ye complain
With a murmur weak and vain
'Tis to see the tyrant's crew
Ride over your wives and you –
Blood is on the grass like dew!

Then it is to feel revenge
Fiercely thirsting to exchange
Blood for blood – and wrong for wrong!
Do not thus when ye are strong.

Birds find rest in narrow nest
When weary of their wingéd quest;
Beasts find fare in woody lair
When storm and snow are in the air;

Asses, swine, have litter spread
And with fitting food are fed;
All things have a home but one –
Thou, oh Englishman, hast none!

'This is Slavery – savage men,
Or wild beasts within a den,
Would endure not as ye do –
But such ills they never knew!

What art thou Freedom? Oh, could slaves
Answer from their living graves
This demand! Tyrants would flee
Like a dream's dim imagery –

Thou art not, as impostors say,
A shadow soon to pass away,
A superstition, and a name
Echoing from the cave of Fame.

For the labourer thou art bread,
And a comely table spread
From his daily labour come
In a neat and happy home.

Thou art clothes, and fire, and food
For the trampled multitude –
No, in countries that are free
Such starvation cannot be
As in England now we see!

To the rich thou art a check,
When his foot is on the neck
Of his victim, thou dost make
That he treads upon a snake.

Thou art justice: ne'er for gold
May thy righteous laws be sold
As laws are in England – thou
Shieldst alike the high and low.

Thou art wisdom: freemen never
Dream that God will damn for ever
All who think those things untrue.
Of which priests make such ado.

Thou art peace: never by thee
Would blood and treasure wasted be
As tyrants wasted them, when all
Leagued to quench thy flame in Gaul

What if English toil and blood
Was poured forth even as a flood?
It availed, oh, Liberty,
To dim, but not extinguish thee!

Thou art Love: the rich have kissed
Thy feet, and like him following Christ,
Give their substance to the free
And through the rough world follow thee –

Or turn their wealth to arms, and make
War for thy beloved sake
On wealth, and war, and fraud – whence they
Drew the power which is their prey.

Science, poetry, and thought
Are thy lamps; they make the lot
Of the dwellers in a cot
So serene, they curse it not.

Spirit, patience, gentleness,
All that can adorn and bless,
Art thou – let deeds, not words, express
Thine exceeding loveliness!

Let a great Assembly be
Of the fearless and the free
On some spot of English ground
Where the plains stretch wide around!

Let the blue sky overhead,
The green earth on which ye tread –
All that must eternal be –
Witness the solemnity!

From the corners uttermost
Of the bounds of English coast;
From every hut, village, and town
Where those who live and suffer moan
For others' misery or their own;

From the workhouse and the prison
Where pale as corpses newly risen,
Women, children, young and old
Groan for pain, and weep for cold;

From the haunts of daily life
Where is waged the daily strife
With common wants and common cares
Which sows the human heart with tares;

Lastly from the palaces
Where the murmur of distress
Echoes, like the distant sound
Of a wind alive around

Those prison halls of wealth and fashion,
Where some few feel such compassion
For those who groan, and toil, and wail
As must make their brethren pale –

Ye who suffer woes untold,
Or to feel, or to behold
Your lost country bought and sold
With a price of blood and gold –

Let a vast assembly be,
And with great solemnity
Declare with measured words that ye
Are, as God has made ye, free!

Be your strong and simple words
Keen to wound as sharpened swords,
And wide as targes let them be,
With their shade to cover ye.

Let the tyrants pour around
With a quick and startling sound,
Like the loosening of a sea,
Troops of armed emblazonry.

Let the charged artillery drive
Till the dead air seems alive
With the clash of clanging wheels,
And the tramp of horses' heels!

Let the fixéd bayonet
Gleam with sharp desire to wet
Its bright point in English blood,
Looking keen as one for food!

Let the horsemen's scimitars
Wheel and flash, like sphereless stars
Thirsting to eclipse their burning
In a sea of death and mourning!

Stand ye calm and resolute,
Like a forest close and mute,
With folded arms and looks which are
Weapons of unvanquished war,

And let Panic, who outspeeds
The career of armèd steeds
Pass, a disregarded shade
Through your phalanx undismayed.

Let the laws of your own land,
Good or ill, between ye stand
Hand to hand, and foot to foot,
Arbiters of the dispute!

The old laws of England – they
Whose reverend heads with age are grey,
Children of a wiser day,
And whose solemn voice must be
Thine own echo – Liberty!

On those who first should violate
Such sacred heralds in their state
Rest the blood that must ensue,
And it will not rest on you.

And if then the tyrants dare,
Let them ride among you there,
Slash, and stab, and maim, and hew –
What they like, that let them do.

With folded arms and steady eyes,
And little fear, and less surprise,
Look upon them as they slay
Till their rage has died away.

Then they will return with shame
To the place from which they came,
And the blood thus shed will speak
In hot blushes on their cheek.

Every woman in the land
Will point at them as they stand –
They will hardly dare to greet
Their acquaintance in the street!

And the bold, true warriors
Who have hugged Danger in wars
Will turn to those who would be free,
Ashamed of such base company.

And that slaughter to the Nation
Shall steam up like inspiration –
Eloquent, oracular –
A volcano heard afar!

And these words shall then become
Like Oppression's thundered doom
Ringing through each heart and brain,
Heard again – again – again:

'Rise like lions after slumber
In unvanquishable number!
Shake your chains to earth like dew
Which in sleep had fallen on you –
Ye are many, they are few!'

(ii) *England in 1819* (23 Dec.; publ. 1839)

An old, mad, blind, despised, and dying king!
Princes, the dregs of their dull race, who flow
Through public scorn – mud from a muddy spring!
Rulers who neither see, nor feel, nor know,
But leech-like to their fainting country cling,

Till they drop, blind in blood, without a blow!
A people starved and stabbed in the untilled field!
An army, which liberticide and prey
Makes as a two-edged sword to all who wield!
Golden and sanguine laws which tempt and slay!
Religion, Christless, Godless – a book sealed!
A senate, time's worst statute unrepealed! –
Are graves, from which a glorious phantom may
Burst, to illumine our tempestuous day.

17. LORD BYRON

from *The Vision of Judgment* (1822)

15

Saint Peter sat by the celestial gate,
   And nodded o'er his keys – when, lo! there came
A wondrous noise he had not heard of late,
   A rushing sound of wind, and stream, and flame,
In short, a roar of things extremely great,
   Which would have made all save a saint exclaim;
But he, with first a start and then a wink,
Said, 'There's another star gone out, I think!'

16

But ere he could return to his repose,
   A cherub flapped his right wing o'er his eyes –
At which Saint Peter yawned, and rubbed his nose.
   'Saint Porter', said the angel, 'prithee rise'
(Waving a goodly wing, which glowed as glows
   An earthly peacock's tale, with heavenly dyes);
To which the saint replied, 'Well, what's the matter?
Is Lucifer come back, with all this clatter?'

17

'No', quoth the cherub, 'George the Third is dead!'
   'And who is George the Third?' replied the apostle –
'What George? what Third?' 'The King of England', said
   The angel. 'Well he won't find kings to jostle

Him on his way! But does he wear his head?
 Because the last we saw here had a tussle,
And ne'er would have got into Heaven's good graces,
Had he not flung his head in all our faces!' . . .

23

While thus they spake, the angelic caravan,
 Arriving like a rush of mighty wind
Cleaving the fields of space, as doth the swan
 Some silver stream (say, Ganges, Nile, or Inde,
Or Thames, or Tweed), and mid them an old man
 With an old soul, and both extremely blind,
Halted before the gate, and in his shroud
Seated their fellow traveller on a cloud.

24

But bringing up the rear of this bright host
 A Spirit of a different aspect waved
His wings, like thunder-clouds above some coast
 Whose barren beach with frequent wrecks is paved.
His brow was like the deep when tempest-tossed –
 Fierce and unfathomable thoughts engraved
Eternal wrath on his immortal face,
And where he gazed a gloom pervaded space.

25

As he drew near he gazed upon the gate,
 Ne'er to be entered more by him or Sin,
With such a glance of supernatural hate
 As made Saint Peter wish himself within –
He pottered with his keys at a great rate,
 And sweated through his apostolic skin
(Of course his perspiration was but ichor,
Or some such other spiritual liquor).

26

The very cherubs huddled all together,
 Like birds when soars the falcon, and they felt
A tingling to the tip of every feather,
 And formed a circle like Orion's Belt
Around their poor old charge – who scarce knew whither
 His guards had led him, though they gently dealt
With royal *manes* (for by many stories,
And true, we learn the angels all are Tories.

27

As things were in this posture, the gate flew
   Asunder, and the flashing of its hinges
Flung over space an universal hue
   Of many-coloured flame, until its tinges
Reached even our speck of Earth, and made a new
   Aurora Borealis spread its fringes
O'er the North Pole – the same seen, when ice-bound,
By Captain Parry's crew in Melville Sound.

28

And from the gate thrown open issued beaming
   A beautiful and mighty Thing of Light,
Radiant with glory, like a banner streaming
   Victorious from some world-o'erthrowing fight
(My poor comparisons must needs be teeming
   With earthly likenesses, for here the night
Of clay obscures our best conceptions – saving
Joanna Southcote, and Bob Southey raving) . . .

30

Michael flew forth in glory and in good,
   A goodly work of Him from whom all glory
And good arise! The portal passed, he stood,
   Before him the young cherubs and saints hoary
(I say 'young', begging to be understood
   By looks, not years, and should be very sorry
To state they were not older than Saint Peter,
But merely that they seemed a little sweeter).

31

The cherubs and the saints bowed down before
   That archangelic Hierarch, the first
Of essences angelical, who wore
   The aspect of a god – but this ne'er nursed
Pride in his heavenly bosom, in whose core
   No thought save for his Maker's service durst
Intrude: however glorified and high,
He knew him but the Viceroy of the sky!

32

He and the sombre silent Spirit met
(They knew each other both for good and ill),
Such was their power that neither could forget
His former friend and future foe – but still
There was a high immortal proud regret
In either's eye, as if 'twere less their will
Than destiny to make the eternal years
Their date of war, and their *champ clos* the spheres . . .

36

The Archangel bowed, not like a modern beau
But with a graceful oriental bend,
Pressing one radiant arm just where below
The heart in good men is supposed to tend.
He turned as to an equal, not too low,
But kindly: Satan met his ancient friend
With more hauteur, as might an old Castilian
Poor noble meet a mushroom-rich civilian.

37

He merely bent his diabolic brow
An instant – and then, raising it, he stood
In act to assert his right or wrong, and show
Cause why King George by no means could or should
Make out a case to be exempt from woe
Eternal more than other kings endued
With better sense and hearts, whom history mentions,
Who long have 'paved Hell with their good intentions'!

38

Michael began: 'What wouldst thou with this man,
Now dead, and brought before the Lord? What ill
Hath he wrought since his mortal race began,
That thou canst claim him? Speak – and do thy will,
If it be just! If in this earthly span
He hath been greatly failing to fulfil
His duties as a king and mortal, say,
And he is thine. If not, let him have way.'

39

'Michael', replied the Price of Air, 'even here,
   Before the gate of Him thou servest, must
I claim my subject – and will make appear
   That as he was my worshipper in dust
So shall he be in spirit! Although dear
   To thee and thine because nor wine, nor lust,
Were of his weaknesses, yet on the throne
He reigned o'er millions to serve me alone! . . .

47

The New World shook him off, the Old yet groans
   Beneath what he and his prepared, if not
Completed. He leaves heirs on many thrones
   To all his vices – without (what begot
Compassion for him) his tame virtues! Drones
   Who sleep, or despots who have now forgot
A lesson which shall be retaught them, wake
Upon the thrones of Earth – but let them quake!

48

Five millions of the primitive, who hold
   The faith which makes thee great on earth, implored
A *part* of that vast *all* they held of old –
   Freedom to worship! Not alone your Lord,
Michael, but you, and you Saint Peter – cold
   Must be your souls if ye have not abhorred
The foe to Catholic participation
In all the license of a Christian nation.

49

True he allowed them to pray God – but, as
   A consequence of prayer, refused the law
Which would have placed them upon the same base
   With those who did not hold the Saints in awe.'
But here Saint Peter started from his place
   And cried, 'You may the prisoner withdraw!
Ere Heaven shall ope her portals to this Guelph
While I am guard, may I be damned myself!' . . .

52

Then Satan turned and waved his swarthy hand,
Which stirred with its electric qualities
Clouds farther off than we can understand
(Although we find him sometimes in our skies).
Infernal thunder shook both sea and land
In all the planets, and Hell's batteries
Let off the artillery which Milton mentions
As one of Satan's most sublime inventions! . . .

57

Upon the verge of space, about the size
Of half-a-crown, a little speck appeared
(I've seen a something like it in the skies
In the Aegean, ere a squall); it neared,
And, growing bigger, took another guise.
Like an aërial ship it tacked and steered –
Or *was* steered (I am doubtful of the grammar
Of the last phrase, which makes the stanza stammer!

58

But take your choice) – and then it grew a cloud –
And so it was! A cloud of witnesses!
But such a cloud! No land ere saw a crowd
Of locusts numerous as the heavens saw these.
They shadowed with their myriads space; their loud
And frequent cries were like those of wild geese
(If nations may be likened to a goose),
And realized the phrase of 'Hell broke loose'! . . .

66

A merry, cockeyed, curious-looking sprite
Upon the instant started from the throng,
Dressed in a fashion now forgotten quite –
For all the fashions of the flesh stick long
By people in the next world, where unite
All the costumes since Adam's (right or wrong),
From Eve's fig-leaf down to the petticoat,
Almost as scanty, of days less remote.

67

The spirit looked around upon the crowds
Assembled, and exclaimed: 'My friends of all
The spheres, we shall catch cold among these clouds,
So let's to business! Why this general call?
If those are freeholders I see in shrouds,
And 'tis for an election that they bawl,
Behold a candidate with unturned coat!
Saint Peter, may I count upon your vote?'

68

'Sir', replied Michael, 'you mistake – these things
Are from a former life, and what we do
Above is more august. To judge of kings
Is this tribunal met: so now you know!'
'Then I presume those gentlemen with wings',
Said Wilkes, 'are cherubs – and that soul below
Looks much like George the Third, but to my mind
A good deal older. Bless me! is he blind?'

69

'He is what you behold him, and his doom
Depends upon his deeds', the Angel said:
'If you have aught to arraign in him, the tomb
Gives license to the humblest beggar's head
To lift itself above the loftiest.' 'Some',
Said Wilkes, 'don't wait to see them laid in lead,
For such a liberty – and I, for one,
Have told them what I thought beneath the sun!' . . .

85

At length, with jostling, elbowing, and the aid
Of cherubim appointed to the post,
The devil Asmodeus to the circle made
His way (and looked as if his journey cost
Some trouble). When his burden down he laid,
'What's this?' cried Michael, 'Why, 'tis not a ghost!'
'I know it', quoth the incubus, 'but he
Shall be one if you leave the affair to me!

86

Confound the renegado! I have sprained
   My left wing, he's so heavy – one would think
Some of his works about his neck were chained.
   But to the point! While hovering o'er the brink
Of Skiddaw (where as usual it still rained),
   I saw a taper far below me wink,
And, stooping, caught this fellow at a libel –
No less on history, than the Holy Bible!

87

The former is the Devil's scripture, and
   The latter yours, good Michael – so the affair
Belongs to all of us, you understand.
   I snatched him up just as you see him there,
And brought him off for sentence out of hand!
   I've scarcely been ten minutes in the air –
At least, a quarter it can hardly be –
I daresay his wife is still at tea!' . . .

94

The varlet was not an ill-favoured knave:
   A good deal like a vulture in the face,
With a hook-nose and a hawk's eye, which gave
   A smart and sharper-looking sort of grace
To his whole aspect, which, though rather grave,
   Was by no means so ugly as his case!
But that, indeed, was hopeless as can be,
Quite a poetic felony *de se*.'

95

Then Michael blew his trump, and stilled the noise
   With one still greater – as is yet the mode
On Earth besides (except some grumbling voice,
   Which now and then will make a slight inroad
Upon a decorous silence, few will twice
   Lift up their lungs when fairly overcrowed) –
And now the Bard could plead his own bad cause,
With all the attitudes of self-applause! . . .

97

He had written praises of a regicide:
   He had written praises of all kings whatever!
He had written for republics far and wide,
   And then against them, bitterer than ever.
For pantisocracy he once had cried
   Aloud (a scheme less moral than 'twas clever),
Then grew a hearty anti-jacobin –
Had turned his coat, and would have turned his skin!

98

He had sung against all battles, and again
   In their high praise and glory. He had called
Reviewing 'the ungentle craft', and then
   Became as base a critic as e'er crawled –
Fed, paid, and pampered by the very men
   By whom his muse and morals had been mauled.
He had written much blank verse, and blanker prose,
And more of both than anybody knows!

99

He had written Wesley's *Life* – here turning round
   To Satan, 'Sir, I'm ready to write yours,
In two octavo volumes, nicely bound,
   With Notes and Preface, all that most allures
The pious purchaser! And there's no ground
   For fear, for I can choose my own reviewers –
So let me have the proper documents
That I may add you to my other Saints.'

100

Satan bowed and was silent. 'Well, if you,
   With amiable modesty, decline
My offer, what says Michael? There are few
   Whose *Memoirs* could be rendered more divine!
Mine is a pen of all work – not so new
   As it was once, but I would make you shine
Like your own trumpet! By the way, my own
Has more of brass in it, and is as well blown.

101

But, talking about trumpets, here's my *Vision*!
   Now you shall judge – all people – yes! You shall
Judge with my judgment, and by my decision
   Be guided who shall enter Heaven, or fall!
I settle all these things by intuition
   (Times present, past, to come – Heaven, Hell, and all),
Like King Alfonso. When I thus see double
I save the Deity some worlds of trouble!

102

He ceased, and drew forth an MS – and no
   Persuasion on the part of devils, saints,
Or angels, now could stop the torrent – so
   He read the first three lines of the Contents;
But at the fourth, the whole spiritual show
   Had vanished, with variety of scents,
Ambrosial and sulphureous, as they sprang
Like lightning off from his 'melodious twang'

103

Those grand heroics acted as a spell:
   The angels stopped their ears, and plied their pinions;
The devils ran howling, deafened, down to Hell;
   The ghosts fled, gibbering, for their own dominions
(For 'tis not yet decided where they dwell,
   And I leave every man to his opinions);
Michael took refuge in his trump – but lo!
His teeth were set on edge, he could not blow.

104

Saint Peter, who has hitherto been known
   For an impetuous saint, upraised his keys,
And at the fifth line knocked the poet down,
   Who fell like Phaeton, but more at ease,
Into his lake – for there he did not drown,
   A different web being by the Destinies
Woven for the Laureate's final wreath, whene'er
Reform shall happen either here or there.

105

He first sank to the bottom (like his *Works*),
But soon rose to the surface (like himself),
For all corrupted things are buoyed like corks
By their own rottenness, light as an elf
Or wisp that flits o'er a morass! He lurks,
It may be, still (like dull books on a shelf)
In his own den, to scrawl some *Life* or *Vision* –
As Welborn says, 'the devil turned precisian'!

106

As for the rest (to come to the conclusion
Of this true dream), the telescope is gone
Which kept my optics free from all delusion,
And showed me what I in my turn have shown.
All I saw farther, in the last confusion,
Was that King George slipped into Heaven, for one,
And when the tumult dwindled to a calm
I left him practising the hundredth psalm.

18. THOMAS HOOD

Ode to H. Bodkin Esq., Secretary to the Society for the Suppression of Mendicity

(1824)

'This is your charge – ye shall comprehend all vagrom men'
Much Ado About Nothing (III iii)

Hail King of Shreds and Patches; hail
Disperser of the poor!
Thou dog in office, set to bark
All beggars from the door!

Great overseer of overseers,
And dealer in old rags,
Thy public duty never fails,
Thy ardour never flags!

Oh, when I take my walks abroad,
How many poor I *miss*!
(Had Doctor Watts walked nowadays,
He would have written this.)

So well the vagrant-catchers prowl,
So clear thy caution keeps
The path – oh Bodkin, sure thou hast
The eye that never sleeps!

No Belisarius pleads for alms,
No Benbow lacketh legs:
The pious man in black is now
The only man that begs!

Street-Handels are disorganized,
Disbanded every band –
The silent *scraper* at the door
Is scarce allowed to stand.

The sweeper brushes with his broom,
The carstairs with his chalk
Retires, the cripple leaves his stand –
But cannot sell his walk!

The old wall-blind resigns the wall,
The camels hide their *humps*,
The witherington without a leg
Mayn't beg upon his stumps!

Poor Jack is gone, that used to doff
His battered, tattered hat,
And show his dangled sleeve – alas,
There seemed no arm in that!

Oh, was it such a sin to air
His true-blue naval rags,
Glory's own trophy, like St Paul,
Hung round with holy flags!

Thou knowest best! I meditate,
My Bodkin, no offence!
Let us, henceforth, but guard our pounds,
Thou dost protect our pence!

Well art thou pointed 'gainst the poor,
   For, when the beggar-crew
Bring their petitions, thou art paid
   Of course to *run 'em through*!

Doubtless thou art what Hamlet meant –
   To wretches the last friend –
What ills can mortals have they can't
   With a bare Bodkin end?

19. LETITIA ELIZABETH LANDON

The Factory (1835)

There rests a shade above yon town,
   A dark funereal shroud –
'Tis not the tempest hurrying down,
   'Tis not a summer cloud.

The smoke that rises on the air
   Is as a type and sign,
A shadow flung by the despair
   Within those streets of thine.

That smoke shuts out the cheerful day,
   The sunset's purple hues,
The moonlight's pure and purple ray,
   The morning's pearly dews.

Such is the moral atmosphere
   Around thy daily life:
Heavy with care and pale with fear,
   With future tumult rife.

There rises on the morning wind
   A low appealing cry –
A thousand children are resigned
   To sicken and to die!

We read of Moloch's sacrifice,
   We sicken at the name,
And seem to hear the infant cries –
   And yet we do the same!

And worse – 'twas but a moment's pain
The heathen altar gave,
But we give years – our idol, Gain,
Demands a living grave!

How precious is the little one
Before his mother's sight,
With bright hair dancing in the sun,
And eyes of azure light.

He sleeps as rosy as the south
(For summer-days are long),
A prayer upon the little mouth,
Lulled by his nurse's song.

Love is around him, and his hours
Are innocent and free:
His mind essays its early powers
Beside his mother's knee.

When after-years of trouble come,
Such as await man's prime,
How will he think of that dear home
And childhood's lovely time!

And such should childhood ever be –
The fairy well – to bring
To life's worn, weary memory
The freshness of its spring!

But here the order is reversed
And infancy, like age,
Knows of existence but its worst –
One dull and darkened page,

Written with tears, and stamped with toil,
Crushed from its earliest hour,
Weeds darkening on the bitter soil
That never knew a flower.

Look on yon child! It droops the head,
Its knees are bowed with pain;
It mutters from its wretched bed,
'Oh let me sleep again!'

Alas 'tis time – the mother's eyes
   Turn mournfully away –
Alas, 'tis time the child must rise,
   And yet it is not day.

The lantern's lit – she hurries forth –
   The spare cloak's scanty fold
Scare screens her from the snowy north;
   The child is pale and cold.

And wearily the little hands
   Their task accustomed ply,
While daily some, mid those pale bands,
   Droop, sicken, pine, and die.

Good God, to think upon a child
   That has no childish days,
No careless play, no frolics wild,
   No words of prayer and praise!

Man from the cradle – 'tis too soon
   To earn their daily bread,
And heap the heat and toil of noon
   Upon an infant's head.

To labour ere their strength be come,
   Or starve – is such the doom
That makes of many an English home
   One long and living tomb?

Is there no pity from above –
   No mercy in those skies –
Hath then the heart of man no love
   To spare such sacrifice?

Oh England, though thy tribute waves
   Proclaim thee great and free,
While those small children pine like slaves
   There is a curse on thee!

20. CAROLINE NORTON

A Voice from the Factories (stanzas 34–48) 1836

34

Fondly familiar is the look she gives
As he returns who forth so lately went,
For they *together* pass their happy lives!
And many a tranquil evening have they spent
Since, blushing, ignorantly innocent,
She vowed, with downcast eyes and changeful hue,
To love him only. Love fulfilled hath lent
Its deep repose; and when he meets her view
Her soft look only says, 'I trust – and I am true!'

35

Scattered like flowers the rosy children play,
Or round her chair a busy crowd they press,
But at the father's coming, start away
With playful struggle for his loved caress,
And jealous of the one he first may bless.
To each a welcoming word is fondly said:
He bends and kisses some; lifts up the less;
Admires the little cheek, so round and red,
Or smoothes with tender hand the curled and shining head.

36

Oh, let us pause, and gaze upon them now!
Is there not one beloved and lovely boy
With Mirth's bright seal upon his open brow,
And sweet fond eyes, brimful of love and joy –
He, whom no measure of delight can cloy,
The daring and the darling of the set –
He who, though pleased with every passing toy
(Thoughtless and buoyant to excess), could yet
Never a gentle word or kindly deed forget.

37

And one, more fragile than the rest, for whom,
As for the weak bird in a crowded nest,
Are needed all the fostering care of home
And the soft comfort of the brooding breast –

One who hath oft the couch of sickness prest
On whom the mother looks, as it goes by,
With tenderness intense, and fear supprest,
While the soft patience of her active eye
Blends with 'God's will be done', 'God grant thou mayst not die!'

38

And is there not the elder of the band,
She with the gentle smile and smooth bright hair,
Waiting, some paces back, content to stand
Till these of love's caresses have their share;
Knowing how soon his fond parental care
Shall seek his violet in her shady nook?
Patient she stands, demure, and brightly fair,
Copying the meekness of her mother's look,
And clasping in her hand the favourite storybook.

39

Wake, dreamer – choose! To labour life away,
Which of these precious little ones shall go
(Debarred of summer-light and cheerful play)
To that receptacle for dreary woe,
The Factory Mill? Shall he, in whom the glow
Of life shines bright, whose free limbs' vigorous tread
Warns us how much of beauty that we know
Would fade when *he* became dispirited
And pined with sickened heart, and bowed his fainting head?

40

Or shall the quiet little one, whose voice
So rarely mingles in their sounds of glee,
Whose life can bid no living thing rejoice,
But rather is a long anxiety –
Shall he go forth to toil? – and keep the free
Frank boy, whose merry shouts and restless grace
Would leave all eyes that used his face to see
Wistfully gazing towards that vacant space
Which makes their fireside seem a lone and dreary place.

41

Or, sparing these, send her whose simplest words
Have power to charm, whose warbled, childish song,
Fluent and clear and bird-like, strikes the chords
Of sympathy among the listening throng –

Whose spirits light, and steps that dance along,
Instinctive modesty and grace restrain –
The fair young innocent who knows no wrong,
Whose slender wrists scarce hold the silken skein
Which the glad mother winds – shall *she* endure this pain?

42

Away! The thought – the *thought* alone – brings tears!
They labour, *they*, the darlings of our lives,
The flowers and sunbeams of our fleeting years,
From whom alone our happiness derives
A lasting strength, which every shock survives –
The green young trees beneath whose arching boughs
(When failing energy no longer strives)
Our wearied age shall find a cool repose –
They toil in torture? No. The painful picture close!

43

Ye shudder – nor behold the vision more!
Oh, fathers! is there then one law for these,
And one for the pale children of the poor –
That to their agony your hearts can freeze,
Deny their pain, their toil, their slow disease,
And deem with false complaining they encroach
Upon your time and thought? Is yours the ease
Which misery vainly struggles to approach,
Whirling unthinking by in Luxury's gilded coach?

44

Examine and decide. Watch through his day
One of these little ones! The sun hath shone
An hour, and by the ruddy morning's ray
(The last and least) he saunters on alone.
See where, still pausing on the threshold-stone
He stands, as loath to lose the bracing wind –
With wistful wandering glances backward thrown
On all the light and glory left behind,
And sighs to think that he must darkly be confined.

45

Enter with him. The stranger who surveys
The little natives of that dreary place
(Where squalid suffering meets his shrinking gaze),
Used to the glory of a young child's face,

Its changeful light, its coloured sparkling grace
(Gleams of Heaven's sunshine on our shadowed Earth),
Starts at each visage, wan, and bold, and base,
Whose smiles have neither innocence nor mirth –
And comprehends the sin, original from birth.

46

There the pale orphan, whose unequal strength
Loathes the incessant toil it *must* pursue,
Pines for the cool sweet evening's twilight length,
The sunny play-hour and the morning's dew –
Worn with its cheerless life's monotonous hue,
Bowed down and faint and stupefied it stands,
Each half-seen object reeling in its view,
While its hot, trembling, languid little hands
Mechanically heed the Taskmaster's commands.

47

There, sounds of wailing grief and painful blows
Offend the ear, and startle it from rest
(While the lungs gasp what air the place bestows),
Or misery's joyless vice, the ribald jest,
Breaks the sick silence. Staring at the guest
Who comes to view their labour, they beguile
The unwatched moment: whispers half-supprest,
And mutterings low, their faded lips defile –
While gleams from face to face a strange and sullen smile.

48

These then are his companions! He, too young
To share their base and saddening merriment,
Sits by, his little head in silence hung,
His limbs cramped up, his body weakly bent,
Toiling obedient till long hours so spent
Produce exhaustion's slumber, dull and deep.
The Watcher's stroke – bold – sudden – violent!
Urges him from that lethargy of sleep,
And bids him wake to life – to labour, and to weep!

XI. Poets in Relationship

Little need be said as introduction to Poets in Relationship. Here we see the writers off guard: Burns writing wonderful songs for an array of different women; Wordsworth addressing his sister in love-poetry of astounding beauty –

Her voice was like a hidden bird that sang;
The thought of her was like a flash of light
Or an unseen companionship, a breath
Or fragrance independent of the wind . . .

– Coleridge addressing Sara Hutchinson in a poem full of awkwardness, emotion and revelation, that was tidied up to form *Dejection: An Ode*; Byron addressing in deeply moving verses both the wife who rejected him, and the half-sister (mother of his child Medora) who almost alone stood by him; Shelley and the tortured emotions of *Epipsychidion*. And here we have Norton addressing her sons in as good a family-poem as has ever been written:

When first thou camest, gentle, shy, and fond,
   My eldest-born, first hope, and dearest treasure,
My heart received thee with a joy beyond
   All that it yet had felt of earthly pleasure –
Nor thought that any love again might be
So deep and strong as that I felt for thee.

1. WILLIAM BLAKE

and Catherine Blake

I Love the Jocund Dance (*Poetical Sketches* 1783)

I love the jocund dance,
The softly-breathing song,
Where innocent eyes do glance,
And where lisps the maiden's tongue.

I love the laughing vale,
I love the echoing hill,
Where mirth does never fail,
And the jolly swain laughs his fill.

I love the pleasant cot,
I love the innocent bower.
Where white and brown is our lot,
Or fruit in the midday hour.

I love the oaken seat
Beneath the oaken tree,
Where all the old villagers meet,
And laugh our sports to see.

I love our neighbours all,
    But, Kitty, I better love thee;
And love them I ever shall;
    But thou art all to me.

2. ROBERT BURNS

(1) and Elizabeth Paton

A Poet's Welcome to his Love-begotten Daughter (May 1785; publ. 1801)

Thou's welcome, wean! Mishanter fa' me
If thoughts o' thee, or yet thy Mamie,
Shall ever daunton me or awe me,
    My bonnie lady,
Or if I blush when thou shalt ca' me
    Tyta, or Daddie!

Tho' now they ca' me fornicator,
And tease my name in kintra clatter,
The mair they talk, I'm kend the better;
    E'en let them clash!
An auld wife's tongue's a feckless matter
    To gie ane fash!

Welcome, my bonnie, sweet, wee dochter!
Tho' ye come here a wee unsought for,
And tho' your comin I hae fought for,
    Baith Kirk and Queir,
Yet by my faith, ye're no unwrought for,
    That I shall swear!

1 *wean* child.
Mishanter fa' me Bad luck to me ('May misadventure fall on me').
8 *tease* make free with. **10** *clash* chatter.
11–12 *a feckless matter . . . fash* an idle matter to worry ('fash') oneself about.

Wee image o' my bonnie Betty,
As fatherly I kiss and daut thee,
As dear and near my heart I set thee,
        Wi' as gude will
As a' the priests had seen me get thee
        That's out o' Hell!

Sweet fruit o' monie a merry dint,
My funny toil is no a' tint;
Tho' ye come to the warld askent,
        Which fools may scoff at,
In my last plack your part's be in't,
        The better half o't!

Tho' I should be the waur bestead,
Thou's be as braw and bienly clad,
And thy young years as nicely bred
        Wi' education,
As ony brat o' wedlock's bed,
        In a' thy station –

For if thou be, what I wad hae thee,
And tak the counsel I shall gie thee,
I'll never rue my trouble wi' thee,
        The cost nor shame o't,
But be a loving Father to thee,
        And brag the name o't!

20 *daut* fondle. **25** *dint* encounter (literally a 'blow').
26 *My funny . . . a' tint* My pleasant labour is not all wasted.
27 *askent* on the side (out of wedlock).
29–30 *In my last plack . . . better half o't* You shall have the better half of my last farthing. **31** *the waur bestead* the worse off for it.
32 *braw and bienly clad* as fine and warmly dressed.
36 *In a' thy station* Among your class as a whole.
42 *And brag the name o't* And boast about it.

(II) and Agnes Craif McLehose

Ae Fond Kiss (Dec. 1787; publ. 1792)

Ae fond kiss, and then we sever –
Ae fareweel, and then for ever!
Deep in heart-wrung tears I'll pledge thee,
Warring sighs and groans I'll wage thee!

Who shall say that Fortune grieves him,
While the star of hope she leaves him:
Me, nae chearful twinkle lights me –
Dark despair around benights me!

I'll ne'er blame my partial fancy,
Naething could resist my Nancy:
But to see her, was to love her –
Love but her, and love for ever!

Had we never loved sae kindly,
Had we never loved sae blindly –
Never met, or never parted –
We had ne'er been broken hearted!

Fare-thee-weel, thou first and fairest!
Fare-thee-weel, thou best and dearest!
Thine be ilka joy and treasure,
Peace, enjoyment, love and pleasure!

Ae fond kiss, and then we sever,
Ae fareweel – alas, for ever!
Deep in heart-wrung tears I'll pledge thee,
Warring sighs and groans I'll wage thee!

(III) and Jean Armour (by now Mrs Burns)

I Love My Jean (April 1788; publ. 1790)

Of a' the airts the wind can blaw,
   I dearly like the west;
For there the bonny lassie lives,
   The lassie I lo'e best:

1 *airts* directions.

There's wild-woods grow, and rivers row,
  And mony a hill between;
But day and night my fancy's flight
  Is ever wi' my Jean!

I see her in the dewy flowers,
  I see her sweet and fair;
I hear her in the tunefu' birds,
  I hear her charm the air –
There's not a bonny flower that springs
  By fountain, shaw, or green;
There's not a bonny bird that sings,
  But minds me o' my Jean!

(IV) and Mary Campbell

Highland Mary (Nov. 1792; publ. 1799)

Ye banks and braes and streams around
  The Castle o' Montgomery,
Green be your woods, and fair your flowers,
  Your waters never drumlie!
There Simmer first unfald her robes,
  And there the langest tarry,
For there I took the last fareweel
  O' my sweet Highland Mary.

How sweetly bloomed the gay green birk,
  How rich the hawthorn's blossom,
As underneath their fragrant shade
  I clasped her to my bosom!
The golden hours, on angel-wings,
  Flew o'er me and my dearie –
For dear to me as light and life
  Was my sweet Highland Mary.

Wi' mony a vow, and lock'd embrace,
  Our parting was fu' tender,
And pledging aft to meet again,
  We tore oursels asunder –

5 *row* roll.

4 *drumlie* muddy, unfit to drink. 5 *Simmer* Summer.

But oh, fell Death's untimely frost
  That nipt my flower sae early,
Now green's the sod, and cauld's the clay,
  That wraps my Highland Mary!

O pale, pale now those rosy lips
  I aft hae kiss'd sae fondly,
And clos'd for ay the sparkling glance
  That dwelt on me sae kindly!
And mouldering now in silent dust
  That heart that lo'ed me dearly,
But still within my bosom's core
  Shall live my Highland Mary.

3. CHARLOTTE SMITH

To My Children (1788)

O'erwhelmed with sorrow, and sustaining long
'The proud man's contumely, the oppressor's wrong',
Languid despondency and vain regret,
Must my exhausted spirit struggle yet?
Yes! Robbed, myself, of all that fortune gave,
Even of all hope (but shelter in the grave),
Still shall the plaintive lyre essay its powers
To dress the Cave of Care with Fancy's flowers –
Maternal love the fiend Despair withstand,
Still animate the heart and guide the hand.
May you, dear objects of my anxious care,
Escape the evils I was born to bear,
Round *my* devoted head while tempests roll!
Yet there, where I have treasured up my soul,
May the soft rays of dawning hope impart
Reviving patience to my fainting heart –
And when its sharp solicitudes shall cease,
May I be conscious in the realms of peace
That every tear which swells my children's eyes,
From sorrows past, not present ills arise.
Then, with some friend who loves to share your pain
(For 'tis my boast that some such friends remain),

By filial grief, and fond remembrance prest,
You'll seek the spot where all my sorrows rest,
Recall my hapless days in sad review
(The long calamities I bore for you),
And – with an happier fate – resolve to prove
How well you merited your mother's love.

4. MARY ROBINSON

and General Sir Banastre Tarleton

Written Between Dover and Calais, July 1792 (1793)

Bounding billow, cease thy motion –
   Bear me not so swiftly o'er!
Cease thy roaring, foamy ocean!
   I will tempt thy rage no more.

Ah! within my bosom beating,
   Varying passions wildly reign.
Love, with proud resentment meeting,
   Throbs by turns of joy and pain!

Joy, that far from foes I wander,
   Where their arts can reach no more;
Pain, that woman's heart grows fonder
   When the dream of bliss is o'er!

Love, by fickle fancy banished,
   Spurned by hope, indignant flies!
Yet, when love and hope are vanished,
   Restless Memory never dies!

Far I go, where fate shall lead me,
   Far across the troubled deep,
Where no stranger's ear shall heed me,
   Where no eye for me shall weep.

Proud has been my fatal passion!
   Proud my injured heart shall be!
While each thought and inclination
   Proves that heart was formed for thee!

Not one sigh shall tell my story,
   Not one tear my cheek shall stain!
Silent grief shall be my glory,
   Grief that stoops not to complain!

Let the bosom, prone to ranging,
   Still, by ranging, seek a cure –
Mine disdains the thought of changing,
   Proudly destined to endure!

Yet ere far from all I treasured,
   Tarleton, ere I bid adieu,
Ere my days of pain are measured,
   Take the song that's still thy due!

Yet believe no servile passions
   Seek to charm thy wandering mind;
Well I know thy inclinations,
   Wavering as the passing wind!

I have loved thee, dearly loved thee,
   Through an age of worldly woe!
How ungrateful I have proved thee,
   Let my mournful exile show!

Ten long years of anxious sorrow,
   Hour by hour I counted o'er;
Looking forward till tomorrow,
   Every day I loved thee more!

Power and splendour could not charm me;
   I no joy in wealth could see;
Nor could threats or fears alarm me –
   Save the fear of losing thee!

When the storms of fortune pressed thee,
   I have sighed to hear thee sigh!
Or when sorrows dire distressed thee,
   I have bid those sorrows fly!

Often hast thou smiling told me
   Wealth and power were trifling things,
While Love, smiling to behold me,
   Mocked cold Time's destructive wings.

When with thee, what ills could harm me?
   Thou could every pang assuage!
Now, alas! what hope shall charm me?
   Every moment seems an age!

Fare thee well, ungrateful rover!
   Welcome Gallia's hostile shore;
Now the breezes waft me over;
   Now we part – to meet no more!

5. WILLIAM COWPER and Mary Unwin

To Mary (autumn 1793; publ. 1803)

The twentieth year is well-nigh past
Since first our sky was overcast –
Ah would that this might be the last,
                                        My Mary!

Thy spirits have a fainter flow,
I see thee daily weaker grow –
'Twas my distress that brought thee low,
                                        My Mary.

Thy needles, once a shining store
(For my sake restless heretofore),
Now rust disused, and shine no more,
                                        My Mary!

For though thou gladly wouldst fulfil
The same kind office for me still,
Thy sight now seconds not thy will,
                                        My Mary.

But well thou playedst the housewife's part,
And all thy threads with magic art
Have wound themselves about this heart,
My Mary.

Thy indistinct expressions seem
Like language uttered in a dream;
Yet me they charm, whate'er the theme,
My Mary.

Thy silver locks, once auburn bright,
Are still more lovely in my sight
Than golden beams of orient light,
My Mary!

For could I view nor them, nor thee,
What sight worth seeing could I see?
The sun would rise in vain for me,
My Mary!

Partakers of the sad decline,
Thy hands their little force resign;
Yet, gently prest, press gently mine,
My Mary.

And then I feel that still I hold
A richer store ten-thousandfold
Than misers fancy in their gold,
My Mary!

Such feebleness of limbs thou prov'st
That now, at every step, thou mov'st
Upheld by two! But still thou lov'st,
My Mary.

And still to love, though prest with ill,
In wintry age to feel no chill,
With me is to be lovely still,
My Mary.

But ah, by constant heed I know
How oft the sadness that I show
Transforms thy smiles to looks of woe,
My Mary!

And should my future lot be cast
With much resemblance to the past,
Thy worn-out heart will break at last,
My Mary!

6. CHARLES LAMB

To Mary Ann Lamb, the Author's Best Friend and Sister (1795; publ. 1797)

If from my lips some angry accents fell,
Peevish complaint, or harsh reproof unkind,
'Twas but the error of a sickly mind
And troubled thoughts, clouding the purer well,
And waters clear, of Reason! And for me,
Let this my verse the poor atonement be –
My verse, which thou to praise wert e'er inclined
Too highly, and with a painful eye to see
No blemish. Thou to me didst ever show
Kindest affection, and wouldst oft-times lend
An ear to the desponding love-sick lay,
Weeping my sorrows with me, who repay
But ill the mighty debt of love I owe,
Mary, to thee, my sister, and my friend.

7. SAMUEL TAYLOR COLERIDGE

(i) *Composed on a Journey Homeward, the Author Having Received Intelligence of the Birth of a Son, September 20, 1796* (1797)

Oft o'er my brain does that strange fancy roll
Which makes the present (while the flesh doth last)
Seem a mere semblance of some unknown past,
Mixed with such feelings as perplex the soul

Self-questioned in her sleep. And some have said
We lived ere yet this fleshly robe we wore.
Oh my sweet baby! when I reach the door,
If heavy looks should tell me thou wert dead
(As sometimes, through excess of hope, I fear),
I think that I should struggle to believe
Thou wert a spirit, to this nether sphere
Sentenced for some more venial crime to grieve –
Didst scream, then spring to meet Heaven's quick reprieve,
While we wept idly o'er thy little bier!

(ii) *Letter to Sara Hutchinson: 4 April 1802, Sunday Evening* (from MS 1936)

Well, if the bard was weatherwise, who made
The grand old *Ballad of Sir Patrick Spens*,
This night, so tranquil now, will not go hence
Unroused by winds, that ply a busier trade
Than that which moulds yon clouds in lazy flakes,
Or the dull sobbing draught, that drones and rakes
Upon the strings of this Eolian lute,
　Which better far were mute.
For lo! the new moon, winter-bright
And overspread with phantom light –
With swimming phantom light o'erspread
But rimmed and circled with a silver thread –
I see the old moon in her lap, foretelling
The coming on of rain and squally blast!
Oh Sara, that the gust even now were swelling,
And the slant night-shower driving loud and fast!

A grief without a pang, void, dark, and drear,
A stifling, drowsy, unimpassioned grief
That finds no natural outlet, no relief
　In word, or sigh, or tear –
This, Sara, well thou knowst,
Is that sore evil which I dread the most,
And oftenest suffer! In this heartless mood,
To other thoughts by yonder throstle wooed,

That pipes within the larch-tree, not unseen
(The larch, which pushes out in tassels green
Its bundled leafits), wooed to mild delights
By all the tender sounds and gentle sights
Of this sweet primrose-month – and vainly wooed!
Oh dearest Sara, in this heartless mood
All this long eve, so balmy and serene,
Have I been gazing on the western sky
And its peculiar tint of yellow-green;
And still I gaze and with how blank an eye!
And those thin clouds above, in flakes and bars,
That give away their motion to the stars;
Those stars, that glide behind them, or between,
Now sparkling, now bedimmed, but always seen;
Yon crescent moon, as fixed as if it grew
In its own cloudless, starless lake of blue –
A boat becalmed, dear William's sky-canoe!
I see them all, so excellently fair!
I *see*, not *feel*, how beautiful they are.

My genial spirits fail –
And what can these avail
To lift the smothering weight from off my breast?
It were a vain endeavour,
Though I should gaze for ever
On that green light which lingers in the west!
I may not hope from outward forms to win
The passion and the life whose fountains are within!
These lifeless shapes, around, below, above,
Oh what can they impart?
When even the gentle thought that thou, my love,
Art gazing now, like me,
And seest the heaven I see –
Sweet thought it is, yet feebly stirs my heart!
Feebly, oh feebly – yet
(I well remember it)
In my first dawn of youth that fancy stole
With many secret yearnings on my soul.
At eve, sky-gazing in 'ecstatic fit',
Alas (for cloistered in a city-school
The sky was all I knew of beautiful),
At the barred window often did I sit,

And oft upon the leaded school-roof lay,
And to myself would say:
There does not live the man so stripped of good affections
As not to love to see a maiden's quiet eyes
Upraised and linking on sweet dreams, by dim connections
To moon, or Evening Star, or glorious western skies –
While yet a boy, this thought would so pursue me
That often it became a kind of vision to me!

Sweet thought, and dear of old
To hearts of finer mould –
Ten thousand times by friends and lovers blest!
I spoke with rash despair,
And, ere I was aware,
The weight was somewhat lifted from my breast.
Oh Sara, in the weather-fended wood –
Thy loved haunt, where the stock-doves coo at noon –
I guess, that thou hast stood
And watched yon crescent, and its ghost-like moon.
And yet, far rather in my present mood
I would that thou'dst been sitting all this while
Upon the sod-built seat of camomile –
And, though thy robin may have ceased to sing,
Yet needs for my sake must thou love to hear
The beehive murmuring near,
That ever-busy and most quiet thing
Which I have heard at midnight murmuring.

I feel my spirit moved,
And, wheresoe'er thou be
Oh Sister, oh beloved,
Those dear mild eyes that see
Even now the heaven I see –
There is a prayer in them – it is for me!
And I, dear Sara, I am blessing thee!

It was as calm as this, that happy night
When Mary, thou, and I together were,
The low decaying fire our only light,
And listened to the stillness of the air!
Oh that affectionate and blameless maid,
Dear Mary – on her lap my head she laid!

Her hand was on my brow
(Even as my own is now),
And on my cheek I felt thy eye-lash play.
Such joy I had that I may truly say,
My spirit was awe-stricken with the excess
And trance-like depth of its brief happiness.

Ah fair remembrances, that so revive
The heart, and fill it with a living power –
Where were they, Sara? Or did I not strive
To win them to me on the fretting hour –
Then when I wrote thee that complaining scroll
Which even to bodily sickness bruised thy soul!
And yet thou blam'st thyself alone – and yet
Forbidd'st me all regret!

And must I not regret that I distressed
Thee, best beloved who lovest me the best?
My better mind had fled I know not whither,
For oh, was this an absent friend's employ
To send from far both pain and sorrow thither
Where still his blessings should have called down joy!
I read thy guileless letter o'er again,
I hear thee of thy blameless self complain,
And only this I learn (and this, alas, I know),
That thou art weak and pale with sickness, grief and pain,
And I – I made thee so!

Oh for my own sake I regret perforce
Whatever turns thee, Sara, from the course
Of calm well-being and a heart at rest!
When thou, and with thee those whom thou lov'st best,
Shall dwell together in one happy home,
One house, the dear abiding home of all,
I too will crown me with a coronal!
Nor shall this heart in idle wishes roam
Morbidly soft!
No! Let me trust that I shall wear away
In no inglorious toils the manly day,
And only now and then, and not too oft,
Some dear and memorable eve will bless
Dreaming of all your loves and quietness.

Be happy, and I need thee not in sight –
Peace in thy heart, and quiet in thy dwelling,
Health in thy limbs, and in thine eyes the light
Of love, and hope, and honourable feeling.
Where'er I am, I shall be well content –
Not near thee, haply shall be more content!
To all things I prefer the permanent!
And better seems it for a heart like mine
Always to know, than sometimes to behold,
   Their happiness and thine;
For change doth trouble me with pangs untold!
To see thee, hear thee, feel thee, then to part,
   Oh, it weighs down the heart!
To visit those I love, as I love thee,
Mary, and William, and dear Dorothy,
It is but a temptation to repine –
The transientness is poison in the wine,
Eats out the pith of joy, makes all joy hollow,
All pleasure a dim dream of pain to follow!
   My own peculiar lot, my household life,
It is, and will remain, indifference or strife –
While ye are well and happy, 'twould but wrong you
If I should fondly yearn to be among you.
Wherefore, oh wherefore, should I wish to be
A withered branch upon a blossoming tree?

But – let me say it, for I vainly strive
To beat away the thought – but if thou pined,
Whate'er the cause, in body or in mind,
I were the miserablest man alive
To know it and be absent! Thy delights
Far off, or near, alike I may partake;
But oh, to mourn for thee, and to forsake
All power, all hope of giving comfort to thee –
To know that thou art weak and worn with pain,
And not to hear thee, Sara, not to view thee,
   Not sit beside thy bed,
   Not press thy aching head,
   Not bring thee health again
   (At least to hope, to try)
By this voice, which thou lov'st, and by this earnest eye!

Nay, wherefore did I let it haunt my mind,
   The dark distressful dream?
I turn from it, and listen to the wind
Which long has raved unnoticed. What a scream
Of agony, by torture lengthened out,
That lute sent forth! Oh thou wild storm without!
Jagg'd rock, or mountain-pond, or blasted tree,
Or pine-grove whither woodman never clomb,
Or lonely house long held the witches' home,
Methinks were fitter instruments for thee,
Mad lutanist, that in this month of showers,
Of dark brown gardens and of peeping flowers,
Mak'st Devil's yule, with worse than wintry song
The blossoms, buds, and timorous leaves among!
Thou actor, perfect in all tragic sounds,
Thou mighty poet, even to frenzy bold!
   What tell'st thou now about?
'Tis of the rushing of an host in rout –
And many groans from men with smarting wounds –
At once they groan with smart, and shudder with the cold!
'Tis hushed: there is a trance of deepest silence.
Again! But all that sound, as of a rushing crowd,
And groans and tremulous shudderings, all are over –
And it has other sounds, and all less deep, less loud –
   A tale of less affright,
   And tempered with delight,
As William's self had made the tender lay:
   'Tis of a little child
   Upon a heathy wild,
Not far from home, but it has lost its way,
And now groans low in utter grief and fear,
And now screams loud, and hopes to make its mother hear!

'Tis midnight, and small thoughts have I of sleep –
Full seldom may my friend such vigils keep –
Oh breathe she softly in her gentle sleep!
Cover her, gentle sleep, with wings of healing.
And be this tempest but a mountain-birth!
May all the stars hang bright about her dwelling,
Silent, as though they watched the sleeping earth!
Healthful and light, my darling, mayst thou rise
   With clear and cheerful eyes –

And of the same good tidings to me send!
For, oh, belovéd friend,
I am not the buoyant thing I was of yore
When, like an own child, I to joy belonged –
For others mourning oft, myself oft sorely wronged,
Yet bearing all things then, as if I nothing bore!

Yes, dearest Sara, yes!
There was a time when, though my path was rough,
The joy within me dallied with distress,
And all misfortunes were but as the stuff
Whence fancy made me dreams of happiness;
For hope grew round me like the climbing vine,
And leaves and fruitage, not my own, seemed mine!
But now ill tidings bow me down to earth –
Nor care I that they rob me of my mirth,
But oh, each visitation
Suspends what nature gave me at my birth,
My shaping spirit of imagination!
I speak not now of those habitual ills
That wear out life, when two unequal minds
Meet in one house, and two discordant wills;
This leaves me where it finds,
Past cure and past complaint – a fate austere,
Too fixed and hopeless to partake of fear!

But thou, dear Sara (dear indeed thou art,
My comforter! A heart within my heart!),
Thou, and the few we love, though few ye be,
Make up a world of hopes and fears for me.
And if affliction, or distempering pain,
Or wayward chance befall you, I complain
Not that I mourn. Oh friends most dear, most true,
Methinks to weep with you
Were better far than to rejoice alone –
But that my coarse domestic life has known
No habits of heart-nursing sympathy,
No griefs but such as dull and deaden me,
No mutual mild enjoyments of its own,
No hopes of its own vintage – none, oh none,
Whence, when I mourned for you, my heart might borrow
Fair forms and living motions for its sorrow.

For not to think of what I needs must feel,
But to be still and patient all I can,
And haply by abstruse research to steal
From my own nature all the natural man –
This was my sole resource, my wisest plan!
And that, which suits a part, infects the whole,
And now is almost grown the temper of my soul.

My little children are a joy, a love,
A good gift from above!
But what is bliss, that still calls up a woe
And makes it doubly keen,
Compelling me to feel, as well as know,
What a most blessèd lot mine might have been.
Those little angel-children – woe is me! –
There have been hours, when feeling how they bind
And pluck out the wing-feathers of my mind,
Turning my error to necessity, I have half
Wished they never had been born!
That, seldom – but sad thoughts they always bring,
And like the poet's Philomel I sing
My love-song with my breast against a thorn.

With no unthankful spirit I confess
This clinging grief too, in its turn, awakes
That love, and father's joy; but oh, it makes
The love the greater, and the joy far less!
These mountains too, these vales, these woods, these lakes,
Scenes full of beauty and of loftiness
Where all my life I fondly hoped to live –
I were sunk low indeed, did they no solace give;
But oft I seem to feel, and evermore I fear,
They are not to me now the things, which once they were.

Oh Sara, we receive but what we give,
And in our life alone does Nature live.
Ours is her wedding garment, ours her shroud –
And would we aught behold of higher worth
Than that inanimate cold world allowed
To the poor loveless ever-anxious crowd,
Ah, from the soul itself must issue forth
A light, a glory, and a luminous cloud

Enveloping the earth!
And from the soul itself must there be sent
A sweet and potent voice, of its own birth,
Of all sweet sounds the life and element.

Oh pure of heart, thou needst not ask of me
What this strong music in the soul may be,
What and wherein it doth exist,
This light, this glory, this fair luminous mist,
This beautiful and beauty-making power!
Joy, innocent Sara! Joy, that ne'er was given
Save to the pure, and in their purest hour –
Joy, Sara, is the spirit and the power
That, wedding Nature to us, gives in dower
A new Earth and new Heaven
Undreamt of by the sensual and the proud!
Joy is that strong voice, joy that luminous cloud –
We, we ourselves rejoice!
And thence flows all that charms or ear or sight –
All melodies the echoes of that voice,
All colours a suffusion of that light.

Sister and friend of my devoutest choice!
Thou being innocent and full of love,
And nested with the darlings of thy love,
And feeling in thy soul, heart, lips, and arms
Even what the conjugal and mother dove,
That borrows genial warmth from those she warms,
Feels in her thrilled wings, blessedly outspread –
Thou, freed awhile from cares and human dread
By the immenseness of the good and fair
Which thou seest everywhere –
Thus, thus shouldst thou rejoice!
To thee would all things live from pole to pole,
Their life the eddying of thy living soul.
Oh dear! Oh innocent! Oh full of love!
A very friend! A sister of my choice –
Oh dear, as light and impulse from above,
Thus mayst thou ever, evermore rejoice!

8. WILLIAM WORDSWORTH

(1) and Dorothy Wordsworth

(i) *To My Sister* (March 1798; publ. *Lyrical Ballads*)

It is the first mild day of March,
Each minute sweeter than before;
The redbreast sings from the tall larch
That stands beside our door.

There is a blessing in the air
Which seems a sense of joy to yield
To the bare trees, and mountains bare,
And grass in the green field.

My sister – 'tis a wish of mine –
Now that our morning-meal is done
Make haste, your morning task resign,
Come forth and feel the sun.

Edward will come with you, and pray
Put on with speed your woodland-dress,
And bring no book – for this one day
We'll give to idleness!

No joyless forms shall regulate
Our living calendar:
We from today, my friend, will date
The opening of the year.

Love, now an universal birth,
From heart to heart is stealing –
From earth to man, from man to earth –
It is the hour of feeling!

One moment now may give us more
Than fifty years of reason;
Our minds shall drink at every pore
The spirit of the season.

Some silent laws our hearts may make,
Which they shall long obey;
We for the year to come may take
Our temper from today.

And from the blessèd power that rolls
About, below, above,
We'll frame the measure of our souls –
They shall be tuned to love.

Then come, my sister, come I pray,
With speed put on your woodland-dress,
And bring no book – for this one day
We'll give to idleness.

(ii) from *Home at Grasmere*

(March 1800; publ. from MS 1888)

Mine eyes did ne'er
Rest on a lovely object, nor my mind
Take pleasure in the midst of happy thoughts,
But either she whom now I have, who now
Divides with me this loved abode, was there
Or not far off. Where'er my footsteps turned,
Her voice was like a hidden bird that sang;
The thought of her was like a flash of light
Or an unseen companionship, a breath
Or fragrance independent of the wind . . .
The boon is absolute: surpassing grace
To me hath been vouchsafed. Among the bowers
Of blissful Eden this was neither given,
Nor could be given – possession of the good
Which had been sighed for, ancient thought fulfilled,
And dear imaginations realized
Up to their highest measure, yea, and more . . .
Long is it since we met to part no more,
Since I and Emma heard each other's call
And were companions once again, like birds
Which by the intruding fowler had been scared –
Two of a scattered brood that could not bear
To live in loneliness! 'Tis long since we,

Remembering much and hoping more, found means
To walk abreast, though in a narrow path,
With undivided steps. Our home was sweet –
Could it be less? If we were forced to change,
Our home again was sweet; but still – for youth,
Strong as it seems and bold, is inly weak
And diffident – the destiny of life
Remained unfixed . . .
    Bleak season was it, turbulent and bleak,
When hitherward we journeyed, and on foot,
Through bursts of sunshine and through flying snows,
Paced the long vales. How long they were, and yet
How fast that length of way was left behind –
Wensley's long vale and Sedbergh's naked heights.
The frosty wind, as if to make amends
For its keen breath, was aiding to our course
And drove us onward like two ships at sea!
Stern was the face of Nature; we rejoiced
In that stern countenance, for our souls had there
A feeling of their strength. The naked trees,
The icy brooks, as on we passed, appeared
To question us. 'Whence come ye? To what end?'
They seemed to say. 'What would ye?' said the shower,
'Wild wanderers, whither through my dark domain?'
The sunbeam said, 'Be happy'. They were moved –
All things were moved – they round us as we went,
We in the midst of them.
                                        And when the trance
Came to us as we stood by Hart-Leap Well,
The intimation of the milder day
Which is to come, the fairer world than this,
And raised us up, dejected as we were
Among the records of that doleful place
By sorrow for the hunted beast who there
Had yielded up his breath – the awful trance,
The vision of humanity and of God
The mourner, God the sufferer, when the heart
Of his poor creatures suffers wrongfully –
Both in the sadness and the joy we found
A promise and an earnest that we twain,
A pair seceding from the common world,
Might in that hallowed spot to which our steps
Were tending, in that individual nook,
Might even thus early for ourselves secure,

And in the midst of these unhappy times,
A portion of the blessedness which love
And knowledge will, we trust, hereafter give
To all the vales of earth and all mankind.

(iii) *To a Butterfly*

('Stay near me') spring 1802; publ. 1807

Stay near me, do not take thy flight!
A little longer stay in sight –
Much reading do I find in thee,
Historian of my infancy.
Float near me, do not yet depart!
Dead times revive in thee;
Thou bringest (gay creature, as thou art)
A solemn image to my heart:
My father's family.

Oh pleasant, pleasant were the days,
The time when in our childish plays
My sister Emmeline and I
Together chased the butterfly.
A very hunter, I did rush
Upon the prey – with leaps and springs
I followed on from brake to bush –
But she, God love her, feared to brush
The dust from off its wings!

(iv) *The Sparrow's Nest* (spring 1802; publ. 1807)

Look, five blue eggs are gleaming there!
Few visions have I seen more fair,
Nor many prospects of delight
More pleasing than that simple sight.
I started, seeming to espy
The home and sheltered bed,
The sparrow's dwelling, which hard by
My father's house in wet or dry,
My sister Emmeline and I
    Together visited.

She looked at it as if she feared it –
Still wishing, dreading to be near it –
Such heart was in her, being then
A little prattler among men.
The blessing of my later years
Was with me when a boy:
She gave me eyes, she gave me ears,
And humble cares, and delicate fears,
A heart, the fountain of sweet tears,
And love, and thought, and joy.

(v) 'Child of My Parents'

(1805 *Prelude* XIII 210–46) publl. 1850/from MS 1926

Child of my parents, sister of my soul,
Elsewhere have strains of gratitude been breathed
To thee for all the early tenderness
Which I from thee imbibed. And true it is
That later seasons owed to thee no less;
For, spite of thy sweet influence and the touch
Of other kindred hands that opened out
The springs of tender thought in infancy,
And spite of all which singly I had watched
Of elegance, and each minuter charm
In Nature and in life, still to the last –
Even to the very going-out of youth,
The period which our story now has reached –
I too exclusively esteemed that love,
And sought that beauty, which (as Milton sings)
Has terror in it. Thou didst soften down
This over-sternness; but for thee, sweet friend,
My soul, too reckless of mild grace, had been
Far longer what by nature it was framed –
Longer retained its countenance severe –
A rock with torrents roaring, with the clouds
Familiar, and a favourite of the stars;
But thou didst plant its crevices with flowers,
Hang it with shrubs that twinkle in the breeze,
And teach the little birds to build their nests
And warble in its chambers.
At a time
When Nature, destined to remain so long

Foremost in my affections, had fallen back
Into second place, well pleased to be
A handmaid to a nobler than herself –
When every day brought with it some new sense
Of exquisite regard for common things,
And all the earth was budding with these gifts
Of more refined humanity – thy breath,
Dear sister, was a kind of gentler spring
That went before my steps.

(II) and Caroline (Vallon) Wordsworth

It Is a Beauteous Evening (Aug. 1802; publ. 1807)

It is a beauteous evening, calm and free:
The holy time is quiet as a nun
Breathless with adoration; the broad sun
Is sinking down in its tranquillity;
The gentleness of heaven is on the sea.
Listen, the mighty being is awake
And doth with his eternal motion make
A sound like thunder – everlastingly!
Dear child, dear girl, that walkest with me here,
If thou appearst untouched by solemn thought
Thy nature is not therefore less divine:
Thou liest in Abraham's bosom all the year,
And worshipst at the temple's inner shrine,
God being with thee when we know it not.

(III) and Mary Wordsworth (née Hutchinson)

(i) *She Was a Phantom of Delight*

(Feb. 1804; publ. 1807)

She was a phantom of delight
When first she gleamed upon my sight;
A lovely apparition, sent
To be a moment's ornament;
Her eyes as stars of twilights fair;
Like twilights, too, her dusky hair;

But all things else about her drawn
From May-time and the cheerful dawn;
A dancing shape, an image gay,
To haunt, to startle, and way-lay.

I saw her upon nearer view,
A spirit, yet a woman too!
Her household motions light and free,
And steps of virgin liberty;
A countenance in which did meet
Sweet records, promises as sweet;
A creature not too bright or good
For human nature's daily food;
For transient sorrows, simple wiles,
Praise, blame, love, kisses, tears, and smiles.

And now I see with eye serene
The very pulse of the machine;
A being breathing thoughtful breath;
A traveller betwixt life and death;
The reason firm, the temperate will,
Endurance, foresight, strength and skill;
A perfect woman; nobly planned,
To warn, to comfort, and command;
And yet a spirit still, and bright
With something of an angel light.

(ii) 'Another Maid There Was'

(1805 *Prelude* VI, 233–9, XI, 215–22) publl. 1850

Another maid there was, who also breathed
A gladness o'er that season, then to me
By her exulting outside look of youth
And placid under-countenance first endeared –
That other spirit, Coleridge, who is now
So near to us, that meek confiding heart
So reverenced by us both . . .
Methought such charm
Of sweetness did her presence breathe around
That all the trees, and all the silent hills,
And everything she looked on, should have had

An intimation how she bore herself
Towards them and to all creatures. God delights
In such a being, for her common thoughts
Are piety, her life is blessedness.

(IV) and Catharine Wordsworth

Surprised by Joy (c. 1813–14; publ. 1815)

Surprised by joy, impatient as the wind,
I wished to share the transport – oh, with whom
But thee, long-buried in the silent tomb,
That spot which no vicissitude can find?
Love, faithful love, recalled thee to my mind –
But how could I forget thee? Through what power
Even for the least division of an hour
Have I been so beguiled as to be blind
To my most grievous loss? That thought's return
Was the worst pang that sorrow ever bore –
Save one, one only, when I stood forlorn,
Knowing my heart's best treasure was no more,
That neither present time, nor years unborn,
Could to my sight that heavenly face restore.

9. PERCY BYSSHE SHELLEY

(I) and Harriet Shelley (née Westbrook)

To Harriet (1812)

Whose is the love that, gleaming through the world,
Wards off the poisonous arrow of its scorn?
    Whose is the warm and partial praise,
    Virtue's most sweet reward?

Beneath whose looks did my reviving soul
Riper in truth and virtuous daring grow?
    Whose eyes have I gazed fondly on,
    And loved mankind the more?

Harriet, on thine! Thou wert my purer mind,
Thou wert the inspiration of my song;
Thine are these early wilding flowers,
Though garlanded by me.

Then press into thy breast this pledge of love,
And know (though time may change, and years may roll)
Each flowret gathered in my heart
It consecrates to thine.

(II) and Mary Shelley (née Godwin)

from Dedication to *Laon and Cythna*

1–46, 91–126 (1817)

So now my summer task is ended, Mary,
And I return to thee, mine own heart's home,
As to his Queen, some victor-knight of Fairy,
Earning bright spoils for her enchanted dome.
Nor thou disdain that ere my fame become
A star among the stars of mortal night
(If it indeed may cleave its natal gloom),
Its doubtful promise thus I would unite
With thy belovéd name, thou child of love and light!

The toil which stole from thee so many an hour
Is ended – and the fruit is at thy feet!
No longer where the woods, to frame a bower,
With interlacéd branches mix and meet,
Or where, with sound like many voices sweet,
Waterfalls leap among wild islands green
(Which framed for my lone boat a lone retreat
Of moss-grown trees and weeds), shall I be seen,
But beside thee, where still my heart has ever been.

Thoughts of great deeds were mine, dear friend, when first
The clouds which wrap this world from youth did pass.
I do remember well the hour which burst
My spirit's sleep. A fresh May-dawn it was
When I walked forth upon the glittering grass,
And wept – I knew not why – until there rose
From the near school-room voices that, alas,
Were but one echo from a world of woes,
The harsh and grating strife of tyrants and of foes.

And then I clasped my hands and looked around –
   But none was near to mock my streaming eyes,
Which poured their warm drops on the sunny ground –
   So without shame I spoke: 'I will be wise,
   And just, and free, and mild, if in me lies
Such power, for I grow weary to behold
   The selfish and the strong still tyrannize
Without reproach or check.' I then controlled
My tears, my heart grew calm, and I was meek and bold.

And from that hour did I with earnest thought
   Heap knowledge from forbidden mines or lore,
Yet nothing that my tyrants knew or taught
   I cared to learn, but from that secret store
   Wrought linkéd armour for my soul, before
It might walk forth to war among mankind!
   Thus power and hope were strengthened more and more
Within me, till there came upon my mind
A sense of loneliness, a thirst with which I pined . . .

And what art thou? I know, but dare not speak –
   Time may interpret to his silent years!
Yet in the paleness of thy thoughtful cheek,
   And in the light thine ample forehead wears,
   And in thy sweetest smiles, and in thy tears,
And in thy gentle speech, a prophecy
   Is whispered to subdue my fondest fears.
And through thine eyes – even in thy soul – I see
A lamp of vestal fire burning internally.

They say that thou wert lovely from thy birth
   (Of glorious parents) thou aspiring child!
I wonder not, for one then left this Earth
   Whose life was like a setting planet mild
   Which clothed thee in the radiance undefiled
Of its departing glory. Still her fame
   Shines on thee, through the tempests dark and wild
Which shake these latter days – and thou canst claim
The shelter from thy sire of an immortal name!

One voice came forth from many a mighty spirit,
   Which was the echo of three thousand years,
And the tumultuous world stood mute to hear it
   As some lone man who in a desert hears

The music of his home! Unwonted fears
Fell on the pale oppressors of our race,
And Faith, and Custom, and low-thoughted cares,
Like thunder-stricken dragons, for a space
Left the torn human heart, their food and dwelling-place.

Truth's deathless voice pauses among mankind!
If there must be no response to my cry –
If men must rise and stamp, with fury blind,
On his pure name who loves them – thou and I,
Sweet friend, can look from our tranquility
Like lamps into the world's tempestuous night,
Two tranquil stars, while clouds are passing by
Which wrap them from the foundering seaman's sight,
That burn from year to year with unextinguished light.

(III) and Teresa [Emilia] Viviani

Epipsychidion: Verses Addressed To The Noble And Unfortunate Lady, Emilia Viviani, Now Imprisoned In The Convent Of St Anna (1821)

L'anima amante si slancia fuori del creato, e si crea nell' infinito un Mondo tutto per essa, diverso assai da questo oscuro e pauroso baratro. (Her own words).

[The loving soul projects itself beyond creation, and in the infinite creates for itself a world wholly its own, far different from this dark and fearful gulf. Teresa Viviani]

ADVERTISEMENT

The writer of the following lines died at Florence, as he was preparing for a voyage to one of the wildest Sporades [Mediterranean islands], which he had bought, and where he had fitted up the ruins of an old building, and where it was his hope to have realised a scheme of life, suited perhaps to that happier and better world of which he is now an inhabitant, but hardly practicable in this. His life was singular; less on account of the romantic vicissitudes which diversified it, than the ideal tinge which it received from his own character and feelings. The present poem, like the *Vita Nuova* of Dante, is sufficiently intelligible to a certain class of readers without a matter-of-fact history of the circumstances to which it relates; and to a certain other class it must ever remain incomprehensible . . .

The stanza [that follows] is almost a literal translation of Dante's famous Canzone, *Voi, ch'intendendo, il terzo ciel movete, etc.* The presumptuous application of the concluding lines to his own composition will raise a smile at the expense of my unfortunate friend. Be it a smile not of contempt, but pity. S.

My song, I fear that thou wilt find but few
Who fitly shall conceive thy reasoning,
Of such hard matter dost thou entertain;
Whence, if by misadventure chance should bring
Thee to base company (as chance may do),
Quite unaware of what thou dost contain,
I prithee, comfort thy sweet self again,
My last delight! Tell them that they are dull,
And bid them own that thou art beautiful.

Sweet spirit! sister of that orphan one
Whose empire is the name thou weepest on,
In my heart's temple I suspend to thee
These votive wreaths of withered memory.
Poor captive bird! – who from thy narrow cage
Pourest such music that it might assuage
The rugged hearts of those who prisoned thee,
Were they not deaf to all sweet melody –
This song shall be thy rose. Its petals pale
Are dead indeed, my adored nightingale,
But soft and fragrant is the faded blossom,
And it has no thorn left to wound thy bosom.
High spirit-wingéd heart! who dost for ever
Beat thine unfeeling bars with vain endeavour,
Till those bright plumes of thought (in which arrayed
It over-soared this low and worldly shade)
Lie shattered, and thy panting, wounded breast
Stains with dear blood its unmaternal nest.
I weep vain tears: blood would less bitter be,
Yet poured forth gladlier, could it profit thee.
Seraph of Heaven! too gentle to be human,
Veiling beneath that radiant form of woman
All that is insupportable in thee
Of light, and love, and immortality.
Sweet benediction in the eternal curse!

Veiled glory of this lampless universe!
Thou moon beyond the clouds! Thou living form
Among the dead! Thou star above the storm!
Thou wonder, and thou beauty, and thou terror!
   Thou harmony of Nature's art! Thou mirror
In whom, as in the splendour of the sun,
All shapes look glorious which thou gazest on!
Aye, even the dim words which obscure thee now
Flash, lightning-like, with unaccustomed glow.
I pray thee that thou blot from this sad song
All of its much mortality and wrong
With those clear drops, which start like sacred dew
From the twin lights thy sweet soul darkens through,
Weeping, till sorrow becomes ecstasy –
Then smile on it, so that it may not die.
I never thought before my death to see
Youth's vision thus made perfect. Emily,
I love thee; though the world by no thin name
Will hide that love from its unvalued shame.
Would we two had been twins of the same mother!
Or that the name my heart lent to another
Could be a sister's bond for her and thee,
Blending two beams of one eternity!
Yet were one lawful and the other true,
These names, though dear, could paint not (as is due)
How beyond refuge I am thine. Ah me,
I am not thine – I am a part of thee!
   Sweet lamp! my moth-like muse has burned its wings
Or, like a dying swan who soars and sings,
Young Love should teach Time, in his own grey style,
All that thou art. Art thou not void of guile,
A lovely soul formed to be blest and bless,
A well of sealed and secret happiness,
Whose waters like blithe light and music are,
Vanquishing dissonance and gloom? A star
Which moves not in the moving heavens, alone?
A smile amid dark frowns? A gentle tone
Amid rude voices? A belovéd light,
A solitude, a refuge, a delight?
A lute, which those whom Love has taught to play
Make music on, to soothe the roughest day
And lull fond grief asleep? A buried treasure?
A cradle of young thoughts of wingless pleasure?
A violet-shrouded grave of woe? I measure

The world of fancies, seeking one like thee,
And find – alas! mine own infirmity.
  She met me, stranger, upon life's rough way,
And lured me towards sweet death – as night by day,
Winter by spring, or sorrow by swift hope,
Led into light, life, peace. An antelope,
In the suspended impulse of its lightness,
Were less aethereally light. The brightness
Of her divinest presence trembles through
Her limbs as underneath a cloud of dew,
Embodied in the windless heaven of June
Amid the splendour-wingéd stars, the Moon
Burns, inextinguishably beautiful –
And from her lips, as from a hyacinth full
Of honey-dew, a liquid murmur drops
Killing the sense with passion, sweet as stops
Of planetary music heard in trance.
In her mild lights the starry spirits dance,
The sunbeams of those wells which ever leap
Under the lightnings of the soul – too deep
For the brief fathom-line of thought or sense.
The glory of her being, issuing thence,
Stains the dead, blank, cold air with a warm shade
Of unentangled intermixture, made
By Love, of light and motion – one intense
Diffusion, one serene omnipresence,
Whose flowing outlines mingle in their flowing,
Around her cheeks and utmost fingers glowing
With the unintermitted blood, which there
Quivers (as in a fleece of snow-like air
The crimson pulse of living morning quiver)
Continuously prolonged, and ending never,
Till they are lost, and in that beauty furled
Which penetrates and clasps and fills the world,
Scarce visible from extreme loveliness.
  Warm fragrance seems to fall from her light dress
And her loose hair, and where some heavy tress
The air of her own speed has disentwined,
The sweetness seems to satiate the faint wind;
And in the soul a wild odour is felt,
Beyond the sense, like fiery dews that melt
Into the bosom of a frozen bud.
See where she stands! a mortal shape indued
With love and life and light and deity,

And motion which may change but cannot die –
An image of some bright eternity;
A shadow of some golden dream; a splendour
Leaving the third sphere pilotless; a tender
Reflection of the eternal moon of love
Under whose motions life's dull billows move;
A metaphor of spring and youth and morning;
A vision like incarnate April, warning,
With smiles and tears, frost the anatomy
Into his summer grave.
Ah, woe is me!
What have I dared? Where am I lifted? How
Shall I descend, and perish not? I know
That love makes all things equal: I have heard
By mine own heart this joyous truth averred:
The spirit of the worm beneath the sod,
In love and worship, blends itself with God.
Spouse! sister! angel! pilot of the fate
Whose course has been so starless! Oh too late
Belovéd! Oh too soon adored, by me!
For in the fields of immortality
My spirit should at first have worshipped thine,
A divine presence in a place divine –
Or should have moved beside it on this earth,
A shadow of that substance, from its birth –
But not as now. I love thee – yes, I feel
That on the fountain of my heart a seal
Is set, to keep its waters pure and bright
For thee, since in those tears thou hast delight.
We – are we not formed, as notes of music are,
For one another, though dissimilar? –
Such difference without discord, as can make
Those sweetest sounds, in which all spirits shake
As trembling leaves in a continuous air?
Thy wisdom speaks in me, and bids me dare
Beacon the rocks on which high hearts are wrecked.
I never was attached to that great sect,
Whose doctrine is, that each one should select
Out of the crowd a mistress or a friend,
And all the rest, though fair and wise, commend
To cold oblivion – though it is in the code
Of modern morals, and the beaten road
Which those poor slaves with weary footsteps tread,
Who travel to their home among the dead

By the broad highway of the world, and so
With one chained friend, perhaps a jealous foe,
The dreariest and the longest journey go.
True love in this differs from gold and clay,
That to divide is not to take away.
Love is like understanding, that grows bright
Gazing on many truths; 'tis like thy light,
Imagination! which from earth and sky,
And from the depths of human fantasy,
As from a thousand prisms and mirrors, fills
The universe with glorious beams, and kills
Error, the worm, with many a sun-like arrow
Of its reverberated lightning. Narrow
The heart that loves, the brain that contemplates,
The life that wears, the spirit that creates
One object and one form, and builds thereby
A sepulchre for its eternity.
Mind from its object differs most in this:
Evil from good; misery from happiness;
The baser from the nobler; the impure
And frail, from what is clear and must endure.
If you divide suffering and dross, you may
Diminish till it is consumed away;
If you divide pleasure and love and thought,
Each part exceeds the whole; and we know not
How much, while any yet remains unshared,
Of pleasure may be gained, of sorrow spared.
This truth is that deep well, whence sages draw
The unenvied light of hope; the eternal law
By which those live, to whom this world of life
Is as a garden ravaged, and whose strife
Tills for the promise of a later birth
The wilderness of this Elysian earth.
There was a being whom my spirit oft
Met on its visioned wanderings, far aloft,
In the clear golden prime of my youth's dawn,
Upon the fairy isles of sunny lawn,
Amid the enchanted mountains and the caves
Of divine sleep, and on the air-like waves
Of wonder-level dream, whose tremulous floor
Paved her light steps. On an imagined shore,
Under the gray beak of some promontory,
She met me, robed in such exceeding glory,
That I beheld her not. In solitudes

Her voice came to me through the whispering woods,
And from the fountains, and the odours deep
Of flowers, which, like lips murmuring in their sleep
Of the sweet kisses which had lulled them there,
Breathed but of her to the enamoured air;
And from the breezes whether low or loud,
And from the rain of every passing cloud,
And from the singing of the summer-birds,
And from all sounds, all silence. In the words
Of antique verse and high romance – in form,
Sound, colour – in whatever checks that storm
Which with the shattered present chokes the past;
And in that best philosophy, whose taste
Makes this cold common Hell, our life, a doom
As glorious as a fiery martyrdom;
Her spirit was the harmony of truth.
 Then, from the caverns of my dreamy youth
I sprang, as one sandalled with plumes of fire,
And towards the lodestar of my one desire,
I flitted, like a dizzy moth, whose flight
Is as a dead leaf's in the owlet-light,
When it would seek in Hesper's setting sphere
A radiant death, a fiery sepulchre,
As if it were a lamp of earthly flame.
But she, whom prayers or tears then could not tame,
Passed, like a god throned on a wingéd planet
Whose burning plumes to tenfold swiftness fan it,
Into the dreary cone of our life's shade;
And as a man with mighty loss dismayed,
I would have followed, though the grave between
Yawned like a gulf whose spectres are unseen –
When a voice said: 'Oh thou of hearts the weakest,
The phantom is beside thee whom thou seekest.'
Then I – 'Where?' The world's echo answered 'where?'
And in that silence, and in my despair,
I questioned every tongueless wind that flew
Over my tower of mourning, if it knew
Whither 'twas fled, this soul out of my soul;
And murmured names and spells which have control
Over the sightless tyrants of our fate;
But neither prayer nor verse could dissipate
The night which closed on her; nor uncreate
That world within this chaos, mine and me,
Of which she was the veiled divinity –

The world I say of thoughts that worshipped her.
   And therefore I went forth, with hope and fear
And every gentle passion sick to death,
Feeding my course with expectation's breath,
Into the wintry forest of our life.
And struggling through its error with vain strife,
And stumbling in my weakness and my haste,
And half bewildered by new forms, I passed,
Seeking among those untaught foresters
If I could find one form resembling hers,
In which she might have masked herself from me.
There, one whose voice was venomed melody
Sat by a well, under blue nightshade bowers;
The breath of her false mouth was like faint flowers,
Her touch was as electric poison – flame
Out of her looks into my vitals came,
And from her living cheeks and bosom flew
A killing air, which pierced like honey-dew
Into the core of my green heart, and lay
Upon its leaves; until, as hair grown gray
O'er a young brow, they hid its unblown prime
With ruins of unseasonable time.
   In many mortal forms I rashly sought
The shadow of that idol of my thought.
And some were fair – but beauty dies away;
Others were wise – but honeyed words betray;
And one was true – oh! why not true to me?
Then, as a hunted deer that could not flee,
I turned upon my thoughts, and stood at bay,
Wounded and weak and panting. The cold day
Trembled, for pity of my strife and pain –
When, like a noonday dawn, there shone again
Deliverance! One stood on my path who seemed
As like the glorious shape which I had dreamed
As is the Moon (whose changes ever run
Into themselves) to the eternal Sun,
The cold chaste Moon, the Queen of Heaven's bright isles,
Who makes all beautiful on which she smiles –
That wandering shrine of soft yet icy flame
Which ever is transformed, yet still the same,
And warms not but illumines. Young and fair
As the descended spirit of that sphere,
She hid me, as the Moon may hide the night
From its own darkness, until all was bright

Between the heaven and earth of my calm mind,
And, as a cloud charioted by the wind,
She led me to a cave in that wild place,
And sat beside me, with her downward face
Illumining my slumbers, like the Moon
Waxing and waning o'er Endymion.
And I was laid asleep, spirit and limb,
And all my being became bright or dim
As the Moon's image in a summer sea,
According as she smiled or frowned on me –
And there I lay, within a chaste cold bed.
Alas, I then was nor alive nor dead –
For at her silver voice came Death and Life,
Unmindful each of their accustomed strife,
Masked like twin babes, a sister and a brother,
The wandering hopes of one abandoned mother,
And through the cavern without wings they flew,
And cried, 'Away, he is not of our crew!'
I wept, and though it be a dream, I weep.
　What storms then shook the ocean of my sleep,
Blotting that Moon, whose pale and waning lips
Then shrank as in the sickness of eclipse;
And how my soul was as a lampless sea,
And who was then its Tempest; and when she,
The Planet of that hour, was quenched, what frost
Crept o'er those waters, till from coast to coast
The moving billows of my being fell
Into a death of ice, immovable;
And then, what earthquakes made it gape and split,
(The white Moon smiling all the while on it)
These words conceal – if not, each word would be
The key of staunchless tears. Weep not for me!
　At length, into the obscure forest came
The Vision I had sought through grief and shame.
Athwart that wintry wilderness of thorns
Flashed from her motion splendour like the morn's,
And from her presence life was radiated
Through the gray earth and branches bare and dead,
So that her way was paved, and roofed above
With flowers as soft as thoughts of budding love,
And music from her respiration spread
Like light. All other sounds were penetrated
By the small, still, sweet spirit of that sound,
So that the savage winds hung mute around;

And odours warm and fresh fell from her hair
Dissolving the dull cold in the frore air.
Soft as an incarnation of the sun,
When light is changed to love, this glorious one
Floated into the cavern where I lay,
And called my spirit, and the dreaming clay
Was lifted by the thing that dreamed below
As smoke by fire, and in her beauty's glow
I stood, and felt the dawn of my long night
Was penetrating me with living light:
I knew it was the Vision veiled from me
So many years – that it was Emily.
   Twin spheres of light who rule this passive earth,
This world of love, this me, and into birth
Awaken all its fruits and flowers, and dart
Magnetic might into its central heart;
And lift its billows and its mists, and guide
By everlasting laws, each wind and tide
To its fit cloud, and its appointed cave;
And lull its storms, each in the craggy grave
Which was its cradle, luring to faint bowers
The armies of the rainbow-wingéd showers;
And, as those married lights, which from the towers
Of heaven look forth and fold the wandering globe
In liquid sleep and splendour, as a robe,
And all their many-mingled influence blend,
(If equal, yet unlike) to one sweet end –
So ye, bright regents, with alternate sway
Govern my sphere of being, night and day!
Thou, not disdaining even a borrowed might;
Thou, not eclipsing a remoter light;
And, through the shadow of the seasons three,
From spring to autumn's sere maturity,
Light it into the winter of the tomb,
Where it may ripen to a brighter bloom.
   Thou too, oh Comet beautiful and fierce,
Who drew the heart of this frail universe
Towards thine own, till, wrecked in that convulsion,
Alternating attraction and repulsion,
Thine went astray and that was rent in twain,
Oh, float into our azure heaven again!
Be there love's folding-star at thy return;
The living sun will feed thee from its urn

Of golden fire; the moon will veil her horn
In thy last smiles; adoring even and morn
Will worship thee with incense of calm breath
And lights and shadows. As the star of death
And birth is worshipped by those sisters wild
Called Hope and Fear – upon the heart are piled
Their offerings – of this sacrifice divine
A world shall be the altar.
                                        Lady mine,
Scorn not these flowers of thought, the fading birth
Which from its heart of hearts that plant puts forth
Whose fruit, made perfect by thy sunny eyes,
Will be as of the trees of Paradise.
The day is come, and thou wilt fly with me.
To whatsoe'er of dull mortality
Is mine, remain a vestal sister still;
To the intense, the deep, the imperishable,
Not mine but me, henceforth be thou united
Even as a bride, delighting and delighted.
The hour is come – the destined star has risen
Which shall descend upon a vacant prison.
The walls are high, the gates are strong, thick set
The sentinels – but true love never yet
Was thus constrained. It overleaps all fence –
Like lightning, with invisible violence
Piercing its continents; like Heaven's free breath,
Which he who grasps can hold not; like Death,
Who rides upon a thought, and makes his way
Through temple, tower, and palace, and the array
Of arms. More strength has love than he or they;
For it can burst his charnel, and make free
The limbs in chains, the heart in agony,
The soul in dust and chaos.
                                        Emily,
A ship is floating in the harbour now,
A wind is hovering o'er the mountain's brow;
There is a path on the sea's azure floor –
No keel has ever ploughed that path before!
The halcyons brood around the foamless isles;
The treacherous ocean has forsworn its wiles;
The merry mariners are bold and free –
Say, my heart's sister, wilt thou sail with me?
Our bark is as an albatross, whose nest
Is a far Eden of the purple east;

And we between her wings will sit, while night,
And day, and storm, and calm, pursue their flight,
Our ministers, along the boundless sea,
Treading each other's heels, unheededly.
It is an isle under Ionian skies,
Beautiful as a wreck of Paradise,
And, for the harbours are not safe and good,
This land would have remained a solitude
But for some pastoral people native there,
Who from the Elysian, clear, and golden air
Draw the last spirit of the age of gold,
Simple and spirited, innocent and bold.
The blue Aegean girds this chosen home,
With ever-changing sound and light and foam,
Kissing the sifted sands, and caverns hoar –
And all the winds wandering along the shore
Undulate with the undulating tide.
There are thick woods where sylvan forms abide;
And many a fountain, rivulet, and pond,
As clear as elemental diamond,
Or serene morning air; and, far beyond,
The mossy tracks made by the goats and deer
(Which the rough shepherd treads but once a year)
Pierce into glades, caverns, and bowers, and halls
Built round with ivy, which, the waterfalls
Illumining, with sound that never fails
Accompany the noonday nightingales,
And all the place is peopled with sweet airs.
  The light clear element which the isle wears
Is heavy with the scent of lemon-flowers,
Which floats like mist, laden with unseen showers,
And falls upon the eyelids like faint sleep;
And from the moss violets and jonquils peep,
And dart their arrowy odour through the brain
Till you might faint with that delicious pain.
And every motion, odour, beam, and tone,
With that deep music is in unison
Which is a soul within the soul – they seem
Like echoes of an antenatal dream.
It is an isle 'twixt heaven, air, earth, and sea,
Cradled, and hung in clear tranquillity;
Bright as that wandering Eden, Lucifer,
Washed by the soft blue oceans of young air.

It is a favoured place. Famine or blight,
Pestilence, war and earthquake, never light
Upon its mountain-peaks – blind vultures, they
Sail onward far upon their fatal way!
The wingéd storms, chanting their thunder-psalm
To other lands, leave azure chasms of calm
Over this isle, or weep themselves in dew,
From which its fields and woods ever renew
Their green and golden immortality.
And from the sea there rise, and from the sky
There fall, clear exhalations, soft and bright,
Veil after veil, each hiding some delight,
Which sun or moon or zephyr draw aside,
Till the isle's beauty, like a naked bride
Glowing at once with love and loveliness,
Blushes and trembles at its own excess!
   Yet, like a buried lamp, a soul no less
Burns in the heart of this delicious isle,
An atom of the Eternal, whose own smile
Unfolds itself, and may be felt, not seen
O'er the gray rocks, blue waves, and forests green,
Filling their bare and void interstices.
But the chief marvel of the wilderness
Is a lone dwelling, built by whom or how
None of the rustic island-people know:
'Tis not a tower of strength, though with its height
It overtops the woods; but, for delight,
Some wise and tender ocean-king, ere crime
Had been invented, in the world's young prime,
Reared it, a wonder of that simple time,
An envy of the isles, a pleasure-house
Made sacred to his sister and his spouse.
It scarce seems now a wreck of human art,
But, as it were titanic; in the heart
Of earth having assumed its form, then grown
Out of the mountains, from the living stone,
Lifting itself in caverns light and high –
For all the antique and learnéd imagery
Has been erased, and in the place of it
The ivy and the wild-vine interknit
The volumes of their many-twining stems.
Parasite flowers illume with dewy gems
The lampless halls, and when they fade, the sky
Peeps through their winter-woof of tracery

With moonlight patches, or star atoms keen,
Or fragments of the day's intense serene,
Working mosaic on their Parian floors.
And, day and night, aloof, from the high towers
And terraces, the earth and ocean seem
To sleep in one another's arms, and dream
Of waves, flowers, clouds, woods, rocks, and all that we
Read in their smiles, and call reality.
    This isle and house are mine, and I have vowed
Thee to be lady of the solitude –
And I have fitted up some chambers there
Looking towards the golden eastern air,
And level with the living winds, which flow
Like waves above the living waves below.
I have sent books and music there, and all
Those instruments with which high spirits call
The future from its cradle, and the past
Out of its grave, and make the present last
In thoughts and joys which sleep, but cannot die,
Folded within their own eternity.
Our simple life wants little, and true taste
Hires not the pale drudge, luxury, to waste
The scene it would adorn – and therefore, still,
Nature with all her children haunts the hill.
The ring-dove, in the embowering ivy, yet
Keeps up her love-lament, and the owls flit
Round the evening tower, and the young stars glance
Between the quick bats in their twilight dance;
The spotted deer bask in the fresh moonlight
Before our gate, and the slow, silent night
Is measured by the pants of their calm sleep.
Be this our home in life, and when years heap
Their withered hours, like leaves, on our decay,
Let us become the overhanging day,
The living soul of this Elysian isle,
Conscious, inseparable, one.
                                        Meanwhile
We two will rise, and sit, and walk together,
Under the roof of blue Ionian weather,
And wander in the meadows, or ascend
The mossy mountains, where the blue heavens bend
With lightest winds, to touch their paramour;
Or linger where the pebble-paven shore,

Under the quick, faint kisses of the sea
Trembles and sparkles as with ecstasy,
Possessing and possessed by all that is
Within that calm circumference of bliss,
And by each other, till to love and live
Be one; or, at the noontide hour, arrive
Where some old cavern hoar seems yet to keep
The moonlight of the expiréd night asleep,
Through which the awakened day can never peep –
A veil for our seclusion, close as night's,
Where secure sleep may kill thine innocent lights –
Sleep, the fresh dew of languid love, the rain
Whose drops quench kisses till they burn again!
And we will talk, until thought's melody
Become too sweet for utterance, and it die
In words, to live again in looks, which dart
With thrilling tone into the voiceless heart,
Harmonizing silence without a sound.
   Our breath shall intermix, our bosoms bound,
And our veins beat together, and our lips
With other eloquence than words eclipse
The soul that burns between them – and the wells
Which boil under our being's inmost cells,
The fountains of our deepest life, shall be
Confused in passion's golden purity,
As mountain-springs under the morning sun.
We shall become the same, we shall be one
Spirit within two frames! – oh, wherefore two? –
One passion in twin-hearts, which grows and grew,
Till like two meteors of expanding flame,
Those spheres instinct with it become the same,
Touch, mingle, are transfigured – ever still
Burning, yet ever inconsumable;
In one another's substance finding food,
Like flames too pure and light and unimbued
To nourish their bright lives with baser prey,
Which point to Heaven and cannot pass away:
One hope within two wills, one will beneath
Two overshadowing minds, one life, one death,
One Heaven, one Hell, one immortality,
And one annihilation. Woe is me!

The wingéd words on which my soul would pierce
Into the height of love's rare universe,
Are chains of lead around its flight of fire –
I pant, I sink, I tremble, I expire!

Weak verses, go, kneel at your Sovereign's feet,
And say: 'We are the masters of thy slave;
What wouldést thou with us and ours and thine?'
Then call your sisters from oblivion's cave,
All singing loud: 'Love's very pain is sweet,
But its reward is in the world divine
Which, if not here, it builds beyond the grave.
So shall ye live when I am there. Then haste
Over the hearts of men, until ye meet
Marina, Vanna, Primus and the rest,
And bid them love each other and be blest:
And leave the troop which errs, and which reproves,
And come and be my guest – for I am Love's!

(IV) and Jane Williams

(i) *To Jane with a Guitar* (June 1822; publ. 1832)

Ariel to Miranda – Take
This slave of music for the sake
Of him who is the slave of thee,
And teach it all the harmony
In which thou canst, and only thou,
Make the delighted spirit glow
Till joy denies itself again
And, too intense, is turned to pain –
For by permission and command
Of thine own Prince Ferdinand
Poor Ariel sends this silent token
Of more than ever can be spoken –
Your guardian-spirit Ariel, who
From life to life must still pursue
Your happiness, for thus alone
Can Ariel ever find his own.
From Prospero's enchanted cell,
As the mighty verses tell,

To the throne of Naples he
Lit you o'er the trackless sea,
Flitting on, your prow before,
Like a living meteor.
  When you die, the silent Moon
In her interlunar swoon
Is not sadder in her cell
Than deserted Ariel:
When you live again on Earth,
Like an unseen star of birth
Ariel guides you o'er the sea
Of life from your nativity!
Many changes have been rung
Since Ferdinand and you begun
Your course of love, and Ariel still
Has tracked your steps and served your will.
Now, in a humbler, happier lot,
This is all remembered not,
And now, alas, the poor sprite is
Imprisoned for some fault of his
In a body like a grave –
From you he only dares to crave
For his service and his sorrow
A smile today, a song tomorrow!
  The artist who this idol wrought
To echo all harmonious thought
Felled a tree, while on the steep
The woods were in their winter sleep,
Rocked in that repose divine
On the wind-swept Apennine
(And dreaming, some, of autumn past,
And some of spring approaching fast,
And some of April buds and showers,
And some of songs in July bowers,
And all, of love), and so this tree –
Oh that such our death may be! –
Died in sleep, and felt no pain,
To live in happier form again,
From which, beneath heaven's fairest star,
The artist wrought this loved guitar,
And taught it justly to reply
To all who question skilfully
In language gentle as their own,
Whispering in enamoured tone

Sweet oracles of woods and dells
And summer-winds in sylvan cells –
For it had learnt all harmonies
Of the plains and of the skies,
Of the forests and the mountains,
And the many-voicéd fountains:
The clearest echoes of the hills,
The softest notes of falling rills,
The melodies of birds and bees,
The murmuring of summer-seas,
And pattering rain, and breathing dew,
And airs of evening.
                    And it knew
That seldom-heard mysterious sound,
Which, driven, on its diurnal round
As it floats through boundless day,
Our world enkindles on its way –
All this it knows, but will not tell
To those who cannot question well
The spirit that inhabits it.
It talks according to the wit
Of its companions, and no more
Is heard than has been felt before
By those who tempt it to betray
These secrets of an elder day –
But sweetly, as it answers, will
Flatter hands of perfect skill:
It keeps its highest holiest tone
For our belovéd Jane alone!

(ii) *To Jane: The Stars Were Twinkling*

(June 1822; publ. 1832)

          The keen stars were twinkling
And the fair moon was rising among them,
               Dear Jane –
          The guitar was tinkling
But the notes were not sweet till you sung them
               Again.

          As the moon's soft splendour
O'er the faint cold starlight of heaven
               Is thrown,

So your voice most tender
To the strings without soul had then given
Its own.

The stars will awaken,
Though the moon sleep a full hour later
Tonight –
No leaf will be shaken
While the dews of your melody scatter
Delight.

Though the sound overpowers
Sing again, with your dear voice revealing
A tone
Of some world far from ours
Where music and moonlight and feeling
Are one.

10. LORD BYRON

(I) and Lady Frances Webster

When We Two Parted (Aug.–Sept. 1815; publ. 1816)

When we two parted
In silence and tears,
Half broken-hearted,
To sever for years,
Pale grew thy cheek and cold,
Colder thy kiss –
Truly that hour foretold
Sorrow to this!

The dew of the morning
Sunk chill on my brow,
It felt like the warning
Of what I feel now.
Thy vows are all broken,
And light is thy fame:
I hear thy name spoken,
And share in its shame.

They name thee before me,
   A knell in mine ear,
A shudder comes o'er me –
   Why wert thou so dear?
They know not I knew thee,
   Who knew thee too well:
Long, long shall I rue thee,
   Too deeply to tell.

In secret we met –
   In silence I grieve
That thy heart could forget,
   Thy spirit deceive!
If I should meet thee
   After long years,
How should I greet thee?
   With silence and tears.

(II) and Lady Byron

Fare Thee Well (1816)

Alas! they had been friends in youth,
But whispering tongues can poison truth,
And constancy lives in realms above,
And life is thorny, and youth is vain,
And to be wrath with one we love,
Doth work like madness in the brain . . .
But never either found another
To free the hollow heart from paining –
They stood aloof, the scars remaining,
Like cliffs which had been rent asunder.
A dreary sea now flows between,
But neither heat, nor frost, nor thunder,
Shall wholly do away, I ween,
The marks of that which once hath been.
(*Christabel*, Part II)

Fare thee well! and if for ever,
   Still for ever, fare thee well!
E'en though unforgiving, never
   'Gainst thee shall my heart rebel.

Would that breast were bared before thee
  Where thy head so oft hath lain,
While that placid sleep came o'er thee
  Which thou ne'er canst know again –

Would that breast, by thee glanced over,
  Every inmost thought could show!
Then thou wouldst at last discover
  'Twas not well to spurn it so.

Though the world for this commend thee,
  Though it smile upon the blow,
Even its praises must offend thee,
  Founded on another's woe.

Though my many faults defaced me,
  Could no other arm be found
Than the one which once embraced me,
  To inflict a cureless wound?

Yet, oh yet, thyself deceive not –
  Love may sink by slow decay,
But by sudden wrench, believe not
  Hearts can thus be torn away!

Still thine own its life retaineth –
  Still must mine, though bleeding, beat!
And the undying thought which paineth
  Is – that we no more may meet.

These are words of deeper sorrow
  Than the wail above the dead:
Both shall live – but every morrow
  Wake us from a widowed bed!

And when thou wouldst solace gather,
  When our child's first accents flow,
Wilt thou teach her to say 'Father!'
  Though his care she must forego?

When her little hands shall press thee,
  When her lip to thine is prest,
Think of him whose prayer shall bless thee –
  Think of him thy love had blest!

Should her lineaments resemble
   Those thou never more mayst see,
Then thy heart will softly tremble
   With a pulse yet true to me.

All my faults perchance thou knowest,
   All my madness, none can know,
All my hopes (where'er thou goest)
   Wither – yet with thee they go.

Every feeling hath been shaken!
   Pride – which not a world could bow –
Bows to thee! By thee forsaken,
   Even my soul forsakes me now.

But 'tis done – all words are idle –
   Words from me are vainer still!
But the thoughts we cannot bridle
   Force their way without the will.

Fare thee well! thus disunited,
   Torn from every nearer tie,
Seared in heart – and lone – and blighted,
   More than this I scarce can die.

(III) and Augusta Leigh

(i) *Stanzas to Augusta* ('When all around') 1816

When all around grew drear and dark,
   And reason half withheld her ray,
And hope but shed a dying spark
   Which more misled my lonely way –

In that deep midnight of the mind,
   And that internal strife of heart,
When, dreading to be deemed too kind,
   The weak despair – the cold depart!

When Fortune changed, and Love fled far,
   And Hatred's shafts flew thick and fast,
Thou wert the solitary star
   Which rose and set not to the last.

Oh, blest be thine unbroken light!
   That watched me as a seraph's eye,
And stood between me and the night,
   For ever shining sweetly nigh.

And when the cloud upon us came,
   Which strove to blacken o'er thy ray –
Then purer spread its gentle flame,
   And dashed the darkness all away!

Still may thy spirit dwell on mine,
   And teach it what to brave or brook:
There's more in one soft word of thine
   Than in the world's defied rebuke.

Thou stoodst as stands a lovely tree,
   That still unbroke, though gently bent,
Still waves with fond fidelity
   Its boughs above a monument.

The winds might rend, the skies might pour,
   But there thou wert – and still wouldst be
Devoted in the stormiest hour
   To shed thy weeping leaves o'er me.

But thou and thine shall know no blight,
   Whatever fate on me may fall;
For Heaven in sunshine will requite
   The kind – and thee the most of all!

Then let the ties of baffled love
   Be broken – thine will never break!
Thy heart can feel, but will not move;
   Thy soul, though soft, will never shake.

And these, when all was lost beside,
   Were found and still are fixed, in thee –
And bearing still a breast so tried,
   Earth is no desert – e'en to me!

(ii) *Stanzas to Augusta*

('Though the day of my destiny') 1816

Though the day of my destiny's over,
  And the star of my fate hath declined,
Thy soft heart refused to discover
  The faults which so many could find;
Though thy soul with my grief was acquainted,
  It shrunk not to share it with me,
And the love which my spirit hath painted
  It never hath found but in thee.

Then when Nature around me is smiling,
  The last smile which answers to mine,
I do not believe it beguiling,
  Because it reminds me of thine;
And when winds are at war with the ocean,
  As the breasts I believed in with me,
If their billows excite an emotion,
  It is that they bear me from thee.

Though the rock of my last hope is shivered,
  And its fragments are sunk in the wave,
Though I feel that my soul is delivered
  To pain – it shall not be its slave!
There is many a pang to pursue me
  (They may crush, but they shall not contemn),
They may torture, but shall not subdue me –
  'Tis of thee that I think – not of them!

Though human, thou didst not deceive me,
  Though woman, thou didst not forsake,
Though loved, thou forborest to grieve me,
  Though slandered, thou never couldst shake;
Though trusted, thou didst not disclaim me,
  Though parted, it was not to fly,
Though watchful, 'twas not to defame me,
  Nor, mute, that the world might belie!

Yet I blame not the world, nor despise it,
  Nor the war of the many with one;
If my soul was not fitted to prize it,
  'Twas folly not sooner to shun –

And if dearly that error hath cost me,
  And more than I once could foresee,
I have found that, whatever it lost me,
  It could not deprive me of thee!

From the wreck of the past, which hath perished,
  Thus much I at least may recall,
It hath taught me that what I most cherished
  Deserved to be dearest of all:
In the desert a fountain is springing,
  In the wide waste there still is a tree,
And a bird in the solitude singing,
  Which speaks to my spirit of thee!

(IV) and the Countess Guiccioli

Stanzas to the River Po (April 1819; publ. 1824)

River, that rollest by the ancient walls
  Where dwells the lady of my love, when she
Walks by thy brink, and there perchance recalls
  A faint and fleeting memory of me,

What if thy deep and ample stream should be
  A mirror of my heart, where she may read
The thousand thoughts I now betray to thee,
  Wild as the wave, and headlong as thy speed!

What do I say – a mirror of my heart?
  Are not thy waters sweeping, dark and strong?
Such as my feelings were, and are, thou art –
  And such as thou art were my passions long.

Time may have somewhat tamed them – not for ever!
  Thou overflow'st thy banks, and not for aye
Thy bosom overboils, congenial river!
  Thy floods subside, and mine have sunk away,

But left long wrecks behind – and now again,
  Borne in our old unchanged career, we move.
Thou tendest wildly onwards to the main,
  And I – to loving *one* I should not love.

The current I behold will sweep beneath
  Her native walls, and murmur at her feet;
Her eyes will look on thee when she shall breathe
  The twilight air, unharmed by summer's heat.

She will look on thee – I have looked on thee,
  Full of that thought! And from that moment, ne'er
Thy waters could I dream of, name, or see,
  Without the inseparable sigh for her.

Her bright eyes will be imaged in thy stream –
  Yes, they will meet the wave I gaze on now –
Mine cannot witness, even in a dream,
  That happy wave repass me in its flow!

The wave that bears my tears returns no more –
  Will she return by whom that wave shall sweep?
Both tread thy banks, both wander on thy shore:
  I by thy source, she by the dark-blue deep.

But that which keepeth us apart is not
  Distance, nor depth of wave, nor space of earth,
But the distraction of a various lot –
  As various as the climates of our birth.

A stranger loves the lady of the land,
  Born far beyond the mountains, but his blood
Is all meridian, as if never fanned
  By that black wind that chills the polar flood.

My blood is all meridian! Were it not,
  I had not left my clime, nor should I be,
In spite of tortures ne'er to be forgot,
  A slave again of love – at least, of thee.

'Tis vain to struggle – let me perish young –
  Live as I lived, and love as I have loved!
To dust if I return, from dust I sprung –
And then, at least my heart can ne'er be moved.

(v) and Loukas Chalandritsanos

I Watched Thee (April 1824; from MS 1887)

I watched thee when the foe was at our side,
  Ready to strike at him – or thee and me,
Were safety hopeless, rather than divide
  Aught with one loved, save love and liberty.

I watched thee on the breakers, when the rock
  Received our prow and all was storm and fear,
And bade thee cling to me through every shock –
  This arm would be thy bark, or breast thy bier!

I watched thee when the fever glazed thine eyes,
  Yielding my couch – and stretched me on the ground
When overworn with watching, ne'er to rise
  From thence if thou an early grave hadst found.

The earthquake came, and rocked the quivering wall,
  And men and Nature reeled as if with wine –
Whom did I seek around the tottering hall?
  For thee! Whose safety first provide for? Thine!

And when convulsive throes denied my breath
  The faintest utterance to my fading thought,
To thee – to thee – e'en in the gasp of death
  My spirit turned, oh! oftener than it ought!

Thus much and more – and yet thou lovst me not,
  And never wilt! Love dwells not in our will.
Nor can I blame thee, though it be my lot
  To strongly, wrongly, vainly, love thee still.

11. JOHN KEATS

and Fanny Brawne

(i) *The Day Is Gone* (10 Oct. 1819; publ. 1838)

The day is gone, and all its sweets are gone!
 Sweet voice, sweet lips, soft hand, and softer breast,
Warm breath, light whisper, tender semitone,
 Bright eyes, accomplished shape, and languorous waist!
Faded the flower and all its budding charms,
 Faded the sight of beauty from my eyes,
Faded the shape of beauty from my arms,
 Faded the voice, warmth, whiteness, paradise!
Vanished unseasonably at shut of eve,
 When the dusk holiday, or holinight,
Of fragrant-curtained love begins to weave
 The woof of darkness thick for hid delight –
But as I've read Love's missal through today,
He'll let me sleep, seeing I fast and pray.

(ii) *I Cry Your Mercy* (mid Oct. 1819; publ. 1848)

I cry your mercy, pity, love – aye love!
 Merciful love that tantalizes not,
One-thoughted, never-wandering, guileless love,
 Unmasked, and, being seen, without a blot.
Oh, let me have thee whole – all, all be mine!
 That shape, that fairness, that sweet minor zest
Of love, your kiss – those hands, those eyes divine,
 That warm, white, lucent, million-pleasured breast –
Yourself, your soul! In pity give me all!
 Withhold no atom's atom, or I die–
Or, living on perhaps, your wretched thrall,
 Forget, in the mist of idle misery,
Life's purposes – the palate of my mind
Losing its gust, and my ambitions blind!

(iii) *Ode to Fanny* (Feb. 1820; publ. 1848)

Physician Nature, let my spirit blood!
   Oh ease my heart of verse and let me rest –
Throw me upon thy tripod till the flood
   Of stifling numbers ebbs from my full breast!
A theme, a theme – great Nature, give a theme!
         Let me begin my dream:
I come. I see thee, as thou standest there,
Beckon me out into the wintry air.

Ah dearest love, sweet home of all my fears
   And hopes, and joys, and panting miseries,
Tonight (if I may guess) thy beauty wears
         A smile of such delight,
         As brilliant and bright,
   As when, with ravished, aching, vassal eyes,
         Lost in soft amaze
         I gaze, I gaze!

Who now, with greedy looks, eats up my feast?
   What stare outfaces now my silver moon?
Ah, keep that hand unravished at the least
         Let, let, the amorous burn,
         But prithee do not turn
The current of your heart from me so soon!
         Oh, save (in charity)
         The quickest pulse for me!

Save it for me, sweet love! Though music breathe
   Voluptuous visions into the warm air,
Though swimming through the dance's dangerous wreath,
         Be like an April day,
         Smiling and cold and gay –
   A temperate lily, temperate as fair,
         Then Heaven, there will be
         A warmer June for me!

'Why, this', you'll say, my Fanny, 'is not true!'
Put your soft hand upon your snowy side
Where the heart beats – confess, 'tis nothing new!
Must not a woman be
A feather on the sea,
Swayed to and fro by every wind and tide?
Of as uncertain speed
As blow-ball from the mead?

I know it – and to know it is despair
To one who loves you as I love, sweet Fanny,
Whose heart goes fluttering for you everywhere,
Nor, when away you roam,
Dare keep its wretched home!
Love, love alone, has pains severe and many –
Then, loveliest, keep me free
From torturing jealousy!

Ah, if you prize my subdued soul above
The poor, the fading, brief pride of an hour,
Let none profane my Holy See of love,
Or with a rude hand break
The sacramental cake –
Let none else touch the just new-budded flower!
If not, may my eyes close,
Love, on their last repose.

12. JOHN CLARE

and Mary Joyce

(i) *Song* ('Mary leave thy lowly cot') 1819–20; publ. 1821

Mary leave thy lowly cot
When thy thickest jobs are done,
When thy friends will miss thee not
Mary to the pastures run –
Where we met the other night
'Neath the bush upon the plain,
Be it dark or be it light
Ye may guess we'll meet again!

Should ye go or should ye not
Never shilly-shally dear,
Leave your work and leave your cot
Nothing need ye doubt or fear:
Chaps may tell ye lies in spite –
Calling me a roving swain –
Think what passed the other night,
Then I'm bound we'll meet again!

(ii) *My Mary* (1820)

Who lives where beggars rarely speed,
And leads a humdrum life indeed
As none beside herself would lead?
                    My Mary.

Who lives where noises never cease,
And, what wi' hogs and ducks and geese,
Can never have a minute's peace?
                    My Mary.

Who, nearly battled to her chin,
Bangs down the yard through thick and thin,
Nor picks a road, nor cares a pin?
                    My Mary.

Who (save in Sunday bib-and-tuck)
Goes daily, waddling like a duck,
O'er head and ears in grease and muck?
                    My Mary.

Unused to pattens or to clogs,
Who takes the swill to serve the hogs,
And steals the milk for cats and dogs?
                    My Mary.

Who (frost and snow as hard as nails)
Stands out o' doors and never fails
To wash up things and scour the pails?
                    My Mary.

Who bustles night and day, in short,
At all catch jobs of every sort
And gains her Mistress' favour for't?
My Mary.

And who is oft repaid wi' praise
In doing what her Mistress says
And yielding to her whimmy ways?
My Mary.

For there's none apter, I believe,
At 'creeping up her Mistress' sleeve'
Than this low kindred stump of Eve,
My Mary!

Who when the baby's all beshit
To please its mamma kisses it,
And vows no rose on earth's so sweet!
My Mary.

But when her Mistress isn't nigh
Who swears and wishes it would die,
And pinches it to make it cry?
My Mary.

Oh rank deceit! What soul could think –
But gently there, revealing ink! –
At faults of thine this friend must wink,
My Mary!

Who (not without a spark o' pride,
Though strong as grunters' bristly hide)
Does keep her hair in papers tied?
My Mary.

And, mimicking the gentry's way,
Who strives to speak as fine as they
And minds but every word they say?
My Mary

And who (though's well bid blind to see
As her to tell the A from B)
Thinks herself none o' low degree?
My Mary.

Who prates, and runs o'er silly stuff,
And 'mong the boys makes sport enough –
So ugly, silly, droll and rough?
My Mary.

Ugly! Muse, for shame 'o thee,
What faults art thou a'going to see
In one that's lotted out to be?
My Mary?

But heedless sayings meaneth nought
Done innocent without a thought –
We humbly ask thy pardon for't,
My Mary.

Who, low in stature, thick and fat,
Turns brown from going without a hat
(Though not a pin the worse for that)?
My Mary.

Who's laughed at, too, by every whelp
For failings which they cannot help –
But silly fools will laugh and chelp,
My Mary!

For though in stature mighty small
And near as thick as thou art tall,
That hand made thee that made us all,
My Mary.

And though thy nose hooks down too much,
And prophesies thy chin to touch,
I'm not so nice to look at such,
My Mary.

No, no! About thy nose and chin,
Its hooking out or bending in,
I never heed nor care a pin,
My Mary!

And though thy skin is brown and rough,
And formed by Nature hard and tough,
All suiteth me – so that's enough,
My Mary!

(iii) *Ballad*

('Mary, fate lent me a moment') 1819–20; publ. 1821

Mary, fate lent me a moment of pleasure
Just to insure me in ages of pain –
Just bid me meet thee and wish for the treasure
To frown back and tell me I wisht it in vain!
Just like spring sunshine I met with thee, Mary,
That shines for a moment and cloudeth again;
But, alas in our love there is one thing contrary
Fate's clouds of that moment cleared never again.

Mary, fond feelings will never forsake me –
Never again though I'm happy with thee –
Hope paints the cure that enraptured could make me
Tho' fate to torment, vows it never shall be!
Mary, hope whispers some chance in our favour,
That still I may gaze on thy beauties once more,
But Fate's bonds are on me, that cruel enslaver,
And love is not lawful to meet as before.

Mary how sweet when love basked in thy feature,
Mary how saddened the sighs rose and fell;
Surely those sighs was the instinct of Nature
Of future forebodings Fate cared no to tell.
Mary thy smiles still endear our departure,
Though they do haunt me in gloomy deform;
Like waining sunbeams the clouds follow after
That just give a glance ere they're lost in the storm.

13. FELICIA HEMANS

The Dreaming Child (1830)

Alas! what kind of grief should thy years know?
Thy brow and cheek are smooth as waters be
When no breath troubles them.
(Beaumont and Fletcher)

And is there sadness in thy dreams, my boy?
What should the cloud be made of? Blessèd child!
Thy spirit, borne upon a breeze of joy,
All day hath ranged through sunshine, clear, yet mild –

And now thou tremblest! Wherefore? In *thy* soul
There lies no past, no future – thou hast heard
No sound of presage from the distance roll,
Thy heart bears traces of no arrowy word!

From thee no love hath gone – thy mind's young eye
Hath looked not into Death's, and thence become
A questioner of mute Eternity,
A weary searcher for a viewless home.

Nor hath thy sense been quickened unto pain,
By feverish watching for some step beloved;
Free are thy thoughts, an ever-changeful train,
Glancing like dewdrops, and as lightly moved!

Yet now, on billows of strange passion tossed,
How art thou wildered in the Cave of Sleep!
My gentle child, midst what dim phantoms lost,
Thus in mysterious anguish dost thou weep?

Awake! They sadden me, those early tears,
First flushings of the strong dark river's flow,
That *must* o'ersweep thy soul with coming years –
The unfathomable flood of human woe!

Awful to watch, e'en rolling through a dream,
Forcing wild spray-drops – but from childhood's eyes!
Wake, wake! as yet *thy* life's transparent stream
Should wear the tinge of none but summer skies.

Come from the shadow of those realms unknown,
Where now thy thoughts dismayed and darkling rove;
Come to the kindly region all thine own,
The home, still bright for thee with guardian love,

Happy, fair child, that yet a mother's voice
Can win thee back from visionary strife!
Oh, shall *my* soul, thus wakened to rejoice,
Start from the dreamlike wilderness of life?

14. CAROLINE NORTON

(1) and her brother

Recollections (1830)

Do you remember all the sunny places
Where in bright days, long past, we played together?
Do you remember all the old home faces
That gathered round the hearth in wintry weather?
Do you remember all the happy meetings,
In summer evenings round the open door –
Kind looks, kind hearts, kind words and tender greetings,
And clasping hands whose pulses beat no more?
  Do you remember them?

Do you remember all the merry laughter,
The voices round the swing in our old garden,
The dog that when we ran still followed after,
The teasing frolic sure of speedy pardon?
We were but children then, young happy creatures,
And hardly knew how much we had to lose –
But now the dreamlike memory of those features
Comes back, and bids my darkened spirit muse:
  Do you remember them?

Do you remember when we first departed
From all the old companions who were round us –
How very soon again we grew light-hearted,
And talked with smiles of all the links which bound us?
And after, when our footsteps were returning
With unfelt weariness o'er hill and plain,
How our young hearts kept boiling up, and burning,
To think how soon we'd be at home again!
   Do you remember this?

Do you remember how the dreams of glory
Kept fading from us like a fairy treasure –
How we thought less of being famed in story,
And more of those to whom our fame gave pleasure?
Do you remember, in far countries, weeping
When a light breeze, a flower, hath brought to mind
Old happy thoughts, which till that hour were sleeping,
And made us yearn for those we left behind?
   Do you remember this?

Do you remember when no sound woke gladly,
But desolate echoes through our home were ringing,
How for a while we talked – then paused full sadly,
Because our voices bitter thoughts were bringing?
Ah me, those days – those days! – my friend, my brother,
Sit down and let us talk of all our woe,
For we have nothing left but one another.
Yet where they went, old playmate, we shall go –
   Let us remember this.

(II) and her children

The Mother's Heart (1836)

When first thou camest, gentle, shy, and fond,
   My eldest-born, first hope, and dearest treasure,
My heart received thee with a joy beyond
   All that it yet had felt of earthly pleasure –
Nor thought that any love again might be
So deep and strong as that I felt for thee.

Faithful and true, with sense beyond thy years
   And natural piety that leaned to Heaven;
Wrung by a harsh word suddenly to tears,
   Yet patient of rebuke when justly given;
Obedient, easy to be reconciled,
And meekly-cheerful – such wert thou, my child!

Not willing to be left – still by my side,
   Haunting my walks, while summer-day was dying –
Nor leaving in thy turn; but pleased to glide
   Through the dark room where I was sadly lying,
Or, by the couch of pain a sitter meek,
Watch the dim eye, and kiss the feverish cheek.

Oh boy, of such as thou are oftenest made
   Earth's fragile idols: like a tender flower
(No strength in all thy freshness) prone to fade,
   And bending weakly to the thunder-shower –
Still, round the loved, thy heart found force to bind,
And clung, like woodbine shaken in the wind!

Then thou, my merry love – bold in thy glee,
   Under the bough, or by the firelight dancing –
With thy sweet temper, and thy spirit free,
   Didst come, as restless as a bird's wing glancing,
Full of a wild and irrepressible mirth,
Like a young sunbeam to the gladdened earth!

Thine was the shout! the song! the burst of joy!
   Which sweet from childhood's rosy lip resoundeth;
Thine was the eager spirit nought could cloy,
   And the glad heart from which all grief reboundeth;
And many a mirthful jest and mock reply,
Lurked in the laughter of thy dark-blue eye!

And thine was many an art to win and bless,
   The cold and stern to joy and fondness warming;
The coaxing smile – the frequent soft caress –
   The earnest tearful prayer all wrath disarming!
Again my heart a new affection found,
But thought that love with thee had reached its bound.

At length thou camest – thou, the last and least –
   Nick-named 'The Emperor' by thy laughing brothers
Because a haughty spirit swelled thy breast,
   And thou didst seek to rule and sway the others,
Mingling with every playful infant wile
A mimic majesty that made us smile!

And oh, most like a regal child wert thou!
   An eye of resolute and successful scheming,
Fair shoulders, curling lip, and dauntless brow –
   Fit for the world's strife, not for Poet's dreaming –
And proud the lifting of thy stately head,
And the firm bearing of thy conscious tread.

Different from both! Yet each succeeding claim,
   I, that all other love had been forswearing,
Forthwith admitted equal and the same –
   Nor injured either, by this love's comparing,
Nor stole a fraction for the newer call,
But in the Mother's Heart, found room for all!

15. LETITIA ELIZABETH LANDON

To My Brother (1835)

Do you recall the fancies of many years ago,
When the pulse danced those light measures that again it cannot
   know?
Ah, we both of us are altered, and now we talk no more
Of all the old creations that haunted us of yore.

Then any favourite volume was a mine of long delight
From whence we took our future to fashion as we might.
We lived again its pages, we were its chiefs and kings,
As actual, but more pleasant, than what the day now brings.

It was an August evening, with sunset in the trees,
When home you brought his *Voyages* who found the fair South Seas
We read it till the sunset amid the boughs grew dim –
All other favourite heroes were nothing beside him!

For weeks he was our idol, we sailed with him at sea,
And the pond amid the willows the ocean seemed to be.
The water-lilies growing beneath the morning smile,
We called the South Sea islands, each flower a different isle.

No golden lot that fortune could draw for human life,
To us seemed like a sailor's, amid the storm and strife.
Our talk was of fair vessels that swept before the breeze,
And new-discovered countries amid the Southern Seas.

Within that lonely garden what happy hours went by,
While we fancied that around us spread foreign sea and sky!
Ah, the dreaming and the distant no longer haunt the mind –
We leave, in leaving childhood, life's fairyland behind.

There is not of that garden a single tree or flower;
They have ploughed its long green grasses, and cut down the
lime-tree bower!
Where are the guelder-roses whose silver used to bring,
With the gold of the laburnums, their tribute to the Spring?

They have vanished with the childhood that with their treasures
played;
The life that cometh after dwells in a darker shade.
Yet the name of that sea-captain it cannot but recall
How much we loved his dangers, and how we mourned his fall!

XII. On Poets and Poetry

'Gie me ae spark 'o Nature's fire', Burns writes in *Epistle to J. Lapraik*, 'My Muse, though hamely in attire, / May touch the heart.' It is a quiet assertion, but, coming as it does in the Kilmarnock edition of 1786, it is revolutionary too – as Wordsworth recognized when he copied the lines ten years later as an epigraph to *The Ruined Cottage* (Narratives of Love), first of his own homely-dressed masterpieces. On Poets and Poetry contains many such insights into the nature and process of Romanticism, from Blake's enchanting claim to inspiration in the Preface to *Europe*, to Tighe's farewell to *Psyche*, and Byron's great lines on the imagination in *Childe Harold*, Canto III:

'Tis to create, and in creating live
A being more intense, that we endow
With form our fancy, gaining as we give
The life we image.

Coleridge's *To William Wordsworth* salutes his fellow-poet 'in the choir / Of ever-enduring men'; Shelley's *Adonais* sees Keats 'like a star, / Beacon[ing] from the abode where the Eternals are'; Hemans touches in *The Grave of a Poetess* on the loss felt by Tighe as she struggles to reconcile the roles of poet and woman – and in her brilliant dramatic monologue, *Properzia Rossi*, portrays her own loss in that of the Roman sculptress:

The bright work grows
Beneath my hand, unfolding, as a rose,
Leaf after leaf, to beauty. Line by line,
I fix my thought, heart, soul, to burn, to shine,
Through the pale marble's veins. It grows – and now
I give my whole life's history to thy brow,
Forsaken Ariadne.

Drawn to Hemans (whom she had never met) as woman-poet, Landon writes one of her greatest poems as a lament for her early death. Wordsworth, meanwhile, in his Lament for the Makers, *Extempore Effusion Upon the Death of James Hogg* (1835), looks back and celebrates his contemporaries: Scott, Hogg, Coleridge, Lamb and Crabbe. Bringing himself up to the moment, it is to Hemans that he turns: 'but why, / O'er ripe fruit, seasonably gathered, / Should frail survivors heave a sigh?'

1. MARY SCOTT

On Anna Laetitia Barbauld (née Aikin),

from *The Female Advocate* (1774)

Fired with the music, Aikin, of thy lays,
To thee the muse a joyful tribute pays –
Transported, dwells on that harmonious line
Where taste and spirit, wit and learning, shine;
Where Fancy's hand her richest colouring lends,
And every shade in just proportion blends.

How fair, how beauteous to our gazing eyes
Thy vivid intellectual paintings rise!
We feel thy feelings, glow with all thy fires,
Adopt thy thoughts, and pant with thy desires!
Proceed bright maid, and may thy polished page
Refine the manners of a trifling age –
Thy sex apprize of Pleasure's treacherous charms,
And woo them from the siren's fatal arms –
Teach them with thee on Fancy's wing to soar,
With thee the paths of science to explore,
With thee the open book of Nature scan,
Yet nobly scorn the little pride of man.
   Man, seated high on Learning's awful throne,
Thinks the fair realms of knowledge his alone;
But you, ye fair, his Salic Law disclaim!
Supreme in science shall the tyrant reign
When every talent all-indulgent Heaven
In lavish bounty to your share hath given?
   With joy ineffable the muse surveys
The orient beams of more resplendent days:
As on she raptured looks to future years,
What a bright throng to Fancy's view appears!
To them see Genius her best gifts impart,
And science raise a throne in every heart!
One turns the moral, one the historic page,
Another glows with all a Shakespeare's rage!
With matchless Newton now one soars on high,
Lost in the boundless wonders of the sky;
Another now (of curious mind) reveals
What treasures in her bowels Earth conceals –
Nature's minuter works attract her eyes,
Their laws, their powers, her deep research descries.
From sense abstracted, some with arduous flight
Explore the realms of intellectual light –
With unremitting study seek to find
How mind on matter, matter acts on mind.
Alike in Nature, arts and manners, read,
In every path of knowledge see them tread –
Whilst men, convinced of female talents, pay
To female worth the tributary lay!

2. ROBERT BURNS

(i) *Epistle to J. Lapraik, An Old Scotch Bard* (April 1785; publ. 1786)

While briers an' woodbines budding green,
An' paitricks scraichen loud at e'en,
An' morning poossie whiddan seen,
Inspire my muse,
This freedom, in an unknown frien',
I pray excuse.

On Fasteneen we had a rockin',
To ca' the crack, and weave our stockin',
And there was muckle fun and jokin'
Ye need na doubt;
At length we had a hearty yokin'
At sang-about!

There was ae sang, amang the rest
(Aboon them a' it pleased me best)
That some kind husband had addrest
To some sweet wife:
It thirled the heart-strings through the breast,
A' to the life.

I've scarce heard ought described sae weel
What generous manly bosoms feel –
Thought I, 'Can this be Pope, or Steele,
Or Beattie's wark?'
They tald me 'twas an odd kind chiel
About Muirkirk!

2 *paitricks* partridges.
3 *poossie whiddan seen* puss-hare seen running nimbly.
7 *Fasteneen* Shrove Tuesday (eve of the Fast), day before Lent, beginning on Ash Wednesday.
rockin' spinning session (from the 'rock', or distaff, used before the spinning-wheel was invented. **8** *ca' the crack* gossip. **11** *yokin'* contest.
13 *ae* one. **17** *thirled* pierced. **19** *ought described* anything that described.
23 *odd kind chiel* strange sort of lad (child).

It pat me fidgean-fain to hear't,
An' sae about him there I spier't;
Then a' that kent him round declare't
He had an ingine –
That nane excelled it, few cam near't,
It was sae fine –

That (set him to a pint of ale,
An' either douse or merry tale,
Or rhymes an' sangs he'd made himsel',
Or witty catches),
'Tween Inverness and Tiviotdale
He had few matches!

Then up I gat, an' swoor an aith:
Though I should pawn my pleugh an' graith,
Or die a cadger-pownie's death,
At some dyke-back,
A pint an' gill I'd gie them baith,
To hear your crack.

But first an' foremost, I should tell:
Amaist as soon as I could spell,
I to the crambo-jingle fell –
Though rude an' rough,
Yet crooning to a body's sel,
Does weel eneugh.

I am nae poet, in a sense,
But just a rhymer like by chance,
An' hae to learning nae pretence –
Yet, what the matter?
Whene'er my Muse does on me glance,
I jingle at her!

25 *It pat me fidgean-fain* It filled me with excitement.
26 *spier't* asked, inquired. **28** *ingine* talent.
32 *douse* sweet (French '*douce*'). **34** *catches* competitive songs, or rounds.
38 *graith* gear, tackle.
39 *a cadger-pownie's death* death of a hawker's [overloaded] pony.
40 *At some dyke-back* behind some wall. **42** *crack* talk, rhyming.
44 *spell* read. **45** *to the crambo-jingle* to making doggerel verses.
49 *in a sense* in the normal sense of the word.

Your critic-folk may cock their nose,
And say, 'How can you e'er propose
(You wha ken hardly verse frae prose)
To mak a sang?'
But by your leaves, my learned foes,
Ye're maybe wrang!

What's a' your jargon o' the schools,
Your Latin names for horns an' stools;
If honest Nature made you fools,
What sairs your grammars?
Ye'd better taen up spades and shools,
Or knappin-hammers.

A set o' dull, conceited hashes
Confuse their brains in colledge-classes!
They gang in stirks, and come out asses
(Plain truth to speak),
An' syne they think to climb Parnassus
By dint o' Greek!

Gie me ae spark o' Nature's fire,
That's a' the learning I desire;
Then though I drudge through dub an' mire
At pleugh or cart,
My Muse, though hamely in attire,
May touch the heart . . .

(ii) *I Am a Bard* (c. autumn 1785; publ. 1799)

I am a bard of no regard
Wi' gentle folks an' a' that,
But Homer-like the glowran byke
Frae town to town I draw that!

61 *the schools* branches of learning.
62 *horns* horn-books (for which the Latin name might be 'primers').
64 *sairs* serves. **65** *shools* shovels.
66 *knappin-hammers* hammers for breaking stone. **67** *hashes* time-wasters.
69 *They gang . . . asses* They go in as bullocks and come out as donkeys.
71 *syne* afterwards. **75** *dub* puddle.

3–4 *But Homer-like . . . draw that* But like Homer I draw the staring crowd.

For a' that, an' a' that,
And twice as muckle's a' that,
I've lost but ane, I've twa behin' –
I've wife eneugh for a' that!

I never drank the Muses' stank,
Castalia's burn, an a' that,
But there is streams, an' richly reams –
My Helicon I ca' that!
For a' that, an a' that . . .

Great love I bear to a' the fair,
Their humble slave, an' a' that –
But lordly will, I hold it still
A mortal sin to thraw that!
For a' that, an' a' that . . .

In raptures sweet this hour we meet,
Wi' mutual love an' a' that,
But for how lang the flie may stang,
Let inclination law that!
For a' that, an' a' that . . .

Their tricks an' craft hae put me daft,
They've ta'en me in an' a' that,
But clear your decks, and here's – 'The Sex!'
I like the jades for a' that!
For 'a that, an' a' that,
An' twice as muckle as a' that,
My dearest bluid to do them guid,
They're welcome till't for a' that!

6 *as muckle's* as much as. **9** *stank* pond.
11 *richly reams* foams delightfully. **20** *thraw* resist, frustrate.
27 *the flie may stang* desire may last (a reference to the 'Spanish fly', regarded as an aphrodisiac). **28** *law* regulate.
34 *ta'en me in* deceived me – but also, welcomed him sexually.
35 *But clear . . . 'The Sex'* Burns' toast to the fair sex is a reminder that this is a drinking-song. **36** *jades* wenches (literally 'mares').
39 *My dearest bluid* my life's blood – but with the implication of semen.
40 *till't* to it.

3. HELEN MARIA WILLIAMS

Sonnet on Reading 'The Mountain Daisy' by Burns (c. 1787; publ. 1791)

While soon the 'garden's flaunting flowers' decay
And (scattered on the earth) neglected lie,
The mountain daisy, cherished by the ray
A poet drew from Heaven, shall never die.
Ah, like that lovely flower the Poet rose
Mid Penury's bare soil and bitter gale!
He felt each storm that on the mountain blows,
Nor ever knew the shelter of the vale.
By Genius in her native vigour nursed,
On Nature with impassioned look he gazed,
Then through the cloud of adverse fortune burst
Indignant, and in light unborrowed blazed!
Scotia, from rude affliction shield thy bard –
His Heaven-taught numbers, Fate herself will guard.

4. JOANNA BAILLIE

An Address to the Muses (lines 49–102) 1790

The youthful poet, pen in hand,
All by the side of blotted stand,
In reverie deep, which none may break,
Sits rubbing of his beardless cheek;
And well his inspiration knows,
E'en by the dewy drops that trickle o'er his nose.

The tuneful sage of riper fame
Perceives you not in heated frame,
But at conclusion of his verse
(Which still his muttering lips rehearse)
Oft waves his hand in grateful pride,
And owns the heavenly power that did his fancy guide.

Oh lovely Sisters! is it true
That they are all inspired by you?
And while they write, with magic charmed
And high enthusiasm warmed,
We may not question heavenly lays,
For well I wot, they give you all the praise.

Oh lovely sisters! well it shows
How wide and far your bounty flows –
Then why from me withhold your beams?
Unvisited of heavenly dreams,
Whene'er I aim at heights sublime,
Still downward am I called to seek some stubborn rhyme!

No hasty lightning breaks the gloom,
Nor flashing thoughts unsought-for come,
Nor fancies wake in time of need –
I labour much with little speed;
And when my studied task is done,
Too well, alas, I mark it for my own! . . .

Ye are the spirits who preside
In earth and air and ocean wide,
In hissing flood and crackling fire,
In horror dread and tumult dire,
In stilly calm and stormy wind,
And rule the answering changes in the human mind.

High on the tempest-beaten hill
Your misty shapes ye shift at will –
The wild fantastic clouds ye form –
Your voice is in the midnight storm,
Whilst in the dark and lonely hour
Oft starts the boldest heart, and owns your secret power!

5. WILLIAM BLAKE

(i) Preface to *Europe, A Prophecy*

(engraved 1794)

'Five windows light the caverned man: through one he breathes the air;
Through one, hears music of the spheres; through one, the eternal vine
Flourishes, that he may receive the grapes; through one, can look
And see small portions of the eternal world that ever groweth;
Through one, himself pass out what time he please (but he will not,
For stolen joys are sweet, and bread eaten in secret pleasant).'

So sang a fairy, mocking, as he sat on a streaked tulip
Thinking none saw him. When he ceased I started from the trees
And caught him in my hat, as boys knock down a butterfly.
'How know you this', said I, 'small sir? Where did you learn this song?'
Seeing himself in my possession, thus he answered me:
'My master, I am yours! Command me, for I must obey.'

'Then tell me, what is the material world – and is it dead?'
He laughing answered: 'I will write a book on leaves of flowers,
If you will feed me on love-thoughts, and give me now and then
A cup of sparkling poetic fancies. So, when I am tipsy
I'll sing to you to this soft lute, and show you all alive
The world, where every particle of dust breathes forth its joy.'

I took him home in my warm bosom: as we went along
Wild flowers I gathered, and he showed me each eternal flower.
He laughed aloud to see them whimper because they were plucked –
They hovered round me like a cloud of incense. When I came
Into my parlour and sat down, and took my pen to write,
My fairy sat upon the table, and dictated *Europe*.

(ii) 'I Come In Self-Annihilation'

(*Milton*, plate 41, 2–28) c. 1804, engraved c. 1808–10

I come in self-annihilation and the grandeur of inspiration
To cast off rational demonstration by faith in the Saviour,
To cast off the rotten rags of memory by inspiration,
To cast off Bacon, Locke and Newton from Albion's covering,
To take off his filthy garments, and clothe him with imagination,
To cast aside from poetry all that is not inspiration,
That it no longer shall dare to mock with the aspersion of madness
Cast on the inspired by the tame high finisher of paltry blots
Indefinite, or paltry rhymes, or paltry harmonies,
Who creeps into state government like a caterpillar to destroy –
To cast off the idiot questioner, who is always questioning,
But never capable of answering; who sits with a sly grin
Silent plotting when to question, like a thief in a cave;
Who publishes doubt, and calls it knowledge; whose science is despair,
Whose pretence to knowledge is envy, whose whole science is
To destroy the wisdom of ages to gratify ravenous envy
That rages round him like a wolf day and night without rest.
He smiles with condescension, he talks of benevolence and virtue
And those who act with benevolence and virtue they murder time on time!
These are the destroyers of Jerusalem, these are the murderers
Of Jesus, who deny the faith and mock at eternal life;
Who pretend to poetry that they may destroy imagination
By imitation of nature's images drawn from remembrance!
These are the sexual garments, the abomination of desolation
Hiding the human lineaments as with an ark and curtains,
Which Jesus rent – and now shall wholly purge away with fire,
Till generation is swallowed up in regeneration . . .

(iii) 'Trembling I Sit'

(*Jerusalem*, plate 5, 16–20) c. 1804–7; engraved c. 1818

Trembling I sit day and night. My friends are astonished at me,
Yet they forgive my wanderings. I rest not from my great task –
To open the eternal worlds, to open the immortal eyes
Of Man inwards into the worlds of thought; into Eternity
Ever expanding in the bosom of God, the human imagination!

6. SAMUEL TAYLOR COLERIDGE

Nehemiah Higginbottom Sonnets (Nov. 1797)

The reader will excuse me for noticing, that I myself was the first to expose *risu honesto* the three sins one or the other of which is the most likely to beset a young writer. So long ago as the publication of the second number of *The Monthly Magazine*, under the name of Nehemiah Higginbottom, I contributed three sonnets, the first of which had for its object to excite a good-natured laugh at 'the spirit of *doleful egotism*', and at the recurrence of favourite phrases, with the double defect of being at once trite and licentious. The second on low, 'low, creeping language and thoughts, under the pretence of *simplicity*'. And the third, the phrases of which were borrowed entirely from my own poems, on the 'indiscriminate use of swelling language and imagery'.

(Coleridge, *Biographia Literaria*, 1817)

(i) 'Pensive at Eve'

PENSIVE at eve, on the *hard* world I mused,
And *my poor* heart was sad; so at the MOON
I gazed, and sighed and sighed – for ah, how soon
Eve saddens into night! Mine eyes perused
With tearful vacancy the *dampy* grass
That wept and glittered in the *paly* ray,
And I *did pause me* on my lonely way
And *mused me* on the *wretched ones* that pass
O'er the black heath of sorrow. But alas!
Most of *myself* I thought – when it befell
That the *soothe* spirit of the *breezy* wood
Breathed in mine ear: 'All this is very well,
But much of ONE thing is for NO thing good.'
Oh *my poor heart's* INEXPLICABLE SWELL!

(ii) 'Oh I Do Love Thee'

Oh I do love thee, meek SIMPLICITY!
For of thy lays the lulling simpleness
Goes to my heart, and soothes each small distress,
Distress though small, yet haply great to me.

'Tis true on Lady Fortune's gentlest pad
I amble on; and yet I know not why
So sad I am! But should a friend and I
Frown, pout, and part, then I am *very sad*.
And then with sonnets and with sympathy
My dreamy bosom's mystic woes I pall;
Now on my false friend plaining plaintively,
Now raving at mankind in general;
But whether sad or fierce, 'tis simple all,
All very simple, meek SIMPLICITY!

(iii) 'And This Reft House'

And this reft house is that, the which he built,
Lamented Jack! and here his malt he piled,
Cautious in vain! these rats, that squeak so wild,
Squeak not unconscious of their father's guilt.
Did he not see her gleaming through the glade!
Belike 'twas she, the maiden all forlorn.
What though she milk no cow with crumpled horn,
Yet, *aye*, she haunts the dale where *erst* she strayed,
And *aye* beside her stalks her amorous knight!
Still on his thighs their wonted brogues are worn,
And through those brogues, still tattered and betorn,
His hindward charms gleam an unearthly white.
Ah! thus through broken clouds, at night's high Noon
Peeps in fair fragments forth the full-orbed harvest-moon!

7. WILLIAM WORDSWORTH

Thoughts on Poetic Imagination, 1798–1806

(i) from the Prologue to *Peter Bell*

(April 1798; publ. 1819)

There's something in a flying horse,
There's something in a huge balloon,
But through the clouds I'll never float
Until I have a little boat
In shape just like the crescent moon.

And now I have a little boat
In shape just like the crescent moon –
Fast through the clouds my boat can sail,
But if perchance your faith should fail,
Look up, and you shall see me soon!

The woods, my friends, are round you roaring,
The woods are roaring like a sea;
The noise of danger's in your ears,
And you have all a thousand fears
Both for my little boat and me . . .

Up goes my boat between the stars
Through many a breathless field of light,
Through many a long blue field of ether,
Leaving ten thousand stars beneath her –
Up goes my little boat so bright!

The towns in Saturn are ill-built,
But Jove has very pretty bowers;
The evening star is not amiss –
But what are all of them to this,
This little earth of ours?

Then back again to our green earth!
What business had I here to roam?
The world for my remarks and me
Will not a whit the better be –
I've left my heart at home.

And that is then the dear green earth
And that's the dear Pacific Ocean
And that is Caucasus so dear,
To think that I again am here –
Oh, my poor heart's commotion!

And there is little Tartary
And there's the famous River Dnieper,
And there, amid the ocean green,
Is that sweet isle, of isles the Queen –
Ye fairies, from all evil keep her!

And there's the town where I was born,
And that's the house of Parson Swan.
My heart is touched, I must avow
(Consider where I've been!), and now
I feel I am a man.

Never did fifty things at once
Appear so lovely, never never;
The woods, how sweetly do they ring –
To hear the earth's sweet murmuring
Thus could I hang for ever.

'Oh shame upon you, cruel shame!
Was ever such a heartless loon
In such a lovely boat to sit,
And make no better use of it? –
A boat that's like the crescent moon!

Out, out, and like a brooding hen
Beside your sooty hearth-stone cower!
Go creep along the dirt, and pick
Your way with your good walking-stick,
Just three good miles an hour.

Sure in the breast of full-grown poet
So faint a heart was ne'er before!
Come to the poets' wild delights –
I have ten thousand lovely sights,
Ten thousand sights in store . . .'

'My pretty little form of light,
My sweet and beautiful canoe,
Now (though it grieves me to the heart)
I feel, I feel that we must part –
I must take leave of you.

You are a pretty little barge,
But while your pleasure you're pursuing
Without impediment or let,
My little barge, you quite forget
What in the world is doing . . .

There is a party in the bower,
Round the stone table in my garden:
The squire is there, and, as I guess,
His pretty little daughter Bess,
With Harry the churchwarden.

They were to come this very evening,
They know not I have been so far;
I see them there, in number nine,
All in the bower of Weymouth pine,
I see them, there they are.

And there's the wife of Parson Swan,
And there's my good friend Stephen Otter –
And, ere the light of evening fail,
To them I must relate the tale
Of Peter Bell the Potter.'

Off flew my pretty little barge
All in a trance of indignation,
And I, as well as I was able,
On two poor legs to my stone table
Limped on with some vexation.

'Oh here he is!' cried little Bess
(She saw me at the garden-door),
'Oh here he is!' cried Mistress Swan –
And all at once around me ran
Full nine of them or more.

'Sit down, I beg you would be seated',
Said I – no doubt with visage pale –
'And if, my friends, it pleases you,
This instant, without more ado,
We'll have the promised tale.'

And so, though somewhat out of breath,
With lips, no doubt, and visage pale,
And sore too from a slight contusion,
Did I, to cover my confusion,
Begin the promised tale.

(ii) *The Glad Preamble*

(c. 18 Nov. 1799; publ. *Prelude* 1850/from MS 1926)

Oh, there is blessing in this gentle breeze,
That blows from the green fields, and from the clouds,
And from the sky; it beats against my cheek,
And seems half-conscious of the joy it gives.
Oh welcome messenger! Oh welcome friend!
A captive greets thee, coming from a house
Of bondage, from yon city's walls set free,
A prison where he hath been long immured.
Now I am free, enfranchised and at large,
May fix my habitation where I will.
What dwelling shall receive me? In what vale
Shall be my harbour ? Underneath what grove
Shall I take up my home, and what sweet stream
Shall with its murmur lull me to my rest?
The earth is all before me – with a heart
Joyous, nor scared at its own liberty,
I look about, and should the guide I choose
Be nothing better than a wandering cloud
I cannot miss my way. I breathe again;
Trances of thought and mountings of the mind
Come fast upon me. It is shaken off –
As by miraculous gift 'tis shaken off –
That burden of my own unnatural self,
The heavy weight of many a weary day
Not mine, and such as were not made for me.
Long months of peace (if such bold word accord
With any promises of human life),
Long months of ease and undisturbed delight
Are mine in prospect. Whither shall I turn,
By road or pathway, or through open field,
Or shall a twig, or any floating thing
Upon the river, point me out my course?
   Enough that I am free, for months to come
May dedicate myself to chosen tasks –
May quit the tiresome sea and dwell on shore
If not a settler on the soil, at least
To drink wild waters, and to pluck green herbs,
And gather fruits fresh from their native tree.
Nay more – if I may trust myself, this hour
Hath brought a gift that consecrates my joy;

For I, methought, while the sweet breath of heaven
Was blowing on my body, felt within
A corresponding, mild, creative breeze,
A vital breeze, which travelled gently on
O'er things which it had made, and is become
A tempest, a redundant energy,
Vexing its own creation. 'Tis a power
That does not come unrecognized, a storm
Which, breaking up a long continued frost,
Brings with it vernal promises, the hope
Of active days, of dignity and thought,
Of prowess in an honourable field,
Pure passions, virtue, knowledge and delight,
The holy life of music and of verse.

(iii) 'A Dedicated Spirit'

(1805 *Prelude* IV, 316–45; publ. 1850)

In a throng,
A festal company of maids and youths,
Old men and matrons staid – promiscuous rout,
A medley of all tempers – I had passed
The night in dancing, gaiety, and mirth,
With din of instruments and shuffling feet
And glancing forms and tapers glittering
And unaimed prattle flying up and down,
Spirits upon the stretch, and here and there
Slight shocks of young love-liking interspersed
That mounted up like joy into the head
And tingled through the veins. Ere we retired
The cock had crowed, the sky was bright with day;
Two miles I had to walk along the fields
Before I reached my home. Magnificent
The morning was, a memorable pomp,
More glorious than I ever had beheld.
The sea was laughing at a distance; all
The solid mountains were as bright as clouds,
Grain-tinctured, drenched in empyrean light;
And in the meadows and the lower grounds
Was all the sweetness of a common dawn –
Dews, vapours, and the melody of birds,
And labourers going forth into the fields.

Ah, need I say, dear friend, that to the brim
My heart was full? I made no vows, but vows
Were then made for me: bond unknown to me
Was given that I should be, else sinning greatly,
A dedicated spirit. On I walked
In blessedness, which even yet remains.

(iv) *Elegiac Stanzas, Suggested by a Picture of Peele Castle in a Storm, Painted by Sir George Beaumont*

(May–June 1806; publ. 1807)

I was thy neighbour once, thou rugged pile –
Four summer weeks I dwelt in sight of thee –
I saw thee every day, and all the while
Thy form was sleeping on a glassy sea.

So pure the sky, so quiet was the air!
So like, so very like, was day to day!
Whene'er I looked, thy image still was there;
It trembled, but it never passed away.

How perfect was the calm! It seemed no sleep –
No mood, which season takes away, or brings –
I could have fancied that the mighty deep
Was even the gentlest of all gentle things.

Ah! then, if mine had been the painter's hand –
To express what then I saw – and add the gleam,
The light that never was on sea or land,
The consecration, and the poet's dream!

I would have planted thee, thou hoary pile,
Amid a world how different from this,
Beside a sea that could not cease to smile;
On tranquil land, beneath a sky of bliss!

Thou shouldst have seemed a treasure-house, a mine
Of peaceful years; a chronicle of Heaven –
Of all the sunbeams that did ever shine
The very sweetest had to thee been given!

A picture had it been of lasting ease,
Elysian quiet, without toil or strife;
No motion but the moving tide, a breeze,
Or merely silent Nature's breathing life.

Such, in the fond delusion of my heart,
Such picture would I at that time have made –
And seen the soul of truth in every part,
A faith, a trust, that could not be betrayed!

So once it would have been – 'tis so no more!
I have submitted to a new control:
A power is gone, which nothing can restore;
A deep distress hath humanized my soul.

Not for a moment could I now behold
A smiling sea, and be what I have been.
The feeling of my loss will ne'er be old –
This, which I know, I speak with mind serene.

Then, Beaumont, friend (who would have been the friend,
If he had lived, of him whom I deplore),
This work of thine I blame not, but commend –
This sea in anger, and that dismal shore!

O 'tis a passionate work – yet wise and well!
Well chosen is the spirit that is here:
That hulk which labours in the deadly swell,
This rueful sky, this pageantry of fear!

And this huge castle, standing here sublime,
I love to see the look with which it braves,
Cased in the unfeeling armour of old time,
The lightning, the fierce wind, and trampling waves.

Farewell, farewell the heart that lives alone,
Housed in a dream, at distance from the kind!
Such happiness, wherever it be known,
Is to be pitied; for 'tis surely blind.

But welcome fortitude, and patient cheer,
And frequent sights of what is to be borne!
Such sights, or worse, as are before me here –
Not without hope we suffer and we mourn.

8. ANNA LAETITIA BARBAULD

To Mr Coleridge (1799)

Midway the Hill of Science, after steep
And rugged paths that tire the unpractised feet,
A grove extends, in tangled mazes wrought,
And filled with strange enchantment. Dubious shapes
Flit through dim glades, and lure the eager foot
Of youthful ardour to eternal chase.
Dreams hang on every leaf; unearthly forms
Glide through the gloom, and mystic visions swim
Before the cheated sense. Athwart the mists,
Far into vacant space, huge shadows stretch
And seem realities; while things of life,
Obvious to sight and touch, all glowing round,
Fade to the hue of shadows.
                                        Scruples here,
With filmy net, most like the autumnal webs
Of floating gossamer, arrest the foot
Of generous enterprise, and palsy Hope
And fair Ambition with the chilling touch
Of sickly hesitation and blank fear.
Nor seldom Indolence these lawns among
Fixes her turf-built seat, and wears the garb
Of deep philosophy, and museful sits
In dreamy twilight of the vacant mind,
Soothed by the whispering shade – for soothing soft
The shades, and vistas lengthening into air
With moonbeam-rainbows tinted. Here each mind
Of finer mould, acute and delicate,
In its high progress to eternal truth
Rests for a space in fairy bowers entranced,
And loves the softened light and tender gloom,
And (pampered with most insubstantial food)
Looks down indignant on the grosser world
And matter's cumbrous shapings!
                                                Youth beloved
Of Science, of the Muse beloved, not here –
Not in the maze of metaphysic lore
Build thou thy place of resting! Lightly tread
The dangerous ground, on noble aims intent,
And be this Circe of the studious cell

Enjoyed but still subservient. Active scenes
Shall soon with healthful spirit brace thy mind,
And fair exertion (for bright fame sustained,
For friends, for country) chase each spleen-fed fog
That blots the wide Creation:
Now Heaven conduct thee with a parent's love!

9. MARY ROBINSON

(i) *Ode Inscribed to the Infant Son of S. T. Coleridge, Esq., Born 14 Sept 1800*

(lines 67–102) Sept. 1800; publ. 1806

Sweet baby boy, accept a stranger's song;
   An untaught minstrel joys to sing of thee!
And, all alone, her forest haunts among,
   Courts the wild tone of mazy harmony!
A stranger's song, babe of the mountain-wild,
Greets thee as Inspiration's darling child!
Oh may the fine-wrought spirit of thy sire
Awake thy soul and breathe upon thy lyre!
And blest, amid thy mountain haunts sublime,
   Be all thy days, thy rosy infant days,
And may the never-tiring steps of time
   Press lightly on with thee o'er life's disastrous maze.

Ye hills, coeval with the birth of time!
   Bleak summits, linked in chains of rosy light!
   Oh may your wonders many a year invite
Your native son the breezy path to climb
Where, in majestic pride of solitude,
   Silent and grand, the hermit thought shall trace,
Far o'er the wild infinity of space,
The sombre horrors of the waving wood;
The misty glen; the river's winding wave;
The last deep blush of summer's lingering day;
The winter storm that, roaming unconfined,
Sails on the broad wings of the impetuous wind.

Oh, whether on the breezy height
Where Skiddaw greets the dawn of light,
Ere the rude sons of labour homage pay
To summer's flaming eye or winter's banner grey;
Whether Lodore its silver torrent flings
The mingling wonders of a thousand springs;
Whether smooth Bassenthwaite, at eve's still hour,
   Reflects the young moon's crescent pale,
Or meditation seeks her silent bower
   Amid the rocks of lonely Borrowdale –
Still may thy name survive, sweet boy, till Time
Shall bend to Keswick's vale thy Skiddaw's brow sublime!

(ii) *To the Poet Coleridge* (Oct. 1800; publ. 1806)

Rapt in the visionary theme,
   Spirit divine, with thee I'll wander,
Where the blue, wavy, lucid stream
   Mid forest-glooms shall slow meander!
With thee I'll trace the circling bounds
   Of thy new paradise, extended,
And listen to the varying sounds
   Of winds and foamy torrents blended.

Now by the source which labouring heaves
   The mystic fountain, bubbling, panting,
While gossamer its network weaves
   Adown the blue lawn slanting –
I'll mark thy 'sunny dome' and view
Thy 'caves of ice', thy fields of dew,
Thy ever-blooming mead, whose flower
Waves to the cold breath of the moonlight hour!
Or when the day-star, peering bright
On the grey wing of parting night,
With more than vegetating power
Throbs, grateful to the burning hour,
As summer's whispered sighs unfold
Her million million buds of gold,
Then will I climb the breezy bounds
   Of thy new paradise, extended,
And listen to the different sounds
   Of winds and foamy torrents blended!

Spirit divine, with thee I'll trace
   Imagination's boundless space!
With thee, beneath thy 'sunny dome'
   I'll listen to the minstrel's lay
   Hymning the gradual close of day,
In 'caves of ice' enchanted roam,
Where on the glittering entrance plays
The moon's beam with its silvery rays,
Or when the glassy stream
   That through the deep dell flows
Flashes the noon's hot beam –
   The noon's hot beam that midway shows
Thy flaming temple, studded o'er
With all Peruvia's lustrous store!
There will I trace the circling bounds
   Of thy new paradise, extended,
And listen to the awful sounds
   Of winds and foamy torrents blended.

And now I'll pause to catch the moan
   Of distant breezes, cavern-pent;
Now, ere the twilight tints are flown,
   Purpling the landscape far and wide
   On the dark promontory's side
   I'll gather wild-flowers dew-besprent
And weave a crown for thee,
Genius of Heaven-taught poesy!
While, opening to my wondering eyes
Thou bidst a new Creation rise,
I'll raptured trace the circling bounds
   Of thy rich paradise, extended,
And listen to the varying sounds
   Of winds and foamy torrents blended.

And now, with lofty tones inviting,
Thy nymph, her dulcimer swift-smiting,
Shall wake me in ecstatic measures,
Far, far removed from mortal pleasures,
In cadence rich, in cadence strong,
Proving the wondrous witcheries of song!
I hear her voice – thy 'sunny dome',
   Thy 'caves of ice', aloud repeat –
   Vibrations maddening, sweet,
Calling the visionary wanderer home!

She sings of thee, oh favoured child
Of minstrelsy, sublimely wild –
Of thee whose soul can feel the tone
Which gives to airy dreams a magic all their own!

10. WILLIAM WORDSWORTH

Portraits of Coleridge

(i) from *The Castle of Indolence Stanzas*

(May 1802; publ. 1807)

With him there often walked in friendly wise,
Or lay upon the moss by brook or tree,
A noticeable man with large dark eyes
And a pale face, that seemed undoubtedly
As if a blooming face it ought to be!
Heavy his low-hung lip did oft appear
(A face divine of heaven-born idiocy);
Profound his forehead was, though not severe –
Yet some did think that he had little business here.

Ah, God forfend – his was a lawful right!
Noisy he was, and gamesome as a boy;
His limbs would toss about him with delight
Like branches when strong winds the trees annoy.
He lacked not implement, device or toy,
To cheat away the hours that silent were;
He would have taught you how you might employ
Yourself, and many did to him repair –
And certés, not in vain – he had inventions rare!

Instruments had he, playthings for the ear
(Long blades of grass, plucked round him as he lay,
These served to catch the wind as it came near);
Glasses he had with many colours gay –
Others that did all little things display:
The beetle with his radiance manifold
(A mailéd angel on a battle day!)
And leaves and flowers, and herbage green and gold,
And all the glorious sights which fairies do behold.

He would entice that other man to hear
His music, and to view his imagery;
And sooth, these two did love each other dear –
As far as love in such a place could be!
There did they lie, from earthly labour free,
Most happy livers as were ever seen!
If but a bird, to keep them company,
Or butterfly sate down, they were, I ween,
As pleased as if the same had been a Maiden Queen!

(ii) 'A Mind Debarred'

(1805 *Prelude* VI, 239–329) 1804; publ. 1850/from MS 1926

O'er paths and fields
In all that neighbourhood, through narrow lanes
Of eglantine and through the shady woods,
And o'er the Border Beacon and the waste
Of naked pools and common crags that lay
Exposed on the bare fell, was scattered love,
A spirit of pleasure and youth's golden gleam.
Oh friend, we had not seen thee at that time,
And yet a power is on me and a strong
Confusion, and I seem to plant thee there!
Far art thou wandered now in search of health
And milder breezes – melancholy lot –
But thou art with us, with us in the past,
The present, with us in the times to come.
There is no grief, no sorrow, no despair,
No languor, no dejection, no dismay,
No absence scarcely can there be, for those
Who love as we do. Speed thee well! Divide
Thy pleasure with us; thy returning strength,
Receive it daily as a joy of ours;
Share with us thy fresh spirits, whether gift
Of gales Etesian or of loving thoughts.
I too have been a wanderer – but alas,
How different is the fate of different men
Though twins almost in genius and in mind!
Unknown unto each other (yea, and breathing
As if in different elements) we were framed
To bend at last to the same discipline,
Predestined if two beings ever were
To seek the same delights, and have one health,

One happiness. Throughout this narrative,
Else sooner ended, I have known full well
For whom I thus record the birth and growth
Of gentleness, simplicity, and truth,
And joyous loves that hallow innocent days
Of peace and self-command. Of rivers, fields,
And groves I speak to thee, my friend – to thee
Who, yet a liveried schoolboy in the depths
Of the huge city, on the leaded roof
Of that wide edifice, thy home and school,
Wast used to lie and gaze upon the clouds
Moving in heaven, or haply, tired of this,
To shut thine eyes and by internal light
See trees, and meadows, and thy native stream,
Far distant, thus beheld from year to year
Of thy long exile.
Nor could I forget
In this late portion of my argument
That scarcely had I finally resigned
My rights among those academic bowers
When thou wert thither guided. From the heart
Of London, and from the cloisters there, thou camest,
And didst sit down in temperance and peace,
A rigorous student. What a stormy course
Then followed! Oh, it is a pang that calls
For utterance to think how small a change
Of circumstances might to thee have spared
A world of pain, ripened ten thousand hopes
For ever withered.
Through this retrospect
Of my own college life I still have had
Thy after-sojourn in the self-same place
Present before my eyes, have played with times
(I speak of private business of the thought)
And accidents as children do with cards,
Or as a man who when his house is built,
A frame locked up in wood and stone, doth still
In impotence of mind by his fireside
Rebuild it to his liking. I have thought
Of thee, thy learning, gorgeous eloquence,
And all the strength and plumage of thy youth,
Thy subtle speculations, toils abstruse
Among the schoolmen, and Platonic forms
Of wild ideal pageantry, shaped out

From things well-matched or ill, and words for things –
The self-created sustenance of a mind
Debarred from Nature's living images,
Compelled to be a life unto itself,
And unrelentingly possessed by thirst
Of greatness, love, and beauty.
Not alone,
Ah, surely not in singleness of heart,
Should I have seen the light of evening fade
Upon the silent Cam, if we had met
Even at that early time. I needs must hope,
Must feel, must trust, that my maturer age
And temperature less willing to be moved,
My calmer habits and more steady voice,
Would with an influence benign have soothed
Or chased away the airy wretchedness
That battened on thy youth. But thou hast trod,
In watchful meditation thou hast trod,
A march of glory, which does put to shame
These vain regrets . . .

(iii) *A Complaint* (c. Dec. 1806; publ. 1807)

There is a change, and I am poor!
Your love hath been, nor long ago,
A fountain at my fond heart's door,
Whose only business was to flow –
And flow it did; not taking heed
Of its own bounty, or my need.

What happy moments did I count –
Blest was I then all bliss above!
Now, for that consecrated fount
Of murmuring, sparkling, living love,
What have I? Shall I dare to tell?
A comfortless and hidden well.

A well of love. It may be deep
(I trust it is), and never dry –
What matter, if the waters sleep
In silence and obscurity?
Such change, and at the very door
Of my fond heart, hath made me poor.

11. MARY TIGHE

'Dreams of Delight, Farewell'

(*Psyche*, concluding stanzas) 1802–3; publ. 1805

58

With fond embrace she clasped her long lost son,
And gracefully received his lovely bride:
'Psyche! thou hardly hast my favour won!'
With roseate smile her Heavenly parent cried,
'Yet hence thy charms immortal, deified,
With the young Joys, thy future offspring fair,
Shall bloom for ever at thy lover's side!
All-ruling Jove's high mandate I declare –
Blest denizen of Heaven, arise its joys to share!'

59

She ceased, and lo! a thousand voices, joined
In sweetest chorus, Love's high triumph sing;
There, with the Graces and the Hours entwined,
His fairy train their rosy garlands bring,
Or round their mistress sport on halcyon wing;
While she enraptured lives in his dear eye,
And drinks immortal love from that pure spring
Of never-failing full felicity,
Bathed in ambrosial showers of bliss eternally!

60

Dreams of delight, farewell – your charms no more
Shall gild the hours of solitary gloom!
The page remains, but can the page restore
The vanished bowers which Fancy taught to bloom?
Ah, no! her smiles no longer can illume
The path my Psyche treads no more for me.
Consigned to dark oblivion's silent tomb,
The visionary scenes no more I see,
Fast from the fading lines the vivid colours flee!

12. SAMUEL TAYLOR COLERIDGE

To William Wordsworth (Jan. 1807; publ. 1817)

Oh friend! Oh teacher! God's great gift to me!
Into my heart have I received that lay
More than historic, that prophetic lay,
Wherein (high theme by thee first sung aright)
Of the foundations and the building-up
Of thy own spirit thou hast loved to tell
What may be told, to the understanding mind
Revealable – and what within the mind
May rise enkindled.
Theme hard as high!
Of smiles spontaneous and mysterious fears:
The firstborn they of Reason, and twin-birth.
Of tides obedient to external force,
And *currents* self-determined (as might seem),
Or by interior power. Of moments awful,
Now in thy hidden life, and now abroad
Mid festive crowds (*thy* brows too garlanded,
A brother of the feast). Of *fancies* fair,
Hyblaean murmurs of poetic thought
Industrious in its joy, by lilied streams
Native or outland, lakes and famous hills.
Of more than fancy: of the hope of man
Amid the tremor of a realm aglow,
Where France in all her towns lay vibrating,
Even as a bark becalmed on sultry seas
Beneath the voice from Heaven – the bursting crash
Of Heaven's immediate thunder, when no cloud
Is visible, or shadow on the main
(Ah, soon night rolled on night, and every cloud
Opened its eye of fire; and Hope aloft
Now fluttered, and now tossed, upon the storm
Floating). Of Hope afflicted and struck down –
Thence summoned homeward, homeward to thy heart,
Oft from the watchtower of man's absolute self
(With light unwaning in her eyes) to look
Far on, herself a glory to behold,
The Angel of the Vision! Then – last strain! –
Of *Duty* (chosen laws controlling choice),
Virtue and Love! An Orphic tale indeed,

A tale divine of high and passionate thoughts
To their own music chanted.
Ah great Bard,
Ere yet that last swell dying awed the air,
With steadfast ken I viewed thee in the choir
Of ever-enduring men! The truly great
Have all one age, and from one visible space
Shed influence, for they – both power, and act –
Are permanent, and time is not with them,
Save as it worketh for them, they in it.
Nor less a sacred roll than those of old
(And to be placed, as they, with gradual fame
Among the archives of mankind), thy work
Makes audible a linkéd song of truth –
Of truth profound, a sweet continuous song,
Not learnt, but native, her own natural notes!
Dear shall it be to every human heart –
To me how more than dearest – me, on whom
Comfort from thee, and utterance of thy love,
Came with such heights and depths of harmony,
Such sense of wings uplifting, that the storm
Scattered and whirled me, till my thoughts
Became a bodily tumult, and thy faithful hopes
(Thy hopes of me, my friend, by me unfelt)
Were troublous to me, almost as a voice
Familiar once, and more than musical,
To one cast forth whose hope had seemed to die –
A wanderer with a worn-out heart,
Mid strangers pining with untended wounds.
Oh friend, too well thou knowst of what sad years
The long suppression had benumbed my soul,
That even as life returns upon the drowned
The unusual joy awoke a throng of pains:
Keen pangs of love (awakening, as a babe,
Turbulent, with an outcry in the heart),
And fears self-willed, that shunned the eye of hope,
And hope that would not know itself from fear –
Sense of past youth, and manhood come in vain,
And genius given, and knowledge won in vain;
And all which I had culled in wood-walks wild,
And all which patient toil had reared, and all,
Commune with thee had opened out, but flowers
Strewed on my corse, and borne upon my bier
In the same coffin, for the self-same grave.

That way no more! And ill beseems it me,
Who came a welcomer, in herald's guise
Singing of glory and futurity,
To wander back on such unhealthful roads
Plucking the poisons of self-harm! And ill
Such intertwine beseems triumphal wreathes
Strewed before thy advancing! Thou too, friend!
Oh injure not the memory of that hour
Of thy communion with my nobler mind
By pity or grief, already felt too long!
Nor let my words import more blame than needs:
The tumult rose, and ceased – for peace is nigh
Where wisdom's voice has found a listening heart.
Amid the howl of more that wintry storms
The halcyon hears the voice of vernal hours
Already on the wing!
Eve following eve
(Dear tranquil time, when the sweet sense of home
Becomes most sweet) – hours for their own sake hailed,
And more desired, more precious, for thy song!
In silence listening, like a devout child,
My soul lay passive: by thy various strain
Driven as in surges now, beneath the stars
(With momentary stars of my own birth –
Fair constellated foam – still darting off
Into the darkness), now a tranquil sea
Outspread and bright, yet swelling to the moon!
And when, oh friend, my comforter, my guide,
Strong in thyself and powerful to give strength,
Thy long sustainéd lay finally closed,
And thy deep voice had ceased (yet thou thyself
Wert still before mine eyes, and round us both
That happy vision of beloved faces –
All whom I deepliest love, in one room, all),
Scarce conscious, and yet conscious of its close,
I sat, my being blended in one thought –
Thought was it, or aspiration, or resolve? –
Absorbed, yet hanging still upon the sound.
And when I rose, I found myself in prayer.

13. LORD BYRON

English Bards and Scotch Reviewers

(lines 1–38, 85–148) 1810

Time was, ere yet in these degenerate days
Ignoble themes obtained mistaken praise,
When sense and wit, with poesy allied –
No fabled graces – flourished side by side,
From the same fount their inspiration drew,
And, reared by taste, bloomed fairer as they grew.
Then in this happy isle a Pope's pure strain
Sought the rapt soul to charm, nor sought in vain –
A polished nation's praise aspired to claim,
And raised the people's, as the poet's, fame.
Like him great Dryden poured the tide of song,
In stream less smooth indeed, yet doubly strong.
Then Congreve's scenes could cheer, or Otway's melt –
For nature then an English audience felt.
   But why these names, or greater still, retrace,
When all to feebler bards resign their place?
Yet to such times our lingering looks are cast,
When taste and reason with those times are past.
No, look around, and turn each trifling page,
Survey the precious works that please the age!
This truth at least let satire's self allow,
No dearth of bards can be complained of now:
The loaded press beneath her labour groans,
And printer's devils shake their weary bones,
While Southey's epics cram the creaking shelves,
And Little's lyrics shine in hot-pressed twelves!
   Behold in various throngs the scribbling crew,
For notice eager, pass in long review:
Each spurs his jaded Pegasus apace,
And rhyme and blank maintain an equal race;
Sonnets on sonnets crowd, and ode on ode,
And Tales of Terror jostle on the road.
Immeasurable measures move along,
For simpering Folly loves a varied song
(To strange, mysterious Dullness still the friend),
Admires the strain she cannot comprehend!
Thus Lays of Minstrels – may they be the last! –
On half-strung harps, whine mournful to the blast . . .

With eagle-pinions soaring to the skies,
Behold the ballad-monger Southey rise –
To him let Camoëns, Milton, Tasso yield –
Whose annual strains like armies take the field.
First in the ranks let Joan of Arc advance,
The scourge of England and the boast of France!
Though burnt by wicked Bedford as a witch,
Behold her statue placed in glory's niche –
Her fetters burst, and just released from prison,
A virgin Phoenix from her ashes risen.
Next see tremendous Thalaba come on,
Arabia's monstrous, wild and wondrous son,
Domdaniel's dread destroyer, who o'erthrew
More mad magicians than the world e'er knew.
Immortal hero, all thy foes o'ercome,
For ever reign – the rival of Tom Thumb!
Since startled metre fled before thy face,
Well wert thou doomed the last of all thy race,
Well might triumphant genii bear thee hence,
Illustrious conqueror of common sense!
Now, last and greatest, Madoc spreads his sails,
Cacique in Mexico, and Prince in Wales;
Tells us strange tales, as other travellers do,
More old than Mandeville's, and not so true!
Oh Southey, Southey, cease thy varied song –
A bard may chant too often and too long!
As thou art strong in verse, in mercy spare –
A fourth, alas, were more than we could bear!
But if, in spite of all the world can say,
Thou still will verseward plod thy weary way,
If still in Berkeley-ballads most uncivil
Thou wilt devote old women to the Devil
(The babe unborn thy dread intent may rue),
'God help thee', Southey, and thy readers too!
Next comes the dull disciple of thy school,
That mild apostate from poetic rule,
The simple Wordsworth, framer of a lay
As soft as evening in his favourite May,
Who warns his friend 'to shake off toil and trouble,
And quit his books, for fear of growing double';
Who both by precept and example shows
That prose is verse, and verse is merely prose,
Convincing all (by demonstration plain)
Poetic souls delight in prose insane,

And Christmas-stories, tortured into rhyme,
Contain the essence of the true sublime.
Thus when he tells the tale of Betty Foy,
The idiot mother of an 'Idiot Boy',
A moon-struck silly lad who lost his way,
And, like his bard, confounded night with day,
So close on each pathetic part he dwells,
And each adventure so sublimely tells,
That all who view the 'idiot in his glory'
Conceive the bard the hero of the story!
Shall gentle Coleridge pass unnoticed here,
To turgid ode and tumid stanza dear?
Though themes of innocence amuse him best,
Yet still obscurity's a welcome guest.
If inspiration should her aid refuse
To him who takes a pixy for a muse,
Yet none in lofty numbers can surpass
The bard who soars to elegize and ass!
How well the subject suits his noble mind –
A fellow-feeling makes us wondrous kind.

14. JAMES LEIGH HUNT

Feast of the Poets (lines 204–41) 1811; expanded 1814

All on a sudden, there rose on the stairs
A noise as of persons with singular airs,
You'd have thought 'twas the Bishops or Judges a-coming,
Or whole court of Aldermen hawing and humming,
Or Abbot at least, with his ushers before,
But 'twas only Bob Southey and two or three more.
As soon as he saw him Apollo seemed pleased,
But as he had settled it not to be teased
By all the vain dreamers from bedroom and brook,
He turned from the rest without even a look!
For Coleridge had vexed him long since I suppose
By his idling, and gabbling, and muddling in prose,
And Wordsworth one day made his very hairs bristle
By going and changing his harp for a whistle!
These heroes however, long used to attack,
Were not by contempt to be so driven back

But followed the God up, and shifting their place
Stood full in his presence and looked in his face –
When one began spouting the cream of orations
In praise of bombarding his friends and relations,
And tother some lines he had made on a straw,
Showing how he had found it and what it was for,
And how, when 'twas balanced, it stood like a spell!
And how, when 'twas balanced no longer, it fell!
A wild thing of scorn he described it to be,
But he said it was patient to Heaven's decree –
Then he gazed upon nothing, and looking forlorn,
Dropped a *natural* tear for *that wild thing of scorn*!
  Apollo half laughed betwixt anger and mirth,
'And cried was there ever such trifling on Earth?
It is not enough that this nonsense, I fear,
Has hurt the fine head of my friend Robert here,
But the very best promise bred up in this school
Must show himself proudest in playing the fool.
What – think ye a bard's a mere gossip, who tells
Of the everyday feelings of everyone else,
And that poetry lies, not in something select,
But in gathering the refuse that others reject.
Must a ballad doled out by a spectacled nurse
About Two-Shoes or Thumb be your model in verse,
And your writings, instead of sound fancy and style,
Look more like the morbid abstractions of bile?
There is one of you here – 'twas of him that I spoke
Who, instead of becoming a byeword and joke,
Should have brought back our fine old pre-eminent way,
And been the first man at my table today . . .

15. LORD BYRON

''Tis to Create'

(*Childe Harold* III, stanzas 3–6) April 1816; publ. 1817

3

In my youth's summer I did sing of one,
  The wandering outlaw of his own dark mind;
  Again I seize the theme, then but begun,
  And bear it with me, as the rushing wind

Bears the cloud onwards. In that tale I find
The furrows of long thought, and dried-up tears
Which, ebbing, leave a sterile track behind,
O'er which all heavily the journeying years
Plod the last sands of life – where not a flower appears.

4

Since my young days of passion – joy, or pain –
Perchance my heart and harp have lost a string,
And both may jar. It may be that in vain
I would essay as I have sung to sing;
Yet, though a dreary strain, to this I cling.
So that it wean me from the weary dream
Of selfish grief or gladness – so it fling
Forgetfulness around me – it shall seem
To me, though to none else, a not ungrateful theme.

5

He who, grown agéd in this world of woe,
In deeds not years piercing the depths of life,
So that no wonder waits him (nor below
Can love or sorrow, fame, ambition, strife,
Cut to his heart again with the keen knife
Of silent, sharp endurance) – he can tell
Why thought seeks refuge in lone caves, yet rife
With airy images, and shapes which dwell
Still unimpaired, though old, in the soul's haunted cell.

6

'Tis to create, and in creating live
A being more intense, that we endow
With form our fancy, gaining as we give
The life we image – even as I do now!
What am I? Nothing. But not so art thou,
Soul of my thought, with whom I traverse earth,
Invisible but gazing, as I glow
Mixed with thy spirit, blended with thy birth,
And feeling still with thee in my crushed feelings' dearth.

16. PERCY BYSSHE SHELLEY

To Wordsworth (1816)

Poet of Nature, thou hast wept to know
That things depart which never may return:
Childhood and youth, friendship and love's first glow,
Have fled like sweet dreams, leaving thee to mourn.
These common woes I feel. One loss is mine
Which thou too feel'st, yet I alone deplore.
Thou wert as a lone star, whose light did shine
On some frail bark in winter's midnight roar;
Thou hast, like to a rock-built refuge, stood
Above the blind and battling multitude;
In honoured poverty thy voice did weave
Songs consecrate to truth and liberty –
Deserting these, thou leavest me to grieve,
Thus having been, that thou shouldst cease to be.

17. JOHN KEATS

(i) *Sleep and Poetry* (lines 96–162) 1817

Oh for ten years, that I may overwhelm
Myself in poesy – so I may do the deed
That my own soul has to itself decreed.
Then will I pass the countries that I see
In long perspective, and continually
Taste their pure fountains. First the realm I'll pass
Of Flora, and old Pan: sleep in the grass,
Feed upon apples red and strawberries,
And choose each pleasure that my fancy sees –
Catch the white-handed nymphs in shady places
To woo sweet kisses from averted faces,
Play with their fingers, touch their shoulders white
Into a pretty shrinking with a bite
As hard as lips can make it, till, agreed,
A lovely tale of human life we'll read.
And one will teach a tame dove how it best
May fan the cool air gently o'er my rest;

Another, bending o'er her nimble tread,
Will set a green robe floating round her head,
And still will dance with ever varied ease,
Smiling upon the flowers and the trees;
Another will entice me on, and on
Through almond blossoms and rich cinnamon,
Till in the bosom of a leafy world
We rest in silence, like two gems upcurled
In the recesses of a pearly shell.
And can I ever bid these joys farewell?
Yes, I must pass them for a nobler life,
Where I may find the agonies, the strife
Of human hearts – for lo, I see afar,
O'ersailing the blue cragginess, a car
And steeds with streamy manes. The charioteer
Looks out upon the winds with glorious fear –
And now the numerous tramplings quiver lightly
Along a huge cloud's ridge; and now, with sprightly
Wheel, downward come they into fresher skies,
Tipt round with silver from the sun's bright eyes.
Still downward with capacious whirl they glide,
And now I see them on a green hillside
In breezy rest among the nodding stalks.
The charioteer with wondrous gesture talks
To the trees and mountains, and there soon appear
Shapes of delight, of mystery, and fear,
Passing along before a dusky space
Made by some mighty oaks. As they would chase
Some ever-fleeting music, on they sweep!
Lo, how they murmur, laugh, and smile, and weep –
Some with upholden hand and mouth severe;
Some with their faces muffled to the ear
Between their arms; some, clear in youthful bloom,
Go glad and smilingly athwart the gloom;
Some looking back, and some with upward gaze.
Yes, thousands in a thousand different ways
Flit onward: now a lovely wreath of girls
Dancing their sleek hair into tangled curls –
And now broad wings! Most awfully intent
The driver of those steeds is forward bent,
And seems to listen – oh that I might know
All that he writes with such a hurrying glow!
The visions all are fled – the car is fled
Into the light of Heaven – and in their stead

A sense of real things comes doubly strong,
And, like a muddy stream, would bear along
My soul to nothingness! But I will strive
Against all doubtings, and will keep alive
The thought of that same chariot, and the strange
Journey it went.

(ii) from *The Fall of Hyperion: A Dream*, Canto I (July–Sept. 1819; from MS 1856)

Fanatics have their dreams, wherewith they weave
A paradise for a sect; the savage too
From forth the loftiest fashion of his sleep
Guesses at Heaven – pity these have not
Traced upon vellum or wild Indian leaf
The shadows of melodious utterance!
But bare of laurel they live, dream, and die –
For poesy alone can tell her dreams –
With the fine spell of words alone can save
Imagination from the sable chain
And dumb enchantment. Who alive can say
'Thou art no poet – mayst not tell thy dreams!'
Since every man whose soul is not a clod
Hath visions, and would speak, if he had loved,
And been well nurtured in, his mother tongue.
Whether the dream now purposed to rehearse
Be poet's or fanatic's will be known
When this warm scribe my hand is in the grave.
   Methought I stood where trees of every clime,
Palm, myrtle, oak, and sycamore, and beech,
With plantain and spice-blossoms, made a screen –
In neighbourhood of fountains (by the noise
Soft-showering in my ears), and (by the touch
Of scent) not far from roses. Turning round
I saw an arbour with a drooping roof
Of trellis-vines, and bells, and larger blooms,
Like floral censers, swinging light in air . . .
Then to the west I looked, and saw far off
An image, huge of feature as a cloud,
At level of whose feet an altar slept,
To be approached on either side by steps
And marble balustrade, and patient travail

To count with toil the innumerable degrees.
Towards the altar sober-paced I went,
Repressing haste as too unholy there,
And, coming nearer, saw beside the shrine
One ministering – and there arose a flame.
   When in mid-May the sickening east wind
Shifts sudden to the south, the small warm rain
Melts out the frozen incense from all flowers,
And fills the air with so much pleasant health
That even the dying man forgets his shroud –
Even so that lofty sacrificial fire,
Sending forth Maian incense, spread around
Forgetfulness of everything but bliss,
And clouded all the altar with soft smoke
From whose white fragrant curtains thus I heard
Language pronounced: 'If thou canst not ascend
These steps, die on that marble where thou art!
Thy flesh, near cousin to the common dust,
Will parch for lack of nutriment – thy bones
Will wither in few years, and vanish so
That not the quickest eye could find a grain
Of what thou now art on that pavement cold.
The sands of thy short life are spent this hour,
And no hand in the universe can turn
Thy hourglass if these gummed leaves be burnt
Ere thou canst mount up these immortal steps.'
   I heard, I looked: two senses – both at once
So fine, so subtle – felt the tyranny
Of that fierce threat and the hard task proposed.
Prodigious seemed the toil! The leaves were yet
Burning, when suddenly a palsied chill
Struck from the pavéd level up my limbs,
And was ascending quick to put cold grasp
Upon those streams that pulse beside the throat –
I shrieked, and the sharp anguish of my shriek
Stung my own ears – I strove hard to escape
The numbness, strove to gain the lowest step!
Slow, heavy, deadly was my pace. The cold
Grew stifling, suffocating at the heart,
And when I clasped my hands I felt them not.
One minute before death, my iced foot touched
The lowest stair, and, as it touched, life seemed
To pour in at the toes – I mounted up,
As once fair angels on a ladder flew

From the green turf to Heaven.
'Holy Power',
Cried I, approaching near the hornéd shrine,
'What am I that should so be saved from death?
What am I that another death come not
To choke my utterance sacrilegious here?'
Then said the veiléd shadow: 'Thou hast felt
What 'tis to die and live again before
Thy fated hour. That thou hadst power to do so
Is thy own safety – thou hast dated on
Thy doom.' 'High Prophetess', said I, 'purge off
Benign, if so it please thee, my mind's film.'
'None can usurp this height', returned that shade,
'But those to whom the miseries of the world
Are misery, and will not let them rest.
All else who find a haven in the world
Where they may thoughtless sleep away their days,
If by a chance into this fane they come,
Rot on the pavement where thou rottedst half!'
'Are there not thousands in the world', said I,
Encouraged by the sooth voice of the shade,
'Who love their fellows even to the death,
Who feel the giant agony of the world,
And more, like slaves to poor humanity
Labour for mortal good? I sure should see
Other men here – but I am here alone.'
'Those whom thou spakest of are no visionaries',
Rejoined that voice, 'they are no dreamers weak,
They seek no wonder but the human face,
No music but a happy-noted voice!
They come not here, they have no thought to come –
And thou art here, for thou art less than they.
What benefit canst thou do, or all thy tribe,
To the great world? Thou art a dreaming thing,
A fever of thyself! Think of the earth –
What bliss even in hope is there for thee?
What haven? Every creature hath its home,
Every sole man hath days of joy and pain,
Whether his labours be sublime or low:
The pain alone, the joy alone – distinct.
Only the dreamer venoms all his days,
Bearing more woe than all his sins deserve.
Therefore – that happiness be somewhat shared –
Such things as thou art are admitted oft

Into like gardens thou didst pass erewhile,
And suffered in these temples! For that cause
Thou standest safe beneath this statue's knees.'
'That I am favoured for unworthiness
By such propitious parley, medicined
In sickness not ignoble, I rejoice –
Aye, and could weep for love of such award.'
So answered I, continuing, 'If it please,
Majestic shadow, tell me: sure not all
Those melodies sung into the world's ear
Are useless – sure a poet is a sage,
A humanist, physician to all men?
That I am none I feel – as vultures feel
They are no birds when eagles are abroad.
What am I then? Thou spakest of my tribe –
What tribe?'
The tall shade veiled in drooping white
Then spake, so much more earnest that the breath
Moved the thin linen folds that drooping hung
About a golden censer from the hand
Pendent: 'Art thou not of the dreamer tribe?
The poet and the dreamer are distinct,
Diverse, sheer opposite, antipodes!
The one pours out a balm upon the world,
The other vexes it.' Then shouted I,
Spite of myself, and with a Pythia's spleen:
'Apollo! Faded, far-flown Apollo!
Where is thy misty pestilence to creep
Into the dwellings, through the door crannies
Of all mock lyrists, large self-worshippers
And careless hectorers in proud bad verse.
Though I breathe death with them it will be life
To see them sprawl before me into graves!
Majestic shadow, tell me where I am –
Whose altar this? for whom this incense curls?
What image this whose face I cannot see
For the broad marble knees? and who thou art,
Of accent feminine so courteous?'
Then the tall shade, in drooping linens veiled,
Spoke out, so much more earnest, that her breath
Stirred the thin folds of gauze that drooping hung
About a golden censer from her hand
Pendent; and by her voice I knew she shed
Long-treasured tears. 'This temple, sad and lone,

Is all spared from the thunder of a war
Foughten long since by giant hierarchy
Against rebellion; this old image here,
Whose carvéd features wrinkled as he fell,
Is Saturn's – I, Moneta, left supreme
Sole priestess of his desolation.'
I had no words to answer, for my tongue,
Useless, could find about its rooféd home
No syllable of a fit majesty
To make rejoinder to Moneta's mourn.
  There was a silence, while the altar's blaze
Was fainting for sweet food: I looked thereon,
And on the pavéd floor, where nigh were piled
Faggots of cinnamon, and many heaps
Of other crispéd spice-wood – then again
I looked upon the altar, and its horns
Whitened with ashes, and its languorous flame –
And then upon the offerings again.
And so by turns, till sad Moneta cried,
'The sacrifice is done! But not the less
Will I be kind to thee for thy good will.
My power, which to me is still a curse,
Shall be to thee a wonder; for the scenes
Still swooning vivid through my globéd brain,
With an electral changing misery,
Thou shalt with these dull mortal eyes behold,
Free from all pain – if wonder pain thee not!'
As near as an immortal's spheréd words
Could to a mother's soften, were these last:
And yet I had a terror of her robes,
And chiefly of the veils, that from her brow
Hung pale, and curtained her in mysteries
That made my heart too small to hold its blood.
  This saw that Goddess, and with sacred hand
Parted the veils. Then saw I a wan face,
Not pined by human sorrows, but bright-blanched
By an immortal sickness which kills not
(It works a constant change, which happy death
Can put no end to). Deathwards progressing
To no death was that visage! It had past
The lily and the snow; and beyond these
I must not think now, though I saw that face –
But for her eyes I should have fled away!
They held me back, with a benignant light

Soft mitigated by divinest lids
Half-closed, and visionless entire they seemed
Of all external things. They saw me not,
But in blank splendour beamed like the mild moon
Who comforts those she sees not – who knows not
What eyes are upward cast. As I had found
A grain of gold upon a mountain's side,
And, twinged with avarice, strained out my eyes
To search its sullen entrails rich with ore,
So at the view of sad Moneta's brow
I asked to see what things the hollow brain
Behind enwombed – what high tragedy
In the dark secret chambers of her skull
Was acting, that could give so dread a stress
To her cold lips, and fill with such a light
Her planetary eyes, and touch her voice
With such a sorrow.
'Shade of Memory',
Cried I, with act adorant at her feet,
'By all the gloom hung round thy fallen house,
By this last temple, by the golden age,
By great Apollo, thy dear foster-child,
And by thyself, forlorn divinity,
The pale omega of a withered race,
Let me behold, according as thou saidst,
What in thy brain so ferments to and fro!'
No sooner had this conjuration passed
My devout lips, than side by side we stood
(Like a stunt bramble by a solemn pine)
Deep in the shady sadness of a vale . . .

18. PERCY BYSSHE SHELLEY

(i) *Julian and Maddalo: A Conversation*

(lines 1–67) Oct. 1818; publ. 1824

Count Maddalo is a Venetian gentleman of ancient family and of great fortune, who, without mixing much in the society of his countrymen, resides chiefly at his magnificent palace in that city. He is a person of the most consummate genius, and capable, if he would direct his energies to such an end, of becoming the redeemer of his degraded country. But it is his weakness to be proud. He derives from acomparison of his own extraordinary mind with the dwarfish intellects that surround him, an intense apprehension of the nothingness of human life. His passions and his powers are incomparably greater than those of other men; and instead of the latter having been employed in curbing the former, they have mutually lent each other strength. His ambition preys upon itself, for want of objects which it can consider worthy of exertion. I say that Maddalo is proud, because I can find no other word to express the concentered and impatient feelings which consume him. But it is on his own hopes and affections only that he seems to trample, for in social life no human-being can be more gentle, patient and unassuming than Maddalo. He is cheerful, frank and witty. His more serious conversation is a sort of intoxication: men are held by it, as by a spell . . .

Julian is an Englishman of good family, passionately attached to those philosophical notions which assert the power of man over his own mind, and the immense improvements of which, by the extinction of certain moral superstitions, human society may yet be susceptible . . . Julian is rather serious.

I rode one evening with Count Maddalo
Upon the bank of land which breaks the flow
Of Adria towards Venice – a bare strand
Of hillocks, heaped from ever-shifting sand,
Matted with thistles and amphibious weeds
Such as from earth's embrace the salt ooze breeds,
Is this – an uninhabitable sea-side
Which the lone fisher, when his nets are dried,
Abandons; and no other objects breaks
The waste, but one dwarf tree and some few stakes
Broken and unrepaired, and the tide makes
A narrow space of level sand thereon,
Where 'twas our wont to ride while day went down.
This ride was my delight.
I love all waste
And solitary places, where we taste
The pleasure of believing what we see
Is boundless, as we wish our souls to be –
And such was this wide ocean, and this shore
More barren than its billows – and yet more
Than all, with a remembered friend I love
To ride as then I rode. For the wind drove
The living spray along the sunny air
Into our faces; the blue heavens were bare,

Stripped to their depths by the awakening north;
And from the waves sound, like delight, broke forth,
Harmonizing with solitude, and sent
Into our hearts aërial merriment!
So, as we rode, we talked, and the swift thought,
Winging itself with laughter, lingered not,
But flew from brain the brain (such glee was ours)
Charged with light memories of remembered hours,
None slow enough for sadness – till we came
Homeward, which always makes the spirit tame.
  This day had been cheerful, but cold, and now
The sun was sinking, and the wind also.
Our talk grew somewhat serious, as may be
Talk interrupted with such raillery
That mocks itself because it cannot scorn
The thoughts it would extinguish – 'twas forlorn
But pleasing, such as once (so poets tell)
The devils held within the dales of Hell
Concerning God, free-will, and destiny!
Of all that Earth has been, or yet may be,
All that vain men imagine or believe,
Or hope can paint, or suffering may achieve,
We descanted, and I (for ever, still,
Is it not wise to make the best of ill?) –
Argued against despondency, but pride
Made my companion take the darker side.
The sense that he was greater than his kind
Had struck, methinks, his eagle-spirit blind
By gazing on its own exceeding light.
  Meanwhile the sun paused ere it should alight,
Over the horizon of the mountains. Oh
How beautiful is sunset, when the glow
Of Heaven descends upon a land like thee,
Thou paradise of exiles, Italy –
Thy mountains, seas and vineyards, and the towers
Of cities they encircle! It was ours
To stand on thee beholding it; and then,
Just where we had dismounted, the Count's men
Were waiting for us with the gondola.
As those who pause on some delightful way
Though bent on pilgrimage, we stood
Looking upon the evening and the flood
Which lay between the city and the shore,
Paved with the image of the sky.

(ii) *Adonais: An Elegy on the Death of John Keats* (stanzas 1–8, 39–58) 1822

John Keats, died at Rome of a consumption, in his twenty-fourth year, on the 23rd of February 1821; and was buried in the romantic and lonely cemetery of the protestants in that city, under the pyramid which is the tomb of Cestius, and the massy walls and towers, now mouldering and desolate, which formed the circuit of ancient Rome. The cemetery is an open space among the ruins, covered in winter with violets and daisies. It might make one in love with death, to think that one should be buried in so sweet a place.

The genius of the lamented person to whose memory I have dedicated these unworthy verses, was not less delicate and fragile than it was beautiful; and where canker-worms abound, what wonder, if its young flower was blighted in the bud? The savage criticism on his *Endymion*, which appeared in the *Quarterly Review*, produced the most violent effect on his susceptible mind; the agitation thus originated ended in the rupture of a blood-vessel in the lungs; a rapid consumption ensued, and the succeeding acknowledgements from more candid critics, of the true greatness of his powers, were ineffectual to heal the wound thus wantonly inflicted.

It may be well said, that these wretched men know not what they do. They scatter their insults and their slanders without heed as to whether the poisoned shaft lights on a heart made callous by many blows, or one, like Keats', composed of more penetrable stuff . . . Against what woman taken in adultery, dares the foremost of these literary prostitutes to cast his opprobrious stone? Miserable man! you, one of the meanest, have wantonly defaced one of the noblest specimens of the workmanship of God. Nor shall it be your excuse, that, murderer as you are, you have spoken daggers, but used none . . . (Shelley)

1

I weep for Adonais – he is dead!
  Oh weep for Adonais – though our tears
  Thaw not the frost which binds so dear a head!
  And thou, sad Hour, selected from all years
  To mourn our loss, rouse thy obscure compeers,
  And teach them thine own sorrow, say: 'With me
  Died Adonais; till the future dares
  Forget the past, his fate and fame shall be
An echo and a light unto eternity!'

2

Where wert thou, mighty Mother, when he lay –
When thy Son lay – pierced by the shaft which flies
In darkness? Where was lorn Urania
When Adonais died? With veiléd eyes,
Mid listening Echoes, in her paradise
She sat while one, with soft enamoured breath,
Rekindled all the fading melodies
With which, like flowers that mock the corse beneath,
He had adorned and hid the coming bulk of death.

3

Oh weep for Adonais – he is dead!
Wake, melancholy Mother, wake and weep!
Yet wherefore? Quench within their burning bed
Thy fiery tears, and let thy loud heart keep
Like his a mute and uncomplaining sleep;
For he is gone, where all things wise and fair
Descend; – oh dream not that the amorous deep
Will yet restore him to the vital air:
Death feeds on his mute voice, and laughs at our despair.

4

Most musical of mourners, weep again!
Lament anew, Urania! He died,
Who was the sire of an immortal strain,
(Blind, old and lonely) when his country's pride,
The priest, the slave, and the liberticide,
Trampled and mocked with many a loathéd rite
Of lust and blood – he went, unterrified,
Into the gulf of death – but his clear sprite
Yet reigns o'er earth, the third among the sons of light.

5

Most musical of mourners, weep anew!
Not all to that bright station dared to climb –
And happier they their happiness who knew,
Whose tapers yet burn through that night of time
In which suns perished; others more sublime,
Struck by the envious wrath of man or god,
Have sunk, extinct in their refulgent prime;
And some yet live, treading the thorny road,
Which leads, through toil and hate, to Fame's serene abode.

6

But now thy youngest, dearest, one has perished –
The nursling of thy widowhood, who grew
Like a pale flower by some sad maiden cherished,
And fed with true-love tears instead of dew –
Most musical of mourners, weep anew!
Thy extreme hope, the loveliest and the last
(The bloom whose petals, nipped before they blew,
Died on the promise of the fruit) is waste!
The broken lily lies – the storm is overpast.

7

To that high capital, where kingly Death
Keeps his pale court in beauty and decay,
He came; and bought, with price of purest breath,
A grave among the eternal. Come away!
Haste, while the vault of blue Italian day
Is yet his fitting charnel-roof – while still
He lies, as if in dewy sleep he lay!
Awake him not – surely he takes his fill
Of deep and liquid rest, forgetful of all ill.

8

He will awake no more, oh never more!
Within the twilight chamber spreads apace
The shadow of white Death, and at the door
Invisible Corruption waits to trace
His extreme way to her dim dwelling-place;
The eternal Hunger sits, but pity and awe
Soothe her pale rage, nor dares she to deface
So fair a prey, till darkness, and the law
Of mortal change, shall fill the grave which is her maw . . .

39

Peace, peace! He is not dead, he doth not sleep –
He hath awakened from the dream of life –
'Tis we who, lost in stormy visions, keep
With phantoms an unprofitable strife,
And in mad trance strike with our spirit's knife
Invulnerable nothings. *We* decay
Like corpses in a charnel; fear and grief
Convulse us and consume us day by day,
And cold hopes swarm like worms within our living clay.

40

He has outsoared the shadow of our night –
Envy and calumny and hate and pain,
And that unrest which men miscall delight,
Can touch him not and torture not again.
From the contagion of the world's slow stain
He is secure, and now can never mourn
A heart grown cold, a head grown grey in vain;
Nor, when the spirit's self has ceased to burn,
With sparkless ashes load an unlamented urn.

41

He lives, he wakes! 'Tis Death is dead, not he –
Mourn not for Adonais. Thou young Dawn,
Turn all thy dew to splendour, for from thee
The spirit thou lamentest is not gone.
Ye caverns and ye forests, cease to moan!
Cease, ye faint flowers and fountains, and thou air,
Which like a mourning veil thy scarf hadst thrown
O'er the abandoned earth, now leave it bare
Even to the joyous stars which smile on its despair!

42

He is made one with Nature: there is heard
His voice in all her music, from the moan
Of thunder, to the song of night's sweet bird;
He is a presence to be felt and known
In darkness and in light, from herb and stone,
Spreading itself where'er that Power may move
Which has withdrawn his being to its own –
Which wields the world with never-wearied love,
Sustains it from beneath, and kindles it above.

43

He is a portion of the loveliness
Which once he made more lovely: he doth bear
His part, while the one Spirit's plastic stress
Sweeps through the dull dense world, compelling there,
All new successions to the forms they wear –
Torturing the unwilling dross that checks its flight
To its own likeness (as each mass may bear)
And bursting in its beauty and its might
From trees and beasts and men into the Heaven's light.

44

The splendours of the firmament of time
May be eclipsed, but are extinguished not;
Like stars to their appointed height they climb,
And death is a low mist which cannot blot
The brightness it may veil. When lofty thought
Lifts a young heart above its mortal lair,
And love and life contend in it for what
Shall be its earthly doom, the dead live there
And move like winds of light on dark and stormy air.

45

The inheritors of unfulfilled renown
Rose from their thrones, built beyond mortal thought,
Far in the unapparent. Chatterton
Rose pale, his solemn agony had not
Yet faded from him; Sidney, as he fought
And as he fell and as he lived and loved
Sublimely mild (a spirit without spot)
Arose; and Lucan, by his death approved –
Oblivion as they rose shrank like a thing reproved.

46

And many more, whose names on earth are dark,
But whose transmitted effluence cannot die
So long as fire outlives the parent spark,
Rose, robed in dazzling immortality.
'Thou art become as one of us', they cry,
'It was for thee yon kingless sphere has long
Swung blind in unascended majesty,
Silent alone amid an heaven of song.
Assume thy wingéd throne, thou Vesper of our throng!'

47

Who mourns for Adonais? Oh come forth,
Fond wretch, and know thyself and him aright!
Clasp with thy panting soul the pendulous earth–
As from a centre, dart thy spirit's light
Beyond all worlds, until its spacious might
Satiate the void circumference; then shrink
Even to a point within our day and night,
And keep thy heart light lest it make thee sink
When hope has kindled hope, and lured thee to the brink.

48

Or go to Rome, which is the sepulchre,
   Oh, not of him, but of our joy! 'Tis nought
   That ages, empires, and religions there
   Lie buried in the ravage they have wrought;
   For such as he, can lend! They borrow not
   Glory from those who made the world their prey –
   And he is gathered to the kings of thought
   Who waged contention with their time's decay,
And of the past are all that cannot pass away.

49

Go thou to Rome – at once the paradise,
   The grave, the city, and the wilderness –
   And where its wrecks like shattered mountains rise,
   And flowering weeds and fragrant copses dress
   The bones of Desolation's nakedness,
   Pass, till the spirit of the spot shall lead
   Thy footsteps to a slope of green access
   Where, like an infant's smile, over the dead
A light of laughing flowers along the grass is spread.

50

And grey walls moulder round, on which dull time
   Feeds, like slow fire upon a hoary brand,
   And one keen pyramid with wedge sublime,
   Pavilioning the dust of him who planned
   This refuge for his memory, doth stand
   Like flame transformed to marble; and beneath,
   A field is spread, on which a newer band
   Have pitched in Heaven's smile their camp of death,
Welcoming him we lose with scarce extinguished breath.

51

Here pause: these graves are all too young as yet
   To have outgrown the sorrow which consigned
   Its charge to each – and if the seal is set,
   Here, on one fountain of a mourning mind,
   Break it not thou! Too surely shalt thou find
   Thine own well full, if thou returnest home,
   Of tears and gall. From the world's bitter wind
   Seek shelter in the shadow of the tomb –
What Adonais is, why fear we to become?

52

The One remains, the many change and pass;
Heaven's light forever shines, Earth's shadows fly;
Life, like a dome of many-coloured glass,
Stains the white radiance of Eternity,
Until Death tramples it to fragments. Die,
If thou wouldst be with that which thou dost seek!
Follow where all is fled! Rome's azure sky,
Flowers, ruins, statues, music, words, are weak
The glory they transfuse with fitting truth to speak.

53

Why linger, why turn back, why shrink, my heart?
Thy hopes are gone before: from all things here
They have departed, thou shouldst now depart!
A light is passed from the revolving year,
And man, and woman – and what still is dear
Attracts to crush, repels to make thee wither.
The soft sky smiles, the low wind whispers near:
'Tis Adonais calls! Oh hasten thither –
No more let Life divide what Death can join together.

54

That Light whose smile kindles the universe,
That Beauty in which all things work and move,
That Benediction which the eclipsing curse
Of birth can quench not, that sustaining Love,
Which through the web of being (blindly wove
By man and beast and earth and air and sea)
Burns bright or dim, as each are mirrors of
The fire for which all thirst – now beams on me,
Consuming the last clouds of cold mortality.

55

The breath whose might I have invoked in song
Descends on me – my spirit's bark is driven
Far from the shore, far from the trembling throng
Whose sails were never to the tempest given.
The massy earth and spheréd skies are riven!
I am borne darkly, fearfully, afar,
Whilst, burning through the inmost veil of Heaven,
The soul of Adonais like a star
Beacons from the abode where the Eternal are.

19. LETITIA ELIZABETH LANDON

Sappho's Song (1824)

Farewell, my lute, and would that I
  Had never waked thy burning chords!
Poison has been upon thy sigh,
  And fever has breathed in thy words.

Yet wherefore, wherefore should I blame
  Thy power, thy spell, my gentlest lute?
I should have been the wretch I am
  Had every chord of thine been mute.

It was my evil star above,
  Not my sweet lute that wrought me wrong;
It was not song that taught me love,
  But it was love that taught me song.

If song be past, and hope undone,
  And pulse, and head, and heart, are flame,
It is thy work, thou faithless one –
  But no, I will not name thy name!

Sun-god! lute, wreath are vowed to thee!
  Long be their light upon my grave,
My glorious grave – yon deep blue sea;
  I shall sleep calm beneath its wave!

20. SAMUEL TAYLOR COLERIDGE

Work Without Hope (21 Feb. 1825; publ. 1828)

All Nature seems at work – slugs leave their lair,
The bees are stirring, birds are on the wing,
And Winter, slumbering in the open air,
Wears on his smiling face a dream of spring!
And I, the while, the sole unbusy thing,
Nor honey make, nor pair, nor build, nor sing.
Yet well I ken the banks where amaranths blow,
Have traced the fount whence streams of nectar flow.

Bloom, oh ye amaranths, bloom for whom ye may –
For me ye bloom not! Glide, rich streams, away!
With lips unbrightened, wreathless brow, I stroll!
And would you learn the spells that drowse my soul?
Work without hope draws nectar in a sieve,
And hope without an object cannot live.

21. THOMAS HOOD

False Poets and True (1827)

Look how the lark soars upward and is gone,
Turning a spirit as he nears the sky
His voice is heard, but body there is none
To fix the vague excursions of the eye.
So poets' songs are with us though they die
Obscured and hid by death's oblivious shroud,
And Earth inherits the rich melody
Like raining music from the morning cloud.
Yet, few there be who pipe so sweet and loud
Their voices reach us through the lapse of space.
The noisy day is deafened by a crowd
Of undistinguished birds, a twittering race –
But only lark and nightingale forlorn
Fill up the silences of night and morn.

22. FELICIA HEMANS

(i) *The Grave of a Poetess*

(*Records of Woman* 1828)

Ne me plaigniez pas – si vous saviez
Combien de peines ce tombeau m'a epargnées

I stood beside thy lowly grave,
  Spring odours breathed around,
And music in the river-wave
  Passed with a lulling sound.

All happy things that love the sun
   In the bright air glanced by,
And a glad murmur seemed to run
   Through the soft azure sky.

Fresh leaves were on the ivy-bough
   That fringed the ruins near;
Young voices were abroad, but thou
   Their sweetness couldst not hear.

And mournful grew my heart for thee,
   Thou in whose woman's mind
The ray that brightens earth and sea,
   The light of song was shrined –

Mournful that thou wert slumbering low
   With a dread curtain drawn
Between thee and the golden glow
   Of this world's vernal dawn.

Parted from all the song and bloom
   Thou wouldst have loved so well,
To thee the sunshine round thy tomb
   Was but a broken spell.

The bird, the insect on the wing,
   In their bright reckless play,
Might feel the flush and life of spring,
   And thou wert past away!

But then, even then, a nobler thought
   O'er my vain sadness came,
The immortal spirit woke, and wrought
   Within my thrilling frame.

Surely on lovelier things, I said,
   Thou must have looked ere now,
Than all that round our pathway shed
   Odours and hues below.

The shadows of the tomb are here,
   Yet beautiful is Earth!
What seest thou then where no dim fear,
   No haunting dream hath birth?

Here a vain love to passing flowers
   Thou gavest, but where thou art
The sway is not with changeful hours:
   There love and death must part.

Thou hast left sorrow in thy song,
   A voice not loud, but deep;
The glorious bowers of Earth among,
   How often didst thou weep!

Where couldst thou fix on mortal ground
   Thy tender thoughts and high?
Now peace the woman's heart hath found,
   And joy the poet's eye.

(ii) *Properzia Rossi* (*Records of Woman* 1828)

Properzia Rossi, a celebrated female sculptor of Bologna, possessed also of talents for poetry and music, died in consequence of an unrequited attachment. A painting by Ducis represents her showing her last work, a basso-relievo of Ariadne, to a Roman knight, the object of her affection, who regards it with indifference.

1

One dream of passion and of beauty more,
And in its bright fulfilment let me pour
My soul away! Let earth retain a trace
Of that which lit my being, though its race
Might have been loftier far. Yet one more dream –
From my deep spirit one victorious gleam
Ere I depart! For thee alone, for thee,
May this last work, this farewell triumph be –
Thou, loved so vainly! I would leave enshrined
Something immortal of my heart and mind,
That yet may speak to thee when I am gone,
Shaking thine inmost bosom with a tone
Of lost affection – something that may prove
What she hath been, whose melancholy love
On thee was lavished: silent pang and tear,
And fervent song, that gushed when none were near,
And dream by night, and weary thought by day,
Stealing the brightness from her life away,
While thou – awake! Not yet within me die
Under the burden and the agony

Of this vain tenderness, my spirit – wake!
Even for thy sorrowful affection's sake,
Live. In thy work breathe out – that he may yet,
Feeling sad mastery there, perchance regret
Thine unrequited gift.

2

It comes – the power
Within me born flows back – my fruitless dower
That could not win me love! Yet once again
I greet it proudly, with its rushing train
Of glorious images: they throng, they press,
A sudden joy lights up my loneliness –
I shall not perish all!
The bright work grows
Beneath my hand, unfolding, as a rose,
Leaf after leaf, to beauty. Line by line,
I fix my thought, heart, soul, to burn, to shine,
Through the pale marble's veins. It grows – and now
I give my own life's history to thy brow,
Forsaken Ariadne! Thou shalt wear
My form, my lineaments; but oh, more fair,
Touched into lovelier being by the glow
Which in me dwells, as by the summer light
All things are glorified. From thee my woe
Shall yet look beautiful to meet his sight,
When I am passed away. Thou art the mould
Wherein I pour the fervent thoughts, the untold,
The self-consuming! Speak to him of me,
Thou, the deserted by the lonely sea,
With the soft sadness of thine earnest eye –
Speak to him, lorn one, deeply, mournfully,
Of all my love and grief! Oh, could I throw
Into thy frame a voice, a sweet, and low,
And thrilling voice of song, when he came nigh,
To send the passion of its melody
Through his pierced bosom – on its tones to bear
My life's deep feeling, as the southern air
Wafts the faint myrtle's breath – to rise, to swell,
To sink away in accents of farewell,
Winning but one, *one* gush of tears, whose flow
Surely my parted spirit yet might know,
If love be strong as death!

3

Now fair thou art,
Thou form, whose life is of my burning heart
Yet all the vision that within me wrought
  I cannot make thee! Oh, I might have given
Birth to creations of far nobler thought;
  I might have kindled, with the fire of Heaven,
Things not of such as die! But I have been
Too much alone. A heart whereon to lean,
With all these deep affections that o'erflow
My aching soul and find no shore below;
An eye to be my star; a voice to bring
Hope o'er my path like sounds that breathe of spring –
These are denied me, dreamt of still in vain!
Therefore my brief aspirings from the chain
Are ever but as some wild fitful song,
Rising triumphantly, to die ere long
In dirge-like echoes.

4

Yet the world will see
Little of this, my parting work, in thee.
  Thou shalt have fame! Oh, mockery! Give the reed
From storms a shelter, give the drooping vine
Something round which its tendrils may entwine,
  Give the parched flower a rain-drop, and the meed
Of love's kind words to woman! Worthless fame!
That in his bosom wins not for my name
The abiding place it asked! Yet how my heart,
In its own fairy-world of song and art,
Once beat for praise! Are those high longings o'er?
That which I have been, can I be no more?
Never, oh never more, though still thy sky
Be blue as then, my glorious Italy!
And though the music, whose rich breathings fill
Thine air with soul, be wandering past me still;
And though the mantle of thy sunlight streams
Unchanged on forms instinct with poet-dreams,
Never, oh never more! Where'er I move,
The shadow of this broken-hearted love
Is on me and around. Too well they know,
  Whose life is all within, too soon and well,
When there the blight hath settled – but I go
  Under the silent wings of peace to dwell.

From the slow-wasting, from the lonely pain,
The inward burning of those words, 'in vain',
Seared on the heart, I go. 'Twill soon be past,
Sunshine, and song, and bright Italian heaven,
And thou, oh thou, on whom my spirit cast
Unvalued wealth – who knowst not what was given
In that devotedness – the sad, and deep,
And unrepaid! Farewell! If I could weep
Once, only once, beloved one, on thy breast,
Pouring my heart forth ere I sink to rest!
But that were happiness, and unto me
Earth's gift is fame. Yet I was formed to be
So richly blest! With thee to watch the sky,
Speaking not, feeling but that thou wert nigh;
With thee to listen, while the tones of song
Swept even as part of our sweet air along –
To listen silently! With thee to gaze
On forms, the deified of olden days,
This had been joy enough! And, hour by hour,
From its glad well-springs drinking life and power,
How had my spirit soared, and made its fame
A glory for thy brow! Dreams, dreams – the fire
Burns faint within me. Yet I leave my name
(As a deep thrill may linger on the lyre
When its full chords are hushed) awhile to live,
And one day haply in thy heart revive
Sad thoughts of me. I leave it with a sound,
A spell o'er memory, mournfully profound –
I leave it, on my country's air to dwell!
Say proudly yet, ' 'Twas hers who loved me well!'

(iii) *To Wordsworth* (1828)

Thine is a strain to read among the hills,
The old and full of voices; by the source
Of some free stream, whose gladdening presence fills
The solitude with sound, for in its course
Even such is thy deep song, that seems a part
Of those high scenes, a fountain from their heart.

Or its calm spirit fitly may be taken
To the still breast in sunny garden-bowers,
Where vernal winds each tree's low tones awaken

And bud and bell with changes mark the hours.
There let thy thoughts be with me, while the day
Sinks with a golden and serene decay;

Or by some hearth where happy faces meet
When night hath hushed the woods with all their birds,
There (from some gentle voice) that lay were sweet
As antique music linked with household-words,
While in pleased murmurs woman's lip might move
And the raised eye of childhood shine in love;

Or where the shadows of dark solemn yews
Brood silently o'er some lone burial-ground
Thy voice hath power that brightly might diffuse
A breath, a kindling as of spring, around
From its own glow of hope and courage high,
And steadfast faith's victorious constancy.

True bard, and holy, thou art even as one
Who, by some secret gift of soul or eye,
In every spot beneath the smiling sun
Sees where the springs of living waters lie –
Unseen they sleep, till, touched by thee,
Bright healthful waves flow forth to each glad wanderer free.

23. WILLIAM WORDSWORTH

Extempore Effusion Upon the Death of James Hogg (1835)

When first, descending from the moorlands,
I saw the Stream of Yarrow glide
Along a bare and open valley,
The Ettrick Shepherd was my guide.

When last along its banks I wandered,
Through groves that had begun to shed
Their golden leaves upon the pathways,
My steps the Border Minstrel led.

The mighty Minstrel breathes no longer,
Mid mouldering ruins low he lies;
And death upon the braes of Yarrow,
Has closed the Shepherd-poet's eyes.

Nor has the rolling year twice measured,
From sign to sign, its steadfast course,
Since every mortal power of Coleridge
Was frozen at its marvellous source –

The rapt one, of the godlike forehead,
The heaven-eyed creature, sleeps in earth:
And Lamb, the frolic and the gentle,
Has vanished from his lonely hearth.

Like clouds that rake the mountain-summits,
Or waves that own no curbing hand,
How fast has brother followed brother,
From sunshine to the sunless land!

Yet I, whose lids from infant slumber
Were earlier raised, remain to hear
A timid voice, that asks in whispers,
'Who next will drop and disappear?'

Our haughty life is crowned with darkness,
Like London with its own black wreath,
On which with thee, oh Crabbe, forth-looking,
I gazed from Hampstead's breezy heath.

As if but yesterday departed,
Thou too art gone before – but why,
O'er ripe fruit, seasonably gathered,
Should frail survivors heave a sigh?

Mourn rather for that holy spirit,
Sweet as the spring, as ocean deep –
For her who, ere her summer faded,
Has sunk into a breathless sleep.

No more of old romantic sorrows,
For slaughtered youth or love-lorn maid!
With sharper grief is Yarrow smitten,
And Ettrick mourns with her their Poet dead.

24. LETITIA ELIZABETH LANDON

(i) *Felicia Hemans* (c. 1835; publ. 1838)

No more, no more, oh never more returning
Will thy belovéd presence gladden earth,
No more wilt thou with sad, yet anxious yearning,
Cling to those hopes which have no mortal birth.
Thou art gone from us, and with thee departed
How many lovely things have vanished too –
Deep thoughts that, at thy will, to being started,
And feelings teaching us our own were true!
Thou hast been round us like a viewless spirit
Known only by the music on the air:
The leaf or flowers which thou hast named inherit
A beauty known but from thy breathing there,
For thou didst on them fling thy strong emotion –
The likeness from itself the fond heart gave,
As planets from afar look down on ocean
And give their own sweet image to the wave.

And thou didst bring from foreign lands their treasures:
As floats thy various melody along,
We know the softness of Italian measures
And the grave cadence of Castilian song.
A general bond of union is the poet:
By its immortal verse is language known,
And for the sake of song do others know it –
One glorious poet makes the world his own!
And thou, how far thy gentle sway extended
The heart's sweet empire over land and sea:
Many a stranger and far flower was blended
In the soft wreath that glory bound for thee.
The echoes of the Susquehanna's waters
Paused in the pinewoods words of thine to hear,
And to the wide Atlantic's younger daughters
Thy name was lovely and thy song was dear.

Was not this purchased all too dearly? Never
Can fame atone for all that fame hath cost.
We see the goal, but know not the endeavour,
Nor what fond hopes have on the way been lost.

What do we know of the unquiet pillow
By the worn cheek and tearful eyelid pressed,
When thoughts chase thoughts like the tumultuous billow
Whose very light and foam reveals unrest.
We say the song is sorrowful, but know not
What may have left that sorrow on the song:
However mournful words may be, they show not
The whole extent of wretchedness and wrong.
They cannot paint the long sad hours past only
In vain regrets o'er what we feel we are.
Alas, the kingdom of the lute is lonely –
Cold is the worship coming from afar!

Yet what is mind in woman but revealing
In sweet clear light the hidden world below,
By quicker fancies and a keener feeling
Than those around, the cold and careless, know?
What is to feel such feeling, but to culture
A soil whence pain will never more depart –
The fable of Prometheus and the vulture
Reveals the poet's and the woman's heart!
Unkindly are they judged, unkindly treated
By careless tongues and by ungenerous words,
While cruel sneer and hard reproach repeated
Jar the fine music of the spirit's chords.
Wert thou not weary, thou whose soothing numbers
Gave other lips the joy thine own had not?
Didst thou not welcome thankfully the slumbers
Which closed around thy mourning human lot?

What on this earth could answer thy requiring
For earnest faith, for love (the deep and true),
The beautiful, which was thy soul's desiring
But only from thyself its being drew!
How is the warm and loving heart requited
In this harsh world, where it awhile must dwell,
Its best affections wronged, betrayed and slighted –
Such is the doom of those who love too well.
Better the weary dove should close its pinion,
Fold up its golden wings and be at peace!
Enter oh lady that serene dominion
Where earthly cares and earthly sorrows cease.

Fame's troubled hour has cleared, and now, replying,
  A thousand hearts their music ask of thine:
Sleep, with a light – the lovely and undying –
  Around thy grave! A grave which is a shrine.

(ii) *The Poet's Lot* (c. 1837; publ. 1841)

The poet's lovely faith creates
  The beauty he believes;
The light which on his footsteps waits,
  He from himself receives.

His lot may be a weary lot,
  His thrall a heavy thrall,
And cares and griefs the crowd know not,
  His heart may know them all.

But still he hath a mighty dower,
  The loveliness that throws
Over the common thought and hour
  The beauty of the rose.

NOTES

I. Romantic Hallmarks

CHARLOTTE SMITH

To the South Downs

2 *'your turf . . . among'*: From Smith's great predecessor among English elegiac poets, Thomas Gray, *A Distant Prospect of Eton College* 8, 'Whose turf, whose shades, whose flowers among'.
6 *this sad breast*: Smith was married off by her father aged fifteen to a feckless husband of twenty-one, who gave her twelve children. It was as a means of raising money that she composed the original *Elegiac Sonnets*, while in prison with her husband for debt.
9 *Aruna*: the River Aruna.
11 *Lethean cup*: a cup of the waters of oblivion in which, according to classical myth, souls were bathed before returning to human existence.

SAMUEL TAYLOR COLERIDGE

Kubla Khan

Preface *summer*: early November, to be accurate.

anodyne: opium presumably.

Here the Khan . . . wall: The words that Coleridge draws from Purchase are closer to the opening lines of his poem than he chooses to suggest: 'In Xamdu did Cublai Cam build a stately Palace, encompassing sixteene miles of plaine ground with a wall, wherein are fertile Meddowes, pleasant Springs, delightfull Streames, and all sort of beasts of chase and of game, and in the middest thereof a sumptuous house of pleasure.'

things: The dreaming mind thus achieves the Coleridgean ideal of language, that words should partake of the nature of the things they evoke or express.

passed away: *Kubla Khan* is a beautifully shaped poem, and many have doubted that Coleridge did indeed dream it; whether he did so or not, the myth of its creation has become inseparable from the poem itself – a part of its magic.
13 *cedarn cover*: copse of cedar trees.
19 *momently*: every moment.
22 *thresher's flail*: hinged stick with which heads of corn (wheat, barley, oats) were beaten on the flat stone threshing-floor, so that the chaff could be 'winnowed' (blown) from the grain.
33 *measure*: music, sometimes dance.
37 *dulcimer*: stringed instrument, originally French.
46 *I would build . . . air*: Inspired by the damsel (who is in some sense a muse), the poet could build the dome in air – as the poem has 'built' it. Standing back from the first thirty-six lines, Coleridge's final paragraph is felt to be a comment on the nature and workings of imagination.

CHARLES LAMB

Old Familiar Faces

2–3 *I had a mother . . . day of horrors*: In September 1796 Lamb's much-loved older sister, Mary, had killed their mother with a kitchen-knife in a moment of insane violence, and wounded their father.
11–12 *I loved a love . . . see her*: Though Lamb is now twenty-two, he regrets still the love of Ann Simmons, his sweetheart when he was fifteen.
14–15 *I have a friend . . . abruptly*: The friend to whom Lamb behaves ungratefully (like an 'ingrate') is Coleridge's disciple Charles Lloyd (see Romantic Sonnet, p. 428, above), who, we learn from a letter, has been playing the piano in Lamb's lodgings, till 'Lamb's feelings were wrought to too high a pitch' and he left the company abruptly and 'rushed into the Temple [area of the Inns of Court], where [he] was born'.
20–21 *Friend of my bosom . . . dwelling*: This time (though there was about to be a two-year estrangement between them) the friend is Coleridge, with whom Lamb had been at school, and to whom he had turned at the time of his mother's death.
24 *And some are taken from me*: Sad allusion to the absence of Mary, who had suffered a relapse on Christmas Eve, and had to go back into the mental hospital – as she did for some part of almost every year till her death in 1847.

WILLIAM WORDSWORTH

Lucy Poems

(i) *Lucy Gray*

1 *Lucy Gray*: Though many have sought to identify her, Lucy, as she develops in the five original 'Lucy Poems' of 1798–9, is a creation of Wordsworth's imagination. Insofar as she is based on any living person, it is the poet's sister Dorothy, who was his companion in the appallingly cold winter when the poems were written in the German medieval city of Goslar.
9 *Yet you may spy*: You may still see.
21 *hook*: bill-hook. Lucy's father is chopping faggots (bundles) of hazel sticks for firewood.
25 *roe*: smallest of the native English deer.
26 *wanton*: exuberant.
30 *She wandered up and down*: Modelled on *The Babes in the Wood* (quoted for its simplicity and emotional power in the Preface to *Lyrical Ballads*):

> Those pretty babes with hand in hand
> Went wandering up and down;
> But never more they saw the man
> Approaching from the town.

40 *furlong*: 220 yards.

56 *And further there were none*: Surprisingly, Wordsworth's source for the ballad of Lucy Gray is a newspaper story, told him by Dorothy, of a child who fell into a canal near Halifax. Looking back, he was proud of the way he had 'spiritualized' the incident, and contrasted it with Crabbe's matter-of-fact style in treating similar material.

(ii) *Strange Fits of Passion I have Known*

16 *All over the wide lea*: All the way across the wide meadow.
19–20 *my eyes . . . descending moon*: Compare the boat-stealing episode of *The Prelude* (Ennobling Interchange, pp. 271–2, above) for the exactly opposite effect: as the child rows *away* from the shore, a mountain *rises* above the near ridge. In each case the viewer is betrayed into disturbing imaginative experience by the intensity of his gaze.
25 *fond*: 'foolish', as well as 'affectionate'.

(iii) *She Dwelt Among the Untrodden Ways*

2 *Dove*: The River Dove in the Peak District of Derbyshire.

(iv) *A Slumber Did My Spirit Seal*

5 *No motion has she now*: Coleridge regarded *A Slumber* as 'a most sublime epitaph', and commented that 'in some gloomier moment' Wordsworth had probably 'fancied the moment in which his sister might die'. *A Slumber* seems to have been written originally as the two closing stanzas of *She Dwelt Among the Untrodden Ways*, hence the use of 'She' in l. 3 where we expect the name Lucy.

(v) *Three Years She Grew*

Title *Three Years She Grew*: Last of the original 1798–9 Lucy Poems. *She Was a Phantom of Delight* (Poets in Relationship, pp. 709–10, above), often thought of as part of the group, belongs to 1804.
8 *impulse*: stimulus, inspiration.
16 *breathing balm*: soothing influence; cf. *Paradise Lost* II 400–402, 'the soft delicious air . . . Shall *breathe* her *balm*.'
18 *insensate*: inanimate.
37–9 *the work was done . . . She died*: It comes as a shock to learn that Nature's claiming of her 'lady' has been a euphemism for death. The poem gives to Lucy the life she never had – a life purely of the poet's imagination.

THOMAS CAMPBELL

Hohenlinden

5–8 *But Linden saw . . . scenery*: Campbell was in Germany (but not as close as is sometimes said to the battle) when on 3 December 1800 the French, under Moreau, defeated the Austrians at Hohenlinden.
31–2 *And every turf . . . sepulchre*: A story is told of Campbell's crossing

the battlefield by coach, and the driver's stopping to cut off the tails of the dead horses.

ROBERT SOUTHEY

The Inchcape Rock

9–12 *The Abbot . . . rung*: Southey bases his poem on a tradition recorded by John Stoddart in his *Remarks on Local Scenery and Manners in Scotland* (1801).

WILLIAM BLAKE

And Did Those Feet

8 *mills*: factories.
13 *mental fight*: spiritual warfare on behalf of imagination: Blake's famous lyric comes from the Preface to his Prophetic Book, *Milton*, where he speaks of 'hirelings in the Camp, the Court, the University, who would, if they could, for ever depress mental, and prolong corporeal war'.

WALTER SCOTT

Lochinvar

6 *Lochinvar*: Sung to the harp by Lady Heron in *Marmion*, Scott's immensely successful poem is about the Battle of Flodden, 1513.
16 *craven*: cowardly.
20 *Solway*: An arm of the sea dividing Cumbria in England from Dumfriesshire in Scotland.
22 *lead but one measure*: dance a single last dance.
32 *galliard*: swift-moving dance.
39 *croup*: horse's rump.
40 *before her*: in front of her.
41 *scar*: crag.

THOMAS MOORE

Oh! Blame Not the Bard (1810)

6 *dart*: arrow.
9 *his country*: Ireland (Erin); Moore was born and brought up in Dublin, and went to Trinity College, arriving in London aged twenty in 1799.
10 *that spirit is broken . . . bend*: Though not an activist himself, Moore had known Robert Emmet, executed for his part in the 1798 uprising.
15 *way*: path – it is of course a flaming torch.
23–4 *the myrtle . . . cover his sword*: Harmodius, who died trying to kill the tyrant

Hippias in 514 BC, is said to have disguised his sword in myrtles (associated for Moore at present only with his 'wreath' as love-poet).

LORD BYRON

'Revelry by Night' (from *Childe Harold* III)

136 *Self-exiled Harold . . . again*: Following Byron's travels in the Mediterranean, 1810–11, *Childe Harold* I–II had been published in 1812, with immediate success. Harold 'wanders forth again' in April 1816, defiantly proclaiming himself 'self-exiled', though failure of his marriage, scandal over his relationship with his half-sister, and (worst of all) large debts, would have made it difficult for Byron to stay in England.
153 *king-making victory*: Rather than literally 'making' kings, victory at Waterloo made safe the monarchies restored after Napoleon's original surrender in 1814, and exile to Elba.
158 *the Eagle*: the French standard.
160 *banded nations*: Waterloo was a victory for the British and Prussian armies, but nations 'banded' against France since the declaration of war in 1793 had included Austria, Russia, Sweden, Portugal, the Ottoman Empire, and a number of German and Italian princedoms.
162 *He*: A reference to Ambition in the previous line, which could as well be a reference to Napoleon.
191 *Or the car rattling*: carriage, clattering over cobbled streets.
200 *Brunswick's fated Chieftain*: The Duke of Brunswick, whose father (Prussian Commander-in-Chief, and author of the monstrous Brunswick Manifesto, 1792) had been killed at Jena in 1806, and who was himself to die at Waterloo. Closely connected with the English royal house of Hanover, the Brunswicks stood for nothing very good, but Byron is moved by the father–son deaths in battle.
227 *Albyn's hills*: Scotland (Byron's imagination is stirred by a Scottish childhood).
228 *her Saxon foes*: The English, against whom the Scots (now fighting in the British army) have fought within living memory in the 1745 Jacobite Rebellion.
229 *pibroch*: bagpipe-music.
234 *Evan's, Donald's*: Heroic leaders of the Cameron clan: Evan who fought for Charles II against Cromwell in 1650, and his grandson, who took the part of Charles Edward Stuart in the equally doomed '45 Rebellion.
252 *blent*: blended.

JOHN KEATS

To Autumn

11 *clammy cells*: sticky 'cells' of the honeycomb.
12 *store*: abundance, plenty.
15 *winnowing wind*: current of air used to blow chaff from the grain after threshing.
17 *hook*: reaping-hook, sickle.

18 *swath*: swathe, uncut corn that is in reach of the reaper's hook.
19 *like a gleaner*: Keats personifies autumn as a villager who has gathered heads of grain, left behind in the harvest-field, and is bringing the bundle home to make flour in the winter.
28 *sallows*: Gray-leaved bushes of the willow family, found near water.
32 *garden-croft*: Small piece of agricultural land attached to house or cottage.
33 *And gathering swallows . . . skies*: Swallows gather in September (Keats is writing on the 19th) before their long migration to North Africa.

PERCY BYSSHE SHELLEY

To a Skylark (1820)

22 *that silver sphere*: the moon.
55 *heavy-wingéd thieves*: the winds (who have 'stolen' the scent of the rose).
61 *sprite*: The old, Miltonic, spelling of 'spirit', useful to later poets as a monosyllable.
66 *Chorus hymeneal*: wedding-song.

JOHN CLARE

The Shepherd's Calendar

114–15 *Hawkweed . . . seedy crowns*: Hawkweed and groundsel (ragwort) have airborne seeds with fluffy canopies to catch the wind.

FELICIA HEMANS

Casabianca

1 *The boy . . . burning deck*: Probably the most famous line in British nineteenth-century poetry – though few would know that the boy was son of the Corsican naval commander, Louis Casabianca, killed at the battle of Aboukir Bay in 1798.
19 *but*: only.

LETITIA ELIZABETH LANDON

Lines of Life

37–8 *And one fear . . . dread*: After a glittering career as poet, novelist and editor of literary journals, Landon was brought down not by ridicule but by gossip. A story was spread that she had had an abortion. Fearing to compromise her fiancé (Dickens' future biographer, John Roberts), she broke off their engagement. To get away from London, she then married the Governor of the Gold Coast, dying three months later from an overdose of prussic acid. Probably she killed herself.
39–40 *A sword . . . o'er the head*: A reference to the courtier, Damocles, whose

fulsome praise of Dionysus the First led to his being symbolically feasted, while a sword hung above his head, suspended by a single hair.
61–4 *I think on that . . . tomb*: Death's gloriousness is the Resurrection, leading to Heaven ('eternal fame', 'The sun of earthly gloom').
67 *A step . . . a look*: So little is needed to discredit, unsettle, the 'earthly future' of unsullied reputation, which prefigures the 'more heavenly one'.
69 *Earth's debasing stain*: original sin.
87–8 *although alloyed . . . divine*: The divine creative spark is present in the poet.
94–6 *Say will my charméd . . . words*: Will the inspired (charmed) music of my verse wake to the dawn of posthumous fame?
103 *From many an antique scroll beside*: From many other ancient books.

II. Narratives of Love

MARY ROBINSON

from *Sappho and Phaon*

Headnote *The story of the Lesbian muse*: Most famous of women poets ('muses'), Sappho was born in the mid seventh century BC on the Greek island of Lesbos. She married early and had a daughter, but later built up a following of young women drawn to poetry and the worship of Aphrodite.

replete with shades . . . poetess: Ovid, though basing his epistle on the late tradition of Sappho's love for Phaon, makes reference also to the lesbianism found in her work, and in her attachment to the poet Erinna (who died when she was nineteen). Pope in his 1712 translation of Ovid allows himself the couplet: 'No more the Lesbian dames my passion move, / Once the dear objects of my guilty love'; Robinson avoids the 'shades' of homosexuality altogether.
Epigraph *Love taught . . . elegies of woe*: Pope's couplet allows us an autobiographical reading of *Sappho and Phaon*, written near the end of Robinson's increasingly sad relationship with Banastre Tarleton.
2 *fancy's fire*: imagination.
5 *numbers*: metre.
11–14 *devours / driven / bowers / heaven*: Robinson sees herself as reintroducing the Petrarchan sonnet, rejected by Shakespeare but used by Milton: 'It must strike every admirer of poetical compositions that the modern sonnet, concluding with two lines winding up the sentiment of the whole, confines the poet's fancy, and frequently occasions an abrupt termination of a beautiful and interesting picture, and that the ancient (or what is generally denominated the "legitimate") sonnet may be carried on in a series of sketches . . . forming in the whole a complete and connected story.'
15 *coëval with*: as old as.
16–17 *A temple stands . . . To chastity divine!*: the Temple of Diana.
21 *Hours*: classical goddesses of the seasons.
31 *dimpled loves*: cupids.

35 *arbitress of night*: the moon.
Title *Discovers* reveals
46 *my chilled breast*: 'Grief chilled my breast, and stopped my freezing blood', Pope, *Sappho to Phaon* 126.
51 *Now on a bank . . . rest*: cf. Feste's song, 'come away, death, / And in sad cypress let me be laid' (*Twelfth Night* IV ii).
53 *dulcet numbers*: sweet music.
90 *rapt*: ecstatic, carried away.
115 *shaggy tribes of mirth*: laughing satyrs.
119 *lord of lustre*: the sun.
139 *sensate*: feeling, sensual.
154 *visionary theme*: delusion.
155 *tesselated pavement*: mosaic.
164 *citrons*: lemons.
172 *chrysolite*: yellow semi-precious stone.
176 *woodbine*: convolvulus, morning glory.
179 *glossy myrtle*: plant with glossy dark-green leaves sacred to Venus.
183–4 *Eolian harp . . . thy strings*: wind harp (placed in a window-frame so as to catch the breeze); for Coleridge an image of the breath of God playing over the strings of Nature.
189 *lorn philomel*: forlorn nightingale.
191 *ether*: substance held by Newton to permeate all space.
198 *To strew the bank where Phaon wakes from rest*: cf. Milton, *Lycidas* 151, 'To strew the laureate hearse where Lycid lies'.
202 *cassia*: cinnamon.
205 *porphyry*: red rock, quarried in Egypt.
482 *black Erebus*: place of darkness between Earth and Hades.
485–7 *'Farewell, my Lesbian love . . . oh Lesbian maid'*: Robinson credits ll. 485 and 487 of her sonnet to Pope (*Sappho to Phaon*, lines 113–14) and points again to Ovid in the background.
491 *Sicilian maids*: Sappho has followed the treacherous Phaon to Sicily.
497 *desert*: wilderness (not always sandy).
505 *mansion of the dead*: the grave.
513 *the Elysian shore*: Elysium, the classical Heaven (as opposed to Hades).
515 *While (doomed . . . no more)*: Pope, *Epistle to Miss Blount* with the works of Voiture (1712), 57–8:

> But, Madam, if the Fates withstand, and you
> Are destined Hymen's willing victim too . . .

528 *Fates*: The goddesses Clotho, Lachesis and Atropos who governed the course of human life.
530 *Lethe*: River of Hades whose waters produced in those who drank forgetfulness of the past.
533 *Aonian maids*: Mounts Olympus and Helicon, associated with the Muses, were both in Aonia (part of Boeotia).
536 *Erato*: 'the lovely one', seventh of the nine Muses, associated with erotic poetry.

the trophies: memorials.
537 *Parian marble*: Special marble from the isle of Paros.
545 *pearls of pity*: tears.
551 *the Leucadian deep*: Sappho's thoughts lure her towards the 2,000-foot cliff on the island of Leuca.
554 *mystic visions*: unearthly apparitions.
558 *phalanx*: company, band (normally used of troops).
563 *the blast yells*: the wind blows loud.
571–2 *the sportive kind / That nip the turf*: birds that fly low over the grass?
574 *prune the painted crest*: preen the colourful crest.
unction: spiritual comfort.
583 *barbarous ire*: cruel anger.
587 *To Phoebus only will I tune my lyre*: If she survives her suicide leap, Sappho will dedicate her life solely to Apollo, god of poetry.
588 *'What suits . . . with thee'*: Borrowed, with acknowledgement, from Pope, *Sappho to Phaon* l. 216. Ovid once more is in the background.
596 *concave*: sky.
599 *the waves Lethean*: the waters of oblivion.
604 *humid*: tearful.
605–6 *Bids the light sylph . . . to bind*: fancy is to cease trying to slow down time with her capricious and transient imaginings.

WILLIAM WORDSWORTH

The Ruined Cottage

79 *Of human passion*: Wordsworth accepts that the poet's elegies are 'pathetic fallacy' (rocks cannot mourn), but values them nonetheless as expressions of human imagination prompted by emotion.
91 *The useless fragment of a wooden bowl*: The broken bowl at Margaret's well brings back to the level of ordinary life the great final image of Ecclesiastes: 'Or ever the silver cord be loosed, or the golden bowl be broken, or the pitcher be broken at the fountain . . .'
98 *passenger*: passer-by.
140 *raiment*: clothing.
144 *And their place knew them not*: cf. Job 7.10: 'He shall return no more to his house, neither shall his place know him any more.'
159 *kite*: Large fork-tailed hawk, once common in England; now successfully reintroduced in Oxfordshire.
269 *Of soldiers going to a distant land*: Robert has accepted the 'bounty' of three guineas paid to men who enlisted in the army.
295 *"trotting brooks"*: A quotation from Burns' *Epistle to William Simpson*. Wordsworth admired Burns, and saw him as his predecessor in writing a poetry of ordinary life and deep-felt emotion.
379 *Her voice was low*: A recollection of Lear's words over the dying Cordelia in the last scene of the play: 'Her voice was ever soft, / Gentle and low, an excellent thing in woman.'

403 *Was comfortless*: A line that Wordsworth never completed.
413–14 *that poverty and grief . . . nearer to her*: To an extraordinary extent the story of Margaret and her feelings is told through her surroundings. Poverty and grief are deduced from her failure to preserve the 'bond of brotherhood' that has existed between the inhabitants of her cottage and an active, but oblivious, Nature.
446 *tract*: region.
446–92 *Five tedious years . . . ruined walls*: Wordsworth's account of Margaret's final years and death was the first part of *The Ruined Cottage* to be written. He was prompted to start work by Southey's vignette of a war widow in the epic poem, *Joan of Arc* (1796):

> At her cottage door
> The wretched one shall sit, and with dim eye
> Gaze o'er the plain, where on his parting steps
> Her last look hung. Nor ever shall she know
> Her husband dead, but tortured with vain hope
> Gaze on . . .

No doubt he had also in mind a particular ruined cottage in the countryside near Racedown in Dorset, where he and Dorothy were living in early summer 1797.
458 *green-sward*: grass.
464 *mendicant*: beggar.
502–6 *traced with milder interest . . . still survived*: The listening poet now is able to perceive the 'secret spirit of humanity' perceptible only to the Pedlar ('I see around me here / Things which you cannot see') at the beginning of the poem.

SAMUEL TAYLOR COLERIDGE

Love

14 *The statue . . . knight*: The knight's statue connects Coleridge's poem with the home of Mary Hutchinson (Wordsworth's future wife) at Stockton-on-Tees, where in November 1799 he fell in love with Mary's young sister, Sara. The poem may thus be seen as a story on three levels: Coleridge woos Sara, by telling her of a minstrel who woos Genevieve, by telling her of a knight who woos the Lady of the Land (see ll. 33–6, below).
95–6 *And so I won . . . bride*: There is an element of wish-fulfilment in these final lines. Coleridge was, and remained (though his passion for Sara lasted ten years and more) a married man. There could be no happy ending to his personal love-story.

WILLIAM BLAKE

(i) *The Crystal Cabinet*

1–4 *The maiden caught me . . . key*: Blake, in the traditional metaphor, is 'captivated', falls in love.
7 *And within it opens into a world*: Love is the entrance to another world where everything seems to be transformed.
15 *Threefold*: Threefold vision, for Blake, is more intense than ordinary imaginative experience, but short of fourfold perfection. It is associated with the land of Beulah, which is feminine, 'moony', not as strenuous as fourfold Eden.
21 *I strove to seize the inmost form*: The poet attempts to go beyond the kiss to an ultimate perfection, but only bursts the cabinet of love. On one level the imagery is sexual, on another it concerns the search for an absolute.

(ii) *The Mental Traveller*

2 *A land of men, and women too*: The fallen world is symbolized for Blake by sexual division: in eternity there would be oneness.
10 *He's given to a woman old*: The 'woman old' is a version of Tirzah, who in Blake's major Prophetic Books (*Vala*, *Milton*, *Jerusalem*) consistently uses cruelty to dominate the male.
12 *cups of gold*: cf. the Scarlet Woman of Revelation with her 'golden cup . . . full of abomination'.
14–16 *She pierces . . . cold and heat*: Crucifixion, which releases the spirit of Christ, here binds the victim down to an earthly existence, makes him a part of the fallen day-to-day world.
20 *And she grows young as he grows old*: Only *The Mental Traveller* shows the sexes in this way feeding on each other.
23–4 *Then he rends up . . . delight*: Orc (representing energy, sexual drives, at times revolution) similarly breaks free from his chains at puberty and ravishes his 'mother' (the nameless female) in *Vala*. It is not difficult to offer a Freudian reading.
29 *agéd shadow*: The female has drained his energies.
37–40 *They are his meat . . . his door*: It is not clear what connection there is between the shadowy male's hospitality to wayfarers and his feeding on human pains.
41–4 *His grief . . . does spring*: The female seems to be reborn in the 'eternal joy' of the travellers' pleasure over the grief of their host.
48 *Or wrap her in his swaddling-band*: To swaddle the child would be to dominate, and the female in this poem is never dominated.
62 *For the eye . . . alters all*: Blake's line amounts to a definition of the transforming of Romantic imagination, but as in *The Crystal Cabinet*, above, it is love (however defined) that alters perception.
64 *the flat earth becomes a ball*: Earth is flat or round according to one's 'eye' – not according to one's belief.
78 *Her fear plants many a thicket wild*: Lovers' moods plant not merely 'thickets', but the entire desert.
87 *many a lover*: As the lovers suddenly become numerous Blake offers an interlude

in the cyclical pattern, which allows of peace and civilization. The 'babe', however, is bound to be reborn, and the horrors will start again.

MARY TIGHE

'A Glimpse of Love'

144 *gale*: breeze
149 *Hours*: goddesses of seasonal change and fulfilment.
154–62 *And in the grassy centre . . . each from other stray*: Many poets of the Romantic period experimented with Spenserian stanzas, but only Tighe is at ease in this allegorical mode.
185–8 *And all its banks . . . ever new*: Lines that Keats clearly had in mind as he wrote in *Ode to a Grecian Urn* of the sacrificial heifer, 'her silken flanks with garlands dressed', the piper forever piping songs 'forever new', and the lover who (like Tighe's young Desire) 'enchanted ever stands'. It is scarcely to Keats' credit that he had written at Christmas 1818 of having grown out of Tighe, and of having decided in general to have no more to do with women 'unless they are handsome'.
190–91 *But not to mortals . . . current bright*: Psyche is mortal, becoming a goddess finally in her marriage to Cupid.
205 *Psyche's punishment*: In her mortal beauty, Psyche has roused the jealousy of Venus, goddess of Love, and mother of Cupid.
206 *From either stream . . . filled*: At each of the two streams he filled an amber vase.
225 *lucid*: translucent, 'see-through'.
231 *the coral gates . . . sweet cell*: Lips are seen as 'coral gates' of the 'cell' (chamber) of the mouth.
252 *breathed celestial air*: returned to Heaven.
261 *owns*: admits.
263 *Still*: ever, always.
268 *dole*: gift
276 *transport*: Psyche is pleasurably 'carried-away' – in an ecstasy.

THOMAS CAMPBELL

Gertrude of Wyoming II

2 *Albert's home*: Scottish by birth, Albert has been forced by poverty to emigrate, and settled in a small colony in Wyoming, Pennsylvania, scene in 1778 of the massacre that brings sadness to the end of Campbell's poem.
20 *Aurora's hills*: eastern hills (hills of the dawn).
32 *Hebe*: Goddess of eternal youth, daughter of Zeus and Hera.
41–2 *when years . . . woman's zone*: when she became a woman (literally, put on the girdle, 'zone', symbolic of virginity).
76 *India's sons*: Indian tribes of North America.
83 *His arms*: Those of the Great Spirit (Campbell probably refers to the American aloe, agave, not the unrelated European plant, source of a purgative drug).

114 *Uplift on*: Lifted up towards.
122 *Nor joyless . . . understood*: Not unhappy at the conversation that seemed to be taking place.
133 *Ausonia*: Poetic name for Italy.
139 *cacique*: Indian chief.
149 *by report*: from what you say.
184 *perfected*: Stressed on the first syllable.
188 *my poor guide*: Chief Outalissi of the Oneyda Indians, who has rescued the child from the Hurons.
203 *There if, oh gentle love . . . aright*: It is the poet speaking.
216 *Coromandel*: Bay of Bengal.
223 *the Hymenean moon*: Moon that presides over the marriage-bed – like the god Hymen.

LORD BYRON

The Bride of Abydos

491 *Zuleika* . . . motionless / stood: Zuleika (whose father, the Giaffir, is about to marry her off to a suitor she has never seen) is on the seashore with her lover Selim. Selim has just told her (i) that he is not her brother, but the son of Abdallah, her father's brother; (ii) that Abdallah has been poisoned by the Giaffir; (iii) that Selim, brought up by the Giaffir as a weakling, is the charismatic leader of a pirate band. In her stillness Zuleika resembles Niobe, turned to stone after her boastfulness had led to the deaths of the six sons and six daughters on whom she prided herself.
499 *wicket-porch*: small sheltered door within the garden's larger entry.
502 *Oh fly . . . brother*: Oh fly, no more [my brother] yet now my more than brother.
513 *'Tis come . . . soon past*: death.
550 *the foremost breakers lave*: are washed by the nearest waves.
565–6 *that fatal gaze . . . chain*: The backward look (fatal to the quest of Orpheus) dooms Selim to be killed or captured.
582 *choked the tone*: stifled the noise.
595 *capote*: cloak.
601 *Sigaeum's steep*: Cape Janissary in the Dardanelles, near which Byron (and Major Ekenhead) swam the Hellespont on 3 May 1810.
602 *Lemnos' shore*: Mountainous island near the Dardanelles, sacred to Vulcan.
603–10 *The sea-birds . . . wave*: Galt recalls that while his ship, the *Salsette*, was off the Dardanelles in 1810, Byron 'saw the body of a man who had been executed . . . floating on the stream to and fro with the trembling of the water, which gave to its arms the effect of scaring away several sea-fowl that were hovering to devour.'
616–17 *Had bled . . . Had seen*: That would have bled . . . That would have seen.
618 *turban-stone*: Carved above Turkish graves.
621 *Helle's stream*: the Hellespont.
627 *The loud wull-wulley*: Turkish lament over the dead.

PERCY BYSSHE SHELLEY

Alastor

153 *Her voice . . . own soul*: Shelley commented in his essay, *On Love* (written in July 1818, after finishing his translation of Plato's *Symposium*), 'there is something within us which, from the instant that we live and move thirsts after its own likeness'. This central vision of *Alastor* shows the Poet creating in dream, and falling in love with, his 'epipsyche', his soul-mate.
163 *wild numbers*: melodies.
168 *an ineffable tale*: one too great for words.
189 *Involved*: enwrapped, enfolded.
194 *garish*: bright (with implication of drawing attention to themselves).
205–7 *He eagerly pursues . . . bounds*: Having created in his dream soul-mate an ideal, the Poet dies questing for a 'prototype of his conception' (Preface, above) – the human original who could not exist.
209–10 *for ever lost . . . sleep*: Shelley has in mind Belial's vision of death in *Paradise Lost* Book II, as being 'swallowed up and lost / In the wide womb of uncreated night'.
221 *insatiate hope*: The unsatisfied ('insatiable'?) hope that in death he may be reunited with the soul-mate of his dream.

JAMES LEIGH HUNT

Paulo and Francesca

483 *Francesca loved*: Hunt derives the episode of Paulo and Francesca from Dante's *Inferno*, regarding it as 'the most cordial and refreshing one in the whole of that singular poem' (Preface). Francesca, daughter of the Count of Ravenna, is to be married to the Prince of Rimini. Her father intrigues to have Rimini's handsome younger brother Paulo sent to claim the bride in place of the Prince, whom she has never seen. At the point, in Canto III, where the excerpt takes up, Francesca is married to the stern and moody elder brother; Paulo, meanwhile, has become aware of her feelings towards him, and fallen in love himself.
496–9 *The gardeners . . . beauty hovered*: Hunt prided himself in his use of the heroic couplet on recurring 'to a freer spirit of versification'. 'Pope and the French school' he saw as having 'mistaken mere smoothness for harmony', and having known 'the least on the subject, of any poets perhaps that ever wrote'. Along with his views on versification went a Wordsworthian belief that 'the proper language of poetry is in fact nothing different from that of real life.' (Preface)
522 *some tree of knowledge*: A tree comparable to the Forbidden Tree of Genesis and *Paradise Lost*, but giving knowledge, not of life and death, good and evil, but of Nature 'primitive and free'.
554 *closing feet*: feet tensed in the action of springing.
560 *inmate*: member of a household.
564 *Queen Genevra*: Guinevere, wife of King Arthur.

THOMAS MOORE

The Fire Worshippers

201 *She . . . loves*: The story of the Fire-Worshippers is told by the minstrel Feramorz to the Princess, Lalla Rookh, daughter of the Indian Emperor, Aurungzebe, who is to marry the King of Bucharia. On their journey they approach the Holy Valley in the minstrel's native Cashmire, and pass the remains of an ancient fire-temple, built by Ghebers who had fled from Persia after the Arab invasion of their country.
212 *kanoon*: Middle Eastern stringed instrument.
224 *in obeisance cast*: bowing to her.
240 *the Day-God*: the sun.
331 *falchion*: sabre.
334 *haram-hours*: hours of relaxation.
351 *Ghebers*: Zoroastrian fire-worshippers, the ancient inhabitants of Persia.
420 *charnel meteors*: lights sent up to mark a burial at sea.

JOHN KEATS

The Eve of St Agnes

1 *ah, bitter chill it was*: St Agnes, fourth-century martyr, and patron saint of virgins, was celebrated on 21 January (regarded as the coldest day of the year).
17–18 *his weak spirit . . . mails*: The kneeling statues, with their 'icy hoods and mails' (armour) are carved in stone.
27 *for sinners' sake to grieve*: Keats sites his romance in a pseudo-medieval Roman Catholic past; the Beadsman is paid to pray ('tell his beads') either for the souls of the living owners of the castle, or, more probably, for those of their dead forebears.
37 *the argent revelry*: The revellers take on the silver ('argent') quality of the trumpets of st. 4.
46–54 *They told her . . . all that they desire*: It was said that if they did everything right virgins would dream of their future husbands. To 'make the *legend* more intelligible', Keats inserted a stanza at this point in revision (but later chose not to print it):

> 'Twas said her future lord would there appear
> Offering as sacrifice – all in the dream –
> Delicious food, even to her lips brought near:
> Viands and wine and fruit and sugared cream,
> To touch her palate with the fine extreme
> Of relish – then to wake again
> Warm in the virgin morn, no weeping Magdalen.

70 *all amort*: 'dead' to all save St Agnes.
71 *St Agnes and her lambs unshorn*: Two white unshorn lambs were presented on

the saint's day at the altar of St Agnes' Basilica in Rome. Their wool was then woven by nuns into a sacred vestment.
86–8 *Hyena foemen . . . his lineage*: Keats writes with the feuds of *Romeo and Juliet* in mind, but his poetry is extravagent, Gothic at times.
105 *Gossip*: Familiar medieval endearment (originally meaning 'godparent').
108 *bier*: Stand on which a coffin is carried to the grave.
117 *St Agnes' wool are weaving piously*: see note to st. 8, l. 17n above.
124 *conjuror*: magician.
126 *mickle*: much, plenty of.
130 *riddle-book*: book of magic.
171 *Since Merlin . . . monstrous debt!*: A reference to Merlin's imprisonment by the Lady of the Lake. There had been two recent editions of Malory, one of which Keats owned.
173 *cates*: delicacies.
174 *tambour-frame*: embroidery frame.
179–80 *Ah! thou must needs . . . the dead*: Angela is aiding a seduction and endangering her soul. At the Day of Judgement the dead will rise from their graves to be rewarded, or punished, for their earthly lives. No one will be overlooked.
185 *fright of dim espial*: fear caused by poor sight.
188 *amain*: extremely.
189 *agues*: fevers.
193 *like a missioned spirit*: as if she were an angel, or spirit, on a mission.
198 *frayed*: frightened.
203 *No uttered syllable . . . betide*: The spell would be broken if she spoke.
216 *A shielded scutcheon . . . kings*: The coat-of-arms blushes because it is blood-red ('gules' in heraldic terms), and at the same time reveals the family's royal connections.
222 *glory*: an aureole, or halo.
237 *poppied*: Sleep overcomes her like an opiate.
241 *Clasped like a missal . . . pray*: Muslims at prayer leave the Christian mass-book clasped and unopened.
268 *Manna*: Thought of by Keats as Syrian fruit (rather than the food supplied by God to the children of Israel).
277 *eremite*: hermit, worshipper.
288 *woofèd*: woven.
292 *La Belle Dame Sans Mercy*: The title of a medieval poem; Keats' own work of the same name was written soon after *The Eve of St Agnes*.
335 *vassal*: retainer.
336 *Thy beauty's shield . . . dyed*: As Madeline's heart-shaped, blood-coloured ('vermeil dyed') shield, Porphyro seems half-way between heraldry and life.
344 *Of haggard seeming . . . indeed!*: seeming wild, but in fact a help.
346 *bloated wassaillers*: Compare *Hamlet* where 'the bloat King', Claudius, 'keeps wassail' as he drains his draughts of Rhenish down' (I iv).
353 *dragons*: Keats enjoys his Gothic extravagence, and does not encourage literal-minded reading. The dragons, after all, exist in 'an elfin-storm from faery land'.
358 *arras*: tapestry.
366 *an inmate owns*: recognizes a member of the household.

377 *avés*: Hail Marys – prayers to the Virgin Mary 'told' by the Beadsman as his fingers moved day after day round the beads of his rosary.

LORD BYRON

Juan and Haidee

881 *in his damp trance*: Juan has been shipwrecked and cast up alone on a Greek island, one of the Cyclades, see below.
988 *your recent poets*: Wordsworth and the Lake School doubtless.
999 *sole*: single survivor.
1000 *piastres*: Spanish silver coins, 'pieces of eight'.
1002 *Like Peter*: 'And Jesus, walking by the sea of Galilee, saw two brethren, Simon called Peter and Andrew his brother, casting a net into the sea; for they were fishers. And he said unto them, "Follow me, and I will make you fishers of men." ' (Matthew 4.19)
1005 *confiscated*: Stressed on the second syllable.
1006 *dished*: served up.
1014 *sad*: morose, gloomy.
1031–2 *As far as in . . . white a skin*: 'I was a stranger, and ye took me in', Matthew 25.35.
1037 *nous*: gumption, intelligence.
1048 *St Paul . . . given*: For Paul's famous celebration of charity, see I Corinthians 13.1–13.
1057 *pelisse*: fur cloak or mantle.
1073 *maid*: maiden (Haidee).
1096 *Narrative*: *A Narrative of the Honourable John Byron, Commodore in a Late Expedition Round the World*, 1768. Commodore Byron and his sailors suffered especially off the coast of Patagonia.
1119–20 *when coffined . . . four*: when you die, aged eighty, engrave on the coffin-plate that you got up at four in the morning.
1132 *Aurora*: dawn.
1153 *victual*: food (pronounced 'vittle').
1160 *Scio*: Turkish island, north-west of Samos.
1170 *hectic*: flush.
1182 *callow*: downy, unfledged.
1197 *pose*: nonplus, baffle.
1351 *Ceres . . . Bacchus* Roman goddess of the harvest and the god of wine.
1360 *Neptune, Pan, or Joves* of the sea, of pastoral life, and of the sky respectively.
1385 *moon*: month.
1389 *prows*: ships.
1391 *Io*: Io, priestess of Hera, was loved by Zeus, who for safety's sake turned her into a heifer, in which form she wandered from country to country plagued by a gadfly that Hera had set on her. In one tradition she is kidnapped by Phoenicians.
1392 *three Ragusan vessels*: Ships from Ragusa, a region of Dalmatia, which traded with Turkey and the eastern Mediterranean.
1400 *kept in garrison*: protected by troops.

1509 *tongues*: languages.
1542 *the Stygian river*: The Styx, over which souls were ferried to the ancient Underworld (Byron's conflation of Christian and Pagan would not have amused his more moral critics).
1555 *fast*: firm.
226 *their siesta took*: Lambro has been long at sea; Haidee has given up concealment and moved her lover from the beach to the house.
319 *lock*: pistol.
328 *more Irish . . . nice*: more fearful, and less fastidious about points of honour?
333 *fatal*: destined (perhaps also 'deadly').
339 *championed*: conquered.
341 *compeers*: partners (men of the same race?).
343 *fairer mark*: better target.
365 *this desolation*: Haidee and Juan have transformed Lambro's austere hall into a place of beauty and feasting, with ivory-inlaid table and satin carpets of crimson and pale blue.
376 *the Frank*: one from the western Mediterranean.
378–9 *while compressed . . . crew*: while *she was* compressed . . . the crew interposed.
398 *galliots*: small fast-sailing galleys.

LETITIA ELIZABETH LANDON

The Indian Bride

14 *Camdeo*: Hindu god of love.
51 *scimitar*: curving single-edged, oriental sword.
56 *atabal*: kettledrum, or tabour.
66 *mandore*: mandolin, lute.

FELICIA HEMANS

Arabella Stuart (*Records of Woman*)

3 *the greenwood-tree*: cf. Amiens' song, 'Under the greenwood tree / Who loves to lie with me' (*As You Like It* II v).
45 *and thou . . . bonds*: Seymour was in the Tower of London.
46–51 *there is one hopeless lot . . . beautiful*: 'Wheresoever you are, or in what state soever you be, it sufficeth me you are mine', writes Arabella Stuart to her husband: 'Rachel wept, and would not be comforted, because her children were no more. And that, indeed, is the remediless sorrow, and none else!' (Hemans)
57 *Could I bear on*: sail on – go on living.
63 Cf. among many biblical parallels, 1 Thessalonians 5.6, 'Therefore let us not sleep as do others, but let us watch'. Hemans is unlikely to know the final words of Coleridge's *The Watchman*, 'O Watchman, thou hast watched in vain.'
65–6 *Thou hast sent . . . thee*: Though imprisoned separately, Arabella and Seymour formed a plan to escape.

87 *from terror*: free from terror.
104 *The dark links . . . again*: the 'chains' of captivity close again.
105–11 *Upon the deck . . . foes*: Arabella's vessel was captured off Calais by a ship which she at first hoped was carrying Seymour to safety. Seymour reached Flanders, but on his own.
111 *What boots it*: What's the profit? (Milton, *Lycidas* 64–5: 'What boots it with uncessant care / To tend the homely slighted shepherd's trade'.)
135 *the stricken deer*: 'I was a stricken deer that left the herd' (Cowper, *Task* III, 108).
160 *proved*: tested. For some reason Hemans in *Records of Woman* offers no stanza number at this point, or in the remaining 100 lines of her poem.
200–203 *Death . . . held no cure*: as if I could not take the law into my own hands (commit suicide).
211 *For human line . . . profound*: too deep by far to be plumbed by a human line.
221–22 *a token sent . . . from home*: Peace is sent to Arabella 'the o'erwearied dust' from her 'home' among the dead.

III. Romantic Solitude, Suffering and Endurance

WILLIAM COWPER

Crazy Kate

537–8 *A serving-maid . . . died*: In the background are Desdemona's words to Emilia:

> My mother had a maid called Barbary;
> She was in love; and he she loved proved mad,
> And did forsake her.
>
> *Othello* IV iii

544 *transports*: pleasures.

JOANNA BAILLIE

The Storm-Beat Maid

10 *yell*: Often used of animal noises at this period.
24 *hind*: labourer.
29 *mill*: watermill, which 'clacks' as the waterwheel turns.
55 *in lily kerchief alight*: dressed in a white kerchief (headscarf).
80 *made obeisance meet*: bowed.
91 *sheeted thorn*: Baillie, *Poems* 1790 (published anonymously, and never reprinted)

reads 'sheeted torn', which has no obvious meaning. Amid her natural imagery, 'thorn' would make good sense, referring to the 'sheets' of white flowers on the blackthorn (appropriate to a winter poem), or perhaps the maybush (hawthorn).
105–6 *Reverse . . . forsook*: The blood goes into reverse, deserts his cheek.
127 *thy love's betrayed*: 'thy love betrayed' (*Poems* 1790).
147 *dizened*: bedecked, dressed up.
160 *covert*: shelter.

CHARLOTTE SMITH

The Female Exile

25 *To fair fortune born*: The stranger is a French aristocrat, waiting with her children at Dover. Smith had spent time in France, and welcomed the Revolution, but had sympathy too for its refugees – especially female ones, left (as she herself had been left) to support a family on their own. *The Female Exile* is expanded in 1793 to form *The Emigrants*.
26 *a once hostile soil*: France had taken the side of the American settlers, 1778–83 (and would be at war with England almost continuously, 1793–1815).
33–6 *I would that my fortune . . . no more*: With money held up by the trustees of her father-in-law's will (settlement took thirty-seven years), and only her writing to feed and educate eight remaining children, Smith was genuinely not in a position to help.

WILLIAM BLAKE

Visions of the Daughters of Albion

Argument Synopsis (as prefaced by Milton to the individual Books of *Paradise Lost*).
5–6 *I plucked . . . the vale*: Leutha presides over a 'vale' that is effectively Innocence. In plucking the flower, and rising from the vale, Oothoon passes into Experience.
Visions 1 *Albion*: Traditional name for England; that Albion's 'daughters' should be represented as 'enslaved' shows the influence of Mary Wollstonecraft whom Blake knew at this period.
3 *the soft soul of America, Oothoon*: Oothoon is not a 'character', or portrayal of a human being, but a figure in Blake's personal myth. Her name and story are suggested by *Oi-thona* in MacPherson's 'translation'. In some sense, however, she stands for America, the country that has emancipated itself as she has done (but which paradoxically is a slave-state). Her chief characteristics are that she is pure (because she can give, and could receive, love), and that she is incredulous of male behaviour (embodied chiefly in the self-tormenting Theotormon).
9–10 *the soul of sweet delight . . . away*: A version of Blake's belief that 'every thing that lives is holy', (l. 215 below), and the theme of his poem.
11–12 *I pluck thee . . . breasts*: Blake's illustration shows Oothoon kneeling, her hands on her breasts, kissing the spirit who leaps from the flower. She has, it seems, accepted her own sexuality.

15 *Theotormon's reign*: Apparently the sea; in her new emancipated mood Oothoon is seeking Theotormon.
16 *Bromion rent her with his thunders*: Bromion's appearance is sudden, but it is he who has in the Argument torn Oothoon's 'virgin mantle' in twain. At this early stage in the poem he is seen as god of winds, and Theotormon as god of the waves.
19 *jealous dolphins*: Like the 'black jealous waters' of l. 27, the dolphins express the mood of Theotormon.
20 *Thy soft American plains*: Bromion addresses Theotormon, to whom Oothoon in some sense 'belongs'. The adjective 'soft' allows Oothoon her femininity despite her being seen in Blake's undeveloped political allegory as America.
21 *Stamped . . . children of the sun*: Having 'possessed' Oothoon, Bromion sees himself as the slave-owner, branding African slaves.
27 *the adulterate pair*: Bromion and Oothoon (with the implication that Oothoon is 'married' to Theotormon).
28 *Bound . . . terror and meekness dwell*: Blake's illustration shows Bromion (Terror) and Oothoon (Meekness) literally bound 'back to back'. Bromion's caves are where, like the classical god Aeolus, he keeps his winds.
30 *secret tears*: Theotormon, who is above all a hypocrite, cannot admit his grief.
30–33 *Beneath him . . . summits of the earth*: Blake's powerful imagery brings together slavery, child prostitution, religious hypocrisy and volcanic lust. The thoughts are prompted by Theotormon, but in what sense voices of slaves and children issue *beneath* him it is difficult to say.
40 *The eagles at her call descend*: Blake has in mind the eagle sent daily by Zeus to eat the liver of Prometheus (which grows again each night).
43 *The Daughters of Albion . . . sighs*: Albion's daughters are throughout witnesses of Oothoon's suffering. They too are 'enslaved', subject to male brutality and hypocrisy.
51 *Arise, my Theotormon, I am pure*: Blake's poem, like Hardy's *Tess of the d'Urbervilles*, is the tale of 'a pure woman' whose inner self has not been affected by rape, yet is rejected by a lover who confuses virginity and innocence.
53–7 *They told me that the night . . . erased*: The message of these unnamed authority figures ('They') is that Oothoon is merely human, her mind restricted to the world of the five senses, and her heart (which has been immortal) now merely a physical 'globe'. It is material that Blake will develop into a myth of the Fall in *The Book of Urizen*, 1794.
58 *Instead of morn . . . an eye*: In place of the sun Oothoon now sees an accusing eye.
63–74 *With what sense is it . . . hid of old*: Early Blake has a tendency to lists and not very answerable questions. Oothoon in this passage is preoccupied with instinct and individuality. Her final question draws attention to man's secrecy and unwillingness to reveal his motivation.
78 *Sweetest the fruit . . . feeds on*: Only ripe apples contain a maggot. Oothoon's point is that slight imperfection is enhancing – she is more, not less, from her experience.
80 *our immortal river*: Effectively the river of life, which marks the swan with its 'red earth', but does not impair it.

I bathe my wings: Oothoon is a spiritual existence, and does seem to fly (see her 'winged exulting swift delight', l. 14 above). Here she takes the form (in thought at least) of a white dove.

82–97 *Then Theotormon . . . the envier*: Oothoon in this context has asked questions that show the drift of her thought; Theotormon tends to make things more abstract and complicated.

98–110 *Then Bromion said . . . eternal life*: Bound back to back with Oothoon, and no longer truculent, Bromion too offers a lament.

108 *And is there not one law . . . ox?*: 'One law for the lion and ox is oppression' (*Marriage of Heaven and Hell*, plate 24).

109–10 *And is there not eternal fire . . . eternal life*: And are there not Hell-fire and the chains of restrictive morality to prevent mankind (fallen 'phantoms of existence') from returning to his unfallen eternal state?

114 *Urizen, creator of men*: Blake's first mention of Urizen ('Your reason'), rationalist Zoa (component of the godhead) whose fall from Eternity creates both man and the world as he knows it.

116 *How can one joy absorb another*: Urizen falls because he becomes selfish – 'self-closed, all-repelling' (*Book of Urizen*, plate 3). It is the nature of Eternity to be expansive, generous.

121 *condemns poverty*: condemns people for being poor.

125–6 *the fat-fed hireling . . . wastes*: the recruiting sergeant, who pays labourers to join the army, leaving the land untilled.

128 *the parson claim the labour of the farmer*: The farmer is bound by law to pay tithes (originally 10 per cent of his produce) to the parson.

129 *nets and gins and traps*: Means by which religion 'entraps' mankind.

132–3 *Till she who burns . . . one she loathes*: Carried away with the thought of priesthood as support for Church and State, Oothoon arrives at the theme of enforced marriage.

136–7 *bound to hold a rod . . . shoulders*: bound to aid the husband she loathes in his cruelties.

139–40 *cherubs in the human form . . . meteor*: Compare *London* ll. 15–16 (Romantic Lyric and Song, p. 368, above), where the 'marriage-hearse' is blighted by 'plagues' of venereal disease. Children who might have been 'cherubs' (unfallen, 'angelic') are born into disease and live lives that go by fast as the flash of a meteor.

142 *the impure scourge*: the child of a loveless marriage, grown up to be himself a 'scourge' (persecutor).

149 *fly*: butterfly.

152–3 *Does not the worm . . . hungry grave*: The worm too is doing his thing, fulfilling his nature, and thus creating a 'place of eternity' from death and decay. Every thing that lives is holy.

176 *happy copulation*: 'Virgin fancies' (l. 173), as long as the mind is innocent, extend to thoughts of happy copulation. By contrast, those who repress their feelings, bound by religion, and yielding to desire in secrecy, will be reduced to 'the self-enjoyings of self-denial' (ll. 183–9 below).

182 *the shadows of his curtains*: Beds were curtained to keep out draughts.

187 *Father of Jealousy*: Urizen.

190 *wailing on the margin of non-entity*: A number of Blake's female figures, Enion and Ahania included, find themselves in this forlorn condition on the edge of non-existence.

199 *girls of mild silver, or of furious gold*: Oothoon is demonstrating her freedom from jealousy. Catching girls for her lover does not seem a very feminist activity, but those formed of silver and 'furious' gold are some way from reality.
209 *thy hard furrow*: Oothoon is still addressing Theotorman, as at ll. 204–5.
210 *king of night*: Perhaps the 'kingly lion' of *Little Girl Lost*, 37.

ROBERT SOUTHEY

Mary the Maid of the Inn

16 *address*: manner.
19 *the Abbey*: Southey claimed to have been told the story of Mary the Maid as a schoolboy, about either Furness Abbey or Kirkstall.
46 *charge*: test.

WILLIAM WORDSWORTH

Wordsworthian Solitaries

(i) *Old Man Travelling*

13–14 *the young behold . . . feels*: Drafted as part of the *Old Cumberland Beggar*, *Old Man Travelling* was published in *Lyrical Ballads* 1798 with six additional lines, designed to create narrative interest, but in the process moving away from its Wordsworthian stillness:

> I asked him whither he was bound, and what
> The object of his journey; he replied
> 'Sir, I am going many miles to take
> A last leave of my son, a mariner,
> Who from a sea-fight has been brought to Falmouth,
> And there is dying in an hospital.'

Recognizing their clash with the poem's original intention, Wordsworth in 1815 removed the inserted lines.

(ii) *The Discharged Soldier*

5 *At such a time*: Though incorporating later detail, *The Discharged Soldier* recalls a walk that took place in the Cambridge Long Vacation of 1789 near Wordsworth's old school at Hawkshead, on the western shore of Lake Windermere. Written eight months before *The Prelude* was conceived in its earliest form, Wordsworth's poem became in 1804 the opening section of Book IV.
38 *an uncouth shape*: Wordsworth's use of the word 'shape' links the Soldier to Milton's apocalyptic portrayal of Death at the gates of Hell, *Paradise Lost* II, 666:

The other shape
If shape it might be called that shape had none
Distinguishable in member, joint, or limb . . .

Milton's lines had been illustrated by Fuseli and others, and cited by Burke as, 'dark, uncertain, confused, terrible, and sublime to the last degree'.
51 *ghastly*: 'Like a ghost; having horror in the countenance; pale, dreadful, dismal' (Johnson, *Dictionary*).
99 *Tropic Isles*: The West Indies, where British soldiers died in great numbers during the French War (declared 1793) from yellow fever. Those who survived were dismissed on their return (l. 101), and reduced to beggary, having sold at below face value the vouchers with which they were paid while overseas.
131 *rang a peal*: Wordsworth recalls *Paradise Lost* II, 656, where hell-hounds round the waist of Sin 'rung a hideous peal'.
133–5 *I do not know . . . stream*: A detail that Wordsworth takes (within days of her recording it on 27 January 1798) from his sister's *Journal*: 'The manufacturer's dog makes a strange, uncouth howl, which it continues many minutes after there is no noise near it but that of the brook. It howls at the murmur of the village stream.'

(iii) *The Mad Mother*

4 *She came far . . . main*: To judge from a Wordsworth letter of 1836, the Mad Mother is an English-speaking North American Indian.
48 *He saves . . . precious soul*: The child prevents her from the deadly sin of suicide.
61 *Thy father cares not . . . breast*: Wordsworth claimed that *The Mad Mother* was suggested by 'a lady of Bristol, who had seen the poor creature', but its development of the theme of the cruel father derives from the Scottish ballad, *Lady Anne Bothwell's Lament*:

Bairne, sin thy cruel father is gane,
Thy winsome smiles maun eise my paine;
My babe and I'll together live,
He'll comfort me when cares do grieve:
My babe and I right soft will ly,
And quite forgeit man's cruelty.
Balow, my babe, ly still and sleipe,
It grieves me sair to see thee weepe.

Wordsworth had been separated for five-and-a-half years by the war from Annette Vallon and their daughter, Caroline. Annette was not strictly speaking deserted, but l. 61 (apart from its sensual awareness) may well imply guilt of a kind.
82 *owlet*: full-grown owl.

(iv) *Complaint of a Forsaken Indian Woman*

3 *I heard the northern gleams*: 'I can positively affirm that in still nights I have frequently heard them [the Aurora Borealis] make a rustling and crackling noise, like the waving of a large flag in a fresh gale of wind.' (Hearne)
21 *you might have dragged me on*: Hearne mentions an Indian woman who three

times managed to catch up with her companions, but on the fourth day fell behind and died.

(v) *Michael*

217 *this good household*: The household consists of Michael (a Grasmere shepherd), his wife Isabel, and Luke, child of their old age.
234 *patrimonial fields*: Land inherited from his fathers – Wordsworth commented, when sending a copy of *Lyrical Ballads* to Charles James Fox in January 1801:

> I have attempted to draw a picture of the domestic affections as I know they exist amongst a class of men who are now almost confined to the North of England. They are small independent proprietors of land, here called 'statesmen' – men of respectable education who daily labour on their own little properties. The domestic affections will always be strong amongst men who live in a country [region] not crowded with population, if these men are placed above poverty. But if they are proprietors of small estates which have descended to them from their ancestors, the power which these affections will acquire amongst such men is inconceivable by those who have only had an opportunity of observing hired labourers, farmers, and the manufacturing poor.

267–79 *There's Richard Bateman . . . foreign lands*: 'The story alluded to here is well known in the country [district]. The chapel is called Ings Chapel, and is on the right-hand side of the road leading from Kendal to Ambleside.' (Wordsworth). NB The road having been moved, it is now on the left.
308 *jocund*: happy, joyful.
333 *a sheepfold*: 'It may be proper to inform some readers that a sheepfold in these mountains is an unroofed building of stone walls, with different divisions. It is generally placed by the side of a brook, for the convenience of washing the sheep'. (Wordsworth)
343 *a promise . . . ere thy birth*: Compare Isaac, Samson and John the Baptist, all of them children of their fathers' old age, and promised (by angels) before their birth.
348–52 *After thou . . . upon thee*: Lines valued by Wordsworth for their 'union of imagination and tenderness'.
379 *mould*: earth – from which man is created (in Genesis), and to which he returns in the grave.
450–53 *Meantime Luke . . . evil courses*: For no obvious reason, Wordsworth's most biased statements about city life all belong to 1800; he knew London well, and always enjoyed his visits.

(vi) *The Leech-Gatherer*

43 *Chatterton*: Thomas Chatterton, author of the fake medieval Rowley Poems, who committed suicide aged seventeen in 1770 (the year of Wordsworth's birth), and was for the Romantic period what Keats has since become, a symbol of the talented poet who died young.
45–6 *Of him who . . . mountain's side*: Robert Burns (1759–96), who also died young, and whose poetry Wordsworth from the first admired.
49 *despondency and madness*: A reference to Burns' *Despondency, An Ode* (Romantic

Odes, p. 325, above), but uppermost in Wordsworth's mind is the future of Coleridge, who has just written the early version of *Dejection, An Ode* (*Letter to Sara Hutchinson*, Poets in Relationship, p. 695, above).

50 *peculiar grace*: 'Some I have chosen', God states in *Paradise Lost* III, 183–4, 'of peculiar grace, / Elect above the rest'.

55 *unawares*: A link with *The Ancient Mariner* 284–7: 'A spring of love gusht from my heart, / And I blest them unaware . . .' where the Mariner's sudden awareness of the beauty of the water-snakes is clearly 'a something given'.

56 *The oldest man . . . grey hairs*: An example of *The Leech-Gatherer*'s underlying humour. Wordsworth has been reading Thomson's *Castle of Indolence* (1749), also in Spenserean stanzas and capable of a subtle blending of seriousness with comedy.

64–84 *As a huge stone . . . move at all*: An early draft of *The Leech-Gatherer* shows that the great imaginative images of the stone, sea beast and cloud, are second thoughts. Wordsworth at first was unable to get away from detail and actuality. Dorothy's *Journal* for 3 October 1800 reveals that the man on whom his poem is based had had his skull run over by a cart, and was the survivor of a wife and ten children, all, with one possible exception, dead.

106–7 *He told me . . . gather leeches*: Leeches (apparently now being used again in medical practice) were employed to lower temperature by sucking blood – often within the patient's mouth.

(vii) The London Beggar

594–7 *How often . . . mystery*: Wordsworth enjoyed the bustle and colour of London, but was frightened by the city-dweller's anonymity. It was the antithesis of the sense of community he had felt growing up in the Lake District. Of his return from Cambridge to Hawkshead (where he had been at school) in summer 1788, he had written: 'The face of every neighbour whom I met / Was as a volume to me' (1805 *Prelude*, IV, 58–9).

601 *second-sight*: ghostly; Wordsworth is thinking of Lake District traditions of spectre-horsemen riding over the fells.

607 *far travelled . . . mood*: The poet has both travelled far (in the London streets) while experiencing such a mood, and travelled far into the mood itself.

615–16 *My mind . . . might of waters*: Before the coming of steam power, water-wheels had driven the Industrial Revolution.

622 *As if admonished . . . world*: From the Leech-Gatherer, two years before, Wordsworth had received 'human strength and strong admonishment'; the 'other world' from which the London Beggar admonishes is less comfortable. Writing the autobiographical *Prelude* ('The story of the man and who he was'), the poet is too like him.

SAMUEL TAYLOR COLERIDGE

'Alone, Alone'

(i) *The Ancient Mariner*

The Ancient Mariner is presented below as the pseudo-medieval ballad published in *Lyrical Ballads* 1798, rather than the tidied up version of 1817. It has been lightly repunctuated, but original spellings and capitalization have been retained.

Argument *Line*: Equator.
15 *Loon*: lunatic, fool; 'The devil damn thee black, / thou cream-faced loon!' (*Macbeth* V iii).
19–20 *And listens . . . his will*: Lines written by Wordsworth in the early phase when he and Coleridge were attempting to collaborate on the poem.
47 *freaks*: tricks.
60 *swound*: swoon, trance.
63 *an it were*: as if it were.
65 *biscuit-worms*: weevils out of the 'ship's biscuit' (the sailor's staple food); a homely touch cut in 1817. It is important that the bird receives hospitality, is indeed treated by the mariners as a 'Christian soul' – one of them.
72 *Came to the Marinere's hollo*: Though fed by the sailors in general, the bird comes specifically to the call of the Ancient Mariner.
73 *shroud*: Set of ropes used to support the mast of a sailing ship.
74 *vespers nine*: evening prayers (why *nine* is not clear).
83 *weft*: piece of woven material.
94 *uprist*: uprose.
108–9 *at noon . . . did stand*: The ship is becalmed on the Equator.
124 *Death-fires*: dead-lights, candles set beside a corpse.
125 *witch's oils*: fluid in a witch's cauldron.
131 *drouth*: drought, lack of moisture.
144 *wist*: observed.
149 *unslacked*: unslaked, unquenched.
160 *to work us weal*: to give us help.
176 *gossameres*: spiders' webs.
180 *Pheere*: companion.
184 *charnel crust*: dried scraps of flesh.
189–90 *And she . . . cold*: Revised in 1817 to make clearer and more powerful the concept of life-in-death:

> The Night-mare LIFE-IN-DEATH was she,
> Who thicks man's blood with cold.

With her red lips, yellow hair, and white leprous face, Life-in-Death is a kind of parody of the naturalness of the Bride who paces into the hall 'red as a rose'.
195 *sterte*: started.
201 *clombe*: climbed.

207 *ee*: eye.
218–19 *And thou art . . . Sea-sand*: Lines written by Wordsworth.
234 *eldritch*: hideous.
237 *or*: e'er, before.
259 *main*: sea.
282–3 *The Albatross . . . sea*: Up to this point the end of each successive section has emphasized the Mariner's guilt by rhyming, or associating, Albatross with Cross (on its own, or as part of the word 'cross-bow'). Now, the Cross is no longer mentioned, the Albatross falls and sinks. The Mariner, it seems, has been redeemed by his spontaneous blessing of the water-snakes (earlier seen as 'slimy things'). Yet he never is entirely forgiven his needless taking of life. The penance of retelling his story, reliving his sufferings, will go on and on.
286 *yeven*: given
289 *silly*: foolish; but perhaps with some implication of Anglo-Saxon 'saelig' (medieval 'sely'), holy, blest.
304 *sere*: dry.
306 *fire-flags*: meteors.
311 *sedge*: rushes, reeds.
317 *with never a jag*: with no zig-zagging.
348 *Lavrock*: Correct medieval spelling of 'lark'.
351 *jargoning*: warbling, twittering (the word's original meaning).
375 *n'old*: would not.
388 *The sun . . . mast*: Again a reference to the Equator. As story-teller, Coleridge still has the problem of returning the ship to England.
404 *By him who died on cross*: Coleridge's most explicit association of the Albatross and Christ as victims of man's cruelty. It is important that at ll. 409–10 the bird is said to 'love' the man 'Who shot him with his bow'.
440 *For a charnel-dungeon fitter*: More suited to being in a burial vault.
490 *rood*: cross.
515 *corse*: corpse.
517 *seraph-man*: angel.
527 *Eftsones*: forthwith.
528 *cheer*: hail.
545 *shrieve*: shrive, give absolution; once again Coleridge returns in the final lines of his section to the Albatross, and the Mariner's guilt – still unassuaged.
566 *lag*: persist (when the 'flesh' of the leaves has rotted).
568 *Ivy-tod*: ivy-head.
569 *Owlet*: full-grown owl (which apparently preys on the wolf puppies).
655 *Turned from the bridegroom's door*: Having lived through the Mariner's tale, the Wedding-Guest is himself 'marked' (like Cain), singled out. Turning from the door, he excludes himself from the festivities that symbolize the well-being, and innocence, of the community.

(ii) *Pains of Sleep*

14–15 *But yester-night . . . agony*: Coleridge had been seriously addicted to opium at least since the spring of 1801. *Notebook* entries show that he was subject to appalling nightmares.

THOMAS CAMPBELL

Lord Ullin's Daughter

26 *water-wraith*: water-spirit, more especially one foreboding death.
46 *discover*: perceive.

MARY BRYAN

The Visit

59 *fearful wrecks . . . endured*: An awkward line, suggesting the strain under which the poet writes. She has been ill herself; barely recovered, she has come to the asylum at Castle Ne Roch to visit a friend. The 'wrecks of storms' that threaten her seem at first to be within the mind, but must on second thoughts apply to the inmates themselves (relics of past internal storms), whom she bravely hugs at l. 67.
63 *Insensate*: unaware, not feeling.
85–6 *past a few . . . ripeness*: When there had been a handful of warm days to show that summer was coming.
92 *for one afar*: for an absent friend; separation is a frequent theme of Bryan's poetry.
94 *Withdrawn the gentle force*: when the bough had been released.
96 *marked the while*: paused awhile to observe.
110 *him who wronged her*: Kate, it seems, has been deserted.
113 *fires not their own*: We should remember that the poet's friend, who tells the story of the encounter with mad Kattern, is an inmate herself of the asylum.
120–21 *a glass / Will show thee*: a 'spy-glass' [telescope] that will reveal you.
126 *Each word . . . oh, farewell*: The poet herself speaks the final line of her poem, thanking her friend for the recollection of Kattern.

LORD BYRON

The Prisoner of Chillon

1 *My hair is grey*: Fraņcois de Bonnivard is speaking, who was imprisoned at Chillon 1530–36, when the fortress was in the possession of the Dukes of Savoy, traditional enemies of the Republic of Geneva. Byron and Shelley visited Chillon on 23 June 1816 (see *Sonnet on Chillon*, Romantic Sonnet, p. 437, above).
11 *my father's faith*: protestantism.
14 *tenets*: beliefs, theological positions.
26 *wreck*: Person of undermined, shattered, or ruined condition (*NED*).
41 *this new day*: Bonnivard has been released.
57 *the pure elements of earth*: sun, wind, rain.
95 *had stood*: would have stood.
102 *Those relics*: Remaining members of the family.
107 *Lake Leman*: Lake Geneva, round which Byron and Shelley sailed in late June

1816, on the occasion when they visited Chillon. Though he was also working on *Childe Harold* III, Byron finished *The Prisoner of Chillon* before his return to the Villa Diodati at the end of the month.
112 *Which round about . . . enthralls*: The prison is itself imprisoned ('enthralled') by water.
167 *race*: family.
230 *a selfish death*: suicide (then regarded as deadly sin).
285 *the while*: for the time.
369 *mote*: dust, obstruction.

JOHN KEATS

Isabella, or The Pot of Basil

261–2 *Their crimes . . . Hinnom's vale*: Isabella's two brothers, rich Florentine merchants, have murdered her lover, Lorenzo, as not worthy of their sister. The smoke in the Vale of Hinnom (here representing guilt) was of human sacrifice (2 Chronicles, 28.3).
270 *Waking an Indian . . . hall*: Keats knew of Indian tortures from Robertson's *History of America*; the cloudy 'hall' appears to be smoke that envelops the brave in his torment.
279 *loaméd*: earthy.
292 *unthread the . . . woof*: unweave the tapestry (reveal the story of the murder).
332 *Portioned us*: portioned out our lives.
342 *the inmost . . . would try*: test the details of the dream.
344 *forest-hearse*: wood that had been turned into a burial ground.
356 *funeral-stole*: shroud.
374 *Those dainties . . . cries*: her breasts (one of Keats' more notorious lines, in a poem where language is often strained).
389 *the old tale*: Keats' source is the sixteenth-century English translation of Boccaccio's *Decameron*.
393–4 *With duller steel . . . head*: Perseus, who beheaded the snake-haired Gorgon Medusa, had a special sword given to him by Mercury.
398 *impersonate*: in human form, incarnate (given that Christ, as Love, died for mankind, Keats' words are close to blasphemy).
411–12 *And divine . . . refreshfully*: The perfumes are distilled.
415 *set*: planted.
432 *leafits*: bunches of young leaves.
436 *Lethean*: steeped in forgetfulness.
442 *Melpomene*: The Muse of Tragedy (celebrated by Spenser, whose effects Keats is imitating, in *Tears of the Muses*).
451 *Baälites*: worshippers of false gods, here money ('pelf').
453 *many a curious elf*: Like the 'deceiving elf' of *Ode to a Nightingale* (and many another in Keats' poetry), present solely for the rhyme with 'self'.
467 *to chapel-shrift*: to be 'shrieved' (given absolution) in chapel.
477 *guerdon*: reward.
503 *burden*: chorus.

PERCY BYSSHE SHELLEY

Final Moments

Shelley based *The Cenci* on a true, and well-known, story of incest and parricide in a noble Roman family of the 1590s. He 'endeavoured as nearly as possible', the Preface claims in 1820, 'to represent the characters as they probably were'. Gentle, loving and devout, Beatrice is raped and humiliated by her father, Count Cenci, who hates his children (partly, it seems, in revenge against their dead mother) and is motivated more by power than by lust. With her brother, Giacomo, and stepmother, Lucrezia, she enters into a plot to kill him. Shelley does not condone this, but Cenci is above the law, buying pardons from the Pope for his murders and debauches. If he lives, Beatrice will be destroyed. The plot is successful (at a second attempt), but immediately found out. Beatrice goes to her death maintaining an innocence that is above the 'cloud of crime and shame' in which she is enveloped.
9 *What, sister . . . sleep* (V iii): Bernardo, Beatrice's younger brother, has played no part in the conspiracy.
11–12 *'Thou / Dost . . .'Tis well'* (V iv): 'You petition for the accused because you are employed to do so – Lucky for you.'
42 *wreck-devoted seaman*: sailor about to be wrecked.
49–50 *So young to go . . . wormy ground*: Shelley is seen at his closest to Shakespeare: Beatrice's speech opens in imitation of Claudio on death – 'Aye, but to die . . . To lie in cold obstruction, and to rot' (*Measure for Measure* III i) – and continues with recollections of Lear on the heath ('Let me not go mad! / Sweet Heaven', ll. 57–8, below) and Hamlet on the bourn from which no traveller returns (ll. 73–4, below). *Macbeth*, it should be said, has been dominant earlier in the play, as the death of Cenci is plotted and carried out. Shelley is perhaps the only Romantic dramatist whose use of Shakespeare is discerning as well as frequent.
54 *familiar thoughts . . . lost*: thoughts that lose their sadness in the thinking.
114 *'twere just*: it would be fair.

LORD BYRON

The Shipwreck

401–8 *At half-past eight . . . short*: Juan, whose relationship with Donna Julia in Canto I has been brought to an abrupt conclusion (see Romantic Comedy and Satire, p. 580, above), has been sent on his travels in the care of his tutor, the priest Pedrillo. Their ship, 'the most holy *Trinidada*', is wrecked in the eastern Mediterranean.
444 *magisterial*: masterful (Latin *magister*, a tutor).
447 *Battista*: Juan's servant.
448 *aqua-vita*: brandy.
518 *And that's their . . . supply*: arranging annuities.
528 *Argo*: The ship in which Jason sets out to discover the Golden Fleece.
531 *like woodcocks . . . suction*: probing soft ground with their long bills, woodcock look as if they could be sucking in their food.

552 *victual*: food (pronounced 'vittle').
559–60 *So Juan's spaniel . . . eating*: Byron is drawing on a number of different shipwreck-narratives, and takes the detail of Juan's dog from his grandfather, Commodore Byron, wrecked in 1740 on the coast of Patagonia (*A Narrative of the Honourable John Byron*, 1768).
592 *Julia's letter*: The letter of farewell written at the end of their relationship as Julia is sent to a convent, and Juan shipped off to mend his morals.
602 *The surgeon . . . instruments*: Again, detail from an actual shipwreck narrative.
624 *pastor . . . master*: chaplain and tutor.
647 *Cadiz*: seaport in Spain (rhyming at the time with 'ladies'); the mate has doubtless been given syphilis.
654–5 *Chewing a piece . . . noddy*: Again, authenticated detail; 'boobies' and 'noddies' are both sea birds, the first a kind of gannet, the second with dark plumage, and resembling a tern.
658–61 *Remember Ugolino . . . His tale*: Count Ugolino, a Guelf leader in Pisa at the end of the thirteenth century, was betrayed by the Ghibelline, Ruggieri degli Ubaldini, and starved to death with two sons and two grandsons. In *The Inferno* he falls to chewing Ruggieri's skull after telling his story to Dante and his guide.

THOMAS HOOD

The Dream of Eugene Aram

10 *They drave the wickets in*: they drove in the stumps (and are going to play cricket).
12 *Lynn*: In Norfolk (where the schoolmaster, Eugene Aram, on whom Hood bases his poem did in fact teach).
17 *Usher*: schoolmaster.
30 *and leaden-eyed*: Keats, *Ode to a Nightingale*, 'And leaden-eyed despairs'.
48 *The Death of Abel*: By Gessner (English translation 1761); killed by his brother Cain, Abel is the first human murder victim.
61 *injured*: wronged.
68 *the curse of Cain*: The 'mark of Cain', stamped on the brow, condemns its bearer to be an outcast and a wanderer.
95 *manhood*: humanity.
97–100 *And lo . . . in blame*: A passage in which the rhythms, tones and language of *The Ancient Mariner* are specially marked: cf. 'The upper air burst into life', and 'a thousand thousand slimy things / Lived on, and so did I' (later text). Hood is no imitator, but writes as if he knows the *Mariner* by heart.
101–2 *I took . . . his name*: A detail from *The Ancient Ballad of Chevy Chase*: 'He tooke the dede man be the hande, / And sayd "Wo ys me for the"' (Percy's *Reliques*).
112 *Was at the Devil's price*: was lost (the Devil could have it for the asking).
121 *dreary*: Was Hood perhaps aware that Anglo-Saxon 'dreorig' means blood-stained?
135–6 *I could not share . . . hymn*: Like both Coleridge's Mariner, unable to pray

as the result of his crime, and the Wedding-Guest, unable to join the marriage festivities as the result of hearing the story.
137 *of the pit*: from Hell.
204 *Like Cranmer's . . . stake*: A grisly image: Thomas Cranmer, Archbishop under the Protestant Edward VI (and responsible for the Anglican Prayer Book), recanted his faith under the Catholic Mary, but then withdrew his recantation, holding the hand that had signed it in the flames as he burned at the stake in what is now Broad Street, Oxford.

FELICIA HEMANS

Indian Woman's Death

33 *lave*: wash.

LETITIA ELIZABETH LANDON

She Sat Alone Beside Her Hearth

34 *fair young stranger*: a European.
100 *the mighty Fall*: Niagara.

IV. Ennobling Interchange: Man and Nature

ANNA LAETITIA BARBAULD

(i) *The Mouse's Petition*

5–6 *For here forlorn . . . wiry grate*: Like the dove in Wright of Derby's famous picture, *An Experiment on a Bird in the Air Pump*, the mouse in his cage ('wiry grate') is assisting Joseph Priestley with experiments that will lead to the discovery of oxygen. Barbauld is writing at Warrington Dissenting Academy, where her father and future husband are colleagues of Priestley, and she herself is his protégée.
25–36 *The well-taught . . . kindred mind*: The mouse (who has apparently been reading Heraclitus on mind as a 'never-dying flame') turns on Priestley, founder of modern Unitarianism, an impeccable Unitarian argument. Barbauld herself, meanwhile, is revealed as holding views on the One Life which twenty-five years later will emerge as central to Coleridge in *Frost at Midnight*, Wordsworth in *Tintern Abbey*.

(ii) *A Summer Evening's Meditation*

26 *ether*: Substance supposed by Newton to permeate all matter and all space.
40 *How soft . . . lucid spheres*: Barbauld, though up-to-date in her scientific thinking, uses a Ptolemaic image of planets attached to revolving translucent 'spheres' that move each within the other.
68 *lawful*: permitted; like the Coleridge of *The Eolian Harp* (below), Barbauld is conscious that her speculations may go too far. Priestley, it seems, came to think they had, and fell out with her.
78 *the suburbs of the system*: Perhaps a recollection of Portia, 'Dwell I but in the suburbs / Of your good pleasure?' (*Julius Caesar* II i)
81 *like an exiled queen*: It is strange to see Saturn, displaced King of the gods, and always a male planet, as female.

WILLIAM COWPER

The Winter Evening

270 *Goliath*: Giant champion of the Philistines, killed by the shepherd-boy David in I Samuel 17, and said to be 'six cubits and a span' (roughly ten foot six!) in height.
282 *mercurial*: quick-witted.
284–5 *I am conscious . . . think*: Cowper's handling of the mock-heroic is elegant and assured.
290 *myself creating what I saw*: Surely the words that prompted Coleridge to the writing of *Frost at Midnight* (below).
292–5 *The sooty films . . . near approach*: Films of thin black carbon that form between the bars of a coal-fire, and are said to predict the arrival of a stranger (drawing on Cowper, Coleridge positively makes a friend of the one that forms on his cottage grate at Nether Stowey).
315 *share*: ploughshare.
316 *fallows*: Fields that are left uncropped for a year to restore fertility to the soil.

ROBERT BURNS

To a Mouse, On Turning Her Up in Her Nest with the Plough, November 1785

8 *Nature's social union*: A mock-heroic touch as Burns (like Barbauld in *The Mouse's Petition*, above, p. 248) turns mice and men into brothers.

SAMUEL TAYLOR COLERIDGE

Conversation Poems A heading used by scholars to bring together four early poems of philosophical blank verse (and sometimes extended to include *Dejection, An Ode* of 1802). Though referring to *The Nightingale* in 1798 as 'A Conversational Poem', Coleridge did not bring the poems together himself.

(i) *The Eolian Harp*

1 *My pensive Sara*: Coleridge dates his poem 20 August 1795, and is addressing Sara Fricker whom he married on 4 October. They were not, in August, living together in either modern sense of the words.
4–5 *jasmine . . . innocence and love*: Myrtle is traditionally sacred to Venus; the association of jasmine and innocence (based merely on the flower's whiteness) is Coleridge's own.
7 *the Star of Eve*: Hesperus, the Evening Star.
12–13 *that simplest lute . . . casement*: The Eolian harp, consisting of an oblong stringed box, placed in the window so that the wind plays over its strings.
25–6 *untamed wing / And thus*: Coleridge inserts at this point in the text of *Sybilline Leaves* (1817) famous lines that give fuller expression to his early Unitarian pantheism. That he should have done so after trying for ten years and more to argue himself into an orthodox Trinitarian view, is a reminder of the emotional power that his more imaginative early positions held for him throughout his life:

> Oh the one life within us and abroad,
> Which meets all motion and becomes its soul –
> A light in sound, a sound-like power in light,
> Rhythm in all thought, and joyance everywhere!
> Methinks, it should have been impossible
> Not to love all things in a world so filled,
> Where the breeze warbles, and the mute still air
> Is Music slumbering on her instrument.

36–40 *And what if . . . God of all*: Central to Coleridge's Conversation Poems is a Unitarian belief in Nature as alive with the presence of God. His image of the harps offers an answer to the question as to how God is present – how seemingly lifeless matter is animated. 'Harps' (units of the natural world) are 'diversely framed' (individually constructed), and doing their own thing, trembling into 'thought' (activity) as the wind (traditionally the breath of God) passes over their 'strings'. The wind is 'plastic' (creative) and 'intellectual' (spiritual, of the mind of God). Because it plays different tunes on different harps, it takes into account individuality, and can be said to be 'At once the soul of each, and God of all.'
42–3 *thoughts / Dim and unhallowed*: Coleridge's thoughts are 'dim' because speculative, and 'unhallowed' because not made holy by guidance from the Scriptures. Whether they would in fact have been reproved by Sara is not clear.
45 *Meek daughter . . . Christ*: Jesus, according to Unitarian doctrine, is a man, son of Joseph the carpenter of Nazareth. He is the Son of God only in the sense in which we are all God's sons and daughters.

47 *unregenerate*: fallen, lacking the means to achieve salvation.
53 *his saving mercies*: The Crucifixion and Resurrection (rising from the dead, Christ for the Unitarians shows not godhead, but humanity perfected, made spiritual).
55 *Wildered and dark*: Lost in the wild (as in 'bewildered', 'wilderness'), and incapable of seeing the light of truth. Coleridge's self-abasement is typical of the posturing we see in this early poetry (he was twenty-two).

(ii) *This Lime-Tree Bower, My Prison*

Headnote *long-expected friends*: Charles Lamb, with whom Coleridge had been at school at Christ's Hospital in London (and who worked there for the East India Company), and William and Dorothy Wordsworth, who had just moved to Alfoxden House, four miles from Coleridge's cottage at Nether Stowey.
6 *whom I may never meet again*: A somewhat exaggerated response to being left behind with a scalded foot. The poem's first draft goes so far as to associate Coleridge with Vulcan, 'lamed by the scathe of fire'.
9 *still*: ever.
17 *long lank weeds*: Identified by Coleridge as adder's tongue or hart's tongue.
30 *In the great city pent*: An allusion to *Paradise Lost* IX, 445, where Satan, newly arrived in Eden, is likened to one 'long in populous city pent', now free to enjoy the 'summer's morn'. Unlike Coleridge, whose early childhood had been spent in Devonshire, Lamb was a Londoner born and bred. He did not see himself as 'gentle-hearted' and 'hungering' after Nature, and, when *The Lime-Tree Bower* was published by Southey in 1800, was very funny about it: 'please to blot out *gentle-hearted*, and substitute, drunken dog, ragged-head, seld-shaven, odd-eyed, stuttering, or any other epithet which truly and properly belongs to the gentleman in question' (to Coleridge, 14 August).
32 *And strange calamity*: Lamb had turned to Coleridge, his two-years-older schoolfriend and fellow Unitarian, when in September 1796 his sister Mary killed their mother, and wounded their father, in a fit of violent madness. Seeing himself as singled out by the 'strange calamity', Lamb remained unmarried, and looked after Mary tenderly for the rest of his life.
35 *heath-flowers*: heather.
37 *So my friend*: So far from being moved by the responses wished onto him, Lamb (Coleridge's best and bluntest critic) referred to ll. 37–44 as an 'unintelligible abstraction-fit'. Though the experience might now seem to us Wordsworthian, Wordsworth nowhere claims to perceive the God in Nature till *The Pedlar* of spring 1798, by which time he had been six months under the influence of Coleridge's Unitarian views.
41 *Less gross than bodily*: spiritualized, lacking the grossness of material existence.

(iii) *Frost at Midnight*

1 *The frost performs . . . ministry*: Coleridge takes as his inspiration Cowper's *Winter Evening* (above), his first line drawing on *Task* IV, 322–5, evoking the transformation of the landscape that is 'performed' by snow:

> Tomorrow brings a change, a total change!
> Which even now, though silently *performed*,
> And slowly, and by most unfelt, the face
> Of universal Nature undergoes.

2 *owlet's cry*: The reference is to a full-grown owl.
10 *extreme*: Stressed, as in Milton, on the first syllable.
15 *Only that film*: A film of soot that forms, and flutters, between the bars of a coal-fire; Coleridge's note draws attention to their superstitious implication: 'In all parts of the kingdom these films are called *strangers*, and supposed to portend the arrival of some absent friend.'
21–4 *the living spirit . . . deep faith*: Cut in later texts of *Frost at Midnight*, but one of the most important statements that Coleridge ever made on the 'living spirit' of imagination, and its tendency (whether in fanciful moods, or in 'deep faith') to perceive the natural world as sharing in its own life-force.
32 *my sweet birth-place*: Ottery St Mary, in Devonshire, where Coleridge was born on 4 October 1772, the eleventh child of the vicar of the parish.
41 *preceptor's*: schoolmaster's.
46–7 *or sister . . . clothed alike*: Coleridge's sister, Anne, who died aged twenty-four when he was nineteen. Boys at this period wore skirts until they were 'breeched', about the age of eight.
57 *In the great city . . . dim*: See *The Lime-Tree Bower*, 30n., above.
67 *Himself in all . . . himself*: An extreme example of Coleridge's early Unitarian pantheism. A month before writing *Frost at Midnight* he had applied for a job as a minister; see Hazlitt's *My First Acquaintance with Poets.*
68 *Great universal Teacher*: God at once teaches through the universe (asking us to read the universal language of Nature), and offers a teaching of universal relevance.
80–5 *Like those . . . eagerness*: Cut in later versions, making a tidier but less personal poem.

(iv) *The Nightingale*

4 *we . . . mossy bridge*: Coleridge, together with William and Dorothy Wordsworth; on 10 May 1798 the newly finished poem is mailed to the Wordsworths: 'I send *per post* my *Nightingale*.'
7 *verdure*: greenness, here green waterweed.
13 *Most . . . melancholy*:

> Sweet bird, that shunnest the noise of folly,
> Most musical, most melancholy!
> (Milton, *Il Peneroso* 60–61)

18 *distemper*: disease, wasting away of the body.
24 *building up the rhyme*: Milton, *Lycidas* 10–11, 'he knew / Himself to sing, and build the lofty rhyme'.
27 *influxes*: influences.
39 *Philomela's . . . strains*: Philomela comes to be the poetic name for a nightingale;

that her songs should plead for pity refers the reader to a legend of violence and metamorphosis. Raped by her brother-in-law, King Tereus of Thrace, she (with her sister, Procne) exacts an appalling revenge. Finally, he is turned into a hoopoe, she into a nightingale, and Procne into a swallow.
41 *A different lore*: cf. *Frost at Midnight* 55–6, above, addressed to Coleridge's infant son Hartley, 'thou shalt learn *far other lore, /* And in far other scenes'.
50 *a castle huge*: Enmore Castle, seat of Lord Egmont.
60 *jug jug*: Sound traditionally associated with the nightingale.
69 *A most gentle maid*: An allusion to Isabella, daughter of Coleridge's friend John Cruikshank (though the 'gentle maid' clearly has qualities in common with Dorothy Wordsworth).
82 *airy harps*: wind harps (as in *The Eolian Harp*, above).
90 *That strain again*: Duke to Musicians, *Twelfth Night* I i, 'That strain again! – it had a dying fall'.
91 *My dear babe*: Hartley Coleridge (as in the conclusion to *Frost at Midnight*).
109 *He may associate joy*: To Coleridge as follower of David Hartley (*Observations on Man*) on whose views Priestleyan Unitarianism was based, associationism was not a mere tendency of the human mind, but a way of thinking ordained by God to bring the individual progressively closer to a spiritual existence.

WILLIAM WORDSWORTH

'Images of a Mighty Mind'

(i) *Tintern Abbey*

1–4 *Five years . . . murmur*: Wordsworth is composing in his head as he and Dorothy walk beside the River Wye in July 1798; the full title of his poem insists that they are 'a Few Miles above Tintern Abbey'. He had hurried through the Wye Valley in very different circumstances in August '93 (see ll. 71–3 below).
20 *as might seem*: The 'wreathes of smoke' come in fact from iron furnaces, but industrialization in this contemplative poem has no relevance to Wordsworth. Harmonizing the landscape, he takes a hint from Gilpin's *Picturesque Tour of the Wye*, which he and Dorothy probably had with them: 'Smoke, which is frequently seen issuing from the sides of the hills . . . beautifully breaks their lines, and unites them with the sky' (cf. the 'steep and lofty cliffs' of ll. 4–8).
24 *forms of beauty*: outward shapes of the Wye landscape, which have been stamped on the mind by the poet's emotions, and carried away as visual images. The process, which gives rise to the central mystical experience of *Tintern Abbey*, had been described by Wordsworth in *The Pedlar* 30–34, three months earlier:

> deep feelings had impressed
> Great objects on his mind with portraiture
> And colour so distinct that on his mind
> They lay like substances, and almost seemed
> To haunt the bodily sense.

43 *affections*: emotions.
57 *sylvan Wye . . . woods*: Wordsworth is playing on Latin *silva*, a wood, and recalling too the Latin name of the Wye, *Vaga*, the Wanderer, which (as Rachel Tricket pointed out to the editors) appears in Pope's Man of Ross (*Epistle to Bathurist* 251).
62 *picture of the mind*: the image which he had carried away with him.
68 *roe*: Smallest of the three native English deer; Wordsworth may also be conscious of Song of Songs 2.17: 'Make haste, my belovéd, and be thou like to a roe, or to a young hart upon the mountain of spices.'
71–3 *more like a man . . . loved*: Travelling through the Wye Valley in August 1793, Wordsworth had been in a distraught state of mind, thinking of politics, France, Annette Vallon and their daughter Caroline (who, because of the war, he had never seen – and wouldn't meet till she was nine).
101 *motion*: Coleridge (on whose thinking *Tintern Abbey* certainly depends) had claimed in 1795 to believe 'in the corporeality of thought, namely that it is motion'. To equate Wordsworth's 'motion and spirit' with what was thought as the immanent mind of God offers a very credible Berkleyan reading.
114 *genial spirits*: vitality, imagination; Wordsworth is thinking of Milton, *Samson Agonistes* 594–6:

> So much I feel my genial spirits droop,
> My hopes all flat; Nature within me
> Seems in all her functions weary of herself . . .

126 *inform*: imbue.
141 *mansion*: resting-place ('In my father's house are many mansions', John 14.2).
145 *portion*: share, fate.

(ii) *There Was a Boy*

1 *There Was a boy*: Despite its impersonal opening, Wordsworth's poem was written originally in the first person. He regarded it as showing 'one of the earliest processes of Nature' in the development of imagination (1815 Preface).
10–11 *Blew mimic hootings . . . answer him*: John Kerrigan points out that Wordsworth's memories of Cumbrian owls are prompted by a passage in Act IV, scene i, of Joanna Baillie's tragedy, *Montfort*, published earlier in the year:

> Oft when a boy, at the still twilight hour,
> I've leant my back against some knotted oak,
> And loudly mimicked him, till to my call
> He answer would return . . .

Though anonymous, Baillie's *Series of Plays* influences at this time both Coleridge and Wordsworth, and provides important elements of the 1798 Advertisement, and 1800 Preface, to *Lyrical Ballads*.
17 *pauses of deep silence*: cf. the 'pause of silence' in Coleridge, *The Nightingale* 76, above, as the birds answer and provoke each other's songs.
20 *far into his heart*: 'This very expression *far*', *De Quincey comments in Recollec-*

tions of the Lakes and Lake Poets, 'by which space and its infinities are attributed to the human heart . . . has always struck me as with a flash of sublime revelation'.
22 *unawares*: unconsciously (as in the comparable moment, *Ancient Mariner* 276–7: 'A spring of love gusht from my heart, / And I blest them unaware').
25 *Into . . . steady lake*: Added at a secondary stage, and presenting the boy, who had been Wordsworth himself in the original draft, as a dead school-friend (John Tyson), are seven lines, designed like the addition to *Old Man Travelling* (p. 157 above) to offer a story element to the poetry:

> Fair are the woods, and beauteous is the spot,
> The vale where he was born: the Church-yard hangs
> Upon a slope above the village school,
> And there along that bank when I have passed
> At evening, I believe, that near his grave
> A full half-hour together I have stood,
> Mute – for he died when he was ten years old.

(iii) *The Two-Part Prelude*

FIRST PART

1 *Was it for this*: Wordsworth, who writes Part I in the German town of Goslar where he and his sister spent the winter of 1798–9, refers to his sense of being unable to make progress on his never completed philosophical poem, *The Recluse*, planned with Coleridge six months before.
8 *'sweet birthplace'*: A quotation from *Frost at Midnight* (above); from the first *The Prelude* was addressed to Coleridge.
14 *earnest*: promise.
23 *groundsel*: ragwort.
34 *springes*: snares; cf. Polonius's metaphor, 'springes to catch woodcocks' (*Hamlet* I iii 115).
35 *fell*: fierce; 'this fell sergeant Death / Is strict in his arrest' (*Hamlet* V ii).
45 *when the deed was done*: The guilt that underlies the poet's memory can (if one chooses) be related to the price of woodcock, which were trapped on the fells during their migration, sold locally, and sent by carriage to London.
58 *Above the raven's nest*: Ravens were (and are) a danger to lambs. A contemporary account shows that the boy would have been roped and let down the cliff-face to remove eggs, or fledglings, for which the parish paid a bounty.
77–80 *Others too . . . was I*: With Burke's distinction in mind, Wordsworth considers himself to have been educated in childhood more by the sublime in Nature (including guilt and terror), than the beautiful.
109 *instinct*: imbued.
135 *vulgar*: common, ordinary.
157–8 *games / Confederate*: games played in groups.
173 *shadow*: reflection.
182 *diurnal*: daily.
183 *train*: succession.
186–9 *Ye powers of earth, ye genii . . . standing pools*: Wordsworth's address to the 'genii' (geniuses of place) and other local gods is an echo of Prospero in *The Tempest*

V i: 'Ye elves of hills, brooks, standing lakes, and groves.' Such attendant-spirits were common in eighteenth-century poetry, occurring for instance in *The Rape of the Lock* and *The Ancient Mariner*. In later versions of *The Prelude*, Wordsworth tended to address Nature directly.
194–5 *Impressed . . . / Of danger or desire*: A key passage in Wordsworth's discussion of education through Nature, and the development of imagination. 'Boyish sports', irrelevant in themselves, lead to the landscapes where they took place being stamped ('impressed') on the mind as visual images. Caves, trees, woods and hills, bear the imprint ('characters' are literally handwriting) of the boy's dangers and enjoyments.
198 *Work*: seethe.
212 *strife too humble . . . verse*: noughts and crosses, tick-tack-toe.
215 *loo*: eighteenth-century card game.
227 *with keen . . . tooth*: From Amiens' song, *As You Like It* II vii, 'Thy tooth is not so keen . . .'
232 *yellings*: Used in Wordsworth's day of animals and objects, as well as human beings.
234 *rehearse*: describe; for the episode that Wordsworth has in mind, see *Nutting* (*Lyrical Ballads* 1800), written originally for *The Prelude*.
249 *Venial*: forgivable.
258–374 *Ere I had seen . . . spirit thence are brought*: The great 'spots of time' sequence of *The Prelude* is seen in its original position (among the other childhood episodes) and original form, only in the two-part poem of 1799.
259 *Eight summers*: Though claiming here to have been seven, Wordsworth was just nine when he was sent in May 1779 to Hawkshead Grammar School.
277–9 *the dead man . . . ghastly face*: The 'half-infant' poet may or may not have given the alarm, but Joseph Jackson, schoolmaster from Sawrey, drowned in Esthwaite Water in June 1779.
287 *like their archetypes*: As the result of local tragic stories, the child's memory is peopled with visual images. The mind revisits these, adding new layers of feeling and association, till they achieve a permanence comparable to that of the natural scenes which are their 'archetypes' (originals).
290 *fructifying virtue*: power (Latin *virtus*) to make fruitful, creative.
302–3 *honest James . . . guide*: The poet, aged five, is staying with grandparents at Penrith; 'honest James' (seen in the child's fantasy as fellow horseman, perhaps his squire) was presumably a servant asked to look after him.
316 *The beacon . . . summit*: Tall bullet-shaped stone signalling beacon (still to be seen above Penrith), built in 1719 to pass on news of Scottish invasions. Last lit in 1745.
322 *visionary dreariness*: Oxymoron modelled on Milton's 'darkness visible'.
331 *The day . . . began*: 19 December 1783; Wordsworth was thirteen.
340 *repaired*: went.
353–60 *The event . . . corrected my desires*: Once again it is misplaced guilt in the child that creates the 'spot of time', charging an unimportant landscape with significance. The child feels that his father has been killed by God as punishment for his too great hopefulness; the adult poet knows well that he wasn't.
367 *indisputable shapes*: Shapes in the mist that seemed 'unquestionably' to be the horses that the poet was expecting; *scan*, indísputáble shapes.

375 *sedulous*: anxious; Milton had described himself as 'Not sedulous by nature to indite / Wars, hitherto the only argument / Heroic deemed' (*Paradise Lost* IX, 27–9).
385 *intellectual*: spiritual.
405–6 *linking . . . associated forms*: The 'innocent' vision of childhood is spoiled, for Wordsworth, the moment associations are brought to bear, comparisons made.
413 *fits of vulgar joy*: moments of ordinary pleasure.
421 *quaint associations*: arbitrary connections within the mind.
430 *substantial lineaments*: Visual memory, on which so much of Wordsworth's poetry depends, had for him extraordinary physicality. In *The Pedlar*, 32–4, he had spoken of landscapes lying 'like substances' on his brain, and almost seeming 'To haunt the bodily sense'.
442 *affections*: emotions.
451 *Reproaches*: Writing Part I has confirmed for Wordsworth his sense of having had a favoured childhood, putting more pressure on him to get on with *The Recluse* (see note to I, l. 1 above).

SECOND PART

1 *my friend*: Coleridge.
18 *monitory*: warning.
33 *our . . . market-village*: Hawkshead, where Wordsworth was at school till the age of seventeen.
44 *huckster*: stall-keeper.
52 *grateful*: pleasing, enjoyable.
56 *bourne*: destination.
59 *umbrageous*: shady.
78 *delicate viands*: fancy food.
81 *Sabine fare*: food such as Horace ate on his frugal Sabine farm.
109 *large abbey*: Furness Abbey, twenty-odd miles from Hawkshead.
136 *we breathed*: allowed our horses to get their breath.
139 *the level sand*: The boys are riding south along Levens Sands, before cutting across to Hawkshead.
146 *gavel-end*: gable; Coniston Hall is Elizabethan, with high gables and immense chimneys.
153 *chafing-dish*: portable charcoal stove to cook the trout, or char, they had caught.
161–74 *And there I said . . . first he rose*: In describing this sentimental phase of boyhood, Wordsworth draws on his first major poem, *The Vale of Esthwaite*, begun when he was fifteen.
191 *characters*: letters.
240 *intervenient*: Nature has so far been valued in the midst of other pleasures.
249–56 *Thou, my friend . . . revealed*: To Coleridge as Unitarian 'the unity of all' is a dogma, where to Wordsworth it is an intuition.
258 *class the cabinet*: set things out as in a display case (the phrase is drawn from Locke, *Essay on Human Understanding*, chap. 2)
262 *Hard task . . . soul*: Raphael (*Paradise Lost* V, 564) speaks of describing the war in Heaven as 'Sad task and hard'; to analyze the human mind, Wordsworth implies, is no less difficult, and no less important.
272 *Claims . . . earthly soul*: when the child's pre-existent soul becomes conscious

of its new earthly condition; cf. Coleridge's sonnet on the birth of Hartley, 1796 (p. 694, above), and Wordsworth's *Immortality Ode*, 1804 (above, p. 327).
286 *apprehensive habitude*: relationship that is especially suited to learning.
321 *now*: Wordsworth returns to the account of adolescence, from which he digressed at l. 242.
324 *The props of my affections*: Boyish sports which have supported 'collaterally' his growing love of Nature.
339 *modes and temporary qualities*: seasonal growth and changes which might have gone unobserved.
344 *'best society'*: 'For solitude sometimes is best society' (*Paradise Lost* IX, 249).
347 *gentle agitations*: Not dependent on 'By' in the previous line, but the last item in a list beginning with 'Hence' in l. 343.
364 *intellectual*: spiritual.
380 *our little lake*: Esthwaite Water.
382–3 *a friend . . . loved*: John Fleming, celebrated in *The Vale of Esthwaite* 1786.
401 *prospect*: view, landscape.
411 *plastic*: creative, formative (the 'power' is imagination at its most dominant).
425 *transport*: rapture.
426 *still*: always.
428 *analytic industry*: rational inquiry.
432 *interminable building*: huge intellectual structure.
463 *O'ercome . . . of that strain*: Overcome by sensual pleasure that forms a prelude to loss of self in the One Life.
478–87 *If, in these times . . . dereliction and dismay*: By 1799 those who continued to support the ideals of the French Revolution were not merely falling away, but sneering at their former friends.
496–7 *Thou, my friend . . . other scenes*: 'For I was reared', Coleridge had written in *Frost at Midnight*, 'In the great city, pent mid cloisters dim' (above, p. 260).
509 *Fare thee well*: Wordsworth is both rounding off his poem and saying a genuine goodbye to Coleridge, who at the end of 1799 has decided to go south and become a journalist in London.

(iv) Statue Horse

16 *A borderer . . . death*: Never published by Wordsworth himself, Statue Horse was written alongside the Climbing of Snowdon (below) for the short-lived five-book *Prelude* of spring 1804, as an example of the transforming power of imagination.

(v) Climbing of Snowdon

10 *It was a summer's night*: The Climbing of Snowdon was written in February 1804, then laid aside to form the conclusion of his new, longer *Prelude*, when Wordsworth decided to break up the five-book version. Lines 66–73 were added as gloss on the original episode in April 1805.
15 *pilot*: guide (the shepherd who conducted visitors up Snowdon to see the sunrise).
45 *their dusky backs upheaved*: As he portrays the sea of mist that is an emblem of human creativity – the transforming power of imagination – Wordsworth recalls

Milton's account of divine Creation: 'the mountains huge appear / Emergent, and their broad bare backs upheave' (*Paradise Lost* VII, 285–6).

65 *The soul, the imagination of the whole*: Tacitly equated in these last words of the 1804 Climbing of Snowdon are the religious principle in man and the creative / perceptive function of imagination, that is his highest human achievement. Both equally are sited by the poet in the cloud-rift through which countless individual voices ('homeless' in the sense of having no distinct source or origin) mount into oneness.

66–73 *A meditation . . . Or vast in its own being*: Wordsworth's gloss on the Snowdon episode brings to its climax his quest for the sublime, evoking a 'mighty mind' that is human in its aspirations, divine in its powers. The 'underpresence' welling up through the cloud-rift of the unconscious (the subconscious, to use the poet's spatial metaphor) may be defined in terms either of the soul ('the sense of God'), or of the imagination (the 'dim / Or vast' within ourselves). Either is a 'feeding upon infinity – the ultimate sublime experience that Wordsworth craves for.

(vi) Crossing the Alps

495 *clomb*: climbed (the strong past participle, known to Wordsworth both as poetic archaism, and in Cumbrian dialect).

494–6 *Upturning . . . to Italy* Wordsworth and his Welsh friend Jones are making a tour on foot during the Cambridge Long Vacation of 1790, through France, into Italy and Switzerland, and back via the Netherlands.

525–9 *Imagination . . . / Athwart me*: Imagination (pleasure at the idea of crossing the Alps) had been disappointed in August 1790 – now fourteen years later the power asserts itself, coming 'athwart' the poet as he writes.

553 *a narrow chasm*: Wordsworth and Jones have crossed the Simplon Pass, and entered the Ravine of Gondo.

568 *workings of one mind*: A reference to the human mind that opens into larger Coleridgean possibilities: 'There is one mind, one omnipresent mind, / Omnific; his most holy name is Love' (1796 *Religious Musings*, 114–15).

569 *blossoms upon one tree*: As he builds up his images of oneness, Wordsworth has in mind not only the expected guides, Milton and the Unitarian Coleridge, but Pope's *Essay on Man* II, 266–72:

> All are but parts of one stupendous whole,
> Whose body Nature is, and God the soul,
> That (changed through all, and yet in all the same) . . .
> Warms in the sun, refreshes in the breeze,
> Glows in the stars, and blossoms in the trees . . .

570 *Characters . . . apocalypse*: Handwriting that implies either past apocalypse (waters of the Flood were considered to have created the Alps), or one that is yet to come.

572 *Of first . . . without end*: A reworking of *Paradise Lost* V, 165, 'Him first, him last, him midst and without end', that leaves out specific reference to God, while allowing for numinous possibility. Coleridge meanwhile had recast the Milton line for Southey's *Joan of Arc* II, 16 (1796) in Berkeleyan/Unitarian terms:

Him first, Him last, to view
Through meaner powers and secondary things
Effulgent, as through clouds that veil his blaze.

WILLIAM LISLE BOWLES

from *Coombe Ellen*

1–2 *Call the strange spirit . . . shaggy solitudes*: 'Coombe Ellen (in Welsh, Cwm Elan) is situated among the most romantic mountains of Radnorshire, about five miles from Rhayader.' (Bowles)
38 *cozenage*: self-delusion.
40 *lapse*: fall.
45 *the wild ash*: the rowan (growing wild in mountainous parts of Britain).
86 *Taste*: elegant landscaping.

CHARLOTTE SMITH

from *Beachy Head*

347 *warrens*: extensive rabbit workings, often with many connected holes.
355 *pagil*: cowslip (common, as are the other flowers in this passage, in the English countryside of downs and hedgerows that Smith knew in her Sussex childhood).
359 *uncultured*: wild, uncultivated.
360 *tumps . . . mosses clad*: anthills, often a foot high or so and overgrown with moss – commonly known as 'emmet-tumps'.
368 *Ah, hills so early loved*: See Smith's sonnet *To the South Downs*, 'Ah, hills beloved', Romantic Hallmarks (above).
374 *calcareous*: chalky.
376–8 *surely the blue ocean . . . never rolled its surge*: Answer (as Smith and informed contemporaries guessed three generations before Darwin and *The Origin of Species*): yes, it did.
380 *volutes*: spiral shells.
382–4 *Or did this range . . . fathomless*: Smith footnotes 'the theory, here slightly hinted' to White of Selborne. Erasmus Darwin (White's contemporary, and Charles Darwin's grandfather) divined from the fossil-record that the earth was 'millions of ages old' – as opposed to the myth of Adam and Eve and the 6,000 years of Creation, which continued to be standard belief.
386 *calx*: lime.
389 *sylvan weald*: lower-lying woodland, protected from the sea by the barrier of chalk downs.
399 *recks*: cares.
401 *wether-flock*: flock of castrated rams.
404–5 *half-obliterated mounds . . . trenches*: Bronze Age burial mounds and earthworks found on the high ground of the southern downs, and beginning in Smith's time to be excavated.

458 *floods of corn*: Much downland was ploughed for the first time during the food shortages of the Napoleonic War.
462 *the pit-falls*: 'Square holes cut in the turf, into which a wire noose is fixed, to catch wheatears' (Smith). Extraordinary numbers of songbirds (most of them, like the wheatear, tiny) were trapped and eaten at this period: Clare records cart-loads of larks being taken daily to market in London.
467–70 *The social bird . . . among them*: 'The yellow wagtail . . . frequents the banks of rivulets in winter . . . but after the breeding-season is over it haunts downs and sheepwalks, and is seen constantly among the flocks, probably for the sake of the insects it picks up.' (Smith)
473 *his white load*: grain being carted to the mill.
477 *matins*: the morning service (medieval and Renaissance poets beautifully regarded the dawn chorus as the birds' daily celebration of God).
478 *dew*: moisture.
484 *mart*: market.
489 *mole*: Usually a man-made breakwater, here probably downland along the cliffs.
491 *Black Down*: 'This is an high ridge, extending between Sussex and Surrey. It is covered with heath [heather], and has almost always a dark appearance. On it is a telegraph [signal beacon].'
497 *that dismantled fortress*: A seemingly specific reference, but Smith notes only that several castles in the district, built under King Stephen (1135–54), have been turned into farmhouses.
what time: The Latin tag, *quo tempore*, as used by Milton, 'What time the gray-fly winds her sultry horn' (*Lycidas* 28).
498 *The Conqueror*: William, Duke of Normandy, victor at the Battle of Hastings (1066), King of England, 1066–87.
504 *yellow meadows*: fields yellow with buttercups.

AMELIA OPIE

Stanzas Written Under Aeolus' Harp

3 *this harp*: a wind-harp (as in Coleridge's *Eolian Harp*, above).
21–4 *So when the lute . . . adored*: Memnon's statue gave off sounds when touched by the sun's rays at dawn, said to be a greeting to Memnon's mother, Aurora. No lute was literally 'hung' upon it.

ISABELLA LICKBARROW

On Esthwaite Water

17 *Tilberthwaite*: Wetherlam, rising above the valley of Tilberthwaite.
22–4 '*Oh may my yielding breast . . . impressed*: There need be no connection between Lickbarrow's images and her fellow Cumbrian Wordsworth's 'solemn imagery' of rocks and woods 'received / Into the bosom of the steady lake' (*There Was a Boy*, above, p. 268), but along with Southey and De Quincey he was a

subscriber to her *Poems* 1814, and she is writing about Esthwaite, the lake of his schooldays.

LORD BYRON

'Concentred in a Life Intense'

(i) Lake Leman

604 *Lake Leman*: The Lake of Geneva, round which Byron and Shelley were sailing as these stanzas were written in June 1816.
609 *the might which I behold*: the power of Nature (from which the poet is distracted by the presence of man).
619 *coil*: turmoil of existence (as in *Hamlet* III i: 'When we have shuffled off this mortal coil').
629–30 *wanderers o'er eternity . . . ne'er shall be*: An appropriate image for poetry written on shipboard – Byron has in mind (also appropriately) Belial in *Paradise Lost* II:

> who would lose,
> Though full of pain, this intellectual being,
> Those thoughts that wander through eternity . . .

636 *froward*: wild.
640–1 *I live not in myself . . . around me*: Byron it seems complained that Shelley was 'dosing' him with Wordsworth at this period. It is with the pantheist affirmations of *Tintern Abbey* that the strongest affinities are felt.
642–3 *the hum / Of human cities*: Milton, *L'Allegro* 117–18, 'Towered cities please us then, / And the busy hum of men'.
654 *spring*: the 'pinion' (wing that enables his spirits to 'soar') 'springs' like a flower from the soil.
662–3 *When elements . . . as it should be*: 'we therefore commit his body to the ground, earth to earth, ashes to ashes, dust to dust . . .' (Burial Service).
670 *contemn*: despise.
785 *your bright leaves*: Byron mingles imagery of the book of fate with that of planetary influence.

(ii) *Epistle to Augusta*

1–2 *My sister! my sweet sister . . . thine*: Compare the exceptional tenderness with which Wordsworth addresses Dorothy in *Tintern Abbey* as 'My dear, dear sister'.
6 *A loved regret . . . resign*: Words that would have carried more than merely general sadness and resilience for Augusta. There can be no doubt that she and her half-brother (younger by five years) had become lovers in 1813, and little that her daughter Medora Leigh was his child.
11 *other claims . . . thou hast*: Augusta was married, and Medora had three elder sisters.

15 *our grandsire's fate of yore*: Admiral Byron was known as 'Foul-weather Jack' for the storms he encountered at sea, and the shipwrecks he endured.
23 *cunning in mine overthrow*: ingenious in bringing troubles upon him.
24 *proper*: own (French '*propre*') – frequent Shakespearean usage (cf. *Hamlet* V ii, 'my proper life').
28 *that walked astray*: A bitter reference to the clubfoot that caused Byron literally as well as metaphorically to 'walk astray'.
39–40 *not in vain . . . we purchase pain*: Compare the final line of Wordsworth's *Elegiac Stanzas*, 'Not without hope we suffer and we mourn.'
58 *admire*: wonder.
59 *of a trivial date*: that cannot last.
63–4 *a lake . . . our own of old*: Byron was writing at the Villa Diodati, on the shores of Lake Geneva. He and Augusta would have shared the lakes at Newstead as lovers in 1813, not as children (their childhoods were separate; he didn't inherit the Abbey till he was ten and she fifteen).
74 *the old Hall . . . no more*: Byron was attempting to sell Newstead to pay off debts.
81 *The world is all before me*: Like Adam and Eve in the closing lines of *Paradise Lost*, Byron is putting a brave face on a new start that has been forced on him: 'The world was all before them, where to choose / Their place of rest, and Providence their guide . . .'
110 *vigils*: periods of watching and waking – Byron was in fact a bad sleeper, and given to nightmares.
121–2 *in thy heart . . . secure*: Byron was justified in his confidence: Annabella would browbeat her into some sort of repentance, but Augusta was always true in her heart to the brother with whom she shared so much that no one else could share.

PERCY BYSSHE SHELLEY

'The Secret Strength of Things'

(i) *Mont Blanc*

1–2 *The everlasting universe . . . mind*: As he stands on the Pont Pelissier above the Ravine of Arve, Shelley's thoughts are on the interaction of mind and Nature. Though claiming to be an atheist, he is Platonist in his intuitions, and attracted by the pantheism of Coleridge's Conversation Poems and Wordsworth's *Tintern Abbey*: 'A motion and a spirit that impels / All thinking things, all objects of all thought, / And rolls through all things.'
5–6 *The source of human thought . . . its own*: Flowing through the mind, the great river of sense-experience meets the 'tributary' stream of human thought. In the circumstances the stream of thought seems to be contributing more (making more noise) than it is, but between them they create the mind's relationship to actuality (whether physical or philosophical).
7–11 *Such as a feeble brook . . . raves*: Standing beside a 'feeble brook' one hears it as making the noise actually made by a 'vast river' in the background.

26–7 *whose veil . . . unsculptured image*: Latent behind the 'veil' of the waterfall (created of spray and rainbows) is an image that is (in Wordsworth's phrase) 'evermore about to be'.
28 *desert*: Used of any desolate or lonely place.
37–8 *which passively . . . influencings*: Rendering and receiving are conceived of as a single 'passive' process.
41–4 *One legion . . . witch Poesy*: The 'wild thoughts' are Shelley's 'separate fantasy' (l. 36, above), floating over the darkness of the Arve, and 'resting' at intervals in the cave of poetry (taking part in the creative process that is making the poem), where the darkness ('that') and Ravine ('thou') are welcome components.
45–8 *Seeking . . . thou art there*: 'Thee' and 'thou' throughout this second verse-paragraph refer to the Ravine. Among 'ghosts of all things that are' (the cave of Poesy seems to have brought to mind the cave of Plato's *Republic*, emblematic of human ability to perceive truth only in shadows), Shelley's wild thoughts pursue the 'shade' of the Arve (said earlier to be an emblem of his imaginative power). Until the thoughts are recalled, they will float above the Ravine, and the Ravine will be a 'guest' in the poet's imagination.
53–4 *Has some unknown . . . life and death*: As Blake, and the early Coleridge, would have agreed, life and death (ordinary human existence) 'unfurled' (let down, like a sail) 'veils' us from perception of higher actuality.
79 *But for such faith*: only through such faith (the wilderness of snow teaches either doubt filled with awe, or a Wordsworthian sense of oneness between man and Nature).
81 *Large codes of fraud and woe*: Christian moral codes, chiefly.
86 *daedal*: cunningly made.
90–91 *the bound . . . they leap*: spring (which enables plants and flowers to leap from the 'detested trance' of winter).
95 *revolve, subside, and swell*: Everything in the previous eleven-and-a-half lines (comprising seasonal existence as we know it) is governed by these three verbs.
100–102 *The glaciers creep . . . rolling on*: The glaciers at Chamouni were much longer in 1816 than they are now. Shelley was deeply impressed by their inexorable advance, and assumed that they would take over the Vale.
120 *And their place . . . known*: cf. Psalm 103.15–16:

> As for man, his days are as grass: as a flower of the field so he flourisheth. / For the wind passeth over it, and it is gone; and the place thereof shall know it no more.

122 *from those secret chasms in tumult welling*: Shelley's portrayal of the River Rhône, which gives to the glaciers and to his poem a positive aspect, owes something to the sacred River Alph in Coleridge's recently published *Kubla Khan*.
139–41 *The secret Strength . . . inhabits thee*: Wordsworth in *Tintern Abbey* had felt a presence 'Whose dwelling is the light of setting suns' (l. 98); Shelley at this moment celebrates a Power that has a 'secret throne' (l. 17, above) and 'dwells apart' (l. 96), and a 'secret Strength of Things' that 'inhabits' Mont Blanc. It is the closest he ever got to portraying (affirmatively) a personalized God.
142–4 *And what were thou . . . vacancy*: Shelley's question, addressed to the Mountain, appears to demand the answer 'Nothing'. With its Platonist intuitions, the poem that he has written refuses to permit this.

(ii) *To Jane: The Invitation*

To Jane: The Williamses (Edward, with whom Shelley drowned in July 1822, and Jane, with whom he had a rather well-matched affair in the last months of his life) were the closest and most understanding friends the Shelleys ever had. Jane was attractive and musical (see Poets in Relationship, p. 729, above), which Shelley always liked. Though not beyond the reach of pain, Mary since the children's deaths and the writing of *Epipsychidion* had been quite distanced from her husband. Publishing *The Invitation* and *A Recollection* (iii, below) in *Posthumous Poems* 1824, Mary made of them a single poem, entitled *The Pine Forest*, removing as she did so the mention of Jane.

6 *brake*: copse, thicket.

38 *stave*: verse.

53 *Of sapless green*: of evergreen pine needles (the pine, of course, is coniferous, not sapless).

59 *wind-flowers*: anemones.

(iii) *To Jane: A Recollection*

33–7 *How calm it was . . . inviolable quietness*: Variations on a theme by Coleridge (Shelley's is after all a Conversation Poem). Cf. *Frost at Midnight* 8–10: ' 'Tis calm indeed – so calm that it disturbs / And vexes meditation with its strange / And extreme silentness.' In Coleridge's night-scene it is the owl that enhances the silence; for Shelley, by day, it is the woodpecker.

45–6 *A spirit interfused . . . silent life*: Shelley's thoughts turn to *Tintern Abbey* (pantheist companion poem to *Frost at Midnight*) and the 'something far more deeply *interfused*, / Whose dwelling is the light of setting suns . . .' As in *Mont Blanc*, the Platonist in Shelley is wistful about this aspect of Coleridge and Wordsworth, but Jane, in the lines that follow, will prove to be the centre of the magic circle, not God or a divine life-force.

52 *The lifeless atmosphere*: The same denial of the One Life that is to be found in Coleridge himself, *Letter to Sara* ll. 52–3 (Poets in Relationship, above): 'These lifeless shapes around, below, above, / Oh what can they impart?'

73 *And . . . interfused beneath*: See ii. 45–6n., above. 'Interfused' is not a common word; to use it twice is to emphasize a connection with Wordsworth.

JOHN KEATS

'A Sort of Oneness'

(i) *Endymion*

777 *becks*: beckons.

780 *alchemized*: rendered fully spiritual (turned to gold); sending the final version of ll. 777–802 to his publisher on 30 January 1818, Keats remarks that the passage has been for him 'a regular steppingstone of the Imagination towards Truth'.

783 *Hist*: Used to claim attention.

783–6 *when the airy stress . . . lucid wombs*: 'Kissed' by music, the winds produce their 'Eolian magic', which proves to be an entry into the world of imagination, releasing the 'buried' poetry of the past.
788 *Old ditties . . . father's grave*: A sort of Last Trump is taking place, in which songs (like souls) rise from their graves.
789–90 *Ghosts . . . Apollo's foot*: At every place associated with Apollo, god of poetry, 'ghosts' of poetic prophecy 'rave' (as did, for instance, the Sybill in *Aeneid* VI).
791 *bruit*: sound.
792 *giant-battle*: battle of the Titans.
794 *Orpheus*: Legendary poet, prophet, musician, son of Apollo and the muse Calliope.
799 *self-destroying*: destructive of selfhood, selfishness.

(ii) *Epistle to J. H. Reynolds*

83 *bourn*: limit, the edge of one's understanding.
87 *The first page*: It is in the Book of Nature that Keats is reading his 'mysterious tale', as he sits on a rock in the Devonshire seaport of Teignmouth.
94 *maw*: stomach.
104 *pard or ounce*: leopard or lynx.

SAMUEL PALMER

Twilight Time

7 *sweet visionary gleam*: 'Whither is fled the visionary gleam', Wordsworth, *Immortality Ode* 56.
12 *this village, safe, and still*: presumably Shoreham, where Palmer lived 1827–33, before moving to Lisson Grove, London.
19 *The wether's bell*: A bell round the neck of the lead sheep (the 'bell-wether') would give notice to the shepherd of their movements.

JOHN CLARE

This Leaning Tree with Ivy Overhung

6 *can heir*: are heir to.
10 *Painting . . . fairy land*: transforming the landscape into a fairy land.
33 *my feet hath trod*: One of many cases where Clare uses a singular verb and plural noun (or vice versa).
37–40 *In Nature's . . . spring*: Clare refers to the wild, magenta-coloured English sweetpea (which does grow like a weed).
51–3 *I pause . . . silence speaks*: Clare has in mind the 'still small voice' of God heard by Elijah on Mount Horeb (1 Kings 19.11–12):

And, behold, the Lord passed by, and a great and strong wind rent the mountains, and brake in pieces the rocks before the Lord; but the Lord was not in the wind: and after the wind an earthquake; but the Lord was not in the earthquake:

And after the earthquake a fire; but the Lord was not in the fire: and after the fire a still small voice.

FELICIA HEMANS

Remembrance of Nature

7 *sparry*: lustrous with crystalline mineral deposits.
11 *Fading I Lie*: Hemans writes on her death-bed.

LETITIA ELIZABETH LANDON

(i) *Scale Force*

1–4 *It sweeps . . . sounding tide*: 'This cascade, distant about a mile and a half from the village of Buttermere, exceeds in extent of fall the renowned Niagara, yet, owing to difficulty of access, it is frequently neglected by the tourist.' (Landon)

(ii) *Fountains Abbey*

10 *fane*: temple

V. Romantic Odes

ROBERT BURNS

Despondency, An Ode

1–6 *Oppressed with grief . . . such as I*: Writing to Coleridge in Feb. 1799, Wordsworth commented: 'Burns . . . is energetic, solemn and sublime in sentiment, and profound in feeling. His *Ode to Despondency* I can never read without the deepest agitation.'

WILLIAM WORDSWORTH

The Immortality Ode

1 *There was a time*: 'At breakfast', Dorothy Wordsworth recorded in her memorable *Journal* entry for 27 March 1802, 'William wrote part of an ode. Mr Gale brought the dung, and we went out to work in the garden.' How different would this greatest of English lyric poems have been, had Mr Gale come another day, or the poet decided not to spread the manure? As it was, ll. 1–57 belong to spring 1802, the rest (including the central myth of pre-existence) was written in February 1804. In 1815 Wordsworth gave his poem (headed simply *Ode* in *Poems* 1807), the weighty title, *Ode, Intimations of Immortality from Recollections of Early Childhood.*

21 *tabor*: small drum, often used in dance music.

23 *A timely utterance . . . relief*: Despite the views of one or two notable critics, the 'utterance' that gives relief to Wordsworth's thought is the Ode that he is writing.

40 *My head . . . coronal*: Wordsworth is consciously imitating Elizabethan pastoral.

54 *pansy*: the small wild viola (American 'Johnny jump-up'); Wordsworth may be playing on the etymology of 'pansy', a '*pensée*', or thought.

59 *our life's star*: the 'sun' of our existence; the work of February 1804 begins (after almost a two-years' rest) at l. 58.

64 *trailing clouds of glory . . . come*: Wordsworth commented late in life that he had based the middle stanzas of the Ode on the Platonic myth of pre-existence, not because he believed in it as dogma, but because it had 'sufficient foundation in humanity' for him to make whatever use he chose of it as a poet.

82 *inmate*: member of a household.

84 *that imperial palace*: Wordsworth is punning on 'empyreal', belonging to the highest heaven, the 'empyrean', or realm of pure fire.

88 *sallies*: bursts.

90–92 *some little plan or chart . . . newly-learnéd art*: Wordsworth, in this least satisfactory stanza of the Ode, portrays the child as imitating adult life, and losing in the process his imaginative power.

103 *'humorous stage'*: A quotation from Daniel, *Musophilus* (1599). As the child acts out the different 'humours' and phases of life, Wordsworth is thinking too of Jaques' 'All the world's a stage' (*As You Like It* II vii).

105 *equipage*: retinue, following.

110–16 *Thou best philosopher . . . fund*: Attacked by Coleridge (in a mood of indignant common sense) as 'mental bombast', 'thoughts and images too great for the subject', *Biographia Literaria*, chapter 22.

120–23 *To whom the grave . . . waiting lie*: Lines that were later cut in response to Coleridge's protest at 'the frightful notion of lying awake in the grave', but which are true to Wordsworth's sense of the peacefulness of death.

148 *worlds not realized*: worlds to which the child's imagination cannot give reality (a hundred years before Freud, Wordsworth values uncomprehended moods of guilt and fear as having been especially formative).

151 *first affections*: early emotions.

157 *Our noisy years*: human life – but also the boisterous years of an individual childhood.

164–70 *Hence in a season . . . evermore*: In the soul's backward look at the waters of pre-existence is contained an intimation of immortality – the thought of mighty waters 'rolling *evermore*'.

193 *one delight*: the child's imaginative pleasure in Nature.

202 *Another race . . . won*: Losing the vision of childhood, the poet has run a different, adult 'race', which (as in *Tintern Abbey*) has its own 'palms' (trophies). In Wordsworth's mind is Milton, *Samson Agonistes* 597, 'My race of glory run, and race of shame'.

205 *blows*: blooms, comes into flower.

SAMUEL TAYLOR COLERIDGE

Dejection, An Ode

1 *Well, if the bard were weather-wise*: For Coleridge's Ode in its longer first version, written in April 1802 as a love letter to Sara Hutchinson, see Poets in Relationship, p. 695, above. The text presented here was published in the *Morning Post* as a tribute to Wordsworth ('Edmund') on his wedding day, 4 October 1802. Fifteen years later the Ode was published with minor revisions in *Sybilline Leaves*, addressed to an anonymous 'Lady'.

7–8 *this Eolian lute . . . mute*: Coleridge's thoughts go back to *The Eolian Harp* of 1795 (Ennobling Interchange, p. 255); there is a new implication now that it might be best if his own 'lute' (poetic voice) were silent.

18 *And sent . . . abroad*: And taken me out of myself (enabled me to respond imaginatively). Lines 17–20 are newly written for *Dejection, An Ode*.

23 *no natural outlet*: Coleridge's poem is a somewhat indignant response to Wordsworth's lament over lost imaginative power in the opening stanzas of *The Immortality Ode* (read to him by Dorothy on the evening of 4 April 1802). Attacked in stanza three by momentary lack of confidence, Wordsworth had recovered at once, and written cheerfully, 'A timely utterance gave that thought relief, / And I again am strong!'

25 *heartless*: depressive, melancholy.

37 *A boat becalmed . . . sky-canoe*: An affectionate reference to Wordsworth's Prologue to *Peter Bell* (On Poets and Poetry, below), written at Alfoxden during the time of the two poets' closest collaboration, spring 1798.

40 *genial*: warm, life-giving; Coleridge's dejection has brought to mind *Samson Agonistes*, 'So much I feel my genial spirits droop, / Nature all flat within me' and Wordsworth's earlier reference to Milton's poem, *Tintern Abbey* 114: 'Nor perchance / If I were not thus taught should I the more / Suffer my genial spirits to decay.'

41 *these*: The beautiful forms of Nature mentioned at the end of stanza II.

82 *And fruits . . . seemed mine*: A self-wounding reference to the period of shared creativity with Wordsworth and Dorothy at Alfoxden, when Coleridge in six months had written his greatest poetry.

87 *imagination!*: A Coleridge note at this point in the *Morning Post* claims that two stanzas have been omitted. *Letter to Sara Hutchinson* contains a great deal of material that he might have thought of as part of the Ode; otherwise he was just masking an abrupt transition in the poem. Seven new lines are incorporated in 1817, and two rewritten.

94 *mountain-tairn*: 'Applied to lakes up in the mountains . . . This address to the wind will not appear extravagant to those who have heard it at night in a mountainous country.' (Coleridge)

95 *clomb*: climbed.

100 *Devils' Yule*: Christmas such as devils keep.

105 *host*: army.

115–19 *'Tis of a little . . . hear*: A tender allusion to Wordsworth's Lucy Gray, lost in the snow (Romantic Hallmarks, above).

PERCY BYSSHE SHELLEY

Hymn to Intellectual Beauty

1 *The awful shadow . . . power*: Shelley's concept of 'intellectual' (spiritual) beauty draws attention to the Platonism so strong at this period also in *Mont Blanc* (Ennobling Interchange, p. 310, above).
20 *shown*: revealed, made known.
28 *their vain endeavour*: that of the sage or poet who wants a supernatural answer to his questions.
33–4 *Or music . . . still instrument*: A reference to the Eolian, or wind-harp, as in Coleridge's earlier poem (p. 255, above).
44–8 *Thou that to human thought . . . dark reality*: 'Spirit of Beauty' cannot (like Christian doctrine) guarantee an afterlife, but mitigates the 'dark reality' of the grave with its sense of man's spiritual nature.
50–51 *ruin . . . pursuing*: A true rhyme ('g' was not sounded).
53 *poisonous names . . . fed*: different names for the Christian God.
65–7 *They have in visioned bowers . . . envious night*: Night would wish to impose its darkness on the scenes of heightened enjoyment ('visioned bowers'), intellectual and erotic.

JOHN KEATS

Odes of Spring

(i) *Ode to Psyche*

2 *sweet enforcement . . . dear*: An imitation of Milton, *Lycidas*: 'Bitter constraint and sad occasion dear.'
4 *conchéd*: shell-like.
14 *Tyrian*: purple.
20 *At tender . . . aurorean love*: when dawn renews their love-making.
24–5 *Oh latest born . . . hierarchy*: Psyche, as Keats knew from Lemprière's *Classical Dictionary*, was not worshipped as a goddess until the second century AD.
26 *Phoebe's sapphire-regioned star*: Keats associates the Titaness, Phoebe, daughter of Heaven and Earth, with the moon in the sapphire-blue sky of night.
27 *Vesper*: the Evening Star.
35 *Of pale-mouthed prophet dreaming*: Keats probably has no specific prophet in mind; why he should be 'pale-mouthed' is unclear.
42 *the faint Olympians*: the gods of Mount Olympus, who succeeded the Titans – now themselves 'faint', or faded (l. 25 above).
50 *fane*: temple.
54–5 *those dark-clustered trees . . . steep*: trees of the mind, 'fledging' (with their implied feathers) the sides of imaginary mountains. In the Lake District, Keats had described the rocks near Keswick as 'fledged with ash, and other beautiful trees'.
66–7 *A bright torch . . . Love in*: Psyche's 'torch' (lamp) is a signal to her lover Eros to come to her

(ii) *Ode to a Nightingale*

4 *Lethe-wards*: into oblivion (like that caused by the waters of Lethe in the classical Underworld).
13 *Flora*: Roman goddess of flowers.
16 *blushful Hippocrene*: The water of Hippocrene (a spring sacred to the muses on Mount Helicon) turns in Keats' fantasy to wine, 'blushing' to redness.
26 *Where youth . . . dies*: Keats had nursed his brother Tom six months earlier, as he died aged nineteen of TB. He had also, though he didn't yet know it, caught the disease himself.
32 *pards*: leopards.
33 *viewless*: invisible.
37 *fays*: fairies.
43 *embalméd darkness*: sweet-smelling, scented (as in *Paradise Lost*), but bringing in a proleptic suggestion of death.
46 *eglantine*: sweetbriar; Keats has in mind Oberon's speech in *A Midsummer Night's Dream*, 'I know a bank . . . With sweet musk-roses and with eglantine'.
64 *clown*: peasant.
65–7 *Perhaps the self-same . . . corn*: The pathos of Ruth is to a large extent created by Keats. The brief book which she has to herself in the Bible shows her gleaning in the harvest-field, but not in tears or homesick (though she has been forced by famine to leave her home in Moab). She catches the eye of the owner of the field (a distant kinsman of her mother-in-law Naomi), marries him, and has a son who establishes the line of Jesse from which David (and ultimately Joseph and his son Jesus) are born.
73–4 *The fancy . . . deceiving elf*: Fancy (not discriminated by Keats from imagination) is the deceiver because despite her powers the poet has to return to reality.

(iii) *Ode on a Grecian Urn*

3 *Sylvan*: pastoral.
7 *Tempe . . . Arcady*: Names chosen to evoke Greek pastoral repose (instantly broken in upon).
11–12 *Heard melodies . . . sweeter*: Music of imagination – the inner ear – has a perfection that performance cannot achieve.
14 *ditties of no tone*: songs that are silent.
33–4 *that heifer . . . drest*: Keats, though he has recently disparaged her in a letter, is drawing on Mary Tighe's *Psyche*, 1805 (Narratives of Love, above). Claude's *Father of Psyche Sacrificing at the Temple of Apollo* is relevant too.
38–40 *And, little town . . . return*: The town for which our sympathy is so beautifully asked exists purely in the imagination and is not present on the Urn.
41–2 *Oh Attic shape . . . overwrought*: After the half-pun of 'Attic' (Athenian) and 'attitude', Keats puns twice more: on 'brede' (braid) and 'breed', and on 'overwrought' as both 'worked' ('sculpted'), and 'distressed'.

(iv) *Ode on Melancholy*

1–2 *No, no . . . poisonous wine*: Keats' draft includes a bizarre gothic first stanza, opening:

> Though you should build a bark of dead men's bones,
> And rear a phantom gibbet for a mast . . .

4 *Proserpine*: Queen of the Underworld.
6–7 *Nor let the beetle . . . mournful Psyche*: do not let the black beetle or the death's-head hawk moth (with its skull and crossbones markings) take the place of Psyche, the soul (with its emblem of the butterfly).
9–10 *For shade to shade . . . soul*: In general it is clear that Keats values the soul's vital anguish and fears lest it be overcome by darkness. But it is far from clear what are the 'shades' he refers to – or indeed whether they are of different kinds.
24 *Turning . . . bee-mouth sips*: as the bee takes nectar from the flowers pleasure turns to poison, as the 'bee mouth' sips its nectar, it experiences fulfilment.
30 *cloudy trophies*: Both, trophies hung in the clouds (heaven), and trophies that partake of Melancholy's darkening of the spirit.

(v) *Ode on Indolence*

Epigraph *They toil not . . . spin*: 'Consider the lilies of the field . . . they toil not, neither do they spin. And yet . . . even Solomon in all his glory was not arrayed like one of these' (Matthew 6.28–9).
9–10 *And they were strange . . . Phidian lore*: Keats had seen Phidias' work in the Elgin Marbles, but it is less than clear why knowing her skills should make the figures 'stranger', less likely to be recognized.
31 *I wanted wings*: I lacked the will to follow; in a different mood Keats had written, 'Give me new Phoenix wings to fly at my desire' (*On Sitting Down to Read 'King Lear' Once Again*).
59 *sprite*: spirit (the Phantoms are creations of the poet's indolent imagination, as it fends off suggestions of activity).
60 'The thing I have most enjoyed this year', Keats remarked on 9 June 1819, 'has been writing an ode to Indolence.'

PERCY BYSSHE SHELLEY

Ode to the West Wind

Headnote *cisalpine regions*: regions on this (the Italian) side of the Alps.
5–7 *Oh thou . . . wingéd seeds*: Shelley is developing images first used in his poem of political revolution, *Laon and Cythna* IX, stanzas 21–4 (1817): 'The blasts of autumn drive the wingéd seeds / Over the earth . . . The seeds are sleeping in the soil; meanwhile / The tyrant peoples dungeons with his prey . . .'
18 *Angels*: messengers.
21 *Maenad*: Frenzied dancing female worshipper of Dionysus.

32 *pumice*: volcanic; Baiae is prononced 'By-ee'.
36–42 *Thou . . . despoil themselves*:

The phenomenon alluded to at the conclusion of the third stanza is well known to naturalists. The vegetation at the bottom of the sea, of rivers, and of lakes, sympathizes with that of the land in the change of seasons, and is consequently influenced by the winds which announce it. (Shelley)

60 *Will take from both*: from both the forest and the poet (as 'lyre', or wind-harp).

VI. Romantic Lyric and Song

WILLIAM BLAKE

Song ('How sweet I roamed') *Poetical Sketches* 1783

3 *Prince of Love*: Cupid.
10 *Phoebus fired . . . rage*: the sun inspired me to sing.
11–12 *He caught . . . cage*: Blake will return to the theme of entrapment by love in *The Crystal Cabinet*, c. 1803 (p. 67, above).

ROBERT BURNS

Songs

(i) *It Was upon a Lammas Night*

1 *Lammas*: Scottish quarter-day, falling in August (originally a harvest festival at which loaves were baked of the new season's corn).
2 *corn rigs*: Parallel ridges in the cornfields, created for drainage, and some twenty feet across (rising in the centre and sloping on each side to a ditch) – Burns, of course, was a ploughman.

(iii) *A Red Red Rose*

1 *O my love's . . . rose*: Seemingly taken down by Burns in 1793 from a country-girl's singing. *Auld Lang Syne*, and many others of his songs, were 'collected' by him and retouched; this one, there is reason to believe, he left alone.

WILLIAM BLAKE

from *Songs of Innocence*

(i) *Introduction*

13–20 *Piper . . . joy to hear*: Blake was commissioned to write the *Songs of Innocence* as a children's book, but as in later works lays claim to inspiration. Critics have heard an ambiguity in his 'staining' of 'the water clear' (is he merely making ink, a process for which the word 'stain' is often neutrally used, or does the act of writing cast a shadow over innocence). The tones and attitudes adopted by Blake in his 1789 collection are those of the child, but imply our awareness of a sophisticated adult poet in the background.

(v) *Laughing Song*

1 *When the green woods . . . joy*: (May 1784) Songs (v) (vi) and (vii) occur in the MS of *An Island of the Moon* and this precede Blake's scheme for *The Songs of Innocence*.

(viii) *The Lamb*

16 *He became a little child*: Jesus is celebrated both as Creator and as the (sacrificial) Lamb of God.

(ix) *The Chimney Sweeper*

3 *weep . . . weep*: The 'cry' of the sweep as he walks the streets looking for work. Boys (sold by parents, or drawn from London orphanages) started work when they were small enough to climb the large open chimneys, and died typically of skin cancer from the heat.

(x) *The Divine Image*

13–16 *Then every man . . . Peace*: As Blake put it in *The Marriage of Heaven and Hell* (1790), 'all deities reside in the human breast'.

SUSANNA BLAMIRE

(i) *The Siller Croun*

1 *'And ye shall . . . attire'*: Blamire, who lived near Carlisle on the border of Cumbria and Scotland, wrote songs in the local Cumbrian dialect, in southern English, and, as in this case, in Scottish. The crown was a heavy silver ('siller') coin, worth five shillings – more than a labourer's weekly wages.
3 *Gin*: If.
20 *waur*: worse.

(ii) *Oh Bid Me Not to Wander*

16 *Which I . . . no more shall see*: Blamire was ill for much of 1792, and not expected to recover; she died in April 1794, aged forty-six.

WILLIAM BLAKE

from *Songs of Experience*

(i) *Introduction*

6 *lapséd*: fallen
10 *And fallen, fallen, light renew*: God, who is all-powerful and might if he wished re-create the universe, descends to Earth to mourn for fallen humanity.

(ii) *Earth's Answer*

11 *Selfish father*: Earth is subject to the repressive forces of Urizen, whose fall into selfhood created the world as we know it, and 'fathered' the human race. See *The Book of Urizen*, published in 1794, where the central figure is characterized by cold rationality, selfishness and jealousy.
13–15 *Can Delight . . . bear*: Can 'the virgins of youth and morning' bear delight to be chained in darkness; cf. *The Daughters of Albion*, Narratives of Love, above.
21–2 *this heavy chain . . . bones around*: jealousy and time are both seen in *The Book of Urizen* as a chain binding man to an earthly existence.

(viii) *London*

1–2 *chartered street . . . chartered Thames does flow*: Blake sees the streets and river as restricted, portioned out, when they ought to be free.
7 *ban*: prohibition.
16 *the marriage-hearse*: The young prostitute gives to the married man the disease that has been given to her, making marriage the vehicle of death.

(x) *The Tyger*

17–18 *When the stars . . . tears*: The stars are weeping, and we should probably see them as defeated. *Four Zoas*, plate 64, shows them as throwing down their spears and fleeing naked away.

(xi) *The Human Abstract*

24 *There grows one in the human brain!*: Mystery and religion (both associated with Urizen) are for Blake the opposite of love and imagination.

(xv) *The Fly*

1 *Little fly*: butterfly (common usage at the time).

ANN BATTEN CRISTALL

Through Springtime Walks

2 *fair*: beauty.
16 *bantered*: teased, made fun of.
18 *pregnant*: ripening.

MARY ROBINSON

A Thousand Torments

9 *blanks to reason's orb*: invisible to the 'eye' of reason.
19–20 *For jealousy . . . more*: Drawn from her novel, *Walsingham*, Robinson's poem reflects the last sad phase of her relationship with Tarleton.

THOMAS CAMPBELL

Written on Visiting a Scene in Argyleshire

4 *the home of my forefathers stood*: 'Kirnan House and garden, in the vale of Glassary, Argyllshire. The last of his race who resided on the family estate of Kirnan was Archibald Campbell, the poet's grandfather.' (Campbell)
17 *night-weed*: deadly nightshade.
33 *front*: forehead; cf. 'to put a bold front on it'.

WILLIAM WORDSWORTH

I. Alfoxden Lyric

6 *The human soul . . . ran*: Wordsworth at this period thinks of the human soul as part of a Platonist World Soul. Once he goes so far as to speak of 'the human soul of the wide earth'.
7–8 *And much it grieved . . . man*: Wordsworth's poem is a sequel to Burns' *Man Was Made to Mourn*:

> Man's inhumanity to man
> Makes countless thousands mourn!

II. Goslar Lyrics

(i) *Two April Mornings*

10 *steaming rills*: streams from which early morning mist is rising.
13 *'Our work . . . begun'*: 'The day began so well'.
51–2 *She seemed . . . on the sea*: The Matthew Poems (*Two April Mornings* and *The*

Fountain) are to be compared with the more famous Lucy Poems of the same period; see Romantic Hallmarks, above.
59–60 *with his bough . . . hand*: Matthew has picked a branch of buds or catkins from the hedge; cf. *Faerie Queene*, II i 60, 'Oft from the forest wildings did he bring'.

(ii) *The Fountain*

7 *fountain*: spring, stream.
11 *Border song or catch*: song, or 'round', from the Scottish Borders.
33 *still*: always.
45 *laws*: obligations, responsibilities.

III. Grasmere Lyrics

(i) *To the Cuckoo*

12 *visionary hours*: dreamlike past experiences.

(ii) *The Rainbow*

1 *My heart . . . behold*: 'While I was getting into bed, [William] wrote *The Rainbow*' (Dorothy Wordsworth, 26 March 1802). Next day Wordsworth wrote the opening stanzas of *The Immortality Ode* (Romantic Odes, p. 327, above).

(iii) *To H.C., Six Years Old*

1 *Oh thou whose fancies . . . brought*: Wordsworth is addressing the young Hartley Coleridge.
24 *A young lamb's heart . . . flocks*: Imagery that strongely suggests that this poem was written originally as part of *The Immortality Ode*.
27–33 *Thou art a dew-drop . . . out of life*: Wordsworth, who copied Andrew Marvell's *Horatian Ode* into his commonplace-book in spring 1804, has in mind *On a Drop of Dew* 19–22, in which 'the soul, that drop, that ray / Of the clear fountain of eternal day' is presented as conscious of pre-existence, 'Remembering still its former height'.

(iv) *The Cock Is Crowing*

8–10 *The cattle . . . like one*: 'When I returned I found William writing a poem descriptive of the sights and sounds we saw and heard. There was the gentle flowing of the stream; the glittering, lively lake; green fields without a living creature to be seen on them; behind us, a flat pasture with forty-two cattle feeding . . .' (Dorothy Wordsworth, 16 April 1802)

(vi) *I Have Thoughts that Are Fed by the Sun*

7 *Dead, without any company*: Wordsworth has in mind Arcite's death in *The Knight's Tale*. Chaucer had written,

What is this world, what asketh men to have,
Now with his love, now in his colde grave,
Allone withouten any compaignye?

IV. Grasmere Lyrics

(i) *Daffodils* (Feb. 1804, expanded c. 1815)

7–12 *Continuous . . . sprightly dance*: Wordsworth's second stanza is added at some point between *Poems* 1807 and the 1815 collection.
14 Wordsworth and Dorothy saw the daffodils beside Ullswater on 15 April 1802. Her moving *Journal* account became later the source of his poetry:

I never saw daffodils so beautiful; they grew among the mossy stones, about and about them. Some rested their heads upon these stones as upon a pillow for weariness, and the rest tossed and reeled and danced, and seemed as if they verily laughed with the wind that blew upon them over the lake, they looked so gay, ever glancing, ever changing.

21–2 *They flash . . . solitude*: Famous lines that are said by Wordsworth to have been written by his wife, Mary.

(ii) *Stepping Westward*

1 *'What . . . stepping westward'*: Dorothy Wordsworth's *Journal of a Scottish Tour* records that in August 1803 she and her brother met, beside Loch Lomond, 'two neatly dressed women without hats, who had probably been taking their Sunday evening's walk':

One of them said to us in a friendly soft tone of voice, 'What, you are stepping westward?' I cannot describe how affecting this simple expression was in that remote place, with the western sky in front, yet glowing in the departed sun.

Dorothy was copying out her *Tour* in June 1805, when her brother wrote his poem.
23–6 *The echo of the voice inwrought . . . endless way*: An image from needlework: 'human sweetness' is the surface, or 'ground', embroidered by the woman's voice with the 'thought' of endlessly travelling into the sunset.

(iii) *The Solitary Reaper*

17 *Will no one . . . sings*: The young woman is singing in Gaelic (Erse).
32 *Long after . . . more*: Wordsworth's poem, he tells us, is suggested 'by a beautiful sentence' from Thomas Wilkinson's *Tours of the British Mountains* (then still in MS):

Passed a female who was reaping alone. She sung in Erse as she bended over her sickle – the sweetest human voice that I ever heard. Her strains were tenderly melancholy, and felt delicious long after they were heard no more.

SAMUEL TAYLOR COLERIDGE

Lyrics 1798–1803

(i) *Something Childish, but Very Natural*

1 *If I had . . . wings*: Coleridge notes that his poem is an imitation of German folksong.

(ii) *The Keepsake*

1 *tedded hay*: grass that has been turned over and spread out to dry.
2–3 *The tedded hay . . . ere come*: Signs of a wet summer: hay still lying in the field unstacked when the corn has been reaped.
4 *or in the gust*: either in the wind.
14 *Emmeline*: One of Wordsworth's pet names for Dorothy, here chosen seemingly for its sound. *The Keepsake* is a fantasy-poem about what it would be like to be able to court Sara Hutchinson and marry her.
17 *And, more beloved . . . hair*: Emmeline is using her auburn hair to embroider for her lover the 'keepsake' picture of forget-me-nots.

CHARLOTTE SMITH

A Walk by the Water

5 *laving*: swimming (literally, bathing).

MARY TIGHE

Address to My Harp

2 *my secret grief*: Tighe's marriage seems to have concealed unhappiness from the first. She accepted a proposal from her first cousin though in love with someone else.
15 *partial*: well-disposed.
29 *Forced . . . this spot*: Tighe and her husband moved between Ireland and London, but *Address to My Harp* was probably written in 1804 when she became seriously ill, and left their home at Woodstock, County Wicklow, for Dublin.

DOROTHY WORDSWORTH

A Cottage in Grasmere Vale

7 *A lowly shed*: Dove Cottage, into which Dorothy and her brother had moved in December 1799; 'shed' was often used poetically of cottages at this period.

LORD BYRON

Lyrics Early and Late

(i) *The Maid of Athens*

6 *My life, I love you*: Byron presents his refrain in Greek, but offers the translation printed here. The Maid of Athens was Theresa Macri, prettiest of three teenage sisters who waited at table on him and Hobhouse in their Athens lodging-house, Christmas 1809–10.
9 *jetty*: black.
11 *the roe*: the roe deer (first seen in Western love-poetry in the Song of Songs).
14 *zone-encircled*: girdled, belted.
15 *token-flowers*: love tokens, in use in the East, 'where ladies are not taught to write, lest they should scribble assignations' (Byron).
22 *Istamboul*: Byron left abruptly for Istanbul in late January 1810; Theresa's mother, on his return to Athens, 'was mad enough to imagine' that he would marry her daughter, and he shifted his lodgings.

(ii) *She Walks in Beauty*

1 *She walks . . . night*: Byron's famous lyric (set to music in *Hebrew Melodies*, 1815) was prompted by the beauty of his young cousin, Lady Wilmot Horton, in a black mourning-dress at a ball.

(iii) *Stanzas for Music* ('There be none of Beauty's daughters')

4 *Is thy sweet voice to me*: Byron is very possibly writing for Mary Shelley's stepsister, Claire Clairmont, who came into his life just before he left England in April 1816, and had a beautiful singing voice.

(iv) *Stanzas for Music* ('There's not a joy')

1 *There's not a joy . . . takes away*: Byron's gloomy thoughts are provoked by the death of his schoolfellow at Harrow, the Duke of Dorset.
7 *magnet of their course*: compass (their sense of direction).
17 *Oh could . . . be what I have been*: Byron is seen echoing Wordsworth – 'Not for a moment could I now behold / A smiling sea, and be what I have been' (*Elegiac Stanzas* 37–8) – at a stage when Shelley's influence (usually thought to have created the Wordsworthian Byron of summer 1816) is not yet a factor.
19 *brackish*: salty, unfit for drinking.

(vi) *The Isles of Greece*

2 *burning Sappho*: For the ardent ('burning') love of the seventh-century BC Greek poetess, Sappho, see Robinson, *Sappho and Phaon* (Narratives of Love, above).
4 *Where Delos . . . Phoebus sprung*: The sun god, Phoebus Apollo, 'springs from'

(is born on) the Isle of Delos, which (with inobtrusive wordplay) 'rises' from the Mediterranean.
7 *The Scian . . . Telan muse*: Homer, and the sixth-century BC lyric-poet, Anacreon, associated respectively with the Ionian island of Chios (Scio) and the town of Telos.
9 *your shores refuse*: that is denied to your shores.
12 *Islands of the Blest*: Elysium, said to lie at the ends of the earth, and inhabited (in Homeric tradition) not by the dead, but by heroes favoured of the gods; Byron's contemporaries associated the Isles with the Canaries or Cape de Verd Islands.
13 *Marathon*: Site of the first Athenian victory over the Persians, 490 BC.
17–18 *standing . . . myself a slave*: Byron, who would fourteen years later die waiting to fight in the cause of Greek independence, visited Marathon with Hobhouse in January 1810. In context, however, *The Isles of Greece* is sung to Juan and Haidee by a Greek poet, who had 'travelled 'mongst the Arabs, Turks and Franks, / And knew the self-love of the different nations'.
19 *A King*: Xerxes.
26 *My country*: Greece (but England too, insofar as one is hearing Byron's voice).
41–2 *Of the three hundred . . . Thermopylae*: The entire Spartan army of 300 men is said to have died in battle with Xerxes' Persians at Thermopylae, 480 BC.
54 *Bacchanal*: drinker (follower of Bacchus, god of wine).
55 *Pyrrhic dance*: a mimic wardance.
56 *phalanx*: body of heavily armed foot-soldiers with linked shields.
59 *Cadmus*: Ancestral god of the Thebans, associated with the invention of agriculture, bronze-working and the alphabet.
64 *Polycrates*: tyrant of Samos from 540 BC (patron of Anacreon and others, known for his public works, encouraging the woollen industry, etc.).
69 *Miltiades*: Absolute, but enlightened, ruler of the Thracian Chersonese (Gallipoli peninsula); forced to abandon his territory to the Persians in 493 BC, Miltiades was to become three years later the victorious Athenian general at Marathon.
74 *Suli's rock and Parga's shore*: Albanian towns, Ionian in origin (the one with a rocky fortress, the other on a peninsula), known for heroic but unavailing resistance to the Turks. Sully was captured by Ali Pasha in 1803, and Parga handed over by the English in 1819.
76 *Doric*: Simplest of the musical and architectural 'modes' of ancient Greece.
78 *The Heracleidan . . . own*: 'Which Hercules might deem his own', MS.
79 *Franks*: Western Europeans; the King of l. 80 is presumably George III, who traded Parga (l. 74n., above).
90 *slaves*: Greeks who are subject to Turkish rule.
91 *Sunium's marbled steep*: Byron in 1810 carved his initials on the temple of Poseidon at Cape Sunion, a rocky promontory north of Athens.

(vii) *On This Day I Complete My Thirty-Sixth Year*

5 *My days . . . yellow leaf*: Macbeth: 'I have lived long enough: my way of life / Is fallen into the sear, the yellow leaf.'
37–40 *Seek out . . . thy rest*: Byron did not find the death in battle for which he had hoped. His last weeks brought disillusion – nothing could persuade the Greek leaders to work together to free their country from Turkish rule – and he died

on 19 April from marsh fever, weakened by repeated bleeding ordered by his doctor.

PERCY BYSSHE SHELLEY

Lyric Poetry, 1817–21

(i) *To Constantia, Singing*

1–4 *Thy voice . . . strings*: Shelley addresses Mary's stepsister, Claire Clairmont, mother of Byron's daughter Allegra, who had a beautiful voice – and for whom Byron probably wrote *Stanzas for Music* (above). If Claire ever became Shelley's mistress, it was at a later stage, in Italy.
27 *cope*: canopy.

(ii) *Stanzas Written in Dejection, December 1818, Near Naples*

22–3 *The sage . . . glory crowned*: Burns in Wordsworth's *The Leech-Gatherer* 'walks' in glory and in joy. Given the verbal link, can it be that Wordsworth (despite Shelley's indignation over his later politics), is the sage who 'walks' with inward glory?
25–6 *Others I see . . . pleasure*: Byron doubtless among them, who in December 1818 was enjoying himself in Venice.
38 *As I*: As I do.

(iii) *The Cloud*

7 *their Mother's*: Mother Earth's.
9 *flail*: implement for threshing grain to part it from the chaff.
20 *at fits*: at intervals.
23–4 *Lured by the love . . . sea*: Shelley's knowledge of clouds derives from Adam Walker, who taught both at Sion Academy and at Eton, and published on the subject in 1803. Shelley domesticates and poeticizes the scientific, as Erasmus Darwin had done in the *Botanic Garden* (1789–91), like him portraying forces of attraction within the natural world in terms of love. Walker saw water vapour as rising due to electricity, and rain as occurring in a reaction between clouds that are positively charged, and the earth that is negative. Thus the 'genii' (seemingly equated with the 'spirit' of l. 28), wherever they may be, draw down the lightning that is 'pilot' to the Cloud.
31 *sanguine*: blood-red.
33 *rack*: formation of clouds driven by the wind.
41 *pall*: rich, usually black, canopy that decks a coffin; here suggesting the dying of day.
51 *woof*: weaving, tapestry.
58 *these*: the stars of l. 52, reflected in water.
81 *I silently laugh . . . cenotaph*: The Cloud (indestructible, because she will always be reconstituted) laughs at the blue dome of the sky, which may seem briefly to be

her cenotaph (memorial), but can never be her tomb; cf. stanza two of *Ode to the West Wind* (Romantic Odes, above), where 'closing night' resembles 'the dome of a vast sepulchre'.

(iv) *Hellas: The Last Chorus*

1060–61 *The world's great age . . . return*: Shelley expected the final chorus of his Aeschylean drama on the Greek War of Independence to remind readers 'of Isaiah and Virgil, whose ardent spirits, overleaping the actual reign of evil which we endure and bewail, already saw the possible, and perhaps approaching, state of society in which *the lion shall lie down with the lamb*'.
1063 *weeds outworn*: old clothes (the snake sheds its skin annually).
1066 *Hellas*: Greece.
1068–70 *A new Peneus . . . Tempes bloom*: The River Peneus flows through the much-celebrated Vale of Tempe in northern Greece.
1071 *young Cyclads*: islands newer (or more recently celebrated) than the Aegean Cyclades.
1072–3 *loftier Argo . . . later prize*: taller ship than that in which Jason sailed, carrying a prize more up-to-date than the golden fleece.
1074 *Orpheus*: legendary poet-musician, said to be son of Apollo, who could charm all things with his music, and tried (unsuccessfully) to bring his wife Euridyce back from Hades; finally torn to pieces by maenads (women followers of Dionysus).
1076–7 *A new Ulysses . . . shore*: On his way back from Troy in Homer's *Odyssey*, Ulysses is held for seven years by the nymph Calypso, who loves him and has turned his shipmates into pigs.
1080 *Laian rage*: Warned by Apollo that he will be killed by his son if he has one, King Laius of Thebes has the infant Oedipus (best known from Sophocles's *Oedipus Rex*) exposed on a hillside to die, with a spike through his feet – hence the child's later name. Years later they meet at a crossroads and the angry Laius is killed by Oedipus, who goes on to answer the riddle of the Sphinx, freeing Thebes from her cruelty, and to marry his mother Jocasta.
1082 *a subtler Sphinx*: a modern tyrant, more skilled in the trade of death.
1090–93 *Saturn and Love . . . unsubdued*: Not one of Shelley's clearer trains of thought. Saturn, who ruled over the golden age, and Love (Eros), will come back to replace (i) their pagan successors (who fell from grace), (ii) Jesus, who rose (came to dominate – with a punning reference to the Resurrection), (iii) the countless other gods still flourishing ('unsubdued') in different parts of the world.

JOHN KEATS

(i) *Where Be Ye Going*

1 *Where be ye . . . maid*: Written at Teignmouth in Devon, and sent in a letter to Benjamin Robert Haydon: 'Here's some doggerel for you.'
15 *the daisy's eye*: A play on 'daisy', etymologically 'day's eye'.

(ii) *The Witching Time*

1 *the 'witching . . . night'*: *Hamlet* III ii.
14 *A pretty lullaby*: Keats' lullaby was written for the expected child of George and Georgiana (his brother and sister-in-law), who had emigrated to Kentucky.
21 *swathe*: swaddling-band; Keats seems to have confused linen (made from flax) and cotton.
23 *silly*: Sheep are traditionally 'silly', the word, in its different phases ('saelig', 'sely', 'silly') diminishing in power: 'sacred', 'innocent', 'foolish'.
32 *a poet evermore*: It was Keats' wish that one of his brother's children might become 'the first American poet'.

(iv) *Hush, Hush! Tread Softly*

4 *padded his nightcap*: made him drowsy with wine.
sweet Isabel: Regarded by many as a reference to Isabella Jones, hinting at an actual situation in which an elderly friend was duped; if so it is surprising that Fanny Brawne should copy the poem into a book that Keats had given her. Lovers outwitting the old and jealous appear in Catullus, Chaucer, Ben Jonson, and others, and are a truism in stage-comedy.
12 *the humming mayfly*: Mayflies don't hum. And though they are found by rivers, they are not nocturnal. Keats is thinking of the much heavier cockchafer, which hums, flies by night, and is often called the maybug.
23 *her soft brace*: Doves lay two eggs (a 'brace') – and hatch two 'soft' fledgelings.

(v) *This Living Hand*

1–3 *This living hand . . . tomb*: Back in the summer Keats had written in *The Fall of Hyperion* (On Poets and Poetry, above, p. 794), 'When this warm scribe my hand is in the grave'.

THOMAS HOOD

(i) *Ruth*

1 *She stood . . . corn*: Hood announces in his first line that this is to be a Keatsian poem, taking as its starting-point the beautiful lines from stanza vii of *Ode to a Nightingale*:

> Perhaps the self-same song that found a path
> Through the sad heart of Ruth, when, sick for home,
> She stood in tears amid the alien corn;

15 *stooks*: triangular piles of sheaves (head-uppermost to throw off rain) that stand in the harvest field until the grain is carried to stack or barn.
17–20 *Sure I said . . . home*: Hood puts himself in the position of Ruth's kinsman, Boaz, who in the Book of Ruth sees her gleaning in the harvest-field, and marries her.
18 *glean*: pick up the heads of grain left behind by the labourers.

CHARLES LAMB

(i) *To Louisa Martin, Whom I Used to Call 'Monkey'*

1–2 *Louisa . . . child*: Lamb at the end of his life was in great demand as a writer of verses in young ladies' albums – the new craze of the 1820s.
12 *The thing . . . been*: Lamb adds a touch of humour by recollecting Wordsworth's *Immortality Ode*: 'The things which I have seen I now can see no more' (l. 9).

(ii) *In My Own Album*

3 *Thou wert . . . album bright*: Lamb, in this very Metaphysical poem (written no doubt in a young lady's album), is playing on Latin *albus*, white – neuter, *album*, a white thing, or blank page.
6 *'written strange defeature'*: 'Careful hours . . . Have written strange defeatures in my face' (*The Comedy of Errors*).
8 *that . . . writing on the wall*: Belshazzar and his court are feasting, and praising 'the gods of gold, and of silver, and of brass': 'In the same hour came forth fingers of a man's hand, and wrote over against the candlestick upon the plaister of the wall of the king's palace: and the king saw the part of the hand that wrote . . .' (Daniel 5.4–5).
9 *recall*: take back again.
19 *numbers*: metre, verses.
22 *no longer brook*: can no longer stand.

FELICIA HEMANS

(i) *The Graves of a Household*

9 *the west*: North America.
20 *a blood-red . . . Spain*: Two of Hemans' brothers, and her ne'er-do-well husband, Captain Alfred, fought against the French in the Peninsular War.

(ii) *A Parting Song*

Epigraph 'Remember my poetry sometimes, my friends! My soul is imprinted upon it.'

JAMES HOGG

When Maggy Gangs Away

1–2 *Oh what . . . gangs away*: Hogg recalls in 1831, 'I heard a girl lilting over the first line to my little daughter Maggy, and forthwith went in and made a song of it'.

VII. *The Romantic Sonnet*

THOMAS WARTON

To the River Loden

14 *the Muse's laurel*: Warton was Professor of Poetry at Oxford, 1757–67, and was to become Poet Laureate in 1785. His work on the sonnet – and *To the River Loden* in particular – did much to reintroduce a form which had almost disappeared in the years since Milton.

CHARLOTTE SMITH

from *Elegiac Sonnets*

(i) *The Partial Muse*

1 *partial*: given to having favourites.
10 *hills*: obstacles.

(ii) *Should the Lone Wanderer*

11 *pencil*: paintbrush.

WILLIAM LISLE BOWLES

from *Fourteen Sonnets*

1 *Oh North . . . vales I leave*: Bowles' *Fourteen Sonnets* coincides with the expanded fifth edition (1789) of Smith's immensely successful *Elegiac Sonnets*. Her influence is seen more in Wordsworth, his pervades the early Coleridge and Lamb. Together, with their frequent reprints, they dominate the Romantic sonnet in its opening phase.

SAMUEL TAYLOR COLERIDGE

(ii) *To the River Otter*

1–5 *Dear native brook . . . light leaps*: Coleridge dedicated *Poems* 1796 to Bowles. It is not difficult to see a tradition, running back to Warton and the Loden, characterized by adult revisiting of a river known to childhood.

MARY ROBINSON

from *Sappho and Phaon*

(i) *Sappho's Conjectures*

1 *To Etna's scorching sands . . . Phaon flies*: The connected narrative of *Sappho and Phaon* is presented above (Narratives of Love). As in 'Etna's shores' (l. 9), Etna is used by Sappho as a synonym for Sicily.
7 *Idalian grove*: A grove sacred to Venus, either in Sicily, or at Idalium in Crete.
10 *A fire, more fierce than Etna's, fills my breast*: Robinson's note points to Ovid, *Heroides* XV, 12: 'Me calor Etnaco non minor igne coquit' ('Heat consumes me no less than the fire of Etna').
12 *cypress wreaths*: Associated with death, as in Feste's song, 'in sad cypress let me be laid' (*Twelfth Night* II iv).

(ii) *Her Address to the Moon*

8 *To tempt the gulf . . . assail*: to commit suicide.

(iii) *To Phaon*

7 *the trembling wire*: lyre-string.
14 *A blighted laurel*: The faded symbol of Sappho's distinction as a poet.

CHARLES LAMB

When Last I Roved

3 *Anna*: Ann Simmons, the 'fair-haired maid' of Lamb's sonnet, had been his sweetheart aged fifteen. He never married, and never ceased to regret her loss.

ROBERT SOUTHEY

To a Brook Near the Village of Corston

5 *descried*: seen.

CHARLES LLOYD

On the Death of Priscilla Farmer

4–5 *On that blest tide . . . gladden*: Charles Lloyd the Poet was eldest of fourteen children of Charles Lloyd the banker, and a favourite of his grandmother Priscilla, whom the children would visit at Bingley, on the outskirts of Birmingham, on Fridays. He became Wordsworth's brother-in-law when his sister Priscilla married Christopher, later Master of Trinity.

ANNA SEWARD

By Derwent's Rapid Stream

1 *Derwent's rapid stream*: Not the Derwent of Wordsworth's Cumbrian childhood, but the smaller river of the same name near Seward's birthplace in the Peak District of Derbyshire. There is also a Yorkshire Derwent.

MARY TIGHE

Written at Scarborough

1 *my silent home*: Tighe, whose health is already failing, has gone to the spa town of Scarborough on the north Yorkshire coast for the mineral waters and sea bathing.

CHARLOTTE SMITH

from *Elegiac Sonnets*

(iii) *To the Earl of Egremont*

5 *domes*: buildings (Latin *domus*).

Science: knowledge (the modern meaning was already current, but is ruled out by context).

WILLIAM WORDSWORTH

Sonnets of 1802

(i) *I Grieved for Bonaparté*

1 *I Grieved for Bonaparté*: Written first of the sonnets of 1802, *I grieved for Bonaparté* was inspired by Dorothy Wordsworth's reading Milton's sonnets to her brother on 21 May. Napoleon had just been declared First Consul, absolute ruler of France. In its unexpected blend of personal and political, the poem sets the tone for the great burst of sonnet writing that occurred during, and immediately after, Wordsworth and Dorothy's visit in July to his French daughter, Caroline, and her mother Annette Vallon.

(ii) *With Ships the Sea Was Sprinkled*

3 *road*: sheltered stretch of water.
8 *Her tackling . . . apparel high*: Wordsworth is drawing on lines from Skelton's *Bouge of Court*:

Methought I saw a shyppe, goodly of sayle,
Come sayling forth into that haven brood,
Her takelynge ryche and of hye apparayle.

12–14 *She will brook . . . journey took*: 'Who is there', Wordsworth commented on his interest in this particular ship, 'who has not felt that the mind can have no rest among a multitude of objects, of which it cannot make one whole, or from which it cannot single out one individual?'

(iii) *Westminster Bridge*

4–8 *This city . . . smokeless air*: Recalling their journey to Dover on 31 July 1802, Dorothy Wordsworth wrote in her *Journal*:

The City, St Paul's, with the River, and a multitude of little boats, made a most beautiful sight as we crossed Westminster Bridge. The houses were not overhung by their cloud of smoke . . . the sun shone so brightly, with such a pure light, that there was even something like the purity of one of Nature's own grand spectacles.

Writing of her brother's poem seems, however, to have been prompted by the return journey in September.

(iv) *Milton, Thou Shouldst Be Living at this Hour*

8 *manners*: moral strength; Wordsworth's revulsion against contemporary materialism is the result of his three weeks' stay in London after returning from France.

(v) *The World Is Too Much with Us*

13–14 *Have sight . . . wreathéd horn*: To form his imaginative conclusion Wordsworth conflates Spenser, *Colin Clout's Come Home Again* 245, 'Triton, blowing loud his wreathéd horn', and Milton *Paradise Lost* II 603–4: 'call up unbound / In various shapes old Proteus from the sea.'

(vi) *Ere We Had Reached the Wished-for Place*

1 *the wished-for place*: Sutton Bank, on the road between Helmsley and Thirsk (in Yorkshire), where the ground falls away suddenly, giving a magnificent view to the west.
13–14 *They . . . fade away*: The sonnet is given additional poignancy by the fact that it is written on Wordsworth's wedding day, 4 October 1802, as he and Mary travel, with Dorothy, back to Grasmere from their marriage at Brompton in Yorkshire.

(vii) *Nuns Fret Not*

3 *pensive citadels*: studies; an allusion to Milton's 'straw-built citadel' (beehive), *Paradise Lost* I, 773.
4 *wheel*: Spinning-wheel.

(viii) *Scorn not the Sonnet*

6 *Camöens . . . exile's grief*: The Portuguese national poet was 'exiled' from home during military expeditions to India and Macao in the 1550s.
11–14 *when a damp . . . too few*: Milton's few, but powerful, sonnets were written during the embattled middle period of his life.

MARY TIGHE

To Death

6 *Thy sad cold javelin*: Tighe is thinking of Death the skeleton, traditionally represented spear in hand.

JAMES LEIGH HUNT

Sonnets, 1814–18

(i) *Written During the Author's Imprisonment, November 1814*

1 *thee*: The poet's home at Hampstead, then a village north of London. Hunt served two years, 1813–15 (in relative comfort, and enjoying the admiration of Byron and others), for libel of the Prince Regent.
13 *loved hill*: Hampstead Heath.

(ii) *Written in the Spring that Succeeded Imprisonment, May 1815*

10 *prime*: dawn.

(iii) *On a Lock of Milton's Hair* (Jan. 1818)

1–4 *It lies before me . . . death*: Compare Keats, *On Seeing a Lock of Milton's Hair*, January 1818, and letter to Bailey: 'I was at Hunt's the other day, and he surprised me with a real authenticated lock of Milton's hair. I know you would like what I wrote thereon . . .'
8 *his own Delphic wreath*: poetic laurels (Delphi being sacred to Apollo, god of poetry).

MARY BRYAN

To My Brother (1815)

1–8 *Oh transient sorrows . . . fear*: An admirer of Smith and Wordsworth, Bryan is conscious of being more experimental than either. At one point she has a 'regular' sonnet of fifteen lines.

LORD BYRON

Sonnets written at the Villa Diodati, July 1816

(i) *Sonnet on Chillon*

9 *Chillon*: Byron and Shelley visited the twelfth-century fortress of Chillon, built where the Rhone enters Lake Geneva between Clarens and Villeneuve, on 23 June 1816.
13 *Bonnivard*: François de Bonnivard (1496–1570), imprisoned at Chillon 1530–36; see Byron's *The Prisoner of Chillon* (Romantic Solitude, Suffering and Endurance, above).

(ii) *Sonnet to Lake Leman*

1–2 *Rousseau, Voltaire . . . shore*: Voltaire, Rousseau, Gibbon, had all lived beside Lake Geneva (Lake Leman), but by now were dead. Madame de Staël was alive and at the height of her fame. Staying at the Villa Diodati, Byron visited her in her chateau at Coppet on the far side of the Lake.

JOHN KEATS

Sonnets of 1816–19

(i) *On First Looking into Chapman's Homer*

1 *realms of gold*: realms of the imagination.
4 *fealty*: allegiance.
6 *demesne*: dominion (pronounced 'demean').
8 *Till I heard Chapman . . . bold*: Keats had been reading Chapman's *Homer* in a folio borrowed by Cowden Clark, and vastly preferring it to Pope's translation.
10 *a new planet*: Uranus had been discovered by Herschel in 1781.
11 *stout Cortez*: It matters not at all that Balboa, not Cortez, was first of the Spanish invaders to see the Pacific. Cortez was similarly awe-struck at the sight of Mexico City.

(ii) *Great Spirits Now on Earth Are Sojourning*

1 *Great spirits . . . sojourning*: Keats celebrates in turn, Wordsworth, Leigh Hunt and the painter Benjamin Robert Haydon.
3 *Helvellyn*: Cumbrian mountain that presides over Grasmere.
5–6 *He of the rose . . . freedom's sake*: Hunt (at this period a major influence on Keats' style); see *Written During the Author's Imprisonment*, above.
7–8 *And lo . . . Raphael's whispering*: Read, 'And *he* whose stature / integrity was such that no lesser painter than Raphael could inspire him.'
9 *spirits*: scanned 'sprites' in this instance (though not in the opening line).

(iii) *To Mrs Reynolds' Cat*

1 *thy grand climacteric*: Probably twenty-one; climacteric years (normally multiples of seven) were regarded as especially critical. The human 'grand climacteric' is sixty-three.
11–12 *though the fists . . . many a maul*: Kitchen-maids have caught the cat thieving.
14 *glass-bottled wall*: Broken glass used to be embedded for protection in the top of garden walls, making them a dangerous place for the cat's 'lists' (tournament).

(iv) *On Sitting Down to Read 'King Lear' Once Again*

1 *Oh golden-tongued Romance . . . lute*: Chiefly in Keats' mind is *The Faerie Queene*; 'serene' is here stressed (as in Milton) on the first syllable.
6 *clay*: flesh – by implication, humanity.
7 *assay*: try, taste.
11 *When through . . . gone*: A draft shows Keats' meaning to be, 'When I finish reading Shakespeare's play'.
13–14 *when I am consumèd . . . my desire*: Keats' hope is that when he has 'burnt' through Shakespeare's great tragedy he will be born anew as a poet.

(v) *When I Have Fears that I May Cease to Be*

3–4 *Before high-pilèd . . . grain*: Before books of his writing ('charactery') hold the ripe produce of his mind as granaries ('garners') hold grain.
8 *the magic hand of chance*: Keats felt (as did his hostile reviewers) that some of his effects were the result of chance rather than choice.
9 *fair creature of an hour*: Apparently a woman whom Keats saw in Vauxhall Gardens.

(vi) *Bright Star*

1 *Bright star . . . thou art*: It is not clear whether Keats is addressing a particular star.
4 *eremite*: hermit, devotee.
6 *pure ablution*: the ritual 'washing' of the waves on the coast.
10 *my fair Love*: Fanny Brawne.

HORACE SMITH

In Egypt's Sandy Silence

1–5 *In Egypt's . . . Kings*: Smith's sonnet is written in competition with Shelley (see below) after visiting the British Museum's newly acquired statue of Ozymandias, Greek name of the Pharaoh, Ramases II, whose refusal (in Exodus) to let the Children of Israel leave Egypt led to Moses calling down the plagues.

9–14 *We wonder . . . place*: Smith's theme goes back to Volney's *Ruins of Empire* (1791) and beyond. Cf. Barbauld, *Eighteen Hundred and Eleven*, where North American tourists wander through deserted London:

> Pensive and thoughtful shall the wanderers greet
> Each splendid square and still, untrodden street,
> Or of some crumbling turret, mined by time,
> The broken stair with perilous step shall climb.
> (p. 13)

PERCY BYSSHE SHELLEY

(i) *Ozymandias*

1–3 *I met . . . desert*: Shelley noticeably gives Ramases II two trunkless legs, Smith only one. Both poets in imagination return the leg(s) to the desert from which the recoverable parts of the Pharaoh's statue had recently been brought to London. Hunt published both sonnets in *The Examiner*.
6–7 *Tell that its sculptor . . . lifeless things*: The 'hand that mocked' the passions of long ago is the sculptor's, 'the heart that fed' them belongs to the Pharaoh. Both are 'survived' by the passions themselves, 'stamped' on the lifeless stone.

(ii) *Lift Not the Painted Veil*

1–4 *Lift not the painted veil . . . spread*: Among the clearest references to the veil of mutability, which for Shelley (as for Blake, and the Berkleyan early Coleridge) masks the world of true realities.
6 *sightless*: out of sight.
12 *A splendour among shadows*: an enlightened spirit.
14 *and like the Preacher . . . not*: 'Vanity of vanities, saith the Preacher . . . ; all is vanity'. (Ecclesiastes 1.2).

WILLIAM WORDSWORTH

The River Duddon: Afterthought

1 *my partner and my guide*: The river has been Wordsworth's 'partner and guide' through a sequence of thirty-two sonnets, tracing the Duddon's course from the spring on Wrynose Pass down to the estuary below Broughton-in-Furness.
6 *The form remains . . . dies*: The 'form' is the river as it is perceived, the 'function' is the action of the water.

THOMAS HOOD

Written in Keats' 'Endymion'

1 *Dian*: the moon, Diana.
4 *Endymion*: the mortal shepherd with whom Diana falls in love.
8 *Tears . . . in the morn*: In the form of dew.
13–14 *Anon . . . dreamlike tale*: Keats' poem becomes, in Hood's image, an echo of the Muse's wings as she flies 'harmonious' through the vale.

HARTLEY COLERIDGE

Long Time a Child

1–5 *Long time a child . . . no fears*: The infant blessed by his father with fervent hope in Coleridge's *Frost at Midnight*, 1798 (Ennobling Interchange, above), grew up to be tiny, brilliant, drunken, much loved, but incapable of sustaining a job or an adult relationship.
12 *rathe*: early (now surviving only in the comparative, 'rather'); cf. Milton, *Lycidas*, 'The rathe primrose that forsaken dies'.

LETITIA ELIZABETH LANDON

The Castle of Chillon

1 *Fair lake*: the Lake of Geneva.
3 *with unsandalled foot*: with feet bare as an act of reverence.
7–9 *Captivity . . . bard*: Of the many distinguished figures with whom Lake Geneva is associated, Landon singles out the patriot Bonnivard (imprisoned at Chillon), Madame de Staël (in exile during the Napoleonic War) and Byron (bard, and author of *The Prisoner of Chillon*, Romantic Solitude, Suffering and Endurance, above).

VIII. The Gothic and Surreal

WILLIAM BLAKE

Fair Elenor

45–8 *My lord . . . flowers*: Blake's tones unexpectedly are those of the Song of Songs: 'My beloved is like a roe, or a young hart' (2. 9).
62–3 *sleeping . . . accurséd Duke*: Drawn from the also murdered ghost in *Hamlet*: 'Thus was I, sleeping, by a brother's hand / Of Life, of crown, of Queen, at once despatch'd' (I v).

HELEN MARIA WILLIAMS

Part of an Irregular Fragment Found in a Dark Passage of the Tower

5 *'Twas on this day*: The poem is spoken by a visitor to the Tower of London, who notices a long-unopened door. Williams notes that it is the anniversary of the murder by Richard III of the Princes, Edward V and Richard, Duke of York.
132 *Rest, troubled form*: A version of Hamlet's words to the ghost of his father on the battlements of Elsinore, 'Rest, rest, perturbéd spirit' (I v). In her gothicizing of *Hamlet*, Williams follows Walpole's *The Castle of Otranto*, and is at once followed by the sixteen-year-old Wordsworth in the beckoning spectre of his unpublished *Vale of Esthwaite*.

ROBERT BURNS

Tam O' Shanter

Epigraph *Of Brownyis . . . this Buke*: Burns' quotation is from Book VI of Gavin Douglas' translation of Virgil's *Aeneid*. Brownies are friendly spirits, bogles are goblins.
7 *lang Scots miles*: Miles (originally 1,000 Roman paces) had not yet been standardized. Scotland was among many countries where they were longer than in England/America.
28 *Kirkton Jean*: Landlady at the Kirkton ale-house.
61–2 *Or like the snow . . . for ever*: Lines singled out by Wordsworth for their beauty.
63 *the borealis race*: The Northern Lights (aurora borealis).
105 *John Barleycorn*: The corn-spirit; here effectively, alcohol (both whisky and beer depending on malted barley).

GOTTFRIED BÜRGER (trans WILLIAM TAYLOR, 1796)

(i) *Lenora*

5–6 *with Richard's host . . . to quell*: with the army of Richard I (on the Third Crusade, 1190) to fight the 'heathen' Mohammedans for the holy places in Palestine.
9–11 *With sowne . . . bydeckt*: Like Chatterton, in the *Rowley Poems*, Taylor creates a fanciful version of medieval English, based partly on the usage of Chaucer's period, partly on distortions of modern spelling.
21 *traine*: succession.
37 *paternoster*: the Lord's Prayer (Latin, 'Our Father').
60 *brings*: will bring (at death).
92 *freeke*: fleck.
98 *pin*: latch.

119 *courser*: warhorse.
145 *sarke*: shirt, nightdress.
191 *thorpe*: village, settlement.
244 *Whylome . . . blee*: once so joyful to look upon.
248 *the scythe and houre-glasse*: Emblems respectively of death and time.

(ii) *The Lass of Fair Wone*

1 *Beside the parson's . . . yew*: Taylor's title has given no clue that the fair 'wone' (dwelling-place) is cursed.
94 *wales*: stripes.
112 *the old one*: her father, the parson.
128 *Our former . . . prove*: enjoy our former pleasures.

MATTHEW 'MONK' LEWIS

Alonzo the Brave and the Fair Imogine

46 *The lights . . . blue*: Sure sign of the presence of a ghost.

WILLIAM WORDSWORTH

The Thorn

32–3 *I've measured . . . wide*: Wordsworth in his 1800 note to *The Thorn* suggested that the story might be told by a retired sea-captain. Whether or not he had this in mind when writing, he does clearly distinguish the narrator's voice from his own. Apart from being credulous and superstitious, the narrator is pedantic in his eye for detail.
49–52 *This heap of moss . . . size*: The narrator is titillated by thoughts of murder. Readers may be too. The poet is concerned rather with psychology. For the crude horror-ballad from which he is working, see Bürger, *The Lass of Fair Wone*, above.
60–3 *For oft there sits . . . scarlet cloak*: Had the poem been the murder story some have taken it to be, the last thing the poet would have done is dress his suspect in scarlet and seat her at the scene of the crime.
78–81 *Now wherefore . . . poor woman go*: The poem at this point becomes a dialogue, a second voice (in some sense Wordsworth himself) anxiously questioning the narrator.
131–2 *cinder / tinder*: Wordsworth's rhyme (presumably designed to be uncomfortable) comes from Bürger, *Lenora* 239–41, where the ghostly lover's armour is 'black as cinder . . . made of tinder'.
148–54 *Last Christmas . . . senses clear*: Farmer Simpson's speculation is not merely innocent gossip. If Martha could be proved to have killed her child when sane, she could be hanged.
232–9 *And some . . . upon the ground*: The unreliability of the narrator is typified at the end of the poem when he reports, as fact, a supernatural stirring of the ground.
243–6 *I cannot tell . . . to the ground*: Wordsworth's motivation in writing *The*

Thorn has been much debated. It may be that his Fenwick Note of 1842 is as good a clue as any:

Arose out of my observing on the ridge of Quantock Hill, on a stormy day, a thorn, which I had often passed in calm and bright weather without noticing it. I said to myself, cannot I by some invention do as much to make this thorn permanently an impressive object as the storm has made it to my eyes at this moment? I began the poem accordingly, and composed it with great rapidity.

SAMUEL TAYLOR COLERIDGE

Christabel, Part I

1–3 *'Tis the middle . . . Tu-whoo!*: 'The metre of *Christabel*', Coleridge writes in the Preface to his 1816 first edition, is not, properly speaking, irregular, though it may seem so from its being founded on a new principle: namely, that of counting in each line the accents, not the syllables. Though the latter may vary from seven to twelve, yet in each line the accents will be found to be only four. Nevertheless, this occasional variation in number of syllables is not introduced wantonly, for the mere ends of convenience, but in correspondence with some transition in the nature of the imagery or passion.
5 *crew*: crowed.
14–15 *Is the night . . . but not dark*: Compare Milton, *Comus* 220–23,

Was I deceived, or did a sable cloud
Turn forth her silver lining on the night?
I did not err, there doth a sable cloud
Turn forth her silver lining on the night . . .

26 *furlong*: 220 yards.
49–52 *The one red leaf . . . the sky*: A detail that Dorothy Wordsworth notes in her *Journal* for 7 March 1798: 'One only leaf upon the top of a tree – the sole remaining leaf – danced round and round like a rag blown by the wind.'
155 *Save the boss . . . tall*: Geraldine's having to be carried over the threshold, her inability to pray, the behaviour of dog and fire, have all implied that she is a supernatural presence; it is less clear how Sir Leoline's shield fits into the pattern.
165 *press down*: Geraldine, it seems, has bodily weight. For all her powers, she is therefore human.
219–24 *All they who live . . . requite you well*: Geraldine's good intentions, like her momentary wish that Christabel's mother should appear, are to be attributed to the 'virtuous powers' of the wild-flower wine, but may none the less reveal an underlying good nature.
247 *Yet Geraldine . . . scorn and pride*: Lines of great importance that were added by Coleridge after the first edition as a replacement for the original l. 247, 'She took two paces and a stride'. Geraldine's reluctance suggests that rather than acting on her own volition, she is herself possessed and has a task to perform.
253–64 *In the touch of this bosom . . . damp air*: With the marvellous sound-effects

of Geraldine's spell, Coleridge's work in 1798 concludes. He couldn't take his poem further – bring it to the point where Geraldine is punished, or more probably redeemed, and Christabel's mother enabled to hear the Castle-bell 'strike twelve upon [her child's] wedding-day'. In autumn 1800 Coleridge did add a second Part (transferring the story to the Lake District, and building up a sinister relationship between Geraldine and Sir Leoline), but once again he was unable to write a conclusion. The unfinished poem was admired in manuscript, and imitated by Scott and Byron, before being published with *Kubla Khan* in 1816. Coleridge offered different accounts as to how the poem would have proceeded, none very convincing.

ROBERT SOUTHEY

The Old Woman of Berkeley

27 *But I secured . . . souls*: By having both son and daughter go into the Church.
30 *The fiends*: Southey cites as 'the original authority' for his story William of Malmesbury, who had it from an eyewitness.
86–9 *To see the priests . . . burning bright*: Clearly based, like the metre of *The Old Woman of Berkeley*, on *The Ancient Mariner* (which Southey had disparaged only weeks before in the *Critical Review* as 'a Dutch attempt at German sublimity'):

> This seraph-band, each waved his hand –
> It was a heavenly sight –
> They stood as signals to the land,
> Each one a lovely light.

105 *told their beads*: said the prayers of the Catholic rosary.

WALTER SCOTT

The Lay of the Last Minstrel

1 *fair Melrose*: Melrose Abbey, thirty miles from Edinburgh; the aged Minstrel is singing to the harp his story of magic and medieval Scottish conflicts.
6 *oriel*: bay window.
16 *St David's ruined pile*: Melrose Abbey was founded by David I of Scotland (1085–1153).
19 *Deloraine*: Sir William of Deloraine has been sent by Lady Margaret of Branksome Hall to bring the magic book of the wizard, Michael Scott, to her in her hour of need.
21 *wicket*: small door cut into the Abbey-gate.
28 *fence*: defend.
29 *rood*: measurement of land (not very accurately defined).
39 *aventayle*: visor of a medieval helmet.
40 *aisle*: Used in this case to mean 'convent'.
54 *scourge of thorn*: For lashing himself in penance.

60 *drie*: suffer; an archaism (normally spelt 'dree') that Scott revived.
66 *Avé Mary*: 'Hail Mary'; a prayer that alternates in the Roman Catholic rosary with the *paternoster* ('Our Father').
67 *foray*: raid.
74 *bye*: pseudo-medieval spelling of 'by'.
87 *glowing north*: the effect of the Northern Lights (aurora borealis).
90 *jennet*: light horseman, or small Spanish horse.
94 *postern-gate*: postern, back way in; there is no warrant for Scott's pseudo-medieval spelling, with 'a' for 'o'.
99 *quatre-feuille*: four-leaved heraldic design.
100 *corbells*: carved projections from the wall to carry floor-beams, or the roof.
104 *scutcheon*: heraldic shield.
106 *pale*: fence, screen.
109 *Otterburne*: Village in Northumberland where a battle took place, which the Scots won, though their leader, Sir William Douglas, was killed by Henry Hotspur
110 *Liddesdale*: Another name chosen for its chivalric colouring.
117 *osier wand*: flexible willow-shoot, used in basket-making.
125 *Triumphant Michael*: the Archangel Michael, triumphant in his fight against Satan (variously seen as the dragon, and an apostate angel).
127–8 *The moonbeam kissed . . . stain*: A passage that Keats has in mind when in *The Eve of St Agnes* moonlight, passing through stained glass, throws 'warm gules on Madeline's fair breast' (Narratives of Love, above).
133 *Paynim countries*: The Monk has been a Crusader in the 'heathen' lands of the Middle East.
138 *Michael Scott*: Famous magician, with whom Walter Scott claims kin.
140 *Salamanca*: Spanish cathedral city.
141 *Him listed*: It pleased him.
145–6 *The words . . . stone*: Folklore has it that magic powers split the hills, and forced the river into a gorge.
163 *his chief of Branksome's need*: Deloraine has come to fetch the magic book because Lady Margaret (present 'chief' of Branksome, and herself a magician) is threatened with marriage to a traditional enemy.
187 *eternal doom*: Last Judgement.
214 *palmer's amice*: pilgrim's garment of white linen.
221 *fellest*: fiercest.
228 *owned*: admitted to, confessed.
241 *yawning stone*: gaping entrance to the grave.
269 *sped*: offered up.

JAMES HOGG

The Wife of Crowle

8 *for a meed*: compulsively, for its own reward.
14 *urn*: grave, resting place.
16 *dead-lights over him burn*: 'corpse-candles' burn over him (figuratively, he is dead).

45 *the flame burnt blue*: Traditional in the presence of a ghost.
51–2 *But each finger's . . . my knee*: A strange detail. Is the Wife's vision blurred? Or does the ghost increase in size? Or could they be *her* fingers?
55 *my blood was boiling*: With extremes of emotion (not anger, as in modern usage).

GEORGE CRABBE

Peter Grimes

7 *in his hand*: by the hand.
26 *the sacrilegious blow*: To strike a parent is 'sacrilege' against the Fifth Commandment: 'Honour thy father and thy mother, that thy days may be long in the land which the Lord God giveth thee.'
32 *inn-settle*: pub bench.
66 *the slave was bound*: The apprentice was 'bound' for seven years to his master, who would be paid a small sum for the child's keep and instruction. London orphanages supplied with 'slaves' the mines and factories of the Industrial Revolution.
67 *trap*: small two-wheeled horse-carriage.
111 *blow*: injury.
138 *draughts*: catches.
140 *mart*: market.
170 *railed*: complained.
181 *neap*: low.
195 *golden-eye*: sea duck with a harsh cry.
197 *bittern*: large marsh bird, now extremely rare in Britain.
220 *bootless labour*: pointless, unavailing.
234 *glasses*: spy-glasses (telescopes).
235 *as anchored for the tide*: as they lay anchored, waiting for high tide to take them up the river.
243 *stations*: points, viewing-places.
251 *Furious*: insane.
up the country: inland.
253 *we*: 'When the reader enters the poem', Crabbe writes in his Preface, 'he will find the author retired from view, and an imaginary personage brought forward to describe his Borough for him.'
300 *paddled*: rowed.
309 *a thin pale boy in either hand*: Presumably the second and third apprentices who (by implication) were murdered, when the first merely died of maltreatment.
346 *villain-sprite*: ill-natured ghost (spirit).

JOHN KEATS

La Belle Dame Sans Merci

1 *Oh, what can . . . knight-at-arms*: Keats writes *La Belle Dame* in April 1819, three months after making what appears to be a reference to the poem in *The Eve of St Agnes*: Porphyro in Madeline's bedroom plays 'an ancient ditty, long since

mute, / In Provence called *La Belle Dame Sans Merci*'. The explanation seems to be that in January he borrowed the title of Porphyro's song from a medieval French poem by Alain Chartier, then in April was inspired by his own evocative lines to write the ballad.
16 *her eyes were wild*: Keats in this beautiful line is probably aware of the opening of Wordsworth's *The Mad Mother*, 'Her eyes are wild . . .', and of the reference to Dorothy Wordsworth's eyes as 'wild' at the end of *Tintern Abbey*.
18 *fragrant zone*: girdle of sweet-smelling flowers – Spenser's enchantresses, 'false' Fidessa (*The Faerie Queene* I) and 'false' Florimel (Book III) both have similar garlands.
32 *kisses four*: Keats' explanation is charming: he was 'obliged to choose an even number that both eyes might have fair play' and might have said 'score' (twenty) without hurting the rhyme, but that would have shown 'headlong impetuosity'.
39–40 *La belle Dame . . . thrall*: To some extent no doubt La Belle Dame represents Keats' sense of being 'enthralled' by Fanny Brawne.
41 *starved lips*: dead or withered, rather than 'hungry' (Anglo-Saxon *steorfan*, to die).
45 *sojourn*: linger (pronounced 'sudgen').

JOHN CLARE

Superstition's Dream

55 *yawing rents*: wide-open gaps.

THOMAS LOVELL BEDDOES

from *The Bride's Tragedy*

6–7 *And made my heart . . . courtship*: The bizarre 'toadish hisses' of l. 3 confirm that in Beddoes' mind is Satan, *Paradise Lost* IV, 800, squatting at the ear of Eve.
11 *out-jetting*: blacker than.
24 *Set in the stitchéd picture*: Embroidered on the bed curtains.
29 *burden*: chorus.
37 *worsted*: woollen thread.
39 *limned so cunningly*: depicted scenes so skilfully.
45 *I thought of once*: who used to be the centre of my thoughts.
54 *this iron aspic*: Literally this 'iron serpent'. Among Beddoes' grandest Gothic phrases. Though writing with Macbeth's airborne (and, at one point, bleeding) dagger in mind, he has powerfully recreated both situation and imagery.
57 *imp*: offspring.
60 *Syren of Acheron*: temptress from Hell (Acheron being one of the rivers of classical Hades, and sirens luring sailors to death with their music).

THOMAS CAMPBELL

The Last Man

19 'Many years ago', Campbell wrote in a letter of September 1823, 'I had the idea of this Last Man in my head and distinctly remember speaking of the subject to Lord Byron. I recognized, when I read his poem *Darkness*, some traits of the picture which I meant to draw, namely, the ships floating without living hands to guide them – the earth being blank – and one or two more circumstances . . . I am entirely disposed to acquit Lord Byron of having intentionally taken the thoughts.'

THOMAS HOOD

The Last Man

5 *the pest*: the plague (which destroys the human race also in Mary Shelley's *The Last Man*, published earlier in 1826 than Hood's poem, and to some degree an influence).
9 *duds*: worn-out clothes.
15 *orts*: leavings.
17 *Newgate-bird*: gaol-bird (Newgate being the London prison famous for its 'new drop').
18 *snaps*: provisions (originally small crisp cakes, as in 'brandysnaps').
40 *case-bottle*: hip-flask.
51 *the very Old One*: the Devil himself.
73 *boused*: drank (boozed).
109 *mumping*: wheedling, coaxing.
131 *kine*: cows.
152 *corals*: teething-toy, made of coral.
164 *bags*: The 'greasy bags' of l. 12?
222 *to pull my legs*: At public executions, friends pulled down on the legs of those who were hanged to enable them to die more quickly.

IX. Romantic Comedy and Satire

WILLIAM BLAKE

Songs from *An Island in the Moon*

(i) *Old Corruption*

1 *When Old Corruption first begun*: Blake (aged twenty-six) presumably wrote *An Island in the Moon* for a small circle of friends, who form part of the cast but cannot now be identified. Certain 'humour' names are readily explained, including Tearguts

(John Hunter, surgeon-extraordinary to George III, 1776, and first to give surgery a considered scientific basis), Inflammable Gas (Joseph Priestley, discoverer of oxygen, polymath, founder of modern Unitarianism), Etruscan Column (Josiah Wedgwood (potter and inventor who brought back antique design, called his factory Etruria, and built a model village for his workmen). Often the satire is broad, and allusions seem to be private jokes. Blake himself would seem to be Cynic. What Plutarch had done to deserve to be operated on is far from clear.
11 *he*: Surgery (who has to be suckled by his father, Corruption, because his mother, Flesh, won't feed him). Blake's allegory seems to be more a case of exuberance than precision.
23 *the father*: surgery.
25 *procured these imps*: begotten these little devils.

(ii) *Lo, the Bat*

5 *Like Doctor Johnson*: Blake's verses seem to have been written a year after Johnson's death in 1784.

(iii) *Village Cricket*

6 *tansey*: cowpat.

ROBERT BURNS

Holy Willie's Prayer

Argument *Mauchline*: Burns' parish at Mossgiel Farm.
Sessional process: Proceedings at the Kirk 'Sessions'; Hamilton, who was Burns' solicitor and friend, was accused of disbelief in 'Effectual Calling' (Predestination, see ll. 15–18n. below).
country: region.
1–2 *Oh thou that in the heavens . . . thysel*: Psalm 115.3, 'As for our God, he is in Heaven; he hath done whatsoever pleased him.' Biblical references in Willie's 'Prayer' are too frequent to be regularly noted.
15–18 *I, wha deserved . . . Adam's cause*: As a Presbyterian (Calvinist), Willie believes not only that all human-beings are guilty of original sin (Adam's Fall), but that from Creation (traditionally computed at 4004 BC), some are predestined to Heaven, others to Hell.
39 *in warldly trust*: In secular matters entrusted to his care (as well as being an Elder of the Parish, ordained 1772, Fisher is a valuer of farm produce).
45 *a living plague*: constant reproach (Proverbs 6.32, 'whoso commiteth adultery with a woman . . . a wound and dishonour shall he get, and his reproach shall not be wiped away').
58 *gifted*: fortunate, favoured (2 Corinthians 12.7, 'lest I should be exalted above measure . . . there was given to me a thorn in the flesh, the messenger of Satan to buffet me').
59–60 *thy hand . . . lift it*: until you lighten the burden that your hand imposes.
62 *here thou hast a chosen race*: Burns was appalled by the doctrine of the elect ('chosen') and the damned.

67 *Gaun Hamilton's deserts*: See Argument, above.
77–8 *Curse thou . . . potatoes*: A traditional curse on the food that is eaten: 'Cursed shall be thy basket and thy store', Deuteronomy 28.17.
80 *that Presbytry of Ayr*: See Argument, above.
81–2 *Lord, make it bare . . . heads*: God is to roll up his sleeves: 'The Lord hath made bare his holy arm in the eyes of all nations', Isaiah 52.10.
85 *glib-tongued Aiken*: Hamilton's Counsel at the Presbytery appeal; see Argument.
89 *Auld*: William Auld, Minister at Mauchline; initially it seems that Auld admired Hamilton and sided against Fisher.
92 *Lord visit . . . employ him*: God is to punish ('visit' with divine justice) both Aiken and his employer, Hamilton.
99 *gear*: Property that will, in Willie's view, show that the grace of God is upon him.
102 *Amen! Amen!*: Though Burns was outlived by Fisher, he wrote him a notable epitaph:

> Here Holy Willie's sair-worn clay
> Taks up its last abode;
> His saul has ta'en some other way –
> I fear, the left-hand road! . . .

MARY ROBINSON

January, 1795

10 *meeting-houses*: chapels.
15 *placemen*: worthless people in government posts.
35 *Odes*: about public figures and public events (often written in hopes of reward).
38 *Generals . . . nurses*: A line that might not have given pleasure to Robinson's lover, General Banastre Tarleton.
44 *art*: cunning.

WILLIAM WORDSWORTH

Ballad Comedies, spring 1798:

(i) *The Idiot Boy*

16 *Him whom she loves, her idiot boy*: Wordsworth's comedy, and the reassuring voice of his narrator, allow us to feel at ease with Betty's love and Johnny's idiocy (the two facts of his poem about which we might feel uncomfortable), creating in the repetitions of this tender line a sort of refrain.
81 *And seems no longer in hurry*: Though Wordsworth late in life commented of *The Idiot Boy*, 'I never wrote anything with so much glee', he writes with the serious purpose of showing 'that people who do not wear fine clothes can feel deeply'. Defending his poem in June 1802 against a correspondent shocked at the one-sidedness of Betty's love, he wrote:

I have indeed often looked upon the conduct of fathers and mothers of the lower classes of society towards idiots as the great triumph of the human heart. It is there that we see the strength, disinterestedness, and grandeur of love . . .

136 *Of Johnny's wit and Johnny's glory*: Clearly Johnny is incapable of wit, but it is not so certain that he has no glory. Wordsworth's 1802 letter comments, 'I have often applied to idiots, in my own mind, that sublime expression of Scripture that *their life is hidden with God.*'
178 *quandary*: Stressed on the second syllable, and repeated, for comic effect.
318 *She thinks no more of deadly sin*: Suicide was regarded as the sin of rejecting God's gift of life.
347–54 *I to the Muses . . . aid bereave me*: Wordsworth has been apprenticed (bound by indentures) to the muses of poetry for twice the normal seven years (taking him back to 1784, date of his first recorded poem written at Hawkshead Grammar School). In his comic reproaches he draws surprisingly on Joanna Baillie's *Address to the Muses*, published anonymously in 1790, and little noticed (see On Poets and Poetry, p. 763, above):

> Oh lovely Sisters! is it true
> That they are all inspired by you? . . .
>
> Oh lovely sisters! well it shows
> How wide and far your bounty flows –
> Then why from me withhold your beams?
> (ll. 61–2, 67–9)

357–61 *Who's yon . . . feeding horse*: With his holly bough and implied oneness with the natural world, Johnny's life has for the poet an element of mystery.
460–61 *'The cocks did crow . . . shine so cold'*: Wordsworth claimed to have heard Johnny's words attributed to a local Down's syndrome child in Somerset, and to have taken them as the starting-point of his poem.

(ii) from *Peter Bell*

531–5 *Is it some party . . . all damned*: Lines described by the normally contemptuous Byron as 'inimitably good', and used by Shelley as epigraph and starting-point in *Peter Bell the Third* (see On Poets and Poetry, above).
536–40 *'Tis no such thing . . . flesh and blood*: Beside the River Swale (in Yorkshire) Peter Bell the Potter has found a donkey hanging its head over the water, and decided to steal it. But it won't budge – though he has beaten it with his staff, and finally knocked it down. He is a shifty and superstitious man, and now his eye has caught sight of something in the river that he doesn't quite like.
618 *transition tragic*: A comic allusion to *peripeteia*, the sudden turn of events in dramatic tragedy.
623 *uncouth*: awkward.
637 *sapling*: staff, made of a young tree.
650 *Uprises like a ghost*: Wordsworth is recalling the drowned schoolmaster of Esthwaite Water, who in the slightly later *Prelude* 'spot of time' (Ennobling

Interchange: Man and Nature, p. 257, above) is said to rise 'bolt upright / . . . with his ghastly face'.

(iii) *We Are Seven*

1–4 *A simple child . . . of death*: Wordsworth began his poem at the end, writing the last line first, and working up to it. When it was complete but for an opening stanza he came in to tea with Coleridge and Dorothy; Coleridge wrote lines 1–4 impromptu, working in the reference to Jim (originally Jem) as a private joke for their friend James Tobin.
5 *I met . . . cottage-girl*: Wordsworth had met the child with whom the conversation (or something like it) occurred, five years before at Goodrich Castle, on the same walk that took him, for the first time, past Tintern Abbey.
47 *porringer*: small basin for soup or porridge.

JOHN HOOKHAM FRERE AND GEORGE CANNING

from *The Rovers*

Author's Headnote *the perfidy of a Monk*: Though broadly a parody of Schiller's *Robbers* (translated into English 1791, and the dominant influence on early Romantic tragedy), *The Rovers* is full of side-references – for instance to Ambrosio in Lewis' Gothic novel, *The Monk* (1795).

chained, coffined, confined: 'Now am I cabined, cribbed, confined . . .' (*Macbeth* III iv 24).
8 *knotting in*: embroidering.
13 *barbs*: steeds.

ROBERT SOUTHEY AND SAMUEL TAYLOR COLERIDGE

The Devil's Thoughts

1–4 *From his brimstone . . . went on*: The first three stanzas, and last four, are by Southey.
12 *the story of Cain and Abel*: First instance of fratricide, as Adam's younger son, Cain, murders his elder brother, Abel.
16 *Death in the Revelation*: 'And I looked, and behold a pale horse: and his name that sat on him was Death' (Revelation 6.8).
19–20 *For I sat myself . . . knowledge*:

> 'So clomb this first grand thief . . .
> Thence up he flew, and on the tree of life . . .
> Sat like a cormorant.'
>
> *Paradise Lost* IV, 194–6

22 *blade*: a gallant, young man-about-town (so-called from his wearing a sword).
27–8 *the long debates . . . abolition*: Debates in Parliament went on until 1807.
39–40 *The pig. . . throat*: Pigs apparently can swim, but strike their throats with their front trotters.
47 *a consecrated flag*: a battle-standard blessed by the Church.
50–51 *Religion . . . W[ilberforce]*: Religion could well be a stab at his friend and fellow-evangelical Hannah More; as well as presenting the anti-slavery bills in Parliament, Wilberforce was famous as an evangelical Christian.
53 *Gascoigne*: Gascoigne seems to have been chosen (by Southey) merely as a red-faced General. In a MS belonging to Coleridge's son Derwent the gap is filled instead by Tarleton, known for bloodthirstiness in the American War, and as the treacherous lover of Mary Robinson, to whom Coleridge was close in 1799, the last year of her life.
57 *general conflagration*: Armageddon, at which the world will be consumed in fire.

GEORGE CRABBE

Procrastination

43 *still*: always.
77 *tabby vest*: watered silk undergarment.
94 *Saw cleaned the plate*: saw that the silver was cleaned.
95 *passion for a shilling*: love of money.
151 *purchase*: acquisition.
159 *culled for wealth by vanity*: created by vanity for the rich.
167 *By hope . . . wealthy maid*: by those hopeful of gaining her favour.
178 *brilliants*: jewels (used in clock-making because they show less wear than metal).
185 *wicked men in scarlet coats*: soldiers.
201 *starch*: prim.
202–3 *Not in her ancient . . . to know*: not playing her 'old' (normal) part, as when she came to ask the instructions she knew she would receive.
243 *For other spousal*: for meeting Christ, as 'Bridegroom', on Judgement Day.
265 *a trimmer spark*: a lover in better shape.
274 *trepanned*: had a circular piece of his skull removed to relieve pressure on the brain.
305 *shares a parish-gift*: became a pauper receiving charity from the parish, and wearing the blue serge coat and badge mentioned in l. 304.
311–12 *her braid / (A costly purchase*: Dinah's hair was professionally braided, perhaps with expensive silks.
345–8 *the way the Levite . . . the other side*: The traveller in Jesus' parable of the Good Samaritan, who fell among thieves and is left naked and bleeding on the side of the road, is famously passed by the Levite on the other side, before the Samaritan tends to him and binds up his wounds (Luke 10.33).

JAMES SMITH

The Baby's Debut, by W. W.

1–2 *My brother Jack . . . New Year's Day*: The most famous of James and Horace Smith's parodies of contemporary poets, *Rejected Addresses* (1812), were inspired by the competition announced by Drury Lane in September for an 'Address' to be spoken when the rebuilt theatre was opened after the fire of 1809. The 'true' Address, written by Byron, was not well received, the 'rejected' ones were enormously popular. Murray turned the copyright down at £20 – and bought it after the eighteenth edition. Smith starts his poem with *We Are Seven* in mind, but is parodying in general what contemporaries thought of as the 'puerility' of *Lyrical Ballads*.
37 *chaise*: two-wheeled carriage, typically drawn by a single horse.
47 *flags*: paving stones.
48 *where I am*: at Drury Lane.
53–4 *But never, never . . . I see*: cf. *The Thorn* ll. 53–4.

> But never, never anywhere,
> An infant's grave was half so fair!

61 *the wing*: edge of the stage, where actors wait for their cue.
83–4 *And if you'll blow . . . to you*: cf. *Simon Lee* 79–80.

> It is no tale, but should you think
> Perhaps a tale you'll make it.

JAMES HOGG

from *The Poetic Mirror*

(i) *James Rigg*

1–4 *On Tuesday morn . . . down stairs*: Wordsworth had published *The Excursion* in 1814 with the words, 'Being a Portion of *The Recluse*' on the title page, and gone on to name sections of the poem that he would never (as it turned out) be able to complete. Hogg fastens on the self-agrandizement and offers a brilliant parody of *Excursion* blank verse, with its weakness of syntax, its blending of matter-of-fact with pomposity and grandiloquence.
26–7 *the frontal glory . . . Child of the desert)*: the brow of the camel?

(ii) *Isabelle*

1 *Can there be . . . tonight*: Though *Isabelle* is a parody of Coleridge's *Christabel* (recently published in 1816), Hogg opens with a reference to Wordsworth, *The Idiot Boy* 161–4: 'As sure as there's a moon in heaven . . . The moon's in heaven, as Betty sees.'
15 *Said Isabelle, 'So let it be'*: *Christabel* I, 227: 'Quoth Christabel, "So let it be."'

16–17 *Why does . . . dewy dell*:

> The lovely lady, Christabel . . .
> What makes her in the wood so late,
> A furlong from the Castle-gate?
> (*Christabel* I, 23–6)

19–24 *And how often the rail . . . hour is near*: Elegant parody of Coleridge's second stanza, as the landrail, or corncrake (now almost extinct in Britain), takes over with its raucous cry from the calibrated howling of the mastiff bitch.
28–9 *Sounds the river . . . but not loud*: Parody of the awkward repetition, *Christabel* I, 14–15,

> Is the night chilly and dark?
> The night is chilly, but not dark

which Coleridge himself imitated from Milton, *Comus* 220–23.
32 *'Tis like a whale*: Shakespeare makes his appearance; cf. *Hamlet* III ii 379–82: *Hamlet* 'Methinks it is like a weasel.' *Polonius* 'It is backed like a weasel.' *Hamlet* 'Or like a whale.' *Polonious* 'Very like a whale.'

JOHN HOOKHAM FRERE

'Irrational Gigantic Anger'

1 *Mr Murray*: Byron's publisher, who no doubt sent him a copy of *Whistlecraft* when it came out, thus storing up trouble for himself. Frere's poem, with its conversational tones and flexible Italian stanza, inspired Byron to the writing first of *Beppo*, then *Don Juan*, which caused the squeamish Murray such anxiety.
9 *Thalia*: Muse of Comedy.
15 *stages*: stagecoaches.
20 *compass*: contrive, accomplish.
24 *Arms and the Monks I sing*: 'Arms and the man I sing' (first words of Virgil's *Aeneid*). Frere's title page proclaims his poem – with a satirical glance at the 'Prospectus to *The Recluse*' in Wordsworth's *Excursion* (1814) – to be 'Prospectus and Specimen of an Intended National Work, by William and Robert Whistlecraft, of Stow Market in Suffolk, Harness and Collar-Makers, intended to comprise The Most Interesting Particulars relating to *King Arthur and His Round Table*'.
31 *exemplary*: stressed éxemplåry (very often at this period the prefix is still stressed).
40 *cut him for the stone*: operated on him to remove a gallstone.
120 *gigantic*: Frere clearly is aware that 'gigantic' comes from Anglo-Saxon 'gigant', a giant.
137–8 *Cader-Gibbrish . . . Loblommon*: Cader Idris, Ben Lomond.
142 *Discussed . . . by reverberation*: Frere's brilliant comedy of the mountains 'discussing by reverberation' owes something to the laughter in Wordsworth's *Joanna*, echoed backwards and forwards among the Cumbrian fells.

JOHN KEATS

Old Meg She Was a Gypsy

1–4 *Old Meg . . . out-of-doors*: Keats is writing for his sister Fanny who is just fifteen, on his Scottish trip of July 1818. 'If you like these sort of ballads', he tells her, 'I will now and then scribble one for you.' Brown, it seems, had been talking on their walk about Scott's *Guy Mannering*, and Keats' imagination got to work on the figure of the gypsy Meg Merriles.
25 *Old Meg . . . Margaret Queen*: In a Scottish context, Queen Margaret suggests Margaret Tudor, daughter of Henry VII, who married James IV in 1503 when she was thirteen, and showed courage when her brother Henry VIII's invading army killed her husband at Flodden ten years later. But what did Keats know of these things?
26 *Amazon[s]*: mythical race of woman warriors (normally thought of as fierce rather than tall).

PERCY BYSSHE SHELLEY

Sin (*Peter Bell the Third* IV, 1–65)

1–2 *Lo, Peter . . . in the Devil's service*: *Peter Bell the Third* is not a parody of Wordsworth's poem, which Shelley almost certainly hadn't read. It is an extravaganza that joins in the fun surrounding the appearance (after twenty years) of *Peter Bell* and its pompous Preface, and that makes en route a brilliantly witty and intelligent assessment of the nature of Wordsworth's mind and art. Learning that *Peter Bell* was going through the press, Keats' friend Reynolds had (in April 1819) beaten it into print by a fortnight with *Peter Bell, A Lyrical Ballad*, parodying Wordsworth's unread poem (on the basis chiefly of *The Idiot Boy*) and claiming to be the original version. Hunt had then reviewed Wordsworth (calling *Peter Bell* unimaginatively a 'didactic little horror') and Keats had reviewed Reynolds. It was on the slender basis of these essays, especially Hunt's (which quoted the 'party in a parlour' stanza, asking whether Wordsworth truly thought his 'fellow-creatures' damned) that Shelley in October embarked on his own poem, showing Peter as 'promoted' by the Devil.
6 *Peter*: Wordsworth (with very little reference to Peter Bell).
57 *And kissed . . . sister's kiss*: Naughty, but entirely relevant, allusion to Dorothy, who did in many ways represent Nature for Wordsworth.
58 *My best Diogenes*: Surely not the fourth-century Cynic philosopher, who was remarkably unWordsworthian, but the less famous earlier Diogenes of Appolonia, who taught that air was the primary substance, rarified and condensed in different forms of matter, but in itself intelligent and divine, and constituting the mind and soul in living creatures. Cf. the divine 'presence' of *Tintern Abbey*, to be found in both 'the living air' and 'the mind of man'.
63–5 *And Burns . . . than you*: Wordsworth's admiration for Buius, seen in *The Leech-Gatherer* and elsewhere, is neatly turned against him.

LORD BYRON

Juan and Julia (*Don Juan* I, stanzas 54–117)

428 *his mother*: The character of Juan's mother, Donna Inez, is based on Lady Byron, from whom the poet separated in 1816 after a year of marriage.
439 *zone*: girdle.
446 *Boabdil*: last Moorish king of Granada, driven out 1492.
450 *hidalgo*: Spanish aristocrat.
483 *bow*: rainbow.
494 *'mi vien in mente'*: it comes to my mind.
510 *in mulct*: as a penalty.
526 *still*: always.
528 *carriage*: conduct, deportment.
567 *Armida*: Beautiful magician who in Tasso's *Gerusalemme Liberata* lured Christian knights into captivity.
598 *Tarquin[s]*: Legendary kings of ancient Rome, expelled by the people when the chastity of Lucretia failed to deter Sextus Tarquinius from rape; cf. Shakespeare, *The Rape of Lucrece*.
637 *utmost list*: furthest limit.
650 *mail of proof*: tested armour.
652 *mole*: man-made pier or breakwater.
670 *inter nos*: between ourselves (Latin).
675 *condition*: social position.
683 *true one*: From the first Byron rhymes his hero's name in English, with 'new un' and 'true un', not in Spanish.
684 *Medea*: mythical Greek lover, magician, revenger, celebrated by Euripides for her passion and cruelty.
696 *grot*: grotto, hermit's cave.
698 *transport*: ecstasy, being 'carried away'.
701 *The bard I quote*: Campbell, *Gertrude of Wyoming* I, iii, 1–4.
719 *So that*: as long as.
754 *Boscan, or Garcilasso*: Spanish sixteenth-century poets.
776 *like all very clever people*: Lady Byron, whom the poet has in mind in his satire of Donna Inez, was a distinguished mathematician.
819 *moon*: month.
824 *post-obits*: loans, to be repaid after the death of a relative from whom the borrower stands to inherit; 'post-obits of theology' would seem to be promises made by religion and called in as history comes to an end.
829 *Anacreon Moore*: Moore (quoted in stanza 88, above) was famous for his *Irish Melodies* and the oriental tales of *Lalla Rookh* (1817), but had translated the Greek odes of Anacreon in 1800.
864 *fifty Louis*: French gold coin.
886 *asp*: small Egyptian poisonous snake, used by Cleopatra in her suicide.
900 *nomenclature*: naming.
1102 *her husband's temples to encumber*: give him cuckold's horns.

1110 *levée*: reception.
1143 *Arras*: tapestry, wall-hangings (Hamlet famously 'pricks' the arras in the queen's bedroom at Elsinore: 'Dead for a ducat, dead!').
1171 *confessor*: Priest to whom the Catholic tells his sins (stressed on the first syllable at this period).
1177 *cortejo*: gallant, cavalier.
1178 *Seville*: A true rhyme with 'revel'.
1180 *rout*: party.
1183–4 *General . . . Who took Algiers*: There was indeed a General Count O'Reilly, and he did (in 1775) attack Algiers, but (as Byron presumably knew – and Julia didn't) he failed to take the city, retreating with heavy losses.
1196 *I wonder . . . the moon is*: Is her husband mad, perhaps, and baying to the moon (a *luna*-tic)?
1217 *toilette*: dressing-table.
1231–2 *since you stain . . . in vain*: since her honour is already stained by her husband's imputations, she may as well give herself to the man they're searching for when he's found.
1270 *Achates*: Known for his friendship to Aeneas.
1271 *So there were . . . cause*: as long as there were disputes of some kind.
1279 *negatives*: pleas of not guilty.
1294 *and thought of Job's*: Job's wife, when he is smitten by Satan with boils, advises her husband cheerfully to 'curse God, and die' (Job 2.9).
1305 *'posse comitatus'*: sheriff's posse (of citizens helping restore order).
1328 *maudlin Clarence . . . butt*: Famous for his prophetic dream, the Duke of Clarence (in *Richard III*) is stabbed, then drowned in a barrel of malmsey-wine.
1336 *a deucéd balance . . . Devil*: The balance of good and evil in one's life 'all-square' (as in tennis), implying probably that the Devil (often called the 'Deuce') holds an advantage. 'Deuced' as a swear word means 'unlucky'.
1368 *My Mistress, all*: 'My Mistress will lose everything' (Antonia is addressing Juan).
1392 *rigmarole*: incoherent, or long-winded speech (not especially a learned term).
1395 *foible*: weakness.
1412–13 *he concluded . . . premises*: he assumed to be hidden on the premises.
1419 *That modern phrase*: 'Tact' is first recorded in its modern sense in 1804.
1487–8 *like Joseph . . . the pair*: Joseph, whose 'coat of many colours' was torn up by his brothers to deceive their father into thinking him dead, lived to be Pharaoh's chief minister and able to do his brothers a favour.

ROBERT SOUTHEY

The Cataract of Lodore (1823)

2 *Lodore*: Waterfall on the southern bank of Derwentwater, in view of the Southeys at Greta Hall, Keswick, and (to judge from pictures and accounts of the period) very much bigger then than it is now.
22–3 *Laureate . . . King*: Southey became Poet Laureate in 1814.
25 *tarn*: mountain lake.

THOMAS LOVE PEACOCK

The Legend of Manor Hall

5 *station*: place, position.
11 *kicked up*: started, provoked.
19 *chapmen*: dealers.
20 *several*: separate.
23–4 *like a good man . . . daily bread*: Peacock's use of submerged Christian implication recalls *The Ancient Mariner* (often invoked by the ballad metre and internal rhyming of *Farmer Wall*): 'Instead of the Cross the Albatross / About my neck was hung' (ll. 137–8). The Farmer would have done well, when 'crossed' (thwarted – but with implied reference to the Crucifixion), to think of the Lord's Prayer: 'Give us this day our daily bread.' God looks after his own, and will provide!
44 *on the nail*: on the spot, at once.
46 *earnest*: pledge, down payment.
57 *the porkling turned*: the suckling-pig – still a delicacy – is roasting on a spit that revolves above the fire. The farmer's gleeful killing of a piglet to celebrate a pact with the Devil is a reminder of the 'killing of the fatted calf' to celebrate the rescue of a soul for Heaven in the parable of the Prodigal Son.
60 *ghostly*: holy, devout.
61 *tirled the pin*: undid the bolt, opened the door.
75 *pelf*: money, riches (like 'elf', in l. 71, a word found almost exclusively when poets need a rhyme for 'self').
79 *tester*: sixpenny bit.
103 *costly mould*: Probably either *NED* 12, 'style, fashion, mode', or 13, 'that which is moulded or fashioned'.
121 *race*: generation.
125 *that all was right*: that all the money was there.

THOMAS HOOD

Mary's Ghost

1–4 *'Twas in the middle . . . bedside*: cf. *Margaret's Ghost* (itself an eighteenth-century reworking of *Fair Margaret and Sweet William*):

> 'Twas at the silent solemn hour,
> When night and morning meet,
> In glided Margaret's grimly ghost
> And stood at William's feet.

11 *my long home*: 'man goeth to his long home, and the mourners go about the streets', Ecclesiastes 12.5.
13 *the body-snatchers*: 'Resurrectionists', who dug up bodies and sold them for dissection – at work throughout the late eighteenth and early nineteenth centuries,

but now best known from the case of Burke and Hare in Edinburgh, 1829, and Dickens' Jerry Cruncher (*A Tale of Two Cities*).
18 *chary*: cherished.
19 *Mary-bone*: the church of St Mary-le-Bone in London.
20 *boned your Mary*: removed her bones (as in filleting).
22 *Doctor Vyse*: Probably Dr Weiss, London maker of surgical instruments.
24 *Guy's*: London hospital, south of the Thames, where Keats studied anatomy as a medical student.
27 *Doctor Bell*: Sir Charles Bell, anatomist and surgeon, famous for neurological discoveries.
31 *Bedford Row*: in Holborn, north of the City (no doubt Hood intends a specific reference, now lost).
34 *Doctor Carpue*: Surgeon at the National Vaccine Institution.
36 *Pickford's*: then as now, a well-known removal company.
39 *the outside place*: unprotected (therefore cheaper) place on the roof, as with carriages of the day.
41 *The cock . . . be gone*: cf. the ghost of Hamlet Senior, which 'faded on the crowing of the cock' (*Hamlet* I i).
44 *Sir Astley*: Sir Astley Cooper, best known surgeon of his day, famous for removing a tumour from the head of George IV.

X. Protest and Politics

WILLIAM COWPER

Sweet Meat has Sour Sauce

1–2 *A trader I am . . . o'er*: A bill was passed in 1788 limiting, but not abolishing, the carrying of slaves in British ships. Cowper's poem (asking ironic sympathy for a trader who may be out of a job) includes detail that comes from John Newton, evangelical curate of Olney, who had been a slaving captain until his conversion-experience.
7 *an electrical knock*: Franklin, Priestley and others had experimented with electricity, and primitive batteries ('Leiden jars') had been developed, but it had as yet no practical uses.
11 *regales*: delicacies (the image of food has an appropriateness as the slave trade exists to bring the luxury of sugar to European tables).
16 *supple-jack . . . rattan*: tropical creepers with strong, pliant stems than can be used for canes.
18 *can*: vessel for carrying milk or other liquid, made like a barrel of wooden staves, hooped for strength.
23 *They sweeten . . . plums*: Cowper's most sardonic line: thumbscrews sweeten the mood of the African, just as sugarplums sweeten that of the European for whose luxuries he is enslaved and tortured.
26 *victuals*: food (pronounced 'vittles').

28 *engine*: implement (in this case for forced feeding).
32 *ware*: goods (auctions took place when the slaves were landed).
46 *awl*: sharp tool for boring holes in wood or leather.
53 *Caesars and Pompeys*: heroic classical names ironically given to slaves.

HANNAH MORE

from *Slavery: A Poem*

68 *though erring*: More (as author of the *Cheap Repository Tracts*, by far the most effective Christian moralist of her period) slips in a reminder that the African soul, however 'firm', is heathen.
77 *conscience*: consciousness.
121 *Tempe's vale*: specially favoured valley of ancient Greece.
parched Angola's sand: region of central Africa, regarded by More as desert.
216 *rifling Gambia's coast*: for slaves.
220 *Cortez*: Spanish sixteenth-century conqueror of Mexico.

ANN YEARSLEY

Death of Luco (from *On the Inhumanity of the Slave Trade*)

247 *maid*: girlfriend.
259 *rude*: barbaric.
265–6 *Rumour . . . blast*: A reference (whether at first or second hand) to Virgil's personification of Rumour in *Aeneid* IV. Yearsley and her fellow Romantic working-class poets were surprisingly well informed.
278 *native*: normal.

ANNA LAETITIA BARBAULD

On the Expected General Rising of the French Nation in 1792

5 *Devoted*: given over to death.
9 *tocsin*: alarm-signal.
10 *Country*: patriotism, the needs of the country.
17 *Briareus*: Mentioned by Homer as son of Poseidon, Briareus had 100 hands.
22–4 *Each deed . . . headlong rage*: Until the sacking of the Tuileries in August 1792, and September Massacres of the following month, the Revolution had been, broadly speaking, peaceful; Barbauld, however, is conscious of sporadic violence.
31–2 *With equal eye . . . ancient laws*: Priests and upholders of the Ancien Régime are to be commemorated alongside heroes of the Revolution.

HELEN MARIA WILLIAMS

France 1792 (from *To Dr Moore*)

48 *the blaze of philosophic day*: The Revolution portrayed as outcome, and triumph, of French Enlightenment philosophy.
49–50 *Those reasoners . . . blest use*: Williams may have others too in mind, but her lines apply most obviously to Burke and his *Reflections on the French Revolution.*
56 *the rude misshapen plan*: The 'plan' of absolute monarchy that has come down, buttressed by 'gothic' precedents and institutions from the past.
64–6 *That fabric . . . fragments fell*: Williams does not name the fortress-prison, symbolic of tyranny, that is invoked in ll. 57–66, but readers would see a reference to the Bastille, sacked in July 1789 and taken down stone by stone.
71 *the witness of those scenes*: Like Wollstonecraft and Wordsworth, Williams was a first-hand witness of the Revolution, and never lost her belief in its ideals. Unlike them, she saw almost the entire process, including being imprisoned by Robespierre during the Terror.
72 *the storied earth*: Earth's history (cf. Gray's *Elegy* 41 'storied urn or animated bust').
74 *friend beloved*: Dr John Moore, Williams' friend and mentor.
76 *idea*: image.

WILLIAM WORDSWORTH

from *The Female Vagrant*

289–90 *Four years . . . supplied*: The speaker is a beggar-woman on Salisbury Plain, who has been driven from her childhood home in Cumbria by a landlord intent on improvements to his property, then (after marriage and a new start) found herself caught up in the horrors of war. Wordsworth's protest is humanitarian, but as he starts his poem in August 1793 he is himself caught up in the early stages of the war with France (declared in February). For political and personal reasons his sympathies are with the French. War has separated him from Annette Vallon and their daughter Caroline, and he has for a month been watching the British fleet arming for battle off the Isle of Wight.
296–7 *The loom . . . unregarding sail*: Jobs (the woman's husband is a weaver) and commerce (merchant shipping) have been made redundant by war.
300–301 *But soon with proud parade . . . pain*: The naval pressgang could seize ('impress') any man it found in the seaports, and take him aboard; army recruiting (here described with heavy irony as to its intentions) was part show, part bribery. Men with starving families could not refuse the bounty of three guineas paid on enlistment.
302 *strain*: hug.
306 *We reached . . . devoted crew*: The woman and her family have followed her husband (as some did) to the theatre of war, in America. They are not merely loving, but in a technical sense 'devoted' (doomed), given over to death.

309 *Want's most lonely cave*: Wordsworth is writing in Spenserian stanzas, and conscious of using Spenserian personification.
311 *car*: chariot.
312 *Obvious*: in the way (Latin *ob via*).
311–13 *dog-like, wading . . . blood*: Wordsworth's vehement language is based on *Julius Caesar* III i, 'Cry "Havoc!" and let slip the dogs of war'.
387 *wanted*: lacked.

ROBERT BURNS

For A' That, and A' That

22 *His ribband . . . that*: In his contempt for titles, Burns is close to Paine, *Rights of Man*, Part I: aristocracy 'talks about its fine *blue ribbon* like a girl, and shows its new *garter* like a child'.

ROBERT SOUTHEY

Poems on the Slave Trade

13–14 *'thunder-tongued . . . deed'*: A powerful adapting of Shakespeare: Duncan's 'virtues' in *Macbeth* I vii, 'Will plead like angels, trumpet-tongued, against / The deep damnation of his taking-off.'

SAMUEL TAYLOR COLERIDGE

(i) *France: An Ode*

20 *still*: ever, always.
28 *disenchanted*: released from a spell.
29 *Like fiends . . . wand*: In Coleridge's image, France has freed herself from the spell of absolute monarchy, which the fiend-like Kings are convened (by a somewhat incongruous wizard) to restore.
31 *And Britain . . . array*: Britain was central to the alliance against France from summer 1793.
39 *partial*: Less than wholehearted.
43 *Blasphemy's loud scream*: Coleridge was concerned not that the Church had been dispossessed, but that the French leaders were irreligious; Robespierre interestingly took the same view, bringing back the concept of the Supreme Being, and sending to the guillotine those who in autumn 1793 had turned Notre-Dame into a Temple of Reason.
50 *The dissonance ceased . . . bright*: The moment of Robespierre's death in July 1793, recorded by Wordsworth too as a time of new hope ('Eternal Justice', *Prelude* Scenes vii).
53–4 *When, insupportably . . . ramp*: Comparatively untrained French armies made a mockery of their professional opponents ('ramp' being perhaps short for

'ramparts'?) as the Republic advanced on its neighbours. It is not clear in what sense the advances were 'insupportable' – from a radical point of view, however, wars of conquest were a betrayal of the Constitution that could not be supported.
56 *Domestic treason*: Royalist counter-revolution, centering in the Vendée (on the Bay of Biscay), and only with great difficulty stamped out.
66 *Helvetia's icy caverns*: French invasion of Switzerland (peaceful, and symbolic of the virtues of a republic) in spring 1798 shocked not only Coleridge, but many remaining supporters of the Revolution, into recantation.
73 *jealous*: watchful, carefully cherished.
77 *bloodless*: non blood-shedding.
79 *toils*: labours, activities (with a possible second reading that France is fatally 'trapped').
82 *murderous prey*: booty obtained as the result of murder.
88 *a heavier chain*: the 'chain' of their own sensuality and ignorance (darkness), from which rebellion has been no escape.
91 *victor's strain*: 'music' of victory, song of triumph.
95 *harpy minions*: rapacious favourites.
97 *subtle pinions*: delicate wings.

(ii) 'Dainty Terms for Fratricide'

118 *translated*: conveyed to Heaven without experiencing death.

ROBERT SOUTHEY

The Battle of Blenheim

18 *the great victory*: The Battle of Blenheim was fought between the French and English in 1704.
55–6 *Great praise . . . Prince Eugene*: Eugene, Prince of Savoy, fought alongside the Duke of Marlborough at Blenheim.

WILLIAM WORDSWORTH

I. Sonnets, 1802 (publ. 1807)

(i) *On the Extinction of the Venetian Republic*

1 *in fee*: in subjection.
4 *eldest . . . Liberty*: Venice had been 500 years a republic when conquered by Napoleon in 1797.
7–8 *And when . . . sea*: A reference to the annual ceremony at which the Doge dropped a gold ring into the sea in token of 'marriage'.

(ii) *To Toussaint L'Ouverture*

1 *Toussaint . . . men*: Leader of a slave rebellion in Haiti in 1791, Toussaint had become successively commander-in-chief of the army, and President. In 1801

Napoleon re-established slavery, and in summer 1802, when Wordsworth was writing, Toussaint had been brought back to France and was imprisoned in the Alps. He died from maltreatment in April 1803.

(iii) *We Had a Fellow-Passenger*

14 *ordinance*: decree.

II. 1805 *Prelude* Scenes from the French Revolution

(i) 'Golden Hours': Calais and the Rhone, July 1790 (VI, 352–69, 380–413)

352–4 *'Twas a time . . . born again*: 'Few persons', Southey wrote, looking back in 1824,

> but those who have lived in it, can conceive or comprehend what the French Revolution was, nor what a visionary world seemed to open upon those who were just entering it. Old things seemed passing away, and nothing was dreamt of but the regeneration of the human race.

355–7 *Bound, as I said . . . Federal Day*: In the Cambridge Long Vacation of 1790, Wordsworth and his friend Jones (Welsh, and a fellow 'mountaineer) made a walking-tour through France, northern Italy, Switzerland, southern Germany and the Netherlands, covering 1,500 miles in three months. They were not politically minded, and it may have been chance that they landed in Calais on 13 July, eve of the anniversary of the fall of the Bastille. At the Fête de la Fédération ('Federal Day') on the 14th, Louis XVI swore an oath of allegiance in Paris to the new Constitution.

359–60 *when joy of one . . . millions*: Helen Maria Williams, who watched Federal Day in Paris, comments in *Letters from France*, 1790, 'It was the triumph of human kind, it was man asserting the noblest privileges of his nature, and it wanted but the common feelings of humanity to become in that moment a citizen of the world.'

384 *Soane*: the River Saône, anglicized as a monosyllable.

396 *the great spousals*: the 'marriage' of King and People. Shortage of money had forced Louis XVI in May 1789 to summon Parliament (the Estates General), a thing which no French king had done since 1611. Now he found himself having to accept the role of constitutional monarch. It is not likely that he ever considered keeping his oath. He had been brought up as an absolute ruler, and had not the imagination to envisage change.

399–401 *Some vapoured . . . saucy air*: Caliban and his companions in *The Tempest* IV i are 'So full of valour' [boastful] that they smote the air / For breathing in their faces'.

403 *Guests welcome*: Not a very close parallel. Abraham is visited by angels, who tell him that Sarah is to have a child. Sarah, who is ninety, laughs, but Isaac is duly born (Genesis 21.2).

409–12 *We bore a name . . . glorious course*: To French eyes it seemed that England had an enviable constitutional monarchy, set up at the 'Glorious Revolution' of 1688, when the Catholic James II was replaced by Parliament with Mary Stuart and her Protestant Dutch husband, William of Orange.

(ii) A Tourist's Unconcern: Paris, Dec. 1791 (IX, 40–71)

40 *Through Paris lay my readiest path*: Wordsworth returned to France in December 1791, chiefly it seems to be out of the way of his family who were pushing him to go into the Church.
43–6 *from the Field of Mars . . .Genevieve*: Wordsworth's list of sites associated with the Revolution includes the Champs de Mars (where Louis XVI had sworn his oath of allegiance), Faubourg St-Antoine, near the dismantled Bastille, and the church of Ste Geneviève (later renamed the Panthéon), where Mirabeau had been buried in April.
47 *The National Synod . . . Jacobins*: The National Assembly and the Jacobin Club, later the basis of Robespierre's power, though at this stage Brissot and the Girondins (whom he guillotined, October 1793) were fellow members.
56 *hubbub wild*: Approaching Chaos in *Paradise Lost* II, 951–2, Satan is greeted by 'a universal hubbub wild / Of stunning sounds, and voices all confused'.
63–7 *Where silent zephyrs . . . enthusiast*: Poetic breezes sport with the dust of the symbolic fortress-prison of the ancien régime, now dismantled; Wordsworth meanwhile still cares so little about politics that he has to act the enthusiast.
68 *strong incumbencies*: tendency to brooding, thoughtfulness.

(iii) Among Royalists: Blois, spring 1792 (IX, 127–68)

131 *seasoned*: in blood.
137 *Were bent upon undoing . . . done*: Though from April 1792 France was at war with Austria (the country of Marie Antoinette), and the Emperor her brother's troops were waiting on the Rhine to 'undo what had been done' (restore absolute monarchy), the French army was staffed, as it always had been, with well-born royalist officers. At one point Lafayette had to appeal to them to leave.
162–4 *his sword was haunted . . . his own body*: Like a child fingering his penis.

(iv) 'A Patriot': Blois, early summer 1792 (IX, 294–9, 511–34)

296 *a patriot*: follower of the Revolution (as many noblemen were). Beaupuy, who became a General in the revolutionary army, and died fighting in 1796, was a major influence on Wordsworth, inspiring his life-long belief in the ideals of 1789.
517 *heartless*: desolate, despairing.
533–4 *whence better days . . . mankind*: Many revolutions did follow the French, as the French had followed the American – in the Netherlands, Poland, Italy, Ireland – but they were put down. And in France the leaders in whom Beaupuy and Wordsworth believed proved weak and were outwitted by Robespierre

(v) 'Sleep No More': Paris, Oct. 1792 (X, 24–82)

29–31 *assumed with joy . . . republic*: After more than three years' attempt to work with the treacherous Louis as a constitutional monarch, France became a republic on 22 September 1792. The King was in prison (and soon to be on trial), and there was little alternative.

31–4 *Lamentable crimes . . . as a judge*: Wordsworth is thinking chiefly of two recent outbreaks of violence in Paris, both set off by the threat of Austrian invasion. Twelve hundred people were killed on 10 August 1792, when the *sans culottes* stormed the Tuileries Palace, including the 400-strong Swiss Guard, who obeyed an order from the King to lay down their arms (bodies were burned in the Place du Carrousel). Three weeks later news that Brunswick's invading army had taken Verdun led to the September Massacres, in which half the inmates in the city's prisons (most of them neither aristocrats, nor priests) were executed by the mob after summary trials.

34–7 *But these were passed . . . and die*: Wordsworth's confidence that violence (like the dragon's teeth sown by Cadmus) has come and gone, stems from the French defeat at Valmy, 19 September, of Brunswick's invading army.

42–4 *The prison . . . bondage*: The Temple, where the King and Queen remained till their executions, respectively on 21 January and 16 October 1793.

64–6 *I thought of those . . . substantial dread*: As Wordsworth reaches out, like Doubting Thomas, to 'feel and touch' the Massacres, the quotation from *Hamlet* – 'a little month' (I ii) – sets up a parallel between his inability to comprehend the violence and Hamlet's to understand his mother's 'o'er hasty marriage'. Poet and Prince equally feel their trust to have been betrayed.

70–74 *'The horse . . . at once'*: Appalled by the thought that violence may be cyclical, Wordsworth creates in five lines a strange apocalyptic poetry, quite unlike anything else he ever wrote. The horse of l. 70 has been schooled ('taught his manage'), and turns full circle standing on his back legs.

76–7 *I seemed to hear a voice . . . Sleep no more*: 'Methought I heard a voice cry, "Sleep no more! Macbeth doth murder sleep!"' (*Macbeth* II ii).

(vi) War and Alienation: London and Wales, 1793–4 (X, 201–74)

204–5 *a contention . . . negro blood*: A bill prohibiting the carrying of slaves in British ships was passed by the House of Commons in 1792, but thrown out by the Lords.

229–30 *And now . . . confederated host*: France and England declared war in February 1793, England concluding alliances in the summer with Austria and Prussia.

233 *Change and subversion*: British followers of the Revolution are 'subverted' (undermined) by having to side with France against their own country; in a different sense, they will be regarded from this moment as themselves 'subversive'.

242–4 *with what ungracious . . . regenerated France*: In fact even Pitt (most determined enemy of France in the years that followed) welcomed the fall of the Bastille.

Opinion was hardening against the French, however, before the publication in November 1790 of Burke's *Reflections on the Revolution.*
257 *station*: position, viewing point.
261–3 *When Englishmen . . . shameful flight*: By autumn 1794 British troops (under the Grand Old Duke of York) had been routed at Hondschoote and Wattignies in the Netherlands.
268–9 *bending all . . . great Father*: 'While each to his great father bends' (*Ancient Mariner,* 641). Compelled to wish for his country's defeat, Wordsworth is as much an alien among the 'simple worshippers' as the Mariner himself.

(vii) 'Eternal Justice': Morecambe Sands, Aug. 1794 (X, 466–76, 515–56)

468–9 *this foul tribe . . . chief regent*: Robespierre and his followers. There is obvious relevance in Wordsworth's allusion to *Paradise Lost* I, 392–3: 'First Moloch, horrid king besmeared with blood / Of human sacrifice.'
472 *a small village*: Rampside, opposite Peele (or Piel) Castle, on the Cumbrian coast.
524–6 *a variegated crowd . . . their guide*: Levens Sands may still be crossed with a guide when the tide is out, but in Wordsworth's day comprised the main north–south route along the coast.
548 *the Augean stable*: Among his 'labours', Hercules cleanses the stable of King Augeus (choked with ox dung) by diverting through it the Rivers Alpheus and Peneus.
549 *their own helper*: the guillotine.
554 *madding*: seething (Gray's *Elegy*, 73, 'Far from the madding crowd's ignoble strife')
556 *the mighty renovation*: Though the Terror ceased, 'renovation' did not proceed as Wordsworth and others hoped. Massive inflation led to wars of conquest (forsworn in the Constitution), and Napoleon was already rising through the ranks; see Coleridge, *France: An Ode*, above.

JOHN CLARE

(i) *Helpstone*

95 *evanished*: vanished (the word in its original form, from French *évanouir*).
101 *pale lilac mean and lowly*: Clare seems to intend a small wild flower, not the garden shrub, *Syringa Vulgaris.*
106 *shepherd's woolly charge*: Poeticism, in the manner of Thomson's *Seasons* (1730), for sheep in the shepherd's care, 'charge'.
115 *But now . . . no more*: A statute for the enclosure of common ground at Helpstone was passed in 1809, the year in which Clare's poem was started. Clare's is not a strictly political response: he does of course resent the village people's loss of rights, but he feels most personally the destruction involved in clearing the land.
119–20 *though Fate's . . . obscurity*: though Fate has hidden away the beauties of Helpstone in a little-known corner of the map.

(ii) *Lamentations of Round-Oak Waters*

174 *moilers*: drudges (as in the phrase, 'toil and moil').
182 *hold*: make for themselves.

JAMES LEIGH HUNT

from *The St James's Phenomenon*

9 *tun*: cask, barrel.
18–19 *shark . . . spark*: swindler, beau (gallant).
22 *this Prince of Shockings*: the Prince Regent (Hunt is writing in Horsemonger Lane Gaol as the result of a previous libel on the Prince; his ballad should be read as an act of defiance).
50 *a start*: an outgrowth?
73–5 *He's got . . . about him*: The judiciary had supported the Prince in his libel suit of February 1813 against Hunt and his brother – hence their both being in gaol.

LORD BYRON

Napoleon's Farewell

3 *She abandons me now*: In April 1814, with the Allied forces storming Montmartre, and about to enter Paris, the Senate (guided by Talleyrand) declared the Emperor and his family to have forfeited the throne. Napoleon was forced to abdicate, and exiled to Elba. Two years later, in April 1816, Byron himself was forced out of England, abandoned (as Napoleon had been) when things went against him. In their grandeur and defiance, his earlier lines (passed off as a translation from the French) could hardly not seem to be his own farewell.
5–6 *which vanquished me . . . too far*: Napoleon's invasion of Russia in 1812 famously weakened him, leading to his downfall two years later.
7–8 *I have coped . . . to millions in war*: As the last prisoner of the War, now over, outnumbered by millions to one, Napoleon is still dreaded, still contends ('copes') with the nations on an equal footing.
11 *leave as I found thee*: Napoleon's rise to power came during the period of economic disaster that followed the death of Robespierre in July 1794, with France hemmed in by enemies on every side. He crowned himself Emperor in December 1804.
20 *Then turn . . . Chief of thy choice*: France did turn again to the 'Chief of [her] choice', during the Hundred Days (March–June 1815), when Napoleon escaped from Elba, resumed power, and came near to winning the decisive battle at Waterloo.

PERCY BYSSHE SHELLEY

(i) *The Mask of Anarchy*

1–4 *As I lay asleep . . . poesy*: The 'voice from over the sea' came in the form of a letter from Peacock telling Shelley of the 'Peterloo Massacre' when six people were killed and eighty injured by mounted militia during a peaceful rally in Manchester, 16 August 1819.
5–6 *I met Murder . . . Castlereagh*: Shelley is thinking chiefly of the part played by Castlereagh (now Tory Foreign Minister) in suppressing the 1798 Irish rebellion; cf. Byron, Dedication to *Don Juan*: 'Cold-blooded, smooth-faced, placid miscreant, / Dabbling its sleek young hands in Erin's gore.'
8 *Seven blood-hounds*: A reference to the seven countries (Austria, France, Portugal, Prussia, Russia, Spain, Sweden) who had in 1815 agreed with Britain to postpone abolition of the slave trade.
15 *Like Eldon . . . gown*: A more personal allusion: following the suicide of Harriet Shelley in November 1816, Eldon as 'ermined' Lord Chancellor (known for weeping in public) had denied Shelley custody of their children, Ianthe and Charles.
24 *Sidmouth*: As Tory Home Secretary, Sidmouth relied on a system of *agents provocateurs* who incited and then reported industrial discontent (punishable in extreme cases by death or transportation).
26 *Destructions*: cf. the 'Slendours' of *Adonais*, similarly half-personified.
30–3 *Last came Anarchy . . . Apocalypse*: An allusion to Benjamin West's *Death on a Pale Horse* as well as to Revelation.
77 *Had cost ten millions . . . nation*: The computed cost of George III's 'education'.
83 *the Bank and Tower*: the Bank of England and Tower of London.
85 *his pensioned Parliament*: the House of Commons and House of Lords are both in the pay of Anarchy.
97 *Misery, oh, misery*: Unexpectedly derived from the cry of that other 'manic maid', Martha Ray, in Wordsworth's *Thorn*: 'Oh misery! Oh misery! / Oh woe is me, oh misery!'
103 *A mist, a light, an image, rose*: As Shelley's mysterious 'shape' emerges, context brings to his mind the spectre bark that drives between ship and sun in *The Ancient Mariner*, 139–45: 'I saw a something in the Sky . . . A speck, a mist, a shape, I wist.'
112–13 *wings whose grain . . . rain*: This time the allusion is to Milton: Raphael's third pair of wings, *Paradise Lost* V, 285, were of 'sky-tinctured grain' ('grain' meaning dye, or colour).
115 *A planet, like the morning's*: Venus, the Morning Star.
142 *throe*: pangs, anguish.
145 *unwithstood*: not to be withstood.
180–83 *that forgery . . . Earth*: Shelley thought of paper money, the 'ghost of gold' (l. 176), as a form of inflation, from which it was the working classes who suffered.
197–204 *birds . . . hast none*: 'And Jesus saith unto him, "The foxes have holes, and the birds of the air have nests; but the Son of man hath not where to lay his head."' (Matthew 8.20).
228–9 *thou dost make . . . upon a snake*: An image that goes back to the coiled rattlesnake on an American revolutionary flag.

240–41 *when all . . . in Gaul*: during the Revolution and the war that followed.
246–8 *the rich have kissed . . . to the free*: For a moment Shelley allows himself a vision of the future, in which the rich kiss the feet of Love, and like the follower of Christ give away their goods.
253 *which is their prey*: against which they are now fighting.
282 *tares*: vetch (pretty weed of the pea family, which in the parable is sown by an enemy among the wheat, Matthew 13.25).
301 *targes*: shields.
306 *Troops of armed emblazonry*: Soldiers gorgeous in their arms.
316 *like sphereless stars*: the scimitars (crescent-shaped eastern swords) flash like stars who have escaped from the sky (their 'sphere').
324 *career*: impetus.
326 *phalanx*: line of battle.
337 *heralds*: heralds of the new political future.
343 *What they like . . . do*: Shelley emerges as an early advocate of passive resistance.
359 *Ashamed . . . base company*: ashamed of consorting with those who have attacked the peaceful rally.
362 *oracular*: prophetic of better times.

(ii) *England in 1819*

1 *An old, mad . . . king*: George III, whose attacks of madness went back to 1763, was continuously insane from 1811; he died aged eighty-one in January 1820.
2–3 *Princes, the dregs . . . muddy spring*: the Prince Regent and his unprepossessing brothers.
7 *A people starved . . . field*: In the disastrous post-war years, the people were 'starved' amid untilled fields in the countryside, and 'stabbed' in the 'Peterloo Massacre', Manchester (August 1819).
10 *sanguine*: bloodthirsty.
12 *A senate . . . unrepealed*: Parliament – seen by Shelley as unrepresentative and an unfortunate legacy from the past.

LORD BYRON

from *The Vision of Judgment*

113 *Saint Peter . . . gate*: Byron's poem is written in response to Southey's *A Vision of Judgment*, written on the death of George III in January 1820. Southey had made himself ridiculous, lauding a king whom he had in more honest early days regarded with contempt, and in the process consigning George to Heaven. To make matters worse, he had used the Preface for an attack on Byron and the 'Satanic School'. Byron broke off work on *Don Juan* to write what is at once the greatest and wittiest lampoon in the language, and a principled Whig rejoinder to the Tory values of the Poet Laureate. He was not unprovoked. 'I have held up that school', Southey writes vaingloriously,

> To public detestation, as enemies, to the religion, the institutions, and the domestic morals of the country. I have given them a designation to which their founder, and leader, answers.

I have sent a stone from my sling which has smitten their Goliath in the forehead. I have fastened his name upon the gibbet, for reproach and ignominy as long as it shall endure. Take it down who can!

132–3 *Well he won't find kings . . . his way*: not too many kings are getting into Heaven.

But does he wear his head: A reference to Louis XVI of France, guillotined in January 1793 – and behind him, to Charles I, who also gained sympathy as martyr which he did not have as king.
177 *caravan*: cavalcade.
180 *Inde*: the River Indus (shortened by Byron for the rhyme, 'Inde' normally meaning India).
183–4 *Halted / Seated*: it is the 'angelic caravan' of l. 177 that halts before the heavenly gate, and seats the king on a cloud.
194 *Sin*: Satan's consort in *Paradise Lost*, and mother of Death.
199 *ichor*: blood of the gods.
204 *Orion's Belt*: stars at the 'waist' of the constellation Orion.
207 *manes*: ghosts.
214 *Aurora Borealis*: the Northern Lights (vividly described by Parry on his return in 1820 from a voyage to discover the non-existent North Passage, linking the Atlantic and Pacific).
222–3 *the night / Of clay*: blindness associated with being human (mortal 'clay').
224 *Joanna Southcote*: Uncharitable reference to the prophet who gave out that she was (at the age of sixty) pregnant with the new Messiah, and who died broken-hearted in 1814 when there proved to be no baby.
233 *Michael*: The Archangel who defeated Lucifer (Satan) in the War in Heaven (*Paradise Lost* VI).
248 *He knew him*: He knew himself to be.
256 *champ clos*: battlefield (used of the enclosed ground of a tournament).
288 *civilian*: commoner (in this case).
296 *paved Hell with . . . intentions*: 'Sir', said Dr Johnson one day, 'Hell is paved with good intentions.' (Boswell)
378 *The faith . . . great on earth*: Roman Catholicism (the single Christian faith in Western Europe until the Protestant Reformation of the sixteenth century).
384 *license*: liberty (no distinction was made between Catholics and Protestant sects who refused to accept the Thirty-nine Articles of the Anglican Church; both being excluded from Oxford and Cambridge, from voting, and from all forms of government office). George III was a consistent opponent of Catholic Emancipation.
385–6 *as / A consequence of prayer*: Catholics had freedom of worship, but not the liberties that might be expected to follow, and that would have placed them on an equal footing with Anglicans (who do not address the saints in prayer).
391 *Guelph*: Family name of the Hanoverian Kings; if Byron is referring also to the Guelph faction in medieval Italy, he ignores the fact that they were supporters of the Pope (as opposed to the Ghibelines, who supported the Emperor).
415 *which Milton mentions*: Cannons are invented by Satan, *Paradise Lost* VI, 484–91, after the first unsuccessful day of the war in Heaven.
449–54 *Upon the verge . . . tacked and steered*: Byron playfully recalls for his readers the arrival of the spectre-ship in *The Ancient Mariner*, 139–48:

> I saw a something in the Sky
> No bigger than my fist;
> At first it seemed a little speck
> And then it seemed a mist . . .
>
> A speck, a mist, a shape, I wist!
> And still it nered and nered;
> And, an it dodged a water-sprite,
> It plunged and tacked and veered.

533 *freeholders*: those with property above a certain value, and therefore entitled to vote.
542 *Wilkes*: The radical Whig satirist and MP (d. 1797), who became Mayor of London, and secured important political reforms with his populist approach.
681 *renegado*: turncoat (original Spanish form of 'renegade').
685 *Skiddaw*: Lake District mountain above Southey's house at Greta Hall, Keswick.
745–7 *The varlet . . . hawk's eye*: It is characteristic of Byron that he should do justice to the rascal ('varlet') Southey's hook-nosed, hawk-eyed impressiveness.
752 *felony de se*: suicide.
769 *praises of a regicide*: Henry Martin signed the death warrant of Charles I, and was imprisoned for life at the Restoration. Southey's sympathetic portrait was a deliberate affront, published in 1797 when (though only twenty-three) he was the best-known poet of the protest movement.
773–4 *For pantisocracy . . . clever*: Byron may be hinting that wives, as well as property, were to be held in common in Southey and Coleridge's projected commune of 1794 on the banks of the Susquehanna. It wasn't so.
775 *anti-jacobin*: right winger, reactionary ('jacobin', though applied in a French context to followers of Robespierre, was in England used as an insult for any voice of the political left). To call the aging Southey an 'anti-jacobin' had especial appropriateness as his early protest-poetry had been repeatedly and brutally travestied by the *Anti-Jacobin* weekly in 1797–8.
777 *He had sung against all battles*: Brilliantly in *The Battle of Blenheim*, above.
780–82 *as base a critic . . . mauled*: From 1809 Southey was one of the most important, and most intolerant, writers for the Tory *Quarterly Review* – a fact that enhanced the pleasure of Byron and others when in 1817 his play *Wat Tyler* (written in 1794 as a republican aged twenty), was pirated by a radical bookseller, and the Lord Chief Justice ruled that publication could not be stopped as the writer had no title in law to seditious work.
801 *Here's my Vision*: Southey, whose turgid and toadying *The Vision of Judgment* is not improved by a decision to write in English hexameters, had welcomed the King into Heaven with a fanfare derived from the Prayer Book:

> Lift up your heads, ye gates, and ye everlasting portals,
> Be ye lift up! For lo! a glorified Monarch approacheth,
> One who in righteousness reigned, and religiously governed his people . . .

807 *Like King Alfonso*: 'Alfonso, speaking of the Ptolomean system, said that "had he been consulted at the Creation of the World, he would have spared the Maker some absurdities".' (Byron)

812 *Contents*: Stressed on the second syllable.

816 *melodious twang*: An 'apparition' near Cirencester, Aubrey records, 'being demanded whether a good spirit or a bad, returned no answer, but disappeared with a curious perfume and a most melodious twang' (*Miscellanies*, 1696).

828 *Phaeton*: Famous for trying to drive the chariot of his father, the sun god Apollo, and falling from the sky.

829 *his lake*: Derwentwater.

830–32 *A different web . . . here or there*: The Fates, who weave the tapestry of Southey's destiny, will make their decision when reform (the cause that he betrayed) comes about, either on Earth or in Heaven. Southey had been Poet Laureate since Scott declined the office in 1814.

840 *turned precisian*: become a pedant (Welborn's phrase comes from Massinger, *A New Way to Pay Old Debts*, c. 1625).

848 *the hundredth psalm*: the *Jubilate*: 'Oh go your way into his gates with thanksgiving, and into his courts with praise!'.

THOMAS HOOD

Ode to H. Bodkin, Esq., Secretary to the Society for the Suppression of Mendicity

1–4 *Hail King . . . the poor*: William Henry Bodkin was appointed Hon. Secretary to the Society for the Suppression of Mendicity (Begging) in 1821. A year later, Lamb published his humane and delightful *Complaint Against the Decay of Beggars in the Metropolis*:

> The all-sweeping besom of societarian reformation . . . is uplift with many-headed sway to extirpate the last fluttering tatters of the bugbear of Mendicity from the metropolis. Scrips, wallets, bags – staves, dogs and crutches – the whole mendicant fraternity, with all their baggage, are fast posting out of the purlieus of this eleventh persecution . . . I do not approve of this wholesale going to work, this impertinent crusado, or *bellum ad exterminationem*, proclaimed against a whole species. Much good might be sucked from these beggars. They were the oldest and honourablest form of pauperism. Their appeals were to our common nature . . .

The Vagrancy Act of 1824, against which Hood protests, divided beggars into 'idle and disorderly persons, rogues and vagabonds, incorrigible rogues and other vagrants'.

1 *King of . . . Patches*: title given by Hamlet to Claudius (I iv).

2 *Disperser . . . poor*: Bodkin 'disp*erses*' the poor (sends them to workhouses, or to distant parishes whence they originally came), when he might disp*ense* charity *to* them.

3 *dog in office*: 'A dog's obeyed in office' (*King Lear* IV vi).

9–10 *Oh, when . . . miss*: Rewriting of Isaac Watts' famous lines in *Divine Songs for Children* (1715): 'Whene'er I take my walks abroad, / How many poor I see.'

16 *The eye . . . sleeps*: God's eye is 'unsleeping' as he works for the good of mankind, Bodkin's as he denies charity to the poor whom God especially protects.
17 *Belisarius*: Roman general who was famously reduced to beggary.
18 *Benbow*: Admiral Benbow had a leg blown off fighting the French in 1701.
19–20 *The pious . . . begs*: The clergy, dependent on tithes from their parishioners, are the only beggars left.
21 *Street-Handels*: street musicians.
23 *scraper*: violinist, fiddler (with pun on foot-scraper).
25 *sweeper*: crossing sweeper, who cleared the road of mud and refuse for the genteel (women especially, in long skirts) to cross over.
26 *The carstairs . . . chalk*: Joseph Carstairs, author of *The Fashionable Penman* (1824), has his name borrowed for artists who drew in chalk on London pavements.
28 *walk*: pitch, territory (unsaleable now as Bodkin has moved potential buyers from the streets).
29 *wall-blind*: beggar, 'wall-eyed' to the point of blindness?
30 *The camels . . . humps*: Perhaps, 'The beasts of burden conceal their ill-temper'.
31 *witherington*: Wetharryngton in Percy's pseudo-medieval *Ballad of Chevy Chase*, fights on legless, 'upon his stumps': 'when both his leggis wear hewyne in to, / Yet he knyled and fought on hys kne.' Lamb in his *Complaint* celebrates at length Samuel Horsey, who 'used to glide his comely upper half over the pavements of London, wheeling along with a most ingenious celerity upon a machine of wood', having lost his legs in the Gordon Riots of 1780.
37–40 *Oh, was it . . . holy flags*: It is Jack who in Hood's conceit is 'Glory's own trophy', decorated with the rags of his once-smart naval uniform, as St Paul's is 'hung round' on special occasions 'with holy flags'.
43 *pounds*: places of confinement, workhouses in this instance (with the pun on pounds sterling).
44 *Thou dost . . . pence*: Locking up the poor saves passers-by the pennies they would otherwise have given to beggars.
45–8 *Well art thou . . . through*: Bodkin (whose name is punned on in Hood's concluding lines) acts towards the poor with sharpness (pointedly), and is, for good measure, *appointed* to do so. He is paid to check through beggars' petitions, but also to run the petitioners through – stab them to the heart.
49–52 *Doubtless . . . Bodkin end?*: 'For who would bear the whips and scorns of time, / The' oppressor's wrong . . . When he himself might his quietus make / With a bare bodkin? (*Hamlet* III i). *NED* gives 'dagger' as the primary meaning of 'bodkin'.

LETITIA ELIZABETH LANDON

The Factory

4 *a summer cloud*: Sir Walter in the opening lines of Wordsworth's *Hart-Leap Well* rides 'down from Wensley moor / With the slow motion of a summer's cloud'.
21 *Moloch's sacrifice*: 'Moloch, horrid king besmeared with blood / Of human sacrifice, and parents' tears' (*Paradise Lost* I, 392–3).
37–8 *and his hours / Are innocent and free*: Wordsworth had written enviously of

the blackbird and lark, 'they see / A happy youth, and their old age / Is beautiful and free' (*The Fountain*, 42–4).
66 *spare*: meagre.
79 *noon*: adulthood.

CAROLINE NORTON

A Voice from the Factories

298–300 *Fondly familiar . . . happy lives*: Norton, whose marriage has been unhappy, and whose children have been removed from her by her husband, portrays a close-knit loving family such as hers might have been, to shock her middle- and upper-class readers into imagining what it must be like for the poor to send a child (for wages of 1/6d. a week) to work in the factories.
318 *With Mirth's bright seal . . . brow*: Turning to *The Mother's Heart* (Poets and Relationship, below), we recognize Norton's second son, her 'Merry love', 'bold in [his] glee, / Under the bough, or by the fire-light dancing'. Her eldest (frail, and tenderly loved from often having to be nursed) finds his place in stanza 37. In 38 we expect her youngest (the 'Emperor' to his brothers), but to avoid too obvious identification he has been replaced by the portrait of a girl – the shy and beautiful daughter that Norton did not have.
405 *comprehends the sin . . . birth*: understands the nature of Original Sin (the Christian dogma that man, since the Fall, is born in sin).
406 *the pale orphan*: Lord Ashley, to whom Norton dedicates her poem (and who led the campaign to reduce children's hours, and improve conditions) pointed out in Parliament that children were sent in barge-loads from orphanages in London to Lancashire factories. Against dogged opposition (Josiah Wedgwood told a Select Committee in 1816 that children's health was not affected by working thirteen-and-a-half hours a day, six days a week), a bill was passed in 1833 reducing the hours of nine- to twelve-year-olds to eight, but left the thirteen to eighteen age-group on twelve hours a day, with nine on Saturday. Norton derives her knowledge from Committee-reports, but spares her readers the more appalling detail.
430–32 *the Watcher's stroke . . . weep*: Flogging of factory children was normal. One witness testified to the 1833 Commission that he 'had seen boys when too late in the mornings dragged out of their beds by the overseers, and even by the Master, with their clothes in their hands to the mill, where they put them on – that he had seen this done oftener than he [could] tell, and the boys were strapped naked as they got out of bed. There was similar treatment for the girls.'

XI. Poets in Relationship

WILLIAM BLAKE

I Love the Jocund Dance

11 *white and brown*: Shorthand apparently for forms of food or drink: water, perhaps (colourless, and therefore 'white') and brown bread (white would be unknown to Blake's class).
18 *But, Kitty . . . thee*: Blake had married Catherine Boucher the previous year.

ROBERT BURNS

(I) *A Poet's Welcome to his Love-begotten Daughter*

6 *Tyta, or Daddie*: Pet names that make Burns' subtitle seem decidedly formal: 'The First Instance that Entitled him to the Venerable Appellation of Father.'
7–8 *ca' me fornicator . . . kintra clatter*: country gossip ('kintra clatter') was not entirely a laughing matter: Burns was forced by the Elders of the Kirk to do public penance for fornication in July 1786.
15–16 *I hae fought . . . Kirk and Queir*: An account of Burns' appearance in front of the Kirk and Choir appears in *The Fornicator: A New Song:*

> Before the Congregation wide
> I passed the muster fairly,
> My handsome Betsy by my side
> We gat our ditty rarely . . .
> With rueful face and signs of grace
> I paid the buttock-hire!

Burns made provision for his 'bastart wean' by a deed of assignment; later his family took care of her.

(II) *Ae Fond Kiss*

1–2 *Ae fond kiss . . . for ever*: In Edinburgh at the beginning of December 1787 Burns enters into a brief romantic affair with the estranged wife of a solicitor, whom he apparently promises (despite Jean Armour and the twins; see iii, 7–8, below) to marry in the event of her husband's death.
10 *Nancy*: Burns' name for Mrs McLehose in the earliest song addressed to her is Clarinda.

(III) *I Love My Jean*

7–8 *But day and night . . . my Jean*: 'Composed', the poet comments, 'out of compliment to Mrs Burns. NB It was during the honeymoon'. Courtship had not been straightforward. Jean had borne twins in September 1786 and again in March 1788, the second pair dying at once. At one stage she had been thrown out by her father, who had a warrant for Burns' arrest. Marriage in late April came after Burns had been distracted by various other women, including the 'polished' Mrs McLehose (with whom in February it had seemed 'prophanity' to compare Jean's 'tasteless insipidity'). Jean, it seems, won through on a fairly basic level: 'I have taken her into my arms; I have given her a mahogany bed; I have given her a guinea; and I have f--d her till she rejoiced with joy unspeakable and full of glory' (early March). 'I have not got polite tattle, modish manners and fashionable dress', Burns concluded in September, but 'I have got the handsomest figure, the sweetest temper, the soundest constitution, and the kindest heart in the county.'

(IV) *Highland Mary*

7–8 *For there I took . . . Highland Mary*: Burns' relationship with Mary Campbell belongs to spring 1786 when James Armour was keeping his pregnant daughter out of sight. It is probable that looking back in 1792 he romanticized it: one contemporary witness certainly went out of his way to dispel the glamour. Burns' own account is tender and circumstantial: 'My Highland lassie was a warm-hearted, charming young creature as ever blessed a man with generous love . . . We met by appointment on the second Sunday of May, in a sequestered spot by the Banks of Ayr, where we spent the day taking a farewell before she should embark for the West Highlands . . .'

9 *birk*: birch.

21–4 *But oh, fell Death's . . . Mary*: 'this fell sergeant, Death, / Is strict in his arrest' (*Hamlet* V ii) 'At the close of the autumn following', Burns writes, 'she crossed the sea to meet me at Greenock, where she had scarce landed when she was seized with a malignant fever, which hurried my dear girl to the grave in a few days, before I could even hear of her illness.'

CHARLOTTE SMITH

To My Children (1788)

2 *contumely*: insolence (the quotation is from 'To be, or not to be', *Hamlet* III i).

5 *Robbed . . . fortune gave*: Legally separated from her husband the previous year, after bearing him twelve children, Smith in 1788 was supporting the eight survivors on her own. As the result of a disputed will she was unable to use the money which her father-in-law had intended for their education, and forced to write a novel a year to make ends meet. *To My Children* was originally to have been published in *Emmeline*.

9 *Maternal love . . . withstand*: Smith's syntax is dependent on 'Still shall' in l. 7.

13 *devoted*: doomed.

17 *solicitudes*: anxieties – over the children.

MARY ROBINSON

Written Between Dover and Calais, July 1792

9 *far from foes*: As official Royal Mistress to the Prince of Wales, 1779–81, Robinson had stirred envy as well as admiration, and forfeited her chance to live a private life.
24 *thee*: Robinson's relationship with Banastre Tarleton (who became a General and Tory MP, and was knighted for his services) lasted sixteen years from 1782. There were a number of partings.
66 *Gallia's hostile shore*: Six months later France and England would be at war; in July 1792 Gallia is merely unwelcoming.

WILLIAM COWPER

To Mary

1–2 *The twentieth . . . overcast*: Cowper and Mrs Unwin had become engaged in 1773, but their sky was darkened at once by his third mental breakdown, and the engagement broken off. To the same year belongs the dream that left Cowper believing for life that he was damned.
21 *indistinct expressions*: Mrs Unwin had had strokes in 1791 and 1792. She lived on till 1796.
53–4 *And should my future lot . . . past*: Cowper's fifth breakdown, from which he never wholly recovered, came in the following year.

CHARLES LAMB

To Mary Ann Lamb

3 *the error of a sickly mind*: Lamb's poem is written a year before Mary's insane killing of their mother in September 1796. He too at this period showed signs of instability.

SAMUEL TAYLOR COLERIDGE

(i) *Composed on a Journey Homeward, the Author Having Received Intelligence of the Birth of a Son, September 20, 1796*

5–6 *And some have said . . . wore*: Platonist belief in pre-existence was relatively common; Coleridge need have no specific authorities in mind.
13 *Didst scream*: The 'spirit' becomes human as a punishment, screams at birth, is pardoned, and returns instantly to Heaven.

(ii) *Letter to Sara Hutchinson: 4 April 1802, Sunday Evening*

1 *Well, if the bard . . . who made*: Coleridge is addressing the younger sister of Mary Hutchinson, whom Wordsworth is engaged to marry in seven months' time. Though married himself, with two young sons, Coleridge has been in love with her since November 1799. His poem is prompted by Dorothy Wordsworth's having read aloud during the afternoon the opening stanzas of her brother's *Immortality Ode*, written the previous week. In October 1802 the *Letter* will be cut down to form *Dejection: An Ode*, and addressed (with its love-poetry removed) to Wordsworth; see Romantic Odes, above.
2 *Sir Patrick Spens*: A traditional Scottish ballad, of which the first four lines are prefixed to *Dejection, An Ode* (Romantic Odes, p. 332, above).
7–8 *this Eolian lute . . . mute*: Coleridge's thoughts go back to *The Eolian Harp* of 1795 (Ennobling Interchange, p. 255, above); there is a new implication now that it might be best if his own 'lute' (poetic voice) were silent.
19 *no natural outlet*: Coleridge's poem begins as a somewhat indignant response to Wordsworth's lament over lost imaginative power. Attacked in stanza three of his Ode by momentary lack of confidence, Wordsworth had written cheerfully, 'A timely utterance gave that thought relief, / And I again am strong!'.
23 *heartless*: depressive, melancholy.
24 *throstle*: song-thrush.
41 *A boat becalmed . . . sky-canoe*: An affectionate reference to Wordsworth's Prologue to *Peter Bell* (On Poets and Poetry, p. 767, above), written at Alfoxden during the time of the two poets' closest collaboration, spring 1798.
44 *genial*: warm, life-giving; Coleridge's dejection has brought to mind *Samson Agonistes*, 'So much I feel my genial spirits droop, / Nature all flat within me', and Wordsworth's earlier reference to Milton's poem, *Tintern Abbey* 114.
45 *these*: the beautiful forms of Nature mentioned in the previous stanza.
52–3 *These lifeless shapes . . . impart?*: Coleridge's denial of the pantheist One Life, in which he and Wordsworth had once so firmly believed – 'that eternal language which [our] God / Utters, who from eternity often teach / Himself in all, and all things in himself' (*Frost at Midnight*, February 1798) – is cut in *Dejection: An Ode*, together with 130 lines of love-poetry and personal reminiscence.
62 *'ecstatic fit'*: Coleridge's quotation marks draw attention to Milton's *Passion*, 'In pensive trance and anguish and ecstatic fit'.
70–71 *linking on . . . skies*: linking sweet dreams of love by dim associative connections to moon, star or sunset.
77–9 *I spoke . . . breast*: An allusion to Wordsworth's Ode, showing that Coleridge too can find relief in 'timely utterance'; see l. 19n, above.
86 *sod-built seat of camomile*: Built by Coleridge and the Wordsworths out of turf in October 1801, and known as 'Sara's seat'.
136 *I too . . . coronal*: A reference to *The Immortality Ode*, stanza III – 'My heart is at your festival, / My head hath its coronal' – that has its undertones of sadness. Coleridge will crown himself, not when he is able to share in the Wordsworth household (of which Sara is increasingly a member), but when they achieve happiness in their 'abiding home' at Dove Cottage, Grasmere, and he is excluded.

191 *clomb*: climbed.
201 *host*: army.
211–15 *'Tis of a little . . . hear*: A tender allusion to Wordsworth's Lucy Gray, lost in the snow. *Dejection, An Ode* reads 'she' for 'it'.
228 *an own child*: Coleridge (who was the youngest in a family of eleven) sees himself poignantly as the 'only child' of joy.
232 *There was a time*: Opening words of *The Immortality Ode*; 'of yore' too (l. 227 above), is from the first stanza of Wordsworth's poem.
237 *leaves and fruitage . . . mine*: A self-wounding reference to the period of shared creativity with Wordsworth and Dorothy at Alfoxden (1797–8), which had produced Coleridge's greatest poetry. Only *The Ancient Mariner* had in fact contained an element of collaboration – and that very little.
244–5 *two unequal minds . . . wills*: Coleridge did little to promote the success of his marriage, writing to his wife (also by chance named Sara) in November 1802:

> Permit me, my dear Sara, without offence to you, as, Heaven knows! it is without any feeling of pride in myself, to say – that in sex, acquirements, and in the quantity and quality of natural endowments, whether of feeling or of intellect, you are the inferior.

267–71 *by abstruse research . . . temper of my soul*: For more than a year Coleridge had been immersed in the complexities of German philosophy, writing in March 1801 'The poet is dead in me', and describing himself ruefully as only 'a species of metaphysician'.
274 *still*: always.
281 *turning my error to necessity*: Making it inevitable that he should stay with his wife.
284 *Philomel*: the nightingale; the tradition that the bird is grieving goes back to Petrarch, and beyond him to the classical legend of Philomel's rape by Tereus. If Coleridge (who scorns the tradition in his own *Nightingale* of 1798) has a specific poet in mind, it is Otway.
295 *They are not . . . were*: 'The things which I have seen I now can see no more', *The Immortality Ode* 7.
296–7 *Oh Sara . . . does Nature live*: Despairing lines that offer the life in Nature as mere projection. At least to some extent this reversal of Coleridge's deepest beliefs is mitigated by his conferring upon Sara (as he had conferred at-oneness with Nature upon the infant Hartley in *Frost at Midnight*) the power of joy, outgoing imagination, that he himself no longer feels.
328 *the conjugal and mother dove*: Coleridge's domestic image of Sara as the mother dove gifts her implicitly with the creative powers of the Holy Spirit, who in *Paradise Lost* broods dove-like over primal Chaos and makes it pregnant.

WILLIAM WORDSWORTH

(1) (i) *To My Sister*

1–4 *It is the first . . . door*: Wordsworth and his sister Dorothy are living at Alfoxden in Somerset, with Coleridge nearby at Nether Stowey. It is the spring of *Lyrical Ballads* and Dorothy's first *Journal*.

13 *Edward*: Six-year-old Basil Montagu, whom the Wordsworths at this period were bringing up.
32 *temper*: disposition.

(I) (ii) from *Home at Grasmere*

108 *this loved abode*: Wordsworth and Dorothy have moved into Dove Cottage, Grasmere (their first true home together), in December 1799.
125–7 *possession of the good . . . realized*: Wordsworth had discovered Grasmere when a schoolboy, and always wished to live there.
171–6 *Long is it . . . loneliness*: It is a major factor in Wordsworth and Dorothy's extraordinary closeness that they had been parted after their mother's death (when he was eight and she was six) and barely saw each other until she was fifteen. They set up house together for six weeks in spring 1794 when she was twenty-two, and permanently from the following autumn. Before coming to Dove Cottage at Christmas 1799, they had lived successively in Dorset, Somerset, Germany and County Durham.
222 *that length of way*: Their walk took them across northern England, from Stockton-on-Tees in the east (home of Dorothy's schoolfriend, and Wordsworth's future wife, Mary Hutchinson) to Grasmere in the west.
237 *Hart-Leap Well*: A spring on the hillside above Wensleydale, which (to judge from Wordsworth's ballad-version of the story) showed signs of a 'pleasure-house' erected to commemorate the death, and amazing final leaps, of a hunted stag. The 'trance' that is shared here by Wordsworth and Dorothy is the one example in his poetry in which spiritual experience is not solitary.
249 *seceding*: In going to live at Grasmere, Wordsworth was not running away from the world, but withdrawing from it to write *The Recluse*, the great philosophical poem which he had planned with Coleridge, and of which *Home at Grasmere* was intended to be part.
252–6 *Might even thus early . . . mankind*: The most outright statement that Wordsworth ever made of belief in a millenarian future. Work on *Home at Grasmere* came to a halt when he had to concede that what seemed a paradise to him didn't seem so to his Cumbrian neighbours. Grasmere shepherds showed small sign of the 'love and knowledge' which he hoped might spread to other vales of earth.

(I) (iii) *To a Butterfly*

12 *Emmeline*: Among Wordsworth's pet names for Dorothy.

(I) (v) 'Child of My Parents'

240 *a nobler than herself*: imagination.

(II) *It Is a Beauteous Evening*

9 *Dear child . . . with me here*: Wordsworth is walking by the sea at Calais with his French daughter, Caroline, in August 1802. Because of the War he had been unable for nine years to meet her, or see again her mother Annette Vallon.
12 *in Abraham's bosom*: colloquial expression used of the afterlife.

(III) (i) *She was a Phantom of Delight*

1–2 *She was a phantom . . . sight*: a delightful illusion, a daydream. Mary had been Dorothy's school friend; Wordsworth was first conscious of her attractiveness in the summer of 1787 when the three of them roamed briefly together on the moors above Penrith.
15–16 *A countenance . . . sweet*: De Quincey (*Reminiscences of the Lake Poets*) saw in Mary's face, 'a sunny benignity, a radiant graciousness, such as in this world [he had] never seen surpassed'.
22 *machine*: 'a structure of any kind, material or inmaterial' (*NED*, first definition, now obsolete).

(III) (ii) 'Another Maid There Was'

234 *that season*: When Mary and the poet were seventeen.

(IV) *Surprised by Joy*

2 *transport*: ecstasy; Wordsworth is addressing his daughter Catharine, who had died in June 1812 aged three.

PERCY BYSSHE SHELLEY

(I) *To Harriet*

11 *Thine . . . wilding flowers*: Shelley wrote *To Harriet* as dedication to a volume of short poems, but found no publisher, and moved the lines to *Queen Mab*.
14 *though time . . . may roll*: Time did change, but for Harriet years did not roll far. After three years of marriage, 1811–14, Shelley eloped with Mary Godwin, and in 1816 Harriet drowned herself in the Serpentine. Mary was to be, if anything, more unhappy, but she survived her husband.

(II) Dedication to *Laon and Cythna*

3 *Fairy*: Fairy Land.
16 *my lone boat*: Shelley writes *Laon and Cythna*, in summer 1817, on the Thames at Marlow.
25 *the near school-room*: Shelley was at Eton.
99 *A lamp of vestal fire*: fire burning in the temple of Vesta, tended by vestal virgins, who were chaste and especially devoted.
102 *for one then left this Earth*: Mary Wollstonecraft, author of the *Rights of Woman* (1792), who died ten days after giving birth to the future Mary Shelley in September 1797.
108 *thy sire*: William Godwin, whom (despite his inconvenient tendency to borrow money) Shelley venerated as author of *Political Justice* (1793).
109–110 *One voice . . . three thousand years*: *Political Justice* is seen as the cumulation of 3,000 years of thinking (which, in some ways, perhaps it is).
113–17 *Unwonted fears . . . and dwelling-place*: On British radicals Godwin had an

immediate and profound effect. The 'pale oppressors' of mankind, however, took the view that as *Political Justice* cost three guineas there was no need to prosecute its author. It wouldn't reach the poor, whom Paine's *Rights of Man* was stirring to revolution at 6d. a copy.

(III) *Epipsychidion* (1821)

1 *Sweet spirit!*: Shelley addresses the soul of Teresa Viviani (Emilia in the poem), nineteen-year-old daughter of the Governor of Pisa, whom the Shelleys and Claire Clairmont met in November 1820 at the convent where she was being kept out of harm's way till she married. Shelley's title could be translated 'Concerning' (Epi) the Little Soul ('Psychidion'); the poetry expresses intense erotic feeling within the framework of Platonic idealism. In the Advertisement Shelley distances himself from the poem through the fiction of his unfortunate friend; it seems that later he came to regret having published it.
1–2 *sister of that orphan one . . . weepest on*: Lines that have never been convincingly explained. Emilia's 'sweet spirit' is 'sister' either to the 'orphan soul' of Shelley himself, or to that of his wife, Mary. On balance, the second seems more probable. Emilia's letters address Mary as '*cara sorella*', and Mary was in a literal sense an orphan, her mother dying at her birth. Mary's 'empire' might in this reading be the name of 'Shelley', over which Emilia weeps because it cannot be hers.
4 *These votive wreaths*: The memories of which Shelley's poem is composed – seen as consecrated offerings.
18 *unmaternal nest*: the 'unmotherly' convent in which Emilia is caged.
21–4 *Seraph of Heaven . . . immortality*: An angel in human form, Emilia 'veils' spiritual qualities too abstract to be 'supportable'.
25 *the eternal curse*: Original sin presumably – though Shelley comes near to seeing Eve's humanity (flesh) as itself the curse.
38 *the twin lights . . . darkens through*: The twin windows (eyes) through which Emily's soul looks into the darkness of human existence.
43–4 *though the world . . . unvalued shame*: though the social world will not be able to conceal with the 'thin name' of marriage the unwarranted shame which it imputes to the poet's love.
46–7 *Or that the name . . . sister's bond*: Shelley wishes complicatedly that if Emilia can't be his twin, she should be Mary's sister.
55 *Young Love should teach . . . grey style*: That 'grey' replaces 'heroic' in the MS suggests a positive reading: 'wise', perhaps.
85–6 *stops / Of planetary music*: the music of the spheres.
90 *fathom-line*: plumb-line for testing depths at sea.
99 *Quivers*: pulses.
116–17 *a splendour . . . pilotless*: Dante's third sphere was reserved for lovers; Shelley uses 'splendour' (which he gets from Dante) to mean a spirit, a power, a dream; cf. *Adonais*, ll. 100, 198.
122 *anatomy*: skeleton.
131 *starless*: uncontrolled, undestined by beneficent 'stars'.
149–59 *I never was attached . . . longest journey go*: Shelley's famous attack on marriage, or at least on monogamy.
167–8 *and kills . . . sun-like arrow*: Apollo, the sun god, was famous for killing the serpent Python.

180–81 *If you divide . . . whole*: An unusually prosaic and didactic Shelley.
221 *owlet light*: twilight, dusk.
222 *Hesper's*: Venus, the Evening Star.
240 *sightless*: invisible; Shelley is thinking of Macbeth's 'sightless couriers of the air' (I vii 23).
256–66 *There, one whose voice . . . unseasonable time*: Shelley's meeting is not with a human being, but with an archetypal temptress, close to Blake's Vala.
268 *The shadow . . . my thought*: Earthly resemblance of his ideal.
271 *And one was true*: Shelley's symbolic allusions in ll. 267–383 have been variously interpreted. It seems likely that the one who 'was true' was Harriet Grove, whom he knew briefly before his marriage to Harriet Westbrook.
272–3 *a hunted deer . . . at bay*: Actaeon (as punishment for seeing Diana bathing) is hunted by his own hounds: Shelley is hunted by his own thoughts.
277–81 *One stood . . . chaste Moon*: Shelley met his cold, chaste moon, Mary Godwin in 1814, and eloped with her despite being married to Harriet. They were married in December 1816 after Harriet's suicide. The stress on her coldness was extremely wounding to Mary. *Epipsychidion* is the one major poem for which she wrote no prefatory note in the edition of 1839.
293–4 *like the Moon . . . Endymion*: The shepherd Endymion (celebrated in Keats' poem of 1818) is given immortality by Jove on condition that he remains asleep. The moon, Diana, falls in love with him and visits him nightly in his cave.
299–304 *there I lay . . . mother*: Who, or what, in Shelley's mind is the 'mother' of Death and Life is far from clear. Specific reference to Harriet Westbrook as 'abandoned mother' seems unlikely in the context.
307 *I weep*: I am still weeping now.
311–19 *And how my soul . . . conceal*: Shelley is, as he says, concealing the details of his autobiography, but it seems likely that the 'Planet of that hour' is Harriet, and that the 'Tempest' is her sister Eliza Westbrook whom Shelley blamed for her suicide. The 'death of ice' and 'earthquakes' experienced by the 'sea-scape' of Shelley's soul are probably to be associated with the Chancery suit (brought by Eliza) that led to his children by Harriet (Ianthe and Charles) being removed from his care.
321 *the obscure forest*: of Shelley's life; cf. Dante's '*selva oscura*'.
322 *The Vision . . . shame*: The soul-mate whom Shelley has failed to discover in previous relationships.
334 *frore*: frosty.
339 *the thing that dreamed below*: Shelley's spirit floats free of his dreaming body.
341 *the dawn of my long night*: Not the 'dawning' of night, but the dawn in which night ends.
345 *Twin spheres of light*: Shelley addresses Emilia as the sun, and Mary as the moon.
362–3 *Thou, not disdaining . . . remoter light*: Mary, as moon, is not to repine that her light is 'borrowed': Emilia, as sun, is not to 'eclipse' the moon.
368 *Comet beautiful and fierce*: Claire Clairmont, Mary's stepsister, who eloped with her and Shelley in 1814, was thrown out after a quarrel in 1816, became pregnant by Byron, and was probably at some stage(s) Shelley's lover.
374 *love's folding-star*: Venus, seen as the Evening Star, by which shepherds 'fold' their sheep.

389–90 *To whatsoe'er . . . a vestal sister*: As the ideal (wholly spirit), Emily shall remain a vestal virgin, a sister – though Shelley has as yet his carnal side.
412 *The halcyons brood . . . isles*: Isles would be 'foamless' because halcyons (kingfishers) were fabled to calm the seas and nest on the water at the time of the winter solstice.
421 *Treading each other's heels*: alternating.
435 *sylvan forms*: spirits of the woods.
442–4 *which, the waterfalls . . . nightingales*: Shelley's syntax is far from clear, but it seems that the waterfalls both illumine the glades and bowers, and with their sound accompany the nightingales.
459 *Bright as . . . Lucifer*: The island to which Shelley in fantasy welcomes Emilia is a paradise bright as the Morning Star (associations of Lucifer with Satan are irrelevant, if ever they can be).
482 *interstices*: gaps.
501 *volumes*: coils.
507 *Parian*: marble.
545 *their paramour*: earth (or the island), seen as lover of the heavens.
557 *thine innocent lights*: Emilia's eyes, extinguished ('killed') by sleep.
568–9 *wells / Which boil*: springs that surge.
577 *instinct*: animated.
581 *unimbued*: spiritual, unpermeated by base matter.
582 *baser prey*: flesh of animals; for a time at least Shelley believed that eating meat was the source of human aggression.
592 *your Sovereign's*: Emily's.
601 *Marina, Vanna, Primus*: Mary Shelley, Jane (Giovanna) Williams, and Shelley's best (first) friend, Edward Williams.

(IV) (i) *To Jane with a Guitar*

1 *Ariel to Miranda*: Shelley, as Ariel (pure spirit, music-maker, and worker of Prospero's magic in *The Tempest*), addresses Jane Williams (Miranda, Shakespeare's most idealized heroine) in the last weeks, or days, of his life. Their relationship seems to have been tender and romantic, and condoned by Edward Williams (Prince Ferdinand in l. 10, who drowned with Shelley on 8 July). Though not beyond the reach of pain, Mary since the children's deaths and the writing of *Epipsychidion* had been quite distanced from her husband.
17–22 *From Prospero's enchanted cell . . . meteor*: Prospero's last charge to Ariel is to calm the seas and give favourable winds for the return to Naples; then he is freed.
24 *interlunar swoon*: daytime; 'The sun to me is dark', Milton writes (*Samson Agonistes* 86–9), 'And silent as the moon / When she deserts the night, / Hid in her vacant interlunar cave.' Shelley's fantasy gives Miranda many lives, all looked after by a devoted Ariel, waiting each time for reincarnation to take place.
31 *Many changes . . . rung*: many new and different earthly lives (the metaphor is of bell-ringing).
38–9 *Imprisoned . . . in a body like a grave*: Shakespeare's Ariel is imprisoned by Sycorax in 'a cloven pine', rescued by Prospero after her death, but then threatened by him with being 'pegged' in 'the knotty entrails' of an oak. Shelley's problem is to give Ariel (and himself) earthly existence.

43 *this idol*: the guitar (not a 'false god', but an image sacred to music, and containing, at l. 81, a 'spirit').
48 *wind-swept Apennine*: Mountains of central Italy.
57 *heaven's fairest star*: Venus presumably.
76 *driven, on its diurnal round*: Like Wordsworth's Lucy, 'Rolled round in earth's diurnal course, / With rocks and stones and trees'.
86 *secrets of an elder day*: Appropriately (when the instrument has been made in such mystical circumstances from a sleeping tree) Shelley has in mind the pines clinging in *Mont Blanc* to the sides of the Ravine of Arve, 'Children of elder time', and worshipped by the winds.

(ii) *To Jane: The Stars Were Twinkling*

22–4 *some world far from ours / Are one*: Wistful lines from a poet so near to his unnecessary death!

LORD BYRON

(I) *When We Two Parted*

7–8 *Truly / Sorrow to this*: Byron had in 1813 been intrigued by the beauty and innocence of Lady Frances, and 'spared' her when she threw herself on his mercy. Three years later he was grieved to hear rumours of her having an amour with the Duke of Wellington.

(II) *Fare Thee Well* (1816)

1–2 *Fare thee well . . . fare thee well*: When repeated, the force of Byron's opening farewell changes. It is as if he had said 'Goodbye, and if it is for always, then for always, God be with you'. Byron had not expected his marriage to break down completely. When it did so he was hurt as well as angry, lashing out at Annabella's advisers, but also showing to the world his pain. As late as 26 February 1816 (three weeks before *Fare Thee Well*, and eight before the legal separation), he wrote to his wife: 'Dearest Pip – I wish you would make it up – for I am dreadfully sick of all this – and cannot foresee any good that can come of it.'
3 *though unforgiving*: though you prove unforgiving.
9 *glanced over*: ignored, rejected.

(III) (i) *Stanzas to Augusta* ('When all around')

11–12 *Thou wert . . . to the last*: Byron and Augusta were half-brother and sister. She was four years older than him, and they had not been brought up together. They had just enough in common, and just enough that was strange, to form the one enduring relationship in Byron's life. When London society turned against her brother, it did not occur to Augusta not to be loyal. That they made a child now seems more natural than shocking.
17 *And when the cloud . . . came*: rumours of incest (few now doubt that Medora Leigh was Byron's daughter).
32 *thy weeping leaves*: By implication Augusta is a weeping willow – love's tree.

37 *the ties of baffled love*: Byron's marriage (legal separation had just come through).
41 *these*: Augusta's resolute heart and soul.

(III) (ii) *Stanzas to Augusta* ('Though the day of my destiny')

7 *painted*: imagined, created as an ideal.
14 *the breasts I believed in*: Annabella and friends who took her side in bringing about separation.

(IV) *Stanzas to the River Po*

1–2 *the ancient walls . . . lady of my love*: After ten days in Byron's company, the nineteen-year-old Countess had been abruptly, and not unreasonably, removed by her husband from Venice to Ravenna.
17 *long wrecks*: Lines of jetsam, thrown up along the river banks.
21–2 *The current . . . native walls*: Byron, though writing in Venice, pictures himself at the source of the Po (l. 36 below), upstream from Teresa, the Countess, in Ravenna.
43 *meridian*: southern, and thus distinct from the nations of 'the moral north'.
51 *To dust . . . I sprung*: 'earth to earth, ashes to ashes, dust to dust' (Burial Service). Byron's relationship to the Countess, which approximated to marriage, but produced no children, lasted till his death.

(V) *I Watched Thee*

1–4 *I watched thee . . . love and liberty*: Loukas, who was fifteen, had been with Byron since late December 1823, sharing various dangers and excitements. At one point, when they were playing cat-and-mouse with Turkish ships along the coast, Byron wrote: 'I am uneasy at being here: not so much on my own account, as on that of a Greek boy with me, for you know what his fate would be – and I would sooner cut him in pieces, and myself too, than have him taken out by those barbarians.'
24 *To strongly . . . love thee still*: Almost certainly this grand and moving line is the last that Byron ever wrote. Loukas too it seems died in the war, but there are no details.

JOHN KEATS

(i) *The Day Is Gone*

4 *accomplished*: perfectly formed.
10 *holinight*: Keats' coinage (the night that is coming – being 'woven' – will be sacred to love).
13 *read Love's missal . . . today*: See Keats' letter to Fanny of 11 October: 'My sweet Girl, I am living today in yesterday. I was in complete fascination all day . . . You dazzled me – there is nothing in the world so bright and delicate!' They had been apart since June.

(ii) *I Cry Your Mercy*

6 *zest*: piquancy, relish (metaphor from the use of orange or lemon peel in flavouring).
10 *or I die*: Keats to Fanny, 19 October 1819, 'I should like to cast the die for love or death – I have no patience with anything else!'
14 *gust*: ability to taste.

(iii) *Ode to Fanny*

1 *let my spirit blood*: Not as gruesome an image to Keats as it is to us. Trained as a medical student, he had no reason to doubt opinion of the day (fatal to Byron among others) that letting blood to bring down a patient's temperature was an effective treatment. Keats bled many patients at Guys, and had been bled himself after his alarming haemorrhage of 3 February 1820.
3–4 *Throw me upon thy tripod . . . full breast*: Keats switches abruptly from contemporary medical practice to an image of the Delphic Oracle, drawn from Lemprière's *Classical Dictionary*. Nature is (somewhat surprisingly) to throw him onto the tripod that supported the seat of the prophetess over a chasm in the inner sanctuary of Apollo, from which vapours rose (or, in Keats' day were held to have risen) inducing a state of ecstasy. Thus inspired, he will get rid of the burden of unwritten verses ('numbers') in his mind
5 *A theme, a theme . . . theme*: 'A horse, a horse – my kingdom for a horse!' (*Richard III*).
7–8 *thou standest . . . wintry air*: Since his haemorrhage Keats had been forbidden by his doctors to excite himself by meeting Fanny, but they were neighbours in Hampstead, and he could see her in the garden. Soon he would be forbidden also to write poetry.
18 *What stare outfaces . . . moon*: What impudent stare makes Fanny turn her eyes away.
19 *unravished*: To Keats in his jealousy the thought even of someone holding Fanny's hand seems a sort of rape. He suggests to her in mid February that she may wish to call off the engagement, but knowing that he is to die brings no calm to his feelings.
27 *dangerous wreath*: 'Many will not allow man and woman to dance together', Burton writes in a passage of *The Anatomy of Melancholy* marked by Keats, but 'it was a pleasant sight to see those pretty knots and swimming figures'.
40 *blow-ball*: Seed-head of the dandelion ('blown' as a children's game, releasing each parachute seed into the air).
51–3 *Let none profane . . . sacramental cake*: Religious images of the Pope's 'throne', seat of power, and the Eucharist, mingle with an allusion to *Lycidas* ('And with forced fingers rude, / Shatter your leaves . . .) to create a poetry of erotic intensity.

JOHN CLARE

(ii) *My Mary*

1 *rarely speed*: have little success.
3–4 *As none beside herself . . . Mary*: Though using the form, refrain and title of Cowper's *My Mary* (above), Clare's poem is broadly satirical, written after his childhood sweetheart, Mary Joyce, has left him, but assuming none the less that they are intended to be together.
9 *battled*: spattered with mud.
17 *Unused to pattens or to clogs*: Both pattens and clogs are heavy wooden-soled overshoes (Mary is an indoor servant, but makes herself useful in the farmyard – without changing her shoes).
26 *catch*: chance, random.
35 *stump*: used satirically where 'offshoot' is to be expected.
50 *grunters*: pigs.
57–9 *And who . . . low degree*: Though illiterate, Mary 'gives herself airs' (which is probably why she ditched Clare).
61 *prates*: chatters.
67 *lotted out*: allotted by fortune.
77 *whelp*: young puppy (human, in this case).
79 *chelp*: gossip.
87 *nice*: fastidious.

FELICIA HEMANS

The Dreaming Child

35–6 *Oh, shall my soul . . . life*: 'Start' into another world.

CAROLINE NORTON

(ii) *The Mother's Heart*

1 *When first thou camest*: Norton addresses in turn her three sons, taken from her by her husband when he charged her with adultery with the Prime Minister, Lord Melbourne.
8 *natural piety* : The child is father to the man, / And I could wish my days to be / Bound each to each by natural piety', Wordsworth, *The Rainbow* (Romantic Lyric and Song, p. 382, above)

LETITIA ELIZABETH LANDON

To My Brother

10 *his Voyages . . . South Seas*: Captain James Cook, *A Voyage Round the World, 1768–71*.
27 *guelder-roses*: the 'snowball tree'.
32 *and how we mourned his fall*: Cook was killed by natives of Hawaii in 1779.

XII. On Poets and Poetry

MARY SCOTT

on Anna Laetitia Barbauld (née Aikin), from *The Female Advocate*

419 *Fired with . . . thy lays*: Scott, aged twenty-two, has been inspired by *Poems* 1773, published by Barbauld (née Aikin) just before her marriage.
423 *Fancy's hand*: imagination.
433 *Teach them . . . to soar*: Barbauld's imagination had soared to outer space, 'Where embryo systems and unkindled suns / Sleep in the womb of chaos' (Ennobling Interchange: p. 252, above).
434 *science*: knowledge, learning (Latin *scientia*).
435–6 *With thee . . . pride of man*: Scott reminds her readers of Pope's famous couplet, 'Know then thyself, presume not God to scan; / The proper study of mankind is Man' (*Essay On Man* II, 1–2), in order to question its settled assumptions – not least, the implication that mankind and man are one.
439 *Salic Law*: Ancient French law alleged to exclude women from succession to the throne.
444 *The orient beams . . . days*: the sun rising (in the east) on a brighter future.
447 *them*: women of the future.
457 *From sense abstracted*: transcending the realms of sense.
460 *How mind on matter . . . mind*: Barbauld had speculated (thinking of Heraclitus, as well as Priestley) that mind, 'A never-dying flame, / Still shifts through matter's varying forms, / In every form the same' in *The Mouse's Petition* (Ennobling Interchange p. 249 above).

ROBERT BURNS

(i) *Epistle to J. Lapraik, An Old Scotch Bard*

51 *An' hae . . . pretence*: Unlike other working-class Romantic poets (Yearsley, Bloomfield, Hogg, Clare), Burns, though unlearned, was by modern standards rather well educated, his father even at one point sending him away to school.

73–8 *Gie me ae spark . . . the heart*: Lines that Wordsworth chose in March 1798 for an epigraph to *The Ruined Cottage*, his first great plain-style poem of the human heart (Narratives of Love, p. 52 above)

(ii) *I Am a Bard*

10 *Castalia's burn*: spring on Mount Parnassus dedicated to Apollo, god of poetry, and the Muses.
12 *Helicon*: Greek mountain, sacred to the Muses.
19 *lordly will*: women's 'lordly' demands; but with a pun (frequent in Shakespeare's *Sonnets*) on the imperious penis.

HELEN MARIA WILLIAMS

Sonnet on Reading 'The Mountain Daisy' by Burns

1 *the 'garden's flaunting flowers'*: Burns, *To a Mountain Daisy* 19, 'The flaunting flowers our gardens yield' (Romantic Hallmarks, p. 5 above).

JOANNA BAILLIE

An Address to the Muses

50 *blotted stand*: stand for pens, ink bottles, etc. on which ink has been spilt (showing the fervour of the young poet's composition).
56 *in heated frame*: with youthful excitement.
61 *lovely Sisters*: The nine classical Muses, daughters of Zeus and Mnemosyne, said to inspire poetry, music and the Arts in general (always shown as young and beautiful), addressed by Wordsworth, with Baillie's poem in mind, at *Idiot Boy*, 347–56, Romantic Comedy and Satire, p. 549, above.
92–102 *Ye are the spirits . . . power*: Lines that inspire Wordsworth's important address to the spirit-world in *Peter Bell*:

> Your presence I have often felt
> In darkness and the stormy night;
> And well I know, if need there be,
> Ye can put forth your agency
> When earth is calm, and heaven is bright.
>
> Then, coming from the wayward world,
> That powerful world in which ye dwell,
> Come, Spirits of the Mind! and try,
> Tonight, beneath the moonlight sky,
> What may be done with Peter Bell!

WILLIAM BLAKE

(i) Preface to *Europe, A Prophecy*

1 *Five windows . . . caverned man*: Fallen man is 'caverned' for Blake in that he is restricted to the evidence of his senses, 'chief inlets of soul in this age' (*Marriage of Heaven and Hell*, plate 4); emblematically the 'cavern' is represented by the human skull, where the mouth, ears, nose and eyes, each have their 'cave-entrances'.
5–6 *Through one, himself pass out . . . pleasant*: Man is not entirely cut off from eternity and eternal vision, but enjoys his deprivation, 'bread eaten in secret'.
13 *what is the material world . . . dead*: The central question for Blake, Coleridge, Wordsworth and Shelley, and also for the scientists of their period.
18 'And 'tis my faith', Wordsworth wrote in *Lines Written in Early Spring* (1798) 'that every flower / Enjoys the air it breathes' (Romantic Lyric and Song, p. 376, above).
24 *and dictated Europe*: A lighthearted, but not unserious, claim for poetic inspiration. Though mischievous (as his kind traditionally are) to the point of laughing at the whimper of plucked flowers, the fairy of *Europe* 'dictates' the poem, as the Eternals dictate Blake's *Book of Urizen* (1794) and Urania dictates to Milton in *Paradise Lost*.

(ii) 'I Come In Self-Annihilation'

2 *I come in self-annihilation*: It is Milton who speaks, near the conclusion of the Prophetic Book named after him, which has seen his return from Heaven to Earth in order to purge away his selfhood and become fully imaginative/spiritual.
9 *the tame . . . blots*: the painter who relies on technique, and records actuality rather than being inspired.
12 *the idiot questioner*: one who cannot accept truth, but must have a reason for everything.
15 *publishes doubt*: proclaims his scepticism.
25–6 *the sexual garments . . . ark and curtains*: Sexuality covers and obscures the soul as the Ark of the Covenant obscured the possibility of regeneration through Jesus. Throughout the passage imagination is the higher spiritual reality, concealed by selfhood, regarded in one form or another as 'clothing' of the nakedness of truth.

SAMUEL TAYLOR COLERIDGE

Nehemiah Higginbottom Sonnets

(ii) 'Oh I Do Love Thee'

1 *Oh, I do love . . . SIMPLICITY!*: Nine months before the publication of *Lyrical Ballads* 1798, assumed by most to bring a new poetry of directness and personal emotion, Coleridge is seen mocking the very qualities on which the volume's fame depends. Far from being new, the cult of simplicity was established enough to have become an affectation. It was geniuneness, sincerity, that mattered.

5 *pad*: slow-pacing horse.
10 *pall*: cover, as with a pall.
7–12 *But should a friend . . . in general*: Coleridge's collaborators in the spring 1797 volume, *Poems by Coleridge, Lamb and Lloyd*, both regarded the *Higginbottom Sonnets* as parodies of their work, as did Southey, with whom Coleridge had quarreled in 1796. Early in 1798 he would quarrel too with Lloyd (who was unstable, and spent August–September 1797 staying with the embittered Southey), and with Lamb, his school friend and life-long correspondent. 'Frowning, pouting and parting' were in the air; Coleridge's claim that he was getting solely at himself is not very credible.

(iii) 'And This Reft House'

1 *And this reft house*: To open a sonnet 'borrowed entirely from [his] own poems' with a direct quotation – Wordsworth, *The Ruined Cottage* 482–3, 'Till this reft house, by frost, and thaw, and rain, / Was sapped' – seems strange. More so, when the Wordsworth line had been transcribed in a Coleridge letter the previous June.
10 *brogues*: breeches.

WILLIAM WORDSWORTH

Thoughts on Poetic Imagination

(i) from the *Prologue to Peter Bell*

1–5 *There's something . . . crescent moon*: The poet's imagination will take flight neither on the legendary Pegasus of the ancient world, nor on the up-to-date scientific invention of the hot-air balloon (first ascent by Montgolfier, 1785), but on a boat of his own making. 'The moon crescent', Dorothy records on 20 April 1798, '*Peter Bell* begun.'
33 *ether*: 'a thin, subtle matter . . . which, commencing from the limits of our atmosphere, possesses the whole heavenly space' (*Encyclopaedia Britannica*, 3rd edn, 1797).
66 *Oh shame . . . shame*: It is the boat that is chiding the poet for his return to earth – and, by implication, for his earth-bound simplicity of style and matter.

(ii) *The Glad Preamble*

6–7 *A captive greets thee . . . set free*: Wordsworth has not literally been a captive. The house of bondage (from Exodus) and city walls are metaphors for a state of mind from which in this exuberant mood he feels liberated. He is composing on foot, en route to Grasmere where he proposes to rent Dove Cottage, the house associated with so much of his greatest poetry. Originally a free-standing effusion, his lines were to become in 1804 the opening of *The Prelude*.
15 *The earth is all before me*: A striking quotation from the final lines of *Paradise Lost*. Adam and Eve, though their human dignity is moving, have been barred from Eden:

> The world was all before them, where to choose
> Their place of rest, and Providence their guide:
> They hand in hand, with wandering steps and slow,
> Through Eden took their solitary way.

Wordsworth, by contrast, is about to enter his Paradise.

17–19 *should the guide . . . my way*: As at ll. 28–31 below, Wordsworth replaces Miltonic Providence with Nature – but at her least solemn and impressive.

40 *a gift that consecrates my joy*: the gift of imagination, which consecrates to poetry an otherwise fleeting joy.

41–7 *For I, methought . . . its own creation*: Wordsworth's famous definition of his sense of imaginative reciprocity – the 'ennobling interchange / Of action from within and from without'. For the breeze as emblem of creative power, akin to divine inspiration (breath), see Coleridge, *The Eolian Harp* (Ennobling Interchange, p. 255, above) and Shelley, *Ode to the West Wind* (Romantic Odes, p. 347, above). Wordsworth was consistent in claiming to be 'vexed', tormented, by his own creativity.

52 *prowess in an honourable field*: To be gained, Wordsworth thought, only by writing the never-to-be-completed philosophical poem, *The Recluse*, wished on him by Coleridge; see opening of *Two-Part Prelude* (Ennobling Interchange, p. 269, above)

(iii) 'A Dedicated Spirit'

318 *promiscuous rout*: mixed company; both noun and adjective are Miltonic in this usage.

319 *tempers*: temperaments.

335 *Grain-tinctured . . . light*: coloured scarlet; Wordsworth is imitating *Paradise Lost* V, 285, 'Sky-tinctured grain' (rather confusingly Milton meant blue); the 'empyrean' was the highest heaven, consisting of pure fire.

338–9 *Dews vapours . . . fields*: Even this simpler style, which we think of as Wordsworthian rather than Miltonic, turns out to have its origins in *Paradise Lost*: 'fruits, and flowers, / Walks, and the melody of birds' (VIII, 527–8).

341–4 *Vows / Were then . . . dedicated spirit*: Wordsworth, by implication, is dedicated – 'called' – to the life of poetry.

(iv) *Elegiac Stanzas, Suggested by a Picture of Peele Castle in a Storm*

1–4 *I was thy neighbour . . . sea*: Wordsworth spent a month in August–September 1794 staying at Rampside, half a mile across the water from Piel Island and the ruin of Piel (or Peele) Castle.

15 *The light that never was . . . land*: One of Wordsworth's most famous definitions of imagination.

36 *A deep distress . . . soul*: Wordsworth's much-loved younger brother John, captain of the largest merchant-ship afloat (the East India Company's *Earl of Abergavenny*), was drowned at sea in February 1805.

42 *deplore*: lament.

53–4 *Farewell . . . kind*: Wordsworth, who sought to reach out to a wider audience with simplicity of language and sincerity of emotion, has come to think the imagination itself elitist in its workings. In his repetition of 'Farewell' he has in mind *Othello* III iii, 'farewell, / Farewell the neighing steed and the shrill trump'.
57–60 *But welcome fortitude . . . mourn*: Wordsworth, after his brother's death, talked himself into a belief in the afterlife, and a Christian stoicism (glimpsed in *The Immortality Ode* and *Ode to Duty*, of 1804), that has some bearing on his poetic decline.

ANNA LAETITIA BARBAULD

To Mr Coleridge

1 *Science*: learning, knowledge.
3 *in tangled mazes wrought*: cf. the fallen angels of *Paradise Lost* II, 561, 'in wandering mazes lost' as they reason of fate and freewill.
4 *Dubious*: dimly visible.
11–13 *while things of life . . . shadows*: Barbauld in her Spenserian allegory beautifully catches the abstractions and temptations of Coleridge's early writing.
15 *gossamer*: spiders' webs.
16 *palsy*: paralyse.
19 *lawns*: forest clearings.
23–4 *for soothing soft / The shades*: 'most soothing sweet it is / To sit beside our cot' (*Eolian Harp*, 2–3, Ennobling Interchange, p. 255).
26 *mould*: substance (the 'clay', or 'dust', from which man was created).
37 *Circe*: the island-enchantress who turned Odysseus' men to pigs while delaying his return journey to Ithaca.
41 *spleen-fed*: melancholy.

MARY ROBINSON

(i) *Ode Inscribed to the Infant Son of S. T. Coleridge, Esq., Born 14 Sept 1800*

69 *her forest haunts among*: Robinson, who in this last phase of her life is contributor of poetry to the *Morning Post* alongside Coleridge, lives in Windsor Great Forest. Derwent Coleridge was born at Greta Hall, Keswick.
95–102 *Whether Lodore . . . sublime*: cf. *Southey's Cataract of Lodore* (see Romantic Comedy and Satire, p. 607, above).

(ii) *To the Poet Coleridge* (Oct 1800; publ 1806)

13–14 *I'll mark . . . 'caves of ice'*: Robinson, who writes this poem, with its allusions to the unpublished *Kubla Khan*, two months before her death, had like Coleridge a contract to produce poetry for the *Morning Post*. No other work of the period shows a knowledge of *Kubla Khan*.
39–40 *Thy flaming temple . . . Peruvia's lustrous store*: A reference that might take

one to Williams (*Conquest of Peru*, 1784), rather than Coleridge. Aside from her brief *Kubla Khan* quotations, Robinson doesn't seem to know his work especially well.
64 *witcheries of song*: Coleridge's 'damsel with a dulcimer' (who at l. 60 has become his 'nymph') produces a music that recollects *The Eolian Harp*, 20, 'soft floating witchery of sound'.
72 *Which gives to airy dreams . . . own*: A touch of *A Midsummer Night's Dream*, where the poet famously gives 'to airy nothing / A local habitation and a name' (V i).

WILLIAM WORDSWORTH

Portraits of Coleridge

(i) from *The Castle of Indolence Stanzas*

37–9 *With him . . . large dark eyes*: Wordsworth's first four stanzas have been a partly comic self-portrait, in the manner of Thomson's pseudo-Spenserian *Castle of Indolence* (1748). The second half of the poem is given over to Coleridge, of whom Dorothy had written on first meeting him in June 1797: 'His eye is large and full, not dark, but grey; such an eye as would receive from a heavy soul the dullest expression, but it speaks every emotion of his animated mind. It has more of the "poet's eye in fine frenzy rolling" [*A Midsummer Night's Dream*] than I ever witnessed.'
43 *A face divine . . . idiocy*: A description that surely comes from Coleridge himself, who had commented in 1796, 'my face, unless when animated by immediate eloquence, expresses great sloth, and great, indeed almost idiotic, good nature'.
46 *forfend*: forbid.
54 *certes*: certainly (pronounced 'sirtease'), cf. *Castle of Indolence* I, 40: 'Certes, who bides his grasp, will that encounter rue!'
58–9 *Glasses he had . . . display*: tinted Claude-glasses (which made landscape look as if it were a painting) and microscopes (which Coleridge ordered in 1802).
67 *As far as love . . . could be*: Surely more a reference to *The Castle of Indolence* (where love would be too strenuous), than to Grasmere, where Coleridge was surrounded by love.
72 *Maiden Queen*: Elizabeth I, to whom Spenser addressed *The Faerie Queene*.

(ii) 'A Mind Debarred'

242 *the Border Beacon*: Penrith Beacon, scene of the child Wordsworth's encounter with the Woman on the Hill, 1799 *Prelude* I, 296–327 (Ennobling Interchange: Man and Nature, pp. 275–6 above), and visited by him with Dorothy, and Mary Hutchinson (whom he was to marry fifteen years later), in the summer of 1787.
246 *we had not . . . time*: Wordsworth and Coleridge met eight years later in September 1795.
249 *Far art thou . . . health*: Wordsworth is writing in March 1804, the month in which Coleridge set off for the Mediterranean and its drier climate.

256 *Speed thee well!*: A private pun – Coleridge is aboard the *Speedwell* brig.
260 *gales Etesian*: Mediterranean winds – included for their half-pun on the phonetic spelling of Coleridge's initials: 'Essteecee'.
276–7 *a liveried schoolboy . . . huge city*: On his father's death when he was nine, Coleridge was sent to Christ's Hospital (the 'Blue-coat' School – hence the reference uf976to 'livery', uniform) in London, 200 miles from his family in Devonshire, whom he saw only in the summers.
286–8 *scarcely had I . . . thither guided*: Wordsworth left Cambridge in January 1791, Coleridge (who was two years younger) matriculated in October.
291–2 *What a stormy . . . followed*: Wordsworth's Cambridge career had been extremely disappointing (he was expected to get a fellowship at St John's, and went down without an honours degree), Coleridge's was disastrous! The most learned and distinguished undergraduate of his generation, he began by winning a University Prize, but then became involved in politics, got into debt, talked of suicide, joined the army, was bailed out, planned to emigrate (*Pantisocracy*), and went down without a degree of any kind. On the positive side, he had begun his career as a writer, and the Unitarian faith that he first experienced at Cambridge was for many years the stable centre of his life.
297 *still*: at all times.
308–11 *toils abstruse . . . words for things*: On the one hand there is medieval scholastic philosophy (Abelard, Aquinas, Ockham), on the other a Platonist idealism which Wordsworth assumes (presumably from what Coleridge told him) had more to do with words than clear thinking.
326 *battened on*: grew fat upon.
326–9 *But thou hast trod . . . vain regrets*: Trying to reassure Coleridge (whose friends assume he may be dying), Wordsworth echoes Milton, *Samson Agonistes* 597–8: My race of glory run, and race of shame, / And I shall shortly be with them that rest.' It was scarcely tactful.

(iii) *A Complaint*

1 *There is a change . . . poor*: Coleridge did not for months go to see the Wordsworths on his return from Malta in 1806. When they did meet he was overweight and painfully distant. Wordsworth, 'not used to make / A present joy the matter of [his] song', on this occasion made from present pain one of the saddest and most emotionally honest of his poems.

MARY TIGHE

'Dreams of Delight, Farewell'

514 *With fond . . . long lost son*: Venus is embracing Cupid, whose marriage to the mortal Psyche she has opposed.
516 *hardly*: with difficulty.
517 *parent*: mother-in-law.
518 *hence*: henceforward.
527 *on halcyon wing*: with wings as blue as the kingfisher's.
538 *Consigned . . . silent tomb*: Probably this despairing line is applied to the poem,

rather than the poet. But Tighe, who was to die of TB in 1810, was already consumptive.

SAMUEL TAYLOR COLERIDGE

To William Wordsworth

1 *Oh friend! . . . gift to me!*: Coleridge's poem is subtitled in the MS, *Lines Composed for the Greater Part on the Night on which he Finished the Recitation of his Poem (in Thirteen Books) Concerning the Growth and History of His own Mind.*
10–11 *Of smiles . . . and twin-birth*: 'Fair seed-time had my soul, and I grew up / Fostered alike by beauty and by fear' (1805 *Prelude* I, 305–6).
12 *Of tides . . . external force*: external pressures that control the mind as tides control the sea.
15 *abroad*: outside, in the social world.
16–17 *thy brows . . . the feast*: Coleridge has in mind Wordsworth's trip down the Rhône in July 1790, dancing hand-in-hand with delegates returning from the Fête de la Fédération (1805 *Prelude* VI, 383–413).
18 *Hyblaean murmurs*: murmurs like those of the bees for which the Sicilian town of Hybla was famous. Bees, in an address to Coleridge (himself in Sicily) at the end of 1805 *Prelude* X, are said to have kept alive the poet Comates 'from month to month', because his lips 'were wet with the muse's nectar'.
20 *Native or outland*: at home or abroad.
23 *Where France . . . vibrating*: A version of Wordsworth's strange image of himself in France, unconcerned as 'a parlour-shrub / When every bush and tree, the country through, / Is shaking to the roots' (1805 *Prelude* IX, 89–91).
24 *a bark becalmed*: 'A boat becalmed, dear William's sky-canoe' (*Letter to Sara Hutchinson*, 41; Poets in Relationship, p. 696, above); situation (the boat becalmed on sultry seas) might take one rather to *The Ancient Mariner*.
29–30 *and Hope . . . upon the storm*: 'I saw the revolutionary power / Toss like a ship at anchor, rocked by storms' (1805 *Prelude* IX, 48–9)
31–5 *Hope afflicted . . . Far on*: Struck down on the political scene, Hope finds a home in Wordsworth's heart, looking out into the future from the 'watchtower' of man's 'absolute' (as opposed to social, political, transitory) self.
36 *Then – last strain*: 'Then, last wish . . . / My last and favourite aspiration' (1805 *Prelude* I, 228–9)
38 *An Orphic tale*: Such as those sung by the legendary musician-king, Orpheus, who could charm equally men and animals.
43–4 *The truly . . . one age*: 'There is / One great society alone on earth, / The noble living and the noble dead' (1805 *Prelude* X, 967–9).
45 *both power and act*: Collectively 'the truly great' constitute power, but with the capacity to act individually.
49 *gradual fame*: fame that comes by stages (Latin *gradus*, a step).
67–8 *of what sad years . . . suppression*: Years of opium addiction, in which the reading of German metaphysics had taken the place of poetry, and relationship had become increasingly difficult.
77 *wood-walks wild*: the natural world (cf. Milton, *L'Allegro* 133–4, 'Or sweetest Shakespeare, fancy's child, / Warble his native wood-noted wild').

87–8 *triumphal wreathes . . . thy advancing*: It is difficult not to have in mind Christ's entry into Jerusalem – more so, as Coleridge in his role of herald so clearly evokes John the Baptist.
90 *my nobler mind*: Coleridge's own mind, in its nobler aspects.
95–7 *Amid the howl . . . wing*: The halcyon (kingfisher) was said to calm the sea and nest at mid-winter on the waves – thus anticipating spring (hearing the approach of 'vernal hours').
104–6 *With momentary stars . . . darkness*: Wordsworth's 'stars' create the patterns and the light that are the poem, Coleridge's are personal associations, started by what he hears, but insubstantial ('constellated foam') and darting off sideways like the wake of a ship.

LORD BYRON

English Bards and Scotch Reviewers

11–12 *Like him great Dryden . . . doubly strong*: Despite his admiration for Pope, Byron has begun his poem in Dryden's stronger, run-on lines. In his mind is the famous opening of *Absolom and Achitophel*: 'In pious times, ere priestcraft did begin . . .'
13 *or Otway's melt*: Remembered now chiefly for *Venice Preserved*, Otway was the great tragic dramatist of the Restoration, who died at the age of thirty-three. For the Romantics his name was synonymous with poignancy (in Smith's sonnets, for instance, and Coleridge's *Dejection, An Ode*).
24 *printer's devils*: juniors in a printing works.
26 *And Little's . . . hot-pressed twelves*: Moore's first volume appeared in duodecimo ('twelves') *The Works of Thomas Little* (1801). 'Hot-pressing' made paper glossy and smooth.
29 *Pegasus*: winged horse who carried poets on 'flights' of imagination.
32 *Tales of Terror*: title of 'Monk' Lewis' second anthology of Gothic verse, 1801.
33 *immeasurable measures*: metres that can't be scanned.
35 *Dullness*: presiding goddess in Pope's *Dunciad*.
37–8 *Thus Lays . . . half-strung harps*: Scott's *The Lay of the Last Minstrel* appeared in 1805, using in part the free four-stress metre of Coleridge's unpublished *Christabel* (which Byron was later to imitate himself).
87 *Camoëns, Milton, Tasso*: Epic poets of the Renaissance, respectively from Portugal, England and Italy.
88 *Whose annual strains . . . take the field*: Southey produces an epic a year (not true!) as armies emerge each spring for a new campaign.
90–1 *The scourge . . . as a witch*: After her success in relieving Orleans in 1428, Joan of Arc was captured by the Burgundians, sold to the English, and burned in 1431 by the Duke of Bedford (Regent during the minority of Henry VI). Southey's epic of 1796 ends with Joan victorious, reflecting Jacobin hopes of the period that revolutionary France would overcome England and her allies.
95–7 *Next see . . . Domdaniel's dread destroyer*: Southey's *Thalaba* (1801) is an arabian spiritual quest in very free verse (admired by Newman as well as Shelley), in which the hero dies avenging his father, and destroying the magicians' training-ground, the 'Domdaniel'.

100 *Tom Thumb*: diminutive hero of Fielding's play.
106 *Cacique . . . Prince in Wales*: Drawing on the legend of Welsh-speaking natives in Central America, Southey creates in *Madoc* (1805) a benign invader who is all that the Spanish conquistadors were not. 'Cacique', chieftain, native prince.
108 *More old than . . . true*: Mandeville's fabulous travel-book appeared in 1356–7, and was immensely famous. Southey drew on it for *The Old Woman of Berkeley* (referred to, ll. 115–6n., below).
112 *A fourth, alas . . . bear*: Southey produced not merely the fourth epic that Byron dreads, *The Curse of Kehama* (1810), but a fifth for good measure, *Roderick, Last of the Goths* (1814).
114 *verseward plod thy weary way*: To show his contempt Byron draws on the marvellous pedestrian third line of Gray's *Elegy*: 'The ploughman homeward plods his weary way.'
115–6 *If still in Berkeley-ballads . . . Devil*: *The Old Woman of Berkeley*, Gothic and Surreal, p. 488, above.
118 *'God help thee', Southey*: Allusion to 'God help thee, silly one', in the widely known *Anti-Jacobin* parody of Southey's *Dactyllics* (1797).
119 *the dull disciple of thy school*: Byron accepts the *Edinburgh Review* casting of Southey as head of the 'Lake School'.
123–4 *Who warns . . . growing double*: *Tables Turned*, 1–4; the friend was Hazlitt, then twenty. Byron, though he had reviewed Wordsworth's *Poems* 1807, attacks in this passage only *Lyrical Ballads*.
129 *Christmas-stories*: A baffling reference till one recalls that Wordsworth's narrator in *The Thorn* has been discussing the story of Martha Ray with Farmer Simpson over Christmas.
137 *the 'idiot in his glory'*: 'Thus answered Johnny in his glory, / And that was all his travel's story' (last lines of *The Idiot Boy*).
140 *To turgid ode . . . dear*: Byron read Coleridge in the 1803 reprint of his 1796–7 volumes. His greatest poems are as yet unknown to his contemporaries. *Kubla Khan* and *Christabel* remain in MS till 1816; *The Ancient Mariner*, though printed in successive editions of *Lyrical Ballads*, doesn't appear over Coleridge's name till *Sibylline Leaves* (1817).
tumid: grandiose, inflated.
144 *a pixy for a muse*: *Songs of the Pixies* (written in 1793, when Coleridge was twenty).
145–8 *Yet none . . . wondrous kind*: Coleridge's 'fellow-feeling', in 1794, had led him to hail a young donkey as a brother, with whom to live 'in the dell / Of peace and mild equality' (*To a Young Ass*, 26–8).

JAMES LEIGH HUNT

Feast of the Poets

204–5 *All on a sudden . . . airs*: Four earthly poets – Campbell, Southey, Scott and Moore – are to dine with Apollo, god of poetry. Others flock in to pay their respects or make their claims to a place at the table. Southey's fellow Lake Poets, Wordsworth and Coleridge, especially give themselves 'singular airs'.

210 *Apollo seemed pleased*: Hunt's selection of Southey to be at Apollo's table is made in 1811, before Southey becomes Poet Laureate and a Tory reviewer for the *Quarterly*.
217 *changing . . . for a whistle*: Hunt may have in mind Wordsworth's claim in *Hart-Leap Well* 'To pipe a simple song to thinking hearts'.
223 *In praise of bombarding . . . relations*: A reference, Hunt makes clear in his Notes, to Coleridge's having defended the French attack on Copenhagen (in *The Friend*, 1810).
224–31 *And tother . . . scorn*: Hunt's parody, he claims in the Notes, has been taken by some of Wordsworth's supporters to be authentic.
246–9 *There is one of you . . . today*: Hunt's anxiety at having in 1811 refused Wordsworth a place at Apollo's table shows itself in 1814 in a twenty-three-page note. Wordsworth, we are told, has 100 times more talent than Southey, but has abused it; Southey has made the best of what he has.

LORD BYRON

''Tis to Create' (*Childe Harold* III, stanzas 3–6)

19–20 *In my youth's summer . . . dark mind*: *Childe Harold* I and II had been published in 1812, when Byron was twenty-three. He takes the poem up again in very different circumstances in April 1816, as debts and scandal make it expedient to resume his travels.
33 *So that it wean*: As long as it weans.

PERCY BYSSHE SHELLEY

To Wordsworth

13–14 *Deserting these . . . cease to be*: It is not clear what prompted Shelley's lament. Mary's journal shows that on a first glance at *The Excursion*, in September 1814, they were 'much disappointed' – 'He is a slave!' was their conclusion – yet *Alastor* (published February 1816) is strongly influenced by *The Excursion*, and summer 1816 is the period at which Shelley famously 'doses' Byron with Wordsworth. In general Wordsworth certainly had become more conservative, forfeiting his 'honoured poverty' in 1813 for the role of Distributor of Stamps for Westmorland (in the gift of Lord Lonsdale) at four hundred pounds a year. But then Shelley had (from 1815) an inherited income of a thousand.

JOHN KEATS

(i) *Sleep and Poetry*

99–101 *Then will I pass . . . fountains*: 'Then will I apply myself in turn to all the species of poetry' (Woodhouse note).
101–2 *the realm . . . of Flora, and old Pan*: pastoral poetry (evoked in sensuous detail, ll. 102–21).
109–10 *till, agreed . . . we'll read*: Presumably the tale is their love (once they've 'agreed'), not a literal storybook.
115 *still*: ever, all the time.
123 *a nobler life*: glossed by Woodhouse as epic poetry.
126–7 *a car . . . streamy manes*: Keats draws the suggestion for his chariot of the imagination from Poussin paintings of Apollo (sun god, but also god of poetry) driving across the sky.
128 *glorious fear*: Woodhouse notes usefully that the charioteer is a personification of the inspired epic-poet.
135 *stalks*: 'poetical expression for trees' (Woodhouse).
137–8 *there soon appear . . . fear*: subjects for the new Keatsian poetry that will encounter 'the strife of human hearts' (evoked in more detail, ll. 138–51)
157–9 *A sense of real things . . . nothingness*: Reality will drag him down, muddying his imagination.

(ii) from *The Fall of Hyperion: A Dream*

1 *Fanatics . . . dreams*: Keats is rewriting as a literary dream his unfinished Miltonic poem *Hyperion*, abandoned in April 1819 (but published as a fragment, in preference to *The Fall*, in 1820). Lines 1–293 are wholly new, as the poet stands back to examine his relation to experience and the materials of his work.
3 *From forth . . . of his sleep*: in his highest dreams.
7 *bare of laurel*: without the reward gained traditionally by poets.
92 *degrees*: steps (Keats probably has in mind the stairs of Mount Purgatory in Carey's translation of Dante, *Purgatory* Canto 9).
96 *One ministering*: Moneta, High Priestess of Saturn (see below).
103 *Maian incense*: scents comparable to the smells of May (it helps little that the goddess Maia was daughter of Atlas, and mother of Hermes – less that the Mayas of Peru were great temple builders).
116 *gummed*: aromatic.
125 *those streams . . . throat*: arteries in the neck.
135 *fair angels on a ladder*: the ladder in Jacob's dream, Genesis 28.12.
137 *hornéd shrine*: Horns were used traditionally to decorate altars.
144 *dated on*: postponed, delayed.
145–6 *purge off / Benign . . . mind's film*: Miltonic trick of style (adjective for adverb) such as Keats was trying to escape from in recasting *Hyperion*.
152 *fane*: building.
167–8 *What benefit . . . dreaming thing*: Keats' fear that he may be a 'dreamer' (one who does not fully accept the responsibility of being human – cannot, in Wordsworth's phrase, hear 'the still, sad music of humanity') goes back to *Sleep*

and Poetry 122 ff., above: 'And can I ever bid these joys farewell? / Yes, I must pass them for a nobler life . . .'
180 *suffered*: allowed.
183–4 *medicined / In . . . not ignoble*: treated for sickness (the dreamer's state of mind) that is conceded to be not wholly unworthy.
189–90 *a poet is a sage . . . all men*: cf. Wordsworth, Preface to *Lyrical Ballads* 1802, '[A Poet] is the rock of defence of human nature; an upholder and preserver, carrying everywhere with him relationship and love'.
202 *The other vexes it*: Presumably by his failure to be fully committed.
203 *a Pythia's spleen*: the rage of the Pythian oracle of Apollo.
204–8 *Apollo . . . proud bad verse*: Thought of more normally as sun god and god of poetry, Apollo brings plague to the Greeks' camp in *Iliad* Book One. Here he is invoked to infect fellow-poets of whom Keats disapproves, Byron especially.
222 *all spared*: all that is spared.
223–4 *Foughten . . . Against rebellion*: fought by Saturn and the giant Titans against the new gods of Olympus.
226 *Moneta*: Latin form of Greek, Mnemosyne, associated with memory, and also warning, admonishment (Latin *monere*).
246 *electral*: electrical.
257 *pined*: tormented.
271 *As*: as if.
282 *Shade of Memory*: Moneta represents memory not merely because her name identifies her with Mnemosyne, but because as sole priestess of Saturn she has vested in her remembrance of the fallen Titans.
284 *house*: family, race (in this case the Titans).
294 *Deep . . . vale*: At this point *The Fall of Hyperion*, with its discussion of Keats' anxieties as a poet, rejoins the text, and story, of *Hyperion* as published in 1820.

PERCY BYSSHE SHELLEY

(i) *Julian and Maddalo*

3 *Adria*: the Adriatic; Shelley's poem in its early phase is based on an evening ride in Venice with Byron on 23 August 1818. Nowhere does he more beautifully show his eye for detail, and his discernment of mood and personality.
34 *cheerful*: To be stressed on the second syllable, 'cheer-ful' (full of cheer).
40–42 *such as once . . . and destiny*: The fallen angels of *Paradise Lost* II, 559 are to be seen 'in wandering mazes lost' as they reason 'Of Providence, foreknowledge, will, and fate'.
46 *descanted*: talked excitedly.
46–7 *for ever . . . best of ill*: for is it not always, even now, wise to make the best . . . (the placing side by side of 'ever' and 'still' has a clumsiness however one punctuates).
50–52 *The sense . . . exceeding light*: The eagle was believed to have sharper vision than other birds because it flew into the sun and burned the scales from before its eyes. Maddalo, by implication, is blinded by solipsism (the pun on Latin *sol* being better than the etymology) – staring into the sun of himself.

62 *gondola*: Apparently pronounced 'gondolay', as, for instance, Africa was pronounced 'Africay'.

(ii) *Adonais: An Elegy on the Death of John Keats*

1 *I weep for Adonais . . . he is dead!*: Shelley, for whom *Lycidas* is a model, begins with a reversal of Milton's famous opening lines, addressed to the shepherds (ll. 165–6):

> Weep no more, woeful shepherds, weep no more,
> For Lycidas your sorrow is not dead . . .

4 *Hour*: the point in time at which Adonais died (offered by Shelley as one of the classical Hours – goddesses of the changing season).
10 *mighty Mother*: Urania, muse of astronomy, invoked by Milton and Wordsworth for her appropriateness to epic poetry, but here a name for Venus in her role as patron of ideal love.
11–12 *the shaft / In darkness*: Croker's anonymous attack on Keats' *Hyperion* (*Quarterly Review*, April 1818).
15 *one*: one of the listening Echoes.
18 *He*: Adonais (Keats) whose poetry, written to disguise the approach of death, is revived as an echo.
25 *amorous deep*: The depths into which Adonais has sunk in death are desirous to retain him.
28 *Most musical of mourners*: Milton (as poet of *Lycidas*), addressed in the next line as 'He'.
33 *many a loathèd rite*: Shelley is characterizing the loose living and repression of Charles II, in whose reign the bulk of *Paradise Lost* was composed,
35 *sprite*: spirit; scanned in *Lycidas* (and in the earlier part of *Adonais*) as a single syllable.
45 *Fame's serene abode*: A major preoccupation of Milton; cf. *Lycidas* 70, 'Fame is the spur which the clear sprite doth raise'.
47 *The nursling of thy widowhood*: Keats is seen as the 'child' of Milton's old age ('widowhood') – his poetic descendant.
49 *fed with true-love tears*: Keats' Isabella waters her pot of basil with tears of love.
55 *that high capital*: Rome.
55–6 *kingly Death . . . pale court*: A recollection of Death acting the King's part in *Richard II*:

> for within the hollow crown
> That rounds the mortal temples of a king
> Keeps Death his court . . .
>
> (III ii)

60 *his fitting charnel-roof*: cf. *Ode to the West Wind*, 25, where the storm 'Will be the dome of a vast sepulchre' (Romantic Odes, p. 348, above).
69 *The eternal Hunger*: Hunger, who is akin to Death and Corruption (but female

where they are male), has the grave for her stomach ('maw'), and seems to be a devouring cosmic principle of change.
361 *'Tis Death is dead, not he*: Compare Donne's Christian version of resurrection, *Death Be Not Proud* 13–14:

> One short sleep past, we wake eternally
> And death shall be no more: Death thou shalt die.

372 *night's sweet bird*: Keats is a part now of the continuity, permanence, that he envied in the nightingale's song:

> The voice I hear this passing night was heard
> In ancient days by Emperor and clown . . .
> (*Ode to a Nightingale*, 63–4)

381 *plastic stress*: creative power.
385 *(as each mass may bear)*: The creative force sweeps through Nature rendering spiritual the material forms that bar its path (insofar as each mass may bear to be spiritualized).
388 *splendours*: splendid achievements – a reference on this occasion to Keats, and others whose imaginative lives transcend death.
399 *the unapparent*: space; compare *Prometheus Unbound* III, iv, 284, 'Pinnacled dim in the intense inane'.
399–400 *Chatterton / Rose pale*: Shelley thinks of Chatterton, Sidney and Lucan as young poets who died too soon to fulfil their potential. Chatterton has special relevance, admired by Keats as 'the purest writer in the English language'. Taking arsenic at the age of seventeen, he had for the Romantics the mythic status that Keats (and Shelley himself) later achieved.
407 *effluence*: outflowing.
414 *Vesper of our throng*: As the Evening Star, Adonais will take charge of a sphere associated with Venus (Urania) but represented as lacking direction ('kingless'). Compare Lycidas' elevation at the end of Milton's poem: 'Henceforth thou art the genius of the shore, / In thy large recompense' (ll. 183–4).
417 *pendulous earth*: A phrase used also by Blake in *The Book of Urizen* 1794 (which Shelley could not have known); the earth does not, of course, *hang* in space, but neither poet is concerned with such precision.
440 *like an infant's smile*: An indirect reference to Shelley's loved child William (Willmouse) who died in Rome in June 1819 and was buried in the Protestant Cemetery, where Keats was buried two years later.
444 *one keen pyramid*: The Pyramid of Cestius, eighteen hundred years old, and on the edge of the Protestant Cemetery.
449 *camp of death*: A playful variant of the Italian *camposanto* (cemetery – literally 'sacred field').
454 *one fountain of a mourning mind*: one source of grief; probably another reference to Willmouse (l. 440n., above).
462 *like a dome of many-coloured glass*: The light of Heaven (traditionally white) is discoloured by human life as sunlight is by a stained-glass window. Shelley has in

mind Keats' *Eve of St Agnes*, where red, rose and amethyst lights are thrown on the praying Madeline.
477 *what Death can join together*: 'Those whom God hath joined, let no man put asunder' (Marriage Service).
480–81 *the eclipsing curse / Of birth*: Shelley writes as a Platonist (and translator of Plato), but the obvious source for this sense of birth as eclipsing earlier blessedness must be Wordsworth's *Immortality Ode.*
492 *I am borne darkly, fearfully, afar*: *Adonais* was printed in Pisa in July 1821. A year later (8 July 1822), Shelley, amid a storm in the Gulf of Spezia, gave the sails of his new 'bark', the *Don Juan*, to the tempest, and drowned with his two companions. In his pocket was a copy of Keats' *Poems* 1820.

SAMUEL TAYLOR COLERIDGE

Work Without Hope

5 *sole unbusy thing*: Coleridge recollects in this self-accusation both the 'stranger' on the grate ('the sole unquiet thing') with which he had identified in *Frost at Midnight* (1798), and the murmuring beehive of *Letter to Sara Hutchinson* (1802), l. 90, 'That ever-busy and most quiet thing' in Poets in Relationship, above, p. 697).
7 *amaranths*: mythical flowers that cannot fade.
11 *wreathless brow*: Coleridge, who has written little verse in the previous twenty years, feels himself now to have no wreaths of unfading amaranths, no poetic 'laurels'.

THOMAS HOOD

False Poets and True

2 *Turning a spirit . . . sky*: A line that both refers to, and avoids, the opening rhyme of Shelley's *To a Skylark*: 'Hail to thee, blithe spirit . . . That from heaven, or near it.'
3 *but body there is none*: 'Like an unbodied joy' (*To a Skylark*, l. 15).
7–8 *Earth inherits . . . morning cloud*: cf. *To a Skylark*, ll. 29–30, 'From one lonely cloud / The moon rains out her beams', and 35, 'from thy presence showers a rain of melody'. Hood is not imitating Shelley, but is enchanted by his poetry. Wordsworth's (much inferior) *To a Skylark* is not in his mind.
13 *But only lark . . . forlorn*: Finally Hood's beautiful sonnet is a lament for Shelley and Keats.

FELICIA HEMANS

(i) *The Grave of a Poetess* (*Records of Woman* 1828)

Epigraph 'Don't grieve for me – if you only knew how many pains this tomb has spared me!'
1–4 *I stood beside . . . lulling sound*: Mary Tighe, author of *Psyche* (see 'Dreams of Delight, Farewell', above, p. 783, and Narratives of Love), died in 1810 and is buried in the churchyard at Woodstock, Kilkenny, beside a stream and close to ruins of the abbey. Hemans knows these details as she writes her poem, but was not in fact able to visit her fellow-poet's grave till three years later, in 1831.
5 *All happy things . . . the sun*: A Wordsworthian touch: 'All things that love the sun are out of doors' (*The Leech-Gatherer*, l. 8).
15–16 *The ray that brightens . . . song*: A version of Wordsworth's 'light that never was on sea or land' *Elegiac Stanzas* 15 (On Poets and Poetry, p. 773, above).
26 *reckless*: unthinking.
32 *thrilling frame*: her body, overcome by a wave, or tremor, of emotion.
43–4 *The sway . . . must part*: Transience and death, which give to love on Earth a Keatsian edge, have no place in Heaven where all is perfect and permanent.

(ii) *Properzia Rossi*

7–9 *For thee alone . . . so vainly*: *Properzia Rossi* is an accomplished dramatic monologue, written five or more years before Tennyson and Browning's earliest experiments with the form. It is addressed to Properzia herself, to her unnamed lover, and to the statue she is making as her last bid for his attention.
36 *my own life's history*: As Properzia gives to her statue the 'history' of her unrequited love we are bound to recognize something of Hemans' own position. Deserted by her husband in 1818 (while carrying his fifth son), she seems never to have accepted that he would not return. She died aged forty-one with twenty-five major publications and collections to her name.
37 *Forsaken Ariadne*: After helping him kill the Minotaur, Ariadne (daughter of Minos and Pasiphae) eloped with Theseus, but was deserted by him on the island of Naxos.
39–42 *glow / light / woe / sight*: At five points in her poem Hemans breaks the pattern of her couplets, introducing an alternating rhyme and two indented lines; on a sixth occasion (ll. 77–80) the variation introduced is *abba*.
60 *Thou form . . . heart*: cf. Byron, ' 'Tis To Create', (On Poets and Poetry, p. 790, above).
86 *That which . . . no more?*: A recollection of Wordsworth, *Immortality Ode*, 9, 'The things which I have seen I now can see no more'.
92 *instinct*: imbued.
121–3 *Yet I leave my name . . . awhile to live*: Wordsworth mourned Hemans at her death alongside Hogg, Scott, Coleridge, Lamb and Crabbe, see *Extempore Effusion*, ll. 34–40, below. Frequent reprintings show that until the Great War, and the reaction against Christian poetry, her work was extremely well known on both sides of the Atlantic.

(iii) *To Wordsworth*

12 *decay*: decline (with none of the modern sense of decomposition).
16 *As antique music . . . household-words*: Words of the present (familiar, personal, domestic) fitted to a tune that has the resonance of the past.
28 *living waters*: A biblical phrase; cf. the Song of Songs 4.15, 'A fountain of gardens, a well of living waters, and streams from Lebanon'.

WILLIAM WORDSWORTH

Extempore Effusion Upon the Death of James Hogg

1–4 *When first . . . guide*: Wordsworth first visited the River Yarrow with James Hogg, shepherd-poet of the Scottish Border district of Ettrick, in September 1814.
5–8 *When last along its banks . . . led*: It was with Sir Walter Scott that Wordsworth revisited the Yarrow in September 1831.
10 *Mid mouldering ruins . . . lies*: Scott died in 1832, and is buried at Dryburgh Abbey.
11–12 *And death . . . Shepherd-poet's eyes*: Hogg, news of whose death prompted Wordsworth's lament for his fellow makers, died in November 1835. The *Effusion* was published in *The Atheneum* on 12 December.
17–18 *The rapt one . . . sleeps in earth*: Coleridge (the 'rapt', or inspired, one) died in July 1834; Wordsworth had known him almost forty years.
19–20 *And Lamb . . . lonely hearth*: Lamb (who adored puns, and would have been delighted after his sad life by Wordsworth's hint of the 'frolicking' lambs of spring) died six months after his schoolfellow and mentor, Coleridge, in December 1834.
23–4 *How fast has brother . . . sunless land*: cf. Dunbar's *Lament for the Makers*:

> Sen he hes all me brether tane,
> He will nocht let me lif alane,
> On fors I mun his nixt prey be,
> Timor mortis conturbat me! (Fear of death does trouble me!)

Looking back over their lives, and celebrating in turn fellow-poets now dead, Wordsworth and Dunbar are identically placed. And Wordsworth owned a copy of Dyce's edition of Dunbar, 1830.
33–4 *As if but yesterday . . . gone before*: Crabbe, whom Wordsworth came to respect, had died in 1832.
37–40 *Mourn rather . . . breathless sleep*: Hemans, who had stayed at Rydal Mount in 1830 (and stirred the jealousy of Wordsworth's household with her accomplished mind and beautiful hair), died of TB, aged forty-one, in May 1835. Wordsworth's lines to her are inserted in the text of 1837.

LETITIA ELIZABETH LANDON

(i) *Felicia Hemans* (c. 1835; publ. 1838)

3–4 *with sad, yet anxious . . . no mortal birth*: Interestingly tentative language to use of Hemans' faith, which always seems enviably secure. Landon in this great celebration of her fellow-poet writes against the background of troubles that will within months bring about her own premature death. No one knows more of the pressures under which women writers had to work.
9 *viewless*: invisible.
11–12 *The leaf . . . breathing there*: Awkward lines with their reference to the singular leaf and plural flowers, but the thought is from Jonson, *Drink To Me Only With Thine Eyes* 9 and 13–16:

> I sent thee late a rosy wreath . . .
> But thou thereon didst only breathe
>   And sent'st it back to me,
> Since when it grows and smells I swear,
>   Not of itself but thee.

17 *And thou didst bring . . . treasures*: Hemans on her mother's side was part German and Italian, she knew half a dozen languages, and published many translations, as well as drawing inspiration for her own work from the 'treasures' of foreign literature. She was writing to feed her family, with constant deadlines, and there is some truth in Wordsworth's comment that she had to find material where she could. His own life by comparison was untroubled.
22 *By its immortal verse . . . known*: As English, for instance, is known through Shakespeare.
27–8 *Many a stranger . . . bound for thee*: Hemans' 'wreath' is made up of 'flowers' that are the response to her poetry of those whom she has never known in distant lands.
29 *the Susquehanna's waters*: River flowing through Pennsylvania (where Coleridge and Southey hoped in 1794 to found their 'pantisocracy').
31 *Atlantic's younger daughters*: American women (from the first Hemans sold widely in the United States).
35 *know not the endeavour*: can't guess the effort required.
53 *culture*: cultivate.
55–6 *The fable of Prometheus . . . heart*: Fastened by Jove to a rock (for doing good to mankind), Prometheus has his liver perpetually eaten by an eagle. Like the woman's, and the poet's heart, the liver constantly regenerates, making inevitable further suffering.
57–8 *Unkindly are they judged . . . ungenerous words*: It was gossip that caused Landon to break off her engagement, and finally to make her desperate marriage and leave the country.
61 *numbers*: verses.
77 *replying*: Beating in unison with the poet's heart.
79–80 *Sleep with a light . . . Around thy grave*: The 'lovely' and undying light

might be expected to be the Christian promise of an afterlife, but seems rather to be the light of an undying recognition in hearts that share her poetry ('music').

(ii) *The Poet's Lot*

3–4 *The light . . . from himself receives*: Landon's poem is a meditation (in a lighter, happier mood) on Coleridge's *Dejection: An Ode*, especially on st. IV: 'Oh Edmund, we receive but what we give, / And in *our* life alone does Nature live.'

SHORT BIOGRAPHIES

BAILLIE, JOANNA (1762–1851) Daughter of Glasgow Divinity Professor; moved with family to London on father's death in 1778. Follower of Burns and of primitivist Scottish critic, Hugh Blair. Author of two important volumes in 1790s, both anonymous, both drawn upon by Wordsworth: *Poems* 1790, including *The Storm-Beat Maid* (connected to Lucy Poems), and *Series of Plays* 1798, extending interest in psychological motivation (source for both the Advertisement and Preface to *Lyrical Ballads*, and owl-hooting of *There Was a Boy*). Built up reputation as leading playwright, though her plays seldom worked on stage. Never married.

BARBAULD, ANNA LAETITIA (1743–1825) Daughter of John Aikin, tutor at Warrington Dissenting Academy; married father's unstable colleague, Rochemont Barbauld, 1774. Protégée of Joseph Priestley; established by *Poems* (five editions 1773, reprinted 1792) as great Unitarian poet of generation before Coleridge. Ran boys' school with husband, wrote *Evenings at Home* with brother (John Aikin, literary editor of *Monthly*). Major literary figure, editing Collins, Akenside, Richardson's *Letters*, and 50-volume edition of *British Novelists* (1810). Returned to poetry with *Eighteen Hundred and Eleven*. No children. Husband committed suicide, 1808.

BEDDOES, THOMAS LOVELL (1803–49) Son of Thomas Beddoes (1760–1808, distinguished Bristol physician, experimenter, early reader of Kant, friend of Coleridge). Trained as doctor; author of *The Bride's Tragedy* (1822), *Death's Jest-Book* (begun c. 1825, published 1850). Follower of Webster, much obsessed by death. Committed suicide.

BLAKE, WILLIAM (1757–1827) Working-class prophet, painter, poet, Londoner, trained as engraver with James Basire. Married 1782 (no children). Friend of Fuseli, follower of Swedish mystic, Emmanuel Swedenborg (rejected 1789 when London Swedenborgians form into 'church', but remains source of much in Blake's prophetic myth). Author of *Songs of Innocence* (1789, three songs complete as early as 1785) and *Experience* (1794, drafted 1792), *Visions of the Daughters of Albion* (1793, showing influence of Wollstonecraft), sequence of mid-length prophetic works, and three major 'epics', *Vala* (1797–1803, revised as *Four Zoas*), *Milton* (1800–1804, engraved c. 1809) and *Jerusalem* (c. 1804–7, engraved 1807 and later). Myth at first despairing, a version of the Fall, later develops redemptive aspect. Group of shorter poems, including *The Crystal Cabinet* and *The Mental Traveller* (written c. 1803, never engraved) employs prophetic myth but cast in lyric metres. Barely known to contemporaries, Blake's writing attracted attention of William Michael Rossetti and Yeats in late nineteenth century; since the 1950s has been valued alongside Coleridge, Wordsworth, Byron, Shelley, Keats.

BLAMIRE, SUSANNA (1747–94) Lived at Thackwood, near Carlisle, composing ballads in Scots, Cumbrian, and southern 'standard' English. Sang to the guitar, and never published. Fell at nineteen for Lord Ossulston (destined by his family for better match), and never married. Led, on Scottish border, the well-to-do maiden aunt's life of good works and humorous observation lived by Austen in Hampshire. Poems collected in 1842.

BLOOMFIELD, ROBERT (1766–1823) Farm labourer in Suffolk, cobbler in London, immensely successful in *The Farmer's Boy* (1800, with Bewick woodcuts), less so with sequels. Died poor.

BOWLES, WILLIAM LISLE (1762–1850) Wiltshire parson, writer of lugubrious revisit-poetry that became vogue in 1790s, influencing early Coleridge, and Wordsworth's *Tintern Abbey*. *Fourteen Sonnets* (1789), though preceded by Charlotte Smith, created for poet a lifetime's reputation.

BRYAN, MARY Author of *Sonnets and Metrical Tales* (1815), follower of Charlotte Smith (who sustained huge family by her pen) and Wordsworth. Wife of Bristol printer who discouraged poetry, left her with six children, and may have been actively unkind.

BÜRGER, GOTTFRIED (1747–94) Author of Gothic ballad, *Lenora*, five times translated (once with Blake illustrations) in 1796, at once admired and reacted against in *The Ancient Mariner* and *Lyrical Ballads*. Translated by William Taylor as *The Lass of Fair Wone*, second Bürger ballad became source of Wordsworth's *Thorn*. A third appeared as *The Chase*, translated anonymously by Scott (alongside a version of *Lenora*).

BURNS, ROBERT (1759–96) Born, and lived, in Ayrshire. Poet, unsuccessful farmer, and (in own words) uncommonly good fornicator, whose love-life and difficult relationship with Presbyterian parish council are celebrated in verse with good claim to be first British Romantic poetry. Kilmarnock *Poems* (1786) an instant success, editions following in Edinburgh, London, Dublin, Belfast, Philadelphia and New York. Major influence on Baillie and Wordsworth (among the first to recognize the greatness of *Tam O'Shanter*), regarded by Lamb as 'god of [his] idolatry'. After two sets of twins (boys who lived, girls who didn't), married in 1788 Jean Armour, whose father had at one point taken out warrant for his arrest. Unable to make a go farming, worked for a time as customs official. 'Collected' (transcribed) in Highlands many unrecorded Scottish songs, including *Auld Lang Syne*. Died young, apparently from rheumatic heart disease.

BYRON, GEORGE GORDON, LORD (1788–1824) Born with clubfoot, and no title, became unexpectedly sixth Baron Byron in 1798, inheriting in process delapidated Newstead Abbey, near Nottingham. Educated at Harrow and Trinity, Cambridge, where he made friendships, dieted fiercely, got into debt, perambulated with tame bear, published early poems (*Hours of Idleness*, 1807), took little notice of university. In 1809 published *English Bards and Scots Reviewers*, set out on tour of Portugal, Spain, Albania, Greece, Turkey (France and Italy inaccessible because of War). 1811: wrote *The Maid of Athens*, swam Hellespont in imitation of Leander, returned to England. 1812: maiden speech in Lords (against death penalty for Nottingham loom-breakers), *Childe Harold*'s startling success, affair with theatrical Lady Caroline Lamb, Lady Oxford's autumnal graces. 1813–14: brilliance of Oriental Tales (*The Bride of Abydos*, *The Corsair*, *Giaour*, *Lara*), closeness to four-years-older half-sister, Augusta Leigh; birth of Medora Leigh (almost certainly Byron's child). 1815: marriage to Annabella Milbanke (beautiful, prudish mathematician, out to tame profligate lord), birth of Ada. 1816: separation from Annabella (unsought by Byron); writes *Fare Thee Well* and other great lyrics; leaves England, forced out by rumour and debt; staunchness of Augusta; meets Shelley, Mary Godwin, on Lake Geneva; writes *Childe Harold* III, *The Prisoner of Chillon*. 1817–18: Venice, various affairs, sells Newstead, publishes *Manfred*, joined in Italy by Shelley and Mary (now married). 1819: beginning of lasting near-marriage with Teresa Guiccioli, appearance of *Don Juan* I–II. 1820–22: Teresa leaves husband, *Don Juan* III–V, *Cain* and other dramas, Shelley drowns in new boat (the *Don Juan*), *The Vision of Judgment*. 1823–4: equips Byron Brigade to fight for Greek independence, *Don Juan* VI–XVI published, dies 19 April 1824 at Missolonghi of marsh fever, while Greek leaders squabble over who does what; buried in family vault close to Newstead.

CAMPBELL, THOMAS (1777–1844) Scottish poet, famous in his day, now almost forgotten; author of *The Pleasures of Hope* (1799), *Gertrude of Wyoming* (1809) and impressive shorter poems, *Hohenlinden* and *Lord Ullin's Daughter* among them.

CANNING, GEORGE (1770–1827) Collaborated with Frere at Eton on Satirical *Microcosm*, and in 1797–8 on *Anti-Jacobin* (thirty-six issues), contributing some of the wittiest parody; Tory Foreign Secretary from 1822; briefly Prime Minister (1827).

CLARE, JOHN (1793–1864) Born at Helpstone in Northamptonshire, worked as farm labourer, but from early age given to reading and writing poetry. Protested against the enclosure of commons (which transformed village c. 1813); went mad in early 1830s after leaving Helpstone to live in nearby Northborough; wrote much poetry in Epping Forest and Northampton asylums, lamenting his loss of the Helpstone landscape and of early sweetheart, Mary Joyce, to whom at times he thought himself married. Taken up by Keats' publisher, Taylor, had short-lived success with *Poems Descriptive of Rural Life* (1820) and *The Village Minstrel* (1821). Held back, and corrected, by Taylor (who saw that the public no longer wanted poetry of natural description), Clare's major work, *The Shepherd's Calendar* (1827) sold less well. His asylum poetry, at its best acute as well as poignant, was unknown till the mid twentieth century, when it provoked a rethinking of his position. Long regarded as unthinkingly descriptive, he is now seen by many as among the great Romantic poets.

COLERIDGE, HARTLEY (1796–1849) Coleridge's eldest child. Inspired great poetry in both his father (*Frost at Midnight*, *The Nightingale*, *Christabel* Conclusion) and Wordsworth (*To H. C., Six Years Old*), but never quite grew up, losing his Oxford fellowship for drunkenness, and seldom being able to hold down a job. Published *Poems, Songs and Sonnets* in 1833, rising to heights of *Long Time a Child*. Supported himself as literary journalist, but chiefly looked after by Lake District cottagers. Went on drunken blinds, several days at a time, on one of which he died.

COLERIDGE, SAMUEL TAYLOR (1772–1834) Tenth and youngest child of Devonshire vicar, who encouraged his precocious reading, but died when he was nine. Sent by mother to Christ's Hospital in faraway London. Lonely (returning home only in summers), but well taught. Began well at Cambridge, with prize for sapphic *Ode on Slave Trade*, but got into debt, and enlisted in Dragoons (as Silas Tomkyn Comberbache); bought out by family. Carried away by idea of founding commune (as many did) in America – 'pantisocracy', the rule of all. Left university without degree, Christmas 1794. Raising money for emigration, wrote series of political sonnets for *Morning Chronicle*, and established himself (aged twenty-two) as lecturer in Bristol, with Jacobin views and Unitarian principles. Married in 1795, in wake of now collapsed American plan (each of twelve male pantisocrats was to have taken with him a wife), and wrote *The Eolian Harp*, first of Conversation Poems. Published in 1796 *Poems on Various Subjects* (second edition, with poems of Lamb and Charles Lloyd, 1797). Wrote in ten-month period, July 1797–April 1798 (spent with William and Dorothy Wordsworth in Somerset) bulk of greatest poetry: *This Lime-Tree Bower My Prison* (July), *Kubla Khan* and early version of *The Ancient Mariner* (Nov.), *Frost at Midnight* (Feb.), full-length *The Ancient Mariner* (March), *Christabel* Part I (April). Short of money, applies for post as Unitarian minister, but given annuity by Wedgwoods (Jan. 1798); publishes slim *Fears in Solitude* quarto, and appears anonymously with Wordsworth in *Lyrical Ballads* (Sept.); spends 1798–9 in Germany; falls in love with Sara Hutchinson, younger sister of Wordsworth's future wife (Nov.); settles (June 1800) at Greta Hall, Keswick, twelve miles from Wordsworths at Dove Cottage, Grasmere. Increasing opium addiction and illness; reading Kant and German metaphysics, feels the poet in him is dead. Writes *Letter to Sara Hutchinson* (April 1802) and *Pains of Sleep* (1803); leaves for Malta (March 1804) in search of health (returns, much changed, Aug. 1806); writes *To William Wordsworth* after reading of *The Prelude* (Jan. 1807). Lectures on poetry at Royal Institution (1808), writes weekly journal, *Friend*, in Grasmere (1809–10); London lectures (1811–12) on Shakespeare and Milton; *Remorse* (written as *Osorio* 1797) performed successfully at Drury Lane (1813); moves in with physician, Gillman, at Highgate, as patient and guest (1816); publication of *Kubla Khan*, *Christabel*, *Pains of Sleep*. *Sybilline Leaves* published (collecting scattered poems, many published in newspapers, and consolidating reputation), 1817, together with *Biographia Literaria* (containing best of Coleridge's criticism, including definitions of imagination). Odd poems still being written, but last years given over to theological speculation. Dies 25 July 1834, aged sixty-one.

COWPER, WILLIAM (1731–1800) Trained as lawyer, suffered repeated nervous breakdowns, believing himself (though there is little sign in his poetry) to be damned. Published in 1785 *The Task*, great blank-verse study of contemplative poet that lies in the background of Coleridge, Wordsworth and the Romantic philosophical tradition. Friend of ex-slave captain, turned evangelical, John Newton; active in anti-slavery protest 1788.

CRABBE, GEORGE (1754–1832) Established reputation, and literary manner, with

The Village (1783), study in heroic couplets of rural poverty and hopelessness, revised by Dr Johnson and written in revulsion against the pastoral. Worked in same idiom throughout Romantic period, producing *The Parish Register* (1807), *Borough* (1810, including his masterpiece, *Peter Grimes*), *Tales in Verse* (1812, including *Procrastination*) and *Tales of the Hall* (1819). Austen's favourite poet; work said (uncharitably) by Wordsworth to have as much to do with imagination as a set of law reports.

CRISTALL, ANN BATTEN (c. 1768–c. 1851) Sister of watercolour-painter Joshua Cristall and friend of Wollstonecraft, Barbauld, Aikin, Dyer and other radical dissenters of the 1790s. Published *Poetical Sketches* in 1795; disappears from view five years later.

FRERE, JOHN HOOKHAM (1769–1846) Witty parodist, with Eton, Cambridge, Foreign Office background, seen (with Canning) at work in the *Anti-Jacobin* (1797–8), notably in *The Rovers*. Co-founder of *Quarterly* (1807), but never part of its Tory bullying. Humour and agreeableness of *Whistlecraft* (1817) has been obscured by discussion of how much Byron's voice and verse derived from it in *Beppo* and *Don Juan*.

HEMANS, FELICIA (1793–1835) Published first volume poems aged fourteen, and went on to become dominant voice for English and American readers of poetry in the decade after Byron's death. Married in 1812 Captain Alfred Hemans, friend of her soldier-brothers, who was put out by her distinction and deserted her when she was pregnant with their fifth son. With mother's help, brought up family on the basis of her writing, providing numerous poems for the annuals then in vogue, and a succession of moving and impressive volumes, notably *Records of Women* (1828). Tennyson and Browning had yet to come on the scene when Hemans explored the dramatic monologue, and the consciousness of her speakers, in *Properzia Rossi* and *Arabella Stuart*.

HOGG, JAMES (1770–1835) Shepherd from age of seven (half-yearly wages, ewe-lamb and pair of shoes); taught himself to read, write, play guitar. Saved £200 in 1790s, but lost all in 1804 scheme to buy Hebrides farm. Gradually built reputation for songs, but still on hillside (without shoes) when visited by Allan Cunningham, 1806. Publishes *The Mountain Bard* (1807); goes to Edinburgh, 1810 (aged almost forty), to make living as writer. Befriended by Scott, publishes *The Queen's Wake* (1813); shows skills and fineness of ear in parodies of Wordsworth and others (*The Poetic Mirror*, 1815). Publishes in *Jacobite Relics* (1819) nationalist songs and music that compare with Moore's *Irish Melodies*; famous as Ettrick Shepherd of *Blackwood*, part author, part butt, of *Noctes Ambrosianae*, 1822–35. Prose masterpiece, *Confessions of a Justified Sinner*, appears in 1824. Farming in Yarrow from 1816. Much that is choice in final collection, *Songs by the Ettrick Shepherd* (1831).

HUNT, JAMES LEIGH (1784–1859) Good writer, whose friends – Hazlitt, Keats, Shelley, Byron – were great ones. Lived through Romantic period, founding, editing journals (*Reflector*, *Examiner*, *Indicator*, *Liberal*); publishing essays, verse, latterly plays; knowing everybody; becoming finally Skimpole in *Bleak House*.

Vilified by reviews as founder of Cockney School; still thought of (unreasonably) as malign influence on Keats. Known as poet only through anthology pieces, but among longer works *Feast of the Poets* (1814), *Rimini* (1816), at least, deserve to be read.

KEATS, JOHN (1795–1821) Lost father when eight, mother (from TB) at fourteen; lower middle-class origins; well taught at Enfield, but at fifteen apprenticed to apothecary, rather than going (like Wordsworth, Coleridge and the aristocrats, Byron and Shelley) to University; transfers, 1815, to train as surgeon at Guy's, quickly becoming 'dresser' (assisting in operations, dressing wounds after surgery, bleeding patients). Turns, against all advice, from surgery to poetry (1816); meets Hunt (who prints *On First Looking into Chapman's Homer* in *Examiner*), Hazlitt and Shelley; *Poems* (March 1817) doesn't sell, but well enough received till Lockhart's autumn attack in *Blackwood's* on Keats and Cockney School; writes *Endymion* (self-imposed task of 4,000 lines at fifty a day). 1818: *Endymion* published; writes *Isabella*; tours Lakes and Scotland; *Blackwood's* and *Quarterly* attacks on *Endymion*, the first, by Lockwood, condescending ('back to the shop Mr John, back to "plasters, pills and ointment boxes" '), the second, by Croker, unfeeling in tone, not wrong in observations; death from TB of Tom Keats, nursed by brother, who contracts disease (writing first *Hyperion*). 1819: moves to Hampstead, falls in love with Fanny Brawne; writes Jan.–Sept. most of great poetry: *The Eve of St Agnes*, *La Belle Dame Sans Merci*, Spring Odes, *Lamia*, *The Fall of Hyperion* (abandoned, Sept. as too Miltonic), *To Autumn*, *Bright Star*. 1820–1: haemorrhage (Feb.), forbidden excitement of writing poetry or seeing Fanny; June, spitting blood, knows he will die; July, *Poems* 1820; 18 Sept., sails for Italy to avoid northern winter; 21 Oct., arrives Naples; 15 Nov., lodged above Spanish Steps in Rome; 23 Feb., dies, aged twenty-four; buried near Pyramid of Cestius in English Cemetery.

LAMB, CHARLES (1775–1834) Like Coleridge and Hunt, a charity-boy at Christ's Hospital. Famous as critic and essayist (*Essays of Elia*, 1823), *Last Essays* (1833), did not think of himself as poet after early days as sonnet-writer and Coleridge disciple (*Poems of Coleridge, Lamb and Lloyd*, 1797; Lamb and Lloyd, *Blank Verse*, 1798). Sad brave devoted life, working as clerk at East India House and looking after older sister, Mary (periodically insane after killing mother with knife, Sept. 1796). Could always write a moving poem, but *Old Familiar Faces* alone shows the poet he might have been. More even than Blake, the true Londoner among the Romantics.

LANDON, LETITIA ELIZABETH (1802–38) Begins career, and ends life, in mystery: first, the five years' anonymity and increasing fame of L. E. L. as poet of the *Literary Gazette*; last, the prussic acid by which she may or may not have intended to kill herself, having made an incongruous and unfortunate marriage. Following success of *Improvisatrice* (7 edns, 1824–5), published eight collections of verse, as well as editing *Drawing-room Scrapbook* and *Book of Beauty*, and contributing liberally to other journals and albums. Persuaded by rumours of abortion to break off engagement with Forster (Dickens' future biographer), marries uncouth Scottish Governor of Gold Coast, dying (probably by suicide, though prussic acid was medically prescribed) after four months in Africa. No active poet save Hemans so well known in last years of Romantic period. Later poetry (*Lines of Life*, *The Factory*, *Felicia Hemans*) adds depth to the charm, skill, liveliness always there. Had the makings (as Elizabeth Barratt observed) of a great writer.

LEWIS, MATTHEW GREGORY (1775–1818) Well-bred opportunist who cashed in on vogue for Gothic, taking Radcliffe's vicarage horrors (*The Mysteries of Udolpho*, 1794) into world with no qualms about supernatural, and unashamedly erotic. Made name with *The Monk* (1796), in which appears comic horror-ballad, *Alonzo the Brave and the Fair Imogine*.

LICKBARROW, ISABELLA (1784–1847) Daughter of Quaker schoolmaster in Kendal, Cumbria, whose talents are only now becoming known. Orphaned (with three sisters) by time of major publication, *Poetical Effusions*, 1814, for which Wordsworth, Southey and De Quincey were subscribers. Contributed much verse to Kendal newspaper, 1811–15, published second book, *Lament upon the Death of Princess Charlotte* in 1818. Latest poems discovered to date, 1820.

LLOYD, CHARLES (1775–1839) Eldest son of Charles Lloyd II, banker and life-long Quaker; couldn't stand banking and never very stable. Tried life of Edinburgh medical student; published first volume of poetry (aged nineteen in 1794); became Coleridge's living-in pupil in Somerset, and through him friend of Lamb, Southey, Wordsworth; wrote Coleridgean sonnets (the best to his grandmother, Priscilla Farmer), and published twice with Lamb 1797–8 (see above). During spell at Cambridge introduced Church of England tutor, Christopher Wordsworth, to sister Priscilla, from whose marriage sprang the *The New Penguin Book of Romantic Poetry*.

MOORE, THOMAS (1779–1852) Witty Irish friend of Byron, educated at Trinity, Dublin; highly rated in his day for verse that now seems talented but slight. Best known for *Irish Melodies* (collections appearing 1808–34); showed versatility in 1817 with *Lalla Rookh*, influenced by Byron's Eastern Tales, but Moore's own version of the Romantic sublime.

MORE, HANNAH (1745–1833) Blue-stocking, friend of Johnson, Garrick, Burke, Horace Walpole, Wilberforce and do-gooder to end all do-gooders. Successful playwright at start of career; towards the end, writes best-selling novel, *Coelebs in Search of a Wife* (1809); in between, becomes abolitionist and evangelical, founds extraordinarily efficient school system in Cheddar for the poor of all ages, and in 1795–6 sells 2,000,000 Cheap Repository tracts in government-backed drive to outdo Paine and *The Rights of Man*.

NORTON, CAROLINE (1808–77) Powerful and original poet who is only now coming to be recognized, leading a life (like so many women writers of the time) dominated by bad marriage. Beautiful and distinguished, she was pressured at nineteen into marrying a weak and spiteful man, who, in 1836, first removed her children (she had left home to avoid his violence), then sued for divorce, citing the Prime Minister, Lord Melbourne, as co-respondent. The case was dismissed, and a separation arranged, but it was four years before she saw her sons again; one died in the interim. As a married woman, she had no legal rights, but almost single-handedly she brought about changes in the law of custody. Meanwhile she went on writing. *The Sorrows of Rosalie* had gone through four editions in 1829, followed by *The Undying One* (1830); in 1833 her *Poems* had been published in Boston. From 1832 she was editor of the *Court Magazine*, and from 1834, of the *English Annual*. *A Voice from the Factories* appeared in 1836, at once part of a protest movement and an example of imaginative sympathy in the dispossessed mother for the sufferings of working-class families.

OPIE, AMELIA (1769–1853) Friend of the bachelor Godwin, whom she teased with her beauty and intelligence, and whose views on marriage she delightfully mocked in *Adeline Mowbray* (1804). Prolific novelist, but merely a weekend poet. Wife of John Opie, the portrait painter, who died young. Devoted Quaker in her later years.

SAMUEL PALMER (1805–63) Follower of Blake and inspired landscape painter; wrote little poetry, but could at times catch in words something of the vision of his Shoreham period drawings.

THOMAS LOVE PEACOCK (1785–1866) Major satirical novelist of the period, who could write accomplished verse when he tried, but remained unresponsive to Romantic ways of thinking. Close friend of Shelley, provoked the *Defence of Poetry* with his *Four Ages* (1820), billing his contemporaries as the age of lead.

ROBINSON, MARY (1758–1800) Best known for catching eye of nineteen-year-old Prince of Wales while acting Perdita in 1779. By this time she had been married off by her family aged fifteen, had a child, gone to debtors' prison with her worthless lawyer-husband and published a volume of poems (1775) under patronage of the Duchess of Devonshire. Official Royal Mistress for a year, she was seduced by Charles James Fox (and probably others) while negotiating a bond for £20,000 given her by the Prince. Though her legs were paralysed as the result of a miscarriage in 1783, she sustained a sixteen-year on-and-off relationship with Banastre Tarleton, bloodthirsty General from the American War and Tory MP, for whom her best lyrics are written. A versatile poet, and author of eight novels, she maintained her independence, and subdued increasing physical pain, by writing. Two volumes of poetry appeared in 1792–3, the first including a poetic correspondence with Merry, leader of the Della Cruscans; her major work, the sonnet sequence *Sappho and Phaon*, came out in 1796, presenting the first, reputedly greatest, of women poets as the injured lover. Responding to new Romantic currents in poetry, Robinson became in her last years (alongside Coleridge) supplier of poems to the *Morning Post*. Just before she died, aged forty-one, at Christmas 1800, *Lyrical Tales* was published, showing her as the disciple of Southey. Her major prose work, *A Letter to the Women of England on the Injustice of Mental Subordination*, belongs to 1799.

SCOTT, MARY (1751–93) Feminist with a dissenting West Country background, whose mission to bring women's writing to wider attention was at least to some extent achieved in *The Female Advocate* (1774). Her epic *Messiah*, with affinities to *Paradise Regained*, appeared in 1788, at the time of her late marriage.

SCOTT, SIR WALTER (1771–1832) Far and away most successful of Romantic poets till the emergence of Byron. Preoccupation with ballad shown in first publication, *The Wild Huntsman* and *Lenora* (1796), translations from Bürger, and in *Minstrelsy of the Scottish Border* (1802–3), leading to the triumphs of Romantic medievalism, *The Lay of the Last Minstrel* (1805), of which 20,000 copies were sold by 1812, *Marmion* (1808) and *The Lady of the Lake* (1810), which did even better. Declined Laureateship in 1813, and next year turned to the novel, achieving again unparalleled success, with the anonymous *Waverley*, first of an extraordinary sequence of best-sellers. Died broken with overwork after heroic attempt to pay off £100,000 debt incurred by the publishers Ballantyne, of which he was a partner.

SEWARD, ANNA (1747–1809) Friend of Erasmus Darwin, the Blue Stockings, and other well-connected literary figures; had distinction of living in Lichfield for more than fifty years, and disliking Dr Johnson (whom her grandfather had taught at the grammar school). Among her varied works as poet are the verse-novel, *Louisa* (4 edns, 1784), *Llangollen Vale* (1797) and *Sonnets* (1799).

SHELLEY, PERCY BYSSHE (1792–1822) Son of Whig baronet, educated at Eton, but sent down from Oxford, 1811, for provocative pamphlet, *The Necessity of Atheism*. Eloped to Scotland with sixteen-year-old Harriet Westbrook, attempted to foment revolution in Ireland, and wrote anti-Establishment *Queen Mab* ('privished' 1813). Eloped once more, 1814, this time to Switzerland with Mary Godwin (also sixteen) plus step-sister, Claire Clairmont (journey recorded, *History of a Six Weeks Tour*, 1817). Returning to Switzerland, spring 1816, sailed with Byron on Lake Geneva, wrote *Hymn to Intellectual Beauty* and *Mont Blanc*, and took part in ghost-story competition at Byron's Villa Diodati that produced Mary's *Frankenstein* and Polidori's *Vampyre*. Married Mary at end of year, distastefully soon after Harriet's suicide (for which he blamed her, not himself), but lost suit for custody of his children, Charles and Ianthe. Published *Alastor* 1816, wrote *Laon and Cythna* 1817 (revised as *The Revolt of Islam*, 1818) and travelled south with Mary and Claire to Italy, translating Plato's *Symposium* at Lucca and writing *Julian and Maddalo* (about himself and Byron) in Venice. Deaths of Clara and Willmouse, Shelley's children by Mary, led to her chronic depression, but did not prevent his writing in 1819–20 *The Cenci* (greatest of Romantic plays), *The Mask of Anarchy*, *Ode to the West Wind*, *Peter Bell the Third* (brilliant parodic insights on Wordsworth), *The Skylark*, *The Cloud* and much else. 1821 saw *Adonais*, great Miltonic elegy for Keats, and the brilliant Platonic, erotic, confusion of *Epipsychidion*, daydream of elopement with Téresa Viviana, seventeen, and bowled over by the poet, but safely immured in a convent. In last months of his life, Shelley found new compelling simplicity in lyrics written for Jane Williams, and ordered new boat, the *Don Juan*, in which he drowned, in July 1822, refusing to lower sails in a Mediterranean storm. Copy of Keats was in his pocket. 'My spirit's bark', he had written in *Adonais*, 'is driven / Far from the shore, far from the trembling throng / Whose sails were never to the tempest given.' He was not quite thirty. Mary, survivor of an appalling marriage, was left to tend remaining child, the pallid Percy Florence, and create for her husband acceptable legend in prefaces to *Posthumous Poems* (1824) and three-volume edition of 1839.

SMITH, CHARLOTTE (1749–1806) Married off at fifteen like Robinson, for father's convenience, and like her wrote first book of poems (*Elegiac Sonnets*, 1784) in debtors' prison. Unlike her, stayed with worthless husband till after their twelfth child (Robinson had only one). Dominant voice in new Romantic development of the sonnet, but forced to write novel a year to feed and educate family. At time of her death, worn out not least by legal suits (settled thirty-seven years later) over money for the children, had embarked on blank-verse poetry of *Beachy Head*, written for herself.

SMITH, HORACE (1779–1849) Famous as joint-author with elder brother James of *Rejected Addresses* (1812), spoof entries by Wordsworth, Coleridge, Byron and others, for competition to write address for opening night at new Drury Lane theatre. Shows stature as poet in sonnet written alongside Shelley's *Ozymandias*, 1878.

SMITH, JAMES (1775–1839) Brother of Horace Smith and co-author of *Rejected Addresses* (see above).

SOUTHEY, ROBERT (1774–1843) Early Jacobin friend of Coleridge, educated at Westminster and Balliol College, Oxford, where in summer 1794 they drew up scheme to found an ideal commune – Pantisocracy (the rule of all) – on the banks of the Susquehanna. Five years later, after publishing volumes of poetry in 1794, 1797 and 1799, and the pro-French epic *Joan of Arc* in 1796, Southey had established himself as the best-known opponent of the Tory government among contemporary poets. Especially impressive was his anti-war poem, *The Battle of Blenheim*, inspired by Wordsworth's *We Are Seven*. Moving to Greta Hall, Keswick, in 1801, Southey took charge of Coleridge's children alongside his own, at the same time publishing a series of epic poems, *Thalaba*, 1801, *Madoc*, 1805, *The Curse of Kehama*, 1810. Conservatism came early. From 1809 he was reviewer on the Tory *Quarterly*, and from 1813, Poet Laureate. In both verse and prose he was immensely prolific. By no means among the great poets of the day, he was perhaps the foremost man of letters. Now he is probably best known from Byron's satirical portrait in *The Vision of Judgment* (1820).

TAYLOR, JANE (1783–1824) Co-author with her sister of *Original Stories for Infant Minds* (1804; fifty edns, many times translated) and *Rhymes for the Nursery* (1806), no less successful, and including 'Twinkle, twinkle, little star'.

TIGHE, MARY (1772–1810) Irish poet, disparaged by Keats, but an influence on *Ode on a Grecian Urn*; to be valued in her own right for six-canto Spenserian allegory, *Psyche*, remarkable in age of free imitation for faithfulness with which movement and atmosphere of *Faerie Queene* are recreated. Died early of TB after empty and childless marriage to first cousin.

WARTON, THOMAS (1728–90) Predecessor of Charlotte Smith and Bowles in re-establishing the sonnet (out of fashion since Milton), especially influential through his revisit-poem *To the River Loden*. Professor of Poetry at Oxford (like his father) and, from 1785, Poet Laureate.

WILLIAMS, HELEN MARIA (1762–1827) Author of *Peru* (1784), and two-volume *Poems*, 1789; accepted by reviewers as among leading British poets till 1790 when she turned to prose as chronicler of the French Revolution (*Letters from France*, 1790–95. Imprisoned during Terror, under daily threat of guillotine, gave her time to translation of Bernardin de St Pierre, *Paul et Virginie*. Never returned to extensive writing of poetry.

WORDSWORTH, DOROTHY (1771–1855) Famous chiefly for her *Alfoxden* and *Grasmere Journals*, 1798, 1800–1803, that tell of the daily lives from which her brother's poetry and Coleridge's emerged. Never thought of herself as writer, and wrote seldom in verse. Declined into Alzheimer's for the last twenty years of her life, but tenderly looked after by poet and family. Poetry published from MS 1987.

WORDSWORTH, WILLIAM (1770–1850) Regarded by Hazlitt as 'pure emanation of the spirit of the age' – his genius and 'levelling' poetic experiments 'carried along with the revolutionary movement' of the day. Born in Cumbria, educated (after mother's death when he was seven) at Hawkshead, formally a tiny but excellent grammar school, informally on the fells. Cambridge career an academic disaster, but produced *Evening Walk* (publ. 1793) and allowed for July 1790 'pedestrian tour' through France (rejoicing at anniversary of Fall of Bastille) to Switzerland and Alps, source of great imaginative poetry. Back in France for a year, 1791–2, Wordsworth falls in love with Annette Vallon, fathers child (christened Anne Caroline Wordsworth, Orleans Cathedral, Dec. 1792), meets republican nobleman, Michel Beaupuy, who converts him to cause. En route for England in Oct. sees Revolution falling into hands of Robespierre and extremists. Trial of Louis XVI (executed Jan. 1793); leads to war, separating Wordsworth from Annette and Caroline till 1802. 1793–6; years of alienation, wishing for British defeat; reunion, Sept. 1795, with sister Dorothy (parted since childhood); first great poetry (*The Ruined Cottage*, 1797); companionship with Coleridge, 1797–8 (writing of *Lyrical Ballads*). Germany, 1798 (Lucy Poems, beginnings of poetic autobiography, *The Prelude*). Returns to Cumbria and landscape of boyhood, Christmas 1799. Creativity of Dove Cottage years (1799–1808): *Home at Grasmere*, *Michael*, *The Leech-Gatherer*, *The Immortality Ode*, thirteen-book *Prelude* of 1805, much else. Marriage, 1802, to Mary Hutchinson, after visit (with Dorothy) to Annette and Caroline during Truce of Amiens. Slow growth of reputation: publication of *The Prelude* (epic of human consciousness, including chronicle of Revolution) deferred – too personal. Moves to Rydal Mount (1813–50); accepts civil service post; *Excursion*, 1814. Poetic genius present now only in moments: *The River Duddon: Afterthought* (1820), *Extempore Effusion* (1835). Periodic revisions of *The Prelude*, mainly for worse. Death, 23 April 1850. *The Prelude* publ. July. (Out of date in year of *In Memoriam*, and best read in early versions: two Parts 1799, 13 Books 1805).

YEARSLEY, ANN (1752–1806) Working-class poet, rescued by Hannah More from extreme poverty, and named by her 'the Bristol Milk Woman'; author of *Poems on Several Occasions* (1785), *Poems on Various Subjects* (1787), poems on slavery and the death of Marie Antoinette, *The Rural Lyre* (1796), a play and part of a novel. Fought More (well-intentioned, but intrusive), successfully and publicly, for right to use earnings to educate her sons.

INDEX OF POETS AND THEIR WORKS

INDEX OF TITLES

INDEX OF FIRST LINES